ALABAMA

HOW TO USE THIS ATLAS

These excerpts from the CONSOLIDATED CHRONOLOGY and the INDIVIDUAL COUNTY CHRONOLOGIES demonstrate the depiction, both textual and cartographic, of county boundary changes and the relationship between these two sections of the atlas.

In addition to the Consolidated Chronology of State and County Boundaries and Individual County Chronologies, Maps, and Areas, the atlas includes the following:

Table of County Creations / Table of Censuses / Census Outline Maps / Bibliography

CONSOLIDATED CHRONOLOGY includes, in chronological order, all boundary changes reported for the state and its counties. Changes for more than one county may appear under one date. Historical sources of information are given in parentheses for every event; more detailed information about sources can be found in the bibliography at the back of the atlas.

Events from the CONSOLIDATED CHRONOLOGY correspond to the events listed in the INDIVIDUAL COUNTY CHRONOLOGY table. These events for Covington are illustrated by maps 4, 5, and 6.

Consolidated Chronology   9

21 January 1824

COVINGTON gained all of BAINBRIDGE; BAINBRIDGE eliminated. (Miss. Laws 1823–1824, 7th sess., ch. 26/p. 35)

JACKSON gained from HANCOCK. (Miss. Laws 1823–1824, 7th sess., ch. 36/pp. 44–45)

23 January 1824

SIMPSON created from COPIAH. (Miss. Laws 1823–1824, 7th sess., ch. 72, sec. 1/p. 87)

1 February 1825

COVINGTON gained from LAWRENCE and WAYNE. Part of COVINGTON's gain from LAWRENCE was unintended; MARION had been authorized to gain from LAWRENCE, but local officials and residents treated the area as part of the territory transferred to COVINGTON. (Miss. Laws 1825, 8th sess., ch. 22/p. 48)

2 February 1825

PIKE gained from LAWRENCE. (Miss. Laws 1825, 8th sess., ch. 33/p. 78)

3 February 1825

PERRY gained from HANCOCK. (Miss. Laws 1825, 8th sess., ch. 43/p. 99)

24 January 1826

JONES created from COVINGTON and WAYNE. (Miss. Laws 1826, 9th sess., p. 59)

4 February 1829

Non-county area (unceded Indian territory) divided into six regions which were attached to: MADISON, MONROE, RANKIN and SIMPSON jointly, WASHINGTON, WAYNE, and YAZOO. (Miss. Laws 1829, 12th sess., ch. 77, secs. 1–2/pp. 81–82)

5 February 1829

MADISON gained from HINDS. (Miss. Laws 1829, 12th sess., ch. 19/p. 17)

30 January 1830

LOWNDES created from MONROE and non-county area attached to MONROE. (Miss. Laws 1830, 13th sess., ch. 14, sec. 1/p. 18)

Part of non-county area detached from RANKIN and SIMPSON, attached to COVINGTON; parts of non-county areas detached from WAYNE and from RANKIN and SIMPSON, attached to JONES. (Miss. Laws 1830, 13th sess., ch. 43/p. 46)

INDIVIDUAL COUNTY CHRONOLOGIES, MAPS, AND AREAS presents boundary changes of a particular county complete with dates of recorded change, a summary of changes, and the resulting area in square miles. When changes cannot be mapped, explanations are provided.

Locator maps identify the county within its state, showing current county configuration. For counties now in other states, the locator map will include appropriate areas.

Numbers in black circles link the maps to the entries in the table.

Map headings show the range of dates for which changes are valid; where more than one range of dates appears, the county was later restored to this configuration.

Heavy lines depict the county boundary during the indicated range of dates.

Underlying map is standard base map drawn by the U.S. Geological Survey.

A standard scale is used throughout unless specifically noted.

When smaller scales are necessary, the alternate scale appears directly beneath small-scale maps.

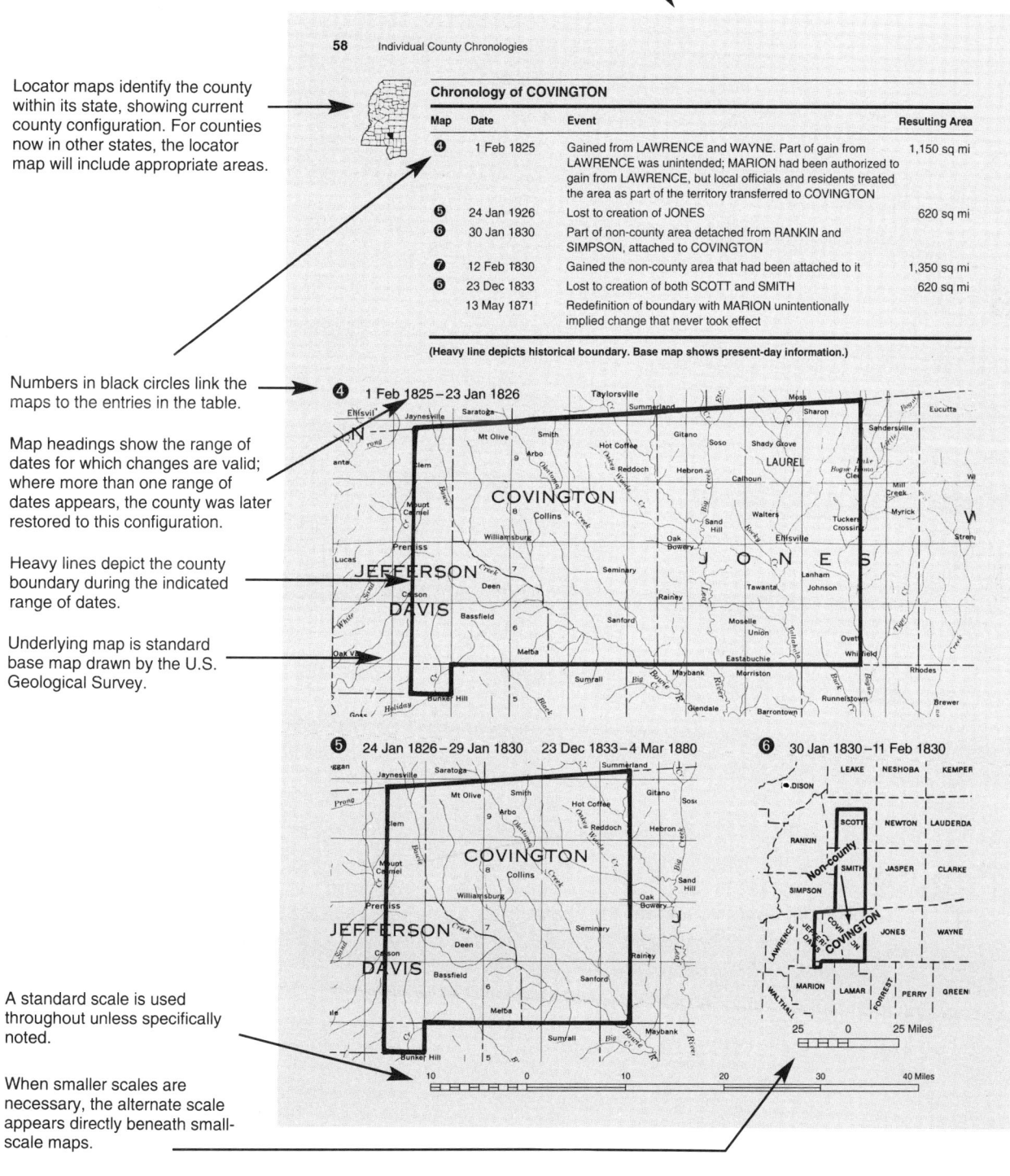

This atlas has been supported by a grant from the
National Endowment for the Humanities, an independent federal agency.

ALABAMA

Atlas of Historical County Boundaries

John H. Long, Editor

Compiled by Peggy Tuck Sinko

A Project of the

Dr. William M. Scholl Center for Family and Community History

The Newberry Library

Charles Scribner's Sons
Macmillan Library Reference USA
Simon & Schuster Macmillan
New York

Simon & Schuster Prentice Hall International
London Mexico City New Delhi Singapore Sydney Toronto

Copyright © 1996 by
The Newberry Library

Charles Scribner's Sons
An Imprint of Simon & Schuster Macmillan
1633 Broadway
New York, New York 10019

All rights reserved. No part of this book may be reproduced or transmitted
in any form or by any means, electronic or mechanical, including photo-
copying, recording, or by any information storage or retrieval system,
without permission in writing from the publisher.

Printed in the United States of America

1 3 5 7 9 11 13 15 17 19 20 18 16 14 12 10 8 6 4 2

Library of Congress Cataloging-in-Publication Data

   Atlas of historical county boundaries. Alabama / John H. Long,
  editor; compiled by Peggy Sinko.
    p. cm.
    Includes bibliography.
    ISBN 0-13-309568-1
    l. Alabama—Administrative and political divisions—Maps.
2. Alabama—Historical geography—Maps. 3. Alabama—History.
I. Sinko, Peggy Tuck.
Gl201.F7A8 1996 Ala. <G&M>
911'.761—dc20   94-15023
                                                  CIP
                                                  MAP

*The paper used in this publication meets the minimum requirements of
American National Standard for Information Sciences—Permanence
of Paper for Printed Library Materials ANSI   Z39.48–1984.*

Contents

Preface and Acknowledgments / vii

Introduction / ix

   History of This Atlas / x

   Sources / xii

   Procedures / xiv

   Special Topics for Alabama / xv

   Base Maps / xvi

   Dates / xvii

Abbreviations / xix

Table of Alabama County Creations / 1

Consolidated Chronology of Alabama State and County Boundaries / 5

Individual County Chronologies, Maps, and Areas for Alabama / 25–377

ADAMS (Miss.) / 26	COLBERT / 116	JACKSON (Miss.) / 192	PASCAGOULA (Orleans Terr., extinct) / 279
AUTAUGA / 27	CONECUH / 117	JACKSON / 193	PERRY / 280
BAINE (extinct) / 36	COOSA / 123	JEFFERSON (Miss., created as PICKERING) / 202	PICKENS / 286
BAKER (see CHILTON)	COTACO (see MORGAN)		PICKERING (see JEFFERSON, Miss.)
BALDWIN / 38	COVINGTON / 126	JEFFERSON / 203	
BARBOUR / 41	CRENSHAW / 133	JONES (extinct) / 217	PIKE / 288
BENTON (see CALHOUN)	CULLMAN / 136	JONES (see COVINGTON)	RANDOLPH / 296
BIBB (created as CAHAWBA) / 46	DALE / 139	LAMAR (created as SANFORD) / 218	RUSSELL / 298
BLOUNT / 56	DALLAS / 143	LAUDERDALE / 219	ST. CLAIR / 300
BULLOCK / 69	DECATUR (extinct) / 151	LAWRENCE / 220	SANFORD (see LAMAR)
BUTLER / 73	DE KALB / 153	LEE / 221	SHELBY / 312
CAHAWBA (see BIBB)	ELMORE / 166	LIMESTONE / 223	SUMTER / 326
CALHOUN (created as BENTON) / 79	ESCAMBIA / 167	LOWNDES / 224	TALLADEGA / 328
CHAMBERS / 88	ETOWAH / 168	MACON / 226	TALLAPOOSA / 336
CHEROKEE / 90	FAYETTE / 172	MADISON / 230	TUSCALOOSA / 339
CHILTON (created as BAKER) / 96	FELICIANA (La., extinct) / 176	MARENGO / 234	WALKER / 353
CHOCTAW / 98	FRANKLIN / 177	MARION / 238	WASHINGTON / 363
CLAIBORNE (Miss.) / 99	GENEVA / 180	MARSHALL / 243	WAYNE (Miss.) / 371
CLARKE / 100	GREENE (Miss.) / 181	MOBILE / 253	WILCOX / 372
CLAY / 104	GREENE / 182	MONROE / 260	WINSTON (created as HANCOCK) / 377
CLEBURNE / 107	HALE / 185	MONTGOMERY / 265	
COFFEE / 114	HANCOCK (see WINSTON)	MORGAN (created as COTACO) / 276	
	HENRY / 186		
	HOUSTON / 191		

Table of Territorial, State, and Federal Censuses in Alabama / 379

Census Outline Maps for Alabama / 381

Bibliography / 397

v

Preface and Acknowledgments

In 1933 the distinguished historian Frederick Merk lamented the lack of "a set of maps tracing the county divisions of the United States," because such maps "would have been of inestimable service to scholars in various fields" (*New England Quarterly*, 6:622). Merk was concerned primarily with outline maps for the plotting of statistics and, knowing that the federal government had published such maps for the census years 1840 to 1900, he was particularly interested in the earlier censuses, 1790 to 1830. This atlas is an attempt not only to satisfy that longstanding need, but also to provide complete and comprehensive information on all changes in all counties, individually and in aggregate.

A single question has focused the preparation of this atlas: at any time in history, what was the legal, effective arrangement of American county jurisdiction? A great number of people seek answers to that question, and, as Merk knew, their fields vary—demography, economics, genealogy, geography, history, law, political science, and other disciplines—and their interests cover a wide spectrum of place and time, from the national level to the local and from the colonial era to the present. The combined needs of this diverse audience shaped the primary goal of this atlas and determined its scope, its content, and its forms.

The geographic scope of the atlas encompasses the historical territory of the forty-eight contiguous states and Hawaii, and the chronological coverage extends to 1990 from the 1630s, when the earliest colonial counties were created. The content is not limited strictly to boundary changes, but also includes such other facets of the jurisdictional issue as unsuccessful authorizations for change and attachments of unorganized counties and non-county areas to operational counties. Data on the many changes in American counties are presented in both text (consolidated and individual county chronologies) and maps (detailed maps of individual counties and outline maps of the entire state's county network). Unlike the offerings of most reference works, these data come not from a synthesis of existing knowledge but are the fruits of original research in primary sources.

The consolidated chronology should be the starting point for readers concerned with a specific period or date, while those interested in particular counties can quickly find their subjects in the section of individual county chronologies and maps. The table of censuses and the set of census outline maps, which cover colonial, territorial, and state enumerations or equivalents, in addition to federal censuses, are designed to serve readers interested in statistical analysis and mapping.

The Newberry Library, Chicago, has been both headquarters and institutional sponsor for this atlas; its rich holdings in old maps and in state and local history, its commitment to scholarship, and its knowledgeable and dedicated staff make it the ideal place to conduct this sort of project. Special thanks are due David Buisseret, Director of the library's Hermon Dunlap Smith Center for the History of Cartography, for his contribution to the continuation of the project, and Richard H. Brown, Academic Vice President, for his stalwart support of the project and his role in bringing the work to fruition. Newberry volunteer Don Burke assisted with measuring county areas and proofreading; Louise Alcorn, from Grinnell College, a Student Fellow of the Newberry Library-Associated Colleges of the Midwest/Great Lakes Colleges Association Humanities Seminar in the fall of 1990, carefully checked many citations; and Elizabeth Worzalla, from Lawrence University, a Student Fellow in the fall 1992 Humanities Seminar, assisted with proofreading, map labeling, checking abbreviations, and other tasks. Adrian Ettlinger helped proofread the maps and pointed out the short-lived attempt in 1810 to extend Orleans Territory eastward along the Gulf coast to the Perdido River. Research Associate Peggy Tuck Sinko compiled all the data on the censuses.

Editorial Assistants Karen Lewak and David Strass merit special recognition. Not only did they format and type (and retype) the chronologies and text for numerous states, they also maintained the master bibliography of over two thousand items, and their editing, proofreading, and checking of the bibliography and citations contributed greatly to the accuracy and readability of the information presented here.

Because the Newberry Library lacks the resources of a full-fledged law library, the atlas staff made frequent use of the Northwestern University Law Library and the Cook County Law Library, which generously facilitated use of their collections. Marsha Selmer, Curator of Maps at the University of Illinois at Chicago, rendered valuable assistance with large-scale topographic maps, both new and old.

Our editors at Simon & Schuster Macmillan, Editorial Director Paul Bernabeo and project editor Dorothy Kachouh, have worked hard to make this atlas the best possible, and they, together with designer Howard Petlack of A Good Thing, Inc., have contributed greatly to the attractive appearance, clarity, and ease of use of this and all other volumes.

County officials, local historians, and librarians throughout Alabama contributed to the completeness and accuracy of the data and maps in this atlas by answering queries regarding dates and the details of local geography. Special thanks are due Yvonne Crumpler, Birmingham Public Library; C. Warren Weaver, Blount County Records Administrator and Archivist; Norwood A. Kerr, Alabama Department of Archives and History; Dan Crittenden, Walker County Mapping Department; Marilyn Davis Barefield, Birmingham; Bette Sue McElroy, Gadsden Public Library; and Deanna M. Slappey, Anniston.

These acknowledgments would be woefully incomplete without special recognition of the important part played by the Reference Materials Program of the National Endowment for the Humanities, an independent federal agency, whose grants have substantially supported the compilation of this atlas. Thanks also to the May Foundation for additional financial support.

Introduction

Counties in the United States are, with few exceptions, administrative subdivisions of their states, not self-governing municipalities, such as cities, towns, and boroughs. Their historical significance lies in their important functions, their nearly universal distribution, and their protean nature. United States counties and their equivalents (i.e., parishes in Louisiana and independent cities in Maryland, Missouri, Nevada, and Virginia) today number more than three thousand and embrace within their bounds every part of the forty-eight conterminous states and Hawaii. (Connecticut abolished its counties as operational institutions in 1960 but retained them as geographical units; Alaska is the only state never to have had counties.) County functions vary from state to state, and there is no standard system of operation. Nonetheless, counties everywhere provide judicial administration, and in most states they are responsible for a number of other important functions and services as well. The county's role is smallest in New England, larger in the Middle Atlantic and North Central states, and greatest in the South and West.

The county system was transplanted to North America by early colonists from England. Following the practice in the home country, colonial laws and policies were administered through a network of county courts by sheriffs, judges, and justices of the peace. The county's judicial functions grew from law enforcement and simple legal proceedings to probating wills and handling a variety of legal instruments, like deeds and certificates of marriage. The recording of births and deaths was a natural addition, and eventually much of the work of census taking was organized around the county. The courthouse, therefore, became both the local seat of justice and the repository of official information concerning every individual within the county's jurisdiction.

Counties also acquired many of the attributes of local government. Welfare administration, road and bridge maintenance, property evaluation and tax collection, and numerous other tasks all became county responsibilities. Although not a product of voluntary action by local inhabitants, the county eventually came under the control of elected officials answerable only to a local constituency. Outside the limits of densely settled urban areas, counties were the obvious geographical units for organizing representation in the provincial, territorial, and state legislatures and for building congressional districts. One result of these developments was that, in the nineteenth century, counties became the grassroots centers for political parties.

Following close on the heels of independence from Great Britain, American settlers began pushing westward onto land formerly occupied only by Indians, and state and territorial governments laid out counties ahead of them. Such acts were more than posturing claims of jurisdiction or fortuitous arrangements; those states and territories were trying to attract settlers with a promise of the orderly provision of governmental services. Unfortunately, a frontier county created in advance of settlement was usually little more than a name and a boundary description in the laws; frequently it was not technically organized and nearly as often was attached to a fully operational county for services and record keeping. Some of these counties remained attached and dependent for years, while others experienced such rapid population growth that they were soon organized and separated from their hosts. This atlas shows not only the territory within each county's prescribed boundaries but also maps the arrangement of any temporary attachments. Attachments are not included in calculations of the host county's area.

The functional importance of counties is not matched by a comparable geographic stability. Few, indeed, are the counties that today have their original shapes and areas. Some boundaries change when existing counties are divided to make new ones; other changes may be intended by legislators to serve the convenience of constituents or to raise the efficiency of government, or sometimes for less admirable purposes. The original counties of any state are few in number and may not even cover all of the state's territory. As population increases and spreads, as industry, agriculture, and transportation grow, so do the counties. Before long no place is outside the jurisdiction of one county or another. County lines form a network that divides the land in numerous ways, sometimes along prominent physical features or sometimes into areas whose sizes and shapes have been designed to optimize travel to the county seat or to facilitate control of the electorate. Most important, regardless of design, is the simple fact of change.

These changes in county shapes and sizes make it difficult to interpret county-level historical data. Did the size of the county's population really change or did the county merely gain or lose territory between census enumerations—or both? Could politicians have gerrymandered the state legislature or congressional delegation without explicitly changing the electoral laws, possibly by unobtrusively rearranging the county lines that underlay the system of electoral districts? There are many issues besides statistical shifts that draw researchers to counties. Genealogists, family historians, and attorneys, among others, often need evidence of specific events at particular locations and times—perhaps the initial gathering of a church, a land sale, a death, or a marriage. Knowing a locality's current county may not be adequate, and discovering which county had jurisdiction in the past may be the key to finding old records. State and local agencies may need to examine past attempts at judicial or administrative reorganization and reform. Nearly everyone concerned with local, state, and national politics of the past needs to know what happened to the county configurations in order to judge the significance, and perhaps the causes, of changes in electoral behavior.

The practice of temporarily attaching some sparsely settled counties and non-county areas to fully operational and self-sustaining counties implies some interesting questions concerning the conduct of research in county records, the administration of county services, the organization of census data, and a number of other issues. For example, how extensive a region did a sheriff have to cover when his county became responsible for one or more attached counties? Researchers investigating an event in county A at the time it was attached to county B may find the records still in the archives of B.

Working with county-based information, especially statistics, has often meant an abundance of topical data and a dearth of information about the configurations of the counties. One can only guess how many researchers have had to interrupt their thematic analyses to piece together the boundary changes of pertinent counties, or how many have revised or abandoned particular projects because compiling the boundary changes loomed as too formidable an obstacle.

History of This Atlas

The impetus for this endeavor came early in the 1970s during the creation of the *Atlas of Early American History: The Revolutionary Era, 1760–1790* (1976) by a team of historians and cartographers, led by editor-in-chief Lester J. Cappon, in Chicago at the Newberry Library. When the staff compiled reference maps of the British North American colonies in 1775, they discovered that, contrary to expectations, there was no authoritative reference source for the historical county lines. There are, instead, a number of separate compilations covering some but not all of the original thirteen states. The quality of those works ranges from superb to unreliable, and they lack anything approaching a common standard or format.

The *Atlas of Early American History* was succeeded by a project to compile the much needed reference work on county development. That original project was conceived as an experiment that would bypass conventional publication by creating a computerized, historical, cartographic data file, thereby making the boundary information available exclusively in a new and flexible format at supposedly reduced costs. The project succeeded in compiling and encoding the data for fourteen eastern and central states, and the data file is distributed by the Inter-university Consortium for Political and Social Research, Ann Arbor, Michigan. The original dissemination plan was broadened to include printing the data in maps and text (e.g., chronology, county code lists), thus providing in addition to the data file both a printed guide for those who had access to computer facilities and a conventional atlas for those without such equipment. The resulting work, the *Historical Atlas and Chronology of County Boundaries, 1788–1980*, edited by John H. Long, was published in five volumes by G.K. Hall in 1984. In the current project, that five-volume work has been treated as any other secondary compilation of county creations and changes (see Sources, below). Except for republication of the data file codes in the appropriate state volumes (as an aid to potential users of the cartographic data file) this *Atlas of Historical County Boundaries*—a projected forty-volume work—is a thoroughly new atlas with a broader range of subject matter than the 1984 work, as well as a different format and completely new maps and text.

Also in 1984, Thomas D. Rabenhorst and Carville V. Earle of the Geography Department at the University of Maryland, Baltimore County, produced the *Historical U.S. County Outline Map Collection, 1840–1980*, an expanded set of fifteen unbound maps derived from county outline maps for the federal census years 1840 to 1900 published in the early twentieth century by the U.S. Department of Agriculture. By the 1980s, those federal maps had been so long out of print that they had become virtually unknown. In 1987 William Thorndale and William Dollarhide published their *Map Guide to the U.S. Federal Censuses, 1790–1920*, which provides well-designed state outline maps of both modern and historical counties and gives sources and a description of the authors' methodology. Both of these publications provide only small-scale outline maps for a limited number of dates, leaving the need for a comprehensive and detailed reference unfilled.

This atlas has been designed to leave no gaps. The chronological range for each state extends back to its earliest county, at least, and runs up to 1990. Geographically the range includes all territory within each state's bounds in 1990, plus (for the relevant historical period) any other territory that may have been within its jurisdiction at an earlier time. Alabama, for example, was originally part of Mississippi Territory. Counties which are now in Mississippi, but once overlapped the current geographical boundaries of Alabama, are shown on maps in this volume. The table of contents lists all counties included in the volume, identifying those created by another state or now located beyond the state's boundaries; cross-references are provided for counties that have been renamed.

A secondary goal of this atlas is to provide a frame of reference for understanding boundary changes. The maps and chronologies in the volumes of this atlas answer questions of what, when, and where. Venturing to explain why and how changes occurred requires more information and a different focus for the research. Readers who undertake that line of inquiry will find value in the information and references provided here.

While the strictly defined purpose and scope of this project preclude additional research and writing for analytical monographs and narrative histories, compilers uncover more information than is needed to draw the maps and describe the boundary changes. None of this information has been ignored. The bibliographies list a wide range of materials that were useful in compiling the changes and drawing the maps. The chronologies cover more than boundary changes alone, including county name changes, unsuccessful authorizations for new counties, and redefinitions and clarifications of existing lines. Line shifts too small to map at the scales employed here are also regularly identified.

The structural heart of this atlas for each state, the component on which all others depend, is the *consolidated chronology* in which all boundary changes and related events for the state are brought together in a single chronological list. The entries not only tell what happened but refer readers to the sources for each event. Following the consolidated chronology is a section that presents the counties one by one. Here the reader will find *individual county chronologies* and complementary sets of *individual county maps* that depict the various configurations of every county. As an aid to readers concerned with statistical densities and other areal data, figures for *county areas* (not including temporary attachments) accompany the individual county chronologies. A final topical section covers all censuses in the state's history, including state and colonial or territorial censuses or equivalents (e.g., tax or poll lists), in addition to the more familiar federal enumerations. In this section the reader will find a *table of censuses* describing the available data and a matching series of *census outline maps*.

The maps are arranged in two series, as indicated above, to serve different purposes. The first series of maps is designed to show the historical jurisdictions of individual counties. With few exceptions there is a separate map for each different configuration of the county lines, so readers can easily see the exact jurisdictional area of the county and the places it encompassed at any time. Most of these maps are derived from the U.S. Geological Survey's State Base series at the scale of 1:500,000 or about eight miles per inch (this atlas's standard base for individual counties), and those maps display considerable detail: water features, cities and towns, state and county boundaries, and, when available, the lines of the federal land survey. Drawing the historical boundary lines on these modern base maps permits a clear comparison of old and new and affords the reader a familiar context and a dependable reference system with which he or she can study the historical boundaries. In most cases, for counties too large to fit on a single page at the standard scale, a small-scale map (1:2,500,000—about one fifth the scale of the standard maps) is used instead. Small-scale maps are also used to show how unorganized counties and non-county areas were temporarily attached to fully functioning host counties.

A second series of maps presents small-scale outline maps that match available census data. Some maps cover more than one census because during the intervening period either there were no territorial changes or changes were too small to show on these maps. Readers should consult the individual county maps for small changes.

Sources

The principal sources for historical county boundary lines in the United States are colonial, territorial, and state laws. Occasionally, in the earliest days of a proprietary colony or a territory, counties were created or changed by executive proclamation; in the nineteenth century a few counties were created by new state constitutions. Courts or special arbitrators sometimes settled jurisdictional disputes at the international, state, and county levels. The number of changes produced outside the legislative process does not, however, represent a large proportion of the total changes for any state.

The compilers have relied upon the provincial, territorial, and state laws because counties are the creatures of their states, created and for the most part controlled by the state legislatures. State laws are authoritative and convenient, relatively compact and coherent as a corpus, and available throughout the country. Session laws are the immediate, official products of each session of the legislature. Sets of statutes at large are authoritative and convenient, though not available for all states or for all periods. Rationalized sets of state laws, usually termed revised codes, pass through the same legislative process as individual session laws and are equally authoritative. Apparent alterations wrought by codifying a state's laws are infrequent and usually accidental. In Alabama the revised and annotated codes usually do not include boundary legislation.

Before codification became a regular feature of the legislative process, a few individuals compiled and published collections of state laws. The most famous is William W. Hening, whose thirteen volumes of *Statutes at Large; Being a Collection of All the Laws of Virginia, from the First Session of the Legislature in the Year 1619 [to 1792]*, published in Richmond, Va., 1819–1823, have become a classic and a standard. Some of these works were commissioned or at least sanctioned by the legislatures, but in all cases they are recognized and accepted as reliable and authoritative. Harry Toulmin's compilations of laws of Mississippi Territory (1807) and laws of Alabama (1823), along with *Statutes of the Mississippi Territory* (the 1816 compilation often attributed to Edward Turner), proved very helpful in reconstructing early boundaries in Alabama.

Collections of pertinent sections of county boundary laws, such as the Historical Records Survey of Mississippi's *State and County Boundaries of Mississippi* (1942) are convenient but demand caution. There is a potential for error in transcription, as well as the possibility that valuable information (e.g., an effective date) may be lost in the editorial process of excerpting the selected passages. Such a compilation can be a marvelous convenience for the researcher, once it has been checked against the session laws and has been found reliable. There are compilations of county creations and changes for a number of states, but they vary greatly in content and in accuracy. It is virtually impossible to judge their reliability until much of the work has been replicated. These secondary sources, therefore, are useful chiefly as guides to the primary laws, proclamations, and decisions.

Although all works used to determine the courses of county boundary lines appear in the bibliography, several deserve special mention. Virginia O. Foscue's *Place Names in Alabama* (1989) and William A. Read's *Indian Place Names in Alabama* (1937, rev. ed., 1984) identify places that have changed names or become extinct. Local histories also were very useful for identifying places and people in Alabama, and sometimes also revealed the events behind boundary changes. Among the most helpful publications were Marilyn Davis Barefield's compilations of Alabama federal land office records. Alabama often used individual residences to delineate county boundary lines. Locating the property of individuals who lived 100 or 150 years ago is frequently unfeasible; Barefield's volumes made it possible to identify dozens of past property owners and to draw historical boundary lines with a much higher degree of accuracy than could otherwise have been achieved.

The histories of United States international and state boundaries, unlike those of county lines, have been thoroughly described and documented in a number of publications. Without the need for further original research at these levels, staff historians have relied heavily upon secondary sources for changes in national, colonial, territorial, and state lines.

Among the most useful modern sources are the large-scale, up-to-date county maps usually published by state departments of transportation or by the individual counties. Used regularly for a number of different purposes, both official and unofficial, such maps normally are extremely reliable compilations of the details of boundaries, roads, natural features, and other landmarks.

Historical maps do not frequently play a large role in this sort of work. Occasionally they are indispensable for lost landmarks and names no longer in use, but seldom for interpretations of boundary descriptions. Throughout the seventeenth and eighteenth centuries, mapmakers knew little about the lay of the land and had to work with relatively inaccurate instruments and data. During the nineteenth century, maps improved with the surveying of the land and advancements in cartography. Nevertheless, maps from the late nineteenth century may have limited research value because boundary landmarks employed at that time often survive on modern maps. In any case, it is important to remember that a map is, by its nature, more like a secondary work than a primary source.

Sometimes errors on old maps can benefit research. When a boundary description cannot be plotted on a modern base map or does not seem to make sense, the flaw may lie not in the description but in the geographic notions upon which it was based. If the errors on an old map accurately reflect accepted ideas and knowledge, however mistaken they may have been, that map may be the key to the true meaning of contemporaneous boundary descriptions.

The historical maps most frequently consulted for place locations were John Melish's *Map of Alabama* (1819), the map of Alabama in *North American Atlas* (1842) compiled by Sidney Edward Morse, and Henry S. Tanner's map of Georgia and Alabama in his *New American Atlas . . .* (c. 1823).

The table of censuses in this atlas does not document the well-known federal enumerations, but it does help readers find extant provincial, territorial, and state statistics and/or records containing the names of individuals, whether in a publication or in an institution. Whenever possible, the citation directs the reader to Henry J. Dubester's widely available *State Censuses: An Annotated Bibliography of Censuses of Population Taken after the Year 1790 by States and Territories of the United States* (1948), rather than to the document (usually a state government publication) in which the data actually appear. For example, for the 1844 Alabama state census, the reader is referred simply to page 1 of Dubester, which provides a detailed reference to the *Tabular Statement of the Census of Alabama, Taken in the Year 1844*, where the statistics were published. This approach, it is hoped, keeps the citations brief and clear.

The manner in which sources are described in the bibliography, the citations of the consolidated chronology, and the table of abbreviations is a composite style fashioned from the guidelines set out in the fourteenth edition of the University of Chicago Press's *Chicago Manual of Style for Authors, Editors, and Copywriters* (Chicago, 1993) and, for legal sources, from the fifteenth edition of *Bluebook: A Uniform System of Citation* (Cambridge, Mass., 1991), compiled jointly by the editors of *Columbia Law Review, Harvard Law Review, University of Pennsylvania Law Review,* and *Yale Law Journal.*

Procedures

There appears to be more than one way to compile the changes in county lines. One attractive approach is starting in the present and working back to the beginning. The most appealing aspect of working from present to past is the apparent logic of the approach—something like following the branches of a family tree back down to its roots or taking down a building brick by brick. But these analogies are misleading. The current array of counties was not constructed by the process of accretion that is at the heart of house-building, nor is it like a genealogical diagram in which changes occur only through the addition of new family members. Trying to dismantle the present to reach the past usually yields little more than frustration or error.

In this project, the compilers map county boundary changes in chronological order, a procedure that provides a built-in checking mechanism. By using a modern map as a base and plotting boundary changes from the past to the present, it is easy to compare the compiler's version of each county's final set of lines with its current configuration. If the two are not the same, there must be an error on the modern map or the compiler has made a mistake, either missing a change or plotting a line incorrectly. Whatever the cause, therefore, a mismatch at the end of research and sketching automatically reveals a problem that must be resolved.

Working directly from originals or photocopies of the verbal boundary descriptions in the laws, the researcher plots the lines on a compilation sheet of tracing paper laid over a base map of the state. These are the graphic equivalents of notes, and the linework is always accompanied by some text, if only the county name, the nature of the change, and the effective date. As each change is plotted, the compiler writes a descriptive entry for the state's boundary chronology and a brief citation to the source of information. Reading straight through the session laws of a state is normally unnecessary; in Alabama, however, it was unavoidable because the titles of acts and the annual indexes do not indicate all changes. Sometimes changes in county boundaries are hidden in laws on other topics, as in laws changing the official status of a place from town to borough, establishing a county seat, or providing for the maintenance of roads and bridges. When it becomes clear that a change has been missed, the compiler broadens the search to include enactments on related subjects.

With few exceptions, all boundary changes have been mapped. Occasionally it has been necessary to use an asterisk or similar device to indicate the approximate location, along the existing boundary, of a change too small to draw with lines. Changes of unusual proportions (one dimension small, the other large) cannot be represented at all on the maps used here, for example, a change that straightens slight irregularities in a long boundary or that shifts a boundary from the center of a stream to one bank or the other. Another unmappable exception is any small change whose location cannot be determined, such as an individual farm identified only by the owner's name or a small area identified only by a landmark now lost. Each unmapped change is noted in the chronology

Areas of counties are calculated by tracing the boundaries on the individual county maps with a digitizer connected to a microcomputer; data from the digitizer are processed by a program that calculates the areas. In order to avoid having the figures appear more precise than is possible, the numbers are rounded to the nearest ten. The county areas published in current reference works commonly are for land area, excluding all bodies of water larger than a certain minimum size. In this atlas figures for present areas normally match those land-only areas; when there is a difference, the number here usually is larger. It is not difficult to avoid counting large water areas by tracing the shorelines of very large lakes and the seacoast, instead of the boundary lines that delineate offshore jurisdiction. No attempt is made to measure and subtract smaller lakes and ponds, nor to add small islands. Thus, for example, the counties of Minnesota are measured without subtracting any of the state's thousands of lakes, but the state's jurisdiction over the waters of Lake Superior is excluded.

Special Topics for Alabama

In 1784 a group of land speculators from Tennessee and North Carolina attempted to create a Georgia county along the north side of the Tennessee River, near Muscle Shoals, in what later became Alabama. They petitioned the Georgia legislature requesting the creation of this county, which they proposed to call Houston (not to be confused with the present Alabama and Georgia counties of the same name). The legislature did not create the county as requested, but authorized the appointment of seven commissioners to "ascertain the Quantity, Quality and Circumstances of the aforesaid lands," and to grant warrants of survey. The unauthorized county of Houston sent a representative to the Georgia legislature in an attempt to legitimize the county, but he was not seated, and in August 1786 a bill to create the county was defeated by a vote of twenty-three to twenty-six.

The first years of the nineteenth century saw the commencement of the federal land survey in present Alabama, and federal survey lines were soon incorporated into county boundary descriptions. Many Alabama county boundaries run along township, range, and section lines and can be drawn with great precision. More difficult are boundaries along mountain ridges, through valleys, along roads, and around individual dwellings.

Surveying errors also played a part in establishing county boundary lines. One example is a portion of the Cherokee-Calhoun boundary that does not match the legal description. First described in 1832 when Benton County (now Calhoun) was created, the boundary was supposed to run due east to the Georgia state line but the surveyor apparently ran it somewhat south of east, and the line continues to follow that southeasterly course today.

A number of Alabama county boundary changes could not be conclusively documented. For example, when Crenshaw County was created in 1866, an entire thirty-six-square-mile township of Montgomery County was assigned to Crenshaw, but all evidence indicates that this provision of Crenshaw's creation was never implemented and that the area actually remained a part of Montgomery County. A similar case is found along the Pike-Bullock line, where boundary descriptions from various laws do not precisely describe the accepted present-day boundary. One of the most puzzling situations involves a three-square-mile area of Walker County along the Tuscaloosa line. This territory was a part of Tuscaloosa at its creation in 1818, but through 1926 both counties assessed taxes there. Even with the assistance of present county officials it was not possible to establish precisely when and by what authority this area shifted to Walker, although the change may date from a badly flawed 1850 law annexing three one-square-mile sections located in the middle of Tuscaloosa County to Walker.

In a couple of instances it has been necessary to date a change based on its appearance on a contemporary map. For instance, around the turn of the century a small section of the Wilcox-Clarke line was changed from its previous course along an old Indian boundary line to run along land survey lines. Maps of the 1880s and 1890s show the boundary following the Indian line, and the annual Rand McNally commercial atlases also show the Indian boundary until the 1902 edition, when the present line first appears. The change to the modern line is thus dated 1901, although it has not been possible to document the exact time and circumstances of the change.

Alabama boundary law has a special term, *liners*, for those people who live on or near a county boundary line. Although people like liners are found in the county boundary descriptions of many states, in Alabama they appear with remarkable frequency, and in 1895 the legislature formally defined them and spelled out procedures for handling their requests for boundary changes (Ala. Acts 1894, bien. sess., no. 199/p. 346). Named liners first appear in legislation in the 1840s. Legislation for liners generally took the form of local relief acts, introduced on behalf of one or more named individuals who wished to establish residence in a particular county. The reasons behind such requests can only be surmised: some changes made it easier for people to fulfill community obligations, such as militia duty or road work, other changes may have saved people from having to cross a difficult river or mountain range to reach the county seat, and in other cases the change may have served the convenience of taxpayers and tax collectors alike by consolidating property in a single county.

Legislation concerning liners varied. In some cases individuals were made citizens of a particular county but the county line was not shifted; in other cases individuals were made citizens of one county but paid taxes in the adjoining county; and in still other cases the boundary line was actually changed. Only those acts that actually altered the boundary line are included in this volume.

No doubt a certain amount of influence was required to persuade a legislator to introduce such a piece of legislation, and it should be no surprise that liners often were local officials, justices of the peace, and major property owners. One interesting case involved H. J. Springfield, a scalawag elected to the state legislature in 1868 from St. Clair County. After the election, someone discovered that Springfield, who resided with his brother Thomas M. Springfield, actually lived over the line in Etowah County. On 17 December 1868 the legislature passed an act "that the boundary line between the counties of Etowah and St. Clair, be changed, so as to include Thomas M. Springfield as a citizen of St. Clair county." Rather than deny H. J. Springfield his seat, the legislature simply shifted the county boundary line, effectively moving him into the correct legislative district. In the few cases when liners' property or homes could not be identified, the chronology indicates "location unknown."

The disruption and disarray that characterized post–Civil War politics in Alabama, as various factions vied for control of the state government, affected the state's county boundaries. The 1866–1867 legislature created Baine, Colbert, and Jones counties, but in November 1867 the constitutional convention abolished all three. Political fortunes soon shifted, and each county was revived in identical or similar form. In 1868 Sanford was created with the same territory as Jones, while Etowah was created in the same general area as Baine. Colbert, named for two Chickasaw Indian brothers, was re-created in 1870.

Alabama also provides the unique instance of a murder case nullifying a county boundary line change. In 1903 Calhoun County gained a little territory from Cleburne County; legislators voting for the change were unaware that this reduced Cleburne County to less than the minimum area of five hundred square miles required by the state constitution. In December 1905 William Kline was arrested for murdering John Phillips in the area that had recently been added to Calhoun County, a crime for which he was subsequently found guilty and sentenced to twenty-five years in prison. Kline appealed the case to the Alabama Supreme Court on the grounds that he was tried in the wrong court since the boundary change was illegal. The Supreme Court agreed (Kline v. The State, *Ala. Rpts.*, 146:1), declaring the boundary change unconstitutional and void and remanding the case to the Circuit Court of Calhoun County. Records indicate that the Calhoun County Sheriff was sent to find Kline and take him to Cleburne County for a new hearing, but the sources are silent regarding the final disposition of the case.

Base Maps

This project relies on maps published by the U.S. Geological Survey. Most of the individual county maps show the historical boundary drawn on a special version of the U.S.G.S. State Base map of Alabama published at the scale of 1:500,000 or eight miles per inch. This map is dated 1966, and there have been only three mappable changes between 1966 and 1990. These special versions of the 1:500,000-scale maps, products of the Geological Survey's custom printing service, are designed to be as uncluttered as possible without losing essential features. The special printing for this atlas has the coastline, rivers, outlines of lakes, and the names of water features, all reduced in blackness by a fifty-percent, bi-angle screen; place names, longitude and latitude lines, state and county boundary lines, and land survey lines (when available) are all in solid black. Omitted from the regular version of the map of Alabama, therefore, are contour lines and miscellaneous symbols.

The small-scale maps used to show counties too large to fit on a single page using the 1:500,000-scale bases are essentially the same as those used to depict both the state's county network for the various censuses and the attachments of unorganized counties and non-county areas. All these maps are redrawings of the pertinent sections of the U.S. Geological Survey's map of the United States at the scale of 1:2,500,000 or about forty miles per inch. This map is dated 1972, and nearly all changes in the county lines since then are too small to show; changes large enough to map have been incorporated into the redrawing.

Although errors on these federal maps are rare, there are two on the Alabama map: one occurs between Cherokee and Calhoun counties where the boundary line actually runs without the "jog" shown on the U.S. Geological Survey map; the other is between Macon and Montgomery counties where the boundary should follow Line Creek all the way to the Bullock County line but is not depicted that way. In both cases the boundary is correctly shown on present county highway maps and in this atlas.

All the maps in this atlas have been reduced from their original size for publication. Determining distances accurately is made possible by the graphic bar scales provided for the maps. While each small-scale map is accompanied by its own scale bar, the standard maps of individual counties have their graphic scale printed across the bottom of the page.

Dates

Every effort has been made to give the day, month, and year (e.g., 25 February 1785) for all county creations, boundary changes, and other events in this atlas. Occasionally it is impossible to date an event so precisely, but a reasonable estimate is possible. When the precise date is not known or an approximate date is more appropriate, the date is generalized to the month and year (e.g., February 1785) or to the year alone. A lack of evidence may make it impossible to give any date at all for a county's creation, and its occurrence can only be confirmed by the record of a later, related happening, such as the appointment of a sheriff. In such a situation, the date of the later event is used with the simple addition of "by" (e.g., by 25 February 1785) to indicate that the county creation or other event occurred no later than that date and probably earlier.

Several dates may be associated with the creation of a county or a change in county lines. To many individuals the date that makes the most sense is the one when people began to observe the change, but in most cases that date is impossible to ascertain. An alternative is the date on which the law effecting the change passed the legislature or was approved by the governor. The date of passage is an important reference because it helps identify the law; now as in the past, references to a law often include the date of passage. Most other compilations of county changes have adopted the date of passage as their standard for when change occurred, but it is not always sufficient.

The dating standard in this atlas is the legally effective date of change, whether it be for the creation of a new county or for the alteration of lines between existing counties. Through the colonial period and into the nineteenth century, the date a law passed was generally the date it went into effect. As the nineteenth century progressed, legislators recognized the importance of preparing for the establishment of a new county organization or for the shift in jurisdiction that accompanies boundary changes. Some laws, therefore, began to carry two dates: one marking the passage of the law and the other specifying when the line change or new county creation would go into effect. If the date of passage and effective date are different, the law gives both.

In Alabama the legally effective date of a county creation is the same as the legislation date in all but three cases. The effective dates of a number of boundary changes between existing counties are not the same as the legislation dates, although in most cases the difference is only a matter of weeks, usually due to a requirement that the prospective change be approved by a local referendum. Voters sometimes rejected a proposed change, thus nullifying the act; in 1879 the legislature authorized Geneva County to gain from Henry, Coffee to gain from Geneva, and the name of Geneva to be changed to Gordon, but no changes actually took place because voters did not approve. In another case, De Kalb was to gain from Jackson in 1870, but there is no evidence that the prescribed election was ever held. In still another case, a transfer of territory from Shelby to Jefferson, authorized in 1831, did not become effective until 1833, after the next state census.

Using effective dates means that many of the dates in this atlas may disagree with dates in other references. As an aid to appreciating how great the differences between the two dates can be and to help correlate the data in this book with other publications, this atlas offers a *table of county creations* that gives both the date of passage and the effective date for all county creations.

Dating events before 1752 is a problem because the calendar then in use is very different from the one in use today. Whereas by 1600 most of Europe had adopted the Gregorian calendar, as the modern system of reckoning the days is called, England observed the Julian calendar until 2 September 1752. For the purposes of this atlas, the chief differences between the two systems are, first, numbering the days and, second, designating the change from one year to the next. There has been no attempt to convert the dates of one system to those of the other. Differences in numbering days, therefore, are effectively ignored; whatever day and month are given in a source are the day and month used here, regardless of whether the document was written in England or some other country, before or after 1752. Under the old Julian calendar the last day of the year was 24 March and the first day was 25 March, which means that in England and its colonies the day after 24 March 1750 was 25 March 1751. This atlas follows the convention of showing both years for dates that fall within the period from 1 January through 24 March when the different calendars call for different years. Thus, successive dates before England's adoption of the Gregorian calendar would occur as follows: the day after 24 March 1688/1689 would be 25 March 1689; the day after 31 December 1689 would be 1 January 1689/1690. About three months later would come 24 March 1689/1690, and the next day after that would be 25 March 1690.

Abbreviations

Abbreviated References in Citations

Many citations identify works by author or by author and short title, but most employ abbreviations. Authors and titles for abbreviated references are given below; see the bibliography at the back of the atlas for full descriptions of these works.

Ala. Acts	Alabama. *Acts of Alabama.*
Ala. Geneal. Reg.	*Alabama Genealogical Register.*
Ala. Hist. Quart.	*Alabama Historical Quarterly.*
Ala. Rpts.	Alabama Supreme Court. *Alabama Reports.*
Ala. Terr. Acts	Alabama Territory. *Acts of Alabama Territory.*
HRS Ala., *Colbert*	Historical Records Survey, Alabama. *Colbert County (Tuscumbia).*
Miss. Terr. Stat.	Mississippi Territory. *Statutes of the Mississippi Territory.*
Orleans Terr. Acts	Orleans Territory. *Acts of the Territory of Orleans.*
Rowland, *Miss. Terr. Arch.*	Rowland, Dunbar, ed. *Mississippi Territorial Archives, 1798–1803.*
Terr. Papers U.S.	*Territorial Papers of the United States.*
U.S. Stat.	United States. *Statutes at Large of the United States of America, 1789–1873.*

Abbreviations to Be Found in This Atlas

Except where noted, plurals are formed by adding s.

A.D.	*anno Domini*, in the year of our Lord	comp.	compiler
adj.	adjourned	Conn.	Connecticut
Ala.	Alabama	corres.	correspondence
Ala. Dept. of Arch. and Hist.	Alabama Department of Archives and History	Cr.	Creek
		D.C.	District of Columbia
ann.	annotated, annual	Dec.	December
Apr.	April	Del.	Delaware
arch.	archives	dept.	department
Ariz.	Arizona	diss.	dissertation
Ark.	Arkansas	doc.	document
art.	article	ed.	edition, editor
assy.	assembly	e.g.	*exempli gratia*, for example
Aug.	August	et al.	*et alii*, and others
bien.	biennial	etc.	*et cetera*, and so forth
bros.	brothers	exec.	executive
c., ca.	*circa*, about	ext.	extra, extraordinary
Calif.	California	Feb.	February
ch.	chapter	Fla.	Florida
co.	company, county	Ft.	Fort
col.	Colonial	Ga.	Georgia
Colo.	Colorado	gen.	general

geneal.	genealogical, genealogy	Ord. of St. Conv.	Ordinances of State Convention
Gov.	Governor	Oreg.	Oregon
hist.	historical, history	p. (plural, pp.)	page
HRS	Historical Records Survey	Pa.	Pennsylvania
I. (plural, Is.)	Island	par.	paragraph
Id.	Idaho	Ph.D.	*Philosophiae Doctor*, Doctor of Philosophy
i.e.	*id est*, that is	pl.	plate
Ill.	Illinois	Ply.	Plymouth
Ind.	Indiana	priv.	private
Jan.	January	pt.	part
jour.	journal	pub.	public
Jr.	Junior	quad.	quadrennial
Jul.	July	quart.	quarter, quarterly
Jun.	June	R.	River
Kans.	Kansas	rec.	record
Ky.	Kentucky	reg.	register, regular
La.	Louisiana	res.	resolution
loc.	local	rev.	revised
Mar.	March	R.I.	Rhode Island
Mass.	Massachusetts	rpt.	report
Md.	Maryland	S.C.	South Carolina
Me.	Maine	S.Dak.	South Dakota
mi.	mile	sec.	section
Mich.	Michigan	Sec. State	Secretary of State
Minn.	Minnesota	Sen.	Senate
misc.	miscellaneous	Sep.	September
Miss.	Mississippi	ser.	series
Mo.	Missouri	sess.	session
Mont.	Montana	spec.	special
MS	manuscript	sq.	square
Mt.	Mount, Mountain	sq. mi.	square miles
n.	north, note	St.	Saint, State, Street
N.C.	North Carolina	stat.	statute, statutes
n.d.	no date	Ste.	Sainte
N.Dak.	North Dakota	Tenn.	Tennessee
Nebr.	Nebraska	terr.	territorial, territory
Nev.	Nevada	Tex.	Texas
N.H.	New Hampshire	Univ.	University
N.J.	New Jersey	U.S.	United States
N.Mex.	New Mexico	U.S.G.S.	United States Geological Survey
no.	number	v.	versus
Nov.	November	Va.	Virginia
n.p.	no place	vol.	volume
n.s.	new series	Vt.	Vermont
N.W. Terr.	Northwest Territory	Wash.	Washington
N.Y.	New York	Wis.	Wisconsin
Oct.	October	W.Va.	West Virginia
Okla.	Oklahoma	Wyo.	Wyoming
opp.	opposite		

Alabama County Creations

County	Source	Dates	
		Authorization	Creation Effective
ADAMS (Miss.)	Rowland, *Miss. Terr. Arch.*, 126–128	2 Apr 1799	same
AUTAUGA	Ala. Terr. Acts 1818, 2d sess., p. 56	21 Nov 1818	same
BAINE (extinct)*	Ala. Acts 1866, reg. sess., no. 92, sec. 1/p. 76	7 Dec 1866	same
BAKER (see CHILTON)			
BALDWIN	Toulmin, *Digest*, ch. 3/pp. 81–82	21 Dec 1809	same
BARBOUR	Ala. Acts 1832, ann. sess., no. 11, sec. 10/p. 10	18 Dec 1832	same
BENTON (see CALHOUN)			
BIBB (created as CAHAWBA)	Ala. Terr. Acts 1818, 1st sess., sec. 2/p. 30	7 Feb 1818	same
BLOUNT	Ala. Terr. Acts 1818, 1st sess., sec. 1/p. 16	6 Feb 1818	same
BULLOCK	Ala. Acts 1866, reg. sess., no. 84, sec. 1/p. 65	5 Dec 1866	same
BUTLER	Ala. Acts 1819, 1st sess., sec. 5/p. 51	13 Dec 1819	same
CAHAWBA (see BIBB)			
CALHOUN (created as BENTON)	Ala. Acts 1832, ann. sess., no. 11, sec. 1/p. 9	18 Dec 1832	same
CHAMBERS	Ala. Acts 1832, ann. sess., no. 11, sec. 6/p. 10	18 Dec 1832	same
CHEROKEE	Ala. Acts 1835, ann. sess., no. 179/p. 170	9 Jan 1836	same
CHILTON (created as BAKER)	Ala. Acts 1868, reg. sess., no. 142, sec. 1/p. 488	30 Dec 1868	same
CHOCTAW	Ala. Acts 1847, 1st bien. sess., no. 213, sec. 1/p. 306	29 Dec 1847	same
CLAIBORNE (Miss.)	Miss. Terr. Stat., p. 88	27 Jan 1802	same
CLARKE	Toulmin, *Digest*, ch. 5/p. 83	10 Dec 1812	same
CLAY	Ala. Acts 1866, reg. sess., no. 110, sec. 1/p. 92	7 Dec 1866	same
CLEBURNE	Ala. Acts 1866, reg. sess., no. 89, sec. 1/p. 71	6 Dec 1866	same
COFFEE	Ala. Acts 1841, ann. sess., no. 190, sec. 1/p. 152	29 Dec 1841	same
COLBERT*	Ala. Acts 1866, reg. sess., no. 321, sec. 1/p. 351	6 Feb 1867	same
COLBERT (re-created)*	Ala. Acts 1869, reg. sess., no. 5/p. 6	9 Dec 1869	24 Jan 1870
CONECUH	Ala. Terr. Acts 1818, 1st sess., sec. 2/p. 96	13 Feb 1818	same
COOSA	Ala. Acts 1832, ann. sess., no. 11, sec. 4/p. 9	18 Dec 1832	same
COTACO (see MORGAN)			
COVINGTON	Ala. Acts 1821, 3d sess., sec. 2/p. 71	7 Dec 1821	same
CRENSHAW	Ala. Acts 1866, reg. sess., no. 39, sec. 1/p. 38	24 Nov 1866	same
CULLMAN	Ala. Acts 1876, bien. sess., no. 56, sec. 1/p. 69	24 Jan 1877	same
DALE	Ala. Acts 1824, 6th sess., secs. 1, 18/pp. 79, 82	22 Dec 1824	17 Oct 1825

County	Source	Dates	
		Authorization	Creation Effective
DALLAS	Ala. Terr. Acts 1818, 1st sess., sec. 1/p. 47	9 Feb 1818	same
DECATUR (extinct)	Ala. Acts 1821, 3d sess., secs. 5–7/p. 72	7 Dec 1821	same
DE KALB	Ala. Acts 1835, ann. sess., no. 179/p. 170	9 Jan 1836	same
ELMORE**	Ala. Acts 1865, reg. sess., no. 312, secs. 1, 4/ pp. 484–485	15 Feb 1866	late Dec 1866
ESCAMBIA	Ala. Acts 1868, reg. sess., no. 34, sec. 1/p. 397	10 Dec 1868	same
ETOWAH*	Ala. Acts 1868, reg. sess., no. 20, sec. 1/p. 359	1 Dec 1868	same
FAYETTE	Ala. Acts 1824, 6th sess., sec. 1/p. 77	20 Dec 1824	same
FELICIANA (La., extinct)	Orleans Terr. Acts 1811, 2d sess., p. 210	7 Dec 1810	same
FRANKLIN	Ala. Terr. Acts 1818, 1st sess., sec. 3/p. 9	6 Feb 1818	same
GENEVA	Ala. Acts 1868, reg. sess., no. 110, sec. 1/p. 446	26 Dec 1868	same
GREENE (Miss.)	Toulmin, *Digest*, ch. 4/p. 82	9 Dec 1811	same
GREENE	Ala. Acts 1819, 1st sess., sec. 8/p. 52	13 Dec 1819	same
HALE	Ala. Acts 1866, reg. sess., no. 418, sec. 1/p. 477	30 Jan 1867	same
HANCOCK (see WINSTON)			
HENRY	Ala. Acts 1819, 1st sess., sec. 6/p. 51	13 Dec 1819	same
HOUSTON	Ala. Acts 1903, bien. sess., gen., no. 27/p. 44	9 Feb 1903	same
JACKSON (Miss.)	Toulmin, *Digest*, ch. 6/p. 83	18 Dec 1812	same
JACKSON	Ala. Acts 1819, 1st sess., sec. 17/p. 54	13 Dec 1819	same
JEFFERSON (Miss., created as PICKERING)	Rowland, *Miss. Terr. Arch.*, 126–128	2 Apr 1799	same
JEFFERSON	Ala. Acts 1819, 1st sess., sec. 9/p. 52	13 Dec 1819	same
JONES (extinct)*+	Ala. Acts 1866, reg. sess., no. 298, sec. 1/p. 323	4 Feb 1867	same
LAMAR (created as SANFORD)*	Ala. Acts 1868, called sess., no. 13/p. 216	8 Oct 1868	same
LAUDERDALE	Ala. Terr. Acts 1818, 1st sess., sec. 3/p. 13	6 Feb 1818	same
LAWRENCE	Ala. Terr. Acts 1818, 1st sess., sec. 2/p. 9	6 Feb 1818	same
LEE	Ala. Acts 1866, reg. sess., no. 61, sec. 1/p. 50	5 Dec 1866	same
LIMESTONE	Ala. Terr. Acts 1818, 1st sess., sec. 2/p. 13	6 Feb 1818	same
LOWNDES	Ala. Acts 1829, 11th sess., p. 25	20 Jan 1830	same
MACON	Ala. Acts 1832, ann. sess., no. 11, sec. 8/p. 10	18 Dec 1832	same
MADISON	Toulmin, *Digest*, ch. 2/pp. 80–81	13 Dec 1808	same
MARENGO	Ala. Terr. Acts 1818, 1st sess., sec. 3/p. 18	6 Feb 1818	same
MARION	Ala. Terr. Acts 1818, 1st sess., sec. 1/p. 96	13 Feb 1818	same
MARSHALL	Ala. Acts 1835, ann. sess., no. 47, sec. 1/p. 47	9 Jan 1836	same
MOBILE	*Terr. Papers U.S.*, 6:305	1 Aug 1812	same

County	Source	Dates	
		Authorization	Creation Effective
MONROE	*Terr. Papers U.S.*, 6:538	29 Jun 1815	same
MONTGOMERY	Toulmin, *Digest*, ch. 8/p. 83	6 Dec 1816	same
MORGAN (created as COTACO)	Ala. Terr. Acts 1818, 1st sess., sec. 1/p. 8	6 Feb 1818	same
PASCAGOULA (Orleans Terr., extinct)	Orleans Terr. Acts 1811, 2d sess., p. 214	4 Jan 1811	same
PERRY	Ala. Acts 1819, 1st sess., sec. 7/p. 52	13 Dec 1819	same
PICKENS	Ala. Acts 1820, 2d sess., sec. 9/p. 92	19 Dec 1820	same
PICKERING (see JEFFERSON, Miss.)			
PIKE	Ala. Acts 1821, 3d sess., sec. 4/p. 71	7 Dec 1821	same
RANDOLPH	Ala. Acts 1832, ann. sess., no. 11, sec. 3/p. 9	18 Dec 1832	same
RUSSELL	Ala. Acts 1832, ann. sess., no. 11, sec. 7/p. 10	18 Dec 1832	same
ST. CLAIR	Ala. Terr. Acts 1818, 2d sess., sec. 2/p. 19	20 Nov 1818	same
SANFORD (see LAMAR)			
SHELBY	Ala. Terr. Acts 1818, 1st sess., sec. 1/p. 29	7 Feb 1818	same
SUMTER	Ala. Acts 1832, ann. sess., no. 11, sec. 13/p. 11	18 Dec 1832	same
TALLADEGA	Ala. Acts 1832, ann. sess., no. 11, sec. 2/p. 9	18 Dec 1832	same
TALLAPOOSA	Ala. Acts 1832, ann. sess., no. 11, sec. 5/p. 9	18 Dec 1832	same
TUSCALOOSA	Ala. Terr. Acts 1818, 1st sess., sec. 2/p. 17	6 Feb 1818	same
WALKER	Ala. Acts 1823, 5th sess., sec. 1/p. 82	26 Dec 1823	same
WASHINGTON	Rowland, *Miss. Terr. Arch.*, 238–239	4 Jun 1800	same
WAYNE (Miss.)	Toulmin, *Digest*, ch. 3/pp. 81–82	21 Dec 1809	same
WILCOX	Ala. Acts 1819, 1st sess., sec. 2/p. 50	13 Dec 1819	same
WINSTON (created as HANCOCK)	Ala. Acts 1849, 2d bien. sess., no. 58/p. 90	12 Feb 1850	same

* BAINE, COLBERT, and JONES were abolished by the 1867 State Constitutional Convention. COLBERT was re-created in 1870 and JONES was re-created in 1868 as SANFORD (now LAMAR). ETOWAH was created in 1868 in the same general area where BAINE existed.

** No record of the exact date of ELMORE's creation was found.

+ JONES became extinct on 13 November 1867. Another county, COVINGTON, was briefly renamed JONES from August to October 1868.

Counties within present Alabama created by other authorities

By Mississippi Territory (1798–1817)	BALDWIN (18090 CLARKE (1812) MADISON (1808) MOBILE (1812) MONROE (1815)	MONTGOMERY (1816) WASHINGTON (1800)

Counties created by other authorities that extended into present Alabama

By Mississippi Territory (1798–1817)	ADAMS (Miss., 1799) CLAIBORNE (Miss., 1802) GREENE (Miss., 1811) JACKSON (Miss., 1812) PICKERING (now JEFFERSON, Miss., 1799) WAYNE (Miss., 1809)
By Orleans Territory (1804–1812)	FELICIANA (La., 1810) PASCAGOULA (Orleans Terr., 1811)

Consolidated Chronology of Alabama State and County Boundaries

24 March 1662/1663

King Charles II created Carolina from earlier range of Virginia territory and granted it as a proprietary colony to eight of his supporters. Limits were: on the north, the north end of Lucke Island and the parallel of 36 degrees north latitude; on the west, the Pacific Ocean; and on the south, the St. Marys R. and, from that river westward, the parallel of 31 degrees north latitude. Included all of present Alabama and Mississippi north of 31 degrees north latitude. (Swindler, 7:357–358)

30 June 1665

King Charles II granted a new charter to the proprietors of Carolina, expanding jurisdiction to north and south. New boundaries were: on the north, a line from the north end of the Currituck R. westward to "Wyonoak" Creek and thence due west along the parallel of 36 degrees, 30 minutes north latitude; on the west, the Pacific Ocean; and on the south, the parallel of 29 degrees north latitude. Included all of present Alabama and Mississippi. (Swindler, 7:375)

January 1701/1702

The French erected Fort Louis de la Louisiane, near present Mobile, the first European settlement in region that became Alabama. (Hamilton, *Colonial Mobile*, 53; Higginbotham, 46–49)

1719

The French commander at New Orleans and the Spanish commander at Pensacola agreed to recognize the Perdido R. as the boundary between their jurisdictions, Louisiana and Florida, and their home governments acquiesced in the arrangement. (Cox, 8)

9 June 1732

King George II created Georgia from South Carolina and granted it as a proprietary colony in trust for 21 years. Boundaries were: on the north, the Savannah R.; on the south, the Altamaha R.; on the west, the Pacific Ocean. Included northern portions of present Alabama and Mississippi. (Swindler, 2:437; Paullin, 27, pl. 42)

10 February 1763

Treaty of Paris, ending the Seven Years' War between Great Britain (the victor) and France and Spain, formally transferred Florida to the British and implicitly set the Mississippi R. as a new western limit for British colonies, including Georgia, whose charter bounds had technically extended to the Pacific Ocean. (Cappon, Petchenik, and Long, 1)

7 October 1763

King George III, by his Proclamation of 1763, created three new royal provinces and settled a dispute between two older ones. Relevant provisions: West Florida was created to cover the territory west of the Apalachicola R., south of 31 degrees north latitude, and east of the Mississippi R., the Iberville R., and Lake Pontchartrain, including southern parts of present Louisiana, Mississippi, Alabama, and Florida; Georgia gained the territory south of the Altamaha R. and north of Florida, thereby settling a dispute between Georgia and South Carolina and confirming Georgia's claim to all of present Alabama and Mississippi north of 31 degrees north latitude. (Cappon, Petchenik, and Long, 1, 77; Shortt and Doughty, 119–120)

July 1764

In the commission to West Florida's first governor, Great Britain redefined West Florida, extending its limits northward to a line running due east from the junction of the Yazoo and Mississippi rivers to the Chattahoochee R.; implicitly reduced western extent of Georgia and added Natchez and much of present Alabama and Mississippi to West Florida. (Cappon, Petchenik, and Long, 87)

8 May 1781

Spain captured Pensacola, successfully concluding a campaign (begun in Aug. 1779) to conquer West Florida from Great Britain during the War of the American Revolution. (Cappon, Petchenik, and Long, 53–54)

3 September 1783

Commissioners from Great Britain and the United States signed the Treaty of Paris ending the War of the American Revolution, recognizing American independence, and generally defining U.S. boundaries as including the Mississippi R. on the west and the Floridas on the south (ratifications exchanged 12 May 1784). Great Britain ceded East and West Florida to Spain by a separate Treaty of Paris but the boundaries of the Floridas were not specified. (Parry, 48:481, 487, 491–492; Van Zandt, 12)

29 July 1784

Spain claimed most of the southwestern United States (north of West Florida, east of the Mississippi R., south of the Tennessee and Hiwassee rivers, and west of the Flint R.), including present Alabama and Mississippi, based upon its conquest of West Florida and the lower Mississippi during the War of the American Revolution. The United States insisted upon the parallel of 31 degrees north latitude, specified in its 1783 peace treaty with Great Britain, as its southern boundary. Neither side actually controlled the interior. (Cappon, Petchenik, and Long, 14, 74, 87; Whitaker, facing 68)

27 October 1795

Pinckney's Treaty with Spain (ratified 25 Apr. 1796) settled the U.S.–Florida boundary along the parallel of 31 degrees north latitude from the Mississippi R. eastward to the Chattahoochee R., thereby ending Spain's 1784 claim to most of present Alabama and Mississippi. (Parry, 53:9, 12–13; Van Zandt, 22)

7 April 1798

The United States created Mississippi Territory. Boundaries were: on the west, the Mississippi R.; on the north, a line running due east from the mouth of the Yazoo R. to the Chattachoochee R.; on the east, the Chattahoochee R.; and on the south, the parallel of 31 degrees north latitude. Covered south-central portions of Alabama and Mississippi. Georgia claimed this area under its colonial charter, and the federal act stated that creation of the territory would not impair Georgia's claim. (U.S. Stat., vol. 1, ch. 28 [1798], secs. 1, 3, 5/pp. 549–550)

2 April 1799

ADAMS (Miss.) and PICKERING (now JEFFERSON, Miss.) created by Mississippi Territory from non-county area; both included part of present Alabama. (Rowland, *Miss. Terr. Arch.*, 126–128; Toulmin, *Statutes*, ch. 1, art. 3/p. 2)

4 June 1800

WASHINGTON created by Mississippi Territory from ADAMS (Miss.) and PICKERING (now JEFFERSON, Miss.); included part of present Mississippi. ADAMS (Miss.) and PICKERING (Miss.) eliminated from present Alabama. (Rowland, *Miss. Terr. Arch.*, 238–239; Toulmin, *Statutes*, ch. 1, art. 4/pp. 3–4)

27 January 1802

CLAIBORNE (Miss.) created by Mississippi Territory from JEFFERSON (Miss.); extended eastward to Georgia, thereby overlapping WASHINGTON. (Miss. Terr. Stat., p. 88)

30 January 1802

Choctaw Indian boundary in present Mississippi implicitly adopted as eastern limit of CLAIBORNE (Miss.), ending overlap of WASHINGTON and eliminating CLAIBORNE (Miss.) from present Alabama [not mapped]. (Miss. Terr. Stat., p. 90)

24 April 1802

Georgia and the United States made a two-part agreement: the United States ceded to Georgia all claims to any territory south of North Carolina and west of the Appalachian watershed that it received in 1787 from South Carolina; Georgia ceded to the United States all territory south of North Carolina and Tennessee, east of the Mississippi R., north of the parallel of 31 degrees north latitude, and west of the present western limit of Georgia, that is, most of present Alabama and Mississippi. (Paullin, 83; *Terr. Papers U.S.*, 5:142–143; Van Zandt, 100)

12 March 1803

CLAIBORNE (Miss.) enlarged eastward to Georgia, apparently by mistake, thereby overlapping non-county area and WASHINGTON [not mapped]. (Miss. Terr. Stat., pp. 90–91)

30 April 1803

The United States purchased Louisiana by treaty from France, taking formal possession 20 December 1803. The United States took advantage of the ambiguous description of the territory to claim all of West Florida west of the Perdido R. (southern portions of present Alabama and Mississippi) as part of the 1719 de facto definition of Louisiana, although Spain actually governed the area. (Parry, 57:27, 30–31; Cox, facing 2, 84–101)

26 March 1804

The United States created Orleans Territory from that portion of Louisiana south of the parallel of 33 degrees north latitude, west of the Mississippi R., and south of Mississippi Territory east of the river; this included part of West Florida between the Mississippi and Perdido rivers (southern portions of present Alabama and Mississippi), claimed by the United States as part of Louisiana but actually governed by Spain. (U.S. Stat., vol. 2, ch. 38 [1804], sec. 1/p. 283; Van Zandt, 107)

27 March 1804

Mississippi Territory gained unorganized territory south of Tennessee, east of the Mississippi R., north of Mississippi Territory, and west of Georgia (i.e., northern portions of present Alabama and Mississippi). (U.S. Stat., vol. 2, ch. 61 [1804], sec. 7/p. 305)

7 February 1807

Boundary separating WASHINGTON from CLAIBORNE (Miss.) clarified, ending overlap of 1803 and eliminating CLAIBORNE (Miss.) from present Alabama. (Miss. Terr. Stat., p. 93)

13 December 1808

MADISON created by Mississippi Territory from non-county area. (Toulmin, *Digest*, ch. 2/pp. 80–81)

21 December 1809

BALDWIN and WAYNE (Miss.) created by Mississippi Territory from WASHINGTON; WAYNE (Miss.) included part of present Alabama. WASHINGTON lost to non-county area. (Toulmin, *Digest*, ch. 3/pp. 81–82; Miss. Terr. Stat., pp. 96–97)

7 December 1810

FELICIANA (La.) created by Orleans Territory from non-county area; extended eastward to the Perdido R., included parts of present Louisiana, Mississippi, and Alabama. Spain actually controlled much of the area. (Orleans Terr. Acts 1811, 2d sess., p. 210)

4 January 1811

PASCAGOULA Parish (Orleans Terr.) created by Orleans Territory within FELICIANA County (La.); included parts of present Mississippi and Alabama. (Orleans Terr. Acts 1811, 2d sess., p. 214)

26 January 1811

PASCAGOULA Parish (Orleans Terr.) gained area within FELICIANA County (La.) in present Alabama. (Orleans Terr. Acts 1811, 2d sess., p. 216)

24 April 1811

PASCAGOULA Parish (Orleans Terr.) gained area within FELICIANA County (La.) in present Alabama. (Orleans Terr. Acts 1811, 2d sess., ch. 28, sec. 6/p. 122)

9 December 1811

GREENE (Miss.) created by Mississippi Territory from WAYNE (Miss.); WAYNE (Miss.) lost to creation of MARION (Miss.). GREENE (Miss.) included part of present Alabama. (Toulmin, *Digest*, ch. 4/p. 82; Miss. Terr. Stat., pp. 104–105)

30 April 1812

State of Louisiana admitted to the Union from Orleans Territory; Orleans Territory eliminated. FELICIANA County (La.) lost all territory between the Pearl and Perdido rivers; PASCAGOULA Parish (Orleans Terr.) eliminated. (U.S. Stat., vol. 2, ch. 50 [1812], secs. 1, 6/pp. 701, 704; ch. 57 [1812]/p. 708)

14 May 1812

Following admission into the Union of the state of Louisiana from Orleans Territory, the United States formally added to Mississippi Territory the remnant of Orleans Territory lying south of 31 degrees north latitude and between the Pearl and Perdido rivers (i.e., the southern portions of present Alabama and Mississippi). Spain retained actual control of the area. (Fuller, 199; U.S. Stat., vol. 2, ch. 84 [1812]/p. 734; Van Zandt, 105)

1 August 1812

MOBILE created by Mississippi Territory from non-county area in present Alabama and Mississippi that was claimed, but not fully controlled, by the United States. (*Terr. Papers U.S.*, 6:305)

10 December 1812

CLARKE created by Mississippi Territory from WASHINGTON. (Toulmin, *Digest*, ch. 5/p. 83; Miss. Terr. Stat., p. 107)

18 December 1812

HANCOCK (Miss.) and JACKSON (Miss.) created by Mississippi Territory from MOBILE; not fully controlled by the United States. JACKSON (Miss.) included part of present Alabama. (Toulmin, *Digest*, ch. 6/p. 83; Miss. Terr. Stat., p. 108)

15 April 1813

American forces captured the city of Mobile from Spain, effectively extending U.S. control over the territory between the Pearl and Perdido rivers, previously claimed by the U.S. as part of Louisiana and where HANCOCK (Miss.), JACKSON (Miss.), and MOBILE had been created. (Cox, facing 2; Fuller, 202)

29 June 1815

MONROE created by Mississippi Territory from non-county area. (*Terr. Papers U.S.*, 6:538)

6 December 1816

MONTGOMERY created by Mississippi Territory from MONROE. (Toulmin, *Digest*, ch. 8/p. 83; Miss. Terr. Stat., p. 464)

3 March 1817

The United States created Alabama Territory from the eastern half of Mississippi Territory. Boundaries were: on the east, Georgia; on the north, Tennessee; on the west, a line up the Tennessee R. to Bear Creek, thence a straight line to the northwest corner of WASHINGTON, and thence due south to the Gulf of Mexico; and on the south, the Gulf, the Perdido R., and thence along the parallel of 31 degrees north latitude to Georgia. BALDWIN, CLARKE, MADISON, MOBILE, MONROE, MONTGOMERY, and WASHINGTON became Alabama counties. GREENE (Miss.), JACKSON (Miss.), and WAYNE (Miss.) eliminated from Alabama, but their eastern ends, which fell east of the new Alabama-Mississippi boundary, became non-county areas in Alabama Territory. (U.S. Stat., vol. 3, ch. 59 [1817], sec. 1/p. 371)

6 February 1818

BLOUNT created from MONTGOMERY and non-county area. MARENGO created from non-county area. TUSCALOOSA created from MONTGOMERY and non-county area; overlapped state of Mississippi. (Ala. Terr. Acts 1818, 1st sess., secs. 1–3/pp. 16–18)

COTACO (now MORGAN) created from non-county area. FRANKLIN and LAWRENCE created from MONTGOMERY and non-county area. (Ala. Terr. Acts 1818, 1st sess., secs. 1–3/pp. 8–9)

LAUDERDALE created from non-county area. LIMESTONE created from MADISON and non-county area. MADISON gained from non-county area. (Ala. Terr. Acts 1818, 1st sess., secs. 1–3/pp. 12–13)

7 February 1818

Parts of Mississippi counties remaining on the Alabama side of the new territorial boundary (3 Mar. 1817) added to Alabama Territory counties: BALDWIN gained eastern part of GREENE (Miss.), MOBILE gained eastern part of JACKSON (Miss.), and WASHINGTON gained eastern part of WAYNE (Miss.). (Ala. Terr. Acts 1818, 1st sess., p. 21)

CAHAWBA (now BIBB) created from MONTGOMERY. SHELBY created from MONTGOMERY and non-county area. (Ala. Terr. Acts 1818, 1st sess., secs. 1–2/pp. 29–30)

9 February 1818

DALLAS created from MONROE and MONTGOMERY. (Ala. Terr. Acts 1818, 1st sess., sec. 1/p. 47)

County boundary lines in Tennessee R. adjusted to run in middle of stream; affected COTACO (now MORGAN), FRANKLIN, LAUDERDALE, LAWRENCE, LIMESTONE, and MADISON [not mapped]. (Ala. Terr. Acts 1818, 1st sess., p. 49)

12 February 1818

MARENGO gained from non-county area. (Ala. Terr. Acts 1818, 1st sess., p. 57)

13 February 1818

CONECUH created from MONROE. MARION created from TUSCALOOSA; included most of TUSCALOOSA's overlap of state of Mississippi. (Ala. Terr. Acts 1818, 1st sess., secs. 1–2/p. 96)

20 November 1818

ST. CLAIR created from SHELBY. SHELBY gained from CAHAWBA (now BIBB) and from non-county area. (Ala. Terr. Acts 1818, 2d sess., secs. 1–2/pp. 18–19)

CAHAWBA (now BIBB) gained from DALLAS and MONTGOMERY; TUSCALOOSA gained from CAHAWBA. (Ala. Terr. Acts 1818, 2d sess., p. 21)

21 November 1818

AUTAUGA created from MONTGOMERY. (Ala. Terr. Acts 1818, 2d sess., p. 56)

DALLAS gained from MONTGOMERY. (Ala. Terr. Acts 1818, 2d sess., p. 76)

Southern boundaries of COTACO (now MORGAN), FRANKLIN, and LAWRENCE clarified [no change]. (Ala. Terr. Acts 1818, 2d sess., p. 39)

13 December 1819

Legislature passed single act creating seven new counties. (*Ala. Rpts.*, 215:640; Ala. Acts 1819, 1st sess., pp. 50–57; for sections of the law on particular counties, see following citations)

BUTLER created from CONECUH, DALLAS, and MONROE (sec. 5/p. 51)

GREENE created from MARENGO and TUSCALOOSA (sec. 8/p. 52)

HENRY created from CONECUH (sec. 6/p. 51)

JACKSON created from non-county area (sec. 17/p. 54)

JEFFERSON created from BLOUNT, ST. CLAIR, and SHELBY (sec. 9/p. 52)

PERRY created from CAHAWBA (now BIBB), DALLAS, MARENGO, and TUSCALOOSA (sec. 7/p. 52)

WILCOX created from DALLAS, MARENGO, MONROE, and MONTGOMERY (sec. 2/p. 50)

BALDWIN gained from CONECUH and MONROE; CAHAWBA (now BIBB) gained from AUTAUGA; DALLAS gained from MONTGOMERY; MADISON gained from non-county area; MARENGO gained from DALLAS. (Ala. Acts 1819, 1st sess., secs. 1, 3–4, 19, 34/pp. 50–51, 54, 56; *Ala. Rpts.*, 215:640).

14 December 1819

State of Alabama admitted to the Union; Alabama Territory eliminated. The southern section of the Alabama-Mississippi line was to be surveyed and adjusted from its original north-south course, if parts of GREENE (Miss.), JACKSON (Miss.), or WAYNE (Miss.) remained east of the interstate line. (U.S. Stat., vol. 3, ch. 47 [1819], secs. 1–3/pp. 489–492 and res. 1 [1819]/p. 608; Van Zandt, 108–109)

17 December 1819

Non-county area belonging to Chickasaw Indians attached to FRANKLIN; non-county area belonging to Choctaw Indians attached to MARENGO; non-county area belonging to Creek Indians attached to MONTGOMERY; non-county area belonging to Cherokee Indians attached to ST. CLAIR. (Ala. Acts 1819, 1st sess., p. 34)

by 29 May 1820

Surveyors demarcated the southern segment of the Alabama-Mississippi line, fixing the end point ten miles east of the mouth of the Pascagoula R. This southern terminus is approximately 3.7 miles east of its prior location, an adjustment authorized in the act admitting Alabama on 14 December 1819. BALDWIN, MOBILE and WASHINGTON lost to Mississippi. (Van Zandt, 108–109)

4 December 1820

CAHAWBA renamed BIBB. (Ala. Acts 1820, 2d sess., p. 63)

13 December 1820

AUTAUGA gained from BIBB. (Ala. Acts 1820, 2d sess., p. 113)

16 December 1820

BALDWIN exchanged with MOBILE; MONROE gained from BALDWIN. (Ala. Acts 1820, 2d sess., p. 104)

19 December 1820

PICKENS created from MARION and TUSCALOOSA; TUSCALOOSA's overlap of state of Mississippi ended. MARION gained from TUSCALOOSA and from part of non-county area attached to FRANKLIN, lost overlap of state of Mississippi, and lost to non-county area. (Ala. Acts 1820, 2d sess., secs. 1, 9/pp. 90, 92)

20 December 1820

BIBB gained from TUSCALOOSA and non-county area, and exchanged with PERRY; GREENE and TUSCALOOSA gained from PERRY. (Ala. Acts 1820, 2d sess., p. 75)

Part of non-county area detached from ST. CLAIR, attached to COTACO (now MORGAN). (Ala. Acts 1820, 2d sess., p. 76; Toulmin, *Digest*, ch. 8/p. 171)

1 April 1821

JEFFERSON exchanged with ST. CLAIR. (Ala. Acts 1820, 2d sess., p. 90)

14 June 1821

COTACO renamed MORGAN. (Ala. Acts 1821, called sess., p. 40)

27 November 1821

LIMESTONE gained from LAUDERDALE. (Ala. Acts 1821, 3d sess., p. 72)

Most of non-county area detached from MORGAN, attached to JACKSON. (Ala. Acts 1821, 3d sess., p. 17)

28 November 1821

CLARKE gained small area from MONROE. (Ala. Acts 1821, 3d sess., p. 68)

7 December 1821

COVINGTON created from HENRY. DECATUR created from JACKSON; non-county area detached from JACKSON, attached to DECATUR. PIKE created from HENRY and MONTGOMERY. (Ala. Acts 1821, 3d sess., p. 71)

17 December 1821

BIBB exchanged with PERRY. (Ala. Acts 1821, 3d sess., p. 56)

27 December 1822

WILCOX gained from DALLAS. (Ala. Acts 1822, 4th sess., p. 96)

30 December 1822

BLOUNT lost to non-county area. (Ala. Acts 1822, 4th sess., p. 96)

PERRY gained from DALLAS. (Ala. Acts 1822, 4th sess., p. 117)

31 December 1822

DECATUR exchanged with JACKSON; northern part of non-county area detached from DECATUR, attached to JACKSON. (Ala. Acts 1822, 4th sess., p. 89)

1 January 1823

MARION and TUSCALOOSA gained from non-county areas. (Ala. Acts 1822, 4th sess., p. 143)

19 December 1823

JEFFERSON gained from ST. CLAIR. (Ala. Acts 1823, 5th sess., p. 85)

26 December 1823

WALKER created from JEFFERSON, MARION, and TUSCALOOSA. (Ala. Acts 1823, 5th sess., sec. 1/p. 82)

20 December 1824

FAYETTE created from MARION, PICKENS, TUSCALOOSA, and WALKER. PICKENS gained from TUSCALOOSA. (Ala. Acts 1824, 6th sess., secs. 1, 12/pp. 77–78)

22 December 1824

MONTGOMERY gained from PIKE. WALKER gained from TUSCALOOSA. (Ala. Acts 1824, 6th sess., p. 87)

17 October 1825

DALE created from COVINGTON and HENRY. (Ala. Acts 1824, 6th sess., secs. 1, 18/pp. 79, 82)

28 December 1825

JACKSON gained all of DECATUR; DECATUR eliminated. Non-county area formerly attached to DECATUR now attached to JACKSON. (Ala. Acts 1825, 7th sess., p. 15)

4 January 1826

DALE gained from HENRY; PIKE gained from DALE. (Ala. Acts 1825, 7th sess., p. 55)

6 January 1826

MADISON gained from JACKSON. (Ala. Acts 1825, 7th sess., p. 10)

12 January 1827

SHELBY gained from AUTAUGA. (Ala. Acts 1826, 8th sess., p. 22)

1 March 1827

Part of non-county area detached from MONTGOMERY, attached to AUTAUGA. (Ala. Acts 1826, 8th sess., p. 32)

28 December 1827

SHELBY gained from AUTAUGA. (Ala. Acts 1827, 9th sess., p. 93)

31 December 1827

JEFFERSON exchanged with TUSCALOOSA. (Ala. Acts 1827, 9th sess., p. 99)

3 January 1828

BIBB gained small area from PERRY. BUTLER gained from PIKE. (Ala. Acts 1827, 9th sess., p. 47)

9 January 1828

ST. CLAIR and SHELBY given concurrent jurisdiction with AUTAUGA over non-county area attached to AUTAUGA on 1 March 1827. (Ala. Acts 1827, 9th sess., p. 30)

15 January 1828

Boundary between BIBB and TUSCALOOSA clarified [no change]. (Ala. Acts 1827, 9th sess., p. 76)

Boundary between BLOUNT and JEFFERSON clarified [no discernible change]. (Ala. Acts 1827, 9th sess., p. 69)

20 December 1828

PIKE gained from DALE. (Ala. Acts 1828, 10th sess., p. 60)

26 January 1829

CLARKE gained from MONROE and WILCOX; MARENGO gained small area from WILCOX. (Ala. Acts 1828, 10th sess., p. 62; *Ala. Rpts.*, 215:640)

27 January 1829

COVINGTON gained from BUTLER; PIKE gained from BUTLER and COVINGTON. (Ala. Acts 1828, 10th sess., p. 44)

WASHINGTON gained from MOBILE. (Ala. Acts 1828, 10th sess., pp. 44–45)

29 January 1829

MONTGOMERY, ST. CLAIR, and SHELBY gained from non-county area that was concurrently attached to AUTAUGA, ST. CLAIR, and SHELBY. MONTGOMERY gained part of non-county attachment. PIKE gained from non-county area attached to MONTGOMERY. (Ala. Acts 1828, 10th sess., p. 65)

20 January 1830

LOWNDES created from BUTLER, DALLAS, MONTGOMERY, PIKE, and WILCOX. WILCOX gained from CLARKE. (Ala. Acts 1829, 11th sess., p. 25)

15 January 1831

BIBB exchanged with TUSCALOOSA. (Ala. Acts 1830, 12th sess., p. 8)

CLARKE gained from WILCOX. (Ala. Acts 1830, 12th sess., p. 30)

FAYETTE gained from MARION. (Ala. Acts 1830, 12th sess., p. 29)

ST. CLAIR exchanged with SHELBY. (Ala. Acts 1830, 12th sess., p. 30)

SHELBY gained from MONTGOMERY. (Ala. Acts 1830, 12th sess., p. 31)

28 December 1831

HENRY gained from PIKE. (Ala. Acts 1831, 13th sess., p. 29)

18 January 1832

BIBB gained from SHELBY. (Ala. Acts 1831, 13th sess., p. 42)

20 January 1832

FAYETTE gained from TUSCALOOSA. (Ala. Acts 1831, 13th sess., p. 95)

21 January 1832

BLOUNT gained from non-county areas attached to JACKSON and MORGAN; FRANKLIN gained from non-county attachment; JACKSON gained from non-county attachment; MORGAN gained from BLOUNT and from non-county areas attached to JACKSON and MORGAN; ST. CLAIR gained non-county attachment and non-county area attached to JACKSON. (Ala. Acts 1831, 13th sess., p. 35)

GREENE gained narrow strip all along PICKENS boundary [not mapped]; PICKENS and TUSCALOOSA gained small areas from GREENE. (Ala. Acts 1831, 13th sess., p. 38)

15 December 1832

Boundary between HENRY and PIKE clarified [no change]. (Ala. Acts 1832, ann. sess., no. 9/p. 66)

18 December 1832

Legislature passed single act creating 10 new counties. (Ala. Acts 1832, ann. sess., no. 11/pp. 9–11; for sections on particular counties, see following citations)

> BARBOUR created from PIKE (sec. 10/p. 10)
>
> BENTON (now CALHOUN) created from ST. CLAIR (sec. 1/p. 9)
>
> CHAMBERS created from MONTGOMERY and SHELBY (sec. 6/p. 10)
>
> COOSA created from MONTGOMERY and SHELBY (sec. 4/p. 9)
>
> MACON created from MONTGOMERY and PIKE (sec. 8/p. 10)
>
> RANDOLPH created from ST. CLAIR and SHELBY (sec. 3/p. 9)
>
> RUSSELL created from MONTGOMERY and PIKE (sec. 7/p. 10)
>
> SUMTER created from non-county area attached to MARENGO (sec. 13/p. 11)
>
> TALLADEGA created from ST. CLAIR and SHELBY (sec. 2/p. 9)
>
> TALLAPOOSA created from MONTGOMERY and SHELBY (secs. 5, 9/pp. 9–10)

PICKENS and WASHINGTON gained from non-county area attached to MARENGO; PIKE gained from MONTGOMERY; FRANKLIN boundaries redefined [no change]; MARION boundaries redefined [no change]. (Ala. Acts 1832, ann. sess., no. 11, secs. 11–12, 14–16/p. 11)

21 December 1832

BALDWIN gained from MOBILE. (Ala. Acts 1832, ann. sess., no. 50/p. 94)

5 January 1833

BUTLER gained small area from MONROE. (Ala. Acts 1832, ann. sess., no. 37/p. 21)

after 1 April 1833

JEFFERSON gained from SHELBY. (Ala. Acts 1830, 12th sess., secs. 3, 6/p. 30; Ala. Acts 1832, ann. sess., no. 53, secs. 1, 8/pp. 30–31)

1 January 1834

MACON gained from MONTGOMERY. (Ala. Acts 1833, ann. sess., no. 10/p. 6)

14 January 1834

JACKSON gained from ST. CLAIR. (Ala. Acts 1833, ann. sess., no. 26/p. 14)

30 December 1834

Part of ST. CLAIR attached to BENTON (now CALHOUN). (Ala. Acts 1834, ann. sess., no. 7/p. 5; repeated as no. 156/p. 148)

9 January 1836

CHEROKEE created from JACKSON, ST. CLAIR, and from that part of ST. CLAIR that was attached to BENTON (now CALHOUN). DE KALB created from JACKSON and ST. CLAIR. (Ala. Acts 1835, ann. sess., no. 179/p. 170)

MARSHALL created from BLOUNT and JACKSON. MADISON gained from JACKSON. (Ala. Acts 1835, ann. sess., no. 47, secs. 1, 13/pp. 47, 49)

23 December 1836

TALLADEGA gained from BENTON (now CALHOUN); BENTON gained from CHEROKEE. (Ala. Acts 1836, ann. sess., no. 149/p. 118)

24 June 1837

COOSA exchanged with MONTGOMERY. (Ala. Acts 1837, called sess., no. 2/p. 3)

2 December 1837

CONECUH gained from BUTLER. (Ala. Acts 1837, ann. sess., no. 90/p. 87)

20 December 1837

MACON gained from PIKE. (Ala. Acts 1837, ann. sess., no. 27/p. 20)

21 December 1837

COOSA gained from MONTGOMERY; remaining boundary between COOSA and MONTGOMERY clarified [no change]. (Ala. Acts 1837, ann. sess., no. 29/p. 21)

23 December 1837

FAYETTE gained from MARION. (Ala. Acts 1837, ann. sess., no. 49/p. 38)

MARSHALL gained from MADISON. (Ala. Acts 1837, ann. sess., no. 44/p. 36)

25 December 1837

RUSSELL gained small area from MACON. (Ala. Acts 1837, ann. sess., no. 84/p. 78)

by 1839

MONROE gained small area from BUTLER. (Morse, pl. 33)

2 February 1839

MONTGOMERY gained from TALLAPOOSA. (Ala. Acts 1838, ann. sess., no. 95/p. 99)

29 January 1840

PIKE gained small area from DALE. (Ala. Acts 1839, ann. sess., no. 43/p. 112)

3 February 1840

JEFFERSON exchanged with TUSCALOOSA. (Ala. Acts 1839, ann. sess., no. 103/p. 142)

4 February 1840

MARENGO gained from DALLAS. (Ala. Acts 1839, ann. sess., no. 60/p. 45)

15 December 1840

MARSHALL gained from MORGAN. (Ala. Acts 1840, ann. sess., no. 6/p. 9)

18 December 1840

BUTLER gained small area from WILCOX. (Ala. Acts 1840, ann. sess., no. 131/p. 98)

2 January 1841

CONECUH gained from BUTLER. (Ala. Acts 1840, ann. sess., no. 5/p. 9)

2 December 1841

JEFFERSON gained small area from SHELBY to accommodate local property owner [location unknown, not mapped]. (Ala. Acts 1841, ann. sess., no. 97/p. 92)

29 December 1841

COFFEE created from DALE. (Ala. Acts 1841, ann. sess., no. 190, sec. 1/p. 152)

LOWNDES gained small area from MONTGOMERY. (Ala. Acts 1841, ann. sess., no. 153/p. 129)

9 January 1843

WALKER gained from FAYETTE. (Ala. Acts 1842, ann. sess., no. 200/p. 158)

27 January 1843

CHEROKEE gained from BENTON (now CALHOUN). (Ala. Acts 1842, ann. sess., no. 196/p. 157)

7 February 1843

DE KALB exchanged with MARSHALL. Boundary between DE KALB and JACKSON adjusted [location unknown, not mapped]. (Ala. Acts 1842, ann. sess., no. 199/p. 158)

11 February 1843

MACON gained small area from RUSSELL to accommodate local property owner. (Ala. Acts 1842, ann. sess., no. 197/p. 157)

13 February 1843

CLARKE gained from MONROE. (Ala. Acts 1842, ann. sess., no. 226/p. 172)

14 February 1843

GREENE gained from PICKENS. (Ala. Acts 1842, ann. sess., no. 227/p. 173)

16 January 1844

DE KALB gained from CHEROKEE. (Ala. Acts 1843, ann. sess., no. 109/p. 69)

17 January 1844

HENRY gained from BARBOUR. (Ala. Acts 1843, ann. sess., no. 135/p. 87)

27 January 1845

BENTON (now CALHOUN) gained small area from CHEROKEE to accommodate local property owners. (Ala. Acts 1844, ann. sess., no. 102/p. 58)

TALLADEGA gained small area from BENTON (now CALHOUN). (Ala. Acts 1844, ann. sess., no. 115/p. 64)

TALLAPOOSA gained from MACON. (Ala. Acts 1844, ann. sess., no. 120/p. 66)

2 February 1846

MACON gained from TALLAPOOSA. (Ala. Acts 1845, ann. sess., no. 178/p. 154)

29 December 1847

CHOCTAW created from SUMTER and WASHINGTON. (Ala. Acts 1847, 1st bien. sess., no. 213, sec. 1/p. 306)

3 March 1848

JACKSON gained from DE KALB. (Ala. Acts 1847, 1st bien. sess., no. 273/p. 363)

5 February 1850

TALLADEGA gained small area from BENTON (now CALHOUN). (Ala. Acts 1849, 2d bien. sess., no. 242/p. 384)

12 February 1850

HANCOCK (now WINSTON) created from WALKER. WALKER authorized to gain from TUSCALOOSA, but apparently faulty description was never implemented [no change]. (Ala. Acts 1849, 2d bien. sess., no. 58/p. 90)

5 February 1852

JACKSON gained small area from MARSHALL. (Ala. Acts 1851, 3d bien. sess., no. 337/p. 441)

9 February 1852

JEFFERSON gained small area from TUSCALOOSA. (Ala. Acts 1851, 3d bien. sess., no. 335/p. 440)

10 February 1852

Boundary between MONROE and CONECUH clarified [no change]. (Ala. Acts 1851, 3d bien. sess., no. 332/p. 439)

14 February 1854

Boundary between BENTON (now CALHOUN) and CHEROKEE adjusted [location unknown, not mapped; mistake in description corrected 1 February 1856]. (Ala. Acts 1853, 4th bien. sess., no. 342/p. 218)

15 February 1854

DE KALB gained from JACKSON. (Ala. Acts 1853, 4th bien. sess., no. 296/p. 184)

18 February 1854

BENTON (now CALHOUN) gained small area from CHEROKEE to accommodate local property owner. (Ala. Acts 1853, 4th bien. sess., no. 311/p. 202)

1 February 1856

Boundary between BENTON (now CALHOUN) and CHEROKEE clarified to correct mistake of 14 February 1854 [no change]. (Ala. Acts 1855, 5th bien. sess., no. 160/p. 120)

22 January 1858

HANCOCK renamed WINSTON. (Ala. Acts 1857, 6th bien. sess., no. 322/p. 327)

29 January 1858

BENTON renamed CALHOUN. (Ala. Acts 1857, 6th bien. sess., no. 306/p. 318)

2 February 1858

DE KALB gained small area from JACKSON to accommodate local property owner; MARSHALL gained from DE KALB. (Ala. Acts 1857, 6th bien. sess., no. 335/p. 337)

6 February 1858

CHEROKEE gained small area from DE KALB [location unknown, not mapped]. (Ala. Acts 1857, 6th bien. sess., no. 308/p. 319)

21 February 1860

WASHINGTON gained small area from MOBILE. (Ala. Acts 1859, 7th bien. sess., no. 416/p. 556)

25 February 1860

DE KALB gained from JACKSON. (Ala. Acts 1859, 7th bien. sess., no. 383/p. 523)

8 February 1861

JEFFERSON gained from SHELBY. (Ala. Acts 1861, called sess., no. 77/p. 67)

11 November 1861

SHELBY gained from JEFFERSON. (Ala. Acts 1861, 1st reg. sess., no. 213/p. 207)

6 December 1861

CLARKE gained small area from MONROE to accommodate local property owner. (Ala. Acts 1861, 1st reg. sess., no. 200/p. 201)

7 November 1862

AUTAUGA gained small area from BIBB to accommodate local property owners [location unknown, not mapped]. (Ala. Acts 1862, 2d reg. sess., no. 128/p. 151)

24 November 1862

BUTLER gained small area from CONECUH to accommodate local property owner [location unknown, not mapped]. (Ala. Acts 1862, 2d reg. sess., no. 129/p. 151)

28 November 1862

MONTGOMERY gained small area from PIKE to accommodate local property owner. (Ala. Acts 1862, 2d reg. sess., no. 153/p. 164)

4 December 1862

JEFFERSON gained small area from SHELBY to accommodate local property owner. (Ala. Acts 1862, 2d reg. sess., no. 137/p. 156)

27 August 1863

MOBILE gained small area from WASHINGTON to accommodate local property owners. (Ala. Acts 1863, called sess., no. 30/p. 31)

28 November 1863

MARENGO gained small area from PERRY to accommodate local property owner. (Ala. Acts 1863, 3d reg. sess., no. 199/p. 151)

30 November 1863

PERRY gained small area from MARENGO to accommodate local property owner. (Ala. Acts 1863, 3d reg. sess., no. 201/p. 152)

3 October 1864

GREENE gained small area from TUSCALOOSA to accommodate local property owner [location unknown, not mapped]. (Ala. Acts 1864, called sess., no. 50/p. 37)

11 December 1865

MONROE gained small area from CONECUH to accommodate local property owner. (Ala. Acts 1865, reg. sess., no. 441/p. 566)

10 February 1866

CHAMBERS gained small area from TALLAPOOSA to accommodate local property owner. (Ala. Acts 1865, reg. sess., no. 416/p. 554)

20 February 1866

MARENGO gained small area from PERRY to accommodate local property owner. (Ala. Acts 1865, reg. sess., no. 450/p. 571)

24 November 1866

CRENSHAW created from BUTLER, COFFEE, COVINGTON, LOWNDES, and PIKE; a provision that would have included part of MONTGOMERY in CRENSHAW was never implemented. BUTLER gained from LOWNDES. (Ala. Acts 1866, reg. sess., no. 39, secs. 1–2/p. 38)

5 December 1866

BULLOCK created from BARBOUR, MACON, MONTGOMERY, and PIKE. (Ala. Acts 1866, reg. sess., no. 84, sec. 1/p. 65)

LEE created from CHAMBERS, MACON, RUSSELL, and TALLAPOOSA. (Ala. Acts 1866, reg. sess., no. 61, sec. 1/ p. 50)

6 December 1866

CLEBURNE created from CALHOUN, RANDOLPH, and TALLADEGA. (Ala. Acts 1866, reg. sess., no. 89, sec. 1 p. 71)

7 December 1866

BAINE created from BLOUNT, CALHOUN, CHEROKEE, DE KALB, MARSHALL, and ST. CLAIR. (Ala. Acts 1866, reg. sess., no. 92, sec. 1/p. 76)

CLAY created from RANDOLPH and TALLADEGA. (Ala. Acts 1866, reg. sess., no. 110, sec. 1/p. 92)

late December 1866

ELMORE created from AUTAUGA, COOSA, MONT-GOMERY, and TALLAPOOSA. (Ala. Acts 1865, reg. sess., no. 312, secs. 1, 4/pp. 484–485)

17 January 1867

LEE gained small area from CHAMBERS to accommodate local property owner. (Ala. Acts 1866, reg. sess., no. 188/ p. 175)

30 January 1867

HALE created from GREENE, MARENGO, PERRY, and TUSCALOOSA. GREENE gained from PICKENS. (Ala. Acts 1866, reg. sess., no. 418, secs. 1, 9/pp. 477, 480)

4 February 1867

JONES created from FAYETTE and MARION. (Ala. Acts 1866, reg. sess., no. 298, sec. 1/p. 323)

FAYETTE gained from MARION. (Ala. Acts 1866, reg. sess., no. 288/p. 317)

LEE gained small area from CHAMBERS to accommodate local property owner. (Ala. Acts 1866, reg. sess., no. 290/ p. 318)

PIKE gained small area from BULLOCK to accommodate local property owner. (Ala. Acts 1866, reg. sess., no. 297/ p. 322)

6 February 1867

COLBERT created from FRANKLIN. (Ala. Acts 1866, reg. sess., no. 321, sec. 1/p. 351)

8 February 1867

BARBOUR exchanged with BULLOCK. (Ala. Acts 1866, reg. sess., no. 335/p. 363)

11 February 1867

BUTLER gained small area from CRENSHAW. (Ala. Acts 1866, reg. sess., no. 355/p. 386)

13 February 1867

Boundary between CHEROKEE and DE KALB redefined [no discernible change]. (Ala. Acts 1866, reg. sess., no. 382/p. 420)

14 February 1867

TALLADEGA gained from CLEBURNE. (Ala. Acts 1866, reg. sess., no. 400/p. 432)

15 February 1867

CLEBURNE gained from CLAY and TALLADEGA; TALLADEGA gained from CLAY. (Ala. Acts 1866, reg. sess., no. 438/p. 496)

16 February 1867

TALLADEGA gained from CLAY. (Ala. Acts 1866, reg. sess., no. 467/p. 528)

TALLAPOOSA gained small area from LEE. (Ala. Acts 1866, reg. sess., no. 480/p. 543)

18 February 1867

CRENSHAW gained from COVINGTON. (Ala. Acts 1866, reg. sess., no. 529/p. 581)

DALLAS gained from PERRY. (Ala. Acts 1866, reg. sess., no. 509/p. 567)

19 February 1867

DE KALB and MARSHALL gained from BAINE. (Ala. Acts 1866, reg. sess., no. 633/p. 677)

LEE gained small area from CHAMBERS to accommodate local property owner. (Ala. Acts 1866, reg. sess., no. 584/p. 632)

LOWNDES gained small area from CRENSHAW. (Ala. Acts 1866, reg. sess., no. 687/p. 747)

PIKE gained from CRENSHAW. (Ala. Acts 1866, reg. sess., no. 540/p. 589)

Change in boundary along BAINE, BLOUNT, and ST. CLAIR lines authorized [cannot be demarcated as described; no change]. (Ala. Acts 1866, reg. sess., no. 566/p. 615)

13 November 1867

FAYETTE and MARION gained all of JONES; JONES eliminated. [On 8 Oct. 1868 SANFORD (now LAMAR) was created with boundaries identical to those of JONES.] (Ala. Acts 1868, Ord. of St. Conv. [1867], no. 1/p. 161)

29 November 1867

FRANKLIN gained all of COLBERT; COLBERT eliminated. (Ala. Acts 1868, Ord. of St. Conv. [1867], no. 5/p. 163)

3 December 1867

BLOUNT, CALHOUN, CHEROKEE, DE KALB, MARSHALL, and ST. CLAIR gained all of BAINE; BAINE eliminated. (Ala. Acts 1868, Ord. of St. Conv. [1867], no. 27/p. 178)

5 August 1868

BUTLER gained small area from CRENSHAW to accommodate local property owner. (Ala. Acts 1868, ext. sess., p. 80)

6 August 1868

COVINGTON renamed JONES. (Ala. Acts 1868, ext. sess., p. 84)

8 October 1868

SANFORD (now LAMAR) created from FAYETTE and MARION; boundaries were identical to those of JONES (extinct). (Ala. Acts 1868, called sess., no. 13/p. 216)

10 October 1868

JONES renamed COVINGTON. (Ala. Acts 1868, called sess., no. 39/p. 257)

1 December 1868

ETOWAH created from BLOUNT, CALHOUN, CHEROKEE, DE KALB, MARSHALL, and ST. CLAIR [ETOWAH boundaries differed from those of BAINE, which had been located in the same area]. MARSHALL apparently gained from DE KALB. (Ala. Acts 1868, reg. sess., no. 20, sec. 1/p. 359)

10 December 1868

ESCAMBIA created from BALDWIN and CONECUH; MONROE apparently gained from BALDWIN. Narrow strip of territory along the state line inadvertently omitted from formal definition of ESCAMBIA [mistake corrected 5 Mar. 1907]. (Ala. Acts 1868, reg. sess., no. 34, sec. 1/p. 397)

ELMORE gained small area from COOSA. (Ala. Acts 1868, reg. sess., no. 44/p. 406)

17 December 1868

ST. CLAIR gained small area from ETOWAH to accommodate local property owner [location unknown, not mapped]. (Ala. Acts 1868, reg. sess., no. 62/p. 417)

24 December 1868

COVINGTON gained from CRENSHAW. (Ala. Acts 1868, reg. sess., no. 95/p. 438)

26 December 1868

GENEVA created from COFFEE, DALE, and HENRY. Strip of territory along the state line inadvertently omitted from formal definition of GENEVA [mistake corrected 11 Feb. 1870]. (Ala. Acts 1868, reg. sess., no. 110, sec. 1/p. 446)

28 December 1868

DALLAS gained small area from PERRY [became a DALLAS exclave on 30 Dec. 1868 and returned to PERRY 28 Feb. 1889]. (Ala. Acts 1868, reg. sess., no. 111/p. 448)

30 December 1868

BAKER (now CHILTON) created from AUTAUGA, BIBB, DALLAS, and SHELBY. Small area gained by DALLAS from PERRY 2 days earlier became a DALLAS exclave [corrected 28 Feb. 1889]. (Ala. Acts 1868, reg. sess., no. 142, sec. 1/p. 488)

31 December 1868

RUSSELL gained from BARBOUR. (Ala. Acts 1868, reg. sess., no. 177/p. 524)

15 December 1869

BAKER (now CHILTON) gained from AUTAUGA. (Ala. Acts 1869, reg. sess., no. 12/p. 18)

DALLAS gained from BAKER (now CHILTON). (Ala. Acts 1869, reg. sess., no. 11/p. 18)

24 January 1870

COLBERT re-created from FRANKLIN. (Ala. Acts 1869, reg. sess., no. 5/p. 6; HRS Ala., *Colbert*, 4)

7 February 1870

MARENGO gained small area from HALE. (Ala. Acts 1869, reg. sess., no. 87/p. 75)

MARENGO gained small area from PERRY to accommodate local property owner. (Ala. Acts 1869, reg. sess., no. 80/p. 69)

ST. CLAIR gained from ETOWAH. (Ala. Acts 1869, reg. sess., no. 74/p. 65)

11 February 1870

Southern boundary of GENEVA clarified to match state line, correcting mistake of 26 December 1868 [no change]. (Ala. Acts 1869, reg. sess., no. 108/p. 97)

14 February 1870

ELMORE gained small area from TALLAPOOSA to accommodate local property owners. (Ala. Acts 1869, reg. sess., no. 125/p. 105)

21 February 1870

COVINGTON gained small area from ESCAMBIA to accommodate local property owner. (Ala. Acts 1869, reg. sess., no. 145/p. 159)

25 February 1870

BLOUNT gained small area from MARSHALL. (Ala. Acts 1869, reg. sess., no. 181/p. 185)

1 March 1870

CHOCTAW authorized to gain from SUMTER, and WASHINGTON authorized to gain from CHOCTAW, dependent on local referendum [local action unknown, no change]. (Ala. Acts 1869, reg. sess., no. 213/p. 234)

3 March 1870

COOSA gained small area from CLAY to accommodate local property owner. (Ala. Acts 1869, reg. sess., no. 333/p. 434)

DE KALB authorized to gain from JACKSON dependent on local referendum [repealed 8 Feb. 1872]; no evidence that referendum was held [no change]. (Ala. Acts 1869, reg. sess., no. 353/p. 449)

15 February 1871

COFFEE gained small area from GENEVA to accommodate local property owner. (Ala. Acts 1870, reg. sess., no. 87/p. 79; Ala. Acts 1869, reg. sess., no. 257/p. 300)

23 February 1871

COFFEE gained small area from CRENSHAW to accommodate local property owners. (Ala. Acts 1870, reg. sess., no. 85/p. 78)

6 March 1871

JEFFERSON gained from SHELBY. (Ala. Acts 1870, reg. sess., no. 84/p. 78)

9 March 1871

BARBOUR gained small area from BULLOCK to accommodate local property owner. (Ala. Acts 1870, reg. sess., no. 86/p. 79)

7 December 1871

BIBB gained small area from PERRY to accommodate local property owners. (Ala. Acts 1871, reg. sess., no. 154/p. 163)

CALHOUN gained from ETOWAH. (Ala. Acts 1871, reg. sess., no. 153/p. 162)

11 December 1871

PIKE gained small area from BULLOCK to accommodate local property owner. (Ala. Acts 1871, reg. sess., no. 152/p. 162)

16 December 1871

CLAY authorized to gain from RANDOLPH [cannot be demarcated as described; no change]. (Ala. Acts 1871, reg. sess., no. 155/p. 163)

8 February 1872

BULLOCK gained small area from BARBOUR. (Ala. Acts 1871, reg. sess., no. 157/p. 164)

Act of 3 March 1870, intended to change boundary between DE KALB and JACKSON, repealed [no change]. (Ala. Acts 1871, reg. sess., no. 151/p. 161)

24 February 1872

LEE gained small area from CHAMBERS to accommodate local property owner. (Ala. Acts 1871, reg. sess., no. 156/p. 164)

15 March 1873

BARBOUR gained small area from RUSSELL to accommodate local property owner. (Ala. Acts 1872, reg. sess., no. 99/p. 137)

17 March 1873

CLAY gained small area from RANDOLPH. (Ala. Acts 1872, reg. sess., no. 100/p. 138)

23 April 1873

SHELBY gained from BAKER (now CHILTON). (Ala. Acts 1872, reg. sess., no. 101/p. 138)

11 December 1874

CONECUH gained from COVINGTON. (Ala. Acts 1874, reg. sess., no. 462/p. 596)

14 December 1874

PIKE gained small area from BULLOCK. (Ala. Acts 1874, reg. sess., no. 464/p. 597)

17 December 1874

BAKER renamed CHILTON. (Ala. Acts 1874, reg. sess., no. 72/p. 179)

29 January 1875

COLBERT exchanged small areas with FRANKLIN. (Ala. Acts 1874, reg. sess., no. 463/p. 597)

10 February 1875

RUSSELL gained small area from BARBOUR to accommodate local property owner. (Ala. Acts 1874, reg. sess., no. 465/p. 598)

13 February 1875

CHILTON gained from DALLAS. (Ala. Acts 1874, reg. sess., no. 73/p. 180)

25 February 1875

CONECUH gained from ESCAMBIA. (Ala. Acts 1874, reg. sess., no. 192/p. 267)

7 March 1876

CHEROKEE exchanged with DE KALB. (Ala. Acts 1875, reg. sess., no. 226/p. 350)

10 January 1877

TALLADEGA gained from CLAY. (Ala. Acts 1876, bien. sess., no. 208/p. 233)

13 January 1877

HALE gained from PERRY. (Ala. Acts 1876, bien. sess., no. 209/p. 235)

24 January 1877

CULLMAN created from BLOUNT, MARSHALL, MORGAN, and WINSTON. (Ala. Acts 1876, bien. sess., no. 56, sec. 1/p. 69)

30 January 1877

DE KALB gained from MARSHALL. (Ala. Acts 1876, bien. sess., no. 210/p. 235)

5 February 1877

MONTGOMERY gained small area from BULLOCK to accommodate local property owner. (Ala. Acts 1876, bien. sess., no. 206/p. 233)

6 February 1877

CRENSHAW gained from PIKE. (Ala. Acts 1876, bien. sess., no. 203/p. 232)

8 February 1877

BLOUNT gained from JEFFERSON and WALKER. (Ala. Acts 1876, bien. sess., no. 201, sec. 1/p. 229)

SANFORD renamed LAMAR. (Ala. Acts 1876, bien. sess., no. 205/p. 232)

9 February 1877

CLAY gained small area from TALLAPOOSA. (Ala. Acts 1876, bien. sess., no. 207/p. 233)

7 December 1878

JEFFERSON gained small area from SHELBY. (Ala. Acts 1878, bien. sess., no. 194/p. 226)

29 January 1879

BLOUNT exchanged with WALKER. (Ala. Acts 1878, bien. sess., no. 186/p. 219)

31 January 1879

ETOWAH gained from DE KALB. (Ala. Acts 1878, bien. sess., no. 193/p. 225)

4 February 1879

MARSHALL gained from DE KALB. (Ala. Acts 1878, bien. sess., no. 191/p. 224)

13 February 1879

BLOUNT gained from CULLMAN. (Ala. Acts 1878, bien. sess., no. 254/p. 280)

GENEVA authorized to change name to GORDON, dependent on local referendum; no evidence that required election was held [no change]. (Ala. Acts 1878, bien. sess., no. 200/p. 230)

GENEVA authorized to gain from HENRY, and COFFEE authorized to gain from GENEVA, dependent on local referendum; no evidence that required election was held [no change]. (Ala. Acts 1878, bien. sess., no. 199/p. 228)

MACON gained small area from LEE. (Ala. Acts 1878, bien. sess., no. 198/p. 227)

28 February 1881

HALE gained from GREENE when boundary line was moved from east bank to middle of Black Warrior R. [not mapped]. (Ala. Acts 1880, bien. sess., no. 139/p. 178)

1 March 1881

CHAMBERS gained small area from LEE to accommodate local property owner. (Ala. Acts 1880, bien. sess., no. 324/p. 467)

10 February 1883

CLEBURNE gained from CALHOUN and CHEROKEE; CHEROKEE gained from CALHOUN. (Ala. Acts 1882, bien. sess., no. 191/p. 347)

12 December 1884

CHEROKEE gained small area from DE KALB. (Ala. Acts 1884, bien. sess., no. 150/p. 261)

JEFFERSON gained from SHELBY. (Ala. Acts 1884, bien. sess., no. 155/p. 267)

17 February 1885

MACON gained small area from TALLAPOOSA. (Ala. Acts 1884, bien. sess., no. 379/p. 676)

11 December 1886

CALHOUN exchanged with CLEBURNE. (Ala. Acts 1886, bien. sess., no. 334/p. 757)

11 February 1887

ST. CLAIR gained from BLOUNT. (Ala. Acts 1886, bien. sess., no. 283/p. 689)

22 February 1887

BULLOCK gained small area from PIKE to accommodate local property owners. (Ala. Acts 1886, bien. sess., no. 437/p. 892)

28 February 1887

BUTLER gained small area from COVINGTON, and exchanged small areas with CRENSHAW. (Ala. Acts 1886, bien. sess., no. 498/p. 988)

CONECUH gained small area from ESCAMBIA. (Ala. Acts 1886, bien. sess., no. 270/p. 662)

CULLMAN gained from BLOUNT. (Ala. Acts 1886, bien. sess., no. 502/p. 990)

12 December 1888

Boundary between LEE and RUSSELL adjusted [location unknown, not mapped]. (Ala. Acts 1888, bien. sess., no. 184/p. 180)

7 February 1889

BULLOCK gained small area from PIKE to accommodate local property owners. (Ala. Acts 1888, bien. sess., no. 232/p. 315)

28 February 1889

PERRY gained the DALLAS exclave of 1868. (Ala. Acts 1888, bien. sess., no. 590/p. 1053)

5 December 1890

COVINGTON gained small area from CRENSHAW. (Ala. Acts 1890, bien. sess., no. 24/p. 34)

9 February 1893

CLAY gained from TALLADEGA. (Ala. Acts 1892, bien. sess., no. 170/p. 343)

21 February 1893

COVINGTON gained small area from CRENSHAW. (Ala. Acts 1892, bien. sess., no. 393/p. 878)

CULLMAN gained from BLOUNT. (Ala. Acts 1892, bien. sess., no. 336/p. 766)

MOBILE exchanged with WASHINGTON. (Ala. Acts 1892, bien. sess., no. 514/p. 1174)

12 December 1894

CLAY exchanged with TALLADEGA. (Ala. Acts 1894, bien. sess., no. 35, secs. 1–2/pp. 55–56)

6 February 1895

FRANKLIN gained from COLBERT; COLBERT gained from LAWRENCE. (Ala. Acts 1894, bien. sess., no. 243/p. 408)

18 February 1895

BLOUNT gained small area from WALKER. (Ala. Acts 1894, bien. sess., no. 422/p. 810)

WASHINGTON gained small area from MOBILE. (Ala. Acts 1894, bien. sess., no. 450/p. 890)

13 February 1897

BULLOCK gained small area from PIKE. (Ala. Acts 1896, bien. sess., no. 359/p. 884)

16 December 1898

JEFFERSON gained small area from BLOUNT and exchanged with WALKER. (Ala. Acts 1898, bien. sess., loc., no. 147/p. 328)

7 February 1899

ST. CLAIR exchanged with SHELBY. (Ala. Acts 1898, bien. sess., loc., no. 320/p. 679)

10 February 1899

ETOWAH gained from CALHOUN. (Ala. Acts 1898, bien. sess., loc., no. 389/p. 798)

1 October 1899

BIBB exchanged with SHELBY. (Ala. Acts 1898, bien. sess., loc., no. 287/p. 580)

1901

CLARKE exchanged small areas with WILCOX. (Rand, McNally, 1902, 154–155)

14 February 1901

DE KALB gained from CHEROKEE. (Ala. Acts 1900, bien. sess., no. 415/p. 1077)

28 February 1901

MOBILE gained small area from WASHINGTON. (Ala. Acts 1900, bien. sess., no. 800/p. 1937)

5 March 1901

WALKER exchanged with WINSTON. (Ala. Acts 1900, bien. sess., no. 1183/p. 2680)

23 April 1901

CULLMAN gained from BLOUNT. (Ala. Acts 1900, bien. sess., no. 881, secs. 1–3, 5, 7/pp. 2051–2053)

1 October 1901

CALHOUN exchanged with ETOWAH. (Ala. Acts 1900, bien. sess., no. 284, sec. 1/p. 789)

9 February 1903

HOUSTON created from DALE, GENEVA, and HENRY. (Ala. Acts 1903, bien. sess., gen., no. 27/p. 44)

30 September 1903

CALHOUN gained from CLEBURNE. (Ala. Acts 1903, bien. sess., loc., no. 389/p. 462)

30 June 1906

CLEBURNE gained from CALHOUN. (*Ala. Rpts.*, 146:1)

2 March 1907

BIBB exchanged with SHELBY. (Ala. Acts 1907, quad. sess., loc., no. 221, secs. 1–2/pp. 390–392)

5 March 1907

Southern boundary of ESCAMBIA clarified to match state line, correcting mistake of 10 December 1868 [no change]. (Ala. Acts 1907, quad. sess., loc., no. 238/p. 403)

25 July 1907

CALHOUN exchanged with CLEBURNE. (Ala. Acts 1907, quad. sess., loc., no. 398/p. 519)

29 July 1907

CLEBURNE exchanged small areas with RANDOLPH. (Ala. Acts 1907, quad. sess., loc., no. 432/p. 553)

9 August 1907

ETOWAH gained small area from CALHOUN. (Ala. Acts 1907, quad. sess., loc., no. 701/p. 866)

6 August 1915

LEE gained small area from TALLAPOOSA. (Ala. Acts 1915, quad. sess., loc., no. 212/p. 170)

10 September 1915

JEFFERSON exchanged with ST. CLAIR. (Ala. Acts 1915, quad. sess., loc., no. 423/p. 322)

28 September 1915

JEFFERSON exchanged with ST. CLAIR. (Ala. Acts 1915, quad. sess., loc., no. 800/p. 490)

JEFFERSON exchanged with TUSCALOOSA. (Ala. Acts 1915, quad. sess., loc., no. 819/p. 491)

9 August 1923

MONTGOMERY gained from ELMORE. (Ala. Acts 1923, quad. sess., loc., no. 128/p. 50)

14 September 1923

CALHOUN gained small area from ETOWAH. (Ala. Acts 1923, quad. sess., loc., no. 285/p. 179)

ETOWAH gained small area from CALHOUN. (Ala. Acts 1923, quad. sess., loc., no. 284/p. 179)

c. 1927

WALKER gained small area from TUSCALOOSA, ending boundary dispute dating from nineteenth century. (Walker County Assessor's Office, correspondence, 10 Feb. 1990; Tuscaloosa County Tax Assessor's Office, correspondence, 1 Feb. 1990)

10 July 1931

ETOWAH gained from CHEROKEE. (Ala. Acts 1931, quad. sess., loc., no. 381/p. 173)

30 September 1932

LEE exchanged with RUSSELL. (Ala. Acts 1932, ext. sess., loc., no. 49/p. 16)

1 October 1943

JEFFERSON exchanged with SHELBY. (Ala. Acts 1943, reg. sess., loc., no. 293, secs. 1, 3/pp. 173, 177)

15 September 1953

CULLMAN gained from WALKER. (Ala. Acts 1953, reg. sess., no. 610/p. 868)

14 September 1963

COOSA exchanged small areas with TALLAPOOSA [mistake in description corrected 20 Apr. 1965]. (Ala. Acts 1963, reg. sess., no. 503/p. 1086)

20 April 1965

Boundary between COOSA and TALLAPOOSA redefined, correcting mistake of 14 September 1963 [no change]. (Ala. Acts 1965, 1st spec. sess., no. 202/p. 271)

6 August 1976

BLOUNT gained from ETOWAH. (Ala. Acts 1976, reg. sess., no. 200/p. 215)

18 July 1979

Boundary between BIBB and CHILTON redefined [no change]. (Ala. Acts 1979, reg. sess., no. 79-364/p. 581)

9 August 1979

JEFFERSON gained small area from SHELBY. (Ala. Acts 1979, reg. sess., no. 79-806/p. 1485; Shelby County Probate Court, correspondence, 15 Nov. 1989)

28 May 1980

BIBB exchanged small areas with TUSCALOOSA [area gained by TUSCALOOSA is too small to map at this scale]. (Ala. Acts 1980, reg. sess., no. 80-622/p. 1064)

18 July 1983

Boundaries of BALDWIN and MOBILE redefined [no change]. (Ala. Acts 1983, reg. sess., no. 83-533, secs. 1–3, 6/pp. 831–832)

Individual County Chronologies, Maps, and Areas for Alabama

ADAMS (Miss.) / 26
AUTAUGA / 27
BAINE (extinct) / 36
BAKER (see CHILTON)
BALDWIN / 38
BARBOUR / 41
BENTON (see CALHOUN)
BIBB (created as CAHAWBA) / 46
BLOUNT / 56
BULLOCK / 69
BUTLER / 73
CAHAWBA (see BIBB)
CALHOUN (created as BENTON) / 79
CHAMBERS / 88
CHEROKEE / 90
CHILTON (created as BAKER) / 96
CHOCTAW / 98
CLAIBORNE (Miss.) / 99
CLARKE / 100
CLAY / 104
CLEBURNE / 107
COFFEE / 114
COLBERT / 116
CONECUH / 117
COOSA / 123
COTACO (see MORGAN)
COVINGTON / 126
CRENSHAW / 133
CULLMAN / 136
DALE / 139
DALLAS / 143
DECATUR (extinct) / 151
DE KALB / 153
ELMORE / 166
ESCAMBIA / 167
ETOWAH / 168
FAYETTE / 172
FELICIANA (La., extinct) / 176
FRANKLIN / 177
GENEVA / 180
GREENE (Miss.) / 181
GREENE / 182
HALE / 185
HANCOCK (see WINSTON)
HENRY / 186
HOUSTON / 191
JACKSON (Miss.) / 192
JACKSON / 193
JEFFERSON (Miss., created as PICKERING) / 202
JEFFERSON / 203
JONES (extinct) / 217
JONES (see COVINGTON)
LAMAR (created as SANFORD) / 218
LAUDERDALE / 219
LAWRENCE / 220
LEE / 221
LIMESTONE / 223
LOWNDES / 224
MACON / 226
MADISON / 230
MARENGO / 234
MARION / 238
MARSHALL / 243
MOBILE / 253
MONROE / 260
MONTGOMERY / 265
MORGAN (created as COTACO) / 276
PASCAGOULA (Orleans Terr., extinct) / 279
PERRY / 280
PICKENS / 286
PICKERING (see JEFFERSON, Miss.)
PIKE / 288
RANDOLPH / 296
RUSSELL / 298
ST. CLAIR / 300
SANFORD (see LAMAR)
SHELBY / 312
SUMTER / 326
TALLADEGA / 328
TALLAPOOSA / 336
TUSCALOOSA / 339
WALKER / 353
WASHINGTON / 363
WAYNE (Miss.) / 371
WILCOX / 372
WINSTON (created as HANCOCK) / 377

ALABAMA

Chronology of ADAMS (Miss.)

Map	Date	Event	Resulting Area
❶	2 Apr 1799	Created by Mississippi Territory from non-county area; included part of present Alabama	14,810 sq mi
	4 Jun 1800	Lost to creation of WASHINGTON; eliminated from present Alabama	

(Heavy line depicts historical boundary. Base map shows present-day information.)

❶ 2 Apr 1799–3 June 1800

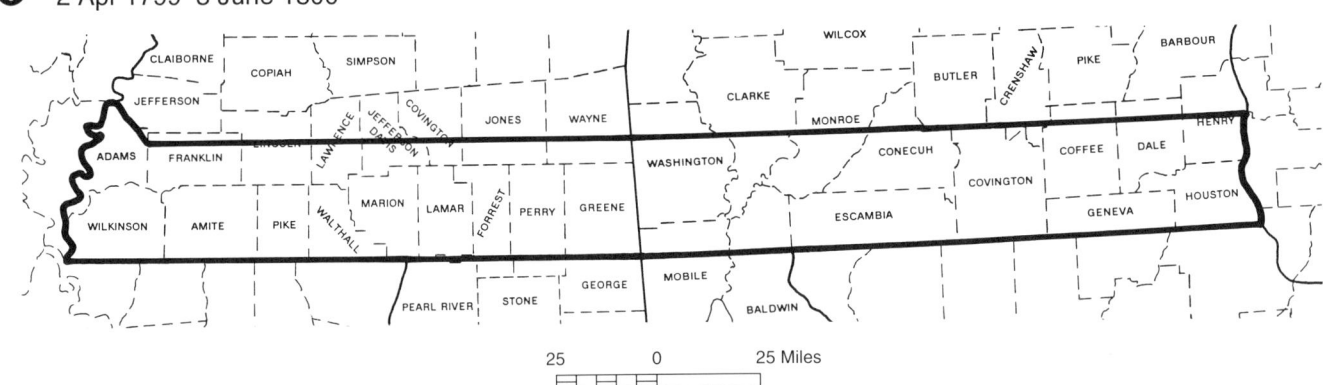

Individual County Chronologies 27

Chronology of AUTAUGA

Map	Date	Event	Resulting Area
❶	21 Nov 1818	Created from MONTGOMERY	1,170 sq mi

(Heavy line depicts historical boundary. Base map shows present-day information.)

❶ 21 Nov 1818–12 Dec 1819

ALABAMA

Chronology of AUTAUGA

Map	Date	Event	Resulting Area
❷	13 Dec 1819	Lost to CAHAWBA (now BIBB)	860 sq mi

(Heavy line depicts historical boundary. Base map shows present-day information.)

❷ 13 Dec 1819–12 Dec 1820

Individual County Chronologies

Chronology of AUTAUGA

Map	Date	Event	Resulting Area
❸	13 Dec 1820	Gained from BIBB	1,040 sq mi

(Heavy line depicts historical boundary. Base map shows present-day information.)

❸ 13 Dec 1820–11 Jan 1827

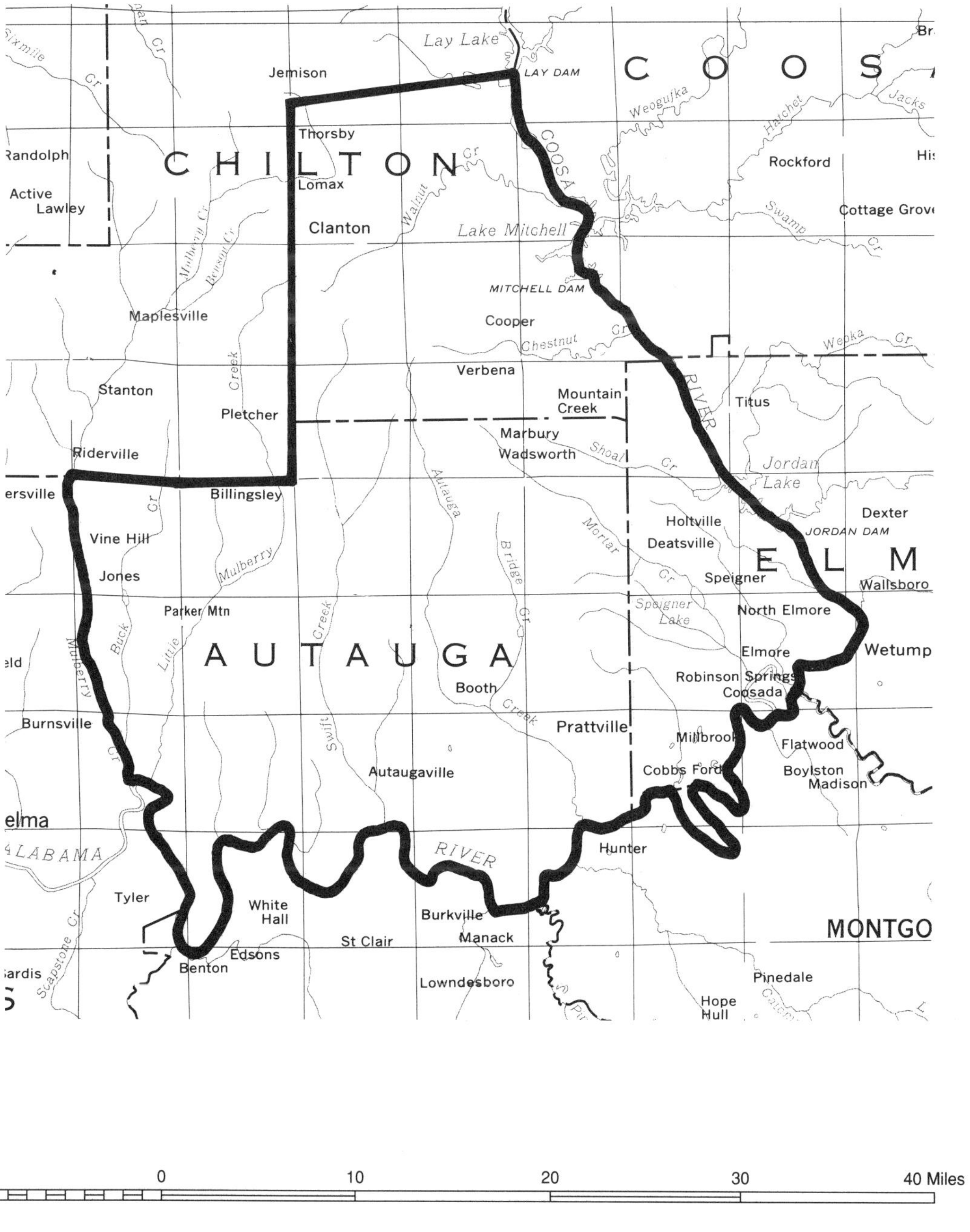

30 ALABAMA

Chronology of AUTAUGA

Map	Date	Event	Resulting Area
④	12 Jan 1827	Lost to SHELBY	1,020 sq mi

(Heavy line depicts historical boundary. Base map shows present-day information.)

④ 12 Jan 1827–27 Dec 1827

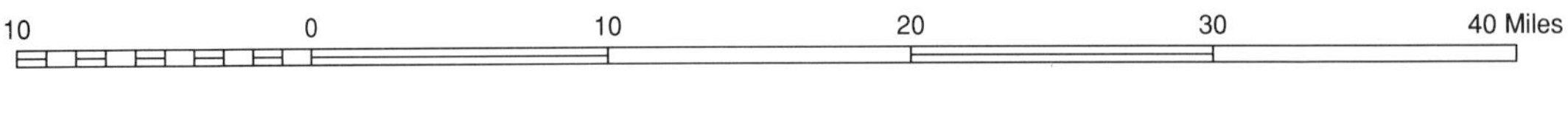

Chronology of AUTAUGA

Map	Date	Event	Resulting Area
❺	1 Mar 1827	Part of non-county area detached from MONTGOMERY, attached to AUTAUGA	

(Heavy line depicts historical boundary. Base map shows present-day information.)

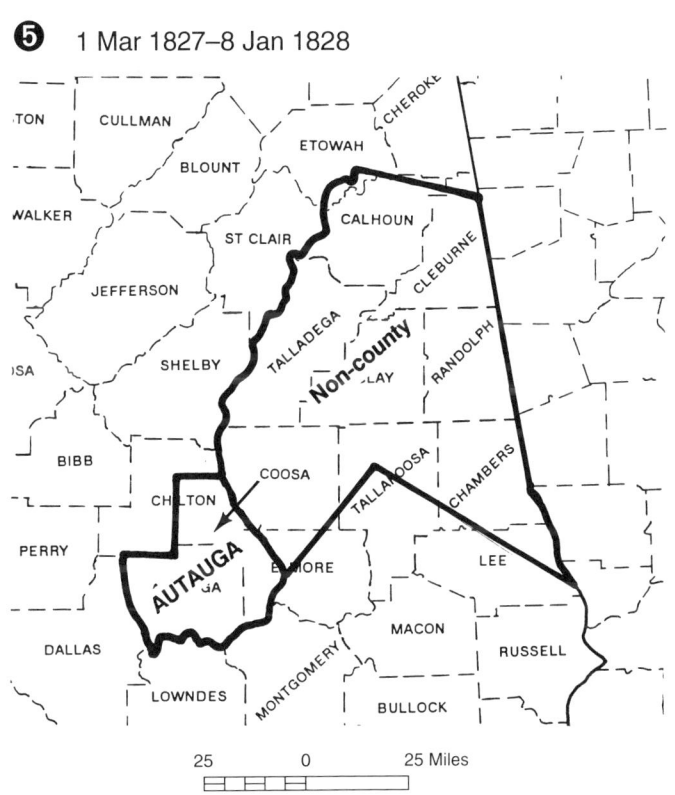

❺ 1 Mar 1827–8 Jan 1828

Chronology of AUTAUGA

Map	Date	Event	Resulting Area
❻	28 Dec 1827	Lost to SHELBY [attachment unchanged; see map 5]	990 sq mi

(Heavy line depicts historical boundary. Base map shows present-day information.)

❻ 28 Dec 1827–late Dec 1866

Chronology of AUTAUGA

Map	Date	Event	Resulting Area
❼	9 Jan 1828	ST. CLAIR and SHELBY given concurrent jurisdiction with AUTAUGA over non-county area attached to AUTAUGA on 1 Mar 1827	
❻	29 Jan 1829	Non-county area detached from concurrent jurisdiction of AUTAUGA, ST. CLAIR, and SHELBY; attached to MONT-GOMERY, ST. CLAIR, and SHELBY	990 sq mi
	7 Nov 1862	Gained small area from BIBB to accommodate local property owners [location unknown, not mapped]	

(Heavy line depicts historical boundary. Base map shows present-day information.)

❼ 9 Jan 1828–28 Jan 1829

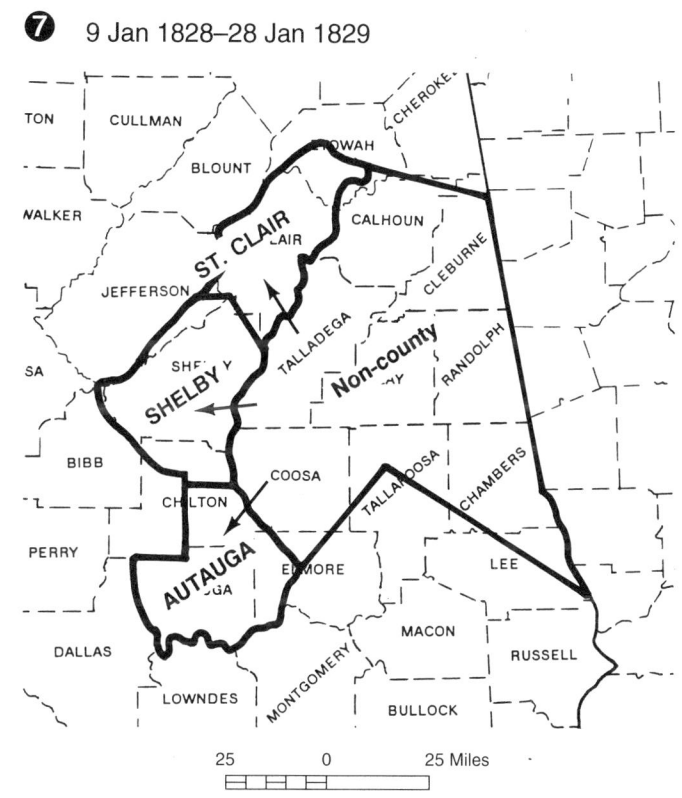

34 ALABAMA

Chronology of AUTAUGA

Map	Date	Event	Resulting Area
⑧	late Dec 1866	Lost to creation of ELMORE	820 sq mi

(Heavy line depicts historical boundary. Base map shows present-day information.)

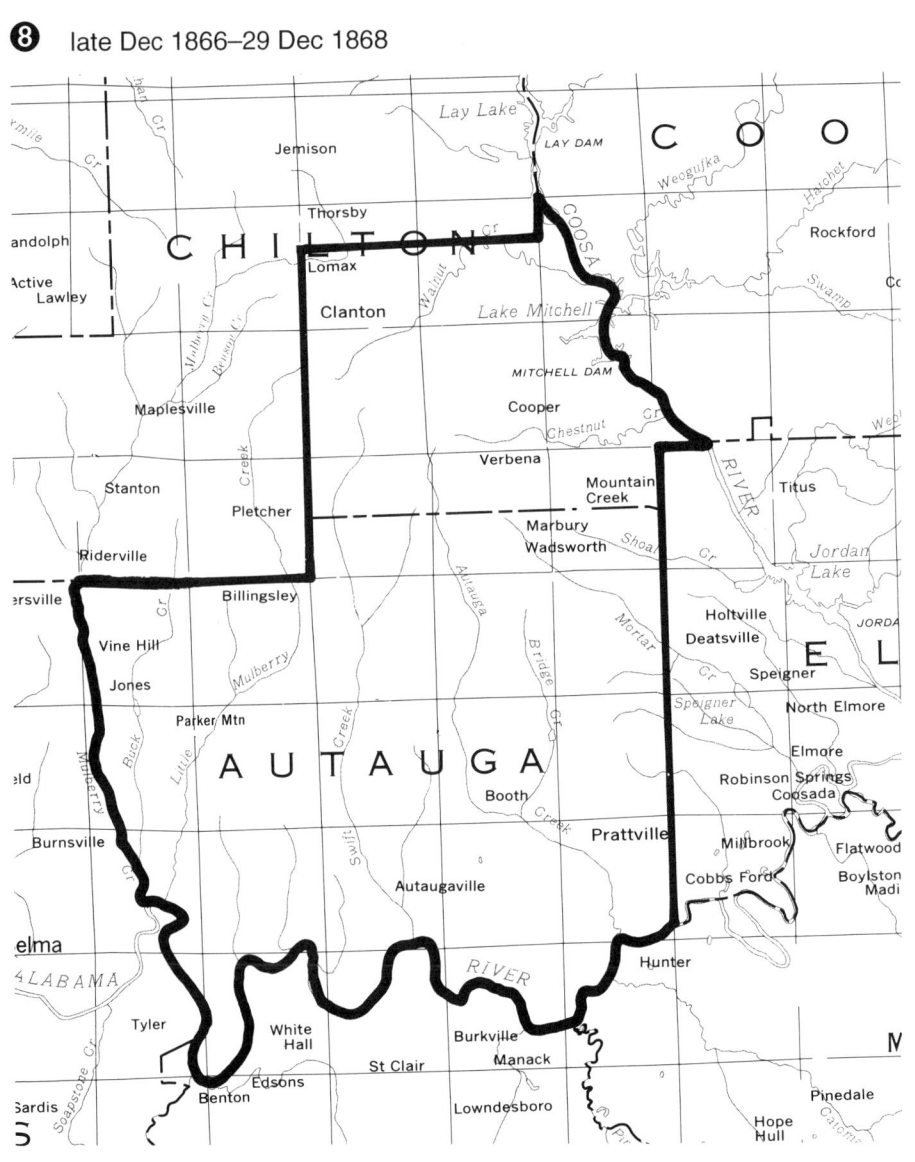

⑧ late Dec 1866–29 Dec 1868

Individual County Chronologies 35

Chronology of AUTAUGA

Map	Date	Event	Resulting Area
⑨	30 Dec 1868	Lost to creation of BAKER (now CHILTON)	660 sq mi
⑩	15 Dec 1869	Lost to BAKER (now CHILTON)	600 sq mi

(Heavy line depicts historical boundary. Base map shows present-day information.)

⑨ 30 Dec 1868–14 Dec 1869

⑩ 15 Dec 1869–1990

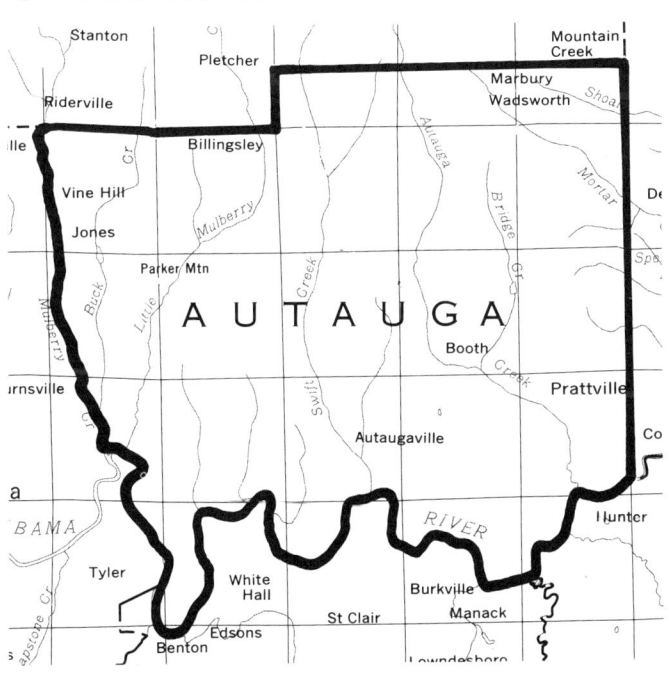

ALABAMA

Chronology of BAINE (extinct)

Map	Date	Event	Resulting Area
❶	7 Dec 1866	Created from BLOUNT, CALHOUN, CHEROKEE, DE KALB, MARSHALL, and ST. CLAIR	860 sq mi

(Heavy line depicts historical boundary. Base map shows present-day information.)

❶ 7 Dec 1866–18 Feb 1867

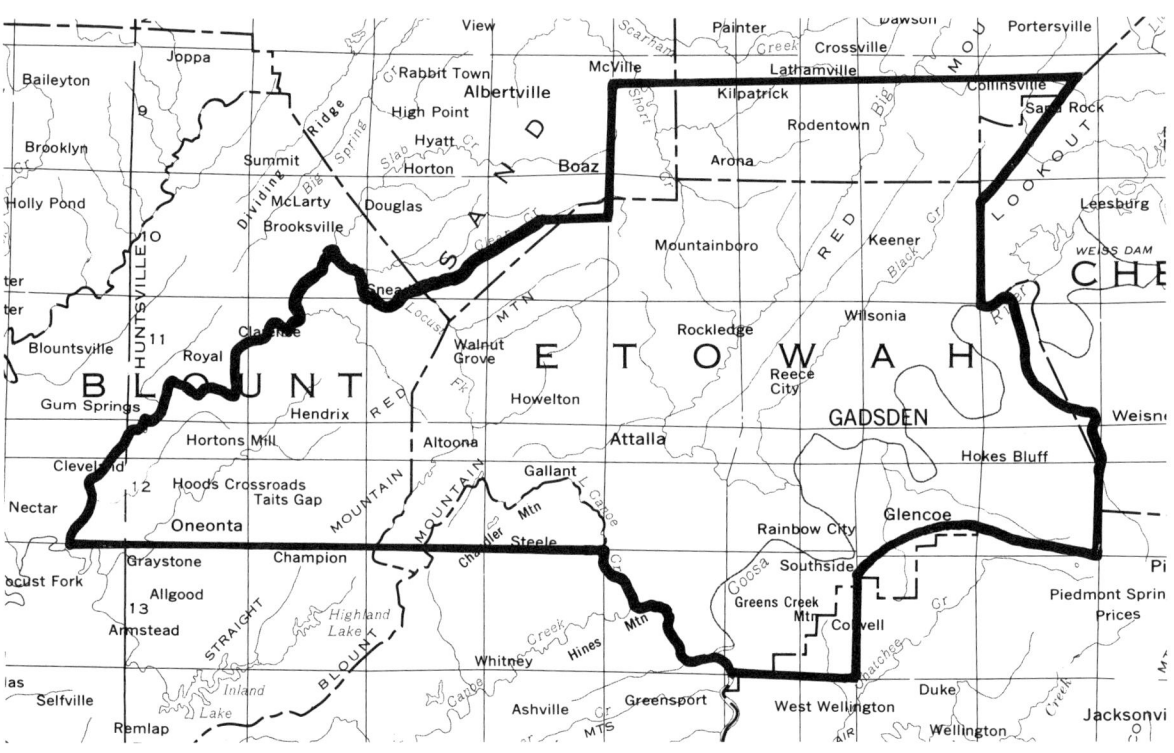

Individual County Chronologies 37

Chronology of BAINE (extinct)

Map	Date	Event	Resulting Area
❷	19 Feb 1867	Lost to DE KALB and MARSHALL Change in boundary with BLOUNT and ST. CLAIR authorized [cannot be demarcated as described, no change]	760 sq mi
	3 Dec 1867	Lost to BLOUNT, CALHOUN, CHEROKEE, DE KALB, MARSHALL, and ST. CLAIR; BAINE eliminated [ETOWAH created 1 Dec 1868 in the same area, but with different boundaries from those of BAINE]	

(Heavy line depicts historical boundary. Base map shows present-day information.)

❷ 19 Feb 1867–2 Dec 1867

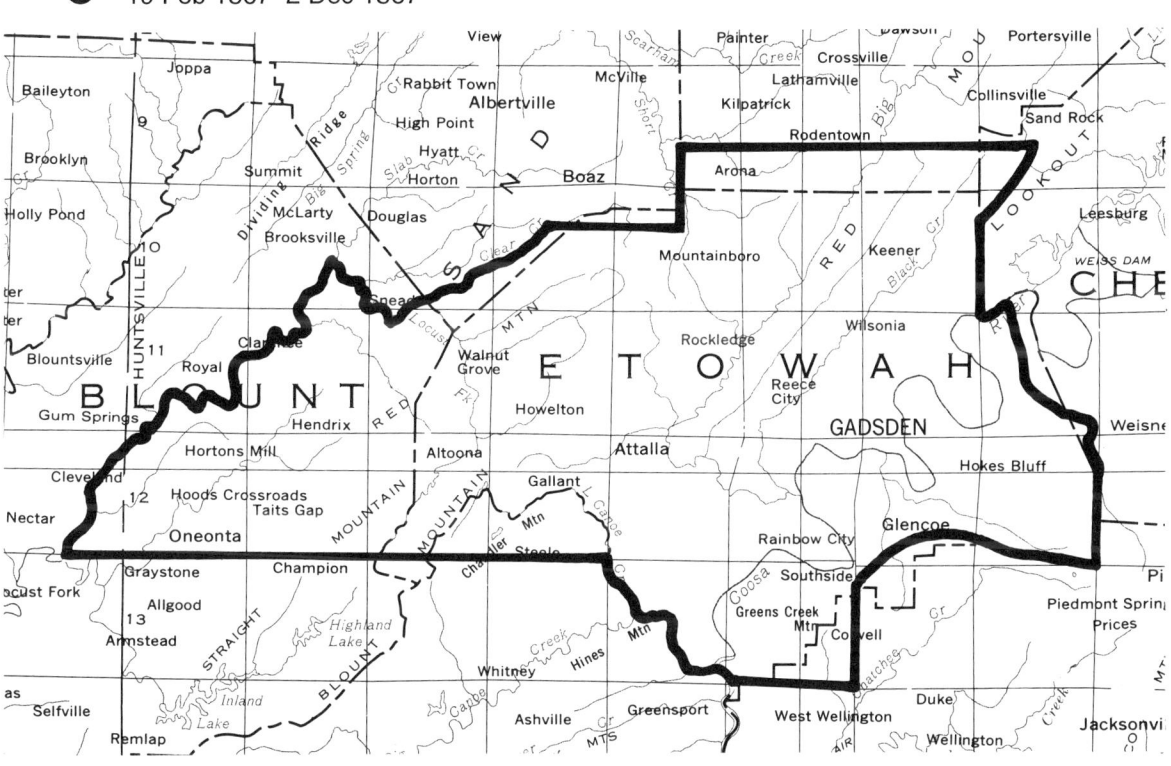

38 ALABAMA

Chronology of BALDWIN

Map	Date	Event	Resulting Area
❶	21 Dec 1809	Created by Mississippi Territory from WASHINGTON	660 sq mi
	3 Mar 1817	Became part of Alabama Territory	
❷	7 Feb 1818	Gained from GREENE (Miss.)	1,020 sq mi

(Heavy line depicts historical boundary. Base map shows present-day information.)

❶ 21 Dec 1809–6 Feb 1818

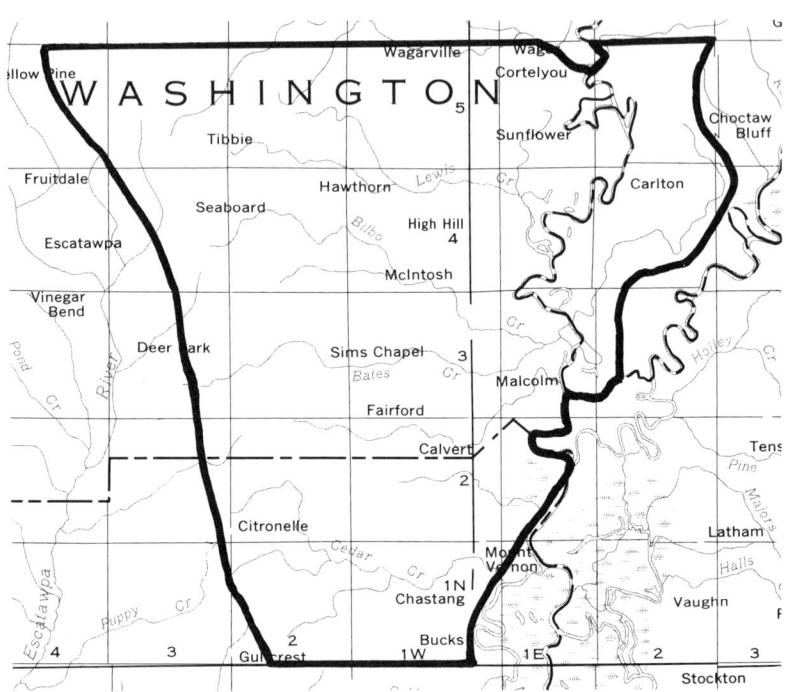

❷ 7 Feb 1818–12 Dec 1819

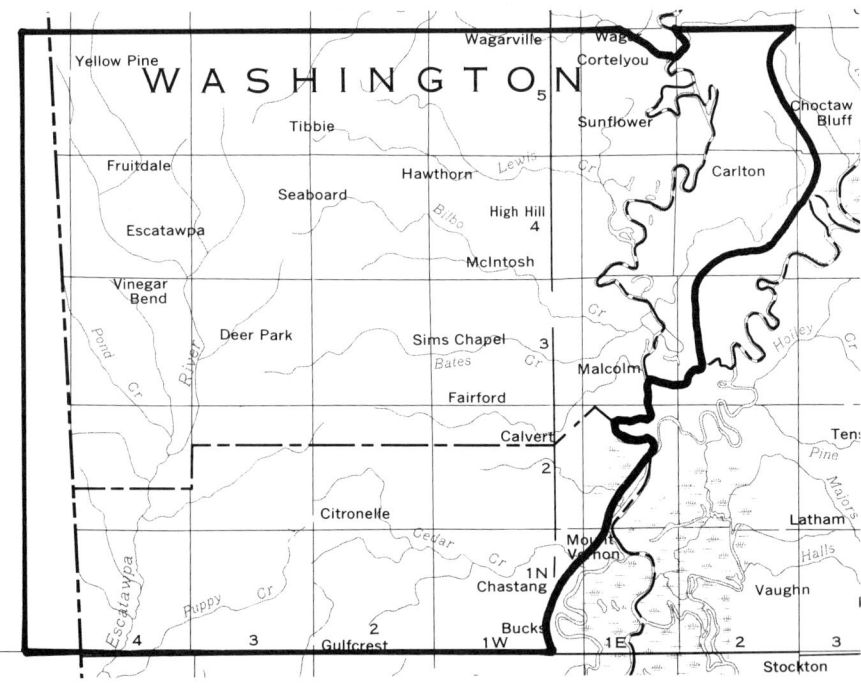

Chronology of BALDWIN

Map	Date	Event	Resulting Area
❸	13 Dec 1819	Gained from CONECUH and MONROE	1,730 sq mi
❹	by 29 May 1820	Lost to Mississippi when surveyors implemented the authorized adjustment of the Mississippi-Alabama line	1,660 sq mi
❺	16 Dec 1820	Exchanged with MOBILE, lost to MONROE	1,890 sq mi
❻	21 Dec 1832	Gained from MOBILE	1,910 sq mi

(Heavy line depicts historical boundary. Base map shows present-day information.)

❸ 13 Dec 1819–before 29 May 1820

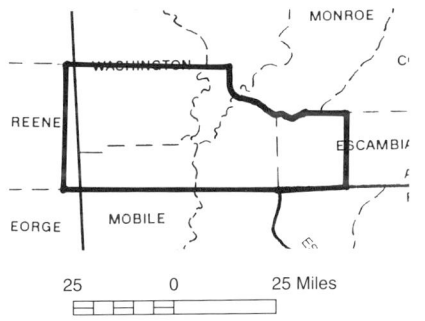

❹ by 29 May 1820–15 Dec 1820

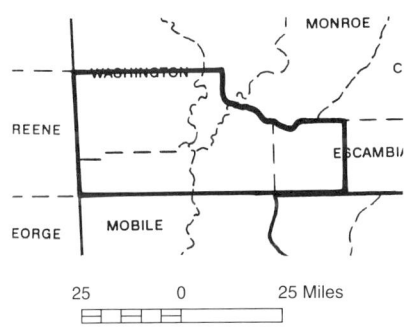

❺ 16 Dec 1820–20 Dec 1832

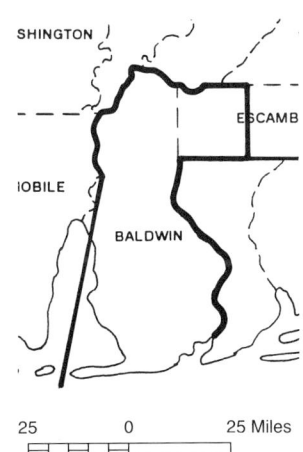

❻ 21 Dec 1832–9 Dec 1868

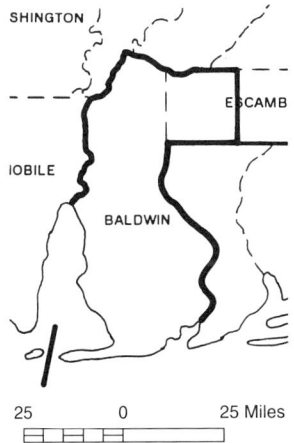

40 ALABAMA

Chronology of BALDWIN

Map	Date	Event	Resulting Area
⑦	10 Dec 1868	Lost to creation of ESCAMBIA, and apparently lost to MONROE	1,590 sq mi
	18 Jul 1983	Boundaries redefined [no change]	

(Heavy line depicts historical boundary. Base map shows present-day information.)

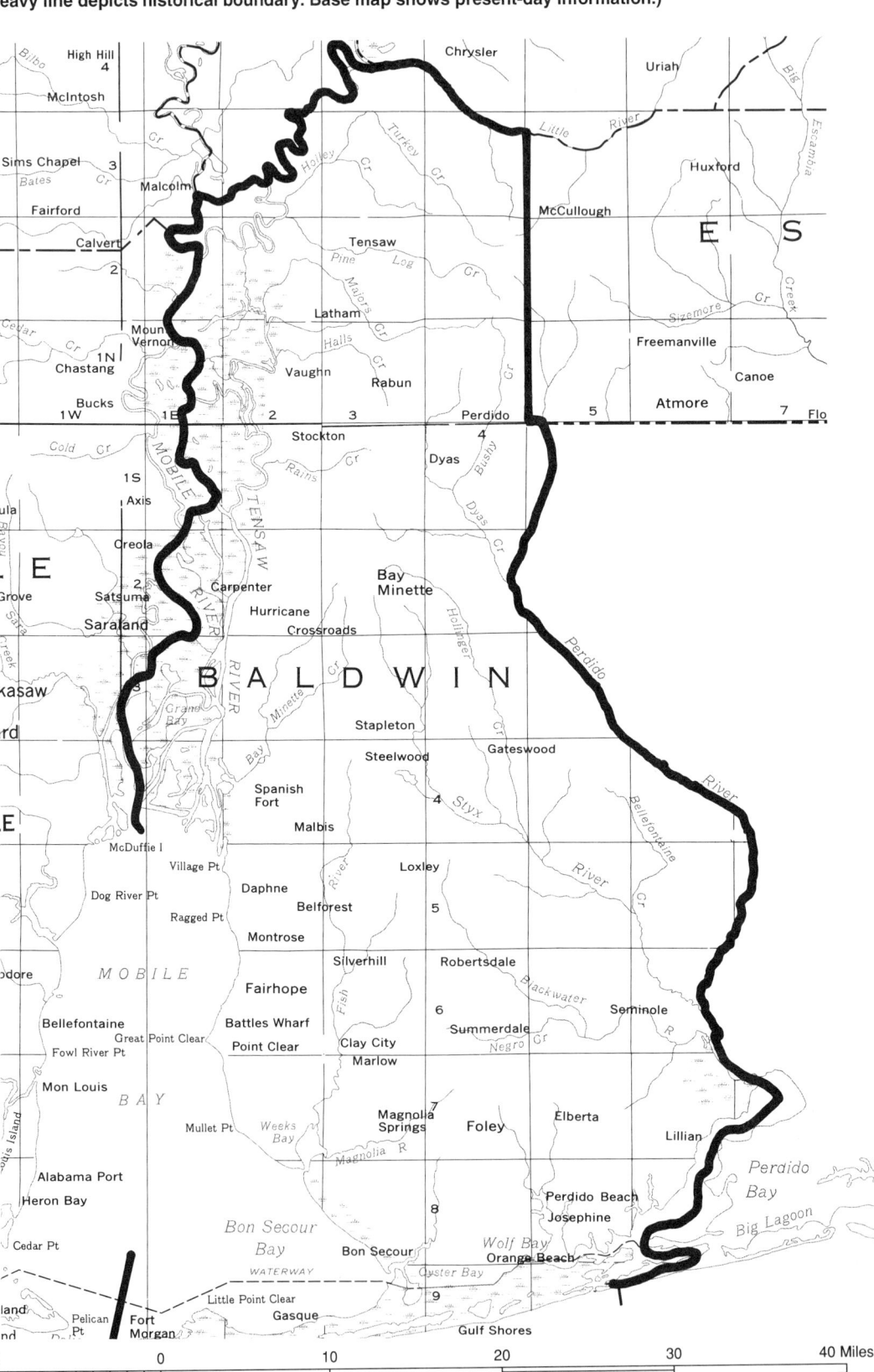

⑦ 10 Dec 1868–1990

Chronology of BARBOUR

Map	Date	Event	Resulting Area
❶	18 Dec 1832	Created from PIKE	990 sq mi
❶	17 Jan 1844	Lost to HENRY	990 sq mi

(Heavy line depicts historical boundary. Base map shows present-day information.)

❶ 18 Dec 1832–4 Dec 1866

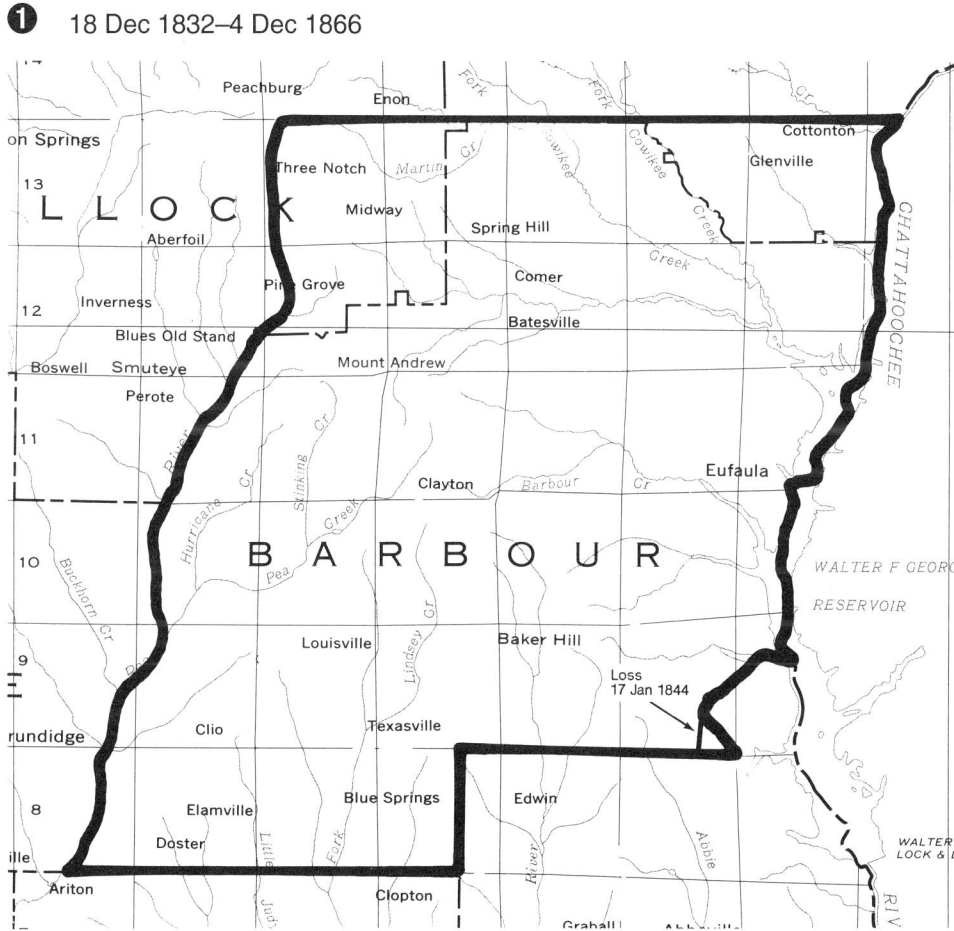

ALABAMA

Chronology of BARBOUR

Map	Date	Event	Resulting Area
❷	5 Dec 1866	Lost to creation of BULLOCK	950 sq mi

(Heavy line depicts historical boundary. Base map shows present-day information.)

❷ 5 Dec 1866–7 Feb 1867

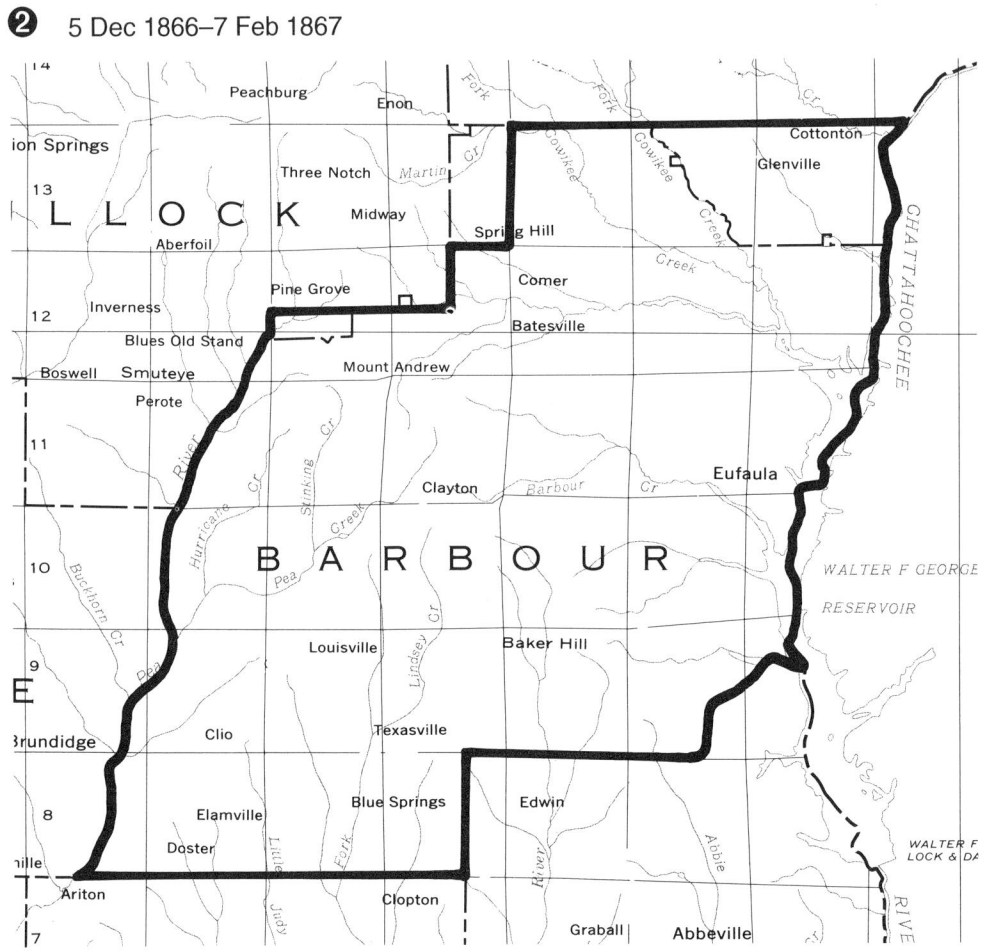

Chronology of BARBOUR

Map	Date	Event	Resulting Area
❸	8 Feb 1867	Exchanged with BULLOCK	970 sq mi

(Heavy line depicts historical boundary. Base map shows present-day information.)

❸ 8 Feb 1867–30 Dec 1868

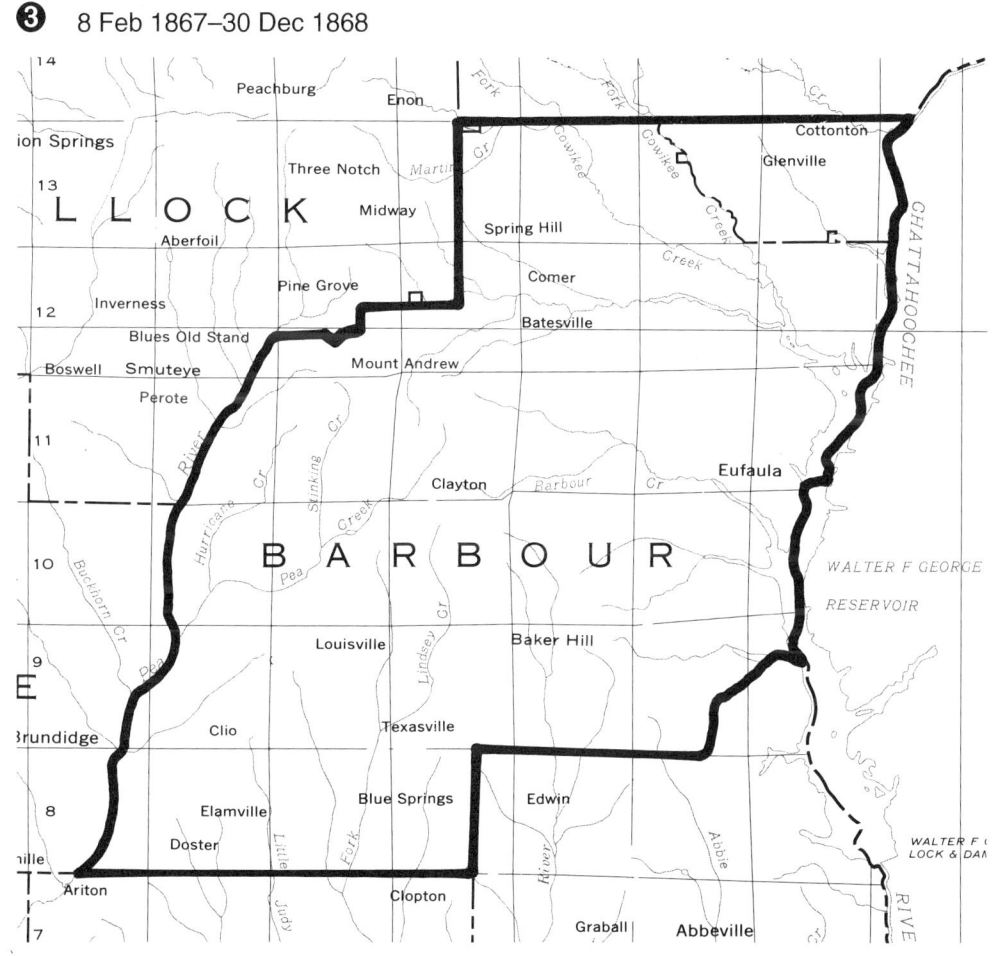

44 ALABAMA

Chronology of BARBOUR

Map	Date	Event	Resulting Area
④	31 Dec 1868	Lost to RUSSELL	900 sq mi
④	9 Mar 1871	Gained small area from BULLOCK to accommodate local property owner	900 sq mi
④	8 Feb 1872	Lost small area to BULLOCK	900 sq mi
④	15 Mar 1873	Gained small area from RUSSELL to accommodate local property owner	900 sq mi

(Heavy line depicts historical boundary. Base map shows present-day information.)

④ 31 Dec 1868–9 Feb 1875

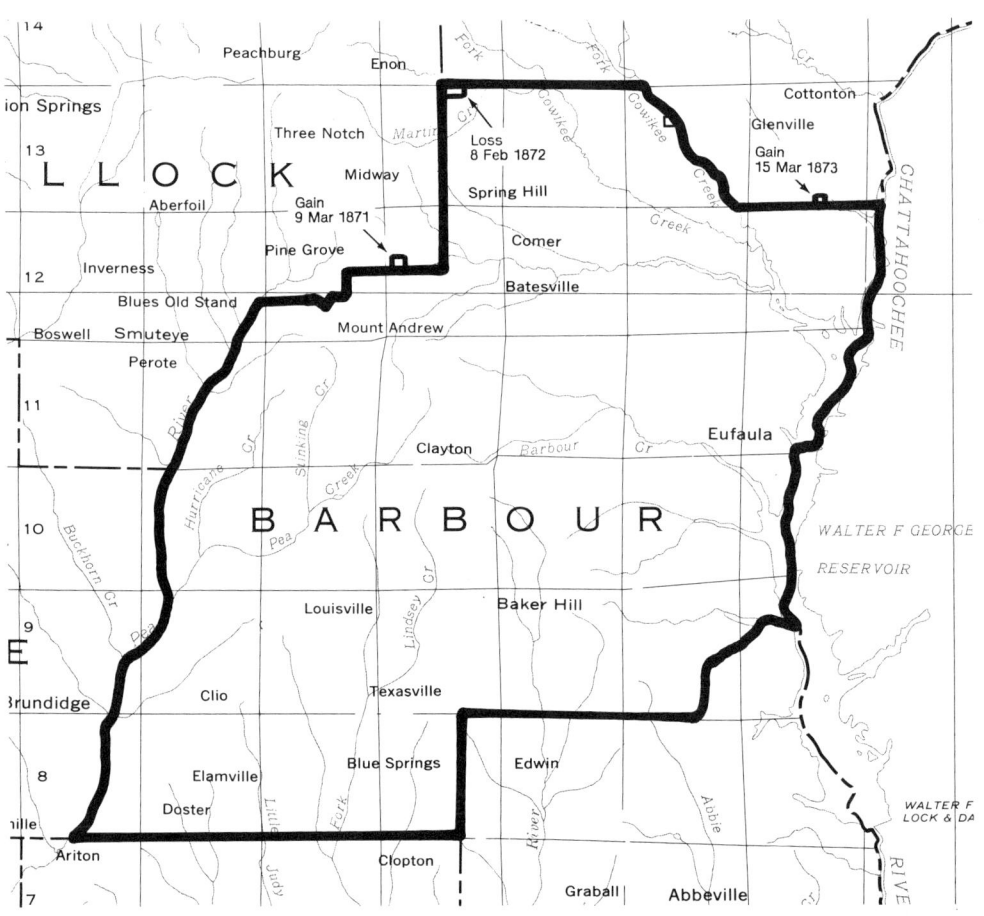

Individual County Chronologies 45

Chronology of BARBOUR

Map	Date	Event	Resulting Area
❺	10 Feb 1875	Lost small area to RUSSELL to accommodate local property owner	900 sq mi

(Heavy line depicts historical boundary. Base map shows present-day information.)

❺ 10 Feb 1875–1990

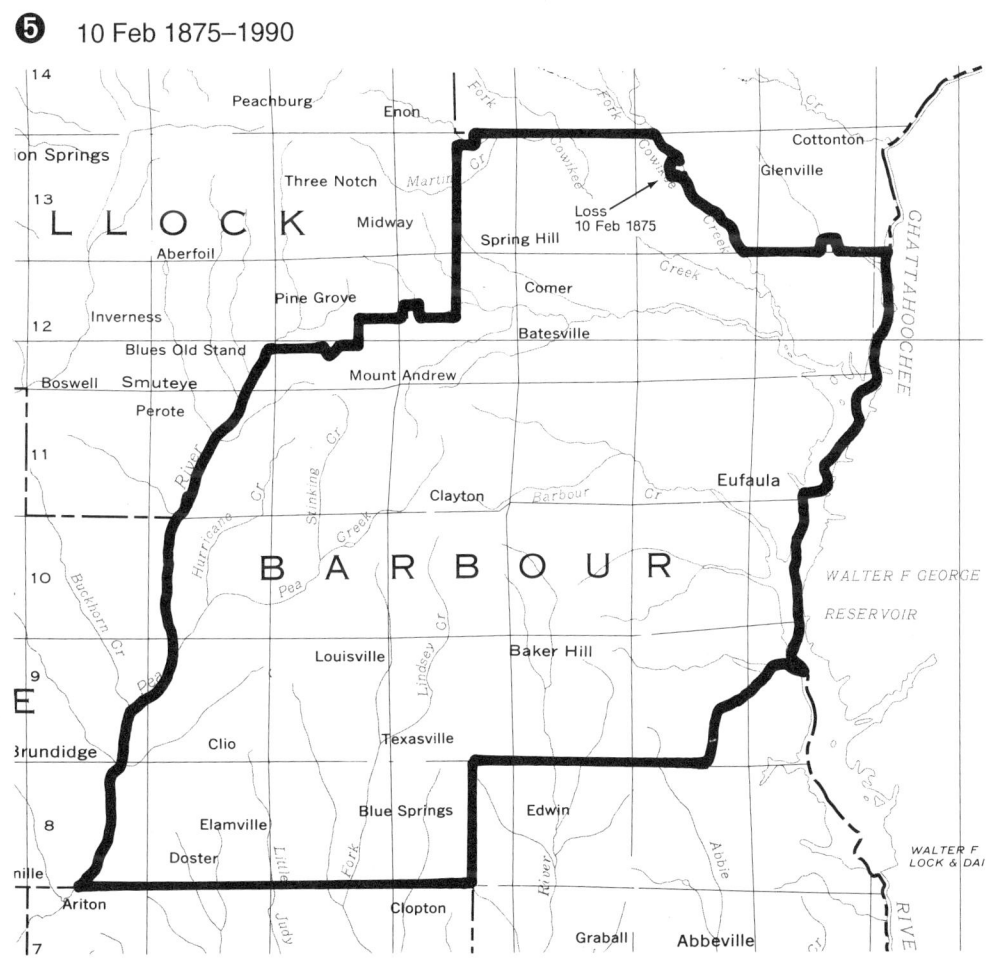

46 ALABAMA

Chronology of BIBB (created as CAHAWBA)

Map	Date	Event	Resulting Area
❶	7 Feb 1818	Created as CAHAWBA from MONTGOMERY	1,320 sq mi
❷	20 Nov 1818	Gained from DALLAS and MONTGOMERY, lost to SHELBY and TUSCALOOSA	910 sq mi

(Heavy line depicts historical boundary. Base map shows present-day information.)

❶ 7 Feb 1818–19 Nov 1818

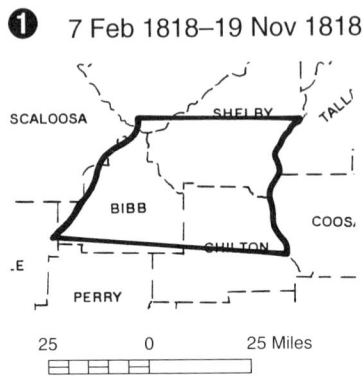

❷ 20 Nov 1818–12 Dec 1819

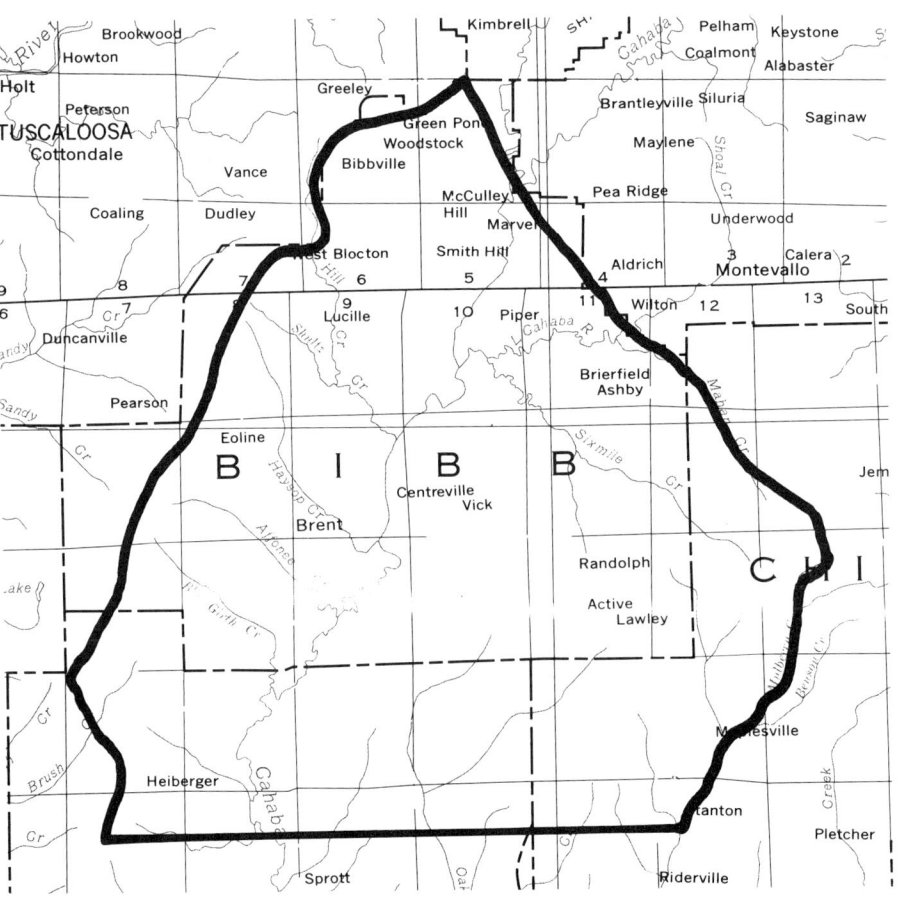

Individual County Chronologies

Chronology of BIBB (created as CAHAWBA)

Map	Date	Event	Resulting Area
❸	13 Dec 1819	Gained from AUTAUGA, lost to creation of PERRY	1,030 sq mi
	4 Dec 1820	Renamed BIBB	

(Heavy line depicts historical boundary. Base map shows present-day information.)

❸ 13 Dec 1819–12 Dec 1820

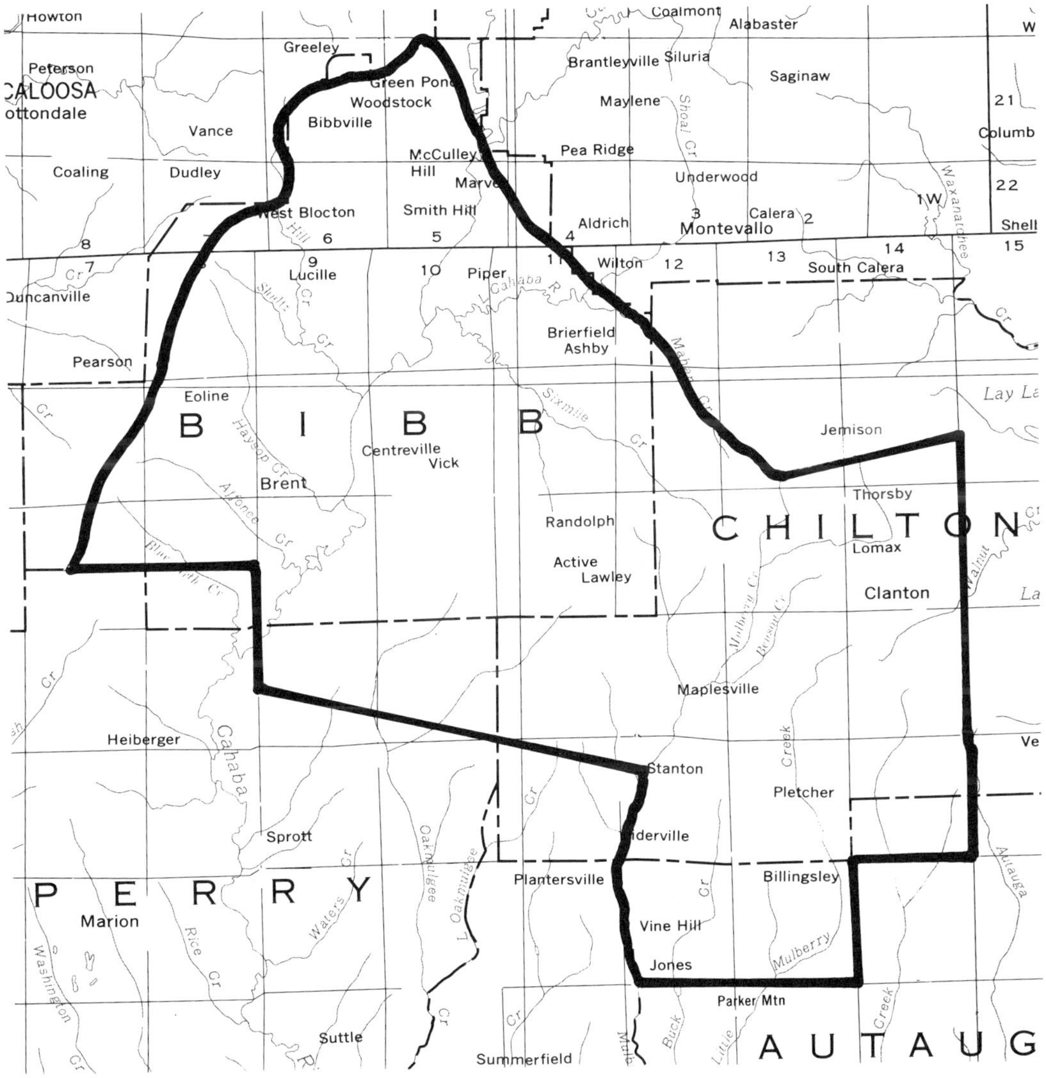

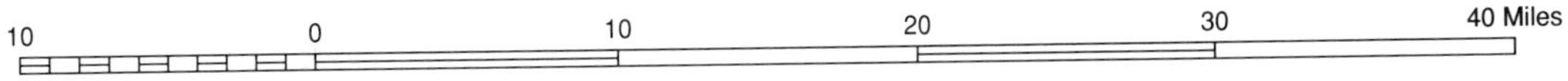

ALABAMA

Chronology of BIBB (created as CAHAWBA)

Map	Date	Event	Resulting Area
④	13 Dec 1820	Lost to AUTAUGA	850 sq mi

(Heavy line depicts historical boundary. Base map shows present-day information.)

④ 13 Dec 1820–19 Dec 1820

Chronology of BIBB (created as CAHAWBA)

Map	Date	Event	Resulting Area
❺	20 Dec 1820	Gained from TUSCALOOSA and from non-county area, exchanged with PERRY	850 sq mi

(Heavy line depicts historical boundary. Base map shows present-day information.)

❺ 20 Dec 1820–16 Dec 1821

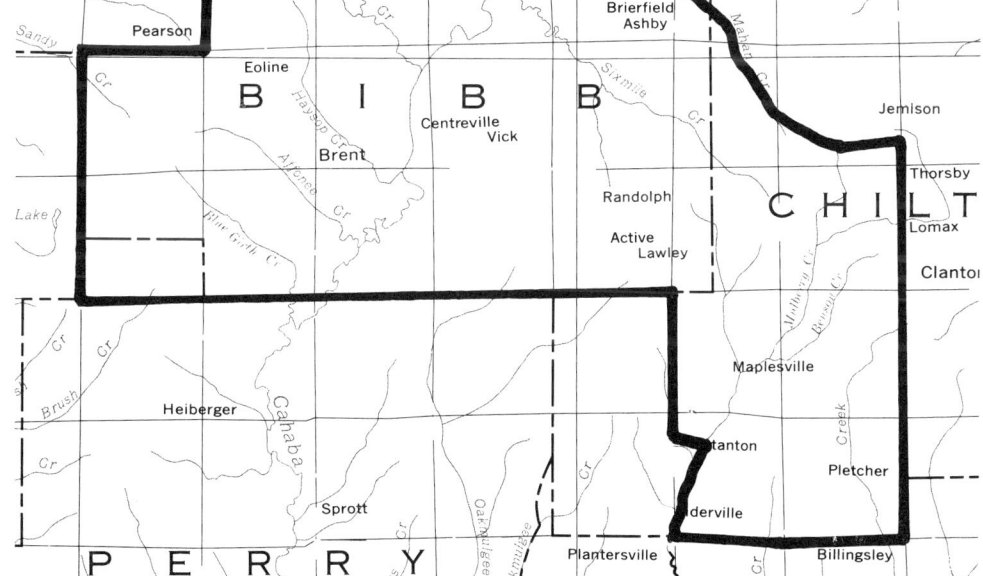

ALABAMA

Chronology of BIBB (created as CAHAWBA)

Map	Date	Event	Resulting Area
⑥	17 Dec 1821	Exchanged with PERRY	850 sq mi
⑥	3 Jan 1828	Gained small area from PERRY	850 sq mi
	15 Jan 1828	Boundary with TUSCALOOSA clarified [no change]	

(Heavy line depicts historical boundary. Base map shows present-day information.)

⑥ 17 Dec 1821–14 Jan 1831

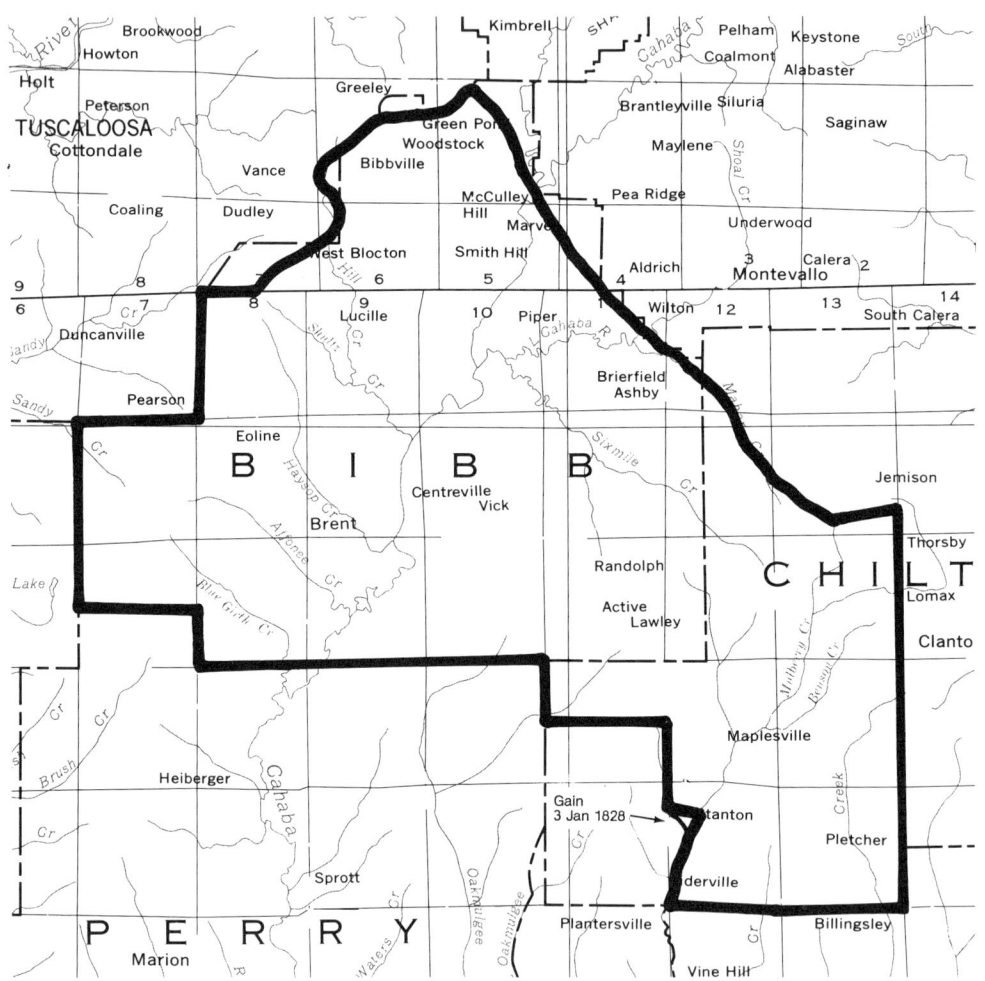

Individual County Chronologies

Chronology of BIBB (created as CAHAWBA)

Map	Date	Event	Resulting Area
❼	15 Jan 1831	Exchanged with TUSCALOOSA	860 sq mi

(Heavy line depicts historical boundary. Base map shows present-day information.)

❼ 15 Jan 1831–17 Jan 1832

ALABAMA

Chronology of BIBB (created as CAHAWBA)

Map	Date	Event	Resulting Area
⑧	18 Jan 1832	Gained from SHELBY	870 sq mi
	7 Nov 1862	Lost small area to AUTAUGA to accommodate local property owners [location unknown, not mapped]	

(Heavy line depicts historical boundary. Base map shows present-day information.)

⑧ 18 Jan 1832–29 Dec 1868

Individual County Chronologies 53

Chronology of BIBB (created as CAHAWBA)

Map	Date	Event	Resulting Area
9	30 Dec 1868	Lost to creation of BAKER (now CHILTON)	620 sq mi
9	7 Dec 1871	Gained small area from PERRY to accommodate local property owners	620 sq mi

(Heavy line depicts historical boundary. Base map shows present-day information.)

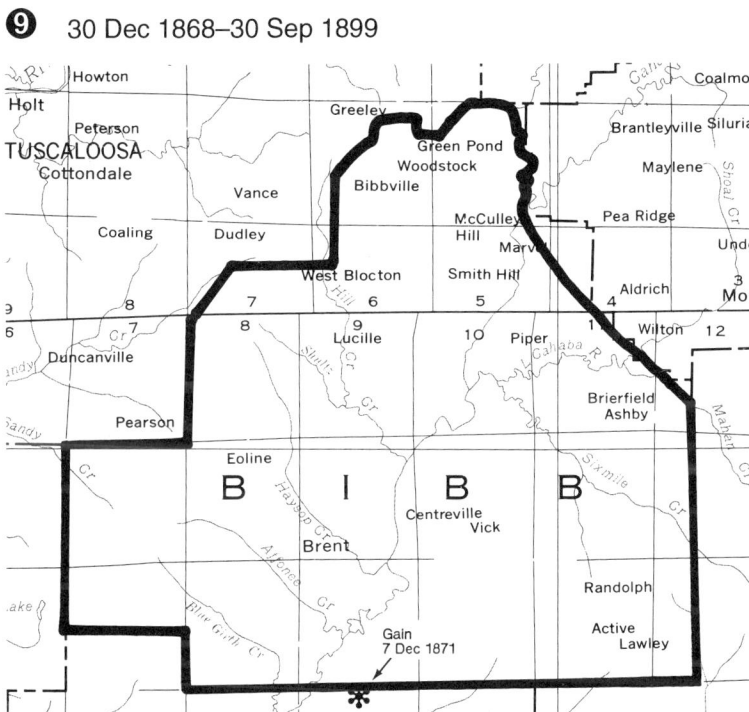

9   30 Dec 1868–30 Sep 1899

54 ALABAMA

Chronology of BIBB (created as CAHAWBA)

Map	Date	Event	Resulting Area
⑩	1 Oct 1899	Exchanged with SHELBY	620 sq mi

(Heavy line depicts historical boundary. Base map shows present-day information.)

⑩ 1 Oct 1899–1 Mar 1907

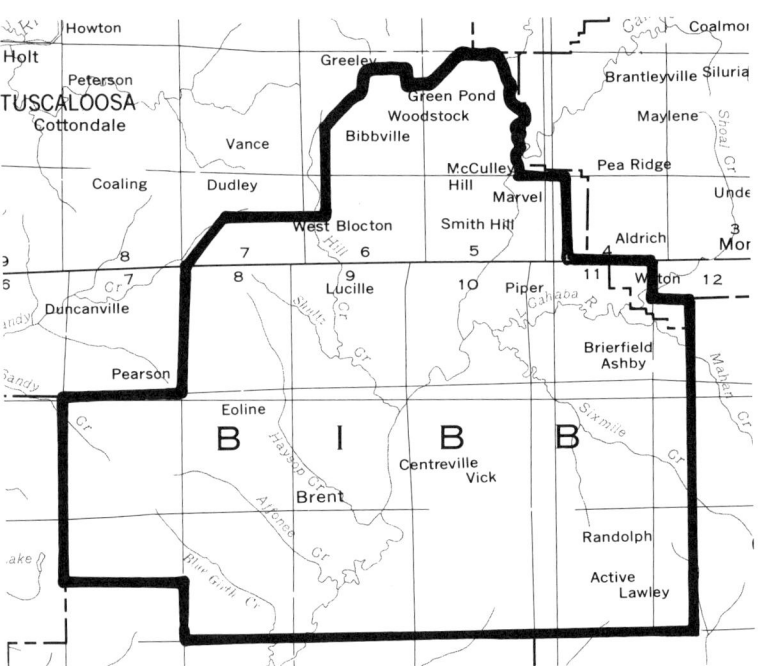

Individual County Chronologies 55

Chronology of BIBB (created as CAHAWBA)

Map	Date	Event	Resulting Area
⑪	2 Mar 1907	Exchanged with SHELBY	620 sq mi
	18 Jul 1979	Boundary with CHILTON redefined [no change]	
⑪	28 May 1980	Exchanged small areas with TUSCALOOSA [area lost to TUSCALOOSA is too small to map at our scale]	620 sq mi

(Heavy line depicts historical boundary. Base map shows present-day information.)

⑪ 2 Mar 1907–1990

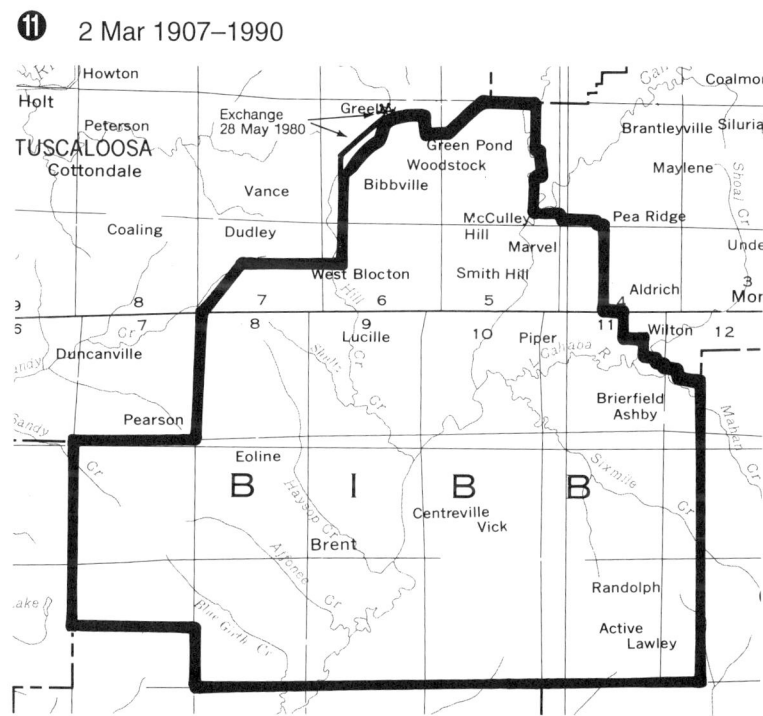

56 ALABAMA

Chronology of BLOUNT

Map	Date	Event	Resulting Area
❶	6 Feb 1818	Created from MONTGOMERY and non-county area	2,650 sq mi
❷	13 Dec 1819	Lost to creation of JEFFERSON	1,730 sq mi

(Heavy line depicts historical boundary. Base map shows present-day information.)

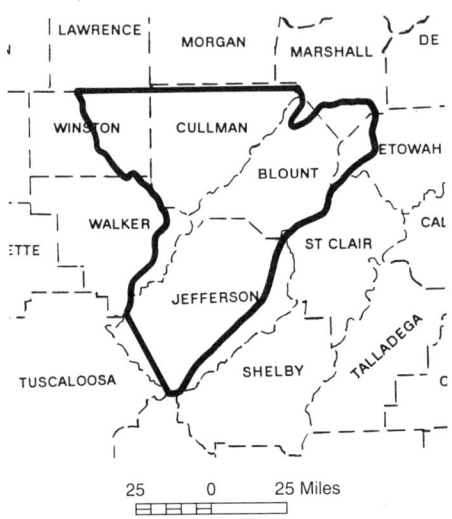

❶ 6 Feb 1818–12 Dec 1819

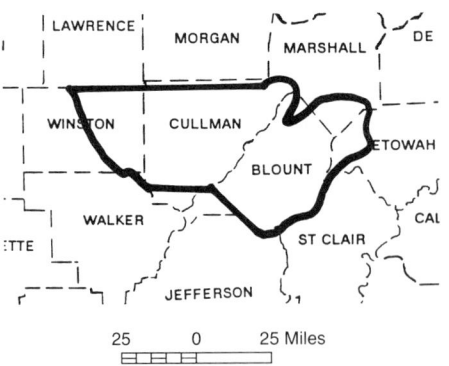

❷ 13 Dec 1819–29 Dec 1822

Chronology of BLOUNT

Map	Date	Event	Resulting Area
❸	30 Dec 1822	Lost to non-county area	1,140 sq mi
	15 Jan 1828	Boundary with JEFFERSON clarified [no discernible change]	

(Heavy line depicts historical boundary. Base map shows present-day information.)

❸ 30 Dec 1822–20 Jan 1832

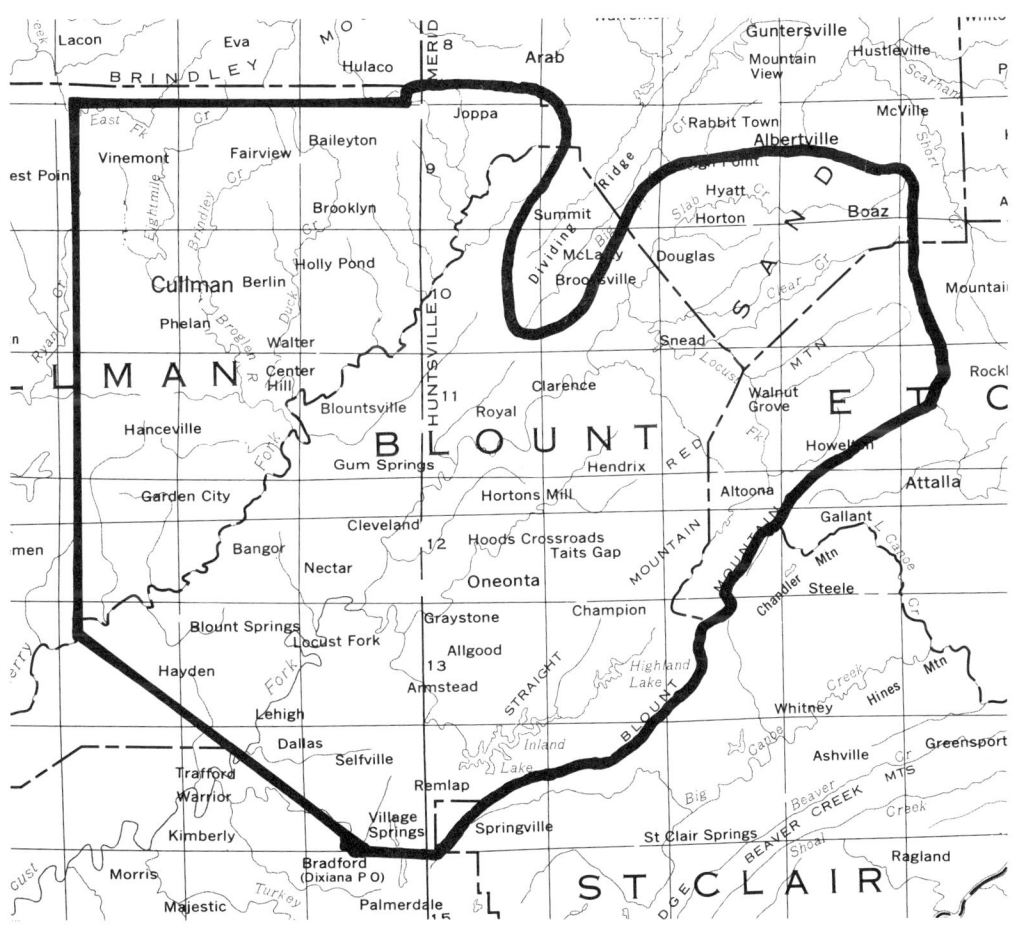

58 ALABAMA

Chronology of BLOUNT

Map	Date	Event	Resulting Area
④	21 Jan 1832	Gained from non-county areas attached to JACKSON and MORGAN, lost to MORGAN	1,330 sq mi

(Heavy line depicts historical boundary. Base map shows present-day information.)

④ 21 Jan 1832–8 Jan 1836

Individual County Chronologies 59

Chronology of BLOUNT

Map	Date	Event	Resulting Area
❺	9 Jan 1836	Lost to creation of MARSHALL	1,010 sq mi

(Heavy line depicts historical boundary. Base map shows present-day information.)

❺ 9 Jan 1836–6 Dec 1866
3 Dec 1867–30 Nov 1868

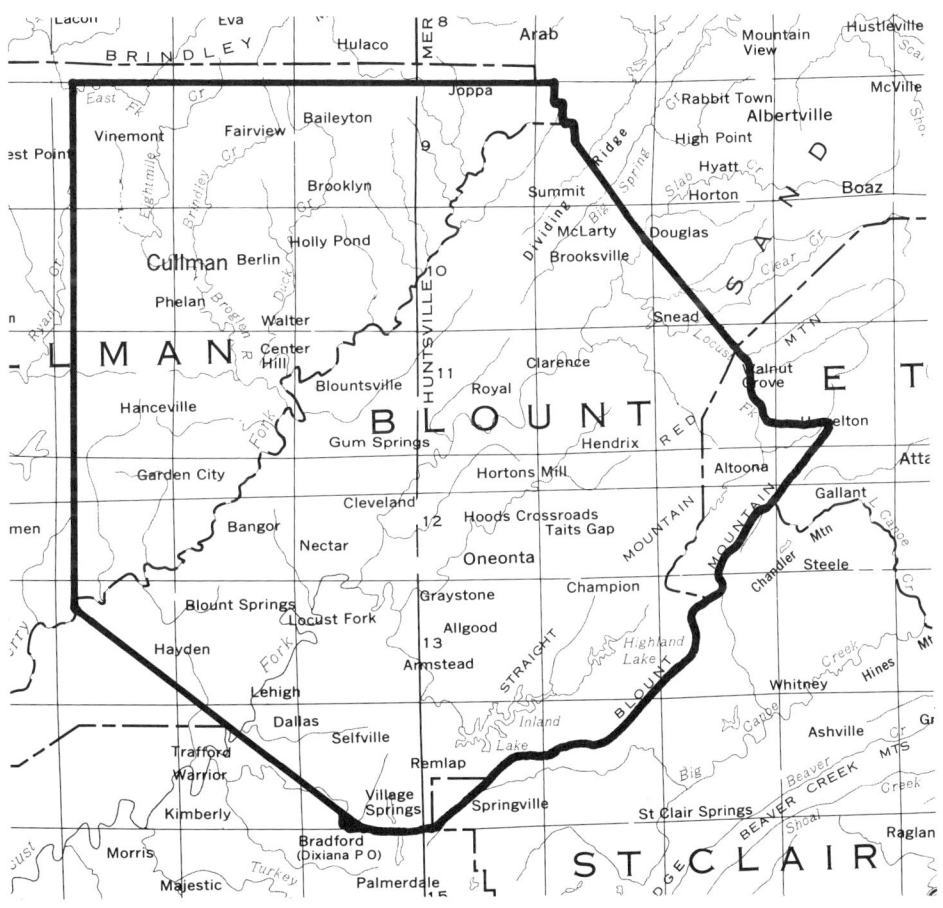

60 ALABAMA

Chronology of BLOUNT

Map	Date	Event	Resulting Area
❻	7 Dec 1866	Lost to creation of BAINE	820 sq mi
	19 Feb 1867	Change in boundary with BAINE and ST. CLAIR authorized [cannot be demarcated as described, no change]	
❺	3 Dec 1867	Gained from BAINE; BAINE eliminated	1,010 sq mi

(Heavy line depicts historical boundary. Base map shows present-day information.)

❻ 7 Dec 1866–2 Dec 1867

Chronology of BLOUNT

Map	Date	Event	Resulting Area
❼	1 Dec 1868	Lost to creation of ETOWAH	980 sq mi
❼	25 Feb 1870	Gained small area from MARSHALL	980 sq mi

(Heavy line depicts historical boundary. Base map shows present-day information.)

❼ 1 Dec 1868–23 Jan 1877

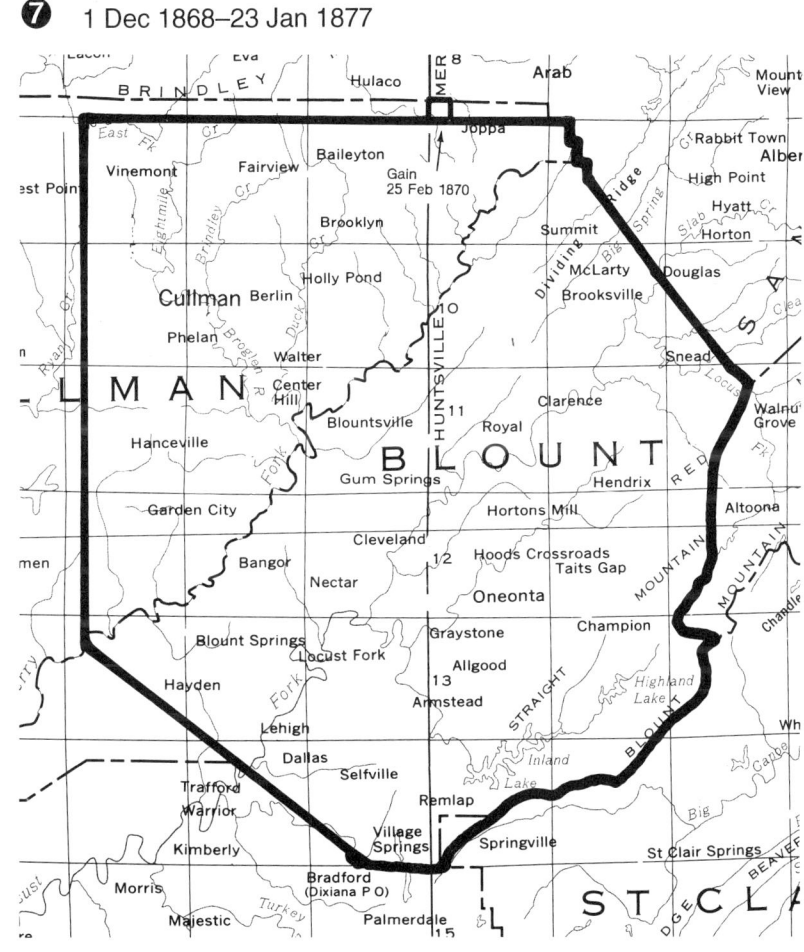

Chronology of BLOUNT

Map	Date	Event	Resulting Area
8	24 Jan 1877	Lost to creation of CULLMAN	670 sq mi

(Heavy line depicts historical boundary. Base map shows present-day information.)

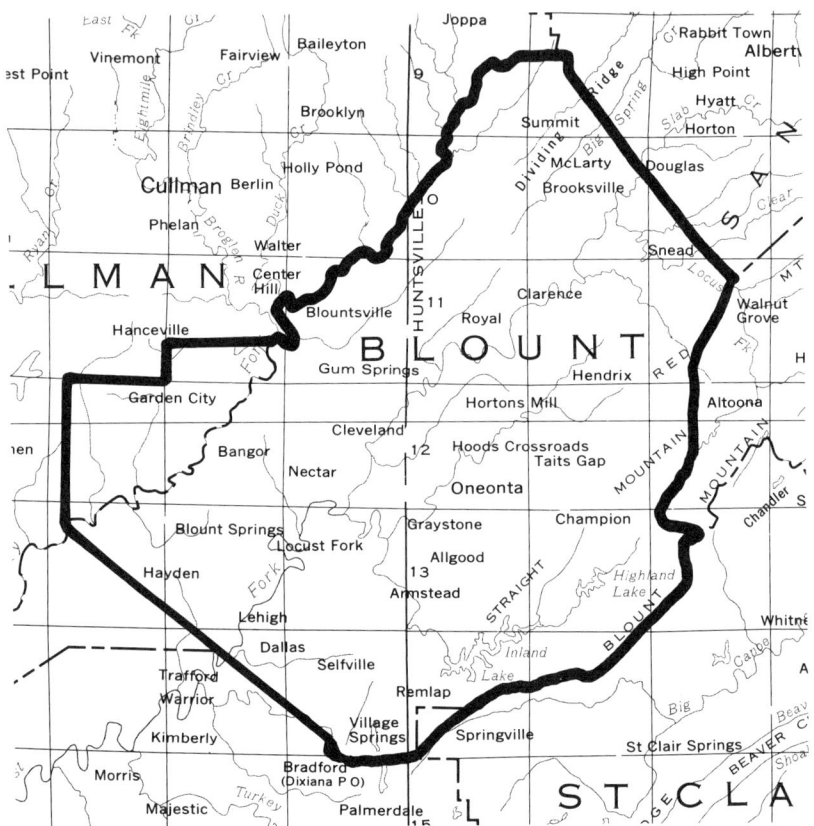

8 24 Jan 1877–7 Feb 1877

Individual County Chronologies 63

Chronology of BLOUNT

Map	Date	Event	Resulting Area
❾	8 Feb 1877	Gained from JEFFERSON and WALKER	770 sq mi

(Heavy line depicts historical boundary. Base map shows present-day information.)

❾ 8 Feb 1877–28 Jan 1879

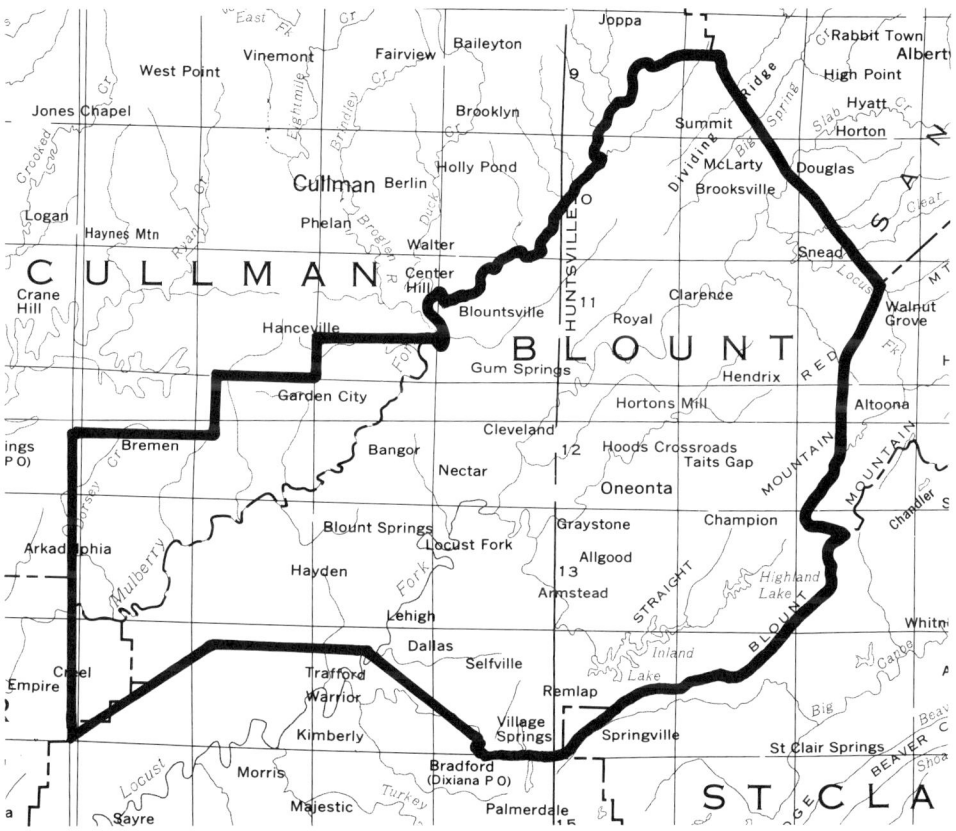

Chronology of BLOUNT

Map	Date	Event	Resulting Area
⑩	29 Jan 1879	Exchanged with WALKER	790 sq mi
⑩	13 Feb 1879	Gained from CULLMAN	790 sq mi
⑩	11 Feb 1887	Lost to ST. CLAIR	790 sq mi

(Heavy line depicts historical boundary. Base map shows present-day information.)

⑩ 29 Jan 1879–27 Feb 1887

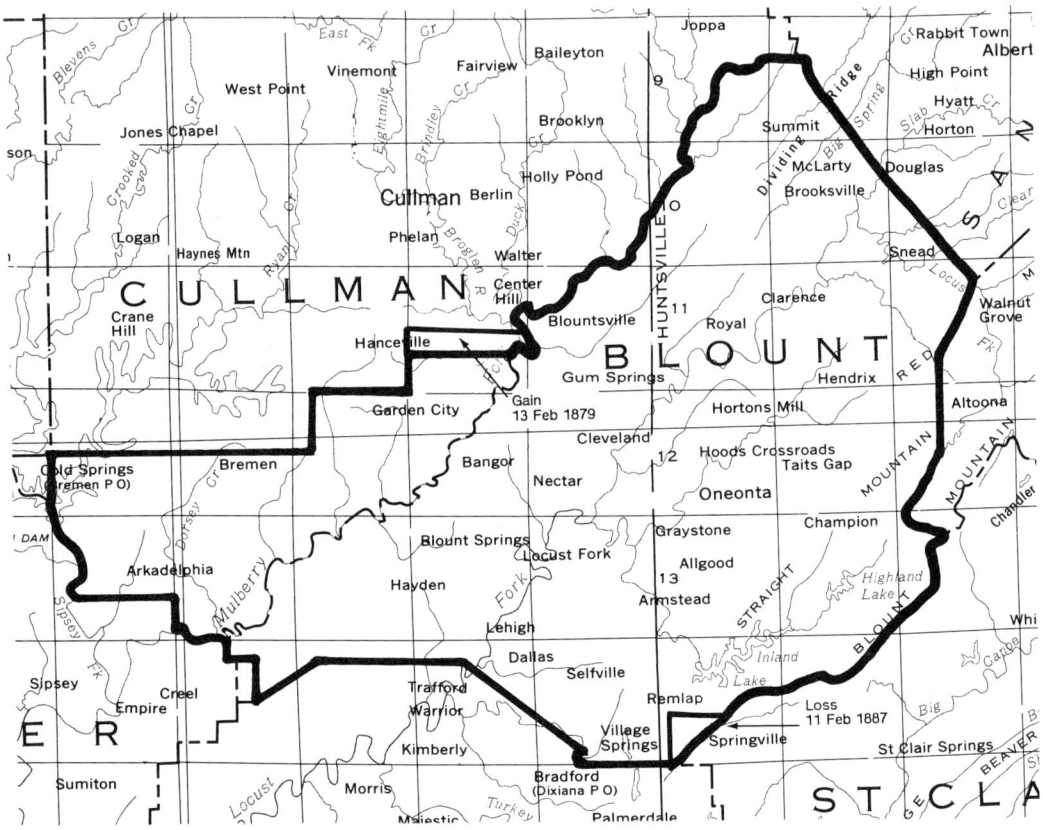

Chronology of BLOUNT

Map	Date	Event	Resulting Area
⑪	28 Feb 1887	Lost to CULLMAN	770 sq mi
⑪	21 Feb 1893	Lost to CULLMAN	770 sq mi
⑪	18 Feb 1895	Gained small area from WALKER	770 sq mi

(Heavy line depicts historical boundary. Base map shows present-day information.)

⑪ 28 Feb 1887–15 Dec 1898

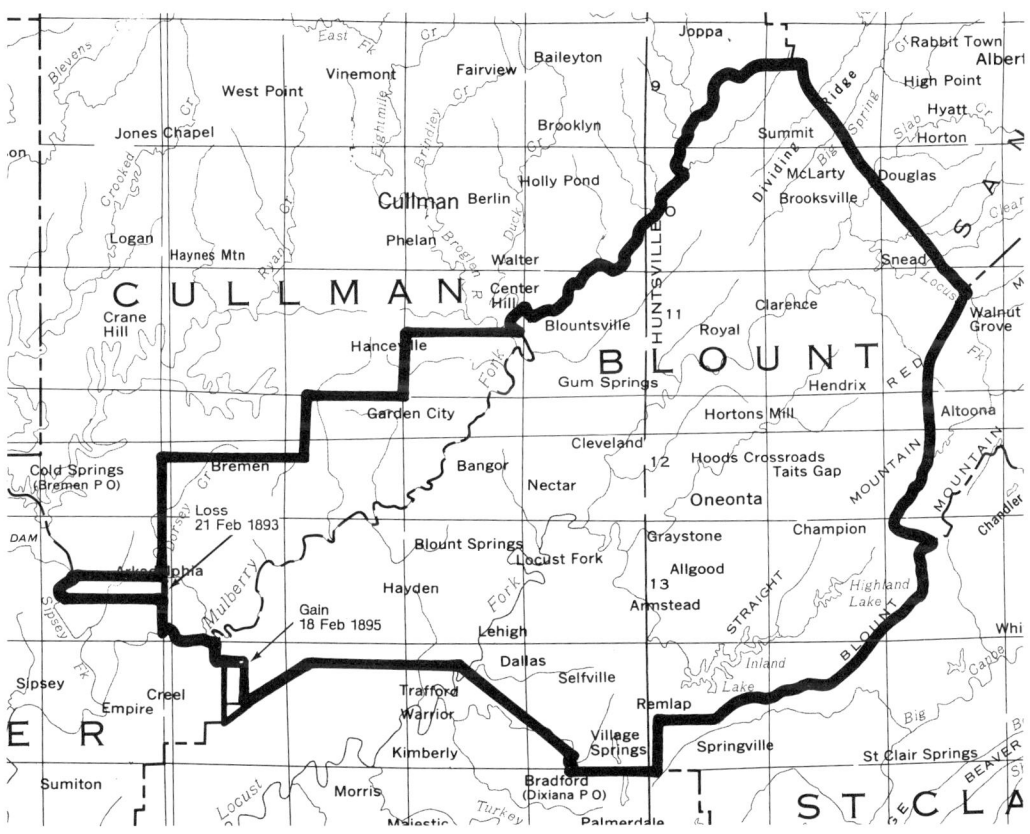

66 ALABAMA

Chronology of BLOUNT

Map	Date	Event	Resulting Area
⑫	16 Dec 1898	Lost small area to JEFFERSON	760 sq mi

(Heavy line depicts historical boundary. Base map shows present-day information.)

⑫ 16 Dec 1898–22 Apr 1901

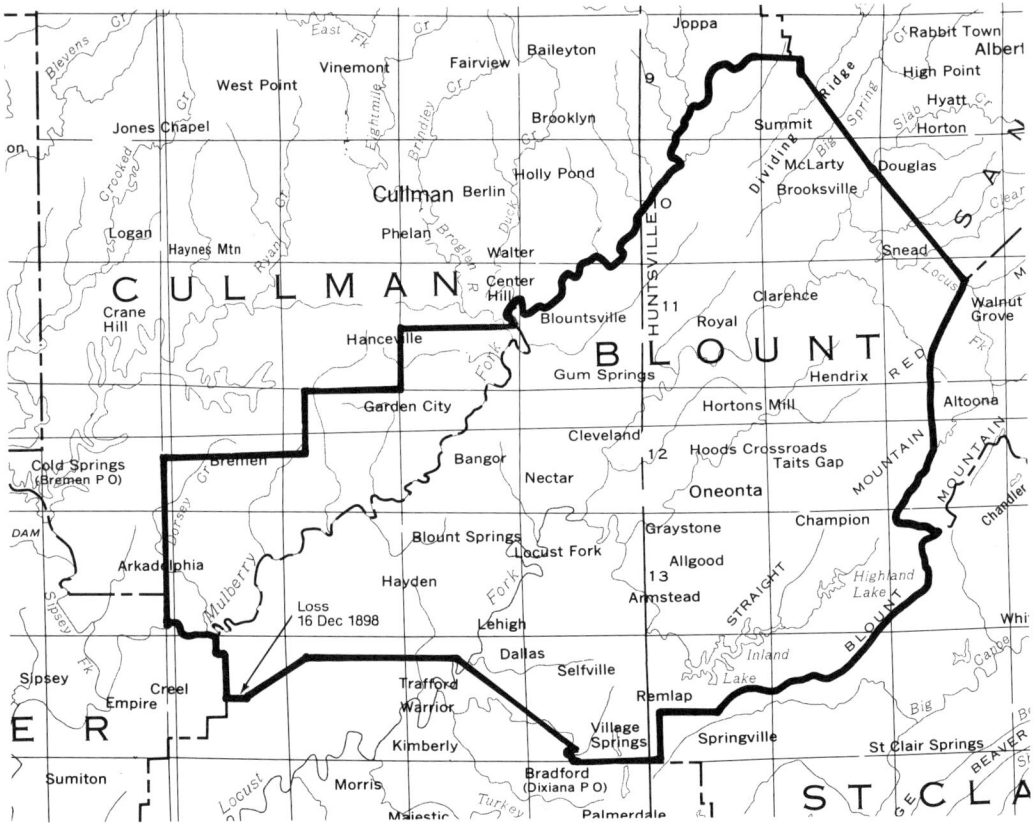

Individual County Chronologies 67

Chronology of BLOUNT

Map	Date	Event	Resulting Area
⑬	23 Apr 1901	Lost to CULLMAN	650 sq mi

(Heavy line depicts historical boundary. Base map shows present-day information.)

⑬ 23 Apr 1901–5 Aug 1976

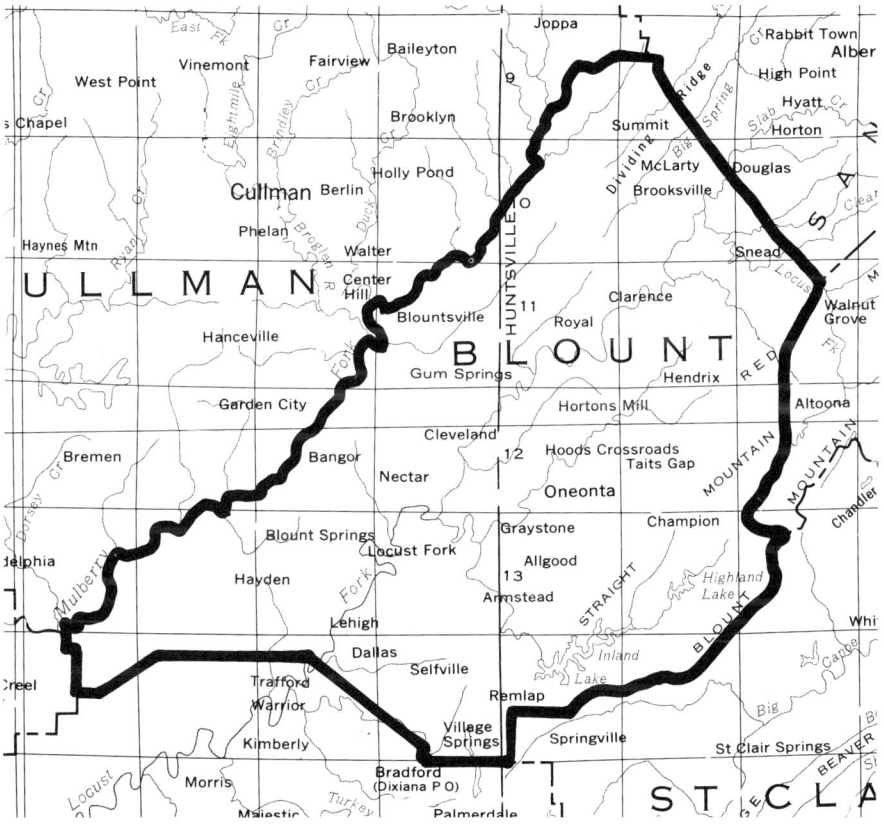

68 ALABAMA

Chronology of BLOUNT

Map	Date	Event	Resulting Area
⑭	6 Aug 1976	Gained from ETOWAH	650 sq mi

(Heavy line depicts historical boundary. Base map shows present-day information.)

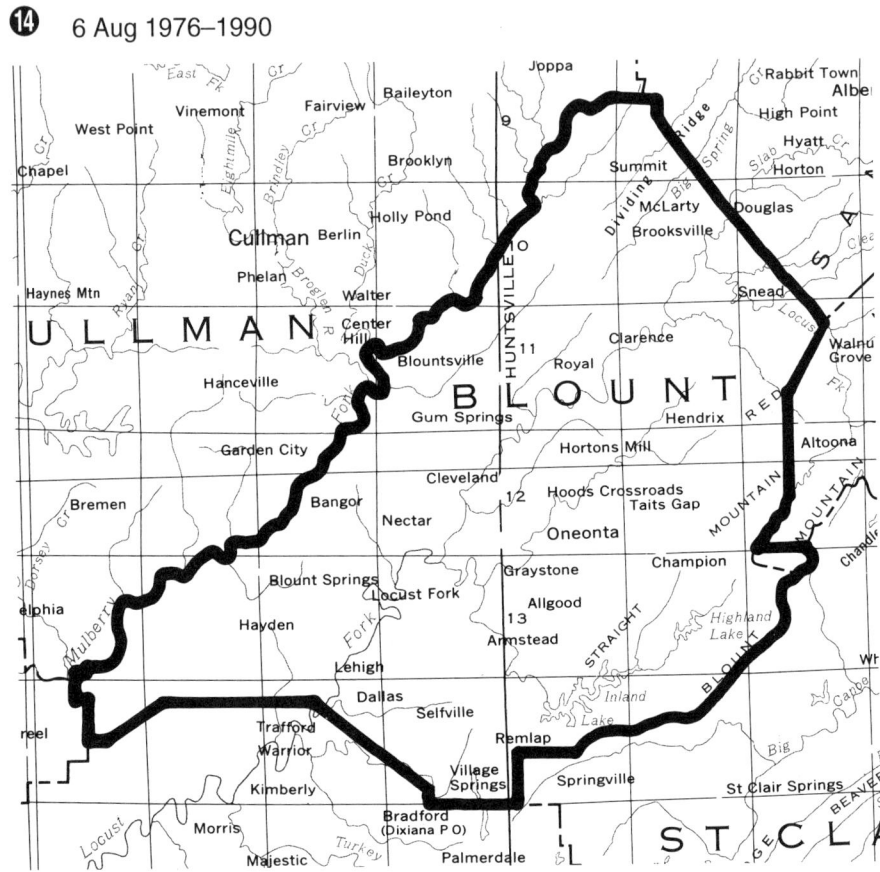

⑭ 6 Aug 1976–1990

Individual County Chronologies 69

Chronology of BULLOCK

Map	Date	Event	Resulting Area
❶	5 Dec 1866	Created from BARBOUR, MACON, MONTGOMERY, and PIKE	640 sq mi
❶	4 Feb 1867	Lost small area to PIKE to accommodate local property owner	640 sq mi

(Heavy line depicts historical boundary. Base map shows present-day information.)

❶ 5 Dec 1866–7 Feb 1867

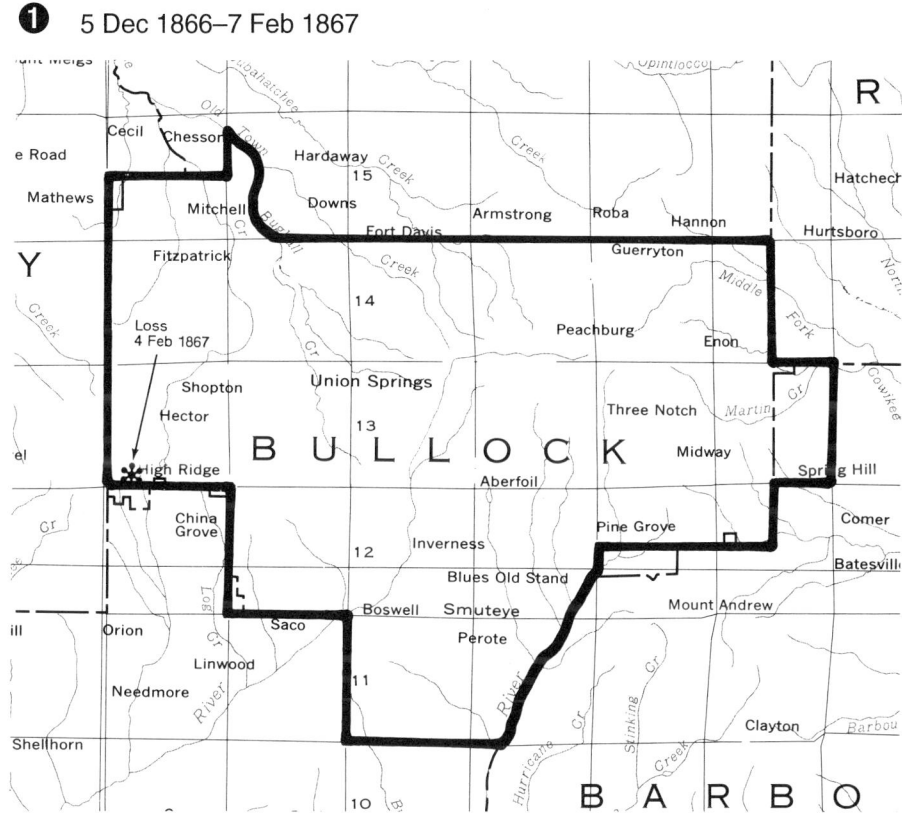

Chronology of BULLOCK

Map	Date	Event	Resulting Area
❷	8 Feb 1867	Exchanged with BARBOUR	630 sq mi
❷	9 Mar 1871	Lost small area to BARBOUR to accommodate local property owner	630 sq mi
❷	11 Dec 1871	Lost small area to PIKE to accommodate local property owner	630 sq mi
❷	8 Feb 1872	Gained small area from BARBOUR	630 sq mi
❷	14 Dec 1874	Lost small area to PIKE	630 sq mi

(Heavy line depicts historical boundary. Base map shows present-day information.)

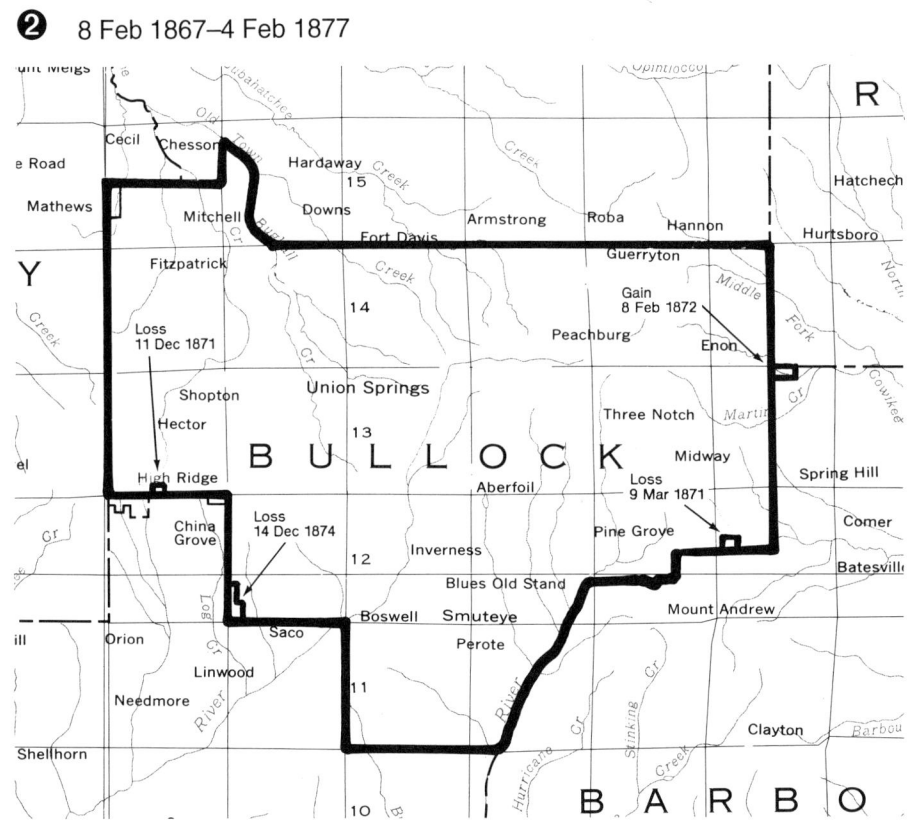

❷ 8 Feb 1867–4 Feb 1877

Individual County Chronologies 71

Chronology of BULLOCK

Map	Date	Event	Resulting Area
❸	5 Feb 1877	Lost small area to MONTGOMERY to accommodate local property owner	630 sq mi
❸	22 Feb 1887	Gained small area from PIKE to accommodate local property owners	630 sq mi
❸	7 Feb 1889	Gained small area from PIKE to accommodate local property owners	630 sq mi

(Heavy line depicts historical boundary. Base map shows present-day information.)

❸ 5 Feb 1877–12 Feb 1897

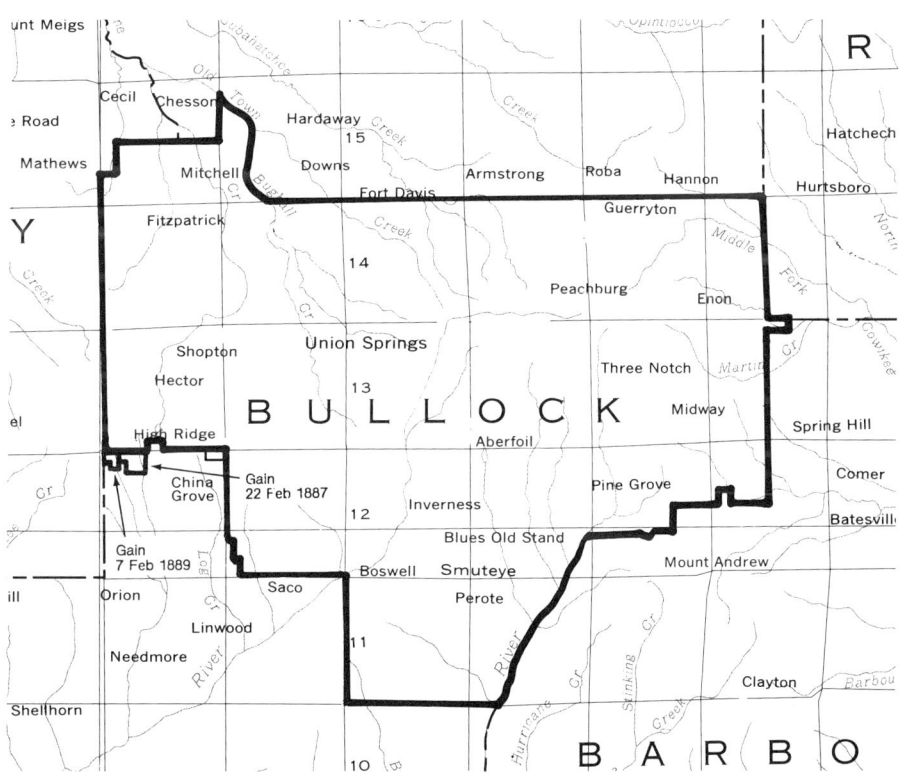

72 ALABAMA

Chronology of BULLOCK

Map	Date	Event	Resulting Area
❹	13 Feb 1897	Gained small area from PIKE	630 sq mi

(Heavy line depicts historical boundary. Base map shows present-day information.)

❹ 13 Feb 1897–1990

Individual County Chronologies 73

Chronology of BUTLER

Map	Date	Event	Resulting Area
❶	13 Dec 1819	Created from CONECUH, DALLAS, and MONROE	1,100 sq mi

(Heavy line depicts historical boundary. Base map shows present-day information.)

❶ 13 Dec 1819–2 Jan 1828

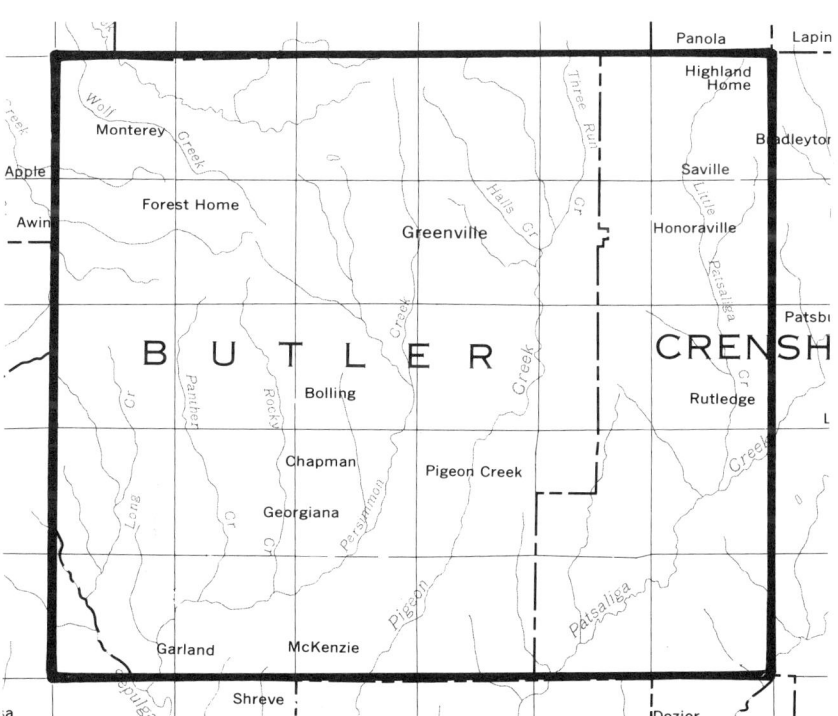

74 ALABAMA

Chronology of BUTLER

Map	Date	Event	Resulting Area
❷	3 Jan 1828	Gained from PIKE	1,150 sq mi
❸	27 Jan 1829	Lost to COVINGTON and PIKE	1,090 sq mi

(Heavy line depicts historical boundary. Base map shows present-day information.)

❷ 3 Jan 1828–26 Jan 1829

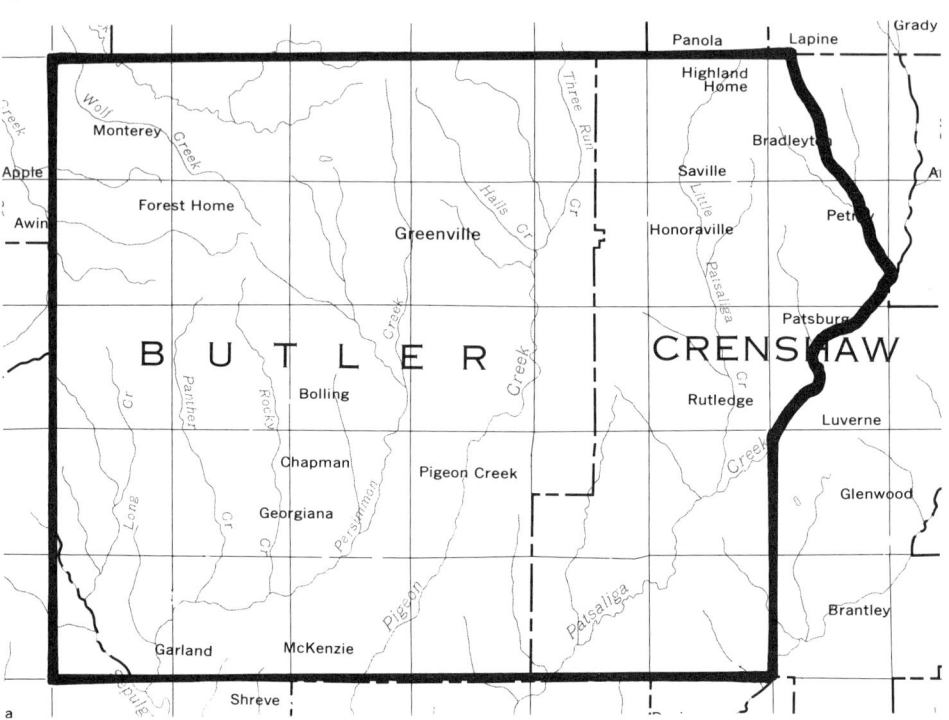

❸ 27 Jan 1829–19 Jan 1830

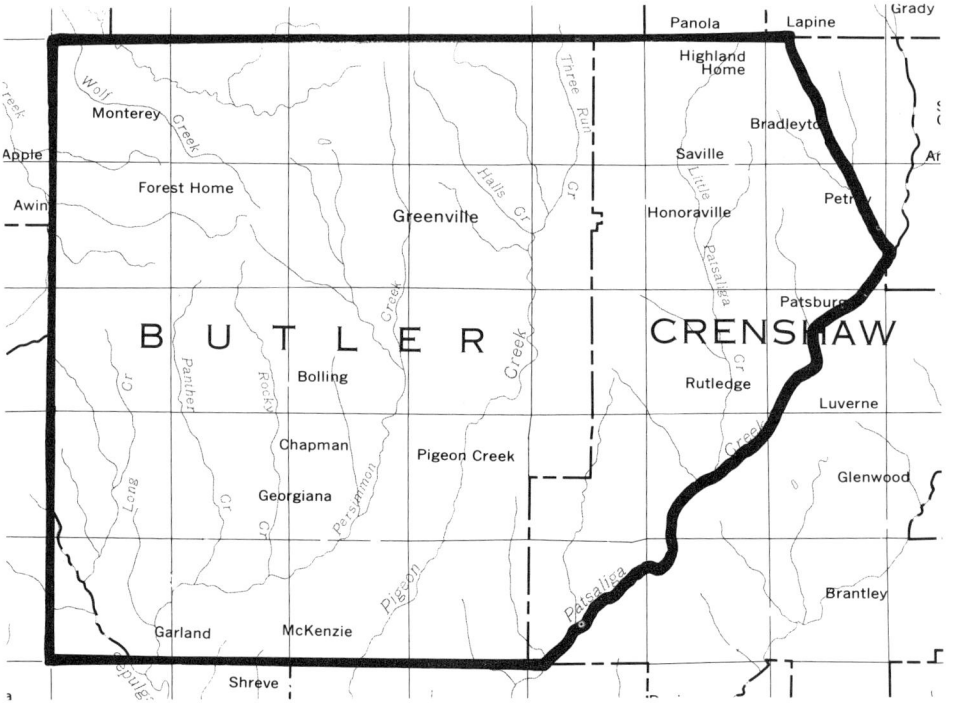

Individual County Chronologies

Chronology of BUTLER

Map	Date	Event	Resulting Area
❹	20 Jan 1830	Lost to creation of LOWNDES	1,020 sq mi
❹	5 Jan 1833	Gained small area from MONROE	1,020 sq mi

(Heavy line depicts historical boundary. Base map shows present-day information.)

❹ 20 Jan 1830–1 Dec 1837

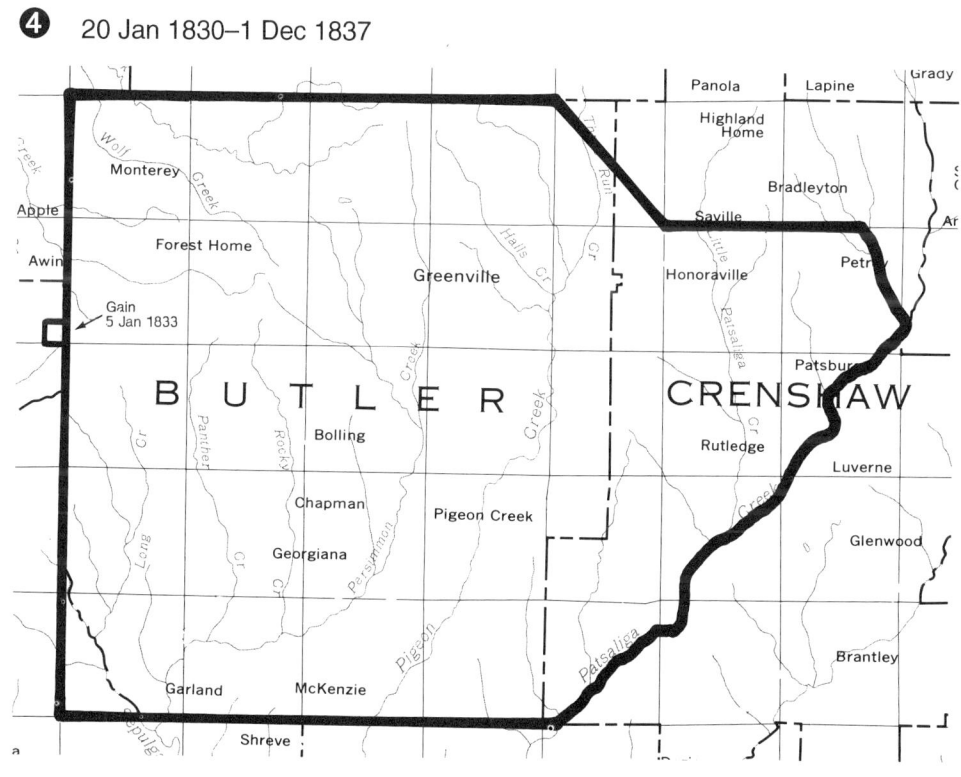

ALABAMA

Chronology of BUTLER

Map	Date	Event	Resulting Area
❺	2 Dec 1837	Lost to CONECUH	1,010 sq mi
❺	by 1839	Lost small area to MONROE	1,010 sq mi
❺	18 Dec 1840	Gained small area from WILCOX	1,010 sq mi

(Heavy line depicts historical boundary. Base map shows present-day information.)

❺ 2 Dec 1837–1 Jan 1841

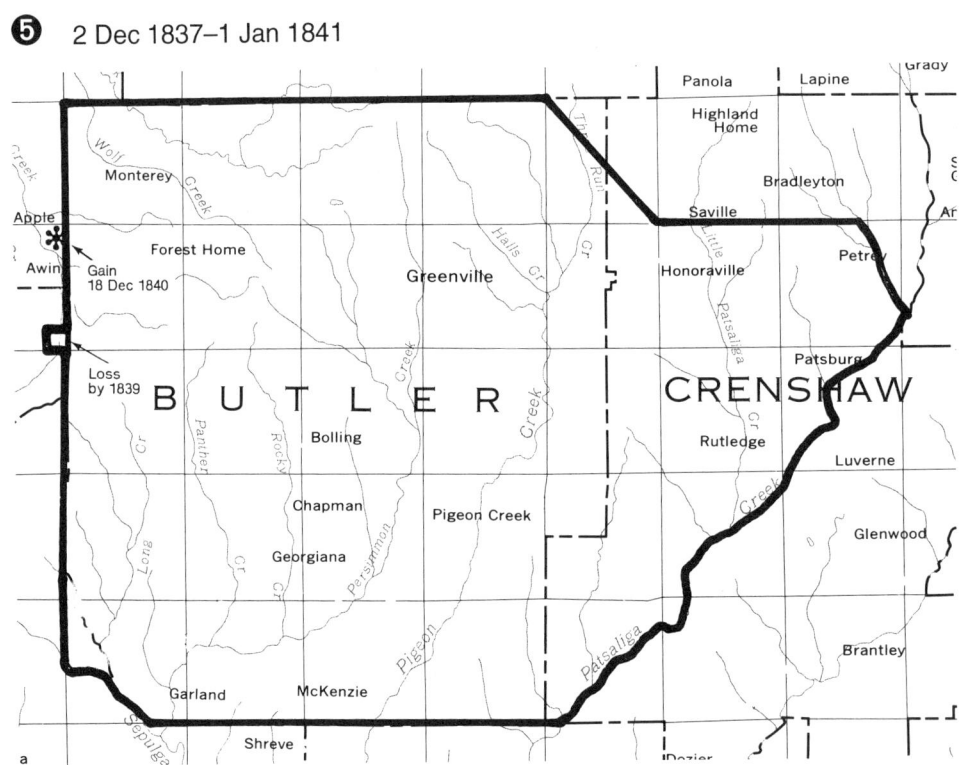

Individual County Chronologies 77

Chronology of BUTLER

Map	Date	Event	Resulting Area
❻	2 Jan 1841	Lost to CONECUH	1,000 sq mi
	24 Nov 1862	Gained small area from CONECUH to accommodate local property owner [location unknown, not mapped]	

(Heavy line depicts historical boundary. Base map shows present-day information.)

❻ 2 Jan 1841–23 Nov 1866

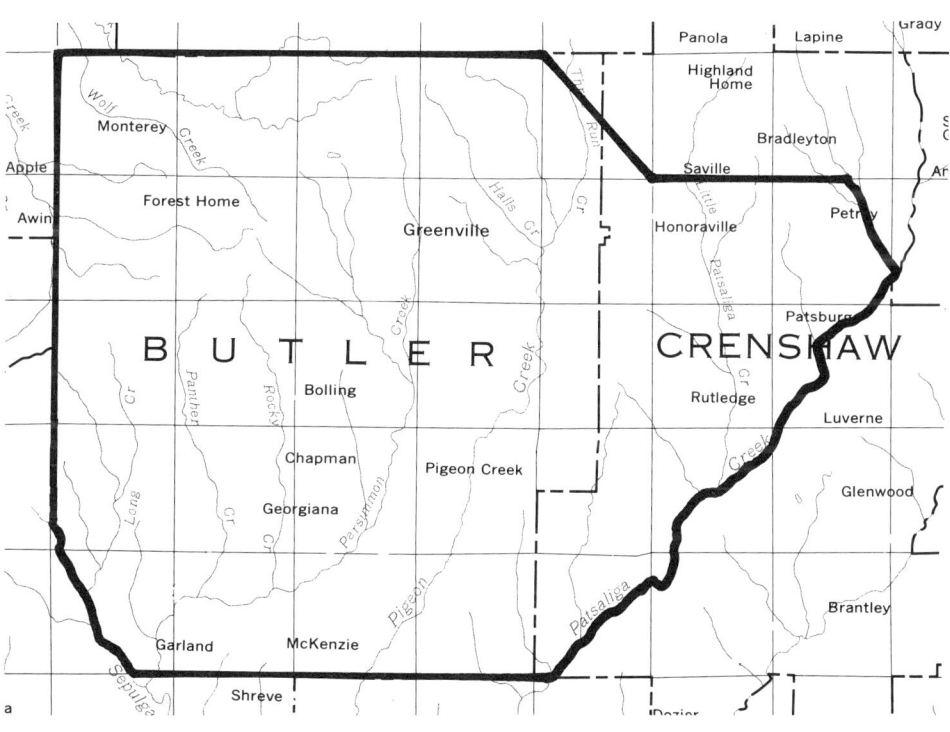

78 ALABAMA

Chronology of BUTLER

Map	Date	Event	Resulting Area
7	24 Nov 1866	Gained from LOWNDES, lost to creation of CRENSHAW	780 sq mi
7	11 Feb 1867	Gained small area from CRENSHAW	780 sq mi
7	5 Aug 1868	Gained small area from CRENSHAW to accommodate local property owner	780 sq mi
7	28 Feb 1887	Gained small area from COVINGTON, exchanged small areas with CRENSHAW	780 sq mi

(Heavy line depicts historical boundary. Base map shows present-day information.)

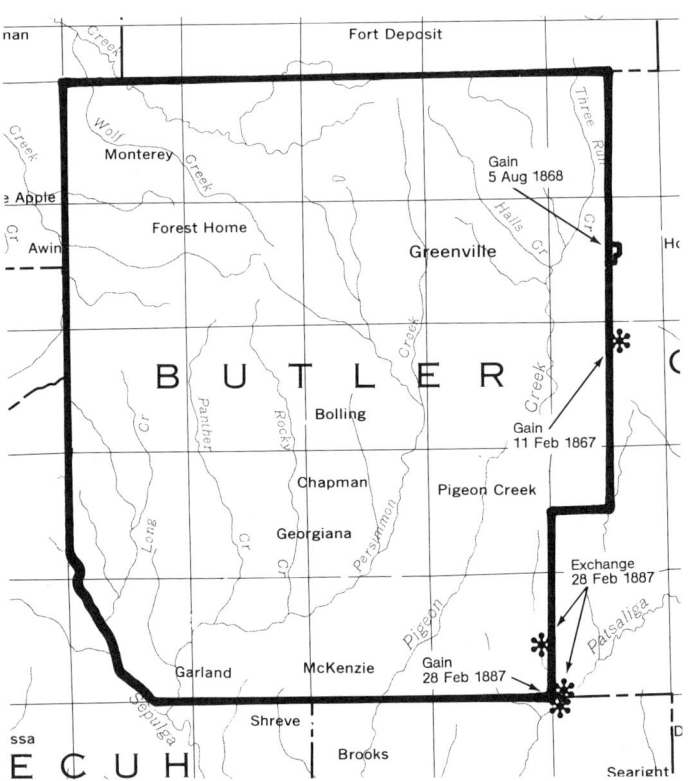

7 24 Nov 1866–1990

Individual County Chronologies 79

Chronology of CALHOUN (created as BENTON)

Map	Date	Event	Resulting Area
❶	18 Dec 1832	Created as BENTON from ST. CLAIR	1,110 sq mi
❷	30 Dec 1834	Part of ST. CLAIR attached to BENTON (now CALHOUN)	
❶	9 Jan 1836	Lost ST. CLAIR attachment to creation of CHEROKEE	1,110 sq mi

(Heavy line depicts historical boundary. Base map shows present-day information.)

❶ 18 Dec 1832–22 Dec 1836

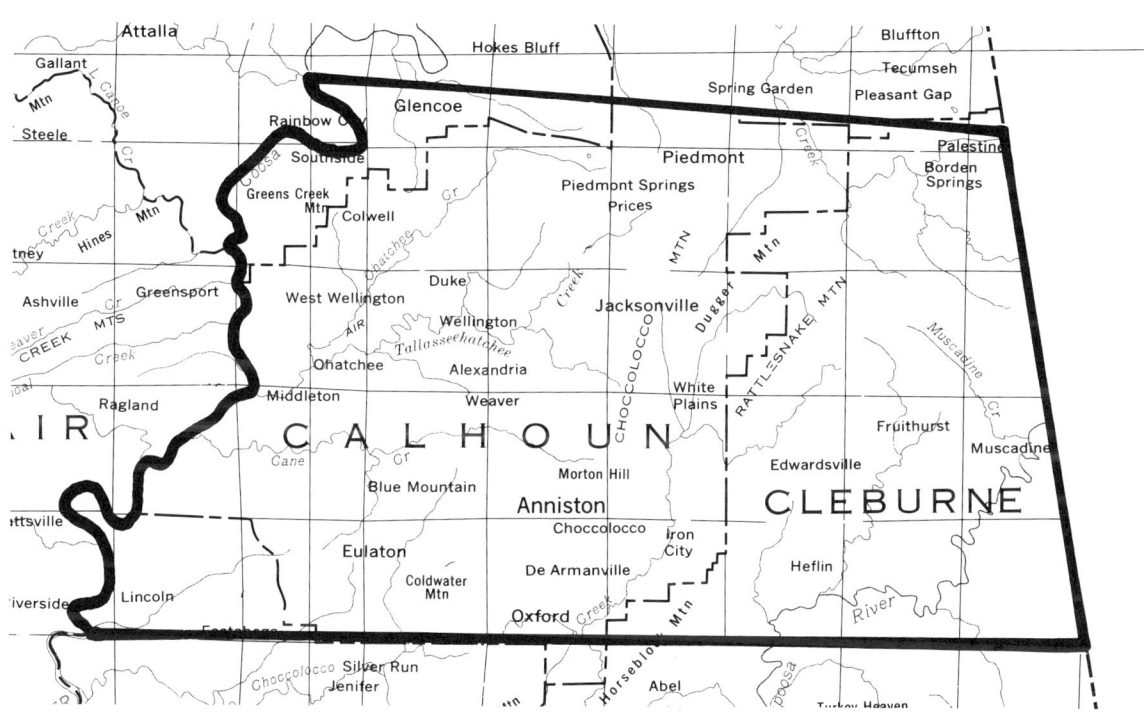

❷ 30 Dec 1834–8 Jan 1836

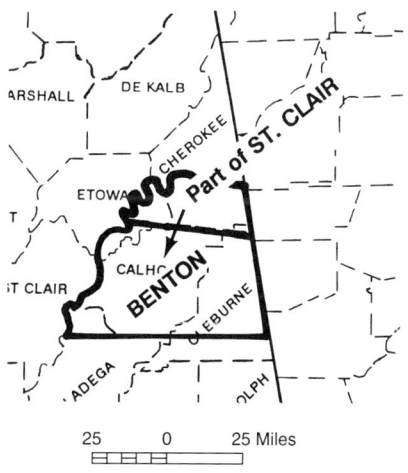

ALABAMA

Chronology of CALHOUN (created as BENTON)

Map	Date	Event	Resulting Area
❸	23 Dec 1836	Gained from CHEROKEE, lost to TALLADEGA	1,160 sq mi

(Heavy line depicts historical boundary. Base map shows present-day information.)

❸ 23 Dec 1836–26 Jan 1843

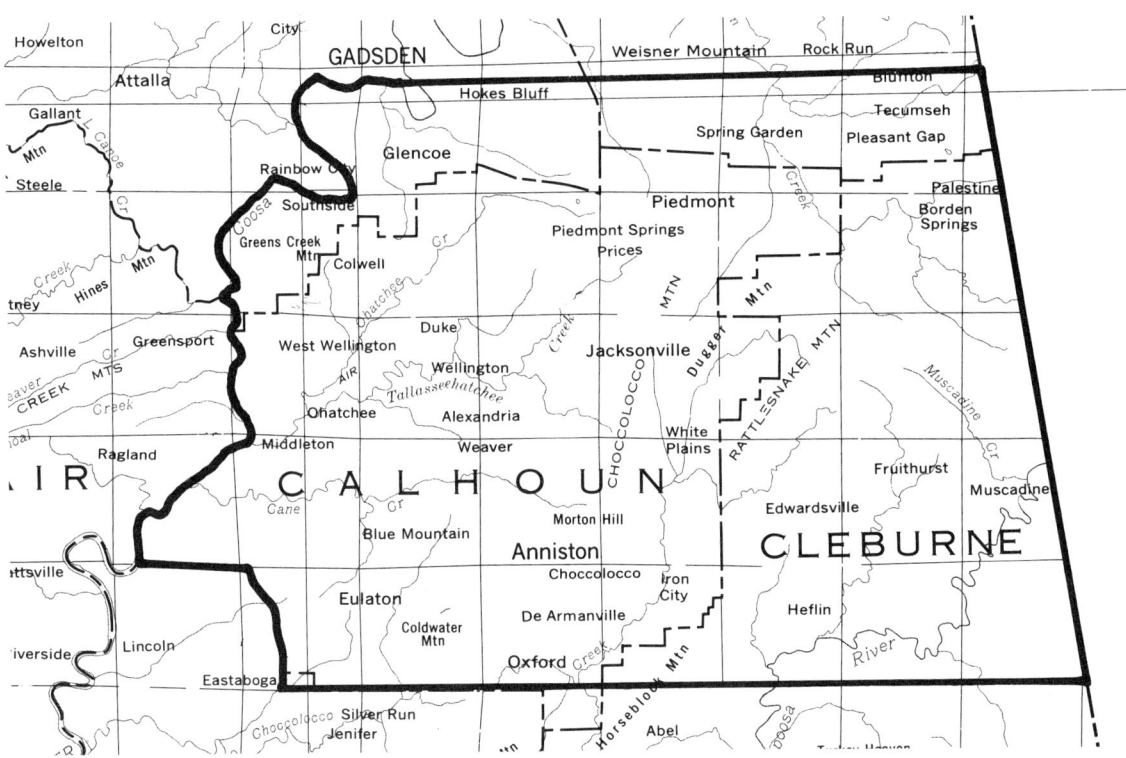

Individual County Chronologies

Chronology of CALHOUN (created as BENTON)

Map	Date	Event	Resulting Area
❹	27 Jan 1843	Lost to CHEROKEE	1,060 sq mi
❹	27 Jan 1845	Gained small area from CHEROKEE to accommodate local property owners, lost small area to TALLADEGA	1,060 sq mi
❹	5 Feb 1850	Lost small area to TALLADEGA	1,060 sq mi
	14 Feb 1854	Boundary with CHEROKEE adjusted [location unknown, not mapped; mistake in description corrected 1 Feb 1856]	
❹	18 Feb 1854	Gained small area from CHEROKEE to accommodate local property owner	1,060 sq mi
	1 Feb 1856	Boundary with CHEROKEE clarified, correcting mistake of 14 Feb 1854 [no change]	
	29 Jan 1858	Renamed CALHOUN	

(Heavy line depicts historical boundary. Base map shows present-day information.)

❹ 27 Jan 1843–5 Dec 1866

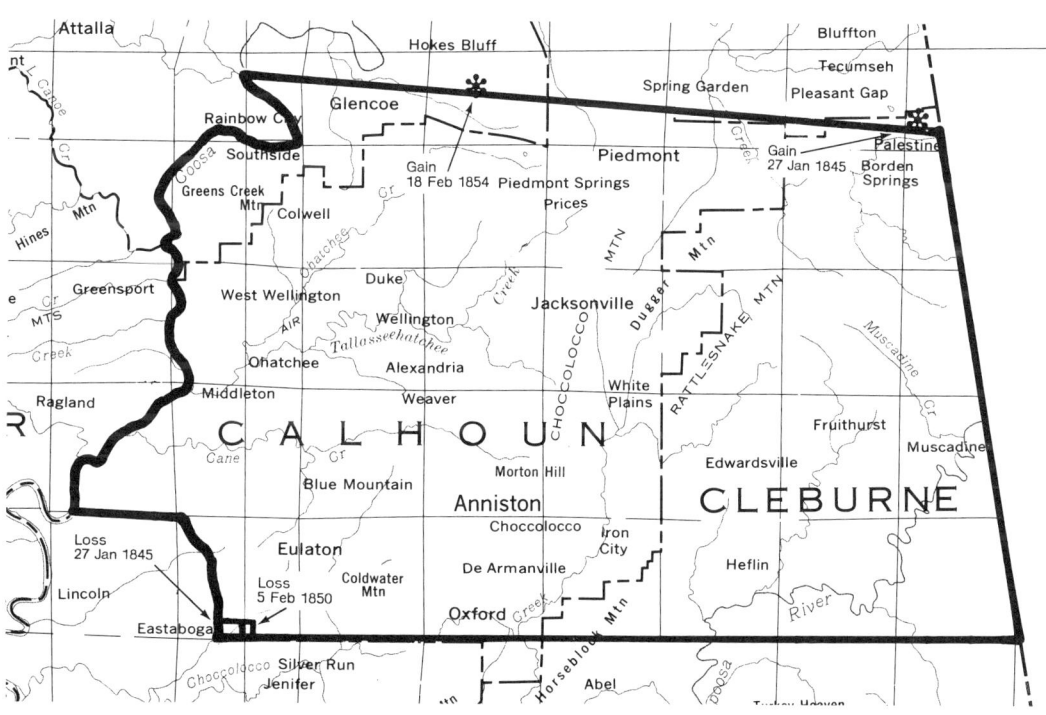

82 ALABAMA

Chronology of CALHOUN (created as BENTON)

Map	Date	Event	Resulting Area
⑤	6 Dec 1866	Lost to creation of CLEBURNE	700 sq mi
⑥	7 Dec 1866	Lost to creation of BAINE	620 sq mi
⑤	3 Dec 1867	Gained from BAINE; BAINE eliminated	700 sq mi

(Heavy line depicts historical boundary. Base map shows present-day information.)

⑤ 6 Dec 1866
3 Dec 1867–30 Nov 1868

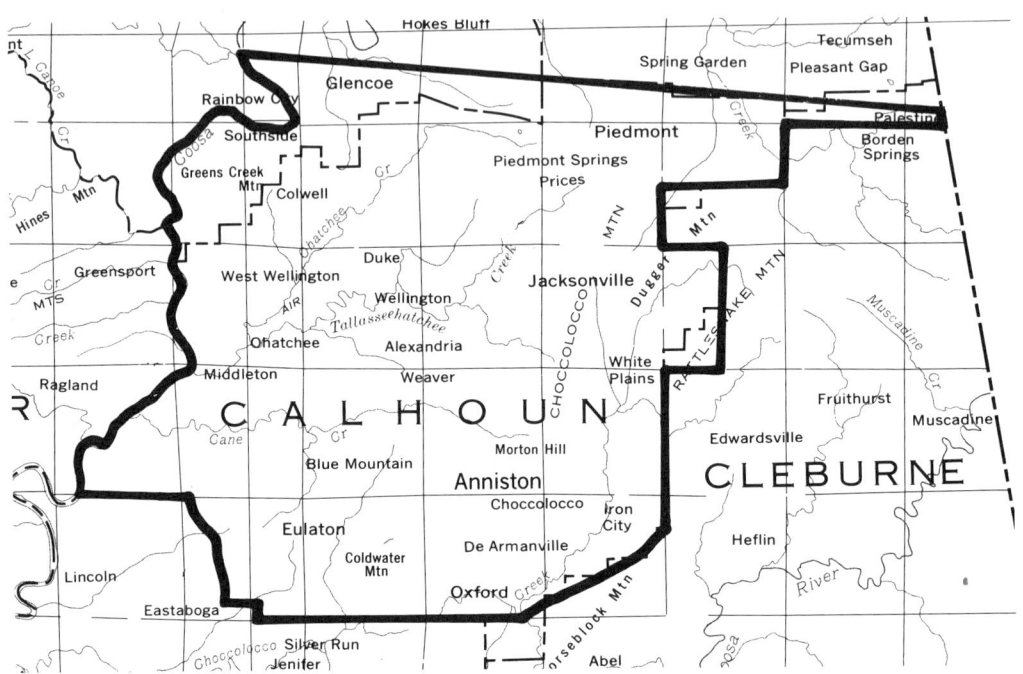

⑥ 7 Dec 1866–2 Dec 1867

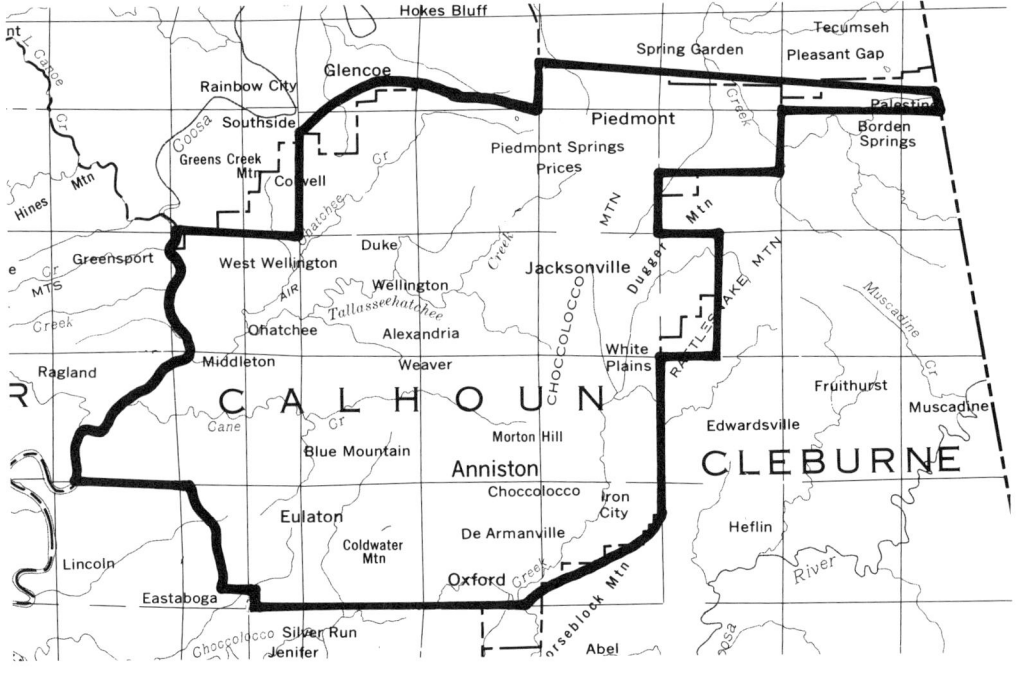

Individual County Chronologies 83

Chronology of CALHOUN (created as BENTON)

Map	Date	Event	Resulting Area
❼	1 Dec 1868	Lost to creation of ETOWAH	640 sq mi
❽	7 Dec 1871	Gained from ETOWAH	650 sq mi

(Heavy line depicts historical boundary. Base map shows present-day information.)

❼ 1 Dec 1868–6 Dec 1871

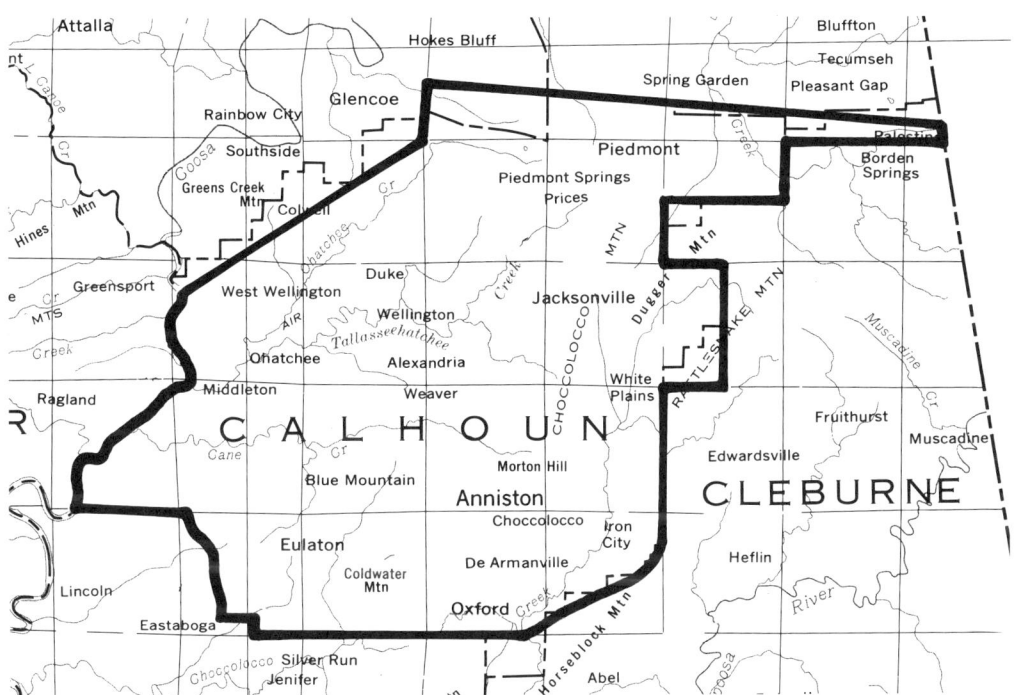

❽ 7 Dec 1871–9 Feb 1883

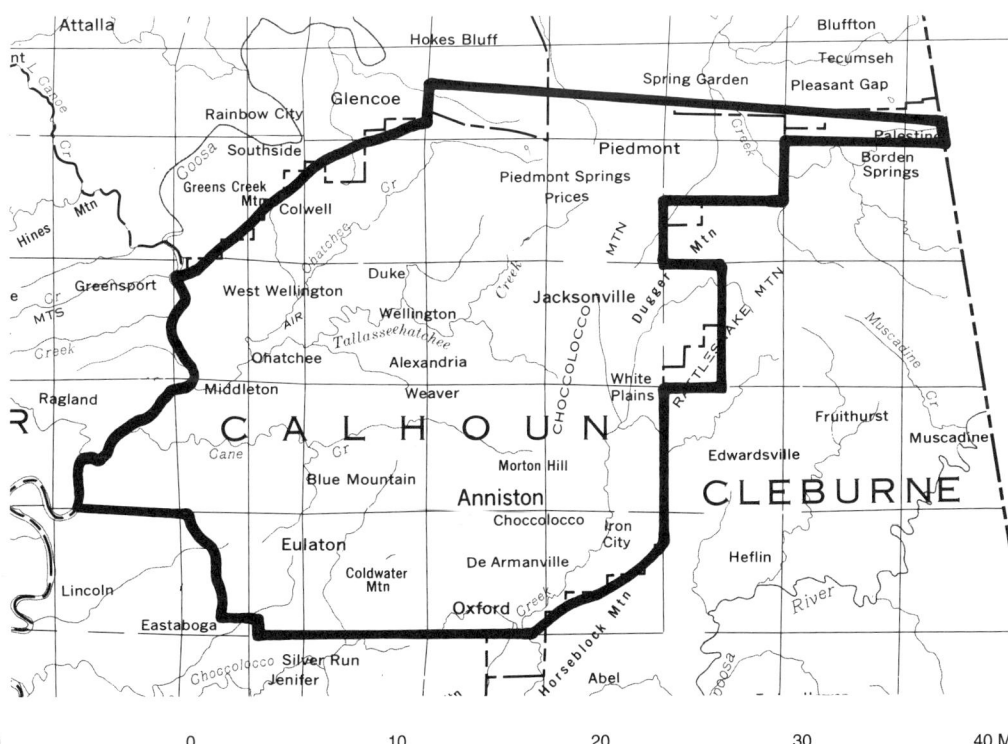

84 ALABAMA

Chronology of CALHOUN (created as BENTON)

Map	Date	Event	Resulting Area
⑨	10 Feb 1883	Lost to CHEROKEE and CLEBURNE	620 sq mi
⑩	11 Dec 1886	Exchanged with CLEBURNE	620 sq mi

(Heavy line depicts historical boundary. Base map shows present-day information.)

⑨ 10 Feb 1883–10 Dec 1886

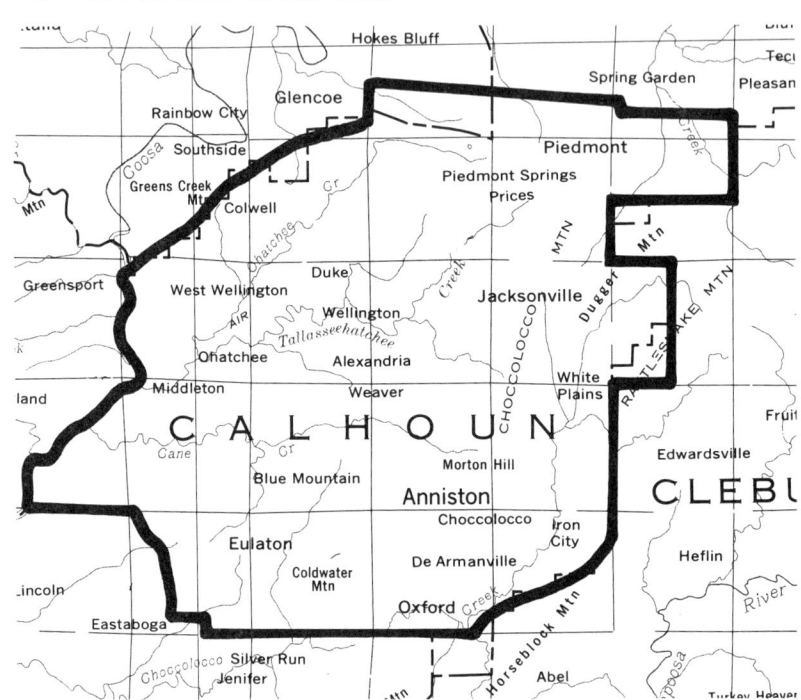

⑩ 11 Dec 1886–9 Feb 1899

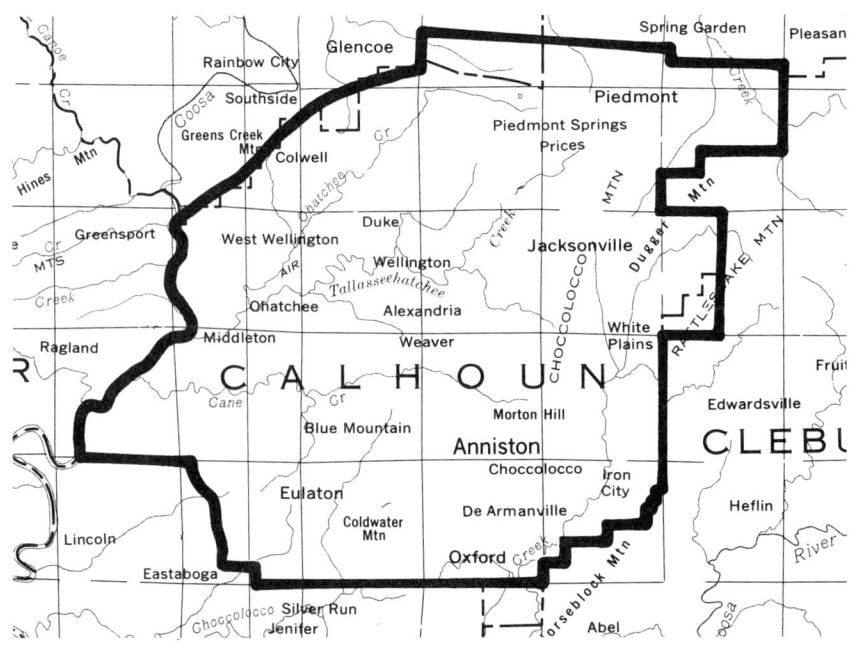

Chronology of CALHOUN (created as BENTON)

Map	Date	Event	Resulting Area
⑪	10 Feb 1899	Lost to ETOWAH	610 sq mi
⑫	1 Oct 1901	Exchanged with ETOWAH	610 sq mi

(Heavy line depicts historical boundary. Base map shows present-day information.)

⑪ 10 Feb 1899–30 Sep 1901

⑫ 1 Oct 1901–29 Sep 1903
30 Jun 1906–24 Jul 1907

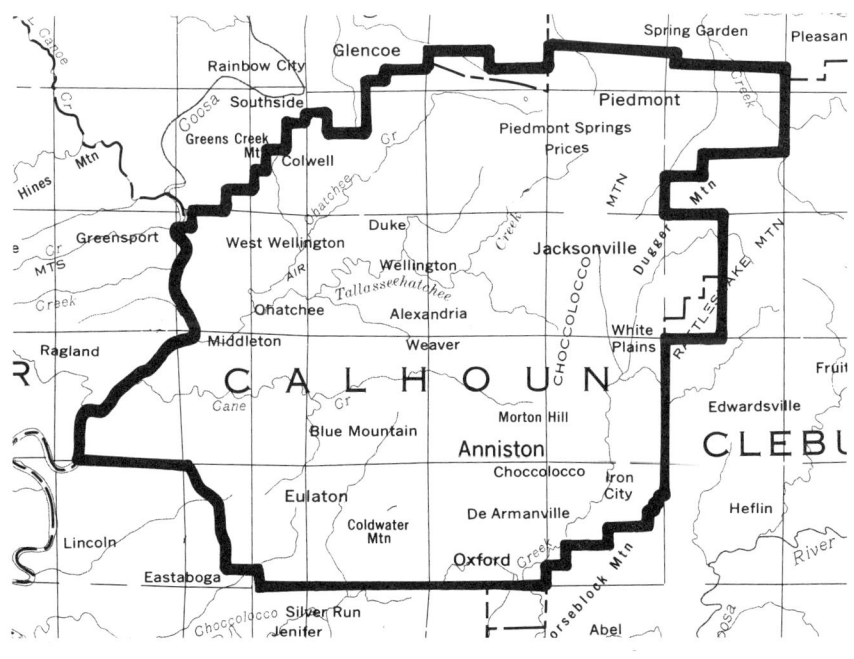

Chronology of CALHOUN (created as BENTON)

Map	Date	Event	Resulting Area
⑬	30 Sep 1903	Gained from CLEBURNE	610 sq mi
⑫	30 Jun 1906	Lost to CLEBURNE	610 sq mi

(Heavy line depicts historical boundary. Base map shows present-day information.)

⑬ 30 Sep 1903–29 Jun 1906

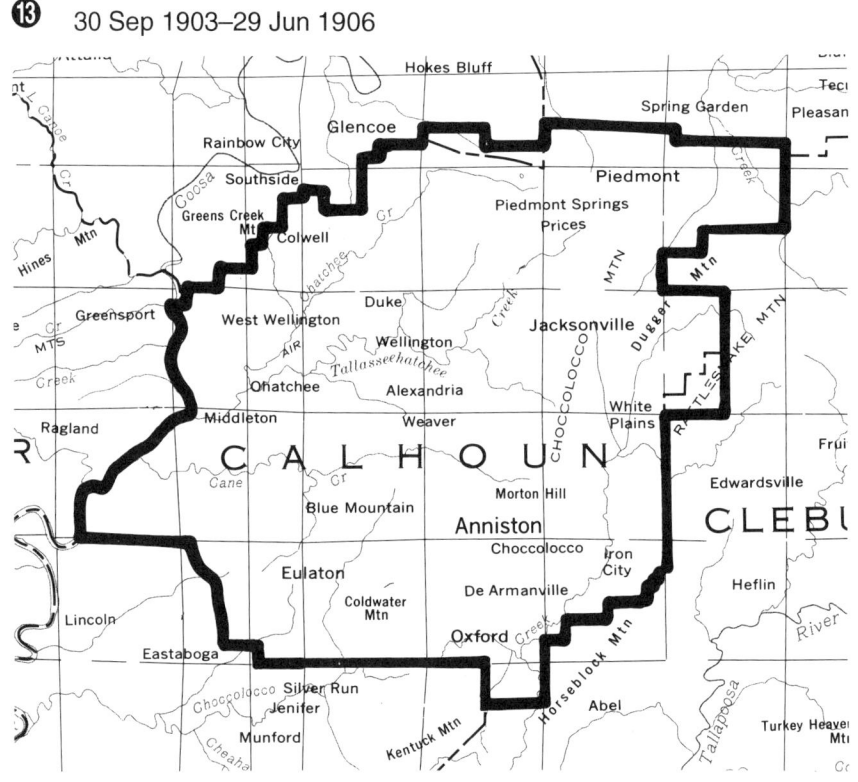

Individual County Chronologies   **87**

Chronology of CALHOUN (created as BENTON)

Map	Date	Event	Resulting Area
⑭	25 Jul 1907	Exchanged with CLEBURNE	610 sq mi
⑭	9 Aug 1907	Lost small area to ETOWAH	610 sq mi
⑮	14 Sep 1923	Exchanged small areas with ETOWAH	610 sq mi

(Heavy line depicts historical boundary. Base map shows present-day information.)

⑭ 25 Jul 1907–13 Sep 1923

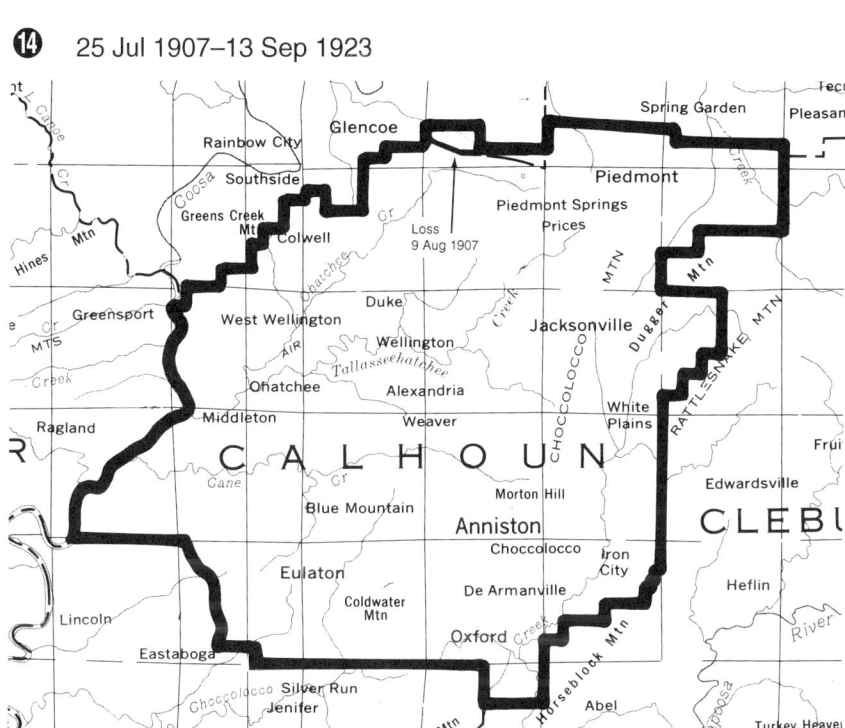

⑮ 14 Sep 1923–1990

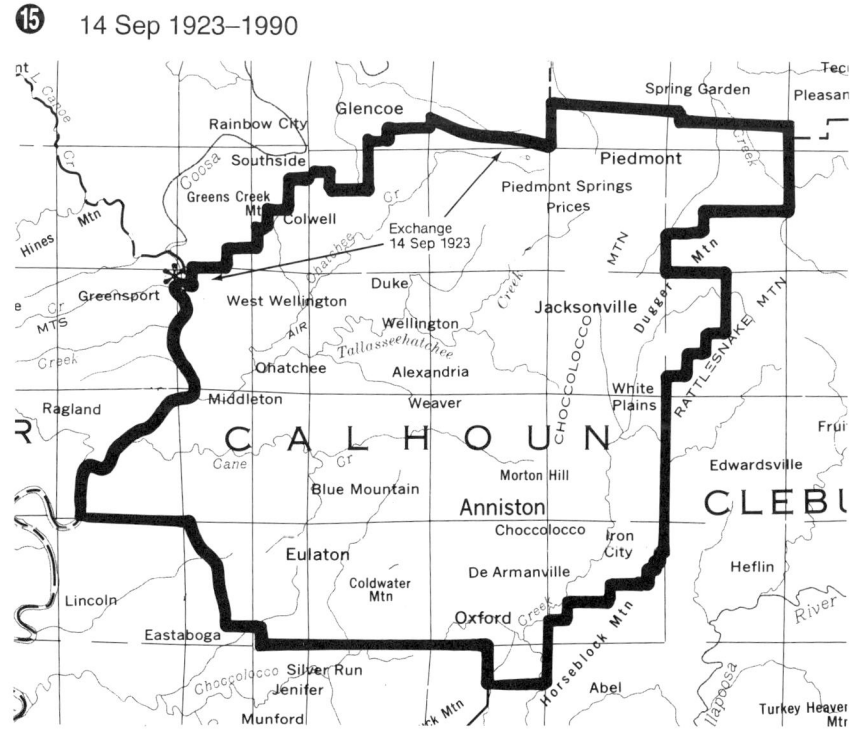

ALABAMA

Chronology of CHAMBERS

Map	Date	Event	Resulting Area
❶	18 Dec 1832	Created from MONTGOMERY and SHELBY	720 sq mi
❶	10 Feb 1866	Gained small area from TALLAPOOSA to accommodate local property owner	720 sq mi
❷	5 Dec 1866	Lost to creation of LEE	600 sq mi
❷	17 Jan 1867	Lost small area to LEE to accommodate local property owner	600 sq mi
❷	4 Feb 1867	Lost small area to LEE to accommodate local property owner	590 sq mi
❷	19 Feb 1867	Lost small area to LEE to accommodate local property owner	590 sq mi
❷	24 Feb 1872	Lost small area to LEE to accommodate local property owner	590 sq mi

(Heavy line depicts historical boundary. Base map shows present-day information.)

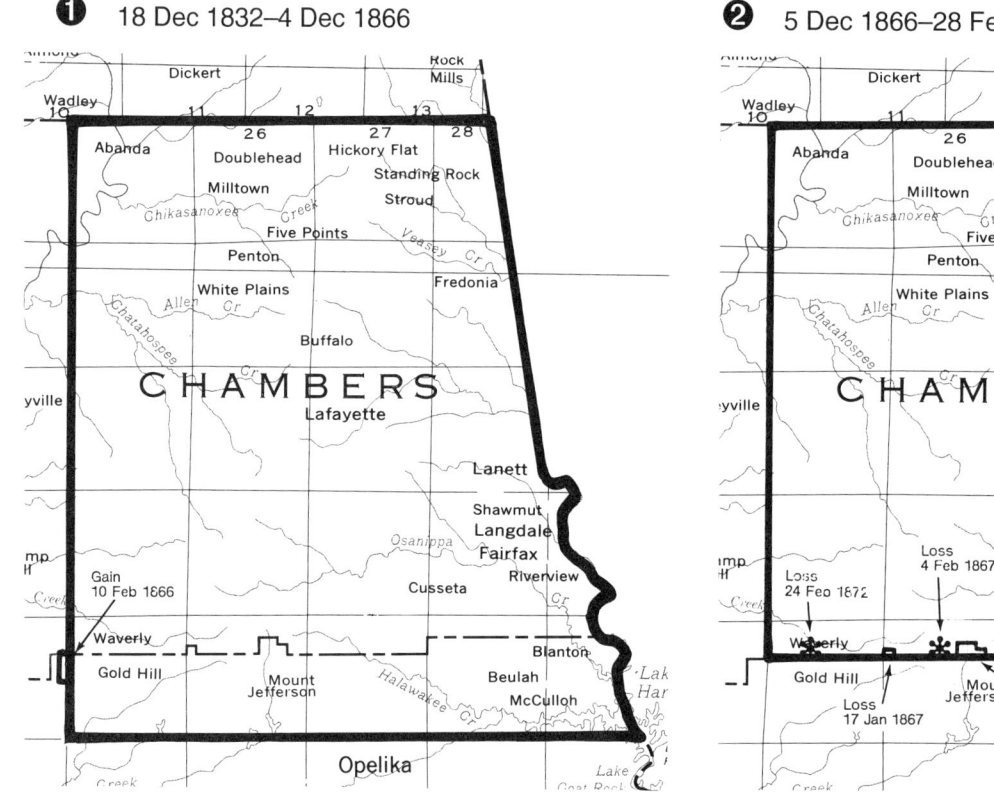

❶ 18 Dec 1832–4 Dec 1866

❷ 5 Dec 1866–28 Feb 1881

Chronology of CHAMBERS

Map	Date	Event	Resulting Area
❸	1 Mar 1881	Gained small area from LEE to accommodate local property owner	590 sq mi

(Heavy line depicts historical boundary. Base map shows present-day information.)

❸ 1 Mar 1881–1990

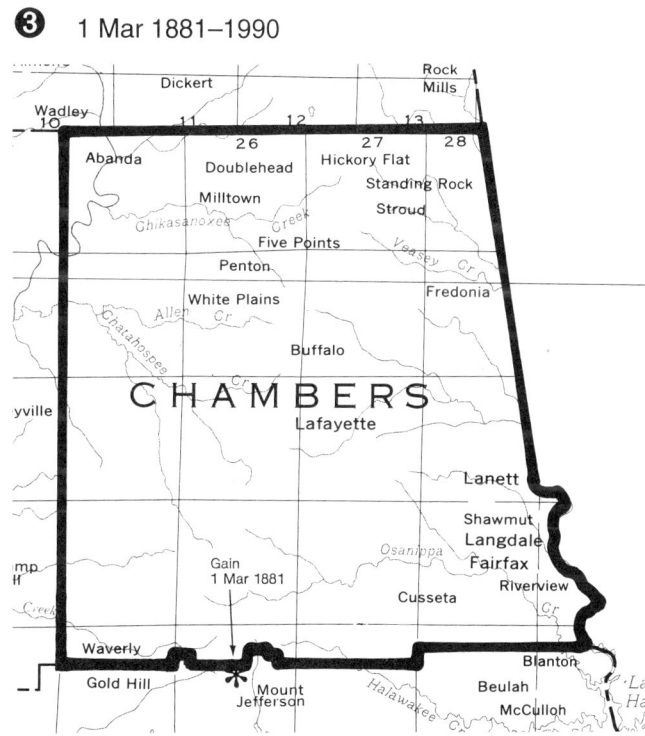

ALABAMA

Chronology of CHEROKEE

Map	Date	Event	Resulting Area
❶	9 Jan 1836	Created from JACKSON, ST. CLAIR, and from that part of ST. CLAIR attached to BENTON (now CALHOUN)	990 sq mi

(Heavy line depicts historical boundary. Base map shows present-day information.)

❶ 9 Jan 1836–22 Dec 1836
27 Jan 1843–15 Jan 1844

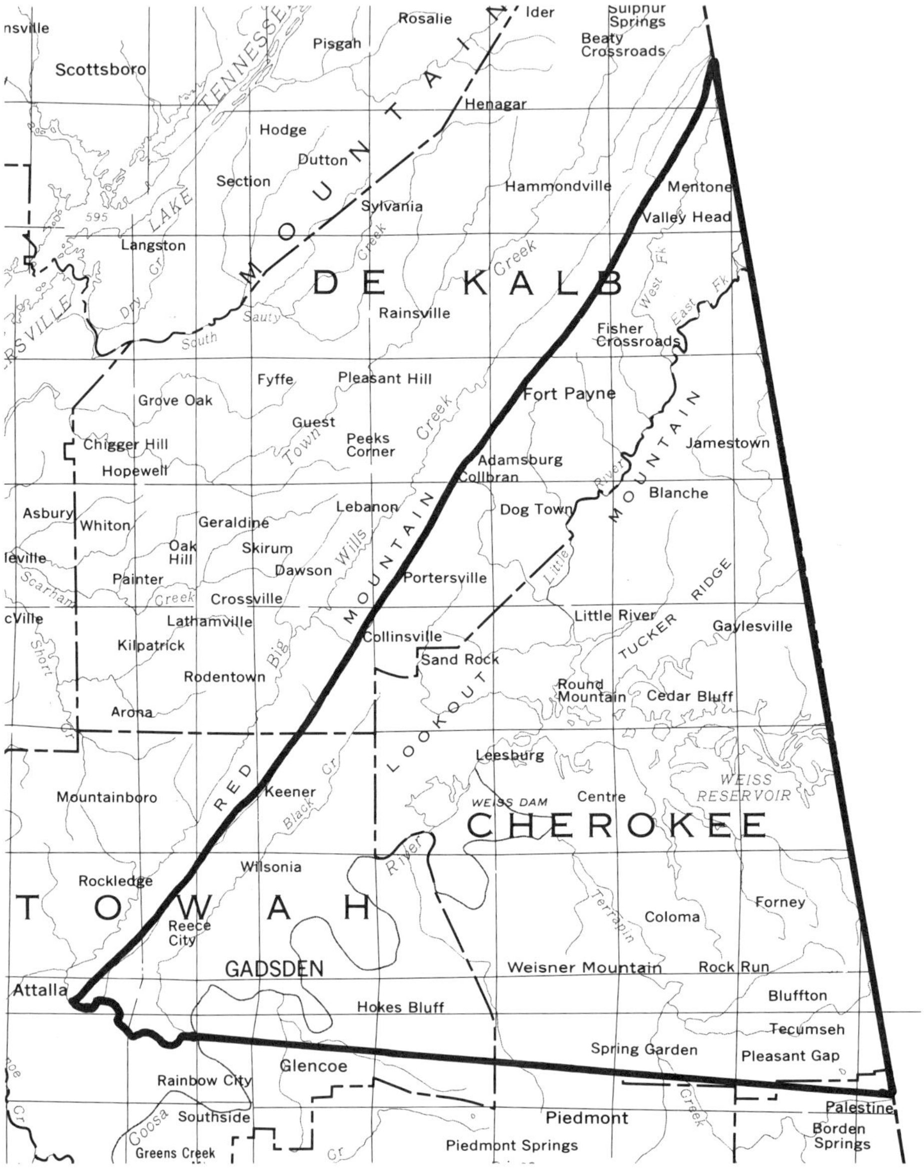

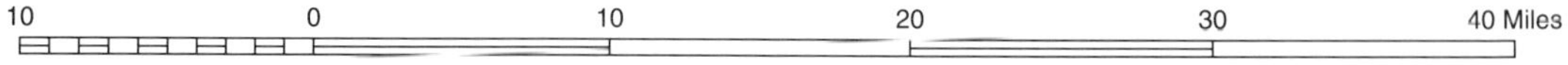

Individual County Chronologies   91

Chronology of CHEROKEE

Map	Date	Event	Resulting Area
❷	23 Dec 1836	Lost to BENTON (now CALHOUN)	850 sq mi
❶	27 Jan 1843	Gained from BENTON (now CALHOUN)	990 sq mi

(Heavy line depicts historical boundary. Base map shows present-day information.)

❷ 23 Dec 1836–26 Jan 1843

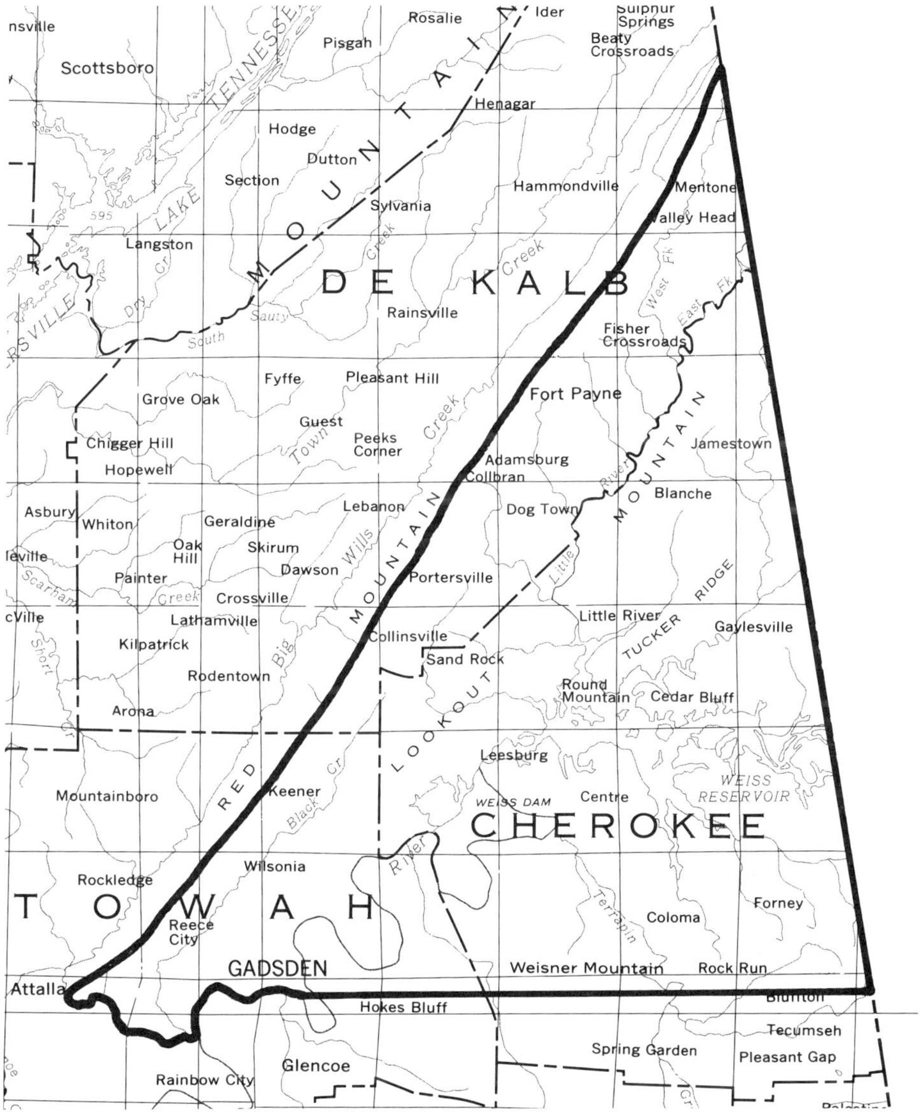

Chronology of CHEROKEE

Map	Date	Event	Resulting Area
❸	16 Jan 1844	Lost to DE KALB	800 sq mi
❸	27 Jan 1845	Lost small area to BENTON (now CALHOUN) to accommodate local property owners	800 sq mi
	14 Feb 1854	Boundary with BENTON (now CALHOUN) adjusted [location unknown, not mapped; mistake in description corrected 1 Feb 1856]	
❸	18 Feb 1854	Lost small area to BENTON (now CALHOUN) to accommodate local property owner	800 sq mi
	1 Feb 1856	Boundary with BENTON (now CALHOUN) clarified, correcting mistake of 14 Feb 1854 [no change]	
	6 Feb 1858	Gained small area from DE KALB [location unknown, not mapped]	

(Heavy line depicts historical boundary. Base map shows present-day information.)

❸ 16 Jan 1844–6 Dec 1866
3 Dec 1867–30 Nov 1868

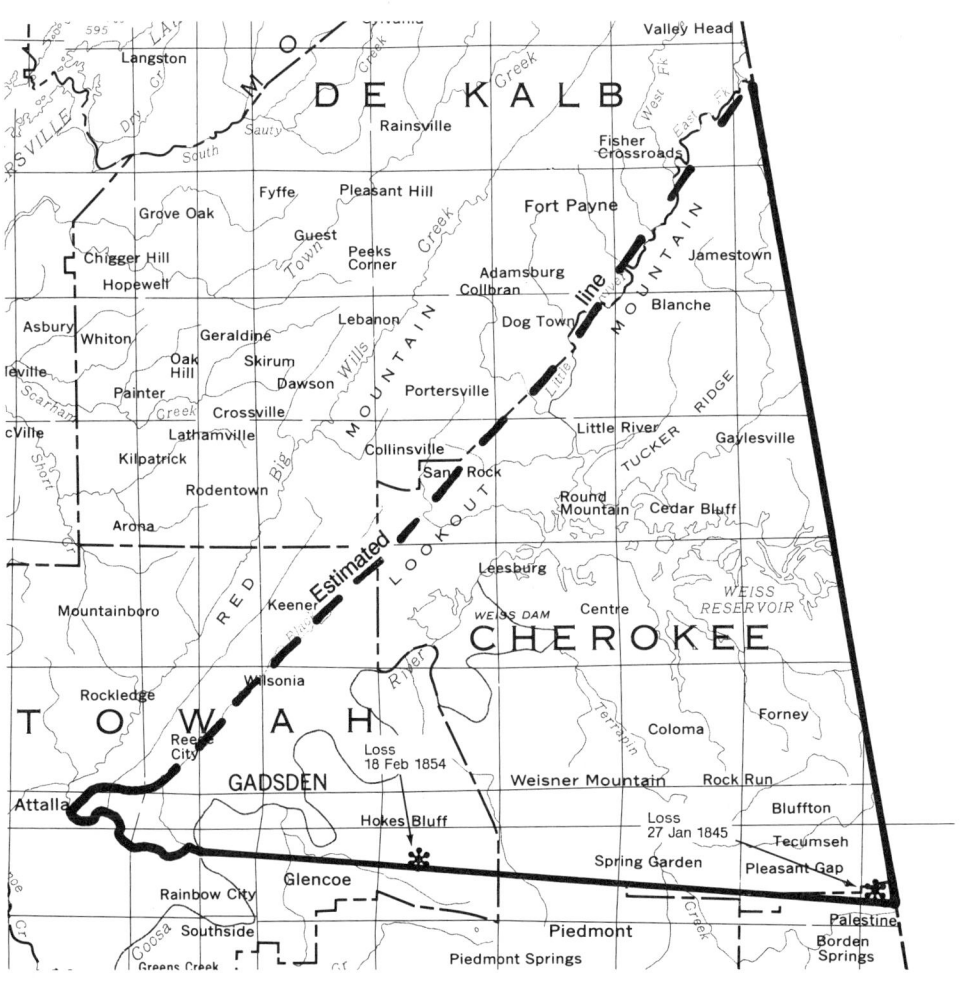

Chronology of CHEROKEE

Map	Date	Event	Resulting Area
❹	7 Dec 1866	Lost to creation of BAINE	630 sq mi
	13 Feb 1867	Boundary with DE KALB redefined [no discernible change]	
❸	3 Dec 1867	Gained from BAINE; BAINE eliminated	800 sq mi
❺	1 Dec 1868	Lost to creation of ETOWAH	600 sq mi

(Heavy line depicts historical boundary. Base map shows present-day information.)

❹ 7 Dec 1866–2 Dec 1867

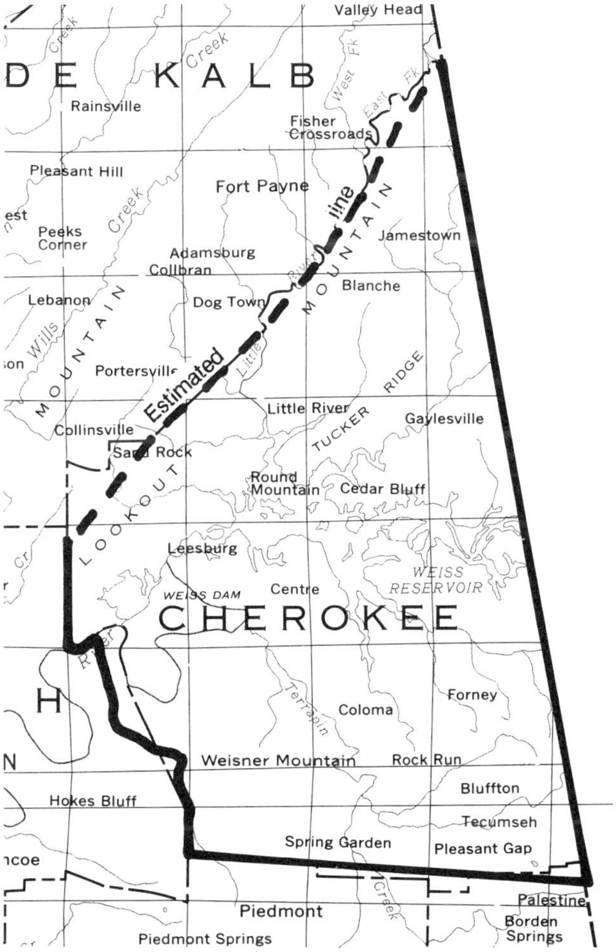

❺ 1 Dec 1868–6 Mar 1876

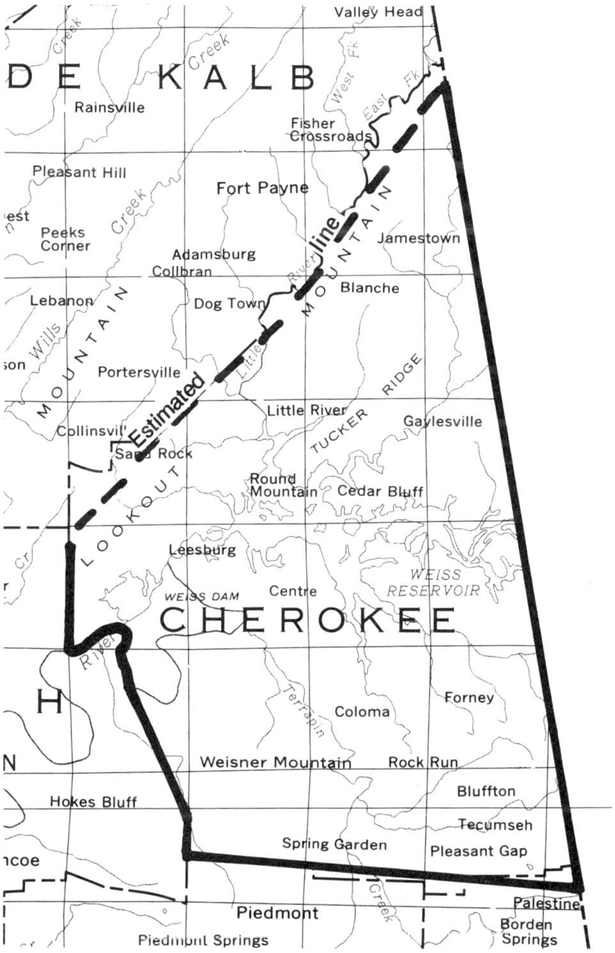

Chronology of CHEROKEE

Map	Date	Event	Resulting Area
⑥	7 Mar 1876	Exchanged with DE KALB	600 sq mi
⑦	10 Feb 1883	Gained from CALHOUN, lost to CLEBURNE	600 sq mi
⑦	12 Dec 1884	Gained small area from DE KALB	600 sq mi

(Heavy line depicts historical boundary. Base map shows present-day information.)

⑥ 7 Mar 1876–9 Feb 1883

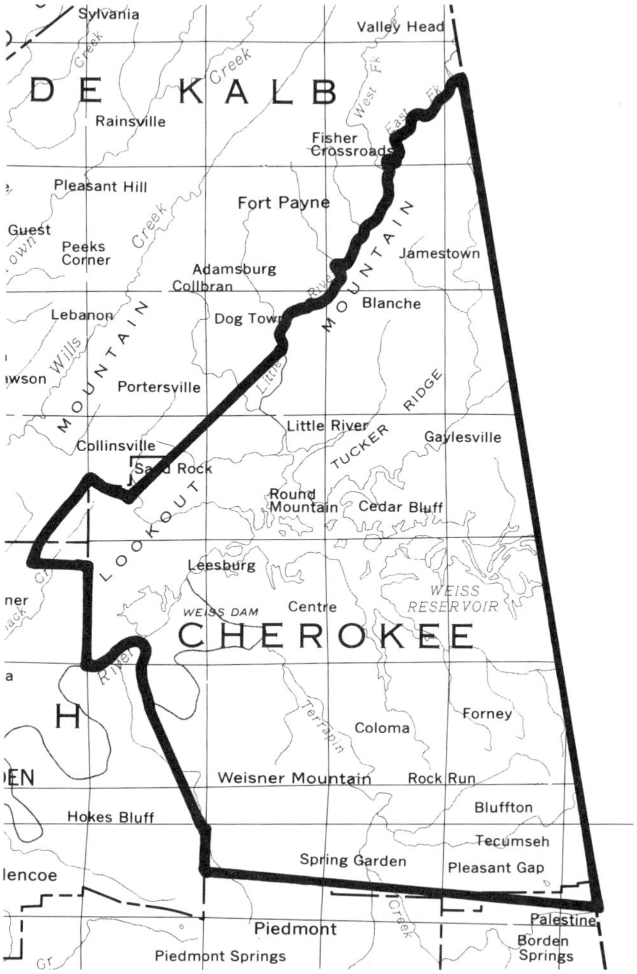

⑦ 10 Feb 1883–13 Feb 1901

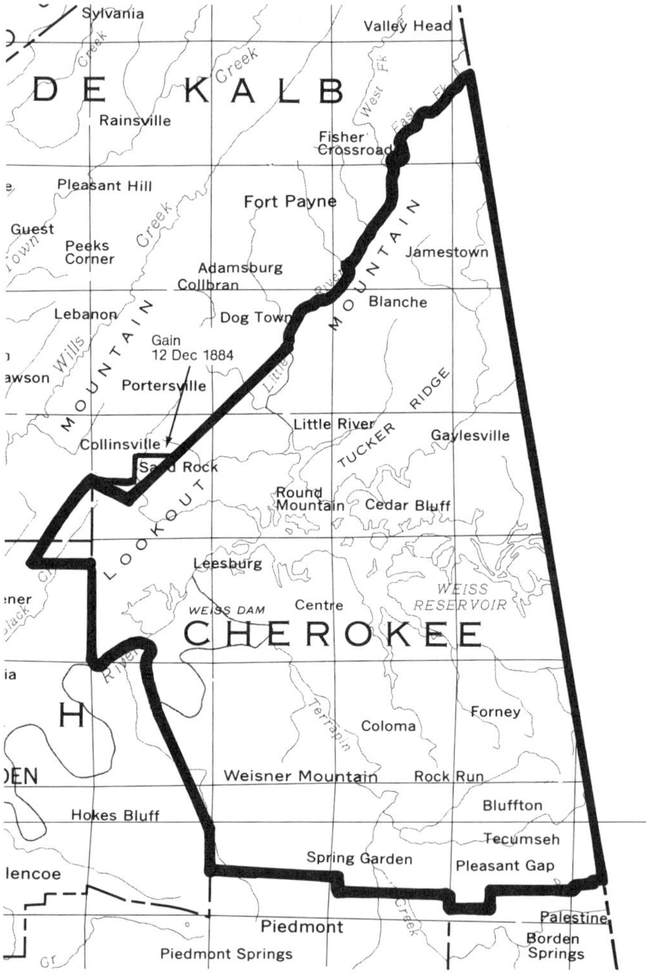

Individual County Chronologies 95

Chronology of CHEROKEE

Map	Date	Event	Resulting Area
❽	14 Feb 1901	Lost to DE KALB	590 sq mi
❾	10 Jul 1931	Lost to ETOWAH	590 sq mi

(Heavy line depicts historical boundary. Base map shows present-day information.)

❽ 14 Feb 1901–9 Jul 1931

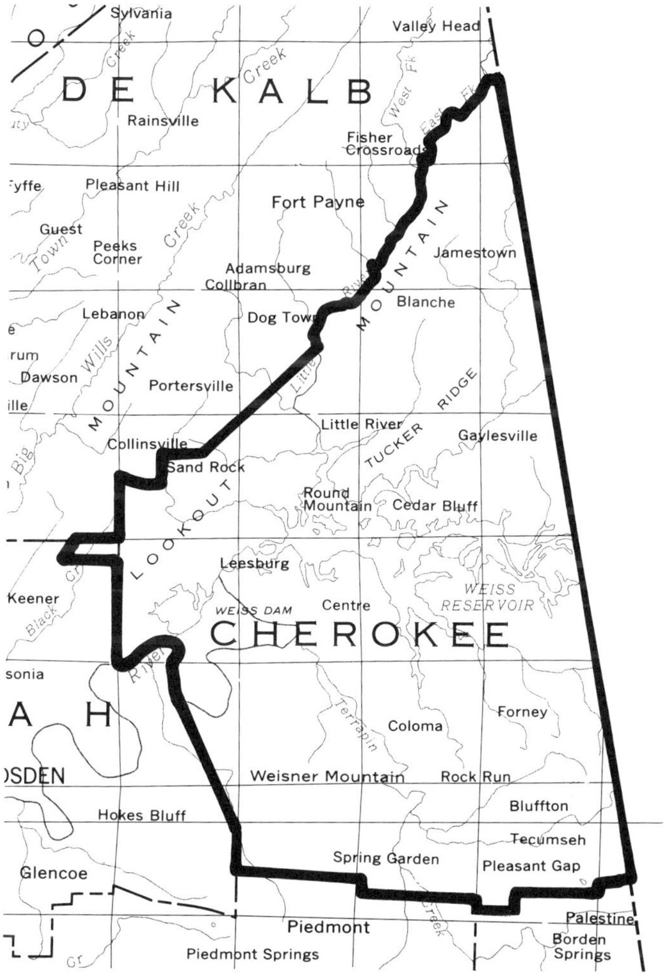

❾ 10 Jul 1931–1990

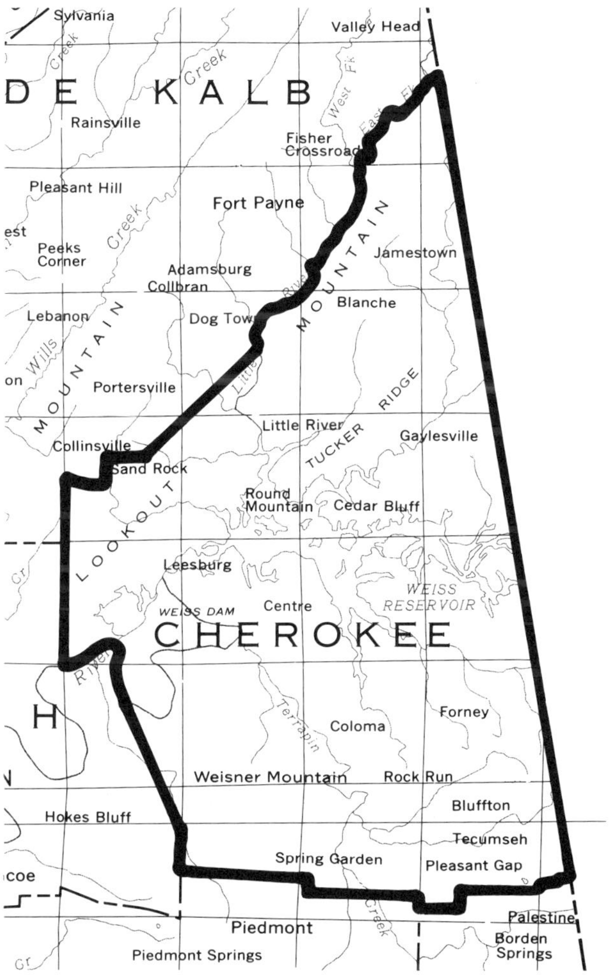

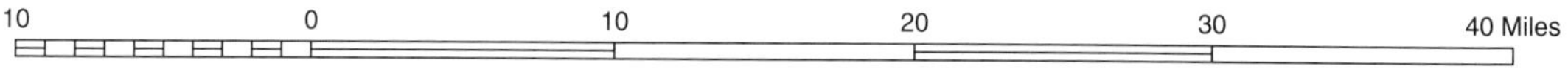

96 ALABAMA

Chronology of CHILTON (created as BAKER)

Map	Date	Event	Resulting Area
❶	30 Dec 1868	Created as BAKER from AUTAUGA, BIBB, DALLAS, and SHELBY	690 sq mi
❷	15 Dec 1869	Gained from AUTAUGA, lost to DALLAS	680 sq mi

(Heavy line depicts historical boundary. Base map shows present-day information.)

❶ 30 Dec 1868–14 Dec 1869

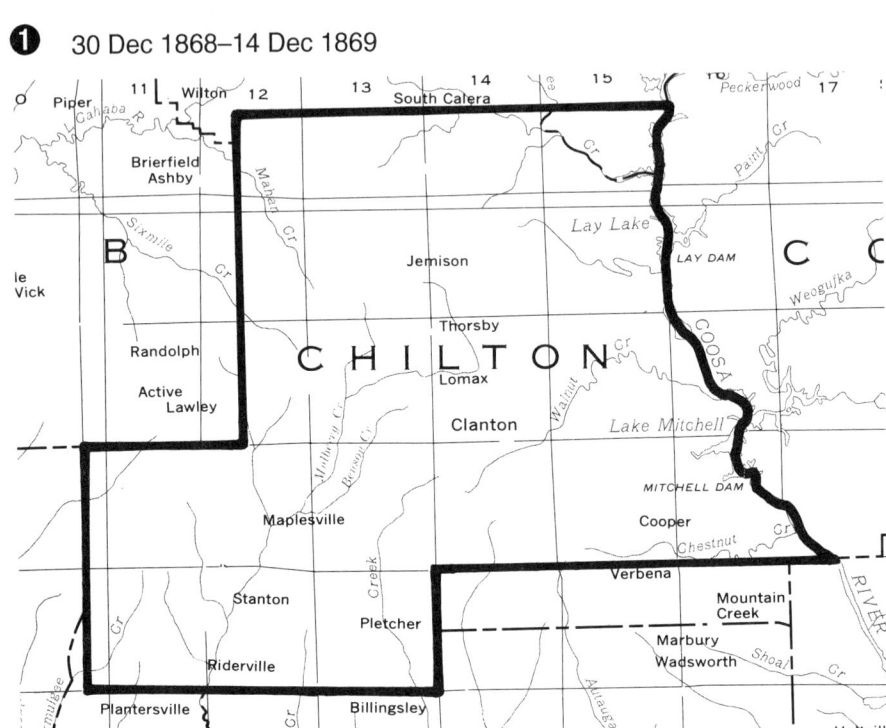

❷ 15 Dec 1869–22 Apr 1873

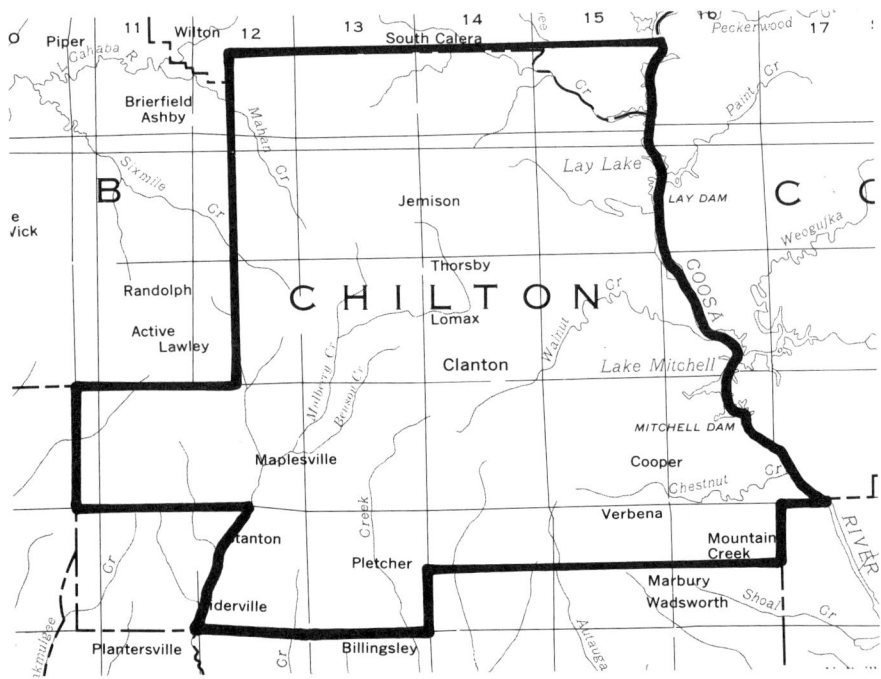

Individual County Chronologies 97

Chronology of CHILTON (created as BAKER)

Map	Date	Event	Resulting Area
❸	23 Apr 1873	Lost to SHELBY	670 sq mi
	17 Dec 1874	Renamed CHILTON	
❹	13 Feb 1875	Gained from DALLAS	710 sq mi
	18 Jul 1979	Boundary with BIBB redefined [no change]	

(Heavy line depicts historical boundary. Base map shows present-day information.)

❸ 23 Apr 1873–12 Feb 1875

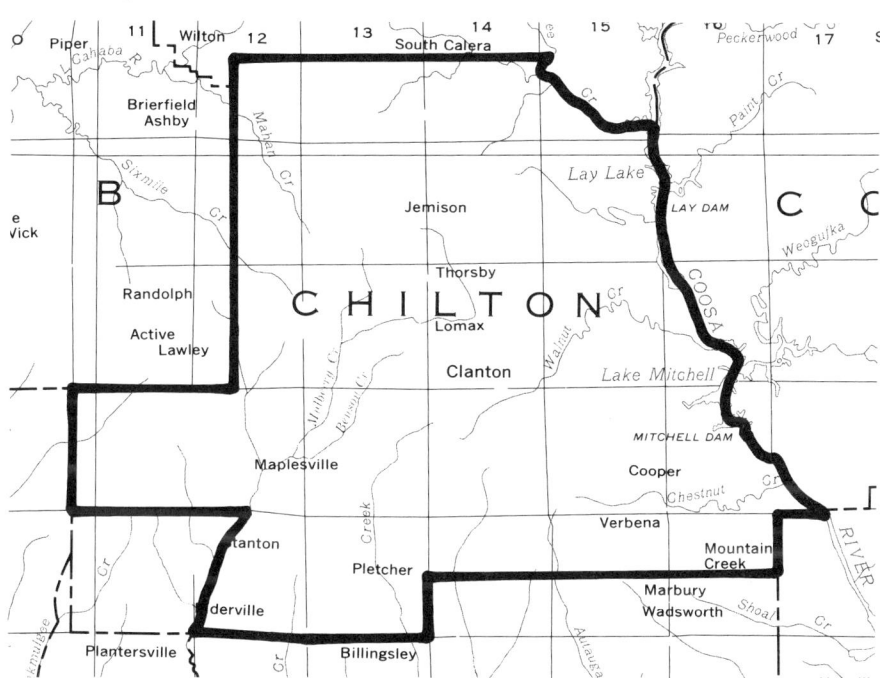

❹ 13 Feb 1875–1990

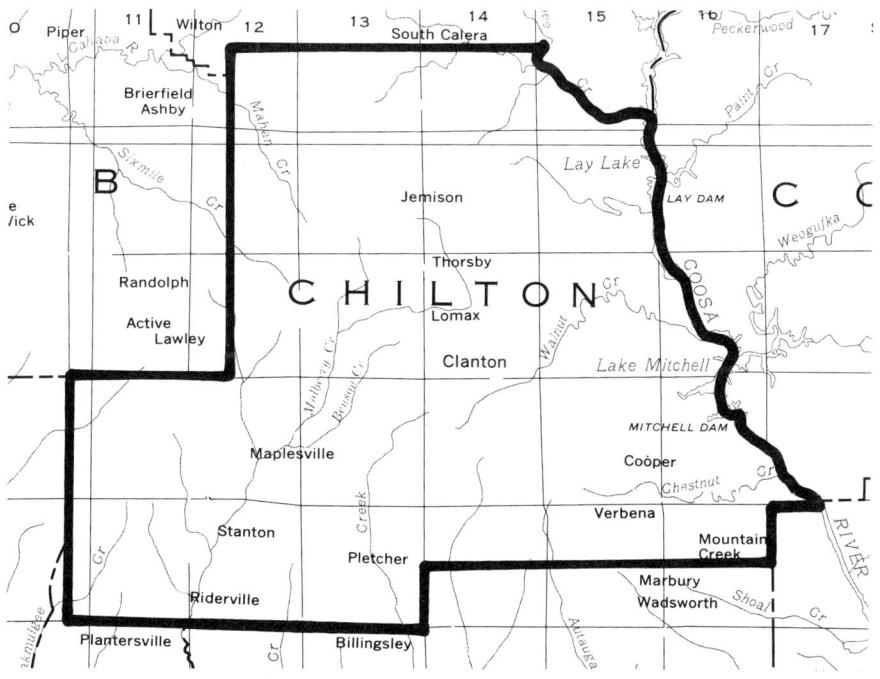

ALABAMA

Chronology of CHOCTAW

Map	Date	Event	Resulting Area
❶	29 Dec 1847	Created from SUMTER and WASHINGTON	910 sq mi
	1 Mar 1870	WASHINGTON authorized to gain from CHOCTAW, and CHOCTAW authorized to gain from SUMTER, dependent on local referendum [local action unknown, no change]	

(Heavy line depicts historical boundary. Base map shows present-day information.)

❶ 29 Dec 1847–1990

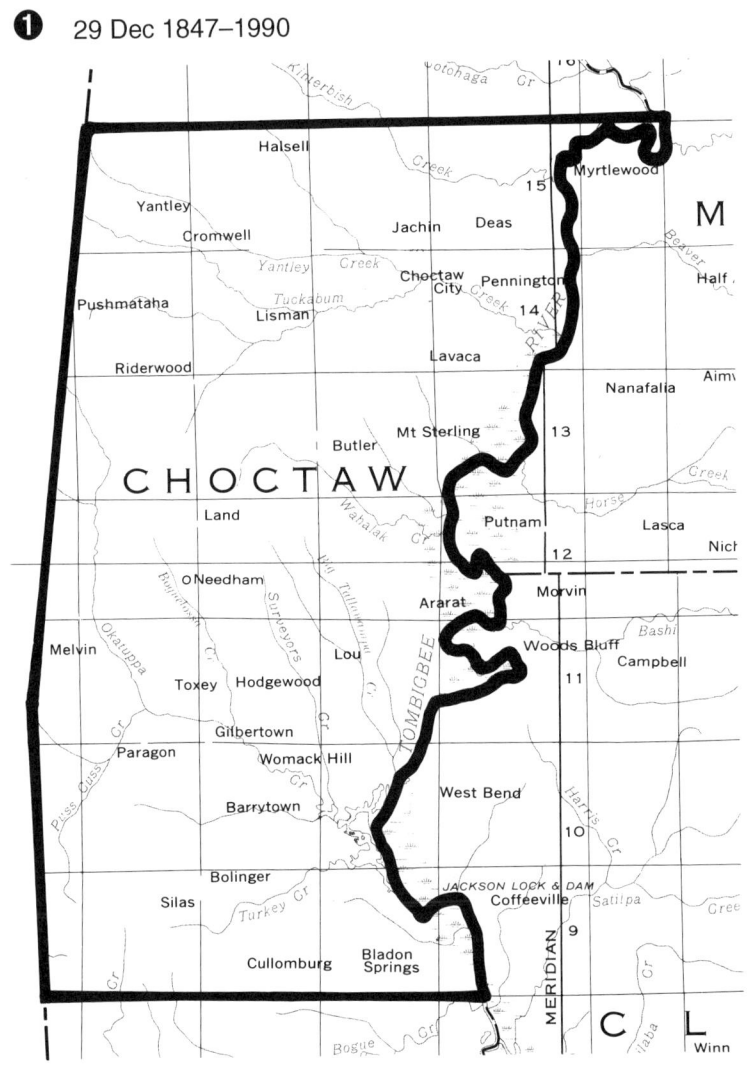

Individual County Chronologies 99

Chronology of CLAIBORNE (Miss.)

Map	Date	Event	Resulting Area
❶	27 Jan 1802	Created by Mississippi Territory from JEFFERSON (Miss.); extended eastward to Georgia, thereby overlapping WASHINGTON	11,300 sq mi
	30 Jan 1802	Lost to non-county area as the Choctaw Indian boundary in present Mississippi was implicitly adopted as eastern limit of CLAIBORNE (Miss.), ending overlap of WASHINGTON; eliminated from present Alabama	
	12 Mar 1803	Enlarged eastward to Georgia, apparently by mistake, thereby overlapping non-county area and WASHINGTON [not mapped]	
	7 Feb 1807	Eastern boundary clarified, ending overlap of 1803; eliminated from present Alabama	

(Heavy line depicts historical boundary. Base map shows present-day information.)

❶ 27 Jan 1802–29 Jan 1802

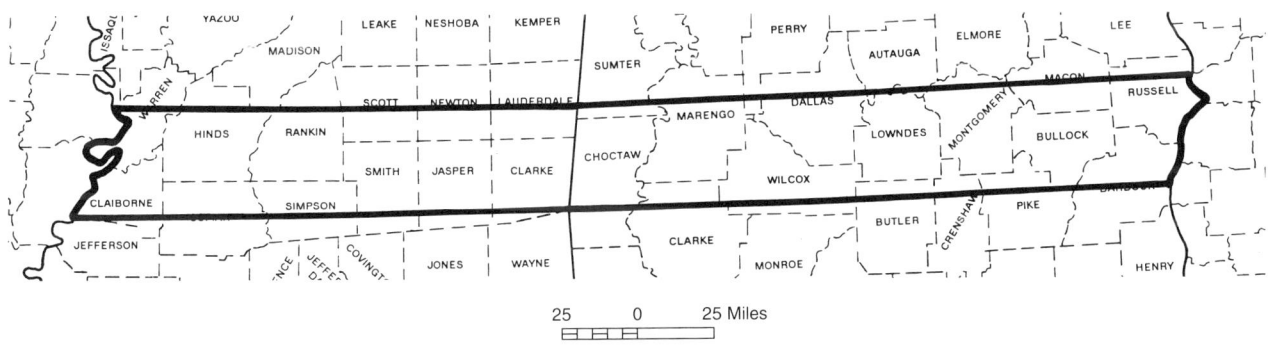

Chronology of CLARKE

Map	Date	Event	Resulting Area
❶	10 Dec 1812	Created by Mississippi Territory from WASHINGTON	880 sq mi
	3 Mar 1817	Became part of Alabama Territory	
❶	28 Nov 1821	Gained small area from MONROE	880 sq mi

(Heavy line depicts historical boundary. Base map shows present-day information.)

❶ 10 Dec 1812–25 Jan 1829

Individual County Chronologies 101

Chronology of CLARKE

Map	Date	Event	Resulting Area
❷	26 Jan 1829	Gained from MONROE and WILCOX	1,250 sq mi

(Heavy line depicts historical boundary. Base map shows present-day information.)

❷ 26 Jan 1829–19 Jan 1830
15 Jan 1831–12 Feb 1843

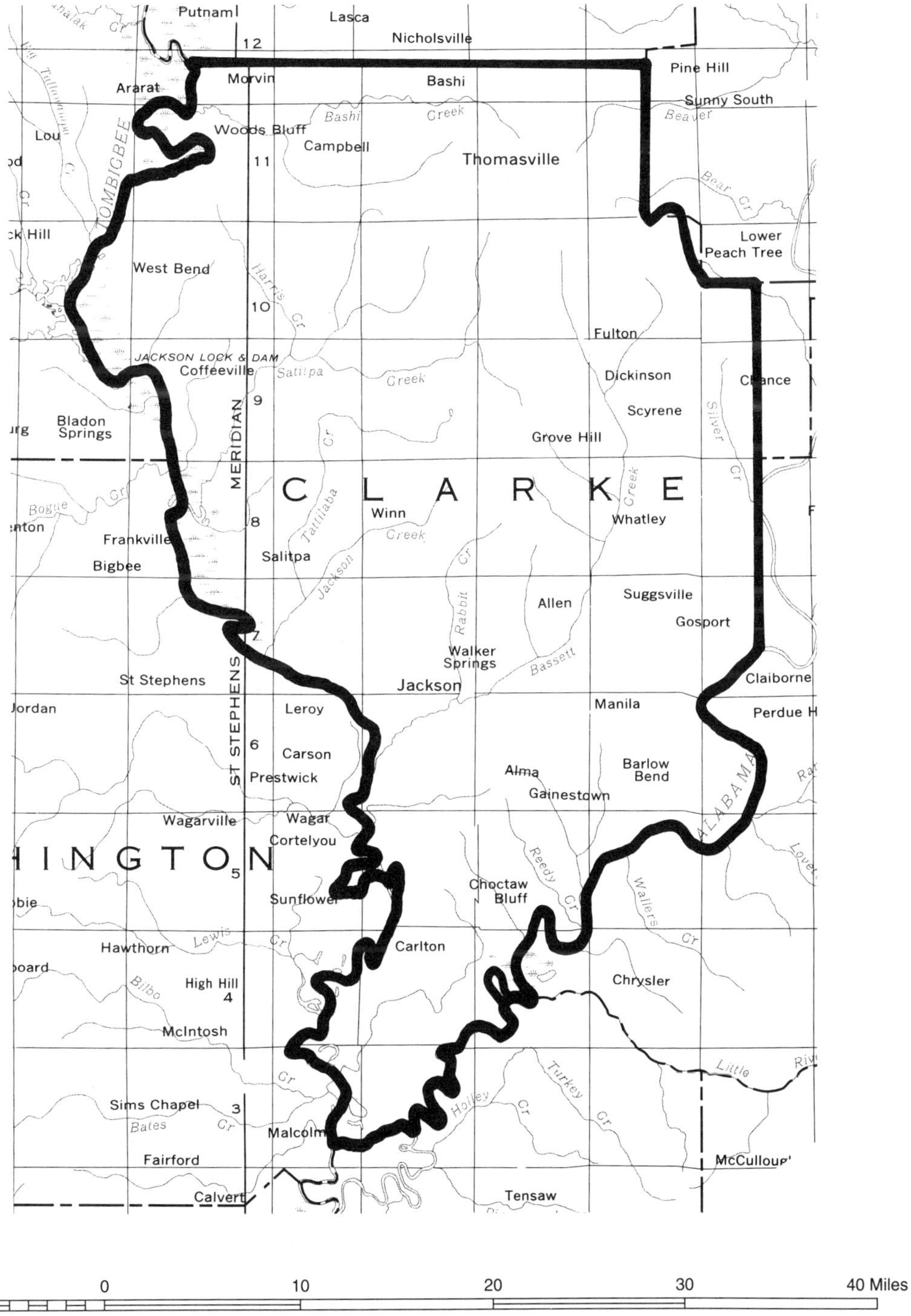

ALABAMA

Chronology of CLARKE

Map	Date	Event	Resulting Area
❸	20 Jan 1830	Lost to WILCOX	1,190 sq mi
❷	15 Jan 1831	Gained from WILCOX	1,250 sq mi

(Heavy line depicts historical boundary. Base map shows present-day information.)

❸ 20 Jan 1830–14 Jan 1831

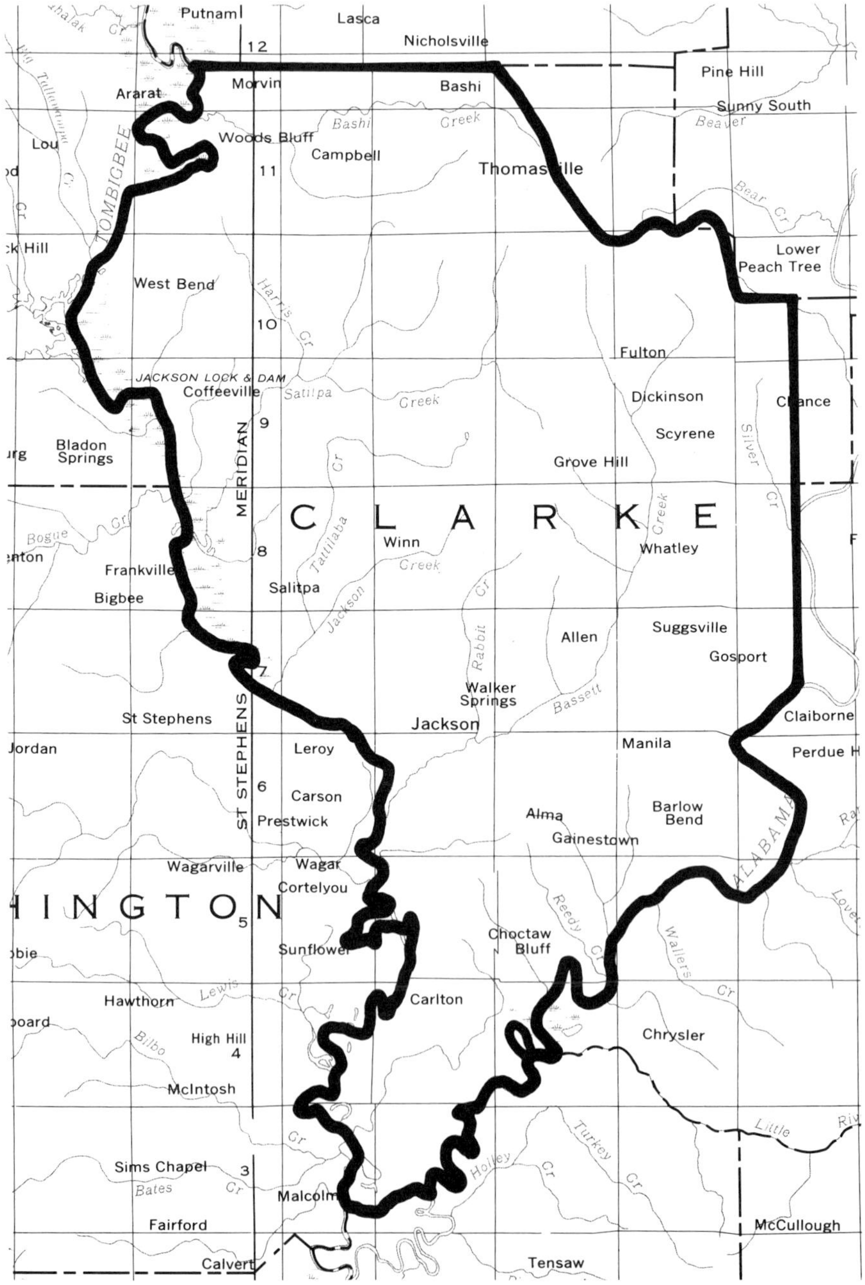

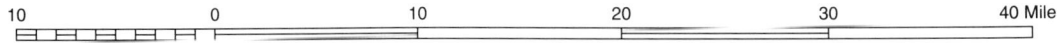

Individual County Chronologies 103

Chronology of CLARKE

Map	Date	Event	Resulting Area
④	13 Feb 1843	Gained from MONROE	1,270 sq mi
④	6 Dec 1861	Gained small area from MONROE to accommodate local property owner	1,270 sq mi
④	1901	Exchanged small areas with WILCOX	1,270 sq mi

(Heavy line depicts historical boundary. Base map shows present-day information.)

④ 13 Feb 1843–1990

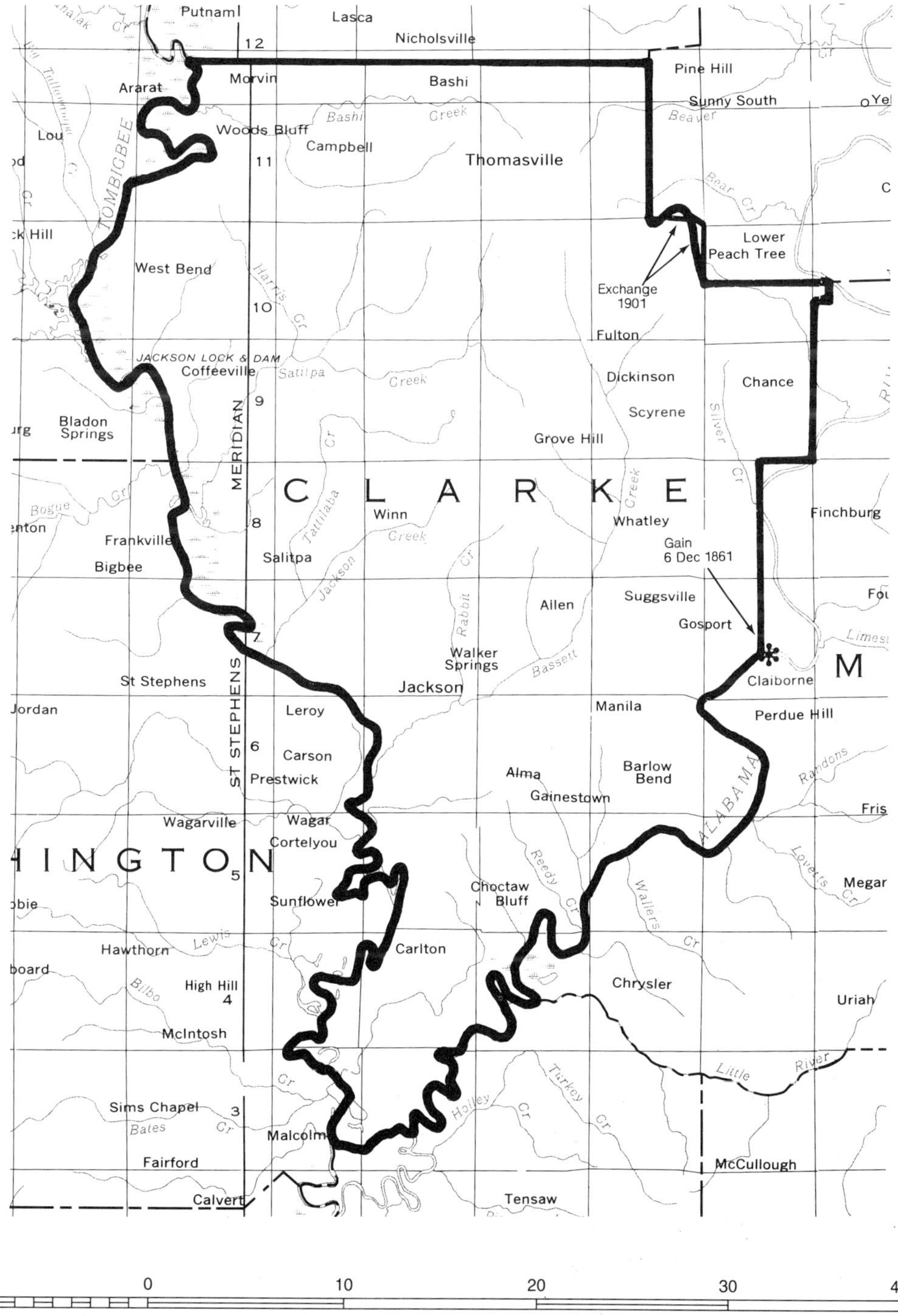

ALABAMA

Chronology of CLAY

Map	Date	Event	Resulting Area
❶	7 Dec 1866	Created from RANDOLPH and TALLADEGA	620 sq mi
❷	15 Feb 1867	Lost to CLEBURNE and TALLADEGA	610 sq mi

(Heavy line depicts historical boundary. Base map shows present-day information.)

❶ 7 Dec 1866–14 Feb 1867

❷ 15 Feb 1867

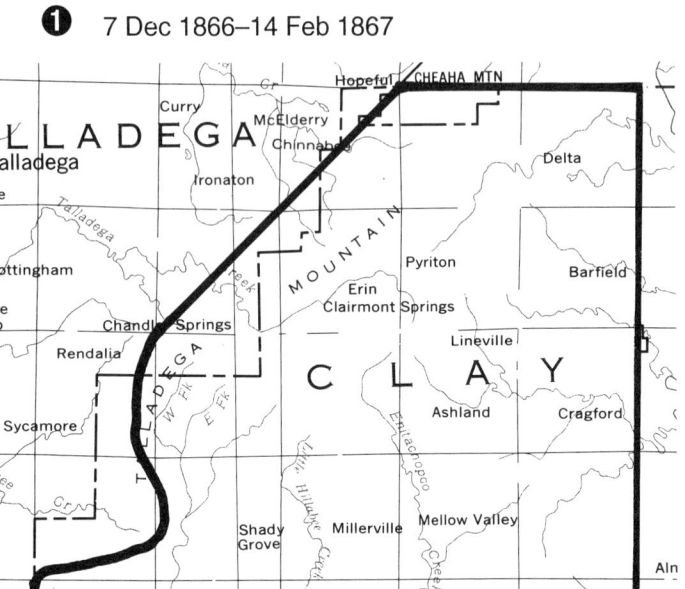

Individual County Chronologies 105

Chronology of CLAY

Map	Date	Event	Resulting Area
❸	16 Feb 1867	Lost to TALLADEGA	580 sq mi
❸	3 Mar 1870	Lost small area to COOSA to accommodate local property owner	580 sq mi
	16 Dec 1871	Gain from RANDOLPH authorized [cannot be demarcated as described, no change]	
❸	17 Mar 1873	Gained small area from RANDOLPH	580 sq mi
❹	10 Jan 1877	Lost to TALLADEGA	550 sq mi
❹	9 Feb 1877	Gained small area from TALLAPOOSA	550 sq mi

(Heavy line depicts historical boundary. Base mapshows present-day information.)

❸ 16 Feb 1867–9 Jan 1877

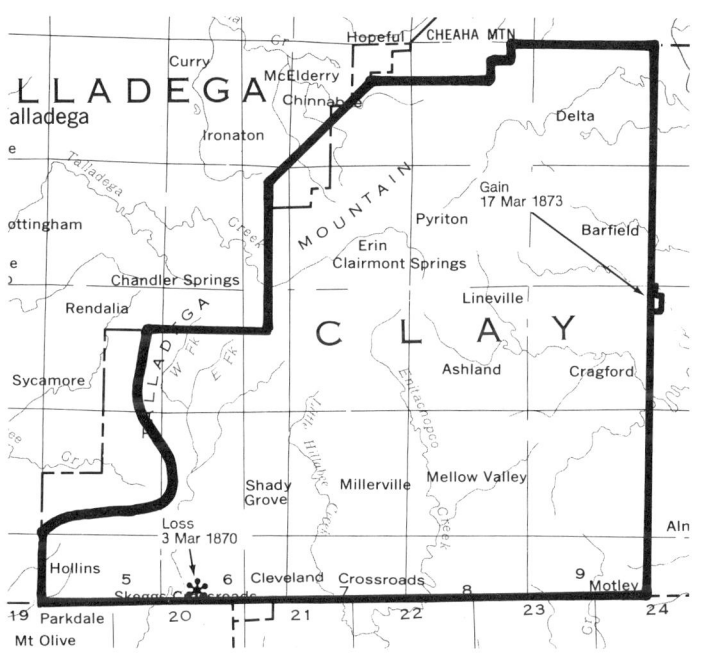

❹ 10 Jan 1877–8 Feb 1893

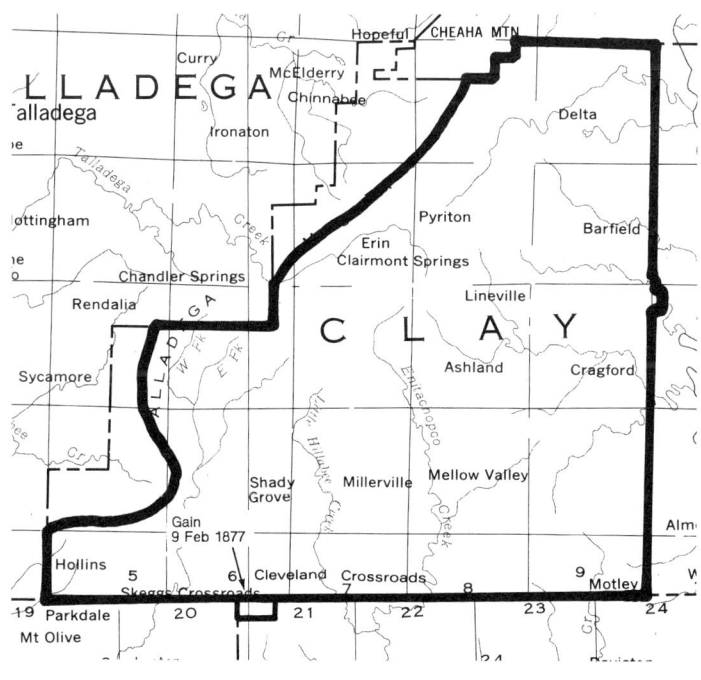

106 ALABAMA

Chronology of CLAY

Map	Date	Event	Resulting Area
❺	9 Feb 1893	Gained from TALLADEGA	590 sq mi
❻	12 Dec 1894	Exchanged with TALLADEGA	600 sq mi

(Heavy line depicts historical boundary. Base map shows present-day information.)

❺ 9 Feb 1893–11 Dec 1894

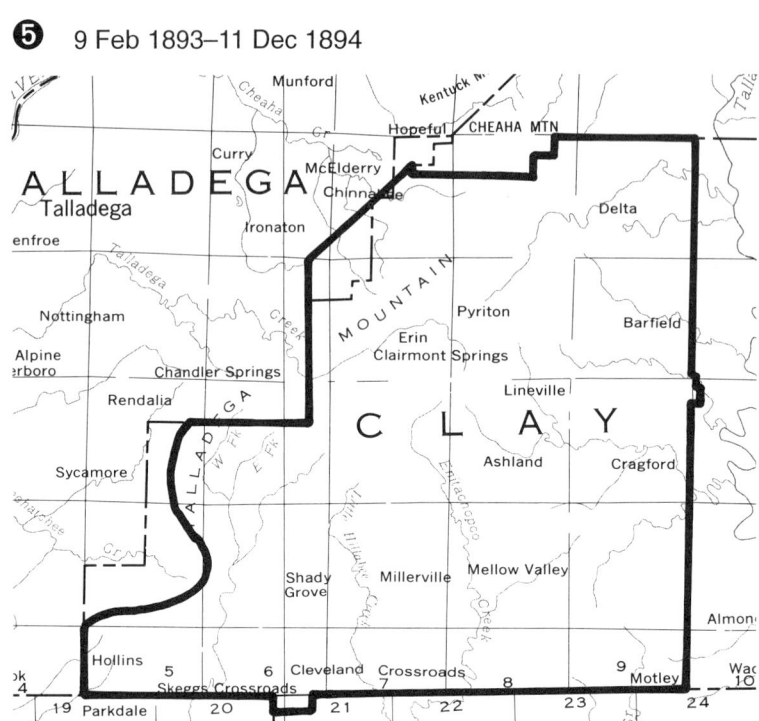

❻ 12 Dec 1894–1990

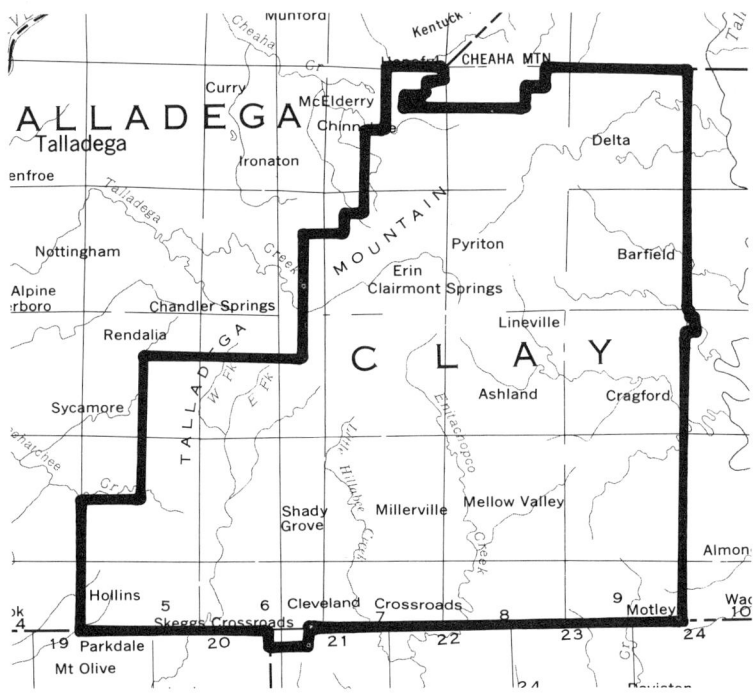

Individual County Chronologies 107

Chronology of CLEBURNE

Map	Date	Event	Resulting Area
❶	6 Dec 1866	Created from CALHOUN, RANDOLPH, and TALLADEGA	550 sq mi

(Heavy line depicts historical boundary. Base map shows present-day information.)

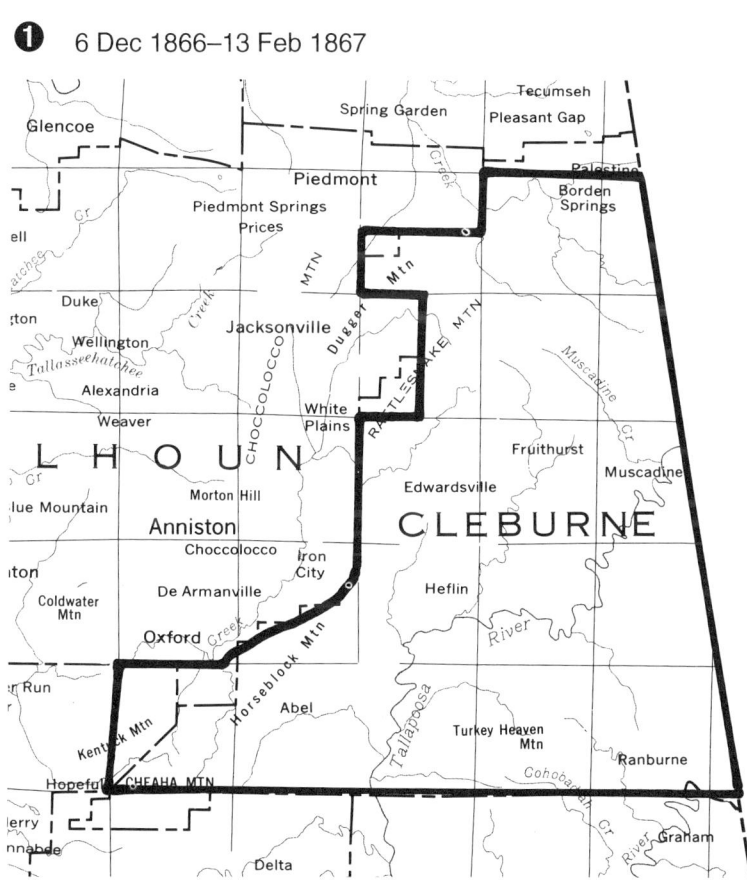

❶ 6 Dec 1866–13 Feb 1867

ALABAMA

Chronology of CLEBURNE

Map	Date	Event	Resulting Area
❷	14 Feb 1867	Lost to TALLADEGA	540 sq mi

(Heavy line depicts historical boundary. Base map shows present-day information.)

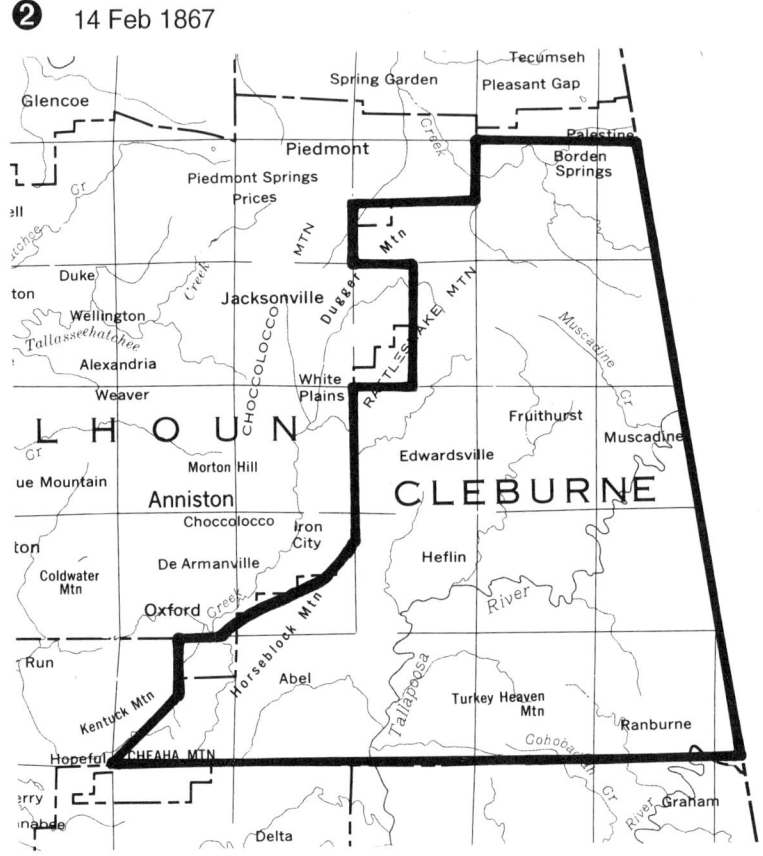

❷ 14 Feb 1867

Chronology of CLEBURNE

Map	Date	Event	Resulting Area
❸	15 Feb 1867	Gained from CLAY and TALLADEGA	550 sq mi

(Heavy line depicts historical boundary. Base map shows present-day information.)

❸ 15 Feb 1867–9 Feb 1883

ALABAMA

Chronology of CLEBURNE

Map	Date	Event	Resulting Area
❹	10 Feb 1883	Gained from CALHOUN and CHEROKEE	560 sq mi

(Heavy line depicts historical boundary. Base map shows present-day information.)

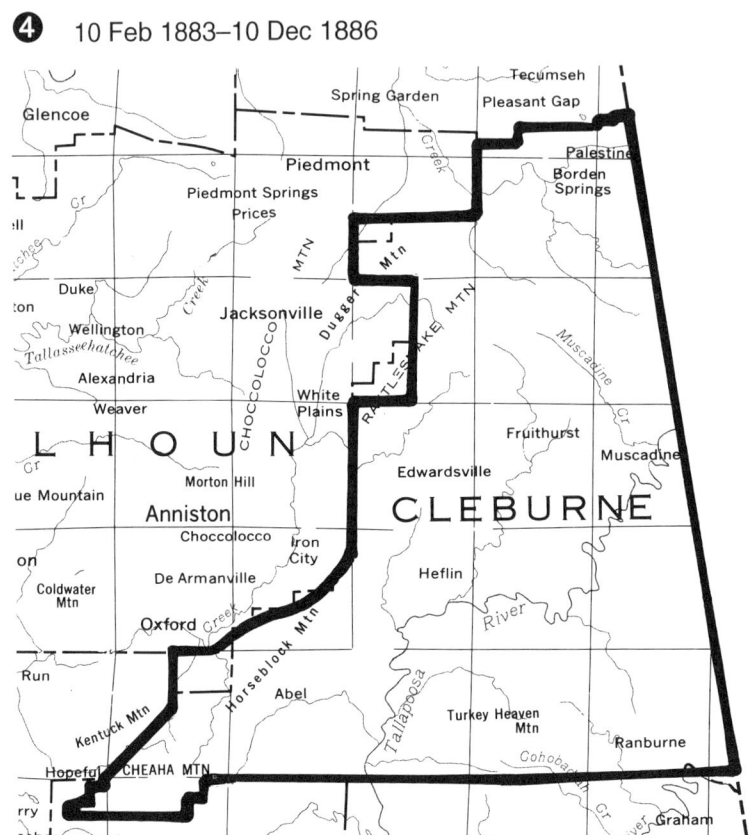

❹ 10 Feb 1883–10 Dec 1886

Individual County Chronologies 111

Chronology of CLEBURNE

Map	Date	Event	Resulting Area
❺	11 Dec 1886	Exchanged with CALHOUN	560 sq mi

(Heavy line depicts historical boundary. Base map shows present-day information.)

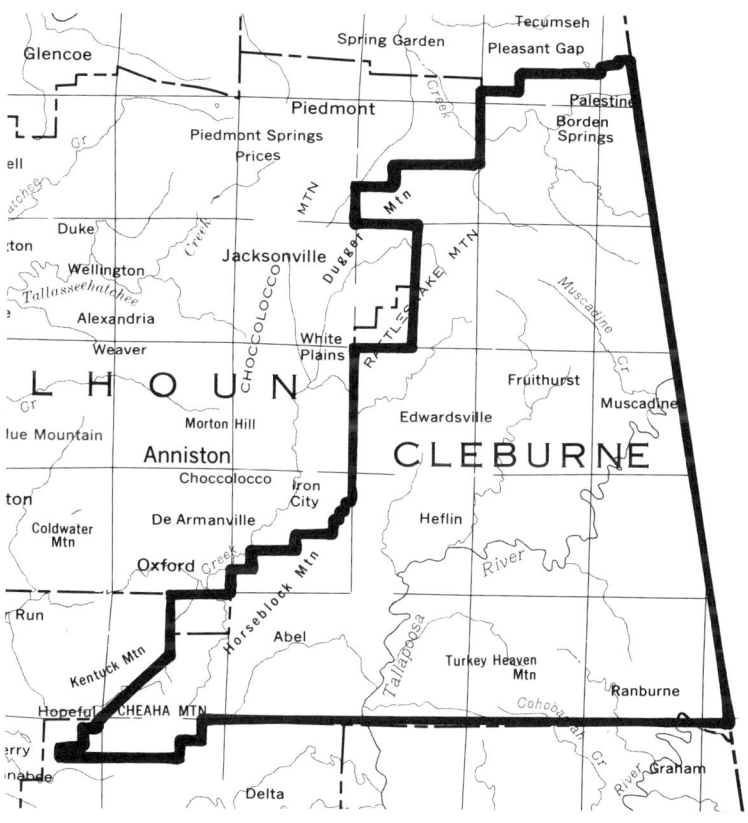

❺ 11 Dec 1886–29 Sep 1903
30 Jun 1906–24 Jul 1907

Chronology of CLEBURNE

Map	Date	Event	Resulting Area
❻	30 Sep 1903	Lost to CALHOUN	550 sq mi
❺	30 Jun 1906	Gained from CALHOUN	560 sq mi

(Heavy line depicts historical boundary. Base map shows present-day information.)

❻ 30 Sep 1903–29 Jun 1906

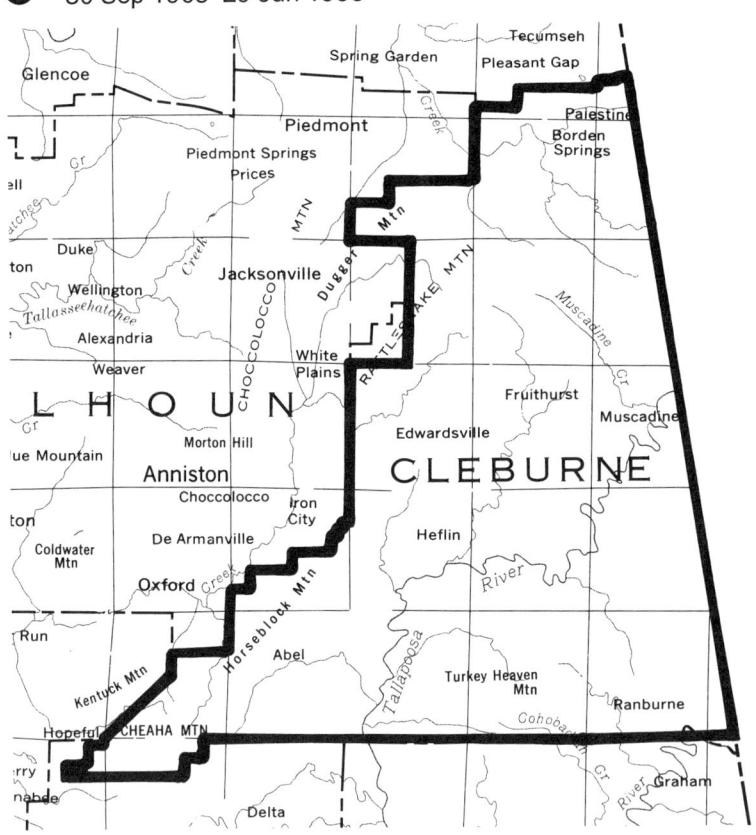

Chronology of CLEBURNE

Map	Date	Event	Resulting Area
❼	25 Jul 1907	Exchanged with CALHOUN	560 sq mi
❼	29 Jul 1907	Exchanged small areas with RANDOLPH	560 sq mi

(Heavy line depicts historical boundary. Base map shows present-day information.)

❼ 25 Jul 1907–1990

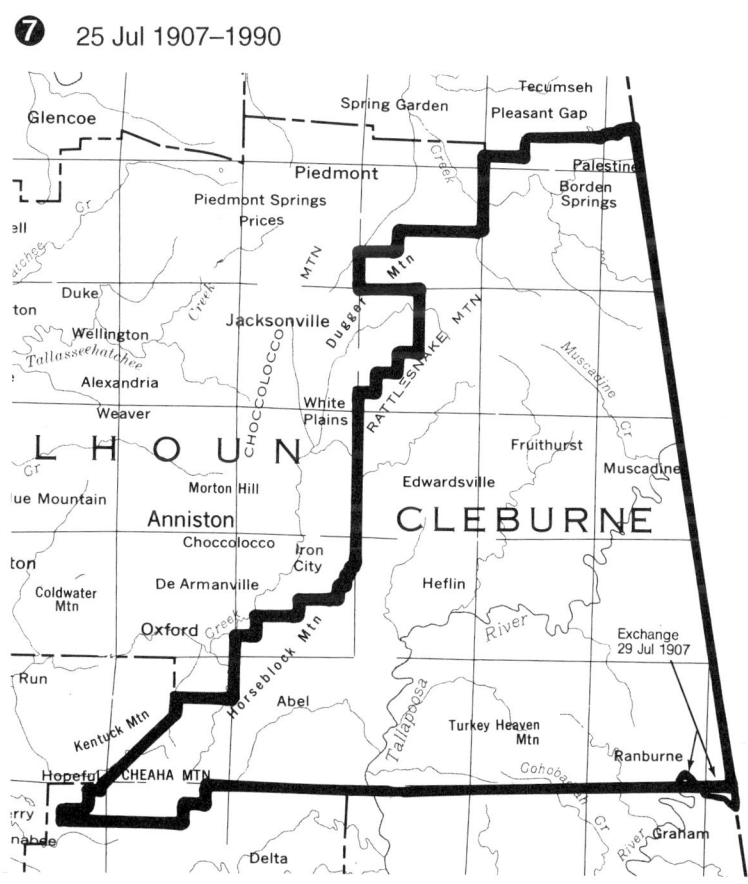

114 ALABAMA

Chronology of COFFEE

Map	Date	Event	Resulting Area
❶	29 Dec 1841	Created from DALE	1,030 sq mi
❷	24 Nov 1866	Lost to creation of CRENSHAW	1,010 sq mi

(Heavy line depicts historical boundary. Base map shows present-day information.)

❶ 29 Dec 1841–23 Nov 1866

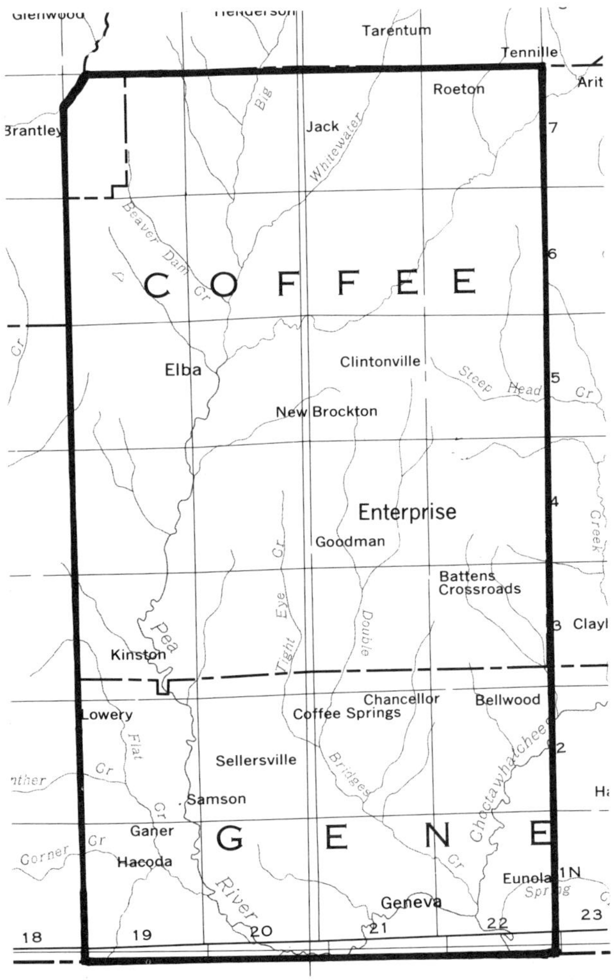

❷ 24 Nov 1866–25 Dec 1868

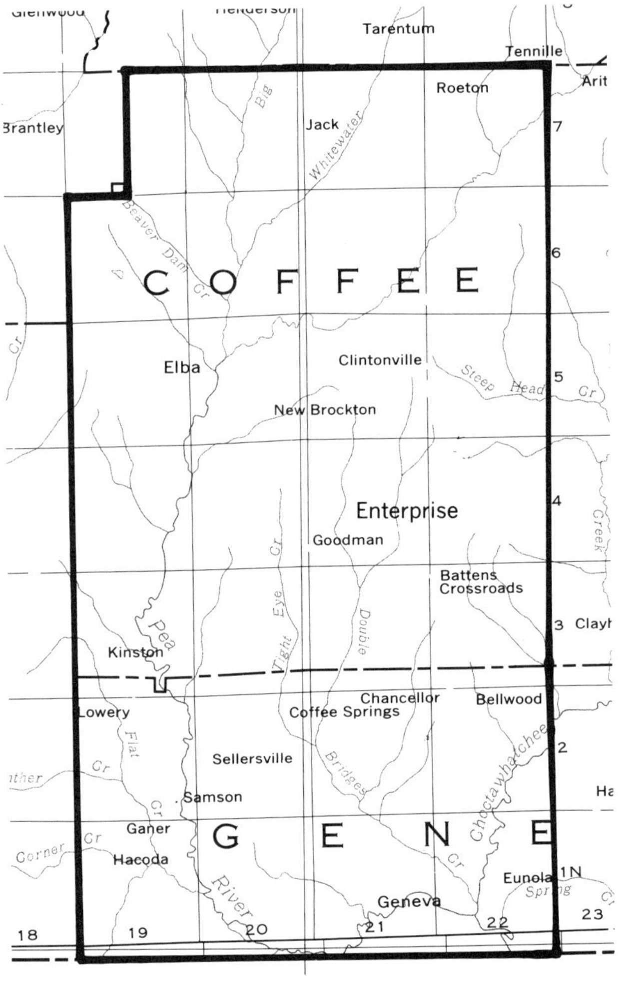

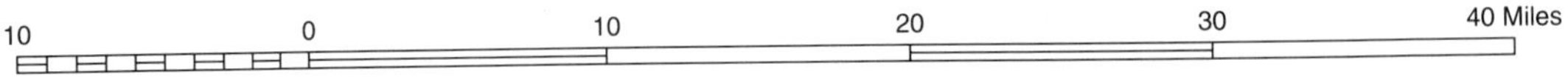

Individual County Chronologies 115

Chronology of COFFEE

Map	Date	Event	Resulting Area
❸	26 Dec 1868	Lost to creation of GENEVA	680 sq mi
❸	15 Feb 1871	Gained small area from GENEVA to accommodate local property owner	680 sq mi
❹	23 Feb 1871	Gained small area from CRENSHAW to accommodate local property owners	680 sq mi
	13 Feb 1879	Gain from GENEVA authorized, dependent on local referendum; no evidence that required election was held [no change]	

(Heavy line depicts historical boundary. Base map shows present-day information.)

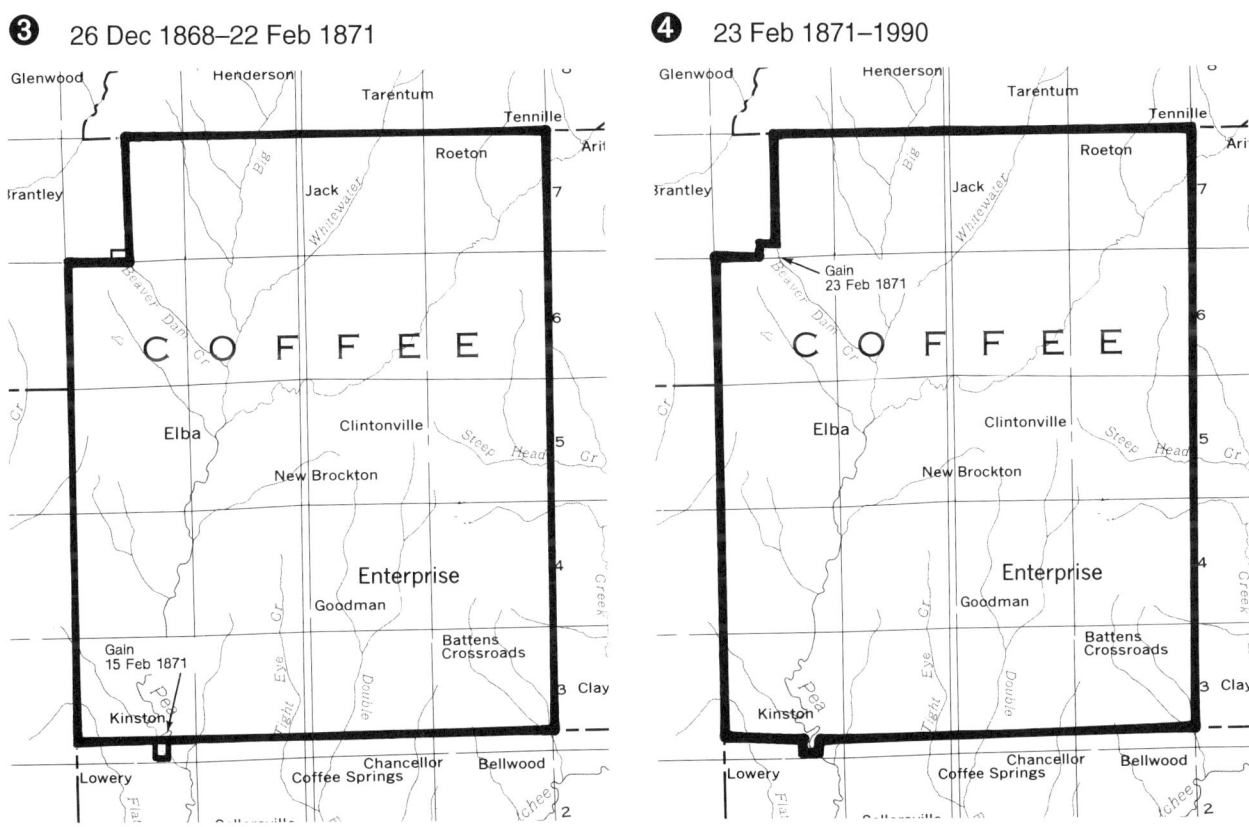

❸ 26 Dec 1868–22 Feb 1871

❹ 23 Feb 1871–1990

116 ALABAMA

Chronology of COLBERT

Map	Date	Event	Resulting Area
❶	6 Feb 1867	Created from FRANKLIN	600 sq mi
	29 Nov 1867	Lost all territory to FRANKLIN; COLBERT eliminated	
❶	24 Jan 1870	Re-created from FRANKLIN	600 sq mi
❶	29 Jan 1875	Exchanged small areas with FRANKLIN	600 sq mi
❷	6 Feb 1895	Gained from LAWRENCE, lost to FRANKLIN	620 sq mi

(Heavy line depicts historical boundary. Base map shows present-day information.)

❶ 6 Feb 1867–28 Nov 1867
24 Jan 1870–5 Feb 1895

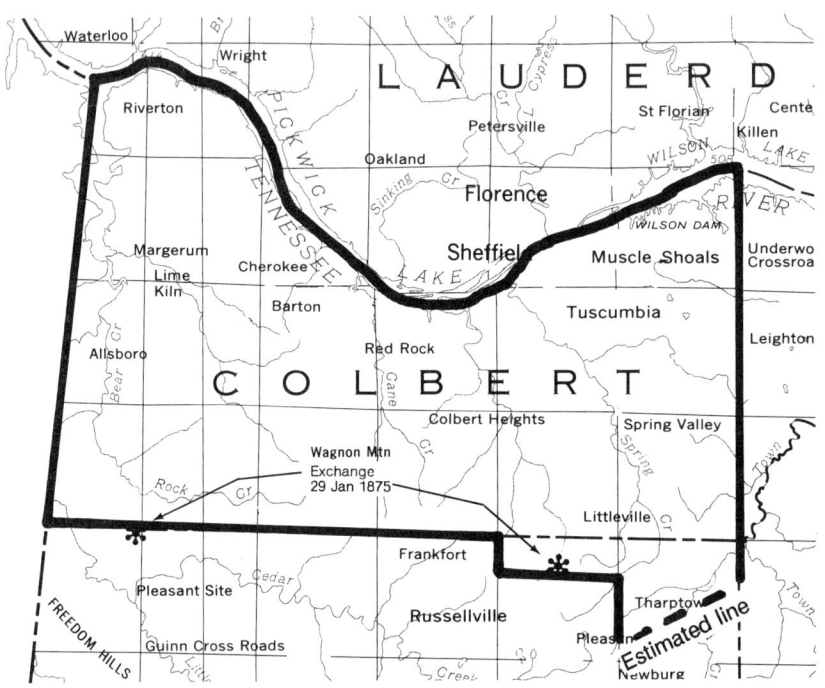

❷ 6 Feb 1895–1990

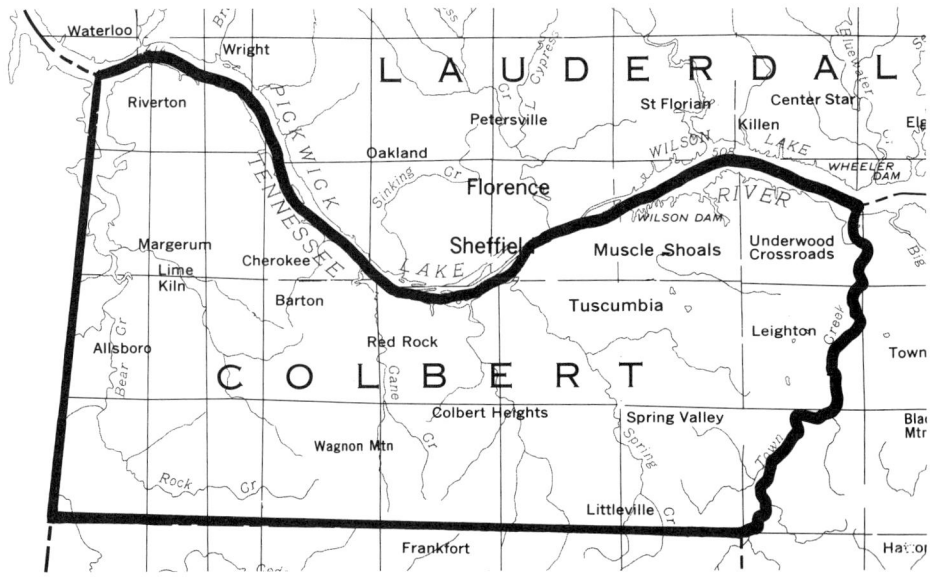

Chronology of CONECUH

Map	Date	Event	Resulting Area
❶	13 Feb 1818	Created from MONROE	8,100 sq mi

(Heavy line depicts historical boundary. Base map shows present-day information.)

❶ 13 Feb 1818–12 Dec 1819

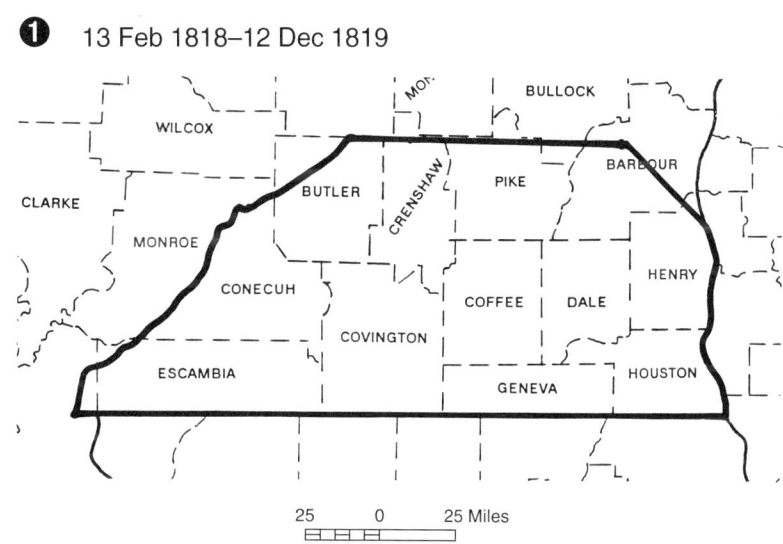

ALABAMA

Chronology of CONECUH

Map	Date	Event	Resulting Area
❷	13 Dec 1819	Lost to BALDWIN and to creation of BUTLER and HENRY	1,480 sq mi

(Heavy line depicts historical boundary. Base map shows present-day information.)

❷ 13 Dec 1819–1 Dec 1837

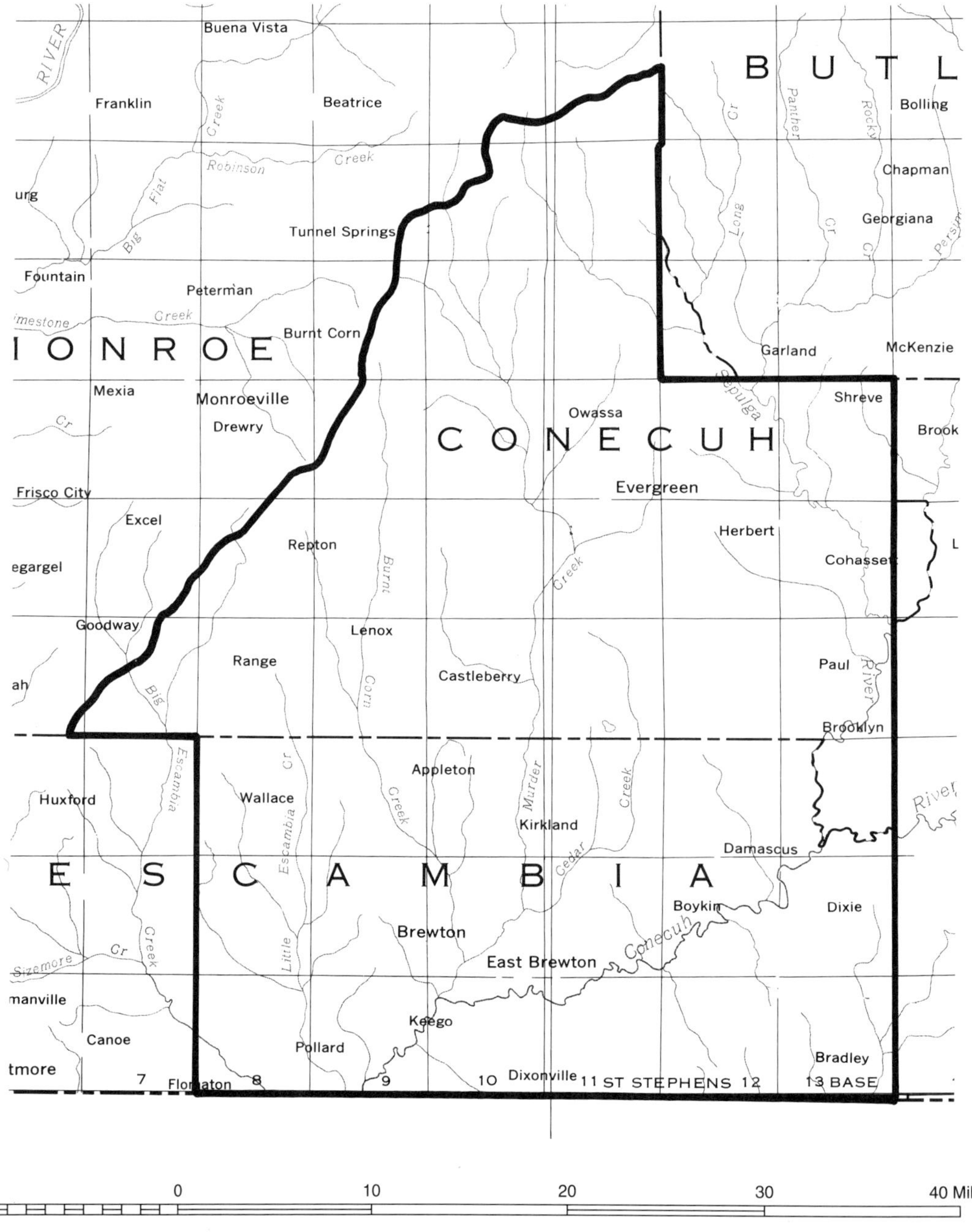

Individual County Chronologies 119

Chronology of CONECUH

Map	Date	Event	Resulting Area
❸	2 Dec 1837	Gained from BUTLER	1,490 sq mi
❸	2 Jan 1841	Gained from BUTLER	1,500 sq mi
	10 Feb 1852	Boundary with MONROE clarified [no change]	
	24 Nov 1862	Lost small area to BUTLER to accommodate local property owner [location unknown, not mapped]	
❸	11 Dec 1865	Lost small area to MONROE to accommodate local property owner	1,500 sq mi

(Heavy line depicts historical boundary. Base map shows present-day information.)

❸ 2 Dec 1837–9 Dec 1868

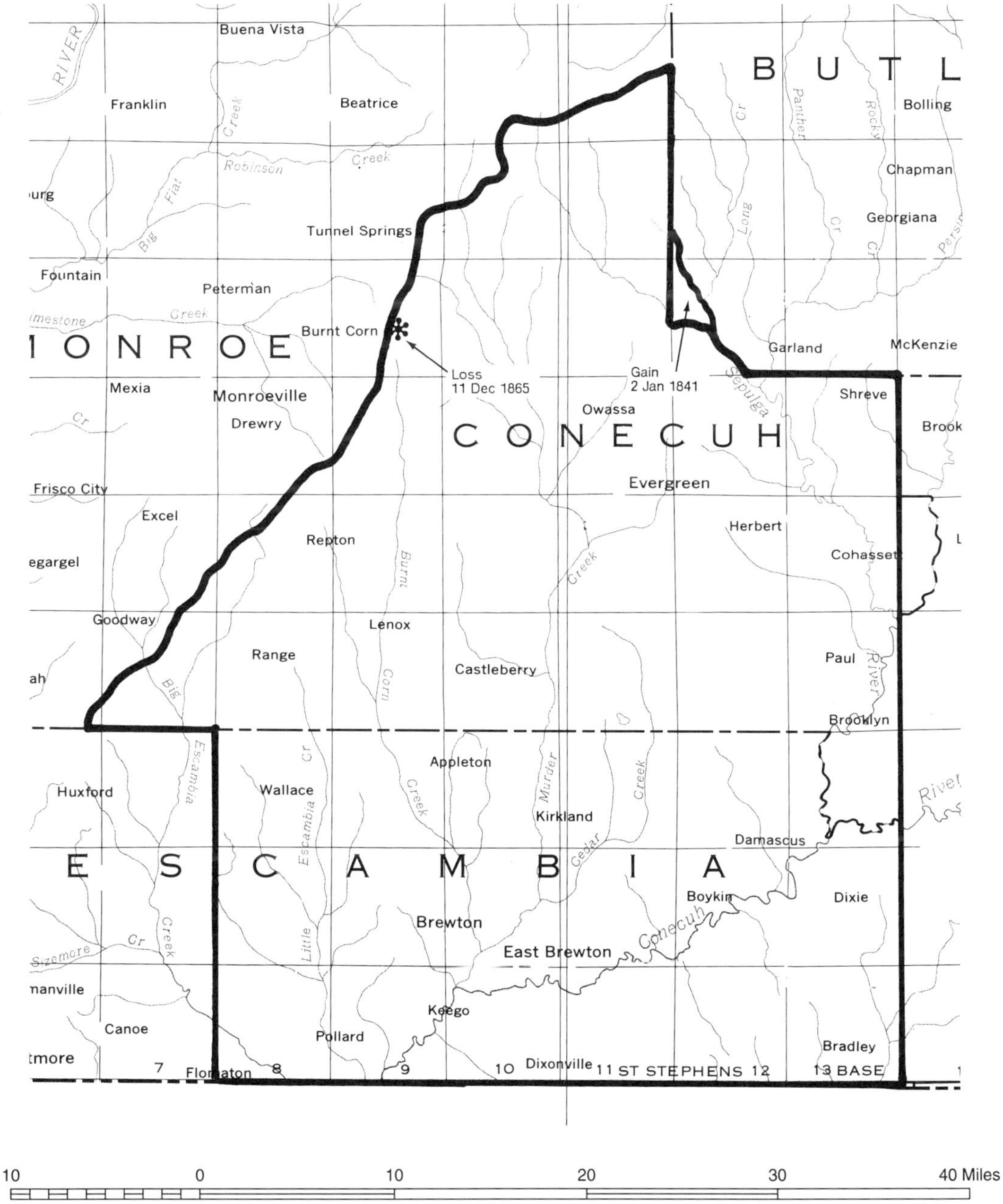

120 ALABAMA

Chronology of CONECUH

Map	Date	Event	Resulting Area
❹	10 Dec 1868	Lost to creation of ESCAMBIA	820 sq mi

(Heavy line depicts historical boundary. Base map shows present-day information.)

❹ 10 Dec 1868–10 Dec 1874

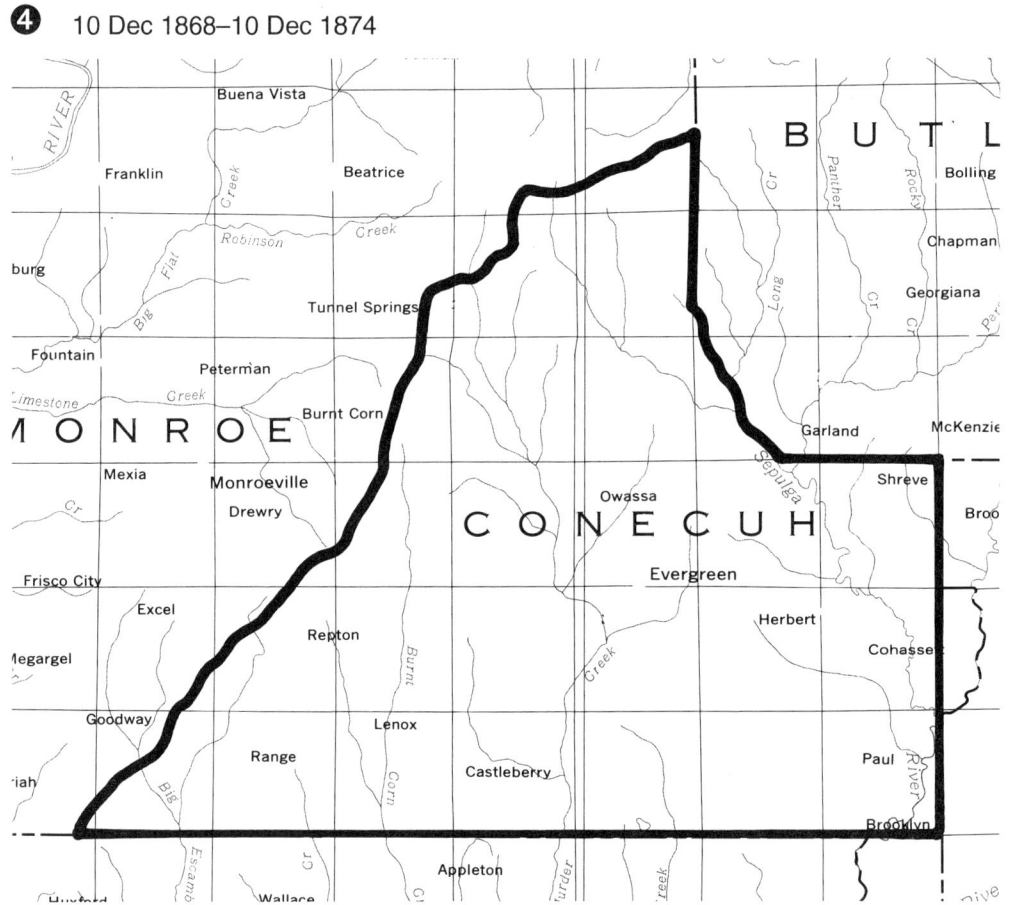

Chronology of CONECUH

Map	Date	Event	Resulting Area
❺	11 Dec 1874	Gained from COVINGTON	830 sq mi

(Heavy line depicts historical boundary. Base map shows present-day information.)

❺ 11 Dec 1874–24 Feb 1875

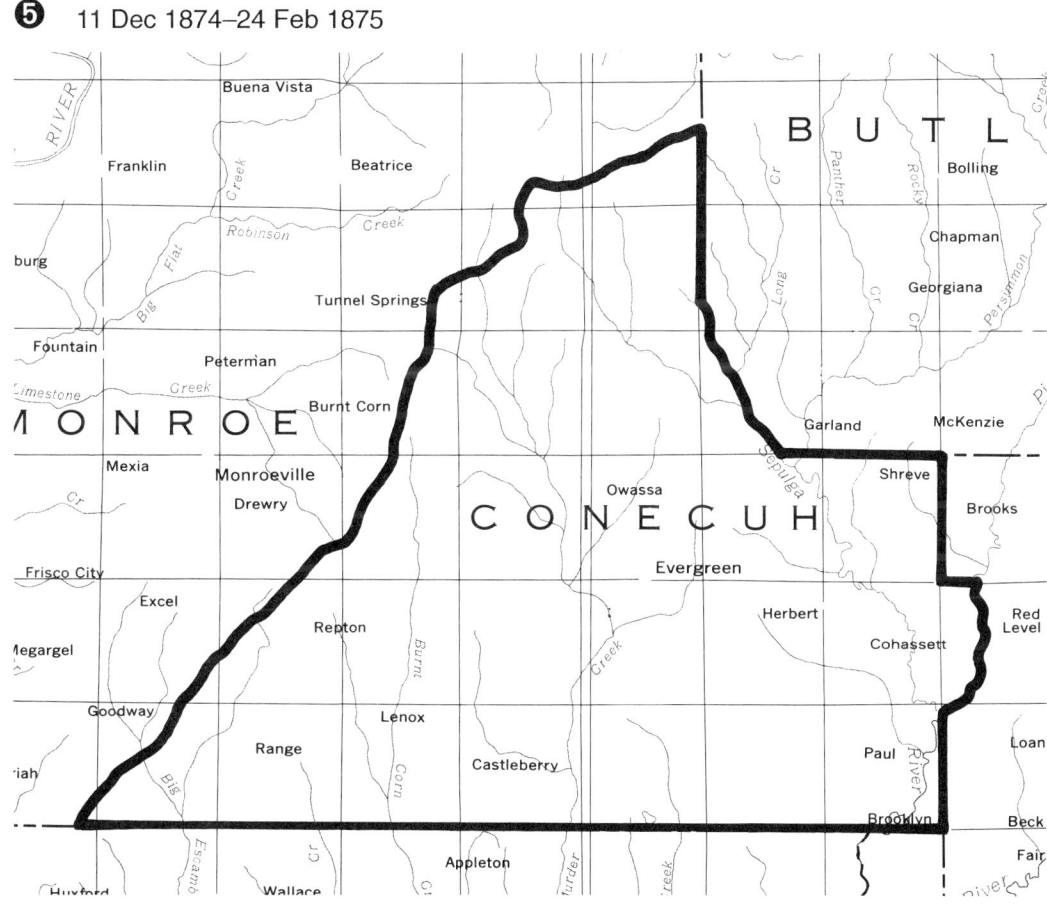

ALABAMA

Chronology of CONECUH

Map	Date	Event	Resulting Area
6	25 Feb 1875	Gained from ESCAMBIA	860 sq mi
6	28 Feb 1887	Gained small area from ESCAMBIA	860 sq mi

(Heavy line depicts historical boundary. Base map shows present-day information.)

6 25 Feb 1875–1990

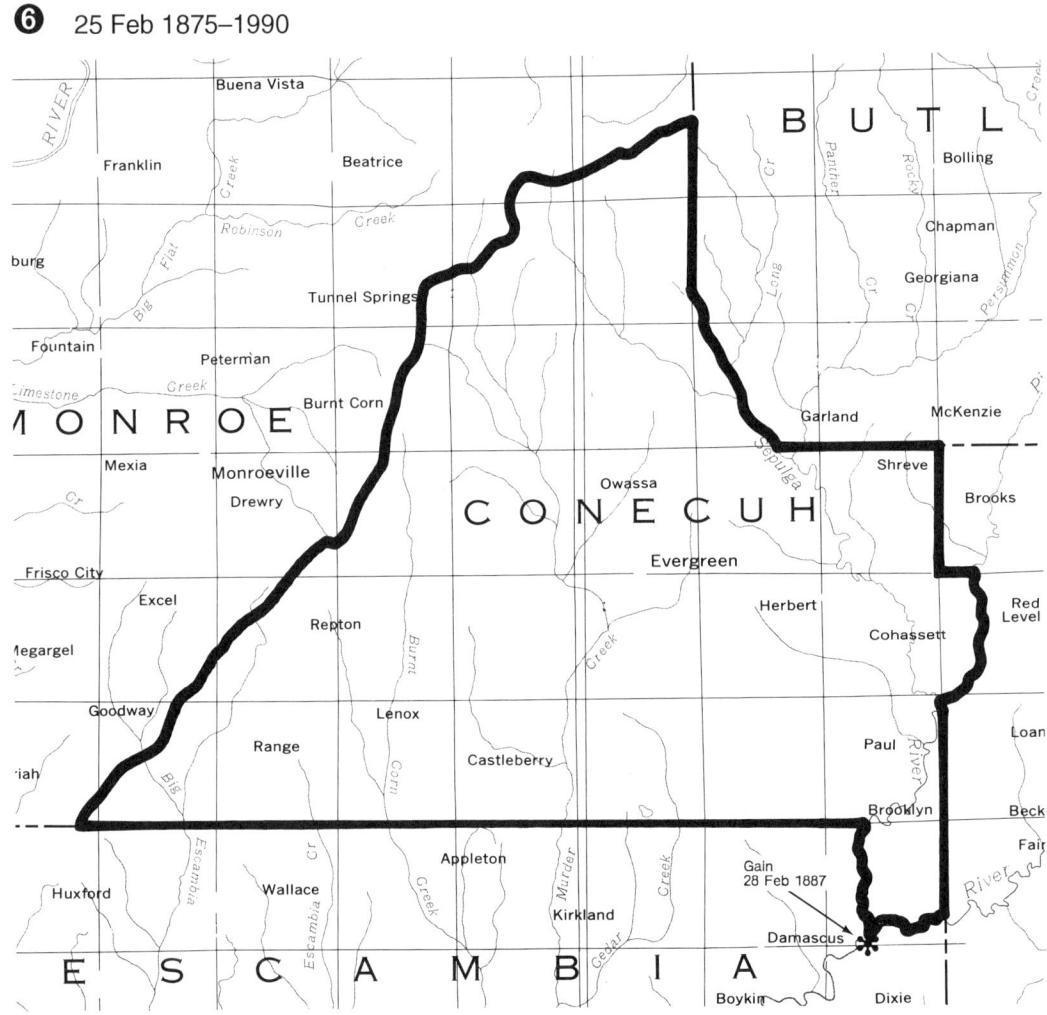

Chronology of COOSA

Map	Date	Event	Resulting Area
❶	18 Dec 1832	Created from MONTGOMERY and SHELBY	930 sq mi

(Heavy line depicts historical boundary. Base map shows present-day information.)

❶ 18 Dec 1832–23 Jun 1837

Chronology of COOSA

Map	Date	Event	Resulting Area
❷	24 Jun 1837	Exchanged with MONTGOMERY	910 sq mi
❷	21 Dec 1837	Gained from MONTGOMERY; remaining boundary with MONTGOMERY clarified [no change]	910 sq mi

(Heavy line depicts historical boundary. Base map shows present-day information.)

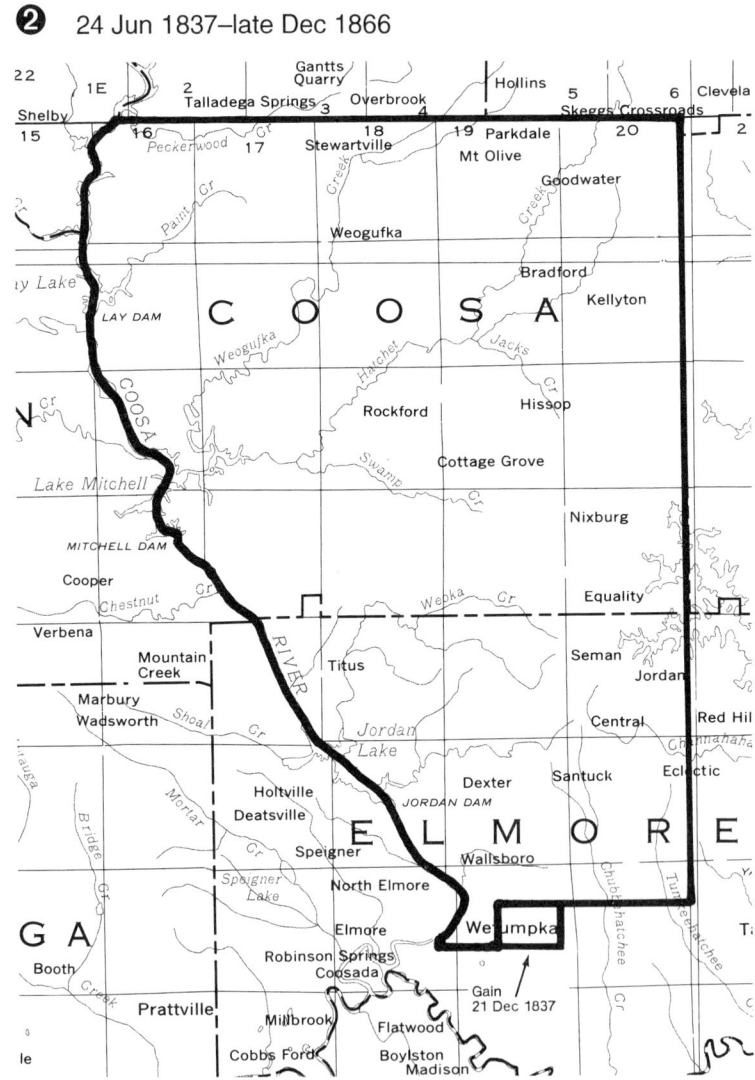

❷ 24 Jun 1837–late Dec 1866

Individual County Chronologies   **125**

Chronology of COOSA

Map	Date	Event	Resulting Area
❸	late Dec 1866	Lost to creation of ELMORE	670 sq mi
❹	10 Dec 1868	Lost small area to ELMORE	670 sq mi
❹	3 Mar 1870	Gained small area from CLAY to accommodate local property owner	670 sq mi
❹	14 Sep 1963	Exchanged small areas with TALLAPOOSA [mistake in description corrected 20 Apr 1965]	670 sq mi
	20 Apr 1965	Boundary with TALLAPOOSA redefined, correcting mistake of 14 Sep 1963 [no change]	

(Heavy line depicts historical boundary. Base map shows present-day information.)

❸ late Dec 1866–9 Dec 1868

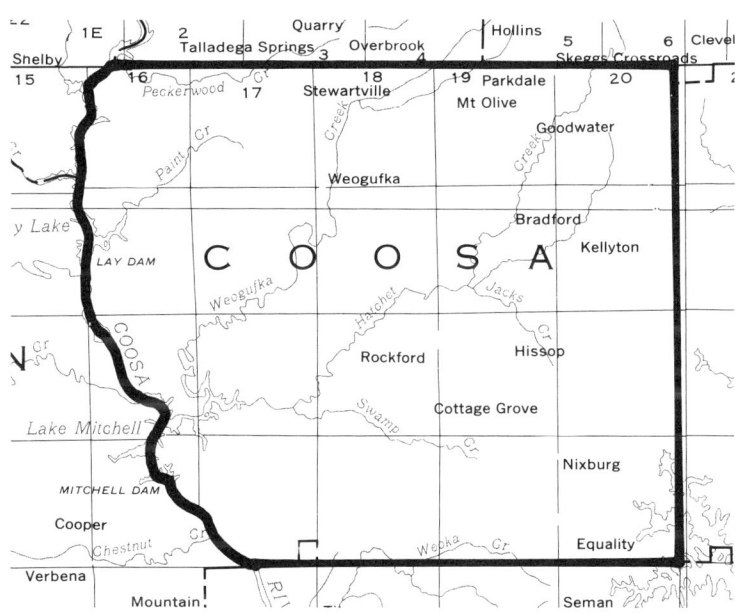

❹ 10 Dec 1868–1990

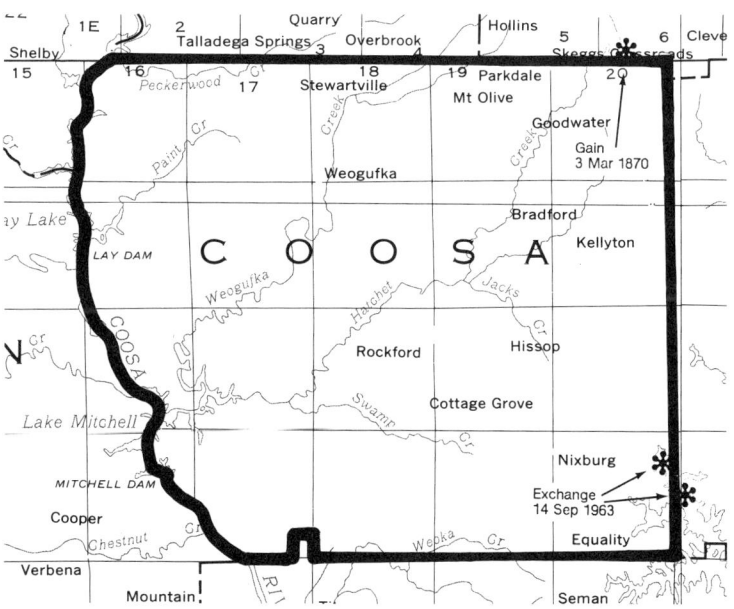

ALABAMA

Chronology of COVINGTON

Map	Date	Event	Resulting Area
❶	7 Dec 1821	Created from HENRY	2,060 sq mi

(Heavy line depicts historical boundary. Base map shows present-day information.)

❶ 7 Dec 1821–16 Oct 1825

Individual County Chronologies   **127**

Chronology of COVINGTON

Map	Date	Event	Resulting Area
❷	17 Oct 1825	Lost to creation of DALE	1,160 sq mi

(Heavy line depicts historical boundary. Base map shows present-day information.)

❷ 17 Oct 1825–26 Jan 1829

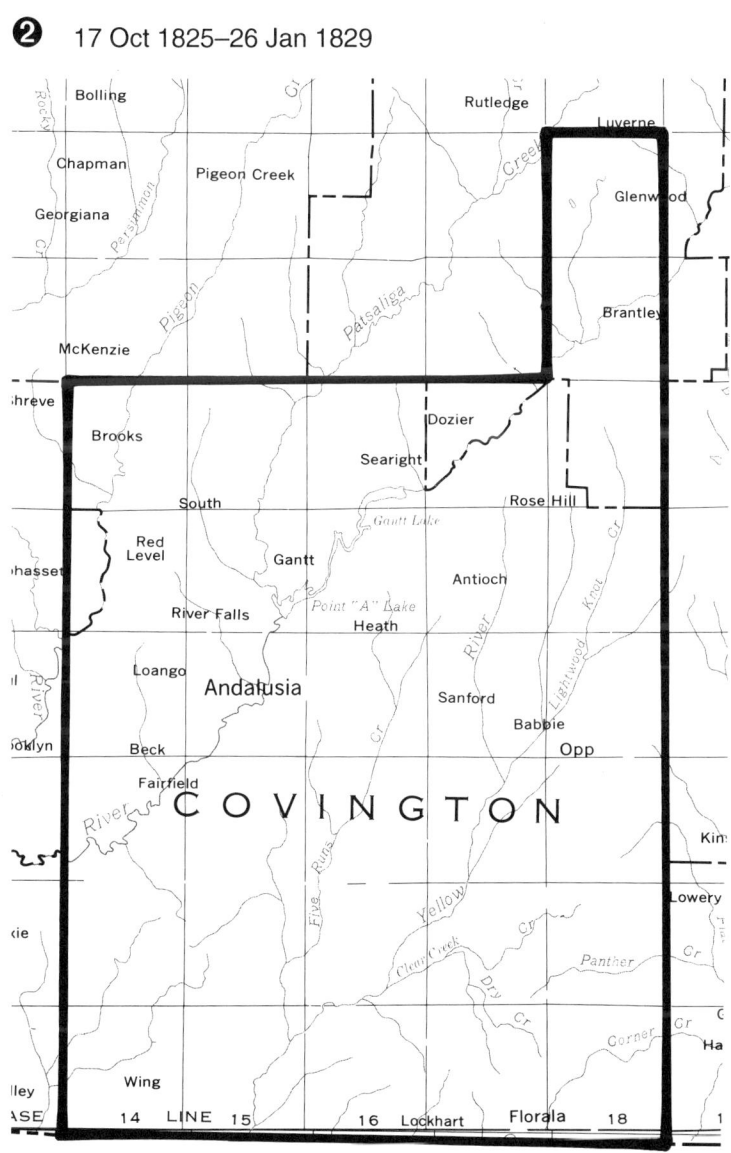

128 ALABAMA

Chronology of COVINGTON

Map	Date	Event	Resulting Area
❸	27 Jan 1829	Gained from BUTLER, lost to PIKE	1,180 sq mi

(Heavy line depicts historical boundary. Base map shows present-day information.)

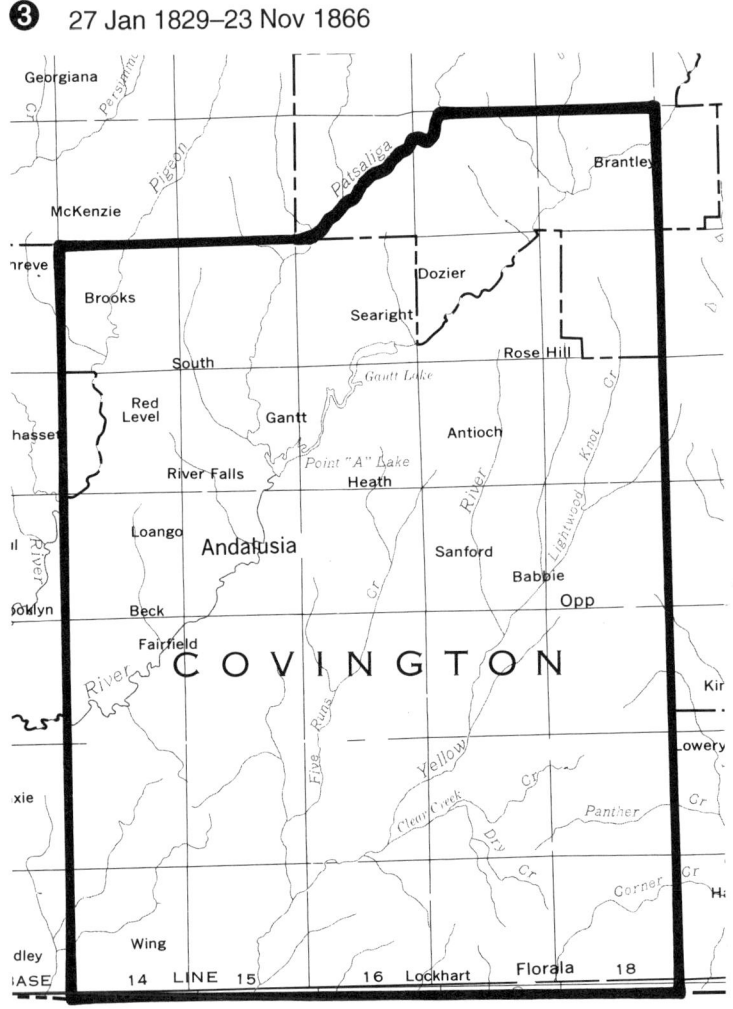

❸ 27 Jan 1829–23 Nov 1866

Chronology of COVINGTON

Map	Date	Event	Resulting Area
❹	24 Nov 1866	Lost to creation of CRENSHAW	1,080 sq mi

(Heavy line depicts historical boundary. Base map shows present-day information.)

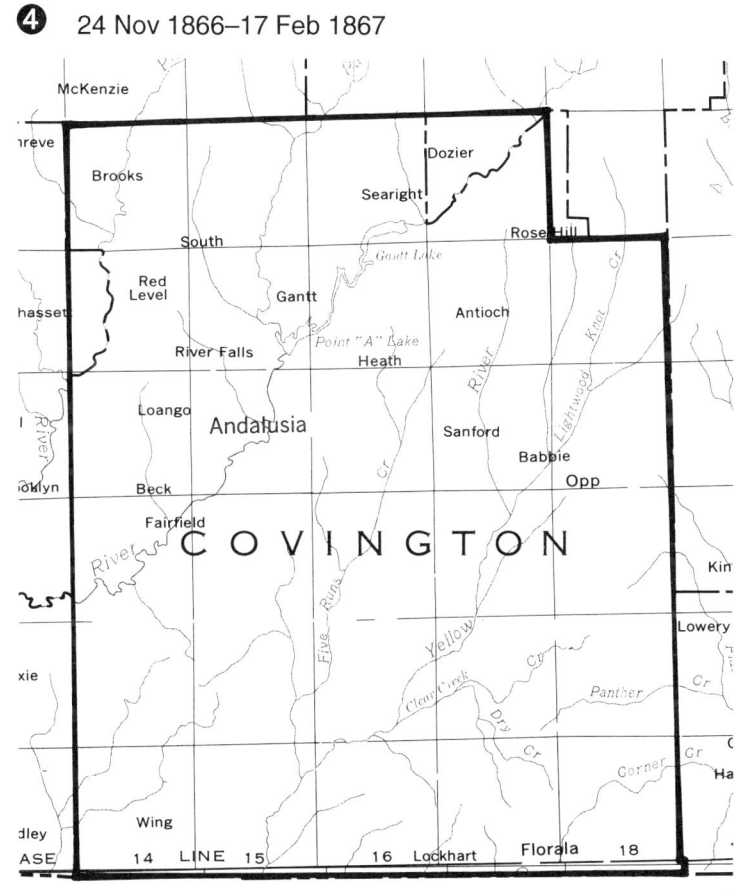

❹ 24 Nov 1866–17 Feb 1867

ALABAMA

Chronology of COVINGTON

Map	Date	Event	Resulting Area
❺	18 Feb 1867	Lost to CRENSHAW	1,060 sq mi
	6 Aug 1868	Renamed JONES	
	10 Oct 1868	Renamed COVINGTON	
❺	24 Dec 1868	Gained from CRENSHAW	1,070 sq mi
❺	21 Feb 1870	Gained small area from ESCAMBIA to accommodate local property owner	1,070 sq mi

(Heavy line depicts historical boundary. Base map shows present-day information.)

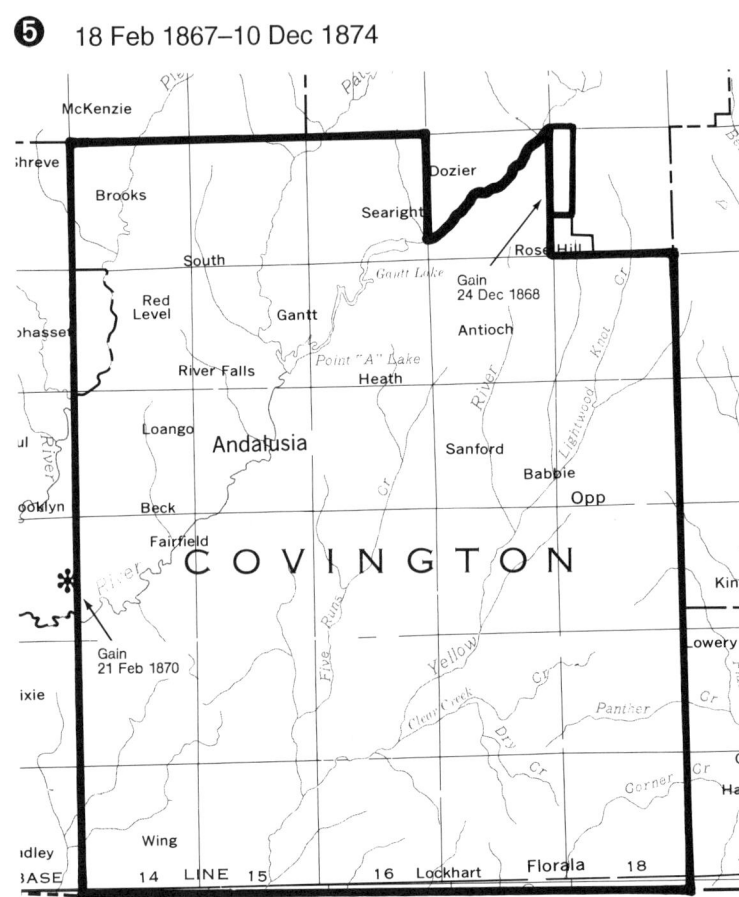

❺ 18 Feb 1867–10 Dec 1874

Chronology of COVINGTON

Map	Date	Event	Resulting Area
❻	11 Dec 1874	Lost to CONECUH	1,060 sq mi
❻	28 Feb 1887	Lost small area to BUTLER	1,060 sq mi
❻	5 Dec 1890	Gained small area from CRENSHAW	1,060 sq mi

(Heavy line depicts historical boundary. Base map shows present-day information.)

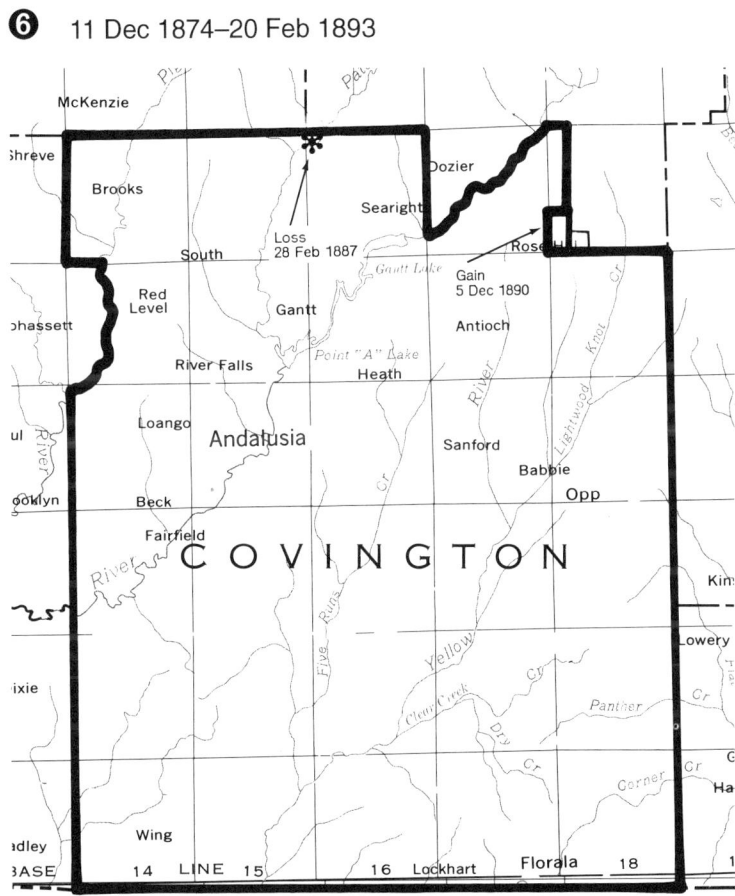

❻ 11 Dec 1874–20 Feb 1893

ALABAMA

Chronology of COVINGTON

Map	Date	Event	Resulting Area
❼	21 Feb 1893	Gained small area from CRENSHAW	1,060 sq mi

(Heavy line depicts historical boundary. Base map shows present-day information.)

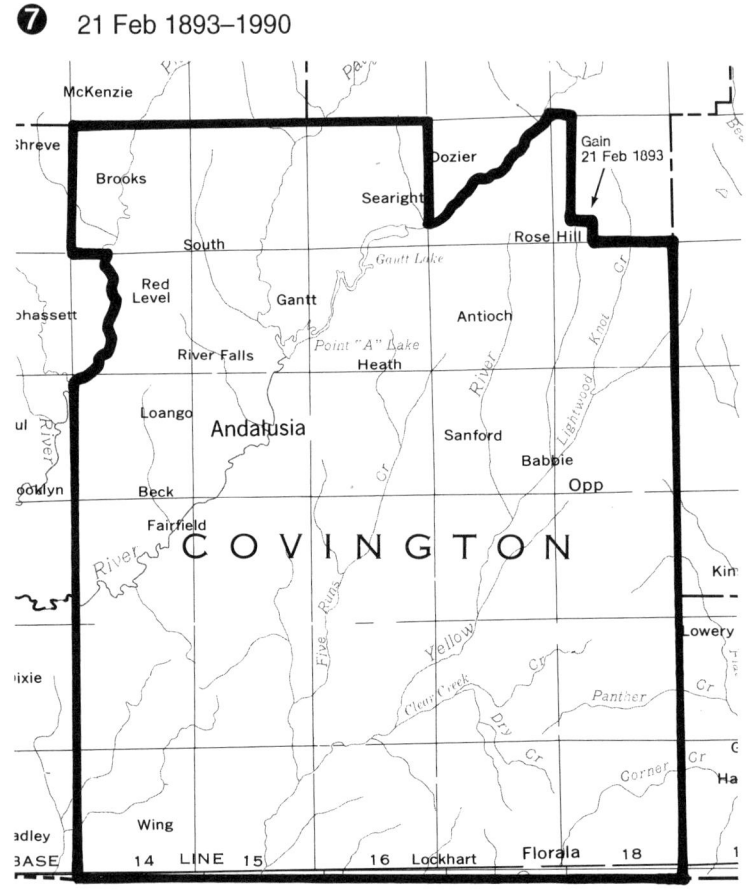

❼ 21 Feb 1893–1990

Chronology of CRENSHAW

Map	Date	Event	Resulting Area
❶	24 Nov 1866	Created from BUTLER, COFFEE, COVINGTON, LOWNDES, and PIKE; a provision would have included part of MONTGOMERY in CRENSHAW but it was never implemented	610 sq mi
❶	11 Feb 1867	Lost small area to BUTLER	610 sq mi
❷	18 Feb 1867	Gained from COVINGTON	620 sq mi
❷	19 Feb 1867	Lost small area to LOWNDES and lost to PIKE	620 sq mi
❷	5 Aug 1868	Lost small area to BUTLER to accommodate local property owner	620 sq mi

(Heavy line depicts historical boundary. Base map shows present-day information.)

❶ 24 Nov 1866–17 Feb 1867

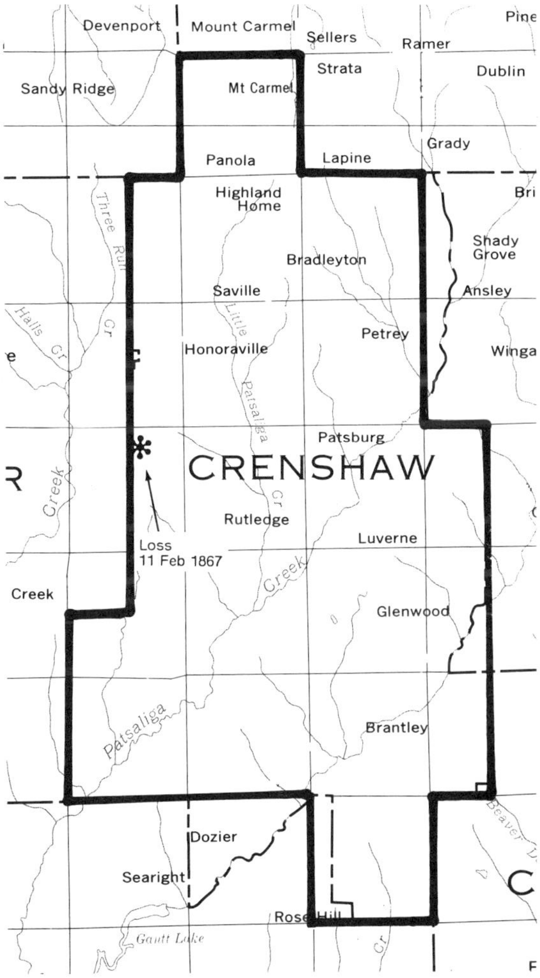

❷ 18 Feb 1867–23 Dec 1868

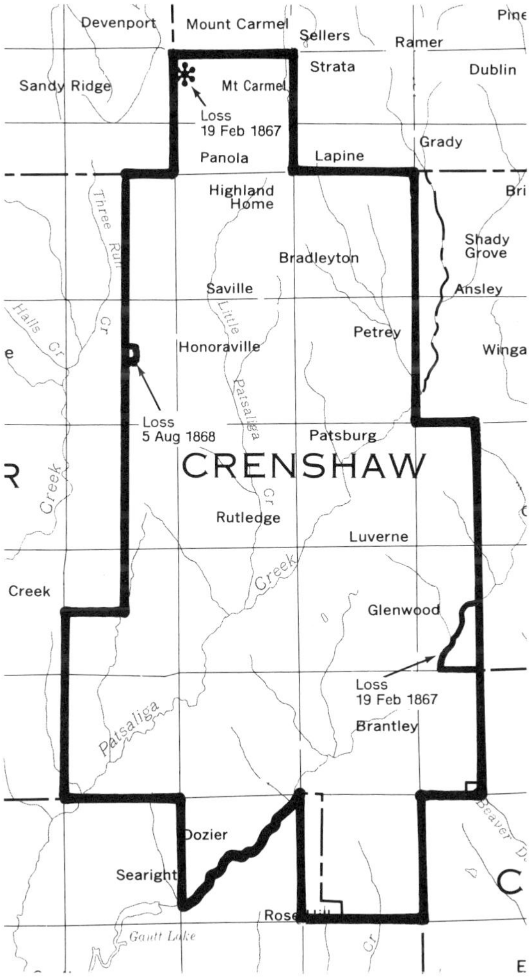

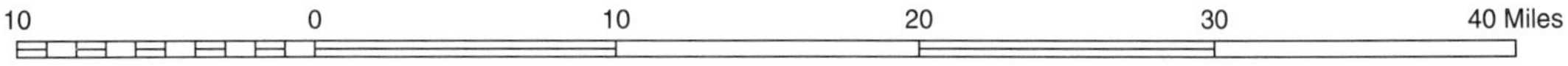

134 ALABAMA

Chronology of CRENSHAW

Map	Date	Event	Resulting Area
❸	24 Dec 1868	Lost to COVINGTON	610 sq mi
❸	23 Feb 1871	Lost small area to COFFEE to accommodate local property owners	610 sq mi
❹	6 Feb 1877	Gained from PIKE	630 sq mi
❹	28 Feb 1887	Exchanged small areas with BUTLER	630 sq mi
❹	5 Dec 1890	Lost small area to COVINGTON	630 sq mi

(Heavy line depicts historical boundary. Base map shows present-day information.)

❸ 24 Dec 1868–5 Feb 1877

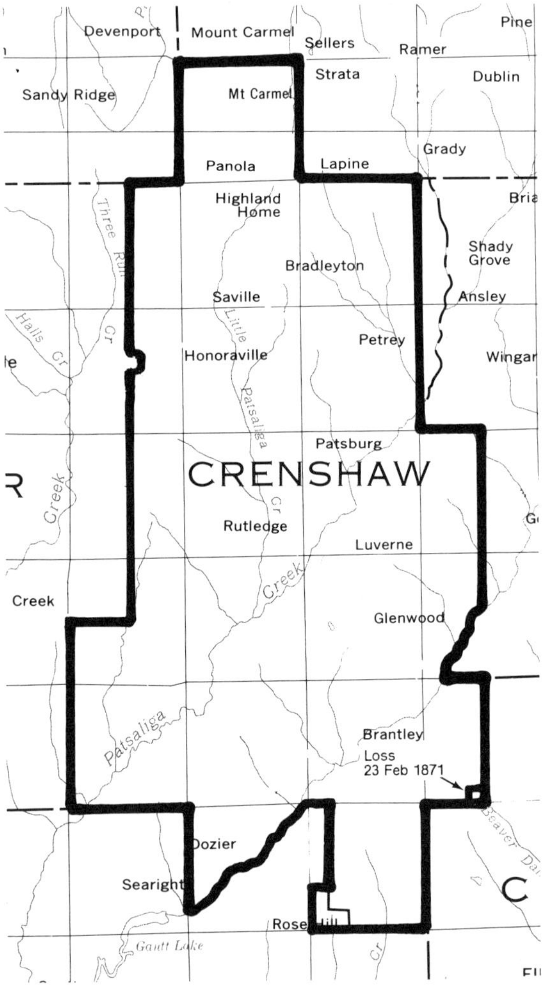

❹ 6 Feb 1877–20 Feb 1893

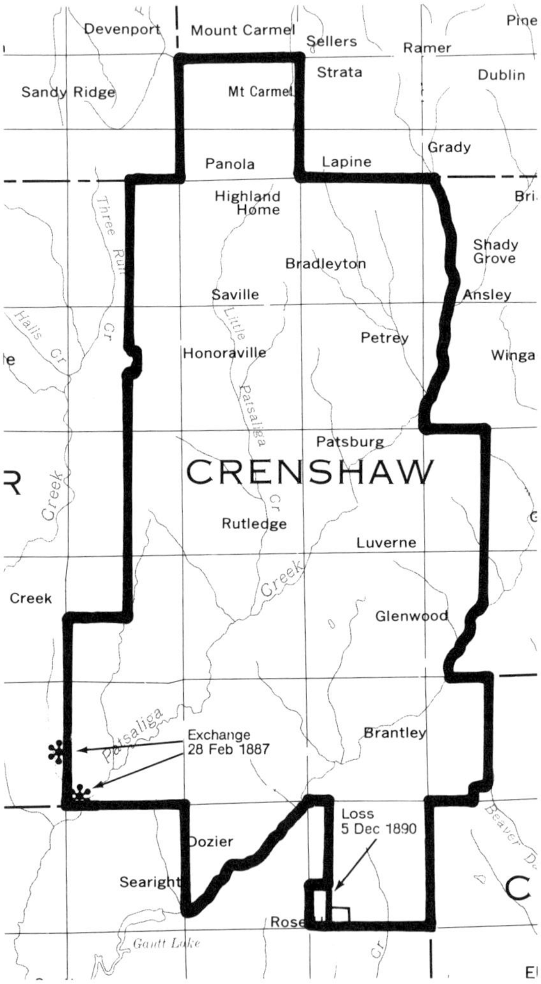

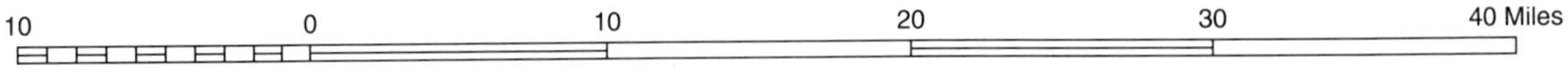

Chronology of CRENSHAW

Map	Date	Event	Resulting Area
❺	21 Feb 1893	Lost small area to COVINGTON	620 sq mi

(Heavy line depicts historical boundary. Base map shows present-day information.)

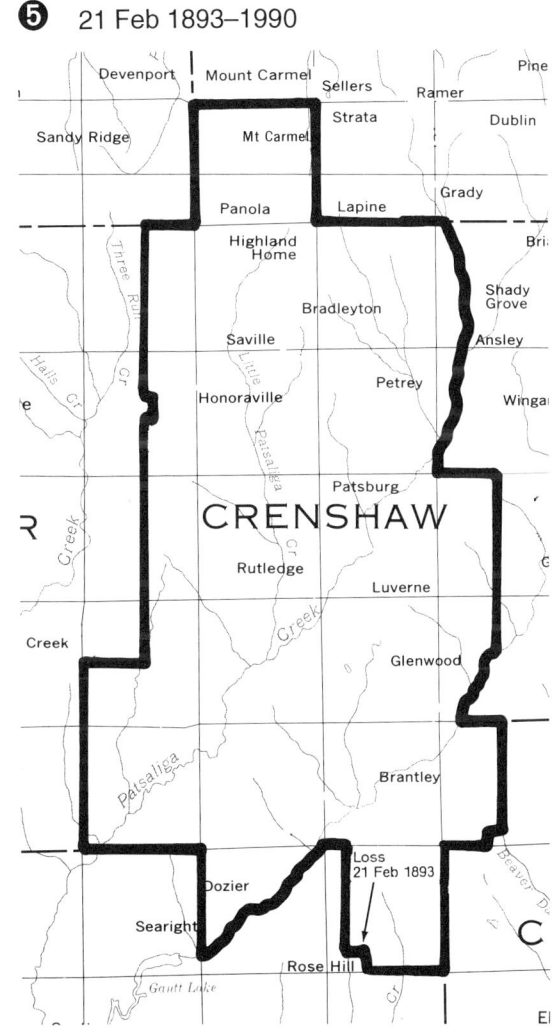

❺ 21 Feb 1893–1990

Chronology of CULLMAN

Map	Date	Event	Resulting Area
❶	24 Jan 1877	Created from BLOUNT, MARSHALL, MORGAN, and WINSTON	610 sq mi
❶	13 Feb 1879	Lost to BLOUNT	610 sq mi
❷	28 Feb 1887	Gained from BLOUNT	630 sq mi
❷	21 Feb 1893	Gained from BLOUNT	640 sq mi

(Heavy line depicts historical boundary. Base map shows present-day information.)

❶ 24 Jan 1877–27 Feb 1887

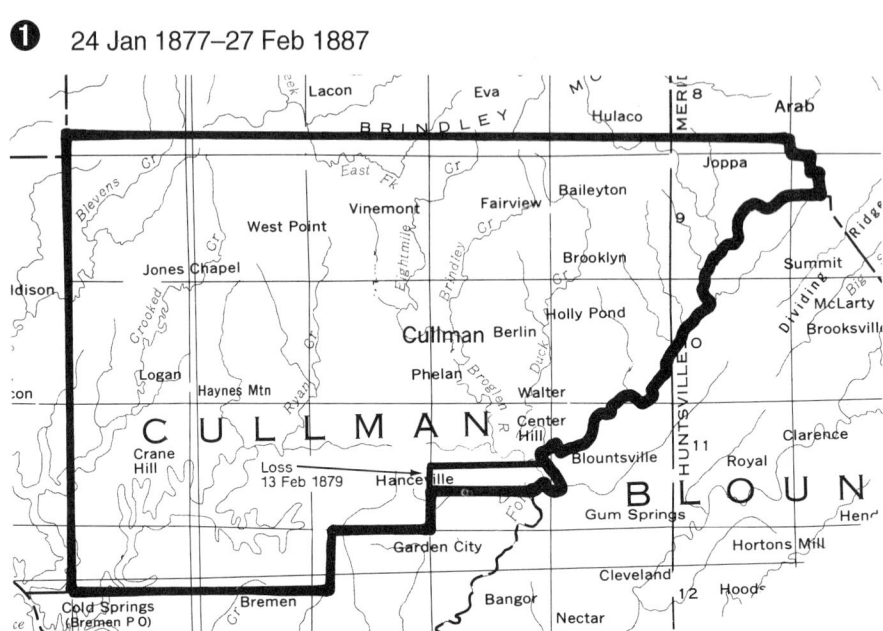

❷ 28 Feb 1887–22 Apr 1901

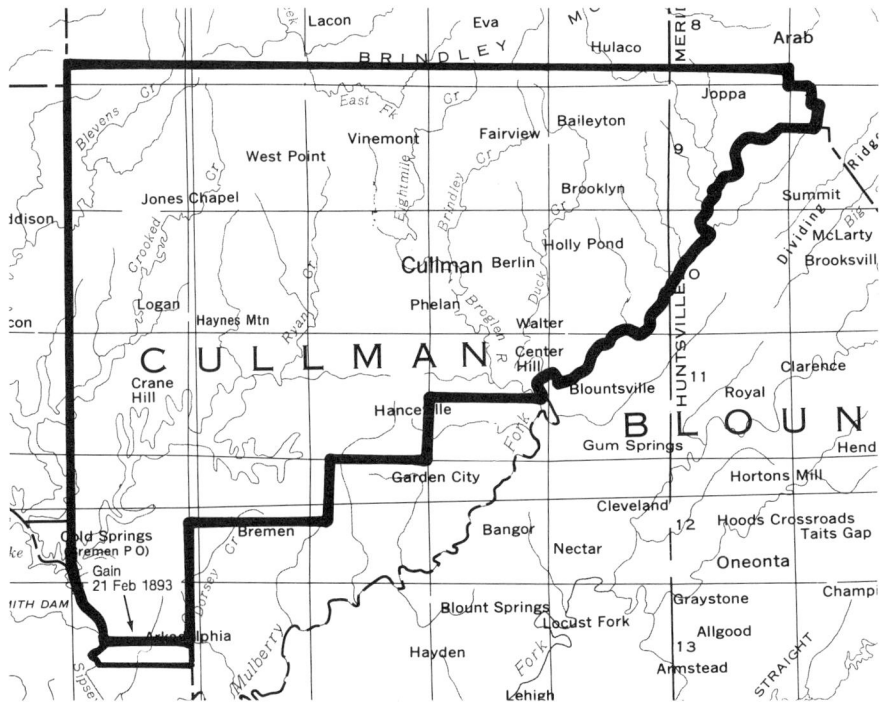

Individual County Chronologies **137**

Chronology of CULLMAN

Map	Date	Event	Resulting Area
❸	23 Apr 1901	Gained from BLOUNT	760 sq mi

(Heavy line depicts historical boundary. Base map shows present-day information.)

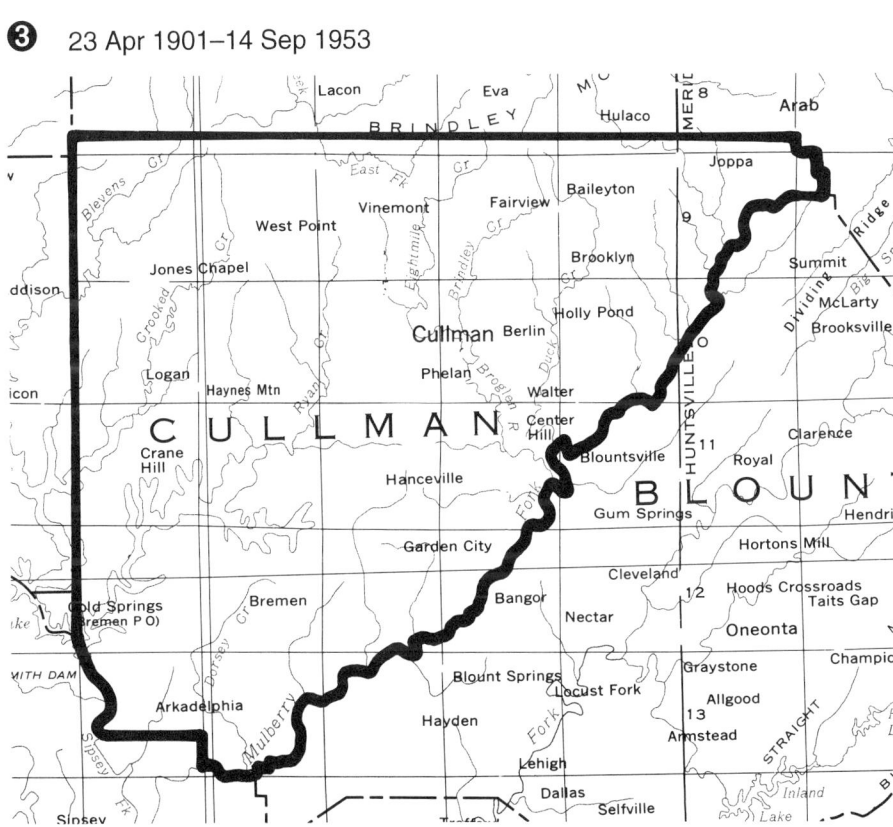

❸ 23 Apr 1901–14 Sep 1953

138 ALABAMA

Chronology of CULLMAN

Map	Date	Event	Resulting Area
④	15 Sep 1953	Gained from WALKER	760 sq mi

(Heavy line depicts historical boundary. Base map shows present-day information.)

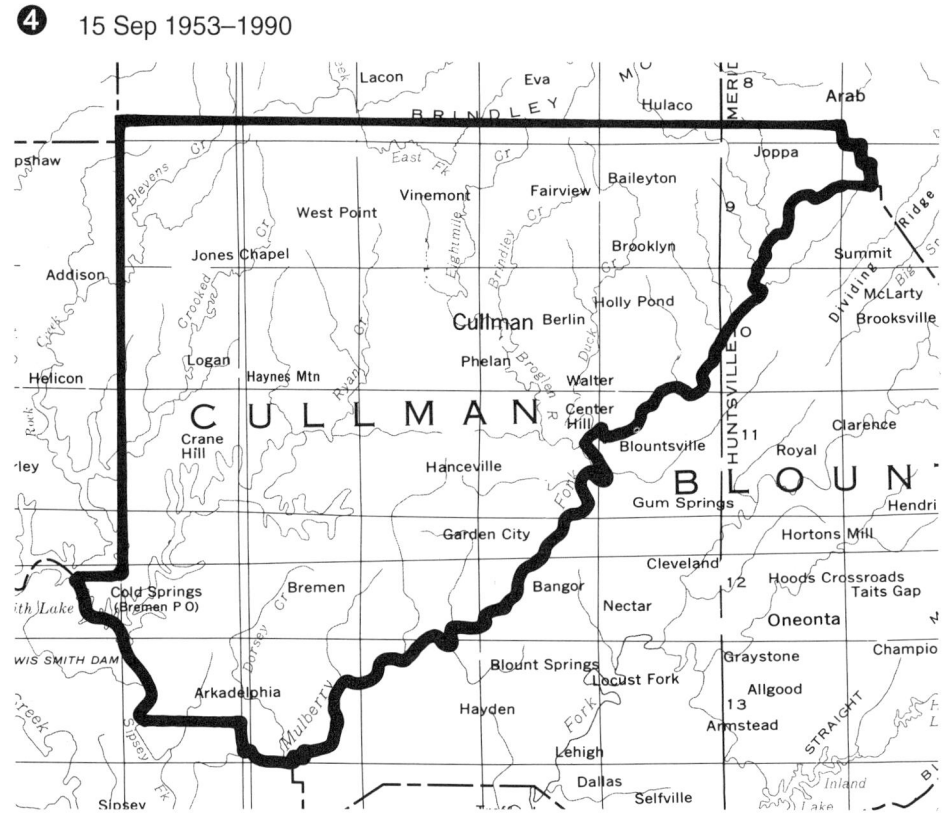

④ 15 Sep 1953–1990

Chronology of DALE

Map	Date	Event	Resulting Area
❶	17 Oct 1825	Created from COVINGTON and HENRY	2,060 sq mi

(Heavy line depicts historical boundary. Base map shows present-day information.)

❶ 17 Oct 1825–3 Jan 1826

ALABAMA

Chronology of DALE

Map	Date	Event	Resulting Area
❷	4 Jan 1826	Gained from HENRY, lost to PIKE	2,030 sq mi

(Heavy line depicts historical boundary. Base map shows present-day information.)

❷ 4 Jan 1826–19 Dec 1828

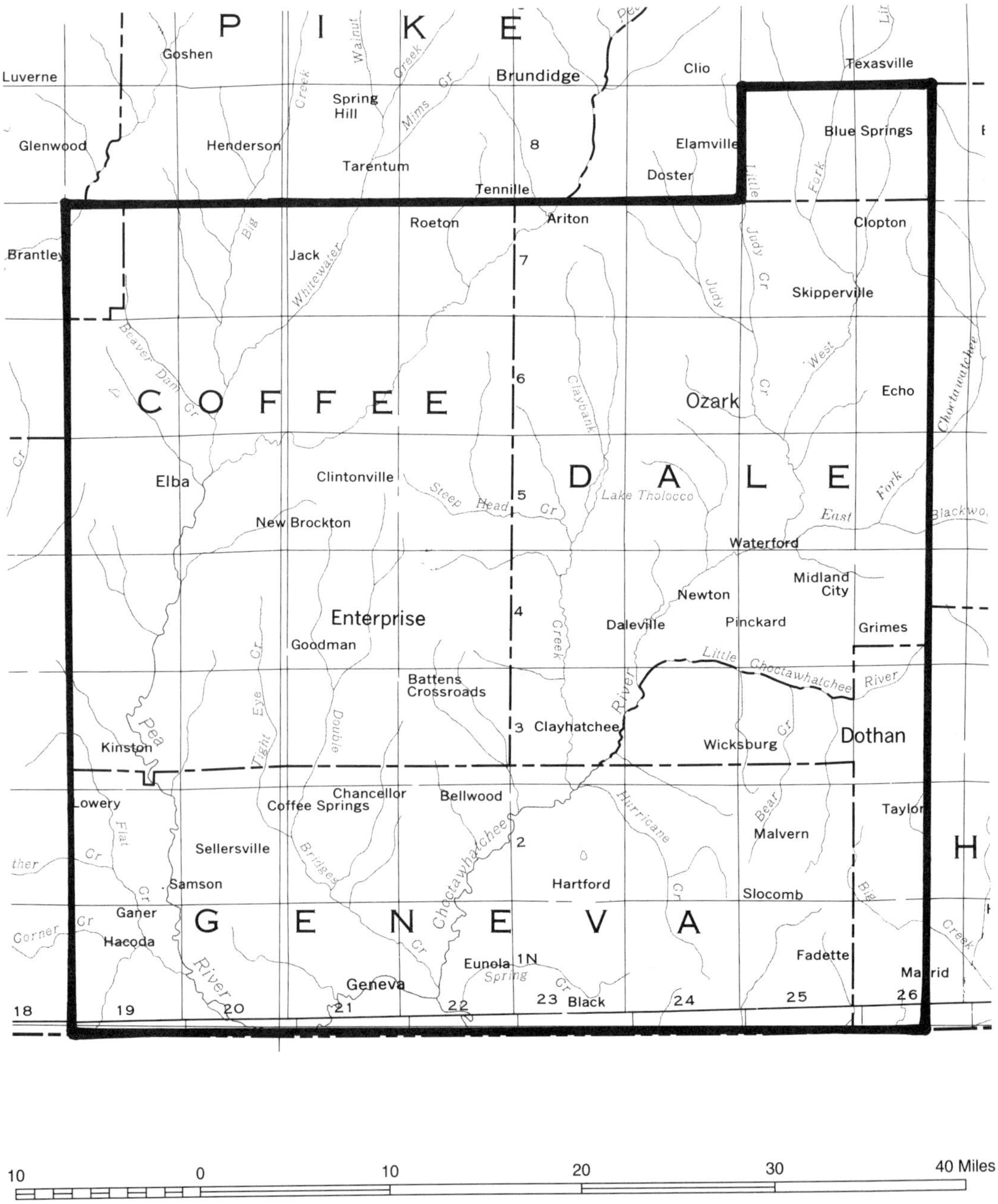

Chronology of DALE

Map	Date	Event	Resulting Area
❸	20 Dec 1828	Lost to PIKE	1,990 sq mi
❸	29 Jan 1840	Lost small area to PIKE	1,990 sq mi

(Heavy line depicts historical boundary. Base map shows present-day information.)

❸ 20 Dec 1828–28 Dec 1841

ALABAMA

Chronology of DALE

Map	Date	Event	Resulting Area
❹	29 Dec 1841	Lost to creation of COFFEE	950 sq mi
❺	26 Dec 1868	Lost to creation of GENEVA	650 sq mi
❻	9 Feb 1903	Lost to creation of HOUSTON	570 sq mi

(Heavy line depicts historical boundary. Base map shows present-day information.)

❹ 29 Dec 1841–25 Dec 1868

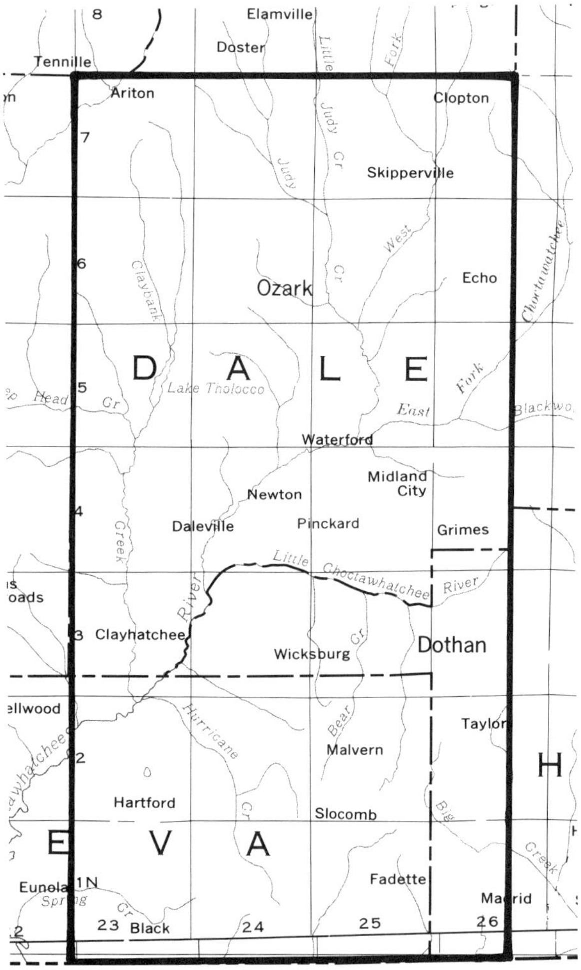

❺ 26 Dec 1868–8 Feb 1903

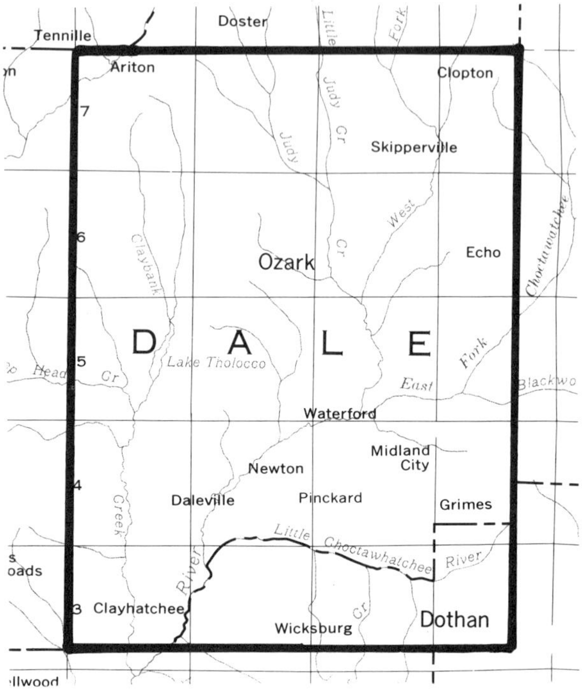

❻ 9 Feb 1903–1990

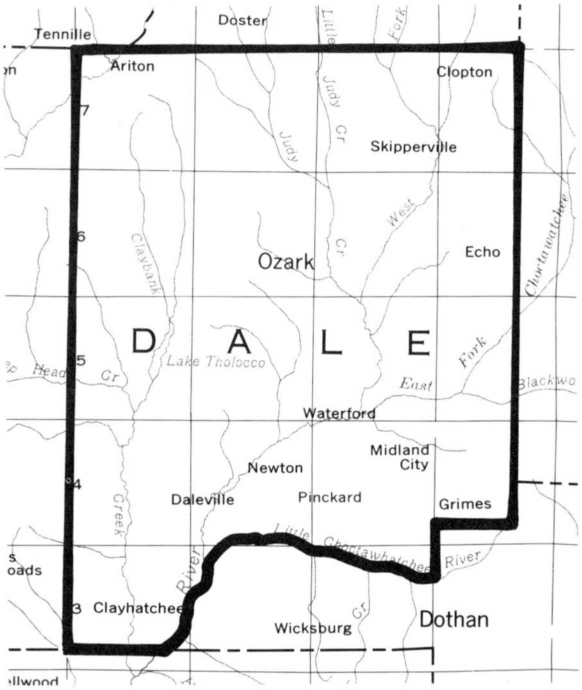

Individual County Chronologies 143

Chronology of DALLAS

Map	Date	Event	Resulting Area
❶	9 Feb 1818	Created from MONROE and MONTGOMERY	2,300 sq mi
❷	20 Nov 1818	Lost to CAHAWBA (now BIBB)	2,000 sq mi
❸	21 Nov 1818	Gained from MONTGOMERY	2,090 sq mi
❹	13 Dec 1819	Gained from MONTGOMERY, lost to MARENGO and lost to creation of BUTLER, PERRY, and WILCOX	1,090 sq mi

(Heavy line depicts historical boundary. Base map shows present-day information.)

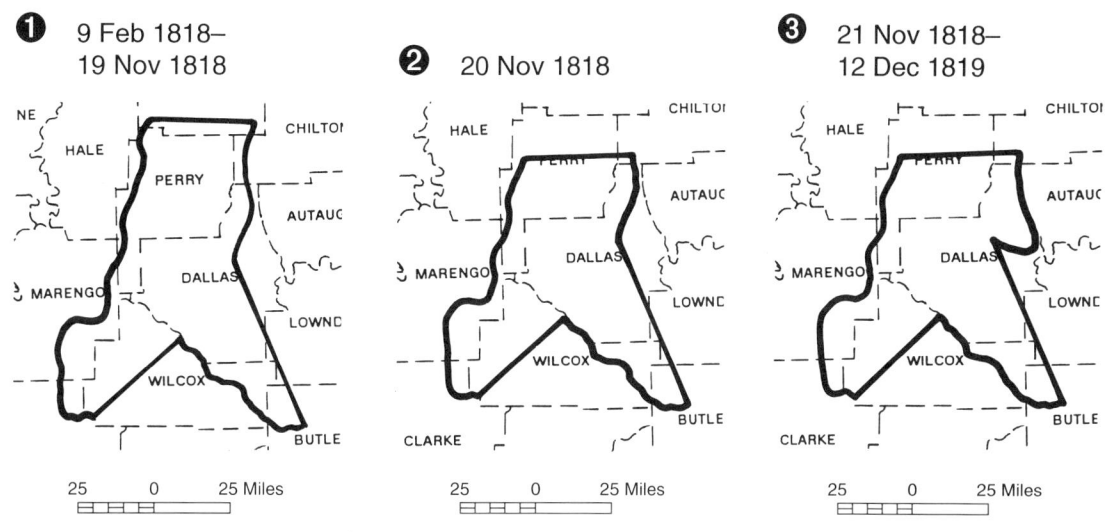

❶ 9 Feb 1818– 19 Nov 1818

❷ 20 Nov 1818

❸ 21 Nov 1818– 12 Dec 1819

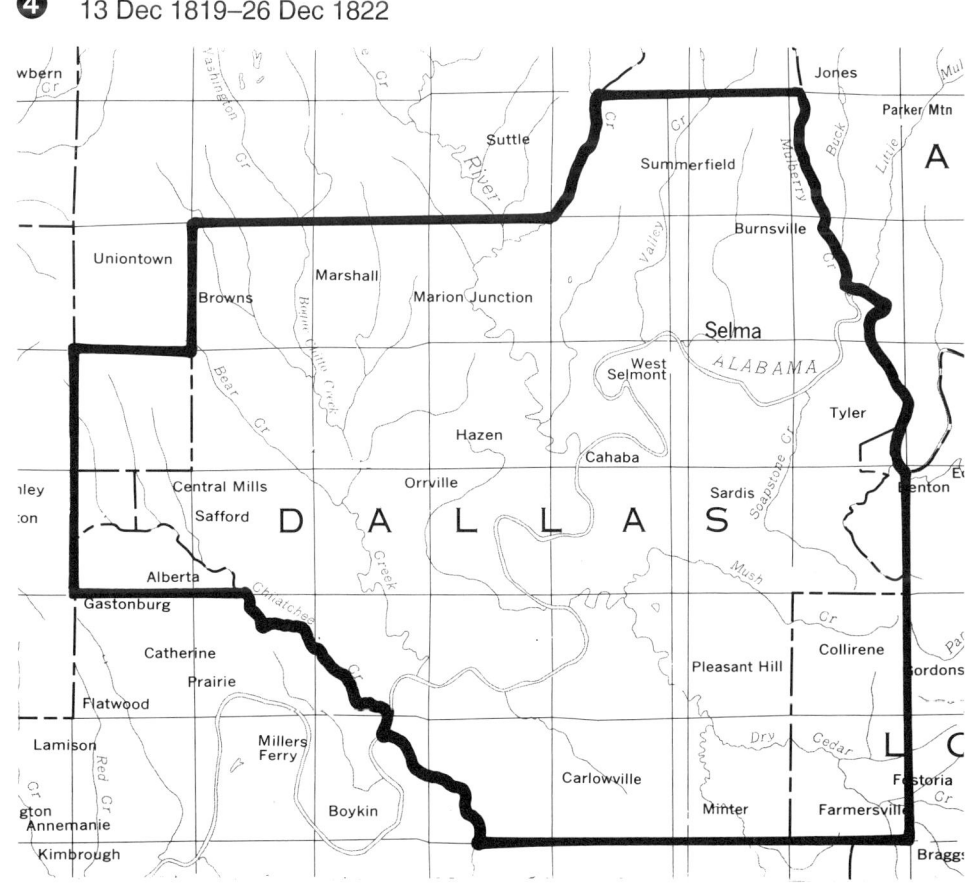

❹ 13 Dec 1819–26 Dec 1822

ALABAMA

Chronology of DALLAS

Map	Date	Event	Resulting Area
⑤	27 Dec 1822	Lost to WILCOX	1,070 sq mi

(Heavy line depicts historical boundary. Base map shows present-day information.)

⑤ 27 Dec 1822–29 Dec 1822

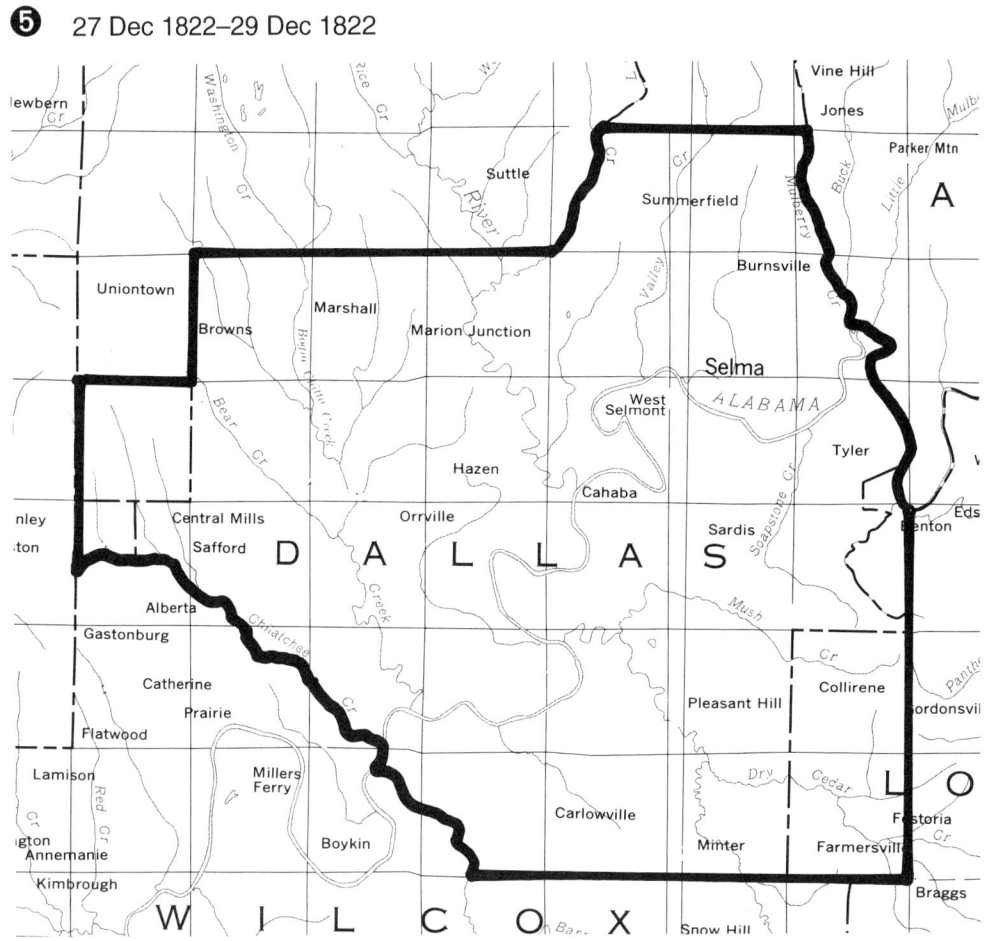

Individual County Chronologies 145

Chronology of DALLAS

Map	Date	Event	Resulting Area
❻	30 Dec 1822	Lost to PERRY	1,030 sq mi

(Heavy line depicts historical boundary. Base map shows present-day information.)

❻ 30 Dec 1822–19 Jan 1830

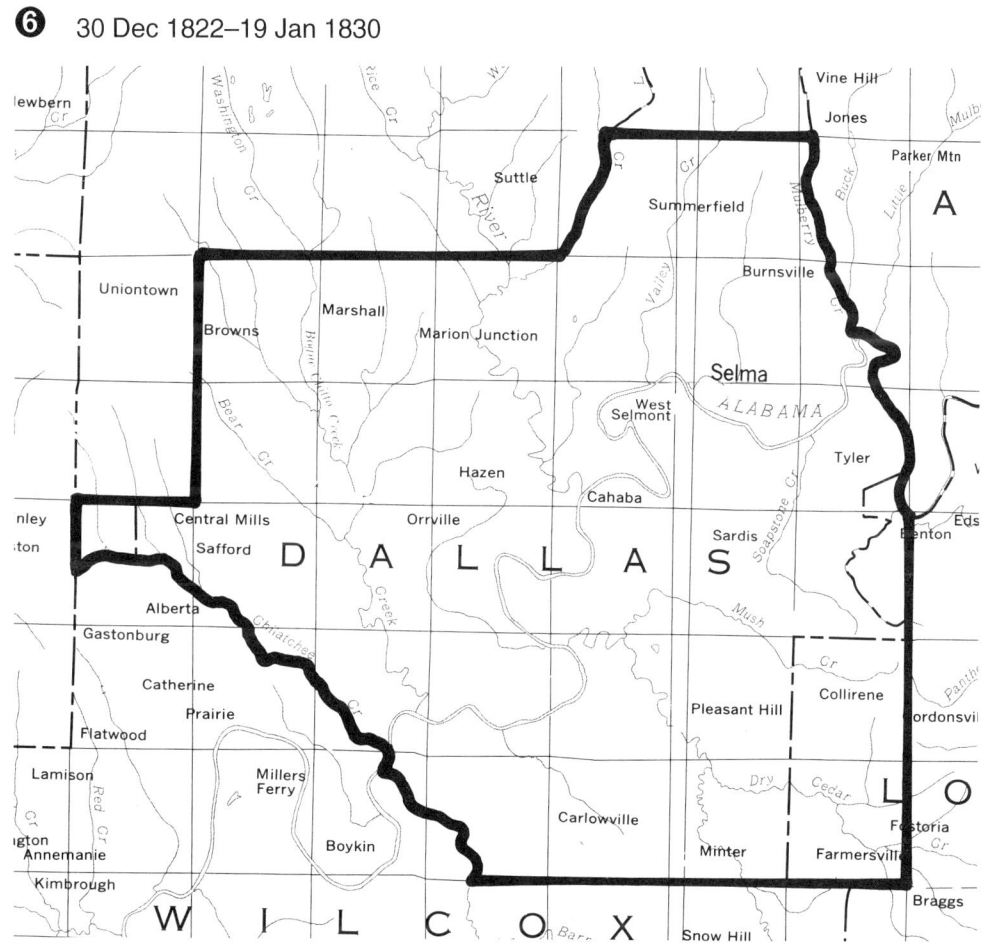

146 ALABAMA

Chronology of DALLAS

Map	Date	Event	Resulting Area
❼	20 Jan 1830	Lost to creation of LOWNDES	960 sq mi

(Heavy line depicts historical boundary. Base map shows present-day information.)

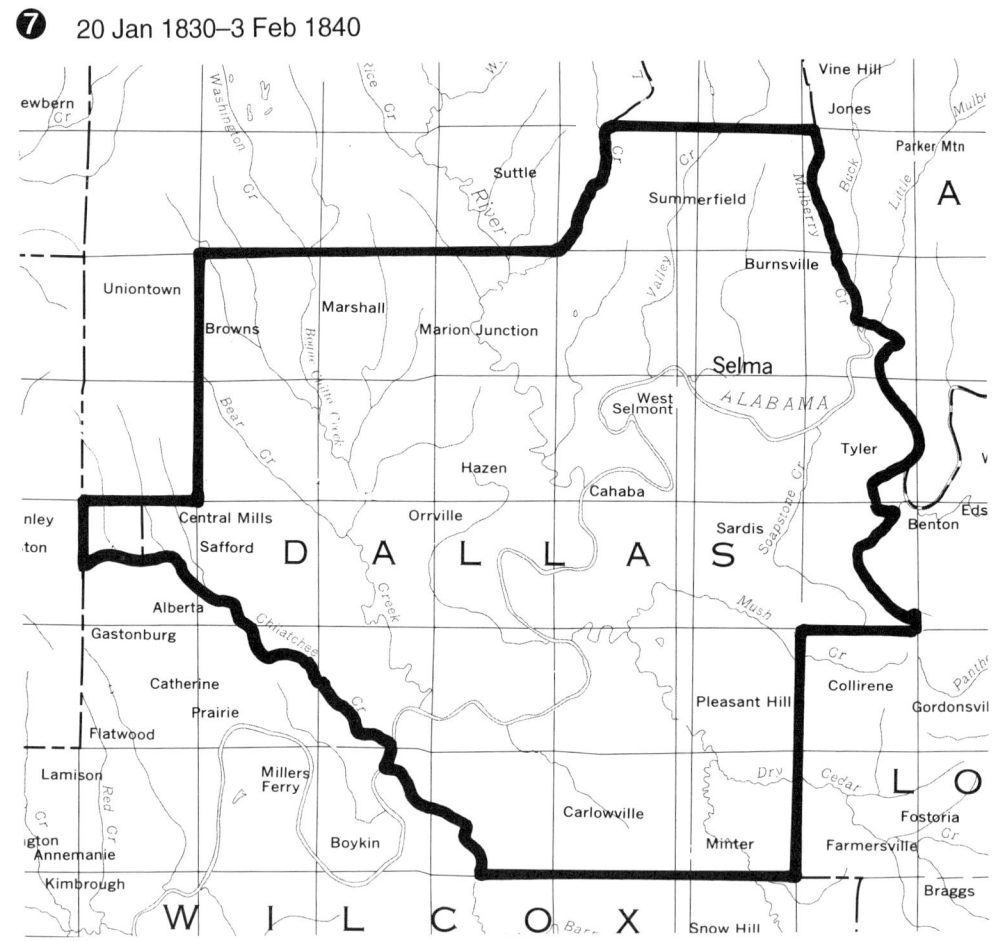

❼ 20 Jan 1830–3 Feb 1840

Individual County Chronologies 147

Chronology of DALLAS

Map	Date	Event	Resulting Area
⑧	4 Feb 1840	Lost to MARENGO	950 sq mi

(Heavy line depicts historical boundary. Base map shows present-day information.)

⑧ 4 Feb 1840–17 Feb 1867

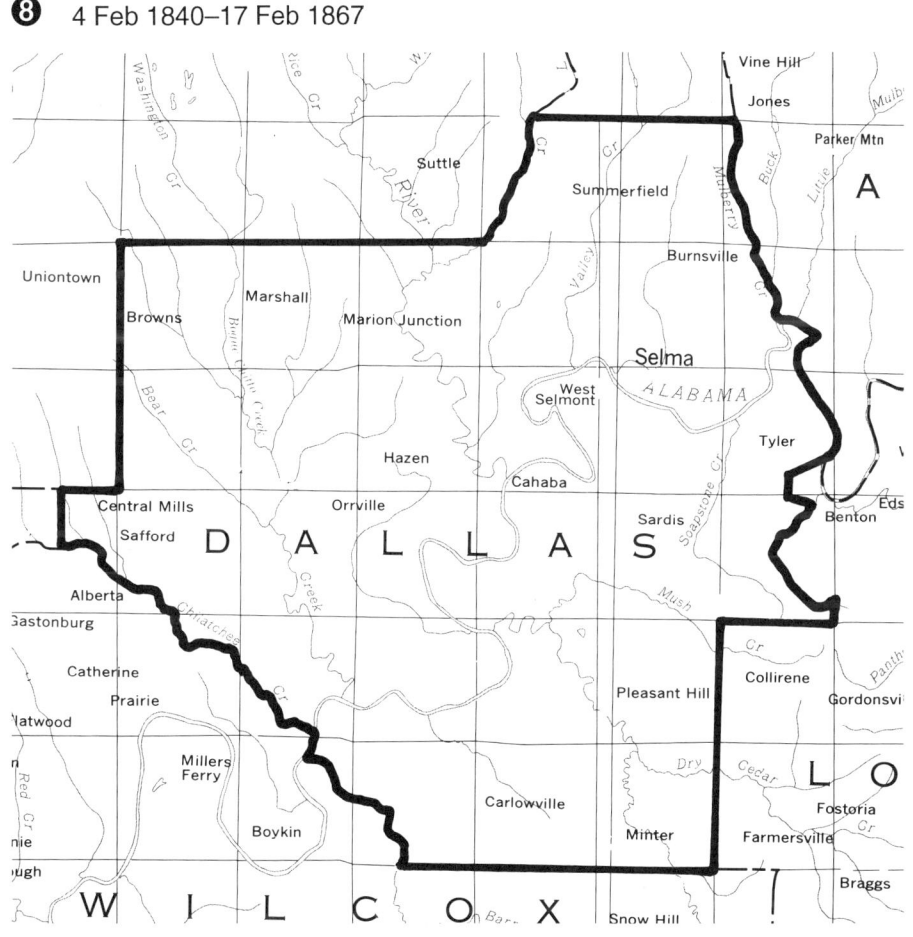

ALABAMA

Chronology of DALLAS

Map	Date	Event	Resulting Area
9	18 Feb 1867	Gained from PERRY	1,060 sq mi
9	28 Dec 1868	Gained small area from PERRY [became a DALLAS exclave on 30 Dec 1868 and returned to PERRY 28 Feb 1889]	1,060 sq mi

(Heavy line depicts historical boundary. Base map shows present-day information.)

9 18 Feb 1867–29 Dec 1868

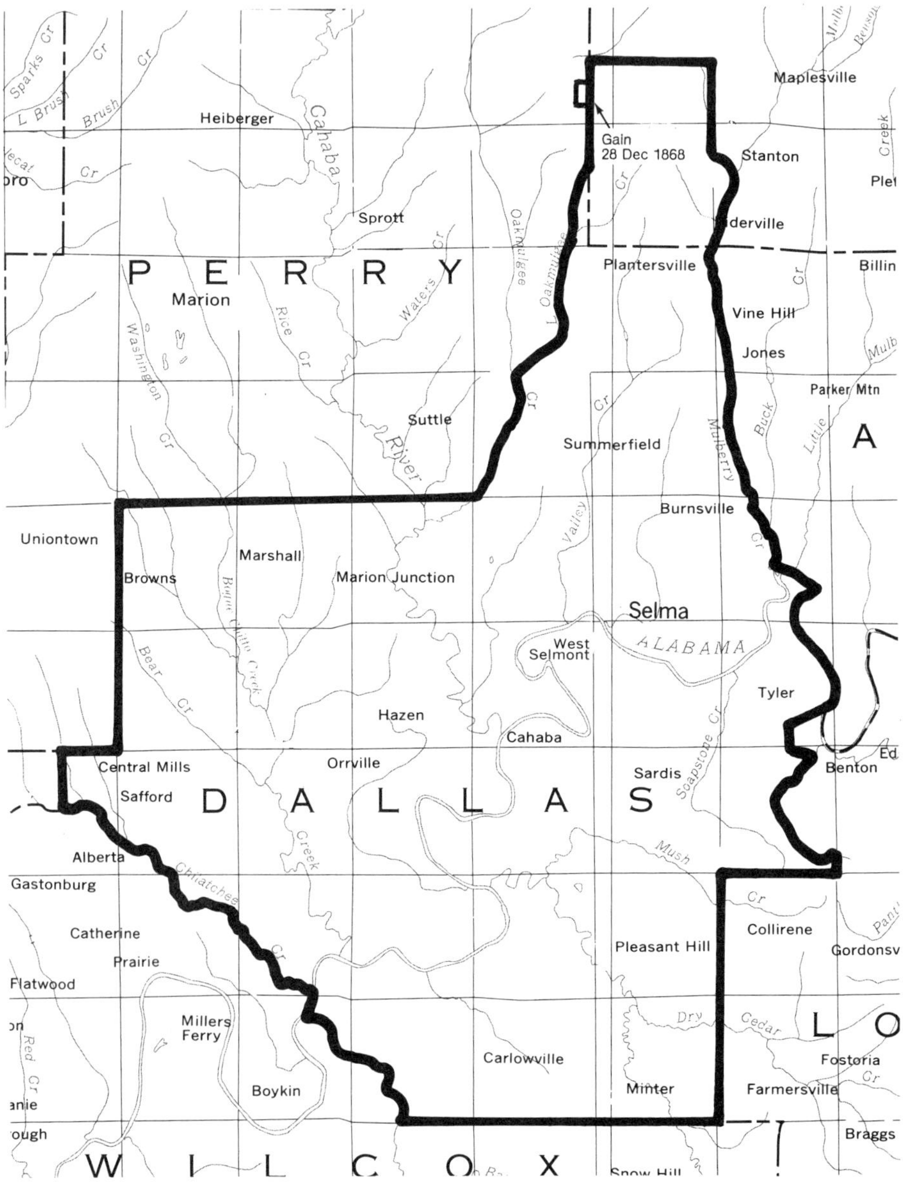

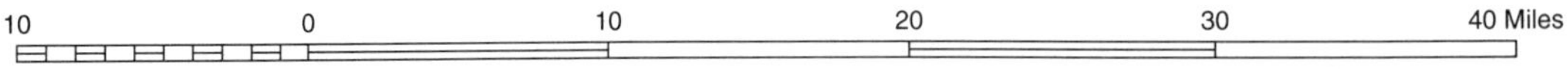

Individual County Chronologies 149

Chronology of DALLAS

Map	Date	Event	Resulting Area
⑩	30 Dec 1868	Lost to creation of BAKER (now CHILTON). Small area, gained by DALLAS from PERRY 2 days earlier, became a DALLAS exclave [corrected 28 Feb 1889]	990 sq mi

(Heavy line depicts historical boundary. Base map shows present-day information.)

⑩ 30 Dec 1868–14 Dec 1869
   13 Feb 1875–1990

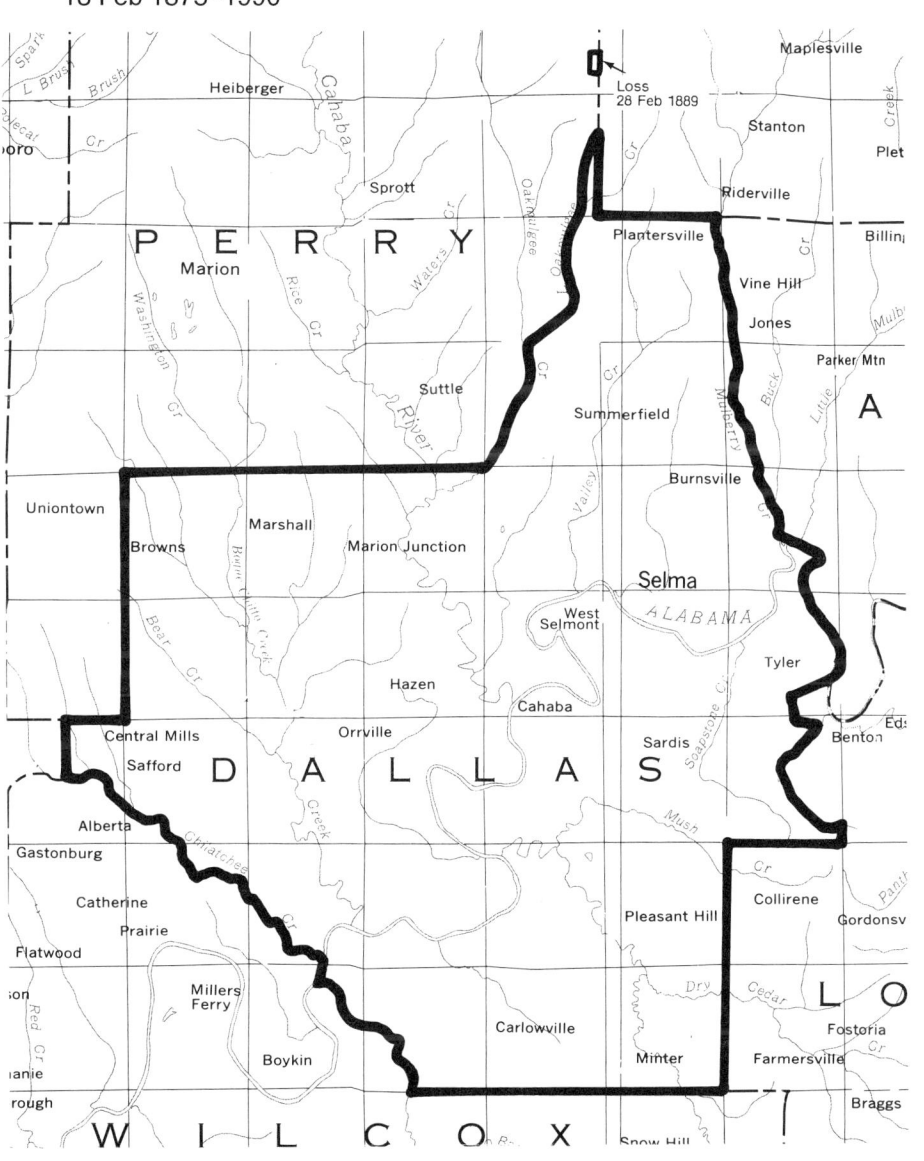

ALABAMA

Chronology of DALLAS

Map	Date	Event	Resulting Area
⑪	15 Dec 1869	Gained from BAKER (now CHILTON)	1,040 sq mi
⑩	13 Feb 1875	Lost to CHILTON	990 sq mi
⑩	28 Feb 1889	Lost exclave of 1868 to PERRY	990 sq mi

(Heavy line depicts historical boundary. Base map shows present-day information.)

⑪ 15 Dec 1869–12 Feb 1875

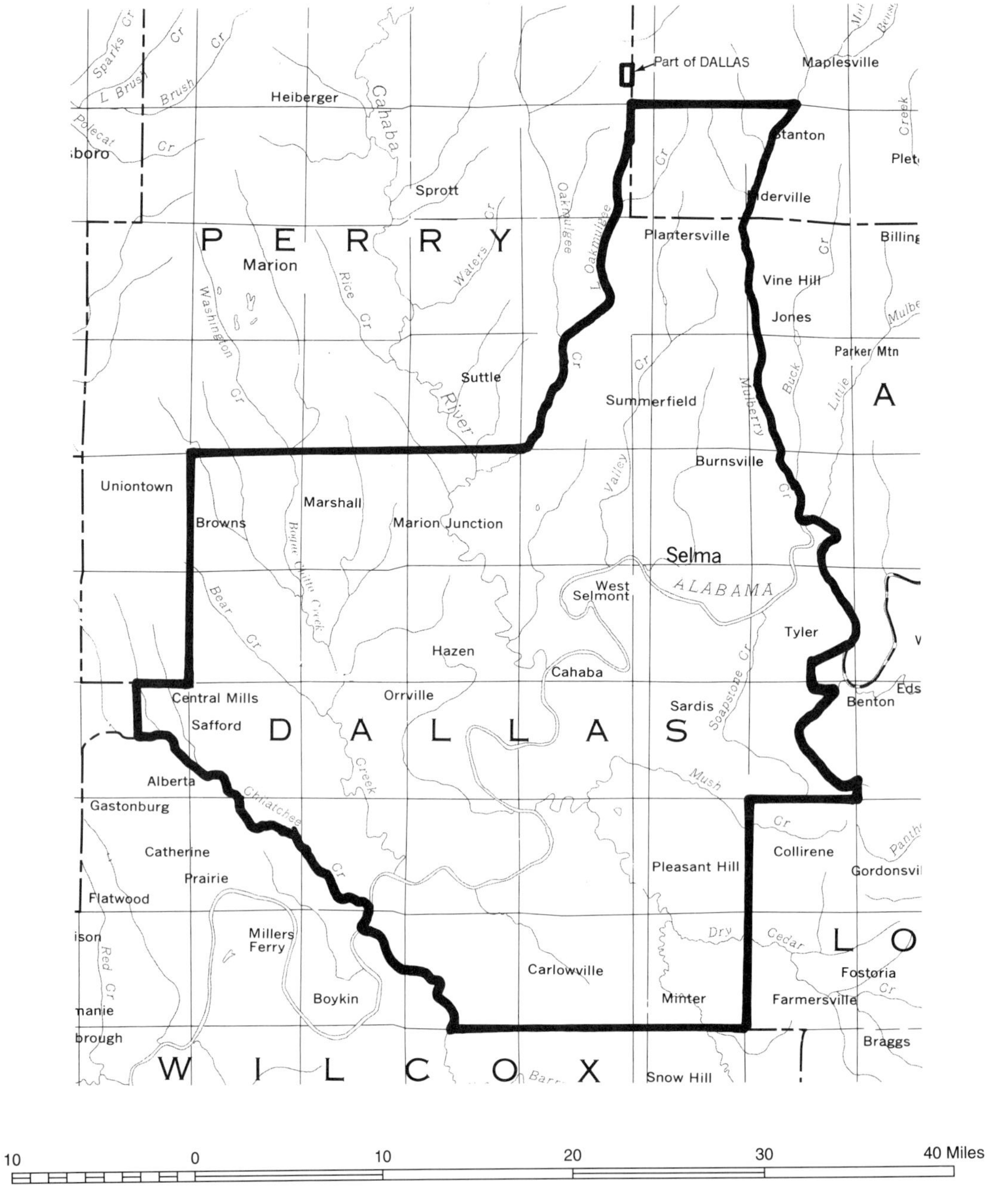

Individual County Chronologies 151

Chronology of DECATUR (extinct)

Map	Date	Event	Resulting Area
❶	7 Dec 1821	Created from JACKSON	540 sq mi
❷		Non-county area detached from JACKSON, attached to DECATUR	

(Heavy line depicts historical boundary. Base map shows present-day information.)

❶ 7 Dec 1821–30 Dec 1822

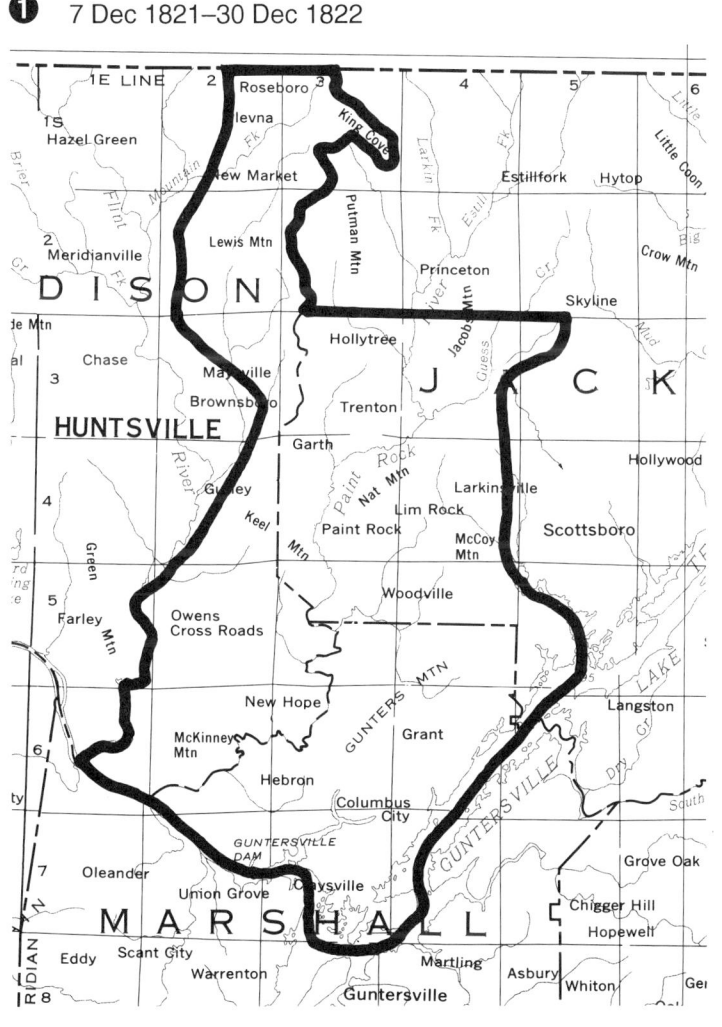

❷ 7 Dec 1821–30 Dec 1822

152 ALABAMA

Chronology of DECATUR (extinct)

Map	Date	Event	Resulting Area
❸ ❹	31 Dec 1822	Exchanged with JACKSON Northern part of non-county area detached, attached to JACKSON	630 sq mi
	28 Dec 1825	Lost all territory to JACKSON; DECATUR eliminated Non-county area formerly attached to DECATUR now attached to JACKSON	

(Heavy line depicts historical boundary. Base map shows present-day information.)

❸ 31 Dec 1822–27 Dec 1825

❹ 31 Dec 1822–27 Dec 1825

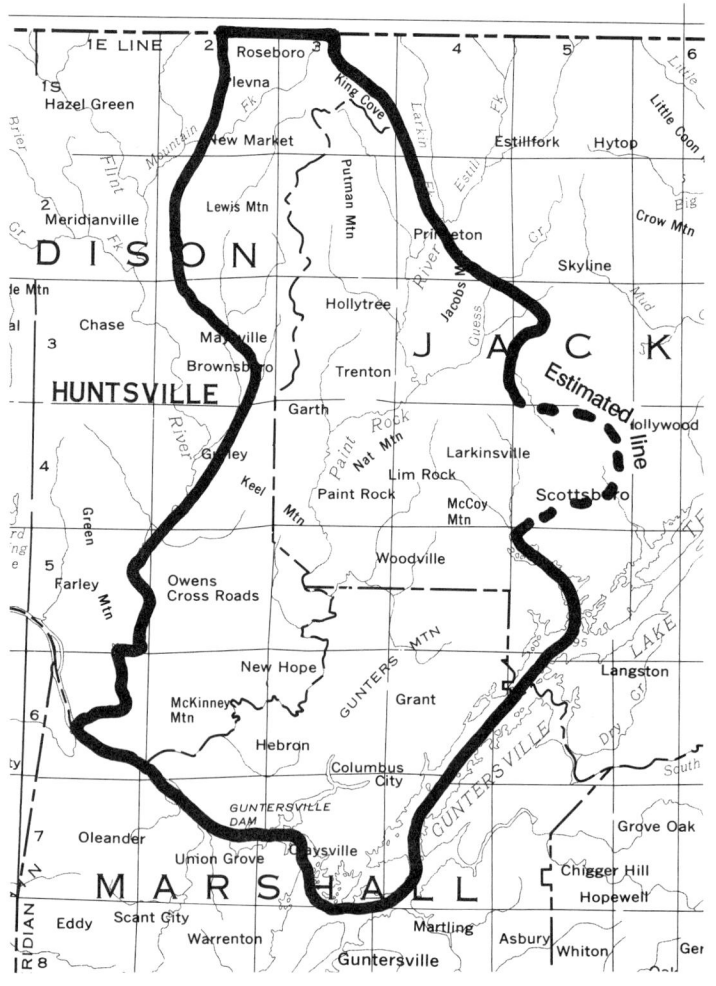

Individual County Chronologies 153

Chronology of DE KALB

Map	Date	Event	Resulting Area
❶	9 Jan 1836	Created from JACKSON and ST. CLAIR	510 sq mi

(Heavy line depicts historical boundary. Base map shows present-day information.)

❶ 9 Jan 1836–6 Feb 1843

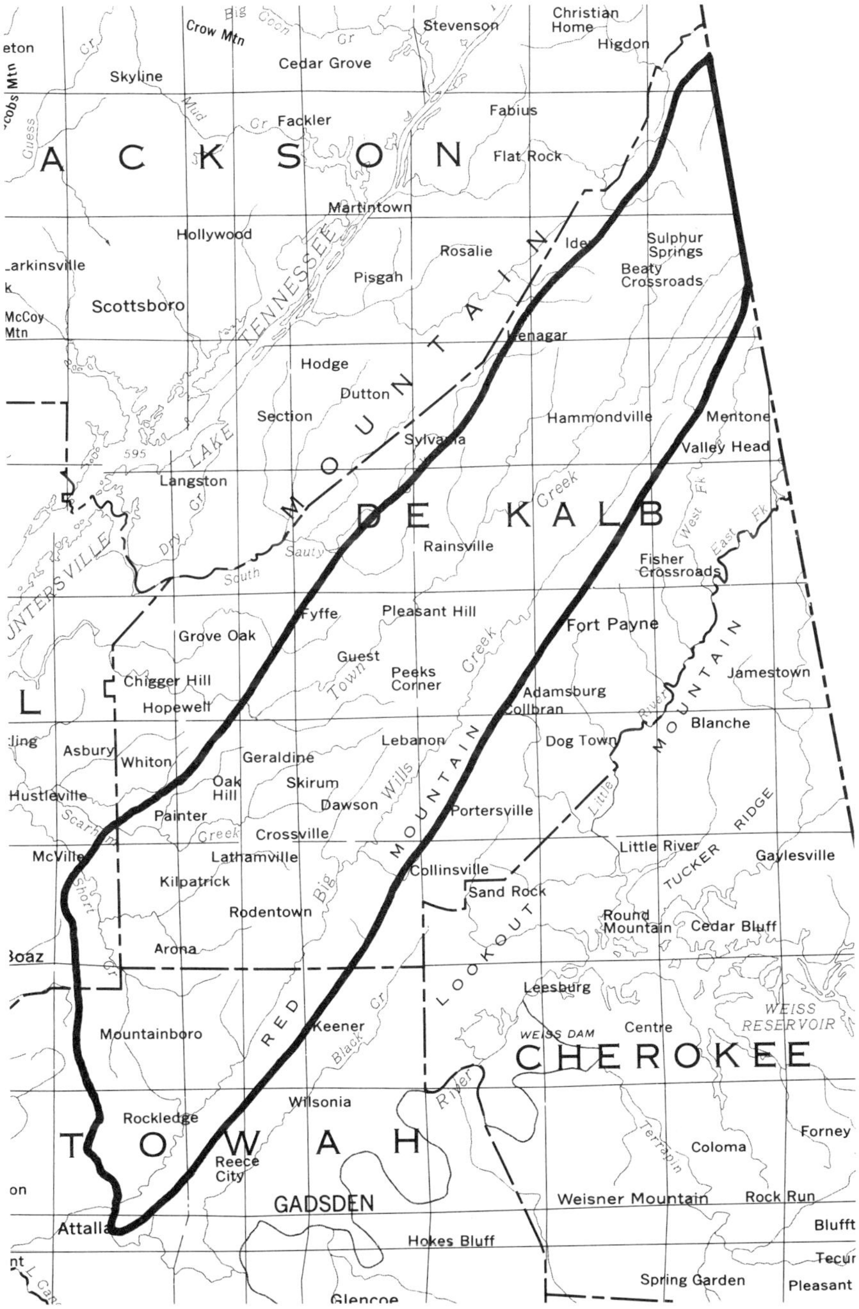

154 ALABAMA

Chronology of DE KALB

Map	Date	Event	Resulting Area
❷	7 Feb 1843	Exchanged with MARSHALL Boundary with JACKSON adjusted [location unknown, not mapped]	630 sq mi

(Heavy line depicts historical boundary. Base map shows present-day information.)

❷ 7 Feb 1843–15 Jan 1844

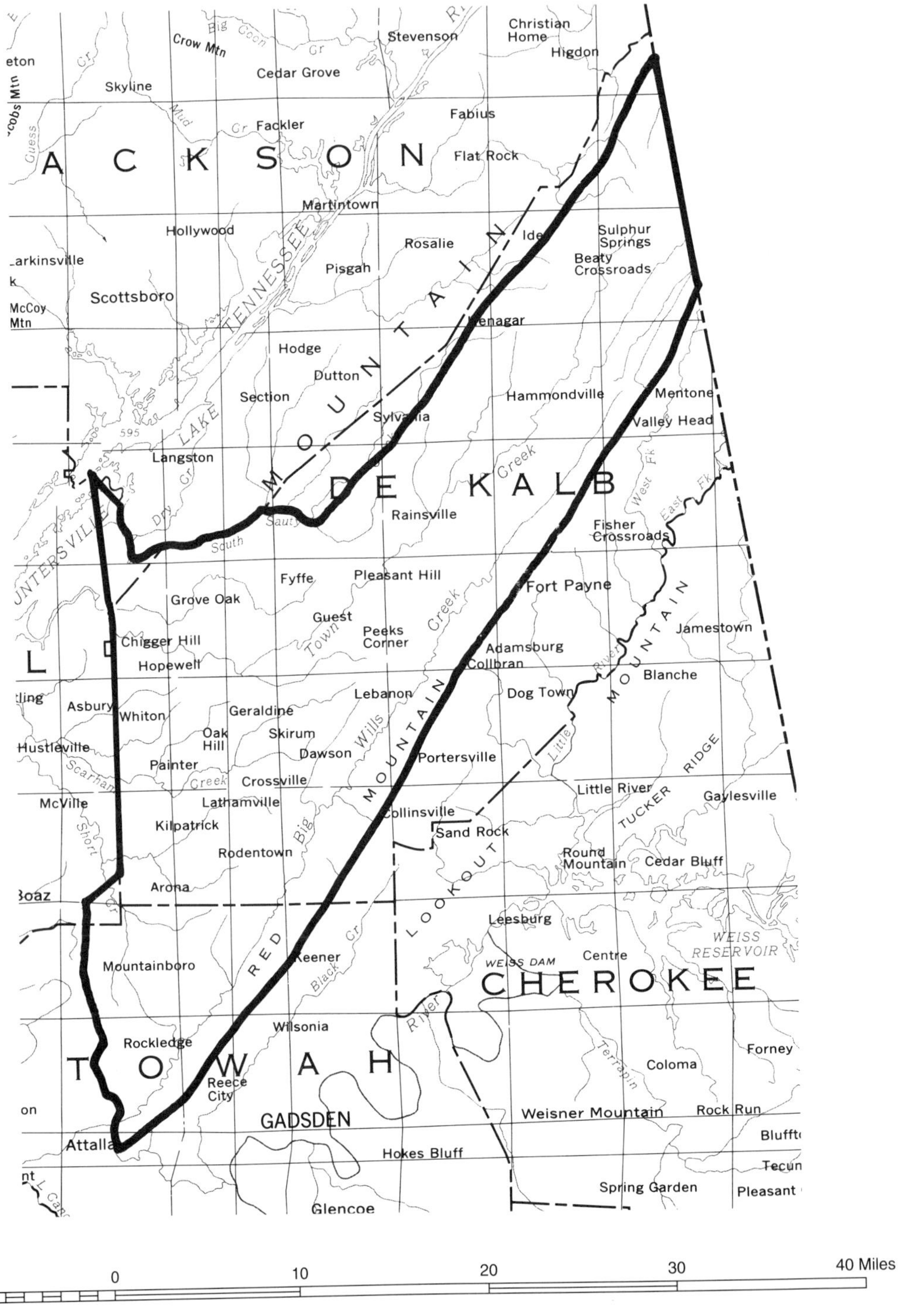

Chronology of DE KALB

Map	Date	Event	Resulting Area
❸	16 Jan 1844	Gained from CHEROKEE	870 sq mi

(Heavy line depicts historical boundary. Base map shows present-day information.)

❸ 16 Jan 1844–2 Mar 1848
15 Feb 1854–1 Feb 1858

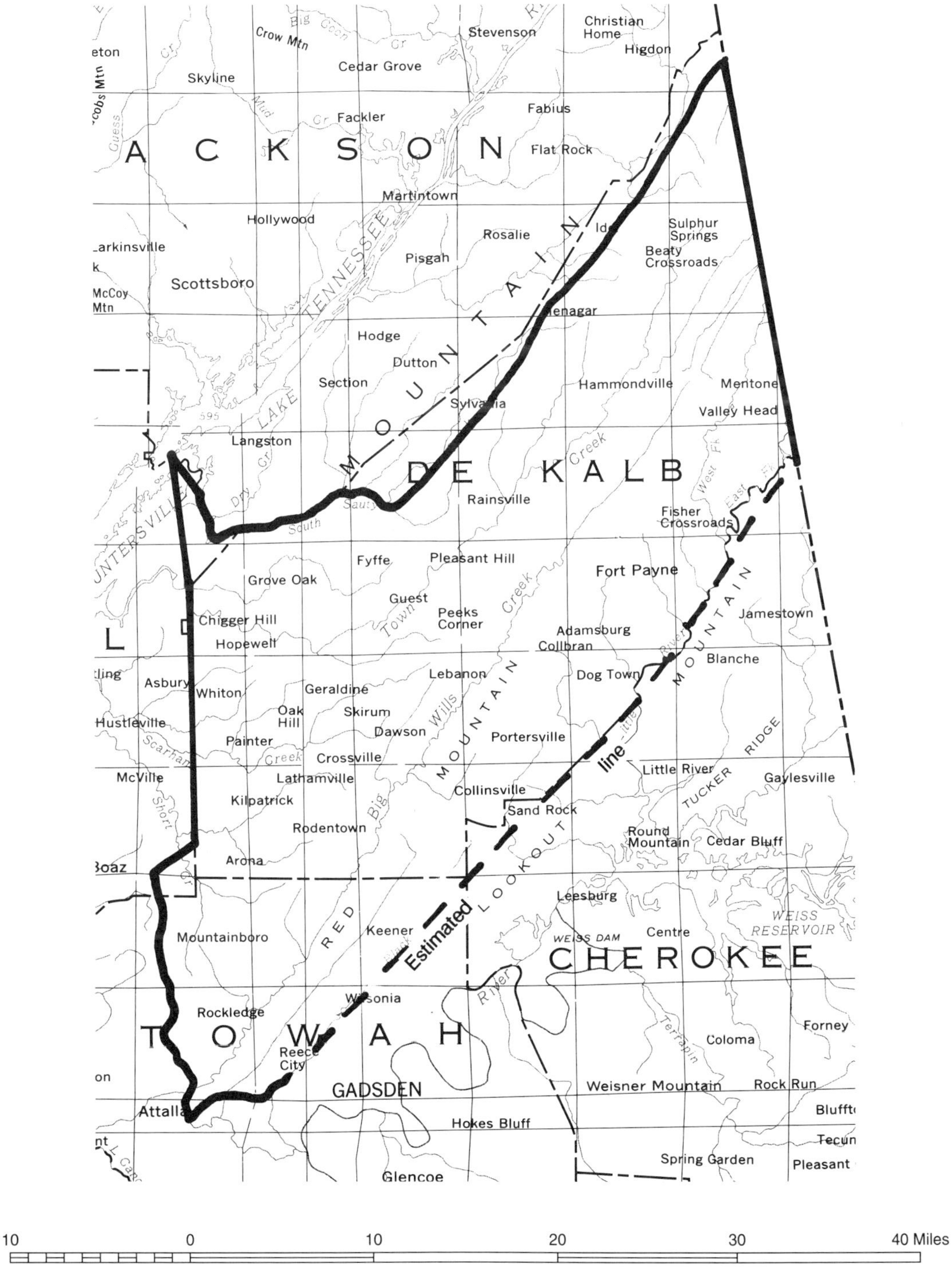

ALABAMA

Chronology of DE KALB

Map	Date	Event	Resulting Area
④	3 Mar 1848	Lost to JACKSON	820 sq mi
③	15 Feb 1854	Gained from JACKSON	870 sq mi

(Heavy line depicts historical boundary. Base map shows present-day information.)

④ 3 Mar 1848–14 Feb 1854

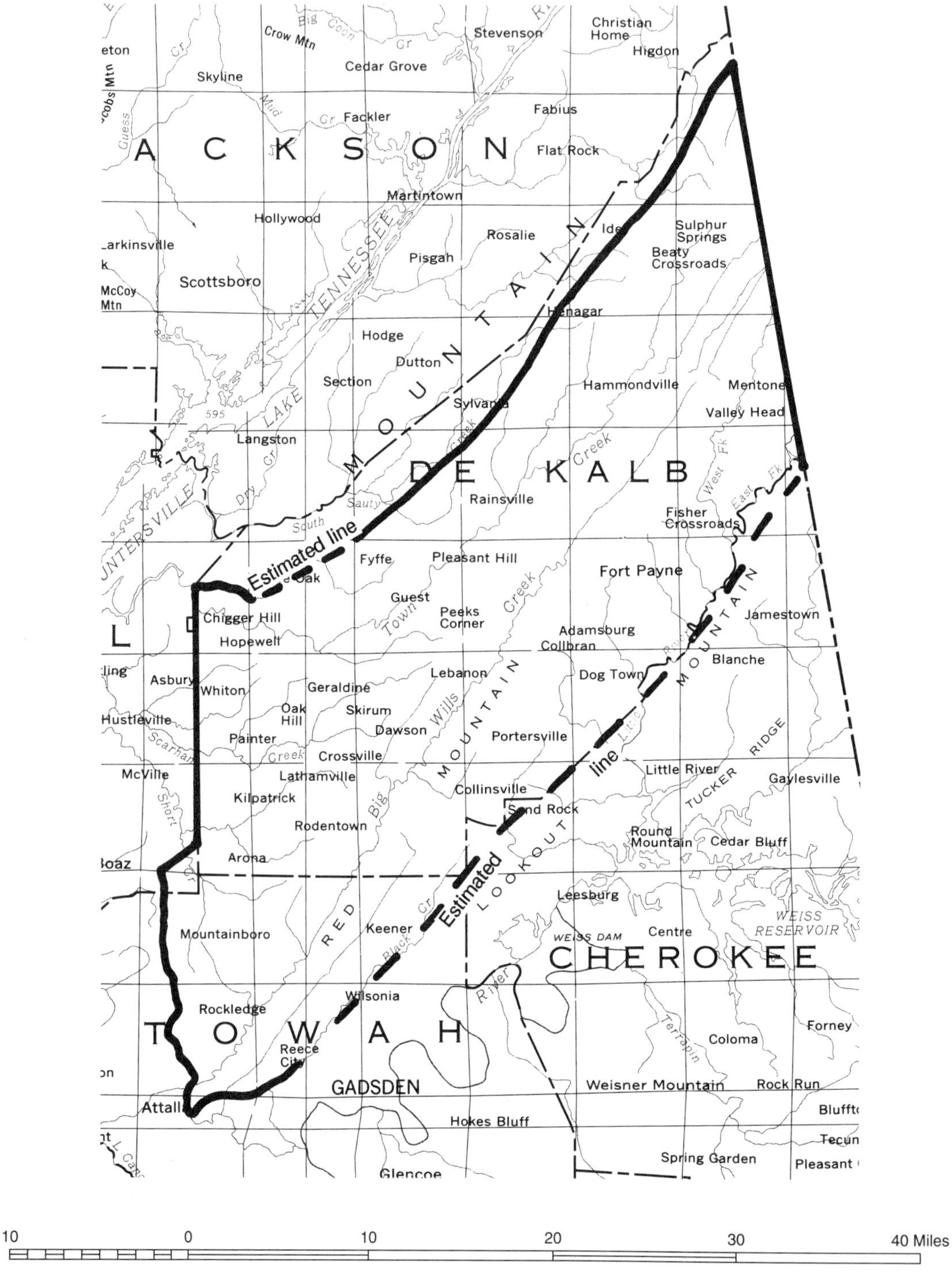

Individual County Chronologies 157

Chronology of DE KALB

Map	Date	Event	Resulting Area
❺	2 Feb 1858	Gained small area from JACKSON to accommodate local property owner, lost to MARSHALL	860 sq mi
	6 Feb 1858	Lost small area to CHEROKEE [location unknown, not mapped]	

(Heavy line depicts historical boundary. Base map shows present-day information.)

❺ 2 Feb 1858–24 Feb 1860

158 ALABAMA

Chronology of DE KALB

Map	Date	Event	Resulting Area
❻	25 Feb 1860	Gained from JACKSON	900 sq mi

(Heavy line depicts historical boundary. Base map shows present-day information.)

❻ 25 Feb 1860–6 Dec 1866
3 Dec 1867–30 Nov 1868

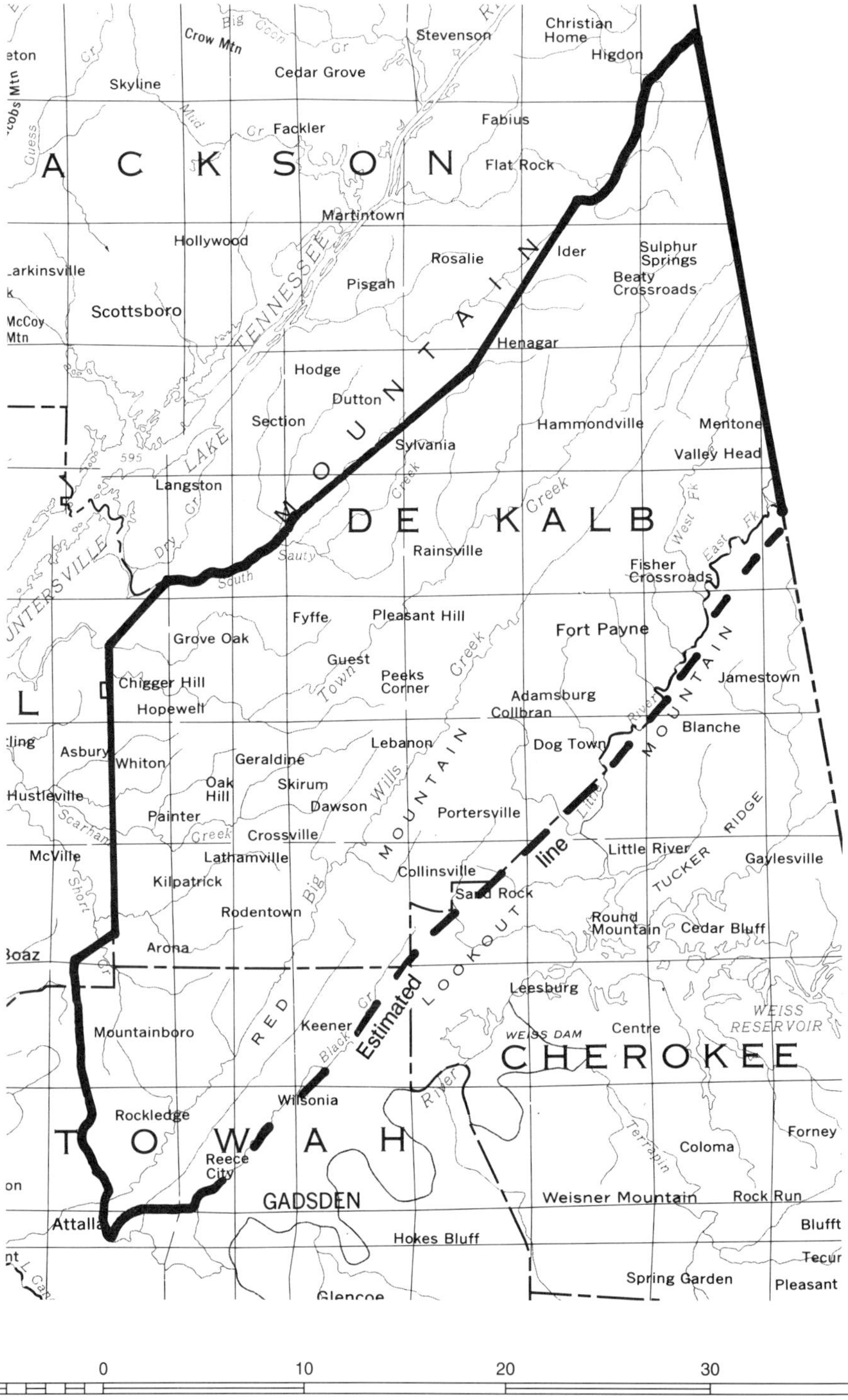

Individual County Chronologies 159

Chronology of DE KALB

Map	Date	Event	Resulting Area
❼	7 Dec 1866	Lost to creation of BAINE	690 sq mi
	13 Feb 1867	Boundary with CHEROKEE redefined [no discernible change]	

(Heavy line depicts historical boundary. Base map shows present-day information.)

❼ 7 Dec 1866–18 Feb 1867

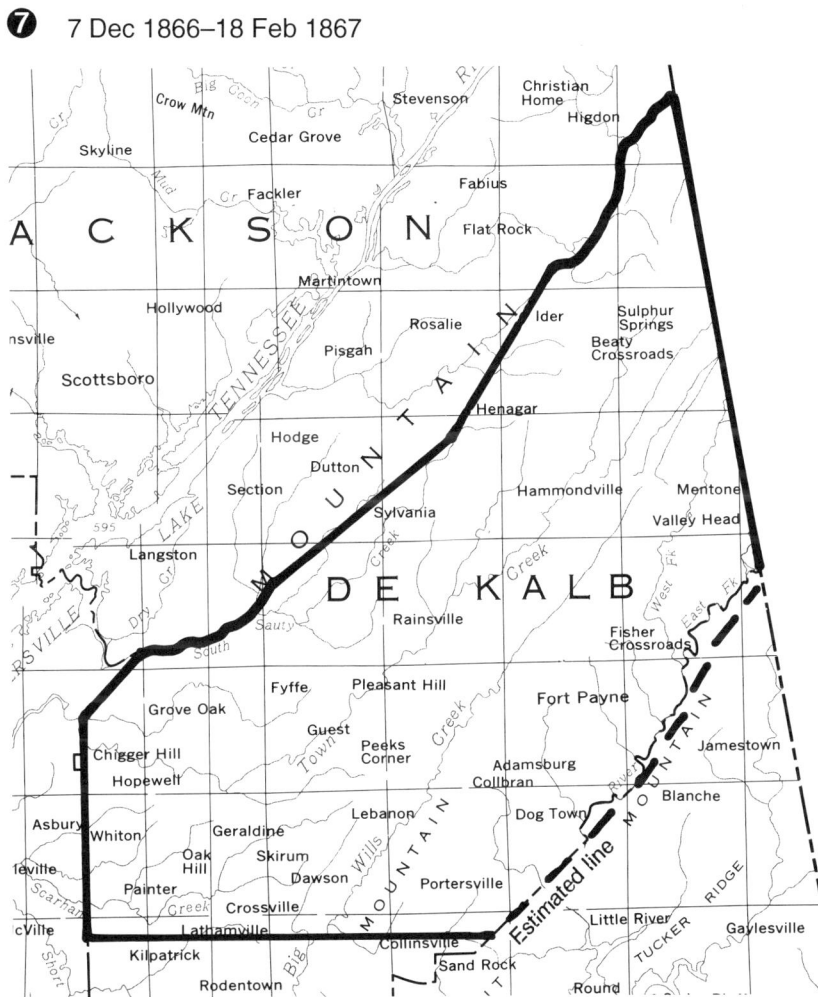

Chronology of DE KALB

Map	Date	Event	Resulting Area
❽	19 Feb 1867	Gained from BAINE	760 sq mi
❻	3 Dec 1867	Gained from BAINE; BAINE eliminated	900 sq mi

(Heavy line depicts historical boundary. Base map shows present-day information.)

❽ 19 Feb 1867–2 Dec 1867

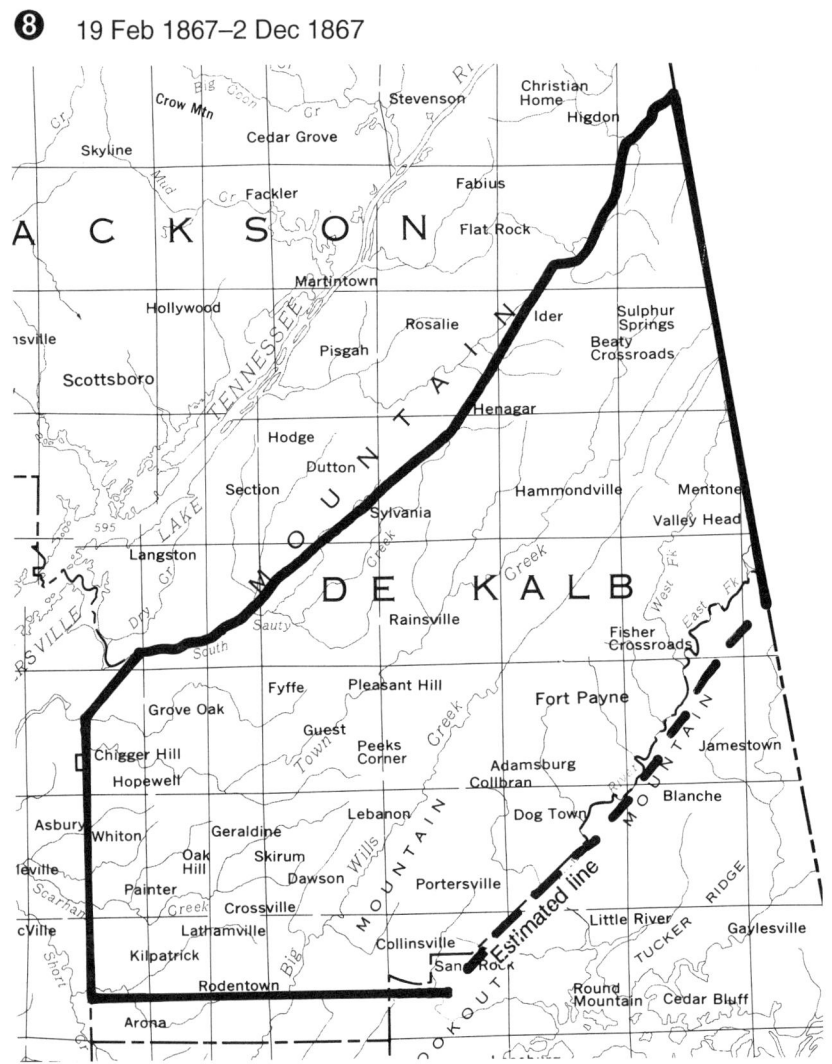

Individual County Chronologies 161

Chronology of DE KALB

Map	Date	Event	Resulting Area
⑨	1 Dec 1868	Lost to creation of ETOWAH and apparently lost to MARSHALL	820 sq mi
	3 Mar 1870	Gain from JACKSON authorized dependent on local referendum [repealed 8 Feb 1872]; no evidence that referendum was held [no change]	
	8 Feb 1872	Act of 3 Mar 1870, intended to change boundary with JACKSON, repealed [no change]	

(Heavy line depicts historical boundary. Base map shows present-day information.)

⑨   1 Dec 1868–6 Mar 1876

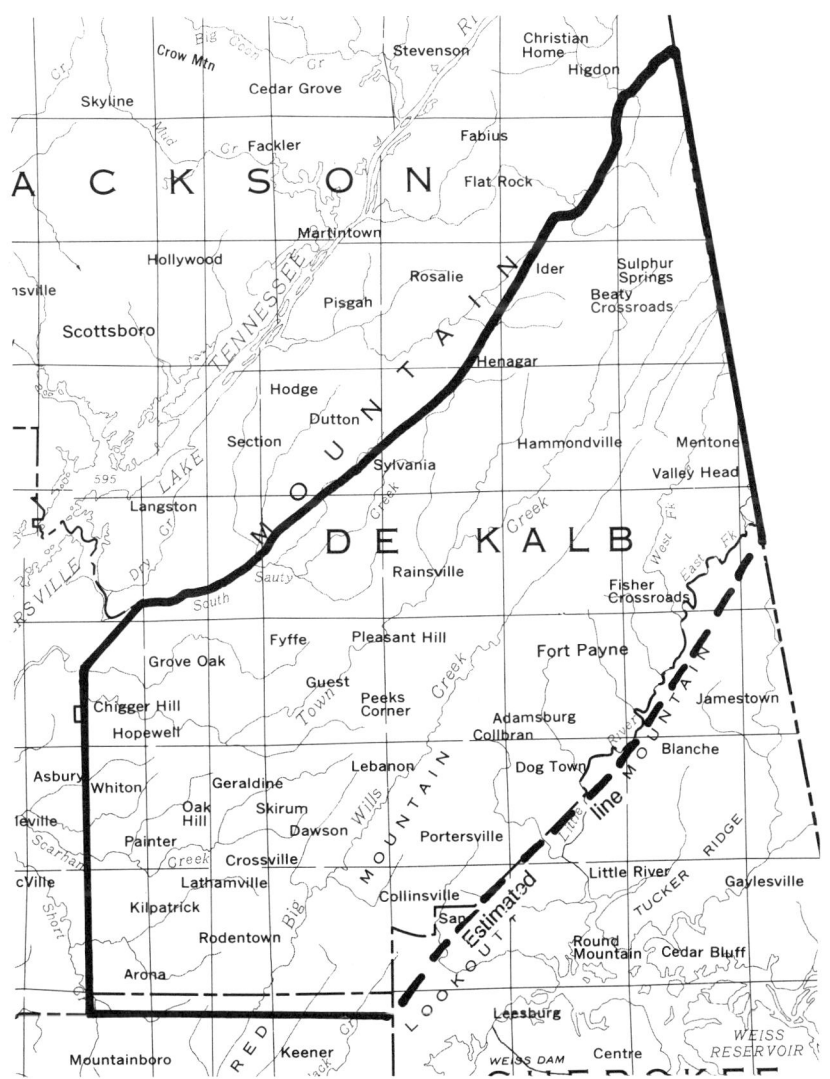

162　　　ALABAMA

Chronology of DE KALB

Map	Date	Event	Resulting Area
⑩	7 Mar 1876	Exchanged with CHEROKEE	800 sq mi
⑩	30 Jan 1877	Gained from MARSHALL	810 sq mi

(Heavy line depicts historical boundary. Base map shows present-day information.)

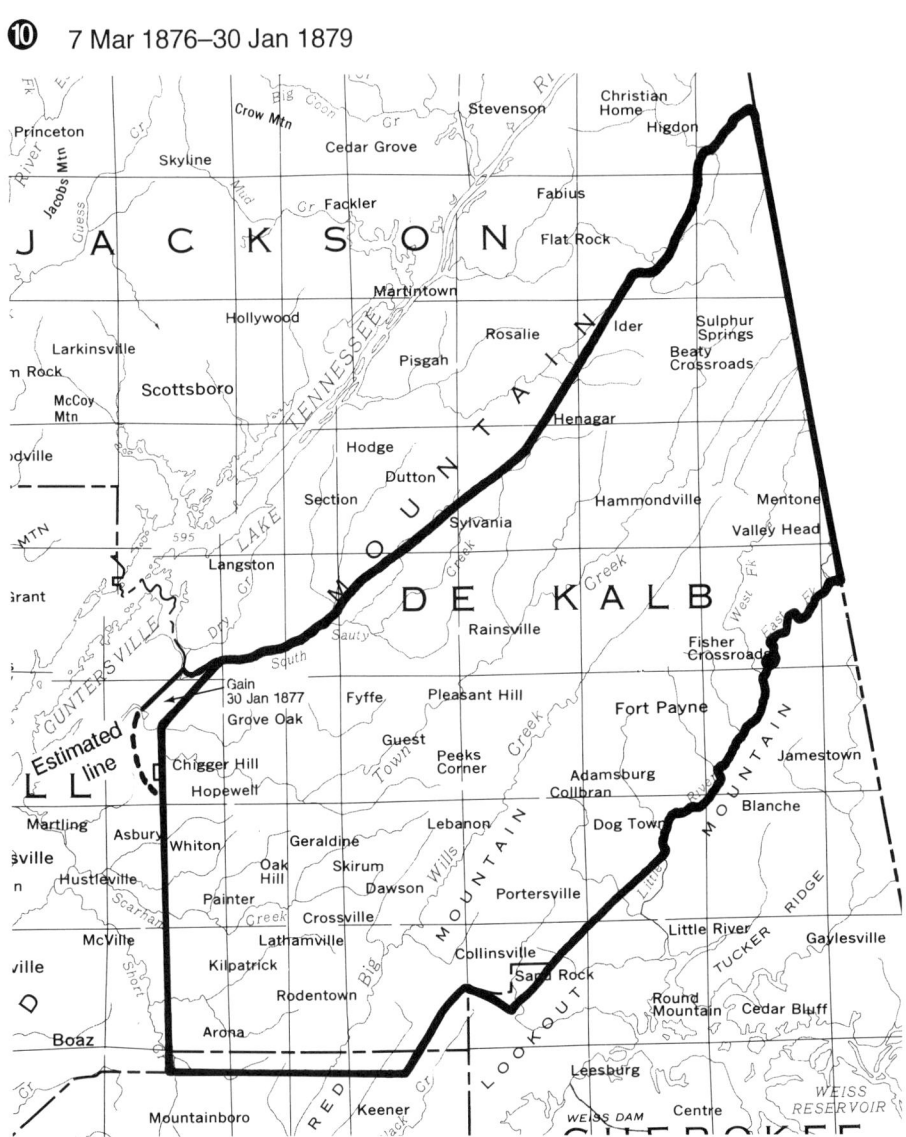

⑩　7 Mar 1876–30 Jan 1879

Individual County Chronologies   **163**

Chronology of DE KALB

Map	Date	Event	Resulting Area
⑪	31 Jan 1879	Lost to ETOWAH	800 sq mi

(Heavy line depicts historical boundary. Base map shows present-day information.)

⑪ 31 Jan 1879–3 Feb 1879

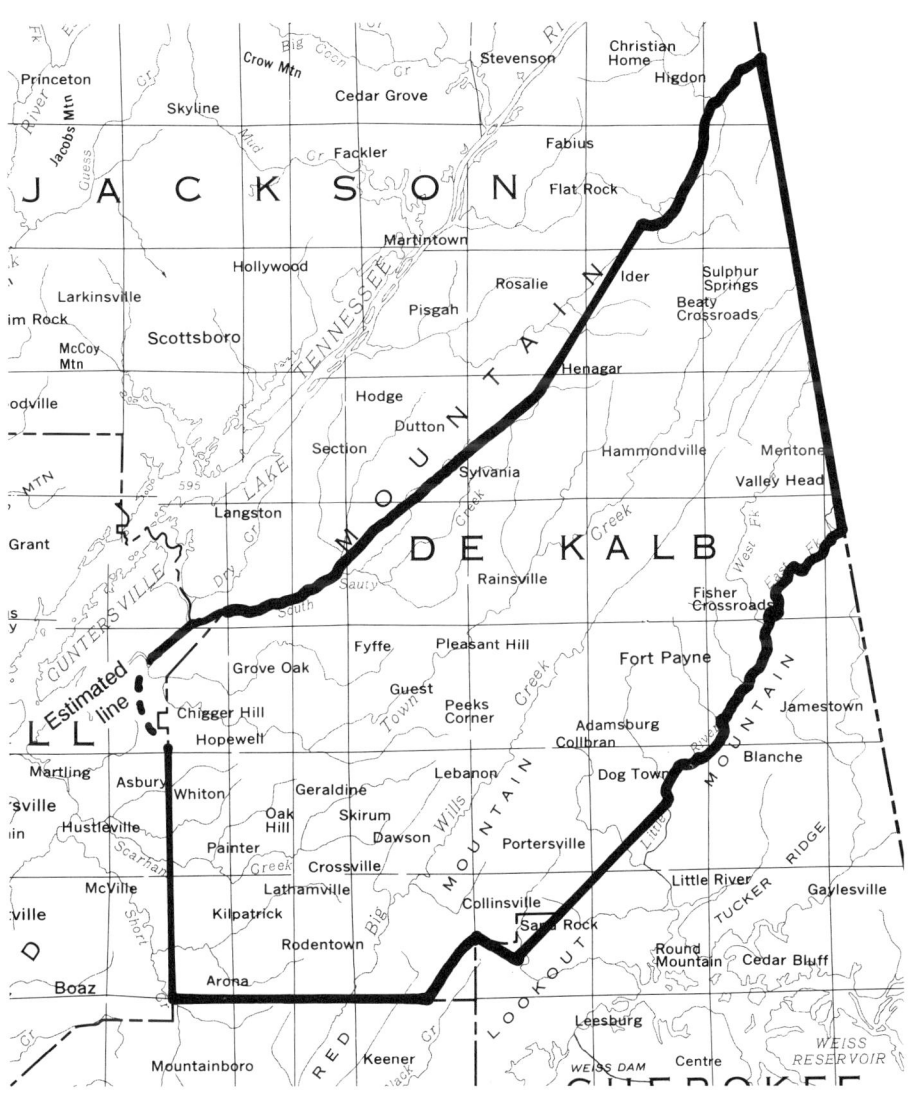

ALABAMA

Chronology of DE KALB

Map	Date	Event	Resulting Area
⑫	4 Feb 1879	Lost to MARSHALL	780 sq mi
⑫	12 Dec 1884	Lost small area to CHEROKEE	780 sq mi

(Heavy line depicts historical boundary. Base map shows present-day information.)

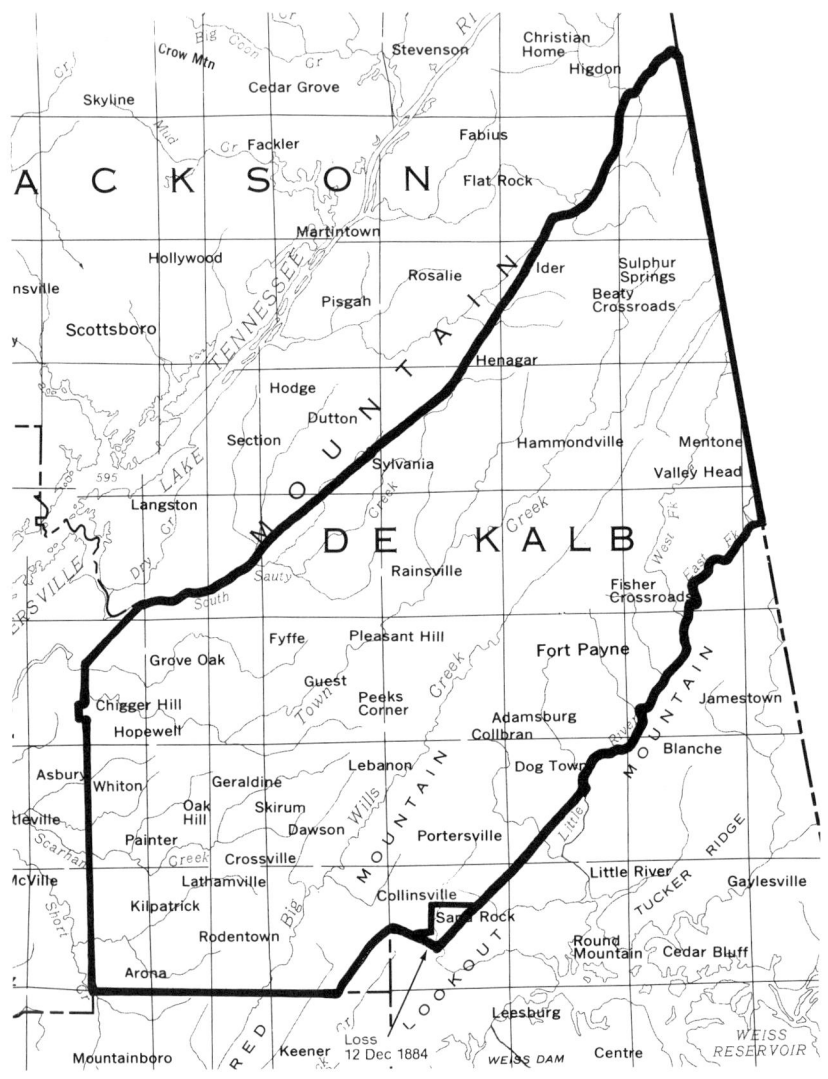

⑫ 4 Feb 1879–13 Feb 1901

Individual County Chronologies 165

Chronology of DE KALB

Map	Date	Event	Resulting Area
⑬	14 Feb 1901	Gained from CHEROKEE	780 sq mi

(Heavy line depicts historical boundary. Base map shows present-day information.)

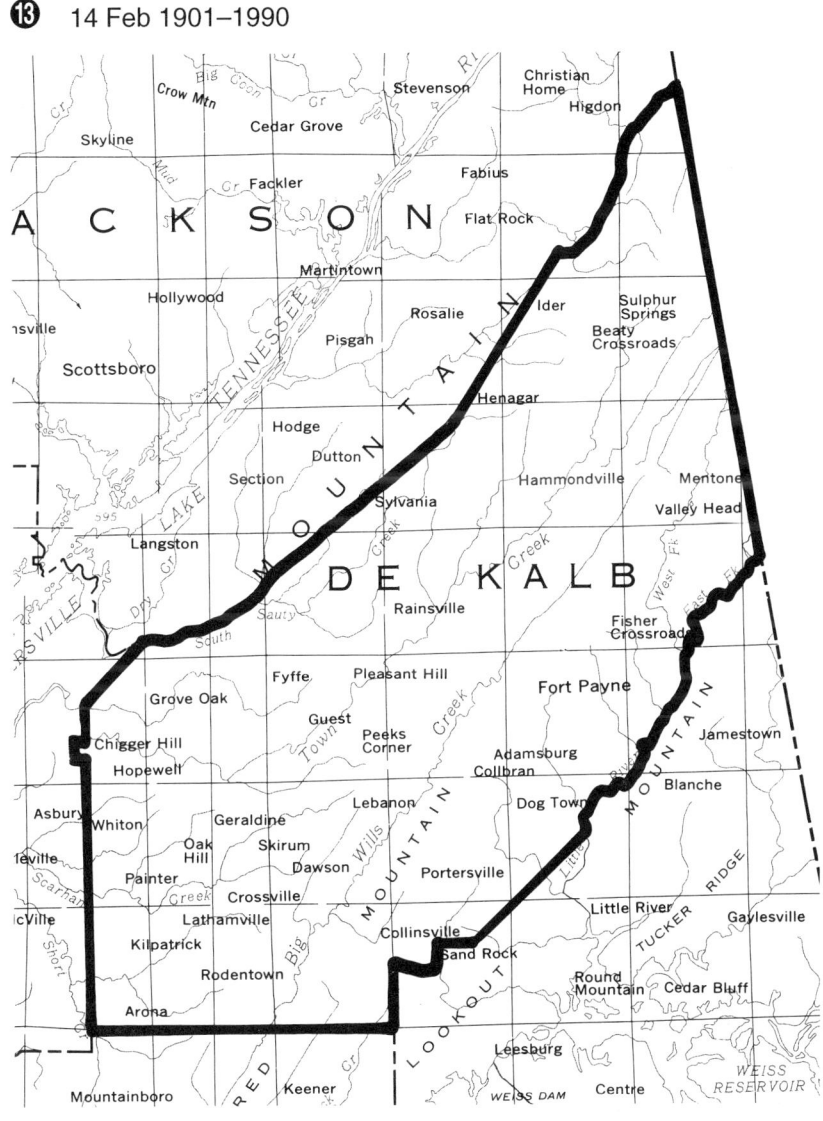

⑬ 14 Feb 1901–1990

166 ALABAMA

Chronology of ELMORE

Map	Date	Event	Resulting Area
❶	late Dec 1866	Created from AUTAUGA, COOSA, MONTGOMERY, and TALLAPOOSA	660 sq mi
❶	10 Dec 1868	Gained small area from COOSA	660 sq mi
❶	14 Feb 1870	Gained small area from TALLAPOOSA to accommodate local property owners	660 sq mi
❷	9 Aug 1923	Lost to MONTGOMERY	660 sq mi

(Heavy line depicts historical boundary. Base map shows present-day information.)

❶ late Dec 1866–8 Aug 1923

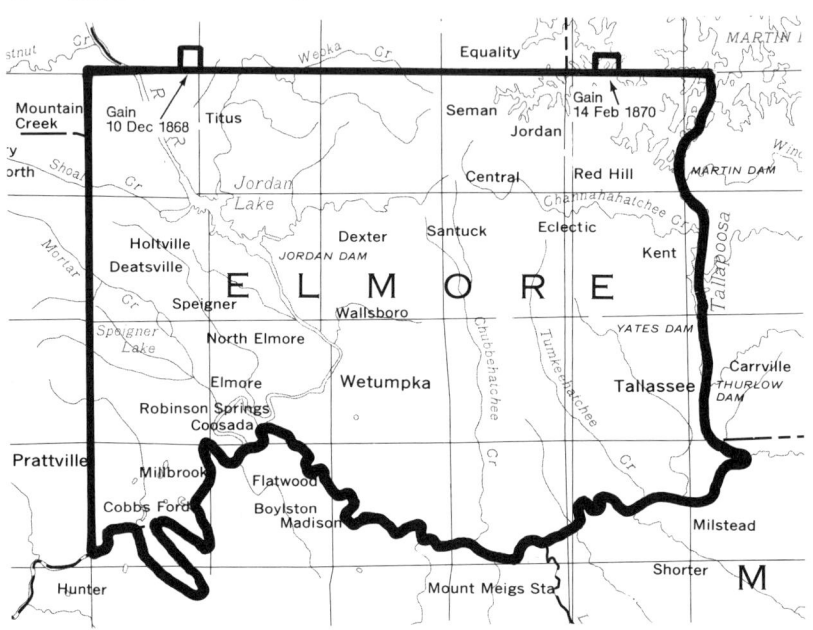

❷ 9 Aug 1923–1990

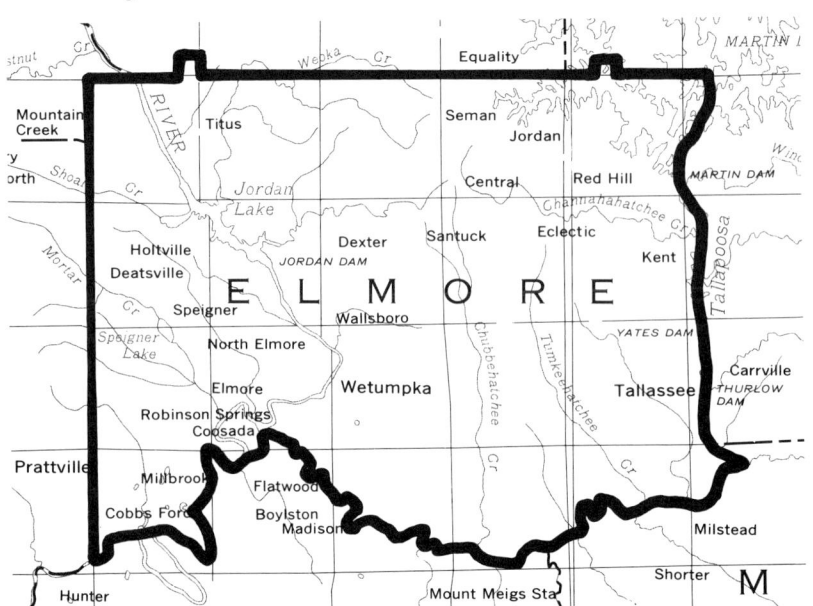

Individual County Chronologies **167**

Chronology of ESCAMBIA

Map	Date	Event	Resulting Area
❶	10 Dec 1868	Created from BALDWIN and CONECUH. Narrow strip of territory along the state line inadvertently omitted from formal definition of ESCAMBIA [mistake corrected 5 Mar 1907]	980 sq mi
❶	21 Feb 1870	Lost small area to COVINGTON to accommodate local property owner	980 sq mi
❷	25 Feb 1875	Lost to CONECUH	960 sq mi
❷	28 Feb 1887	Lost small area to CONECUH	960 sq mi
	5 Mar 1907	Southern boundary clarified to match state line, correcting mistake of 10 Dec 1868 [no change]	

(Heavy line depicts historical boundary. Base map shows present-day information.)

❶ 10 Dec 1868–24 Feb 1875

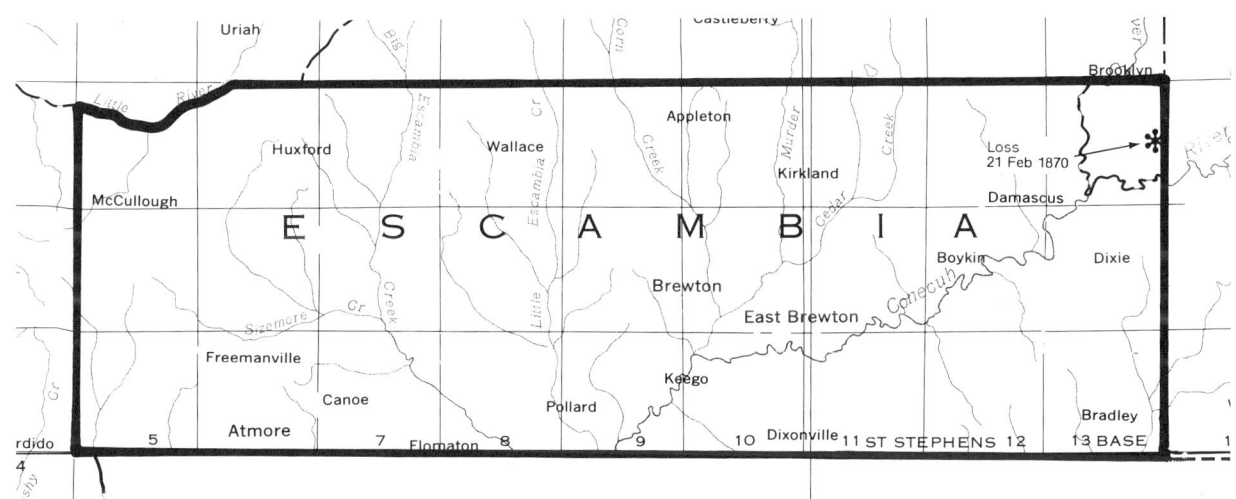

❷ 25 Feb 1875–1990

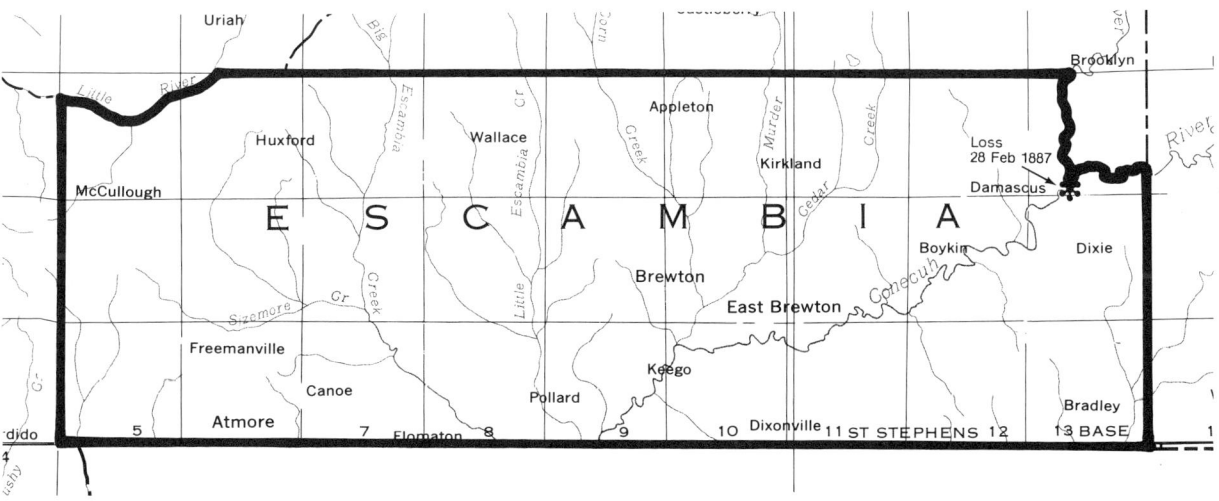

ALABAMA

Chronology of ETOWAH

Map	Date	Event	Resulting Area
❶	1 Dec 1868	Created from BLOUNT, CALHOUN, CHEROKEE, DE KALB, MARSHALL, and ST. CLAIR [ETOWAH boundaries different from those of BAINE, which had been located in the same area]	570 sq mi
	17 Dec 1868	Lost small area to ST. CLAIR to accommodate local property owner [location unknown, not mapped]	
❷	7 Feb 1870	Lost to ST. CLAIR	550 sq mi

(Heavy line depicts historical boundary. Base map shows present-day information.)

❶ 1 Dec 1868–6 Feb 1870

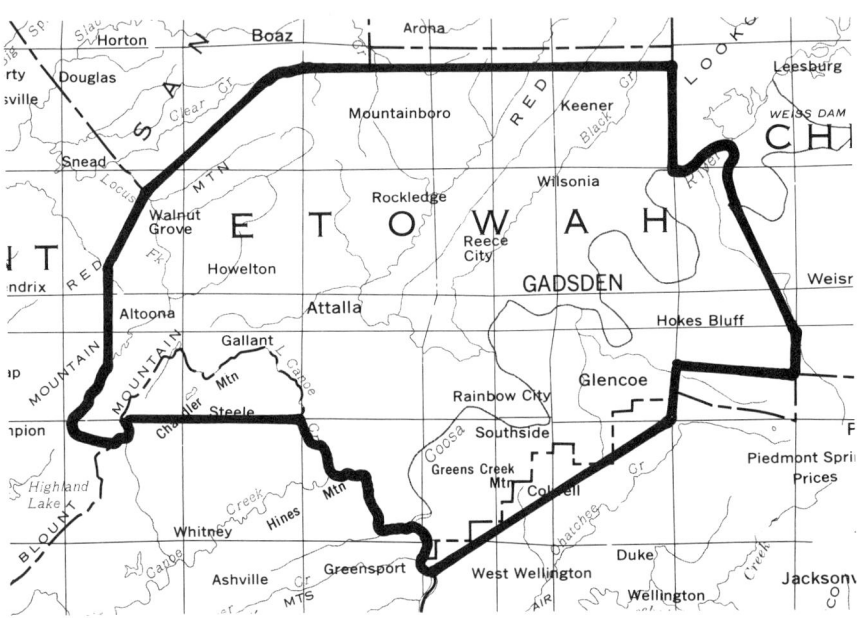

❷ 7 Feb 1870–6 Dec 1871

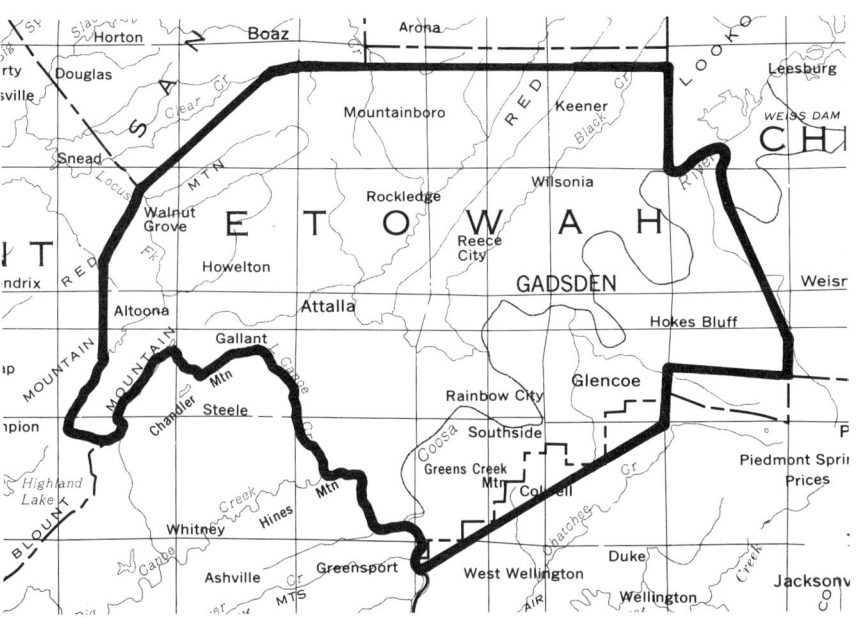

Individual County Chronologies 169

Chronology of ETOWAH

Map	Date	Event	Resulting Area
❸	7 Dec 1871	Lost to CALHOUN	540 sq mi
❹	31 Jan 1879	Gained from DE KALB	550 sq mi

(Heavy line depicts historical boundary. Base map shows present-day information.)

❸ 7 Dec 1871–30 Jan 1879

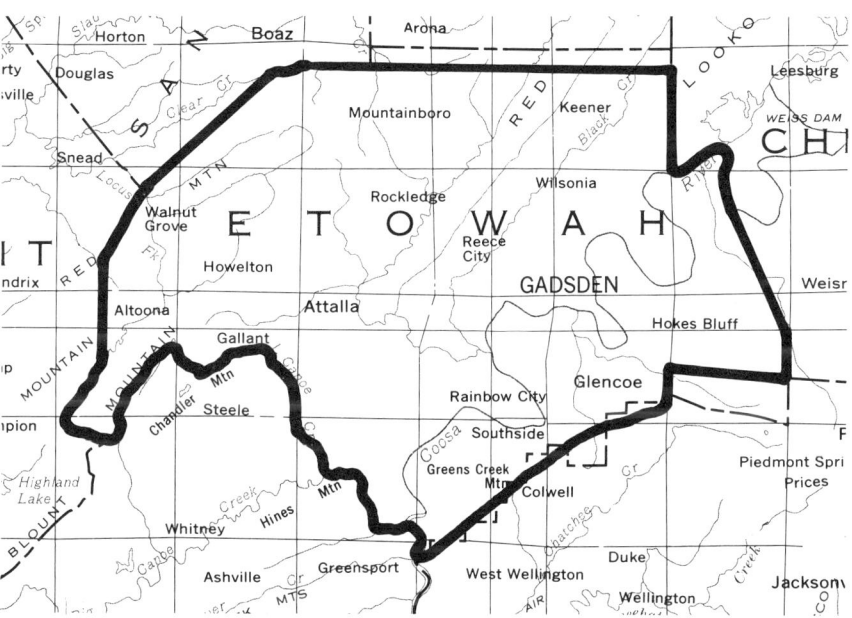

❹ 31 Jan 1879–9 Feb 1899

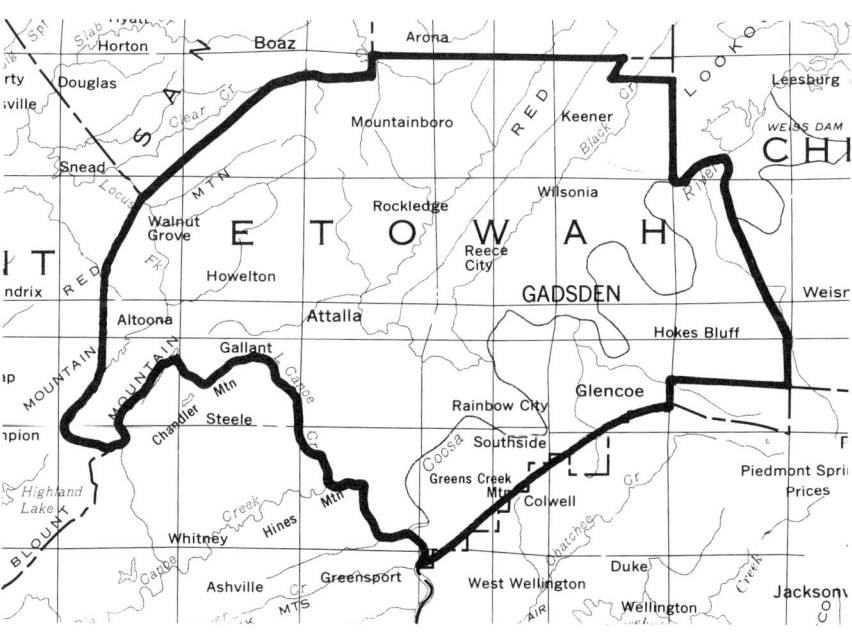

ALABAMA

Chronology of ETOWAH

Map	Date	Event	Resulting Area
❺	10 Feb 1899	Gained from CALHOUN	560 sq mi
❻	1 Oct 1901	Exchanged with CALHOUN	560 sq mi
❻	9 Aug 1907	Gained small area from CALHOUN	560 sq mi

(Heavy line depicts historical boundary. Base map shows present-day information.)

❺ 10 Feb 1899–30 Sep 1901

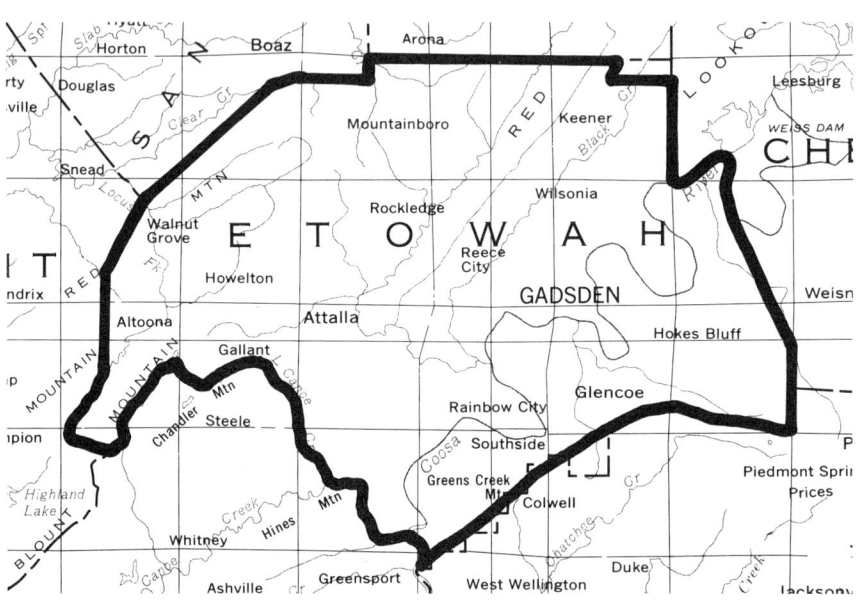

❻ 1 Oct 1901–13 Sep 1923

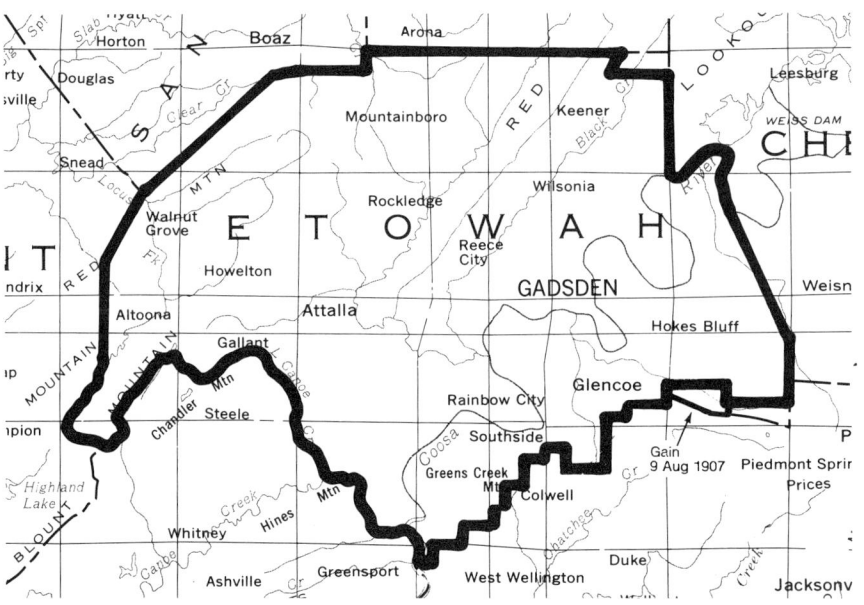

Individual County Chronologies 171

Chronology of ETOWAH

Map	Date	Event	Resulting Area
❼	14 Sep 1923	Exchanged small areas with CALHOUN	570 sq mi
❼	10 Jul 1931	Gained from CHEROKEE	570 sq mi
❽	6 Aug 1976	Lost to BLOUNT	560 sq mi

(Heavy line depicts historical boundary. Base map shows present-day information.)

❼ 14 Sep 1923–5 Aug 1976

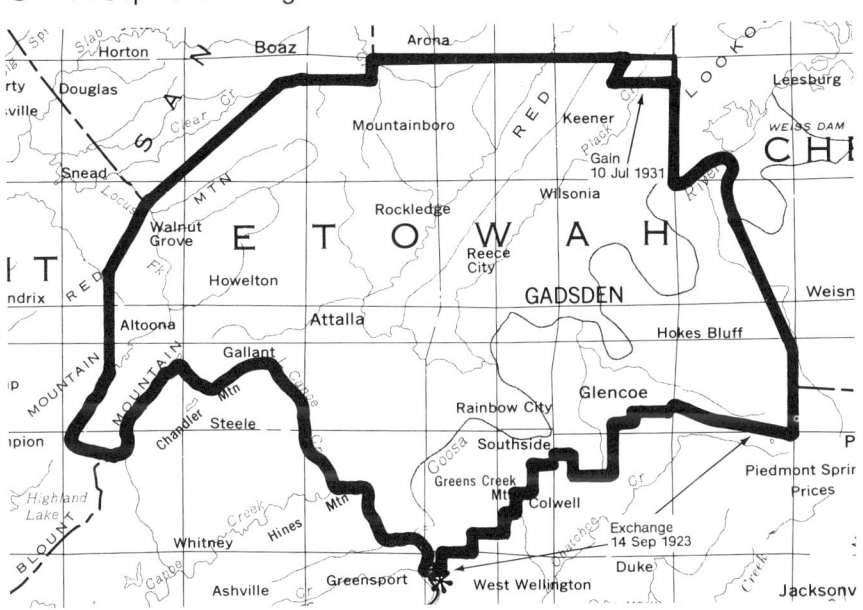

❽ 6 Aug 1976–1990

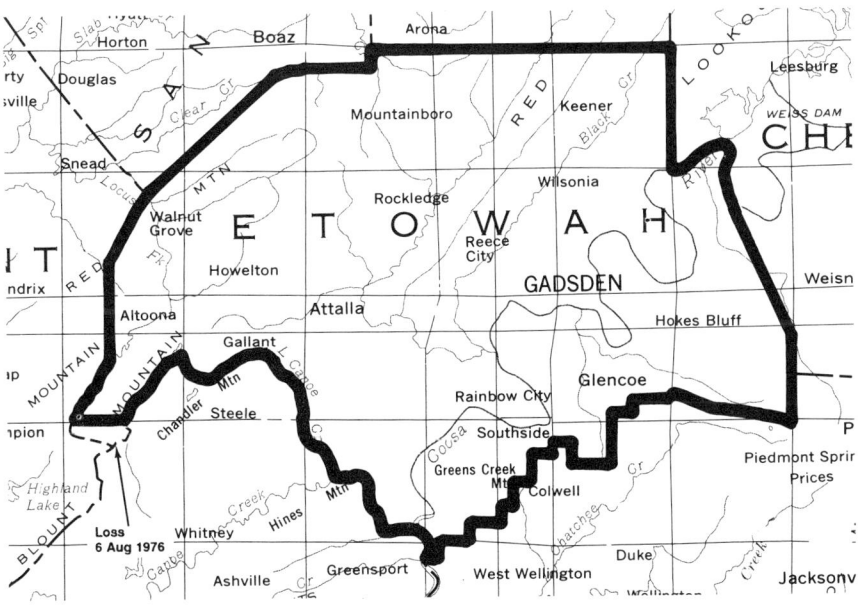

ALABAMA

Chronology of FAYETTE

Map	Date	Event	Resulting Area
❶	20 Dec 1824	Created from MARION, PICKENS, TUSCALOOSA, and WALKER	930 sq mi
❷	15 Jan 1831	Gained from MARION	950 sq mi

(Heavy line depicts historical boundary. Base map shows present-day information.)

❶ 20 Dec 1824–14 Jan 1831

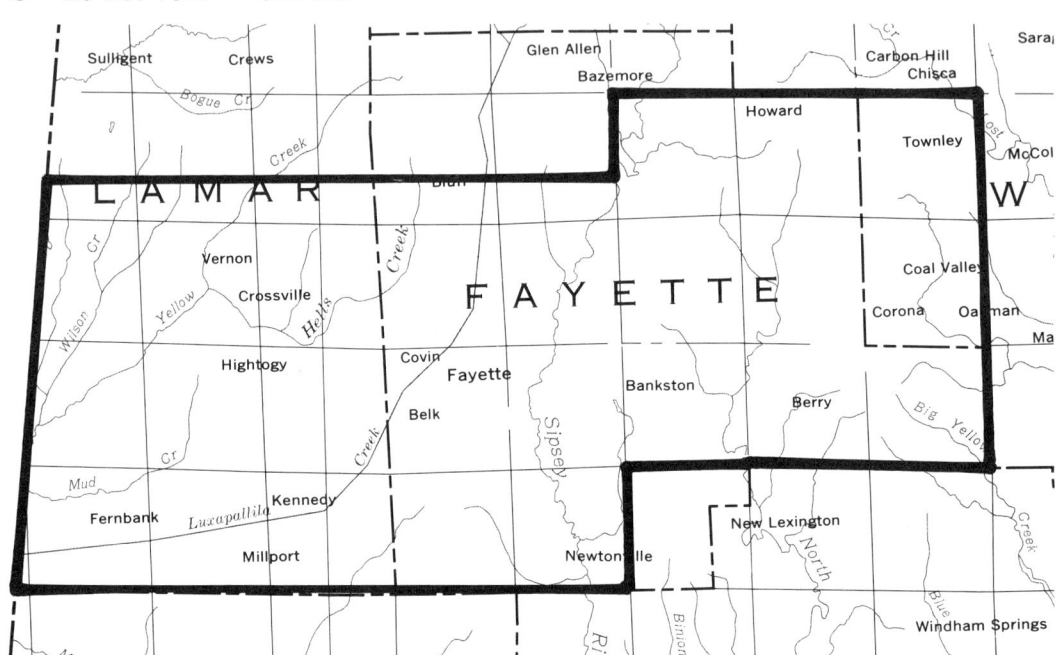

❷ 15 Jan 1831–19 Jan 1832

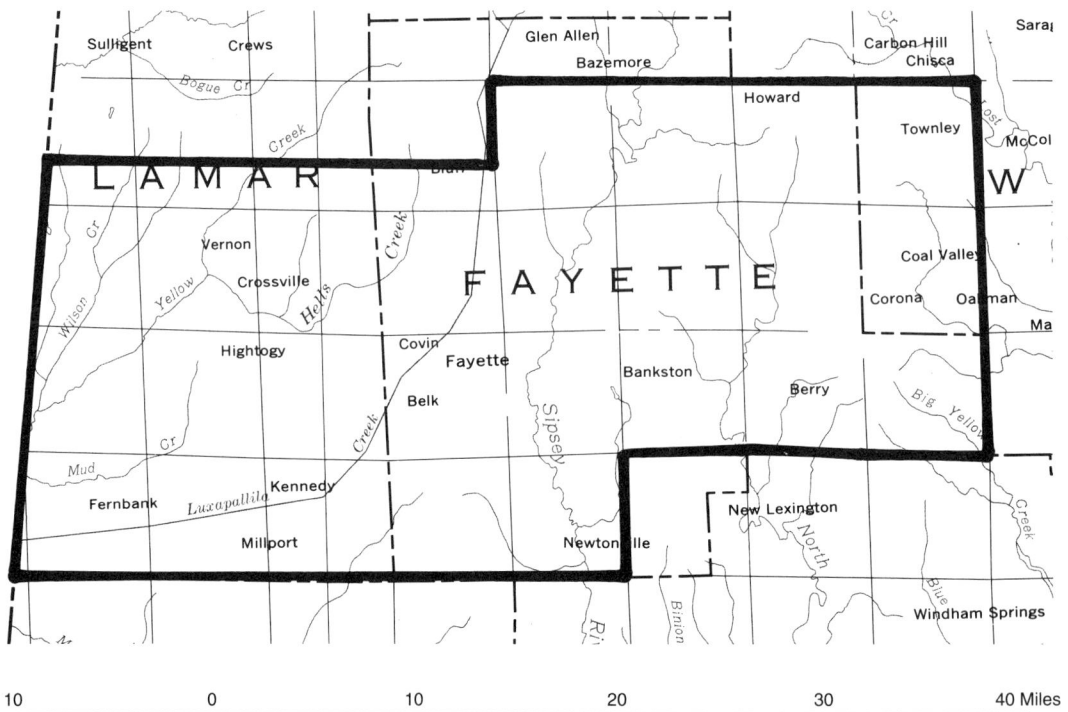

Individual County Chronologies 173

Chronology of FAYETTE

Map	Date	Event	Resulting Area
❸	20 Jan 1832	Gained from TUSCALOOSA	980 sq mi
❹	23 Dec 1837	Gained from MARION	1,010 sq mi

(Heavy line depicts historical boundary. Base map shows present-day information.)

❸ 20 Jan 1832–22 Dec 1837

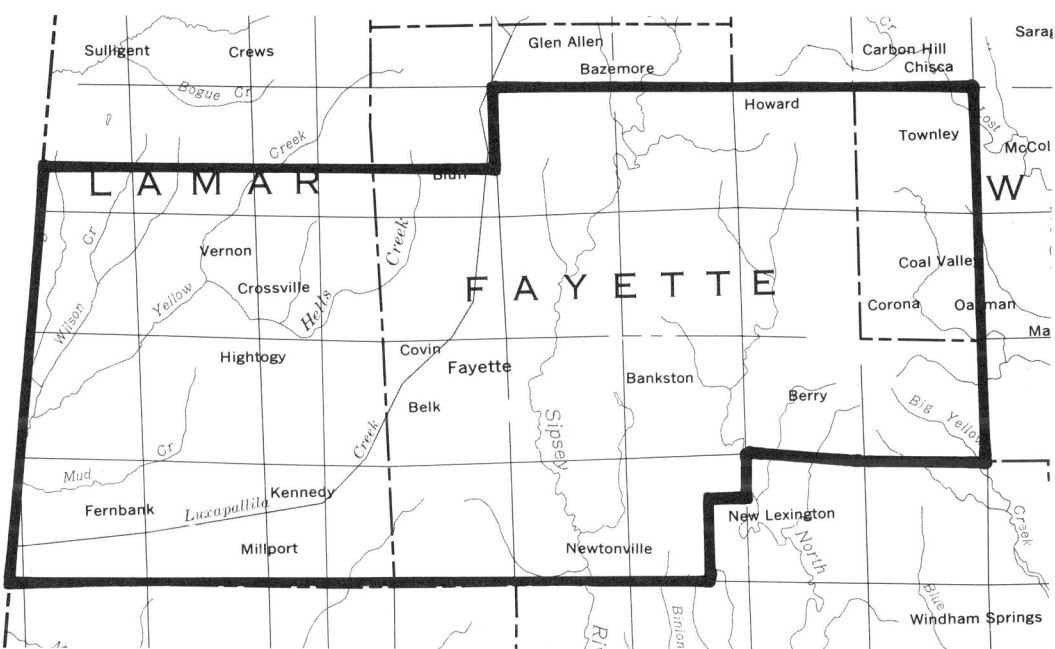

❹ 23 Dec 1837–8 Jan 1843

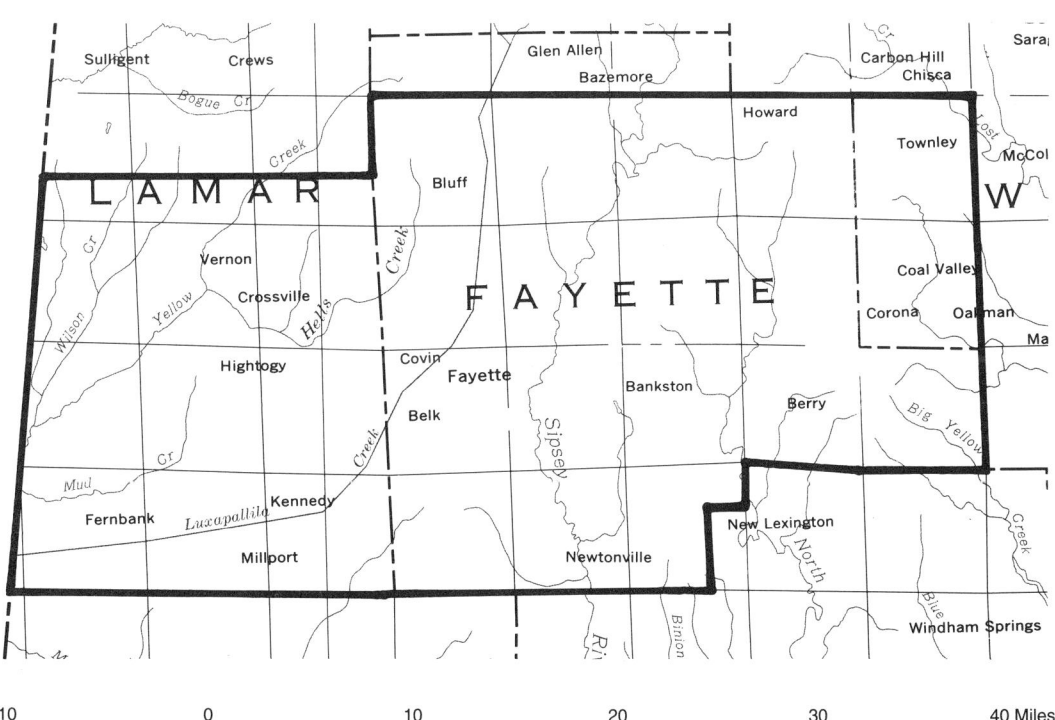

174 ALABAMA

Chronology of FAYETTE

Map	Date	Event	Resulting Area
❺	9 Jan 1843	Lost to WALKER	930 sq mi
❻	4 Feb 1867	Gained from MARION, lost to creation of JONES	620 sq mi

(Heavy line depicts historical boundary. Base map shows present-day information.)

❺ 9 Jan 1843–3 Feb 1867

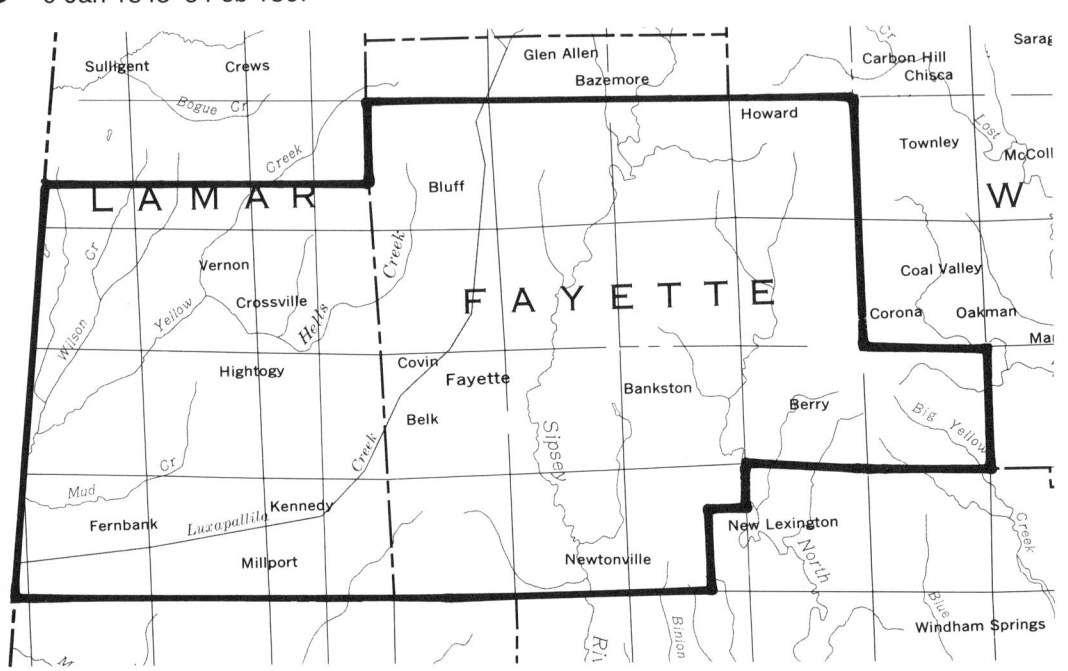

❻ 4 Feb 1867–12 Nov 1867
   8 Oct 1868–1990

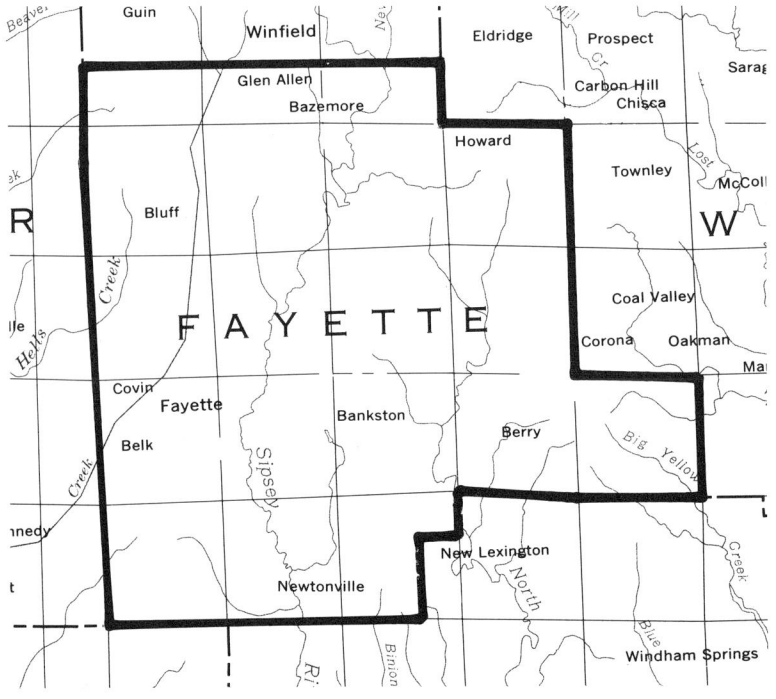

Chronology of FAYETTE

Map	Date	Event	Resulting Area
❼	13 Nov 1867	Gained from JONES; JONES eliminated	980 sq mi
❻	8 Oct 1868	Lost to creation of SANFORD (now LAMAR)	620 sq mi

(Heavy line depicts historical boundary. Base map shows present-day information.)

❼ 13 Nov 1867–7 Oct 1868

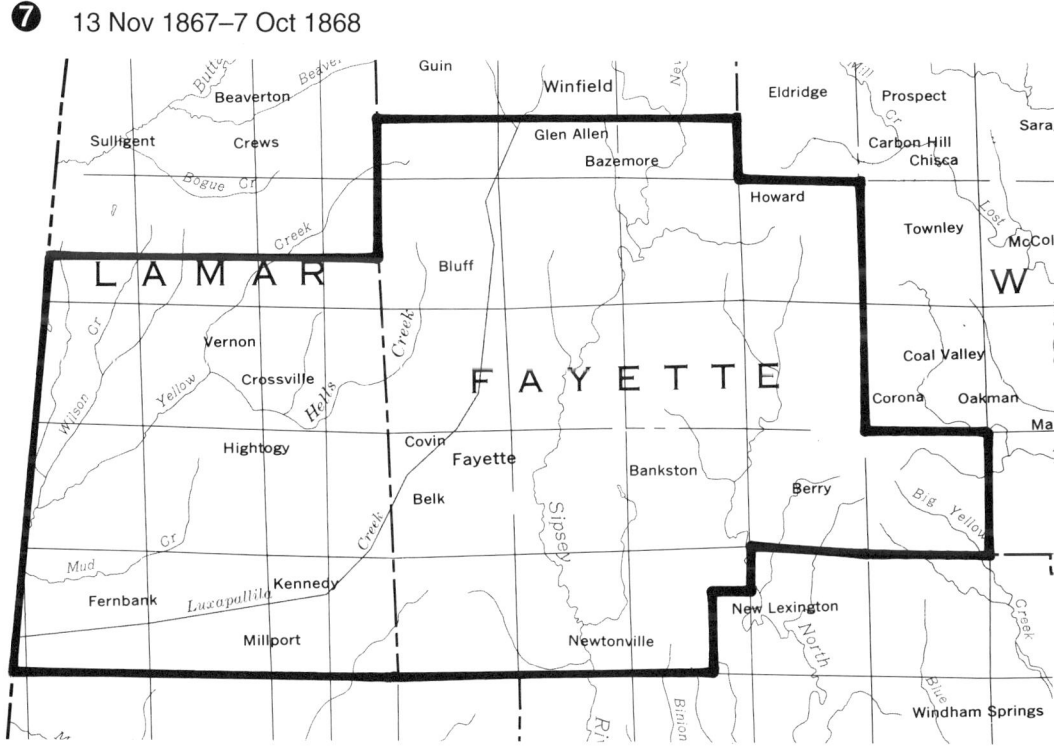

176 ALABAMA

Chronology of FELICIANA (La., extinct)

Map	Date	Event	Resulting Area
❶	7 Dec 1810	Created by Orleans Territory from non-county area; included parts of present Louisiana, Mississippi, and Alabama. Spain actually controlled part of the area	15,000 sq mi
	30 Apr 1812	Eliminated from present Alabama when Louisiana was admitted to the Union	

(Heavy line depicts historical boundary. Base map shows present-day information.)

❶ 7 Dec 1810–29 Apr 1812

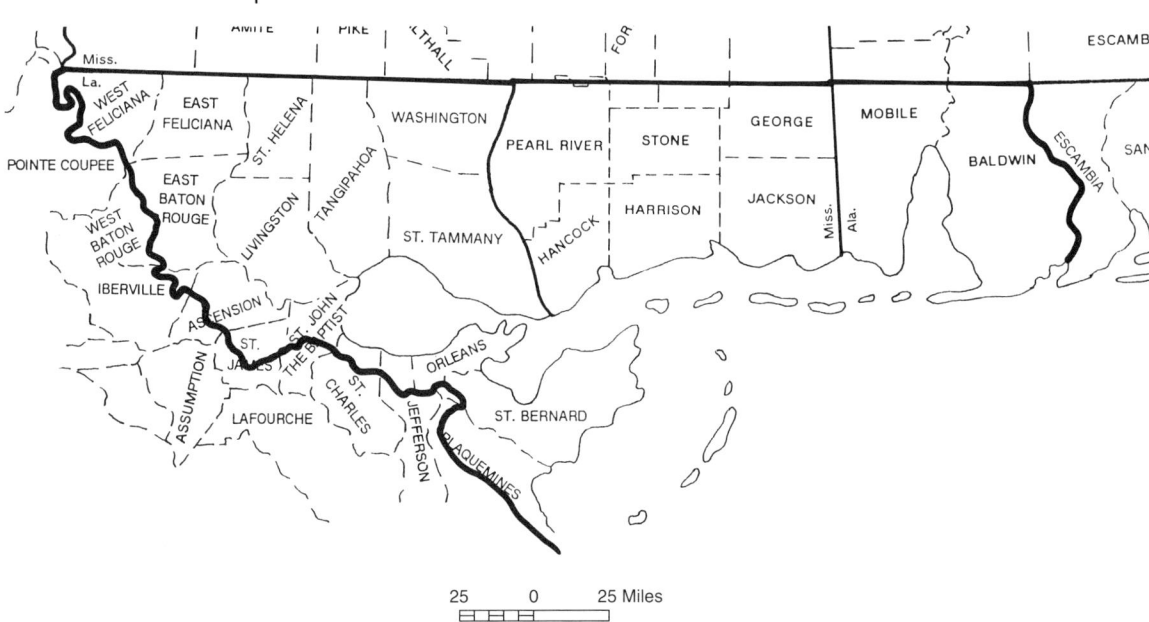

Chronology of FRANKLIN

Map	Date	Event	Resulting Area
❶	6 Feb 1818	Created from MONTGOMERY and non-county area	630 sq mi
	9 Feb 1818	County boundary line in Tennessee R. adjusted to run in middle of stream [not mapped]	
	21 Nov 1818	Southern boundary clarified [no change]	
❷	17 Dec 1819	Non-county area belonging to Chickasaw Indians attached to FRANKLIN	

(Heavy line depicts historical boundary. Base map shows present-day information.)

❶ 6 Feb 1818–20 Jan 1832

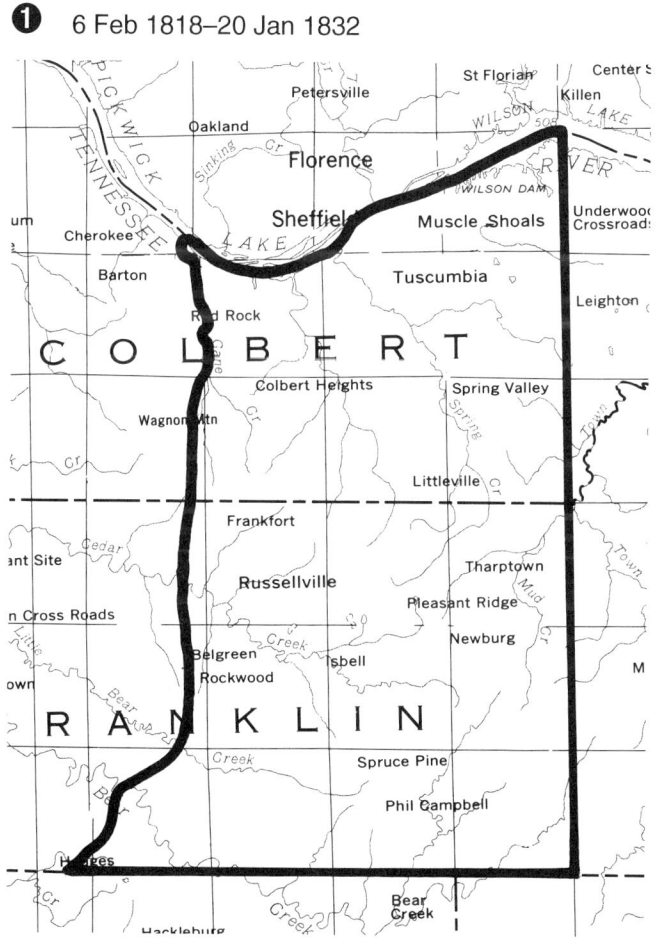

❷ 17 Dec 1819–18 Dec 1820

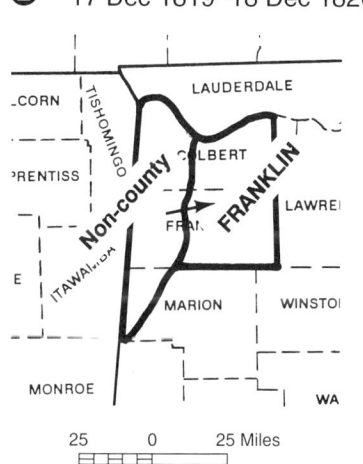

178 ALABAMA

Chronology of FRANKLIN

Map	Date	Event	Resulting Area
❸	19 Dec 1820	Lost part of non-county attachment to MARION	
❹	21 Jan 1832	Gained non-county attachment	1,190 sq mi
	18 Dec 1832	Boundaries redefined [no change]	

(Heavy line depicts historical boundary. Base map shows present-day information.)

❸ 19 Dec 1820–
20 Jan 1832

❹ 21 Jan 1832–5 Feb 1867
29 Nov 1867–23 Jan 1870

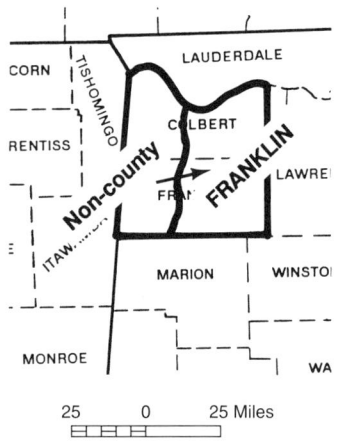

Chronology of FRANKLIN

Map	Date	Event	Resulting Area
❺	6 Feb 1867	Lost to creation of COLBERT	600 sq mi
❹	29 Nov 1867	Gained all of COLBERT; COLBERT eliminated	1,190 sq mi
❺	24 Jan 1870	Lost to re-creation of COLBERT	600 sq mi
❺	29 Jan 1875	Exchanged small areas with COLBERT	600 sq mi
❻	6 Feb 1895	Gained from COLBERT	640 sq mi

(Heavy line depicts historical boundary. Base map shows present-day information.)

❺ 6 Feb 1867–28 Nov 1867
24 Jan 1870–5 Feb 1895

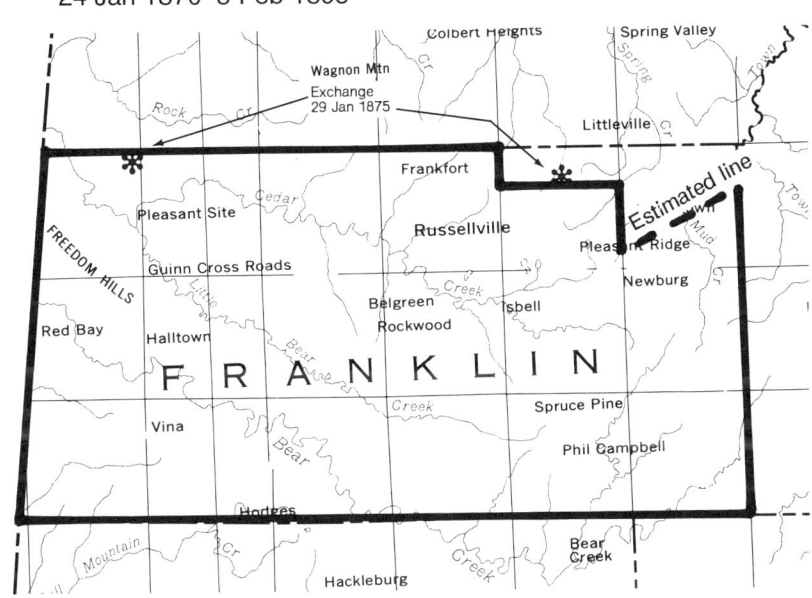

❻ 6 Feb 1895–1990

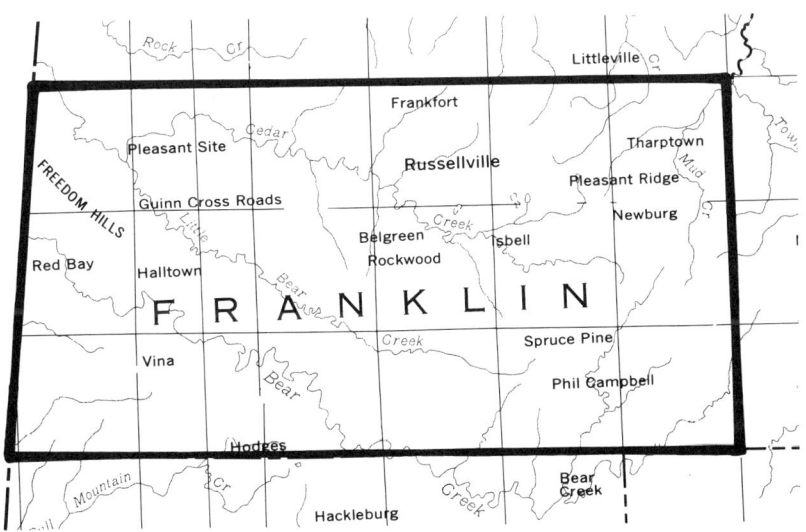

ALABAMA

Chronology of GENEVA

Map	Date	Event	Resulting Area
❶	26 Dec 1868	Created from COFFEE, DALE, and HENRY. Strip of territory along the state line inadvertently omitted from formal definition of GENEVA [mistake corrected 11 Feb 1870]	670 sq mi
	11 Feb 1870	Southern boundary clarified to match state line, correcting mistake of 26 Dec 1868 [no change]	
❶	15 Feb 1871	Lost small area to COFFEE to accommodate local property owner	670 sq mi
	13 Feb 1879	Name change to GORDON authorized, dependent on local referendum; no evidence that required election was held [no change]. Gain from HENRY and loss to COFFEE authorized, dependent on local referendum; no evidence that required election was held [no change]	
❷	9 Feb 1903	Lost to creation of HOUSTON	580 sq mi

(Heavy line depicts historical boundary. Base map shows present-day information.)

❶ 26 Dec 1868–8 Feb 1903

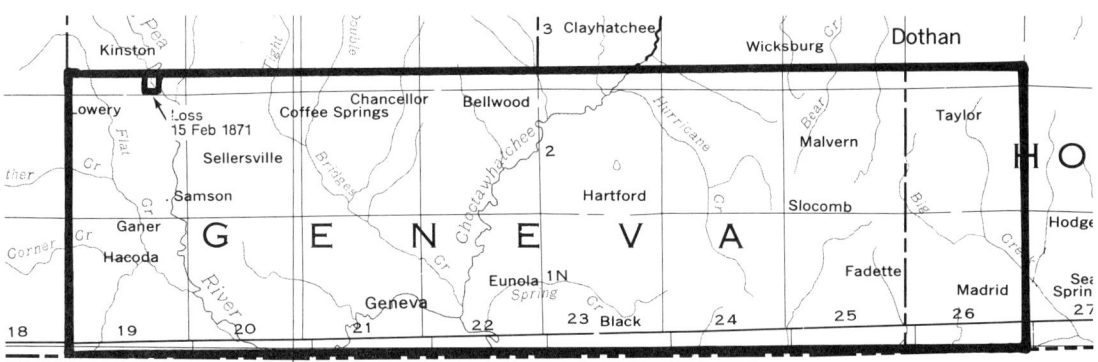

❷ 9 Feb 1903–1990

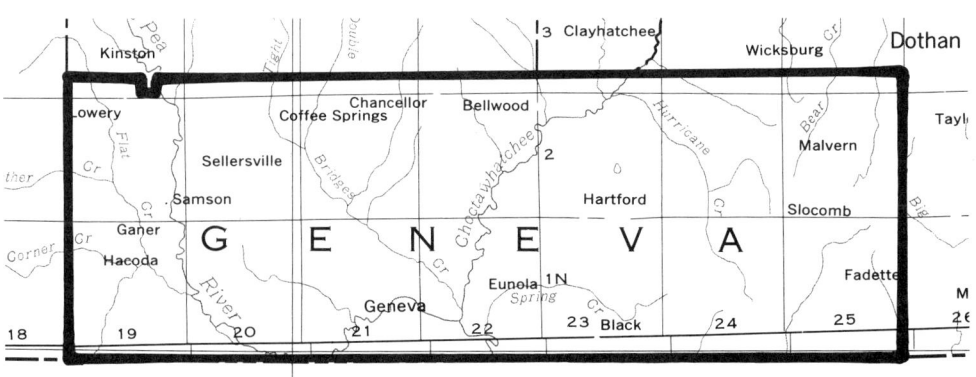

Chronology of GREENE (Miss.)

Map	Date	Event	Resulting Area
❶	9 Dec 1811	Created by Mississippi Territory from WAYNE (Miss.); included part of present Alabama	1,860 sq mi
	3 Mar 1817	Eliminated from present Alabama when Alabama Territory was created; eastern end fell within Alabama Territory and became non-county area	
	7 Feb 1818	Remnant in Alabama Territory was added to BALDWIN	

(Heavy line depicts historical boundary. Base map shows present-day information.)

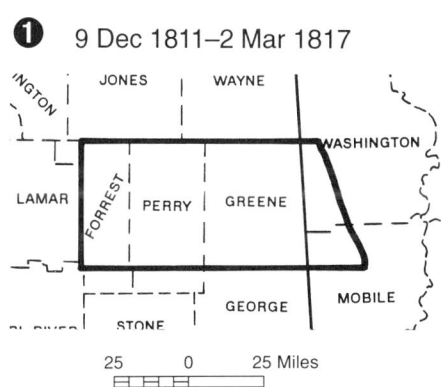

❶ 9 Dec 1811–2 Mar 1817

ALABAMA

Chronology of GREENE

Map	Date	Event	Resulting Area
❶	13 Dec 1819	Created from MARENGO and TUSCALOOSA	950 sq mi

(Heavy line depicts historical boundary. Base map shows present-day information.)

❶ 13 Dec 1819–19 Dec 1820

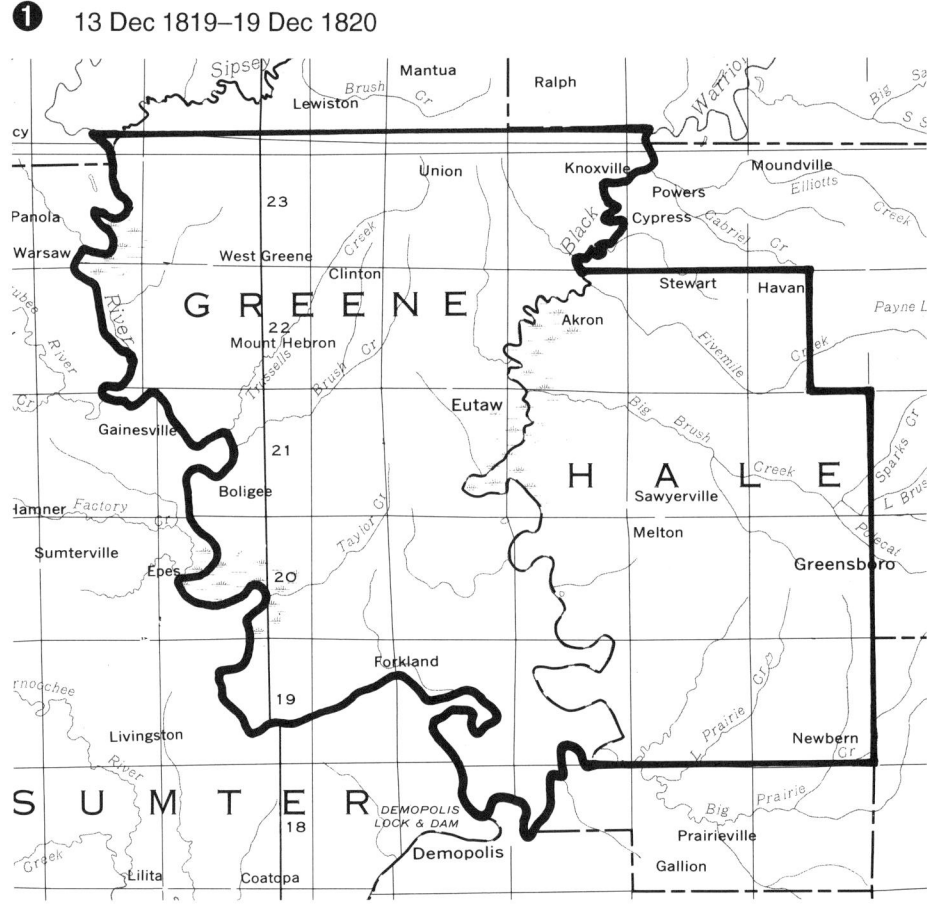

Chronology of GREENE

Map	Date	Event	Resulting Area
❷	20 Dec 1820	Gained from PERRY	980 sq mi
❷	21 Jan 1832	Gained narrow strip all along PICKENS boundary [not mapped]; lost small areas to PICKENS and TUSCALOOSA	980 sq mi
❷	14 Feb 1843	Gained from PICKENS	990 sq mi
	3 Oct 1864	Gained small area from TUSCALOOSA to accommodate local property owner [location unknown, not mapped]	

(Heavy line depicts historical boundary. Base map shows present-day information.)

❷ 20 Dec 1820–29 Jan 1867

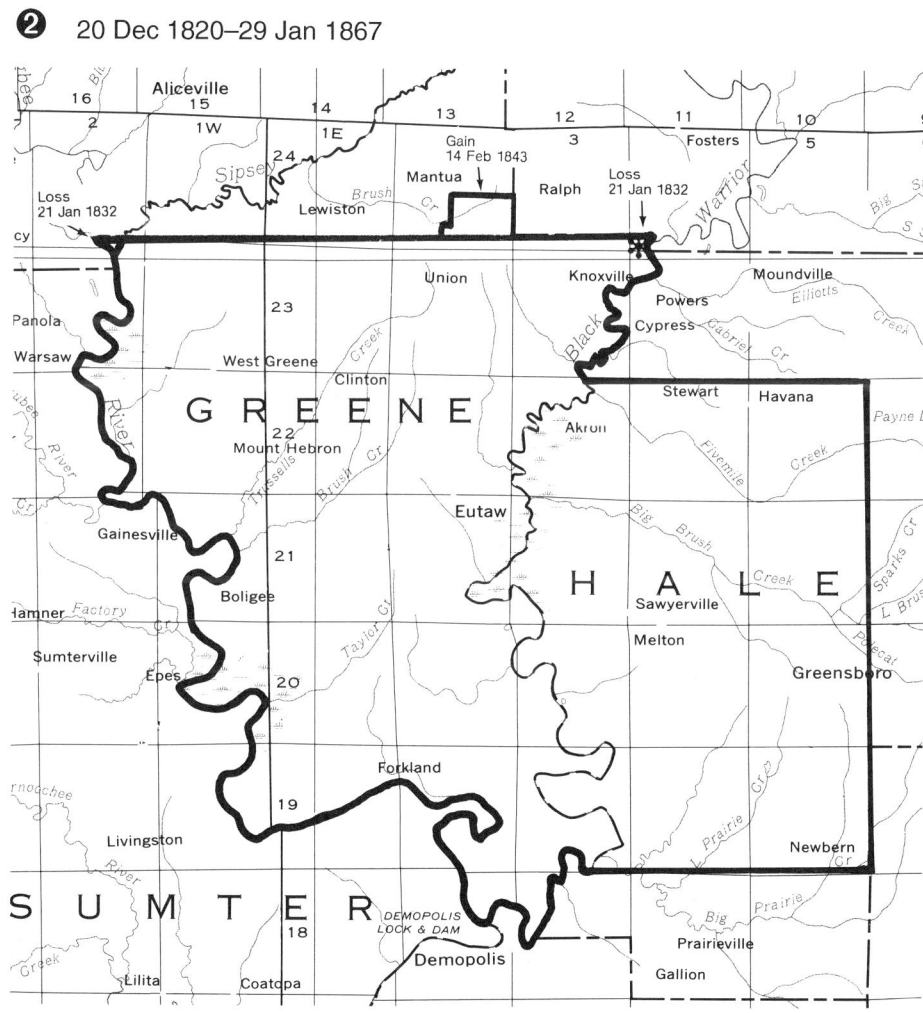

184 ALABAMA

Chronology of GREENE

Map	Date	Event	Resulting Area
❸	30 Jan 1867	Gained from PICKENS, lost to creation of HALE	660 sq mi
	28 Feb 1881	Lost to HALE when boundary line was moved from east bank to middle of Black Warrior R. [not mapped]	

(Heavy line depicts historical boundary. Base map shows present-day information.)

❸ 30 Jan 1867–1990

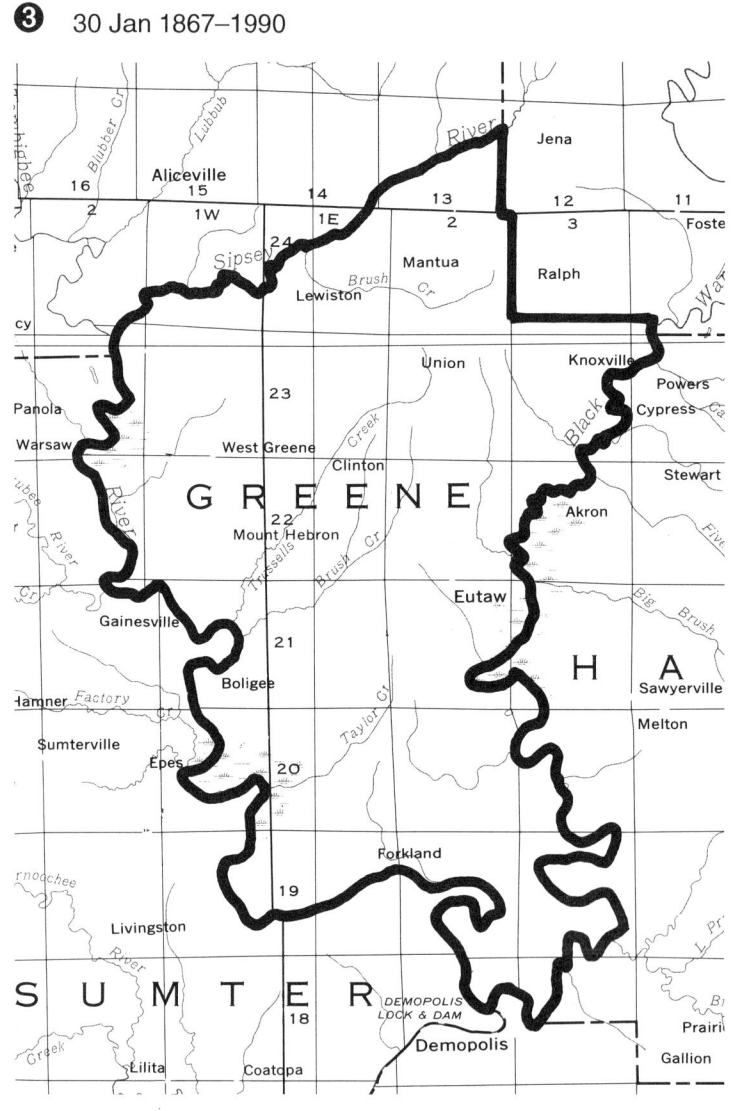

Chronology of HALE

Map	Date	Event	Resulting Area
❶	30 Jan 1867	Created from GREENE, MARENGO, PERRY, and TUSCALOOSA	640 sq mi
❶	7 Feb 1870	Lost small area to MARENGO	640 sq mi
❷	13 Jan 1877	Gained from PERRY	660 sq mi
	28 Feb 1881	Gained from GREENE when boundary line was moved from east bank to middle of Black Warrior R. [not mapped]	

(Heavy line depicts historical boundary. Base map shows present-day information.)

❶ 30 Jan 1867–12 Jan 1877

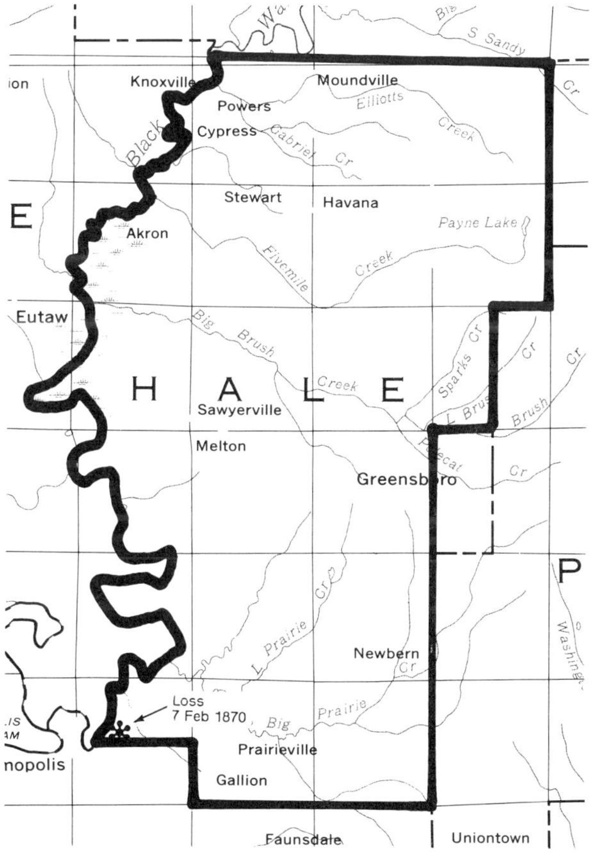

❷ 13 Jan 1877–1990

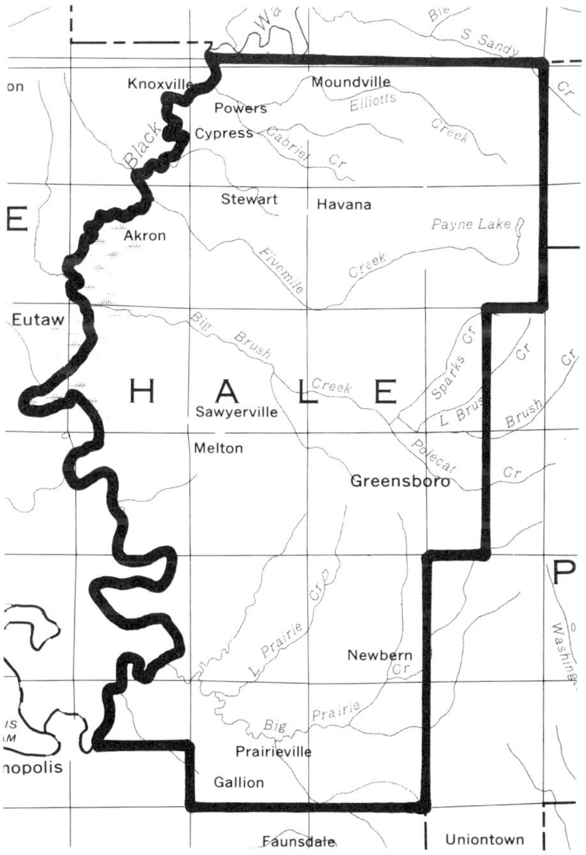

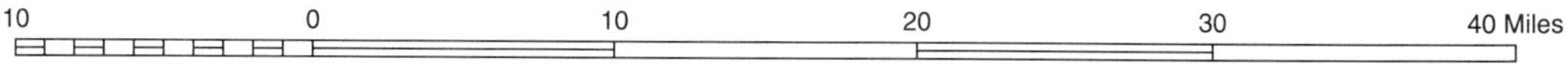

ALABAMA

Chronology of HENRY

Map	Date	Event	Resulting Area
❶	13 Dec 1819	Created from CONECUH	5,470 sq mi

(Heavy line depicts historical boundary. Base map shows present-day information.)

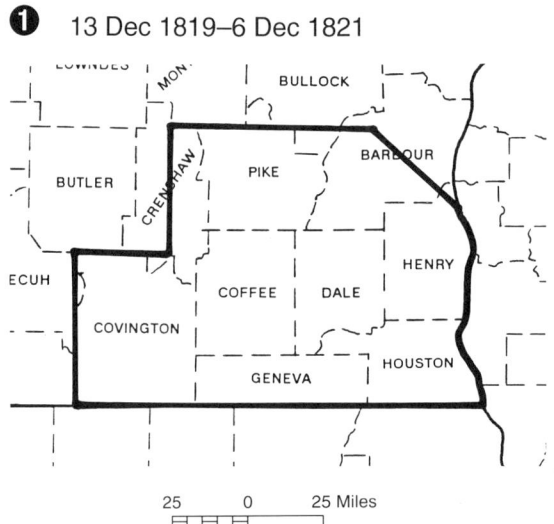

❶ 13 Dec 1819–6 Dec 1821

Individual County Chronologies 187

Chronology of HENRY

Map	Date	Event	Resulting Area
❷	7 Dec 1821	Lost to creation of both COVINGTON and PIKE	2,360 sq mi

(Heavy line depicts historical boundary. Base map shows present-day information.)

❷ 7 Dec 1821–16 Oct 1825

ALABAMA

Chronology of HENRY

Map	Date	Event	Resulting Area
❸	17 Oct 1825	Lost to creation of DALE	1,230 sq mi
❹	4 Jan 1826	Lost to DALE	990 sq mi

(Heavy line depicts historical boundary. Base map shows present-day information.)

❸ 17 Oct 1825–3 Jan 1826

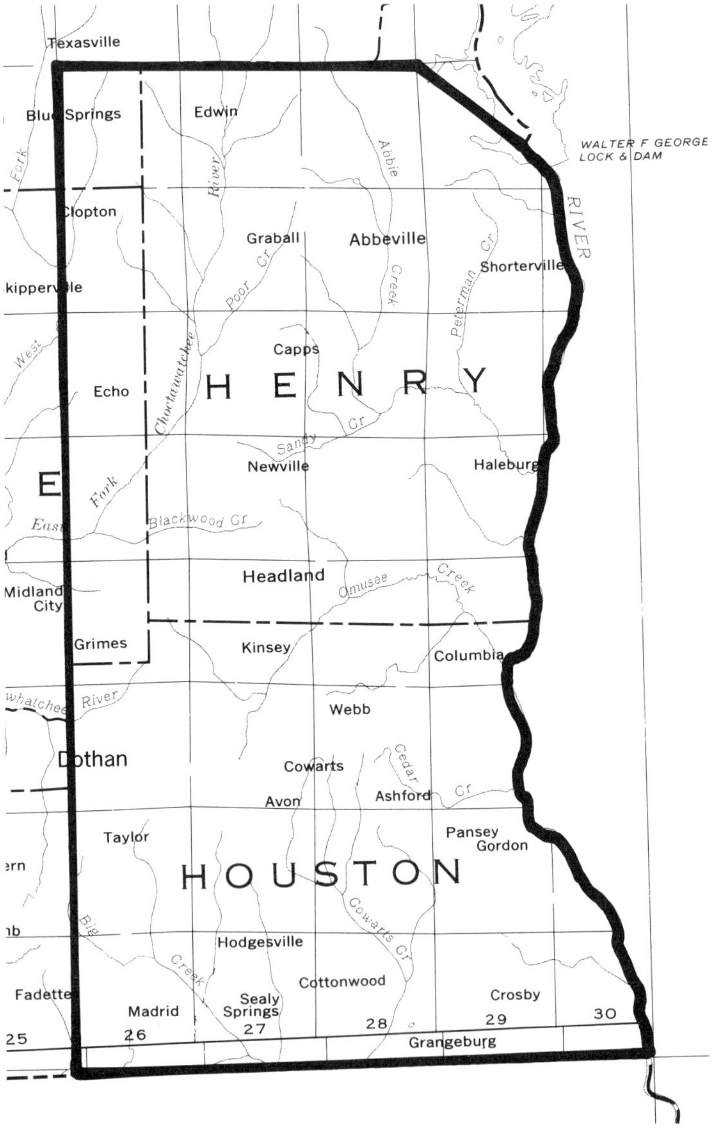

❹ 4 Jan 1826–27 Dec 1831

Chronology of HENRY

Map	Date	Event	Resulting Area
❺	28 Dec 1831	Gained from PIKE	1,020 sq mi
	15 Dec 1832	Boundary with PIKE clarified [no change]	
❺	17 Jan 1844	Gained from BARBOUR	1,020 sq mi
❻	26 Dec 1868	Lost to creation of GENEVA	1,000 sq mi
	13 Feb 1879	GENEVA authorized to gain from HENRY, dependent on local referendum; no evidence that required election was held [no change]	

(Heavy line depicts historical boundary. Base map shows present-day information.)

❺ 28 Dec 1831–25 Dec 1868

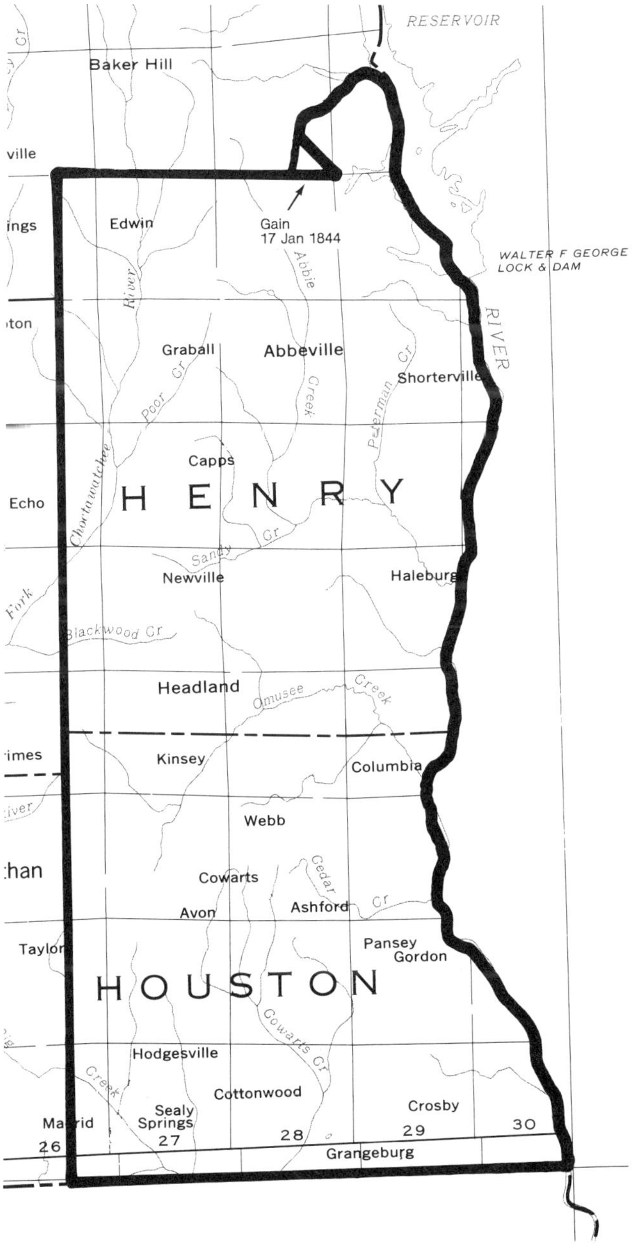

❻ 26 Dec 1868–8 Feb 1903

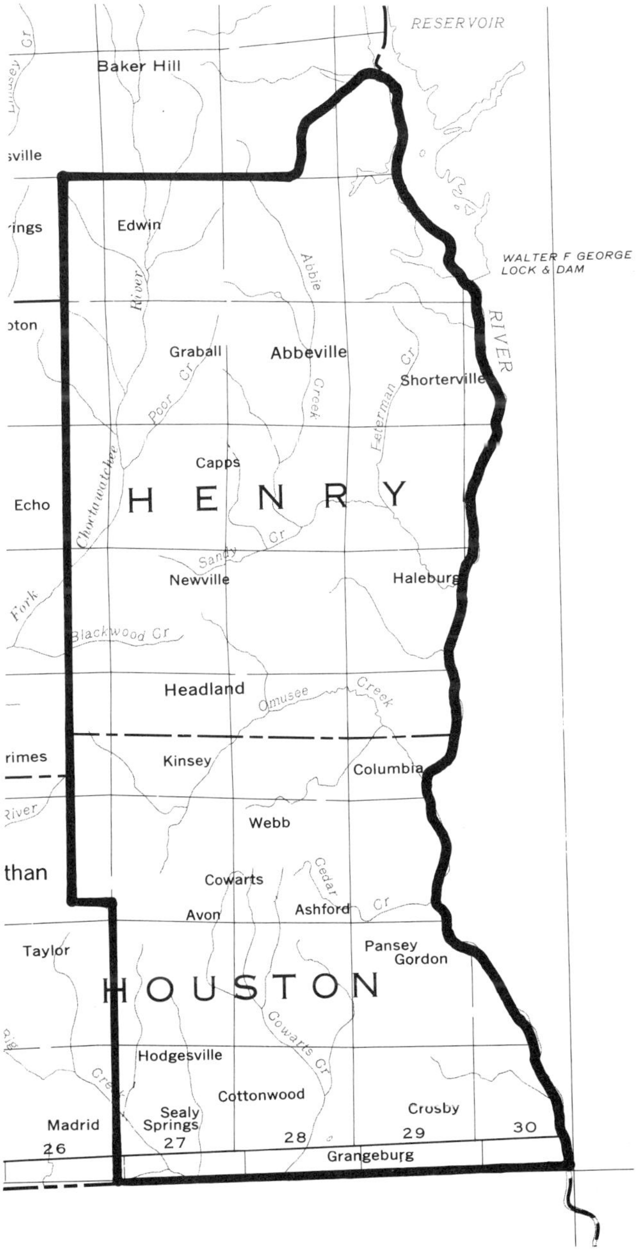

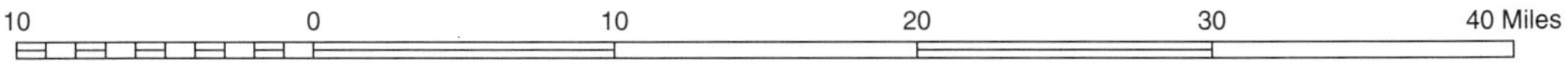

ALABAMA

Chronology of HENRY

Map	Date	Event	Resulting Area
❼	9 Feb 1903	Lost to creation of HOUSTON	570 sq mi

(Heavy line depicts historical boundary. Base map shows present-day information.)

❼ 9 Feb 1903–1990

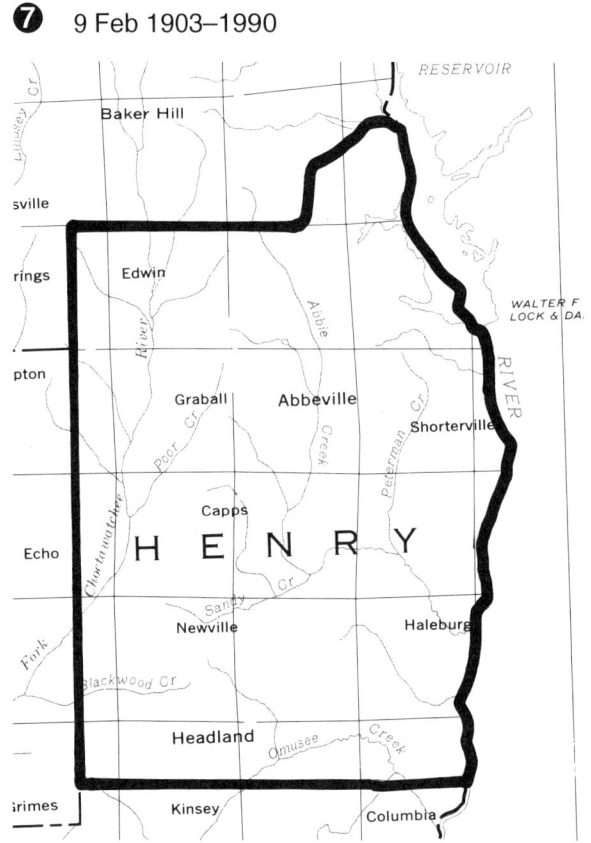

Chronology of HOUSTON

Map	Date	Event	Resulting Area
❶	9 Feb 1903	Created from DALE, GENEVA, and HENRY	590 sq mi

(Heavy line depicts historical boundary. Base map shows present-day information.)

❶ 9 Feb 1903–1990

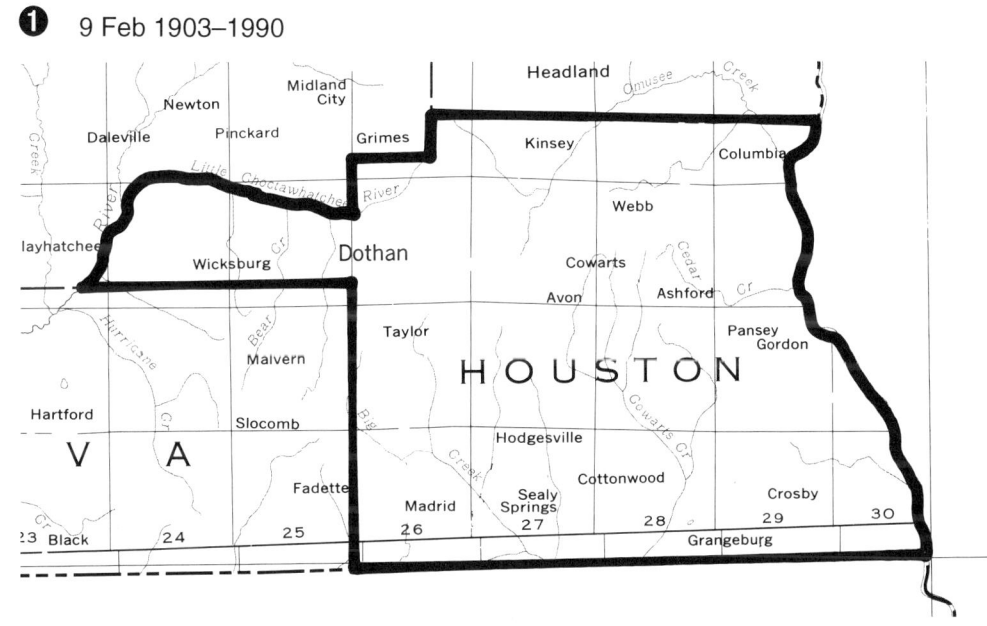

Chronology of JACKSON (Miss.)

Map	Date	Event	Resulting Area
❶	18 Dec 1812	Created by Mississippi Territory from MOBILE; included part of present Alabama; not fully controlled by the United States	1,720 sq mi
	15 Apr 1813	American forces captured city of Mobile from Spain, effectively adding to the United States the territory between the Pearl and Perdido rivers previously claimed by the United States as part of Louisiana and where JACKSON (Miss.) had been created	
	3 Mar 1817	Eliminated from present Alabama when Alabama Territory was created; eastern end fell within Alabama Territory and became non-county area	
	7 Feb 1818	Remnant in Alabama Territory added to MOBILE	

(Heavy line depicts historical boundary. Base map shows present-day information.)

❶ 18 Dec 1812–2 Mar 1817

Individual County Chronologies 193

Chronology of JACKSON

Map	Date	Event	Resulting Area
❶	13 Dec 1819	Created from non-county area	1,130 sq mi
❷	27 Nov 1821	Most of non-county area detached from MORGAN, attached to JACKSON	

(Heavy line depicts historical boundary. Base map shows present-day information.)

❶ 13 Dec 1819–6 Dec 1821
28 Dec 1825–5 Jan 1826

❷ 27 Nov 1821–6 Dec 1821
28 Dec 1825–20 Jan 1832

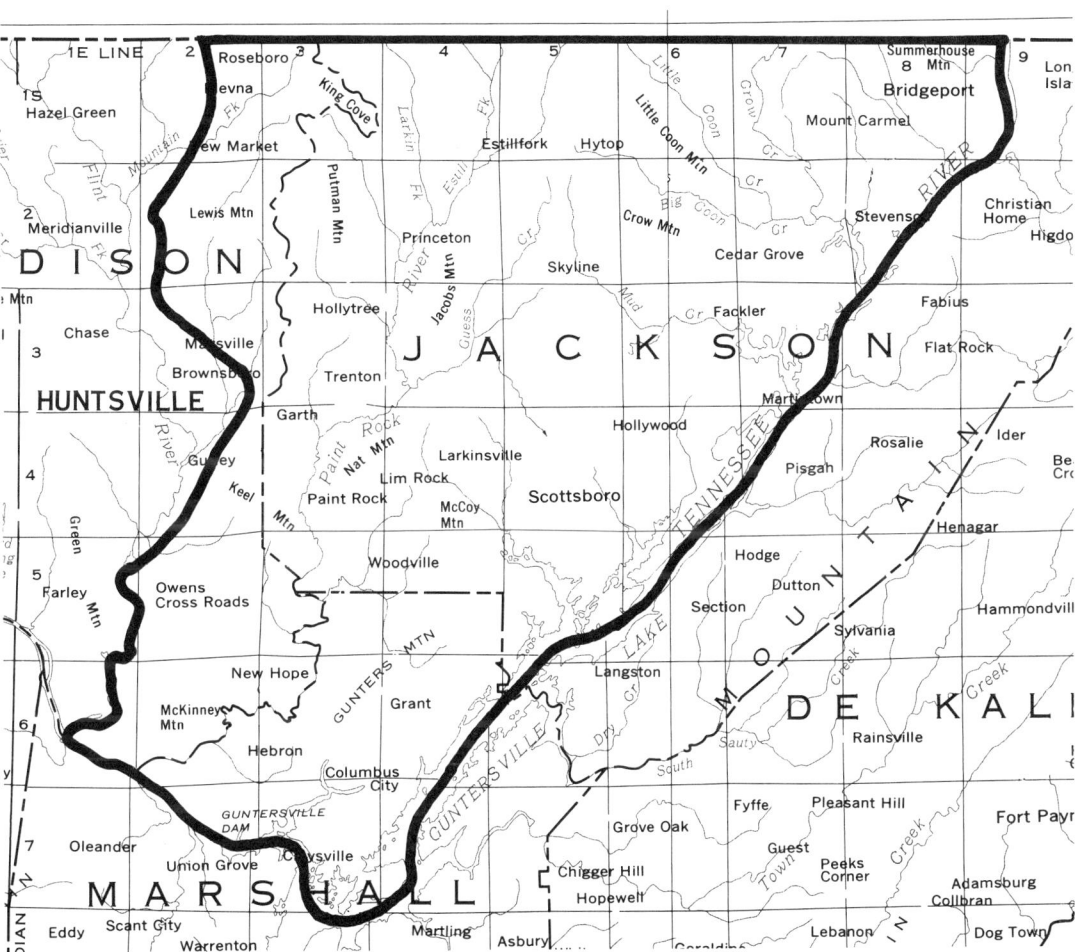
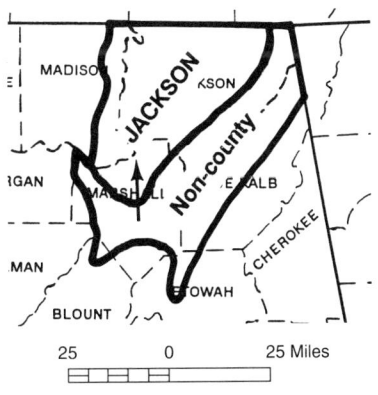

194 ALABAMA

Chronology of JACKSON

Map	Date	Event	Resulting Area
❸	7 Dec 1821	Lost to creation of DECATUR Non-county area detached, attached to DECATUR	600 sq mi
❹ ❺	31 Dec 1822	Exchanged with DECATUR Northern part of non-county area detached from DECATUR, attached to JACKSON	520 sq mi

(Heavy line depicts historical boundary. Base map shows present-day information.)

❺ 31 Dec 1822–27 Dec 1825

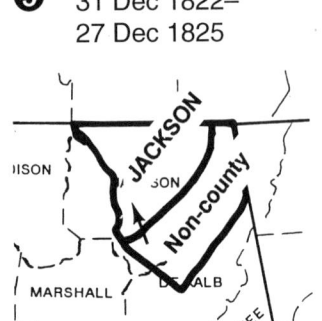

❸ 7 Dec 1821–30 Dec 1822

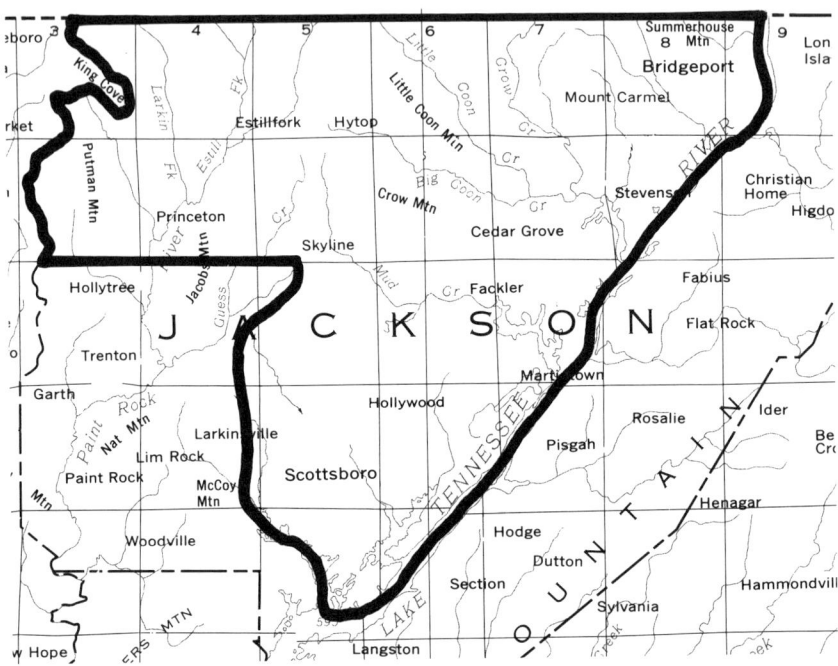

❹ 31 Dec 1822–27 Dec 1825

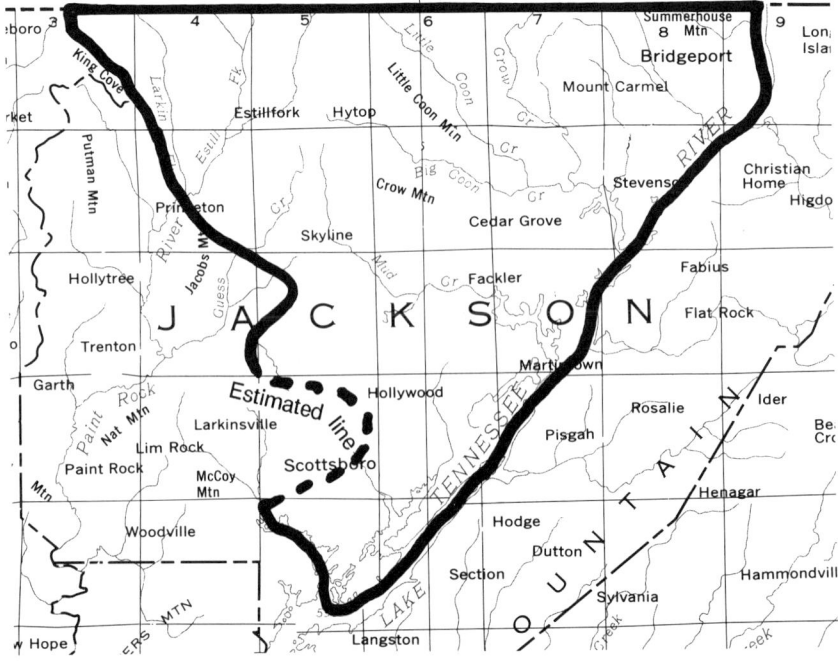

Chronology of JACKSON

Map	Date	Event	Resulting Area
❶ ❷	28 Dec 1825	Gained all of DECATUR; DECATUR eliminated. Non-county area formerly attached to DECATUR now attached to JACKSON	1,130 sq mi
❻	6 Jan 1826	Lost to MADISON [attachment unchanged; see map 2]	960 sq mi

(Heavy line depicts historical boundary. Base map shows present-day information.)

❻ 6 Jan 1826–20 Jan 1832

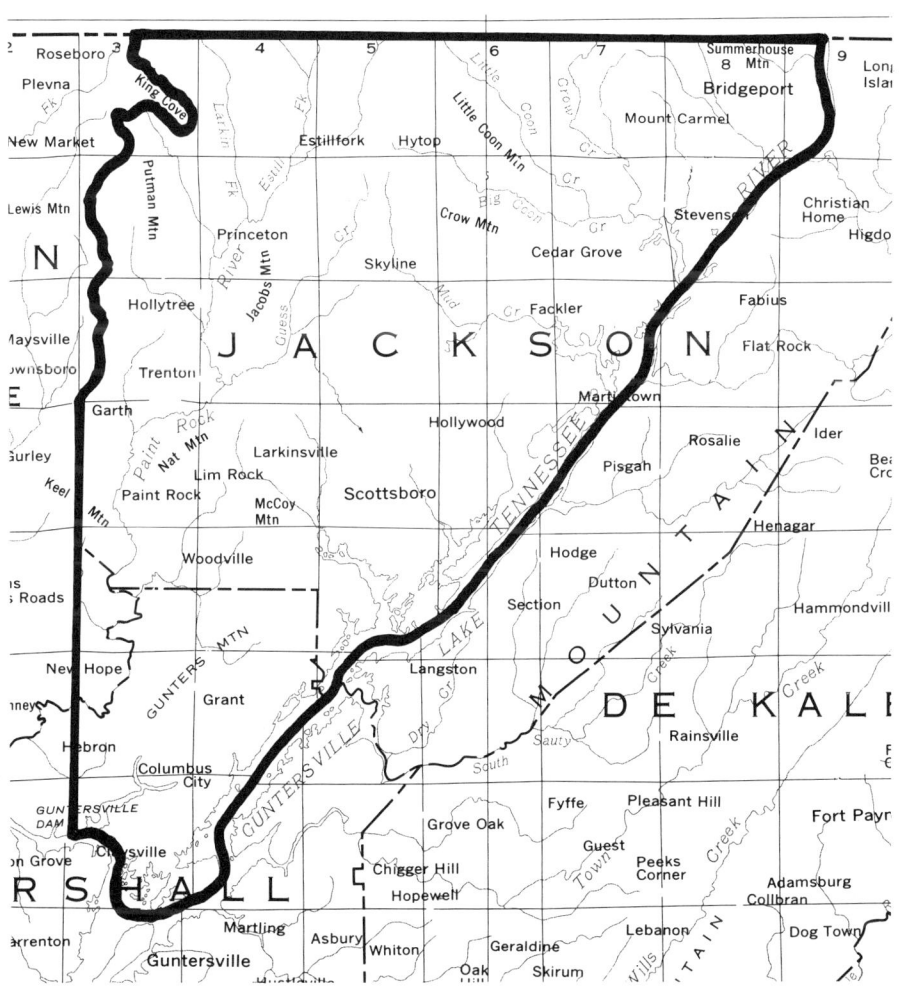

ALABAMA

Chronology of JACKSON

Map	Date	Event	Resulting Area
❼	21 Jan 1832	Gained part of non-county attachment; lost remaining non-county attachment to BLOUNT, MORGAN, and ST. CLAIR	1,550 sq mi

(Heavy line depicts historical boundary. Base map shows present-day information.)

❼ 21 Jan 1832–13 Jan 1834

Individual County Chronologies 197

Chronology of JACKSON

Map	Date	Event	Resulting Area
❽	14 Jan 1834	Gained from ST. CLAIR	2,330 sq mi

(Heavy line depicts historical boundary. Base map shows present-day information.)

❽ 14 Jan 1834–8 Jan 1836

Chronology of JACKSON

Map	Date	Event	Resulting Area
⑨	9 Jan 1836	Lost to MADISON and to creation of CHEROKEE, DE KALB, and MARSHALL	1,190 sq mi
	7 Feb 1843	Boundary with DE KALB adjusted [location unknown, not mapped]	

(Heavy line depicts historical boundary. Base map shows present-day information.)

⑨ 9 Jan 1836–2 Mar 1848

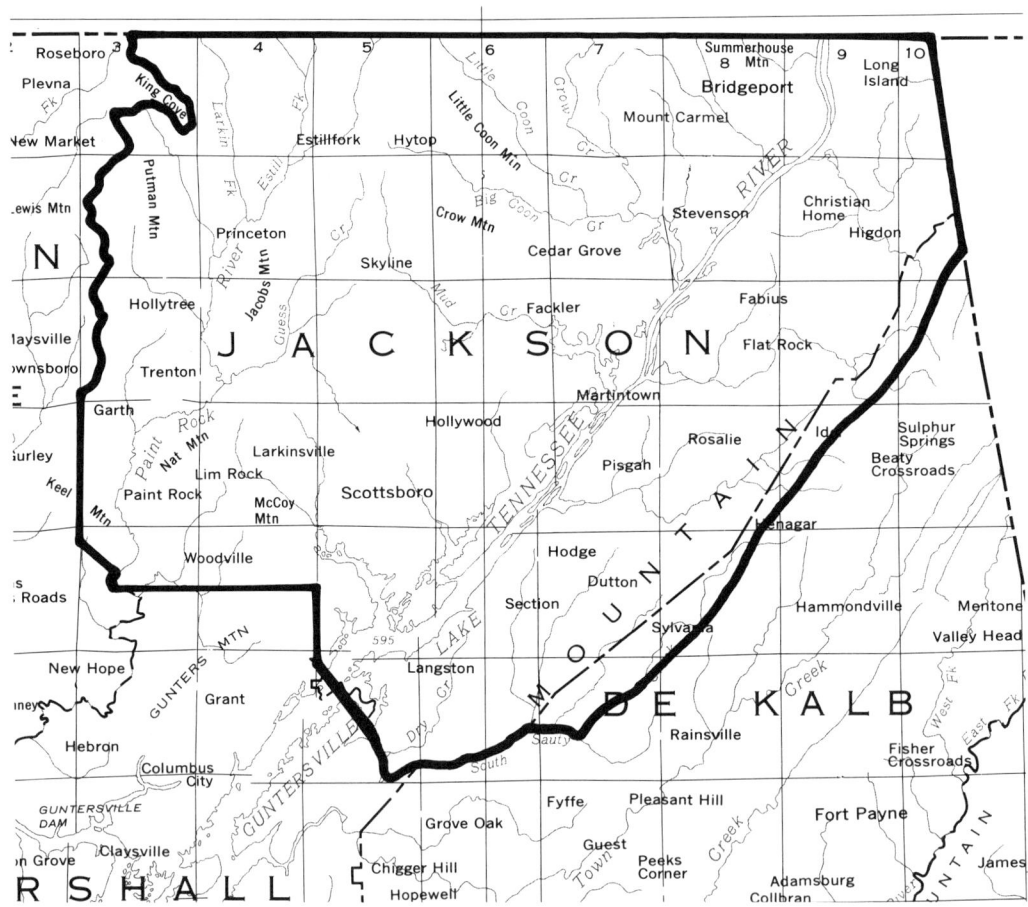

Chronology of JACKSON

Map	Date	Event	Resulting Area
⑩	3 Mar 1848	Gained from DE KALB	1,230 sq mi
⑩	5 Feb 1852	Gained small area from MARSHALL	1,230 sq mi

(Heavy line depicts historical boundary. Base map shows present-day information.)

⑩   3 Mar 1848–14 Feb 1854

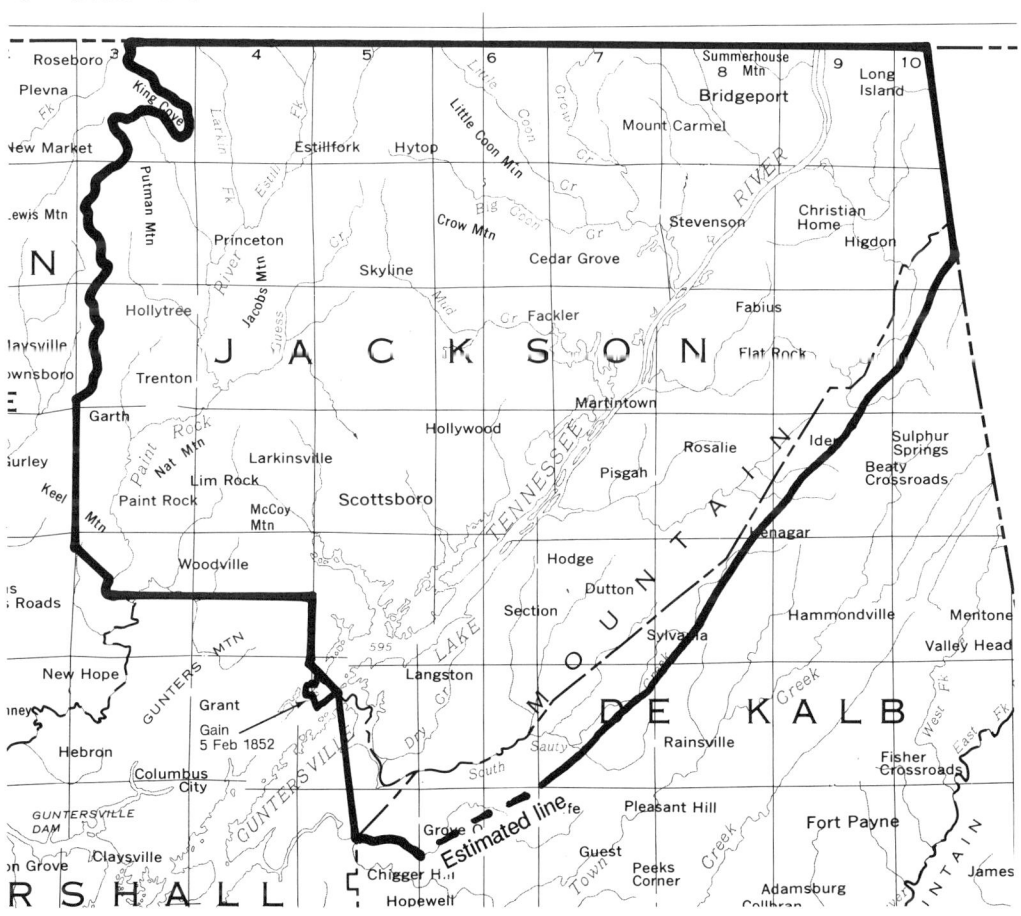

Chronology of JACKSON

Map	Date	Event	Resulting Area
⑪	15 Feb 1854	Lost to DE KALB	1,190 sq mi
⑪	2 Feb 1858	Lost small area to DE KALB to accommodate local property owner	1,190 sq mi

(Heavy line depicts historical boundary. Base map shows present-day information.)

⑪ 15 Feb 1854–24 Feb 1860

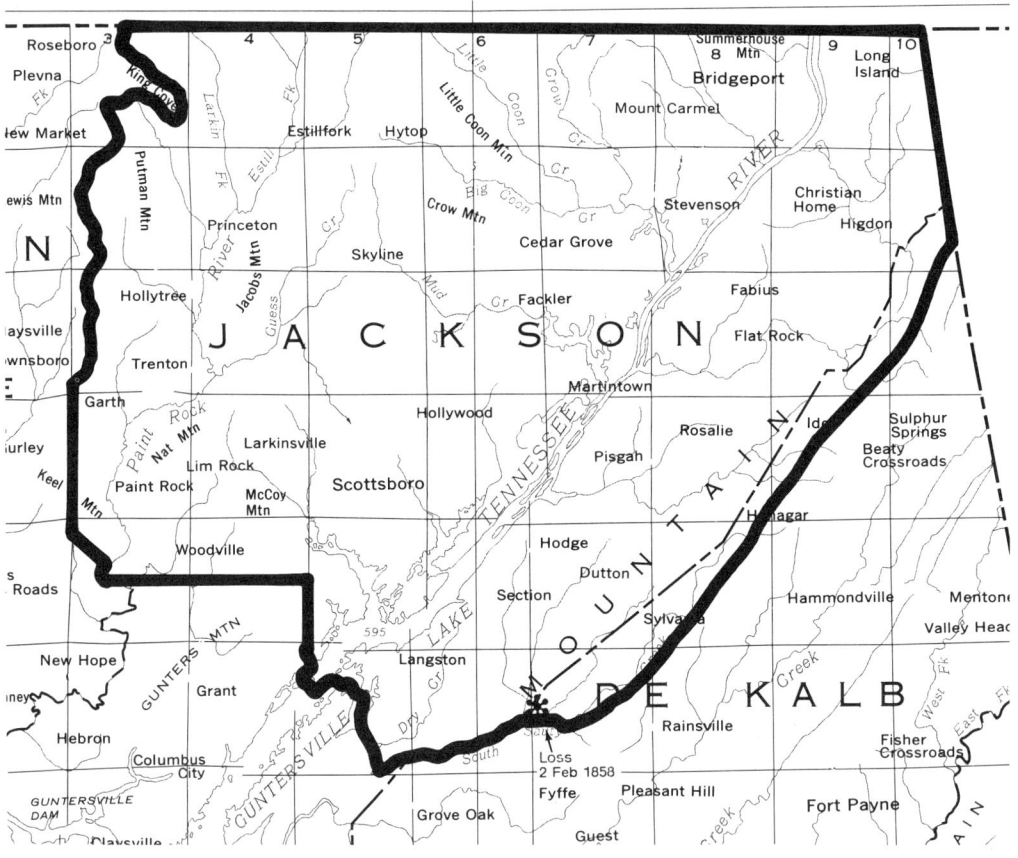

Individual County Chronologies 201

Chronology of JACKSON

Map	Date	Event	Resulting Area
⑫	25 Feb 1860	Lost to DE KALB	1,130 sq mi
	3 Mar 1870	DE KALB authorized to gain from JACKSON, dependent on local referendum [repealed 8 Feb 1872]; no evidence that referendum was held [no change]	
	8 Feb 1872	Act of 3 Mar 1870, intended to change boundary with DE KALB, repealed [no change]	

(Heavy line depicts historical boundary. Base map shows present-day information.)

⑫ 25 Feb 1860–1990

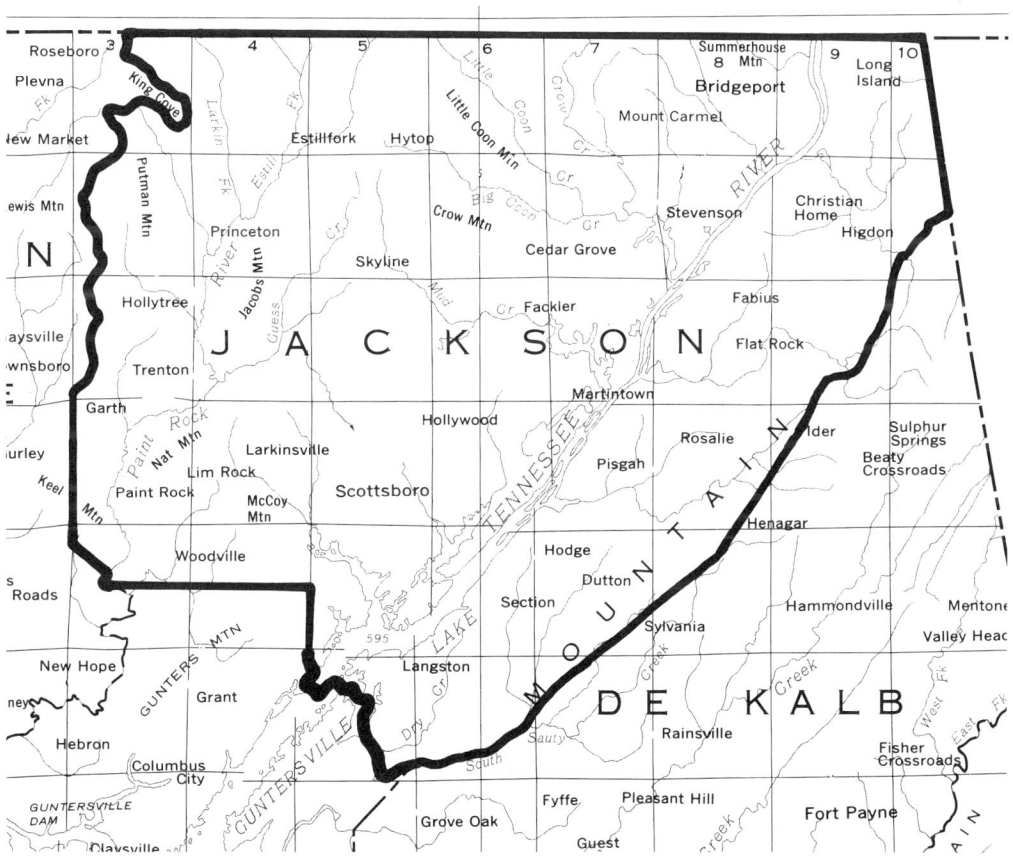

202 ALABAMA

Chronology of JEFFERSON (Miss., created as PICKERING)

Map	Date	Event	Resulting Area
❶	2 Apr 1799	Created as PICKERING by Mississippi Territory from non-county area; included part of present Alabama	19,870 sq mi
	4 Jun 1800	Lost to creation of WASHINGTON; eliminated from present Alabama	

(Heavy line depicts historical boundary. Base map shows present-day information.)

❶ 2 Apr 1799–3 Jun 1800

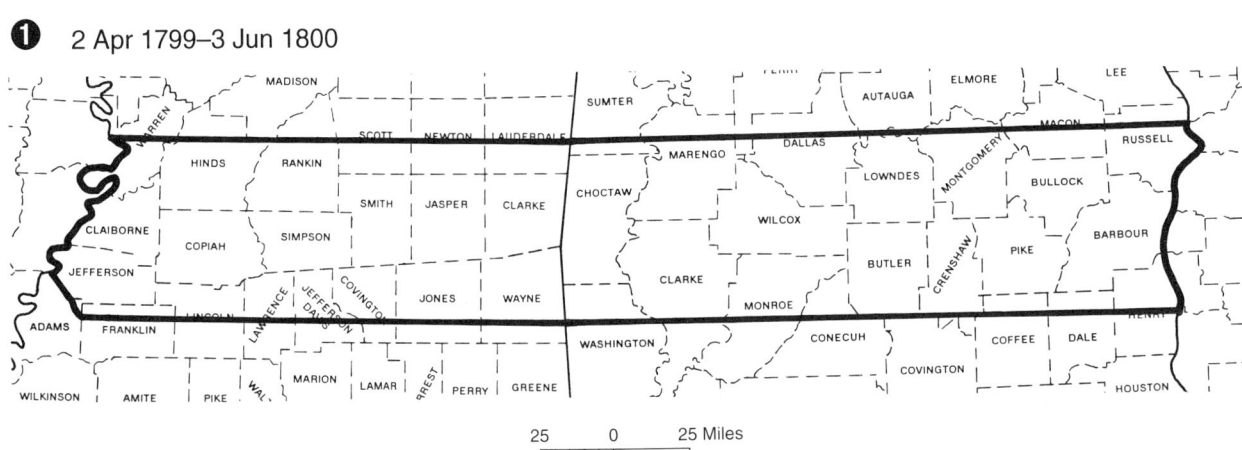

Chronology of JEFFERSON

Map	Date	Event	Resulting Area
❶	13 Dec 1819	Created from BLOUNT, ST. CLAIR, and SHELBY	1,110 sq mi

(Heavy line depicts historical boundary. Base map shows present-day information.)

❶ 13 Dec 1819–31 Mar 1821

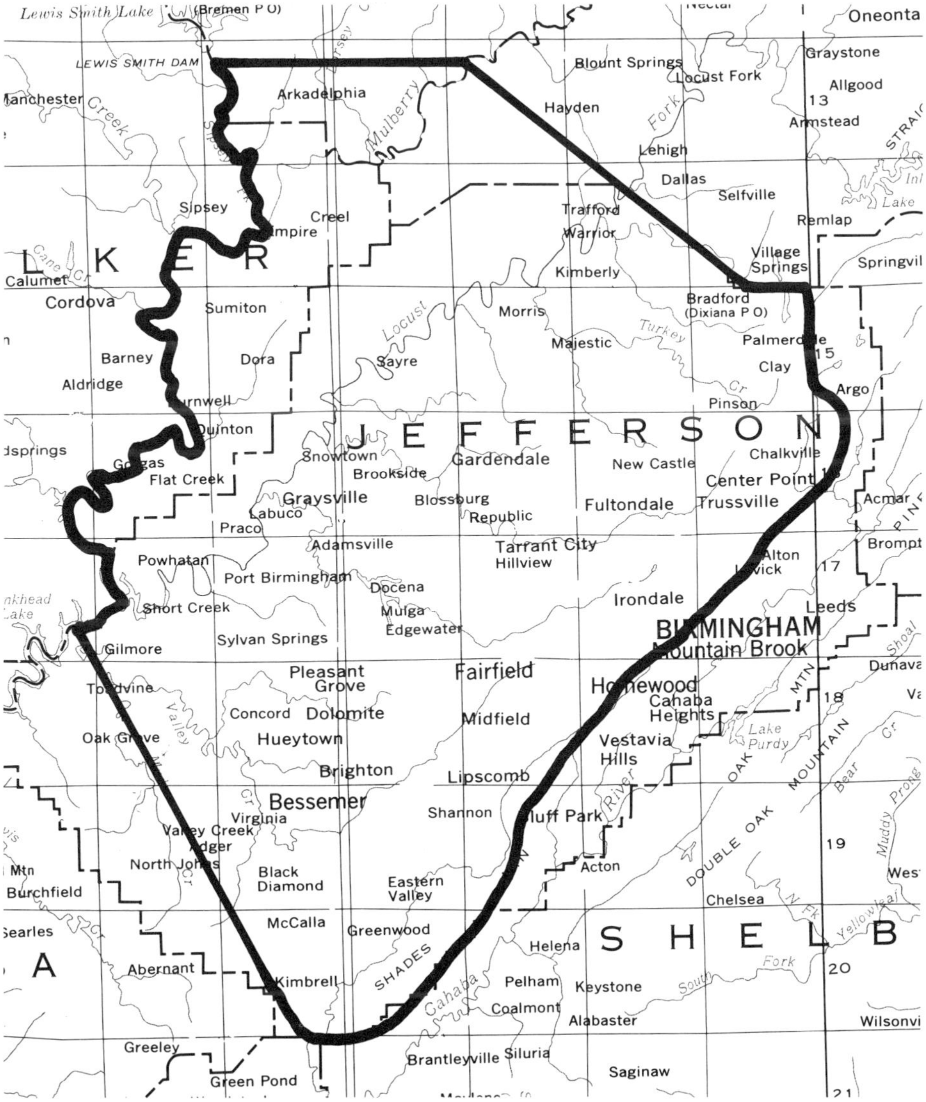

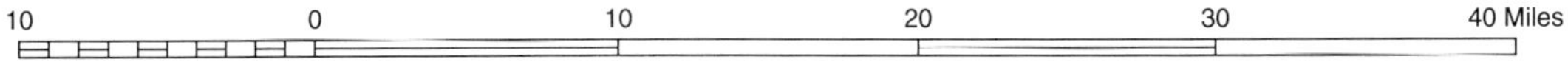

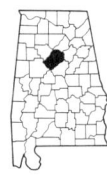

Chronology of JEFFERSON

Map	Date	Event	Resulting Area
❷	1 Apr 1821	Exchanged with ST. CLAIR	1,110 sq mi

(Heavy line depicts historical boundary. Base map shows present-day information.)

❷ 1 Apr 1821–18 Dec 1823

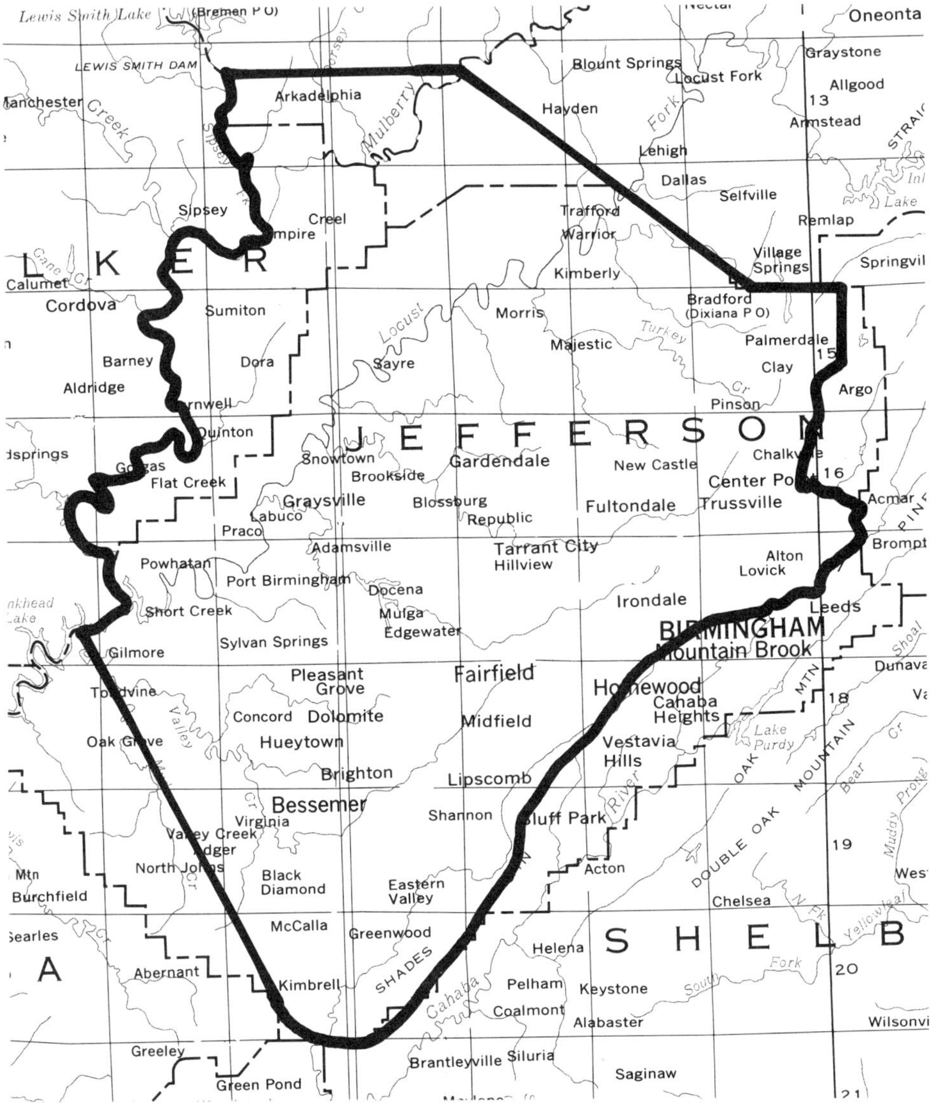

10 0 10 20 30 40 Miles

Individual County Chronologies 205

Chronology of JEFFERSON

Map	Date	Event	Resulting Area
❸	19 Dec 1823	Gained from ST. CLAIR	1,140 sq mi

(Heavy line depicts historical boundary. Base map shows present-day information.)

❸ 19 Dec 1823–25 Dec 1823

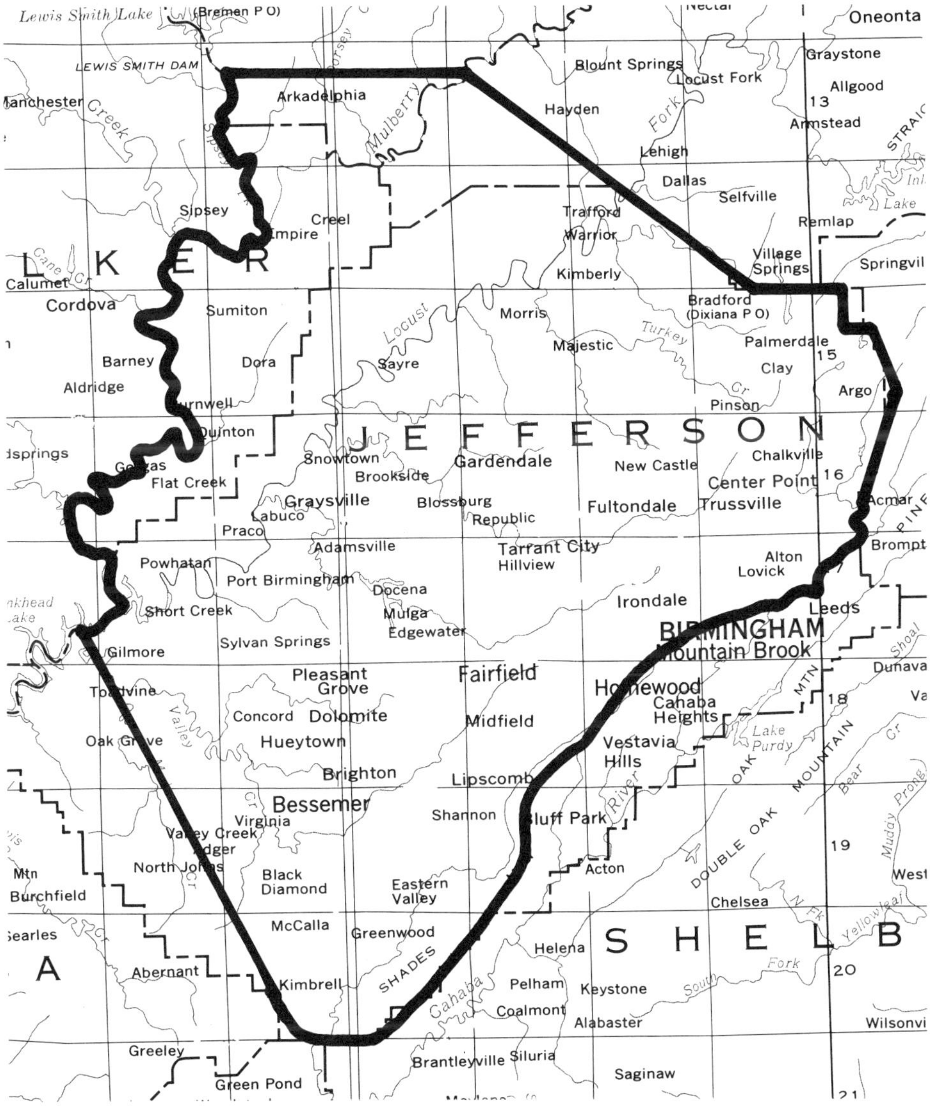

ALABAMA

Chronology of JEFFERSON

Map	Date	Event	Resulting Area
④	26 Dec 1823	Lost to creation of WALKER	930 sq mi

(Heavy line depicts historical boundary. Base map shows present-day information.)

④ 26 Dec 1823–30 Dec 1827

Chronology of JEFFERSON

Map	Date	Event	Resulting Area
❺	31 Dec 1827	Exchanged with TUSCALOOSA	950 sq mi
	15 Jan 1828	Boundary with BLOUNT clarified [no discernible change]	

(Heavy line depicts historical boundary. Base map shows present-day information.)

❺ 31 Dec 1827–c. Apr 1833

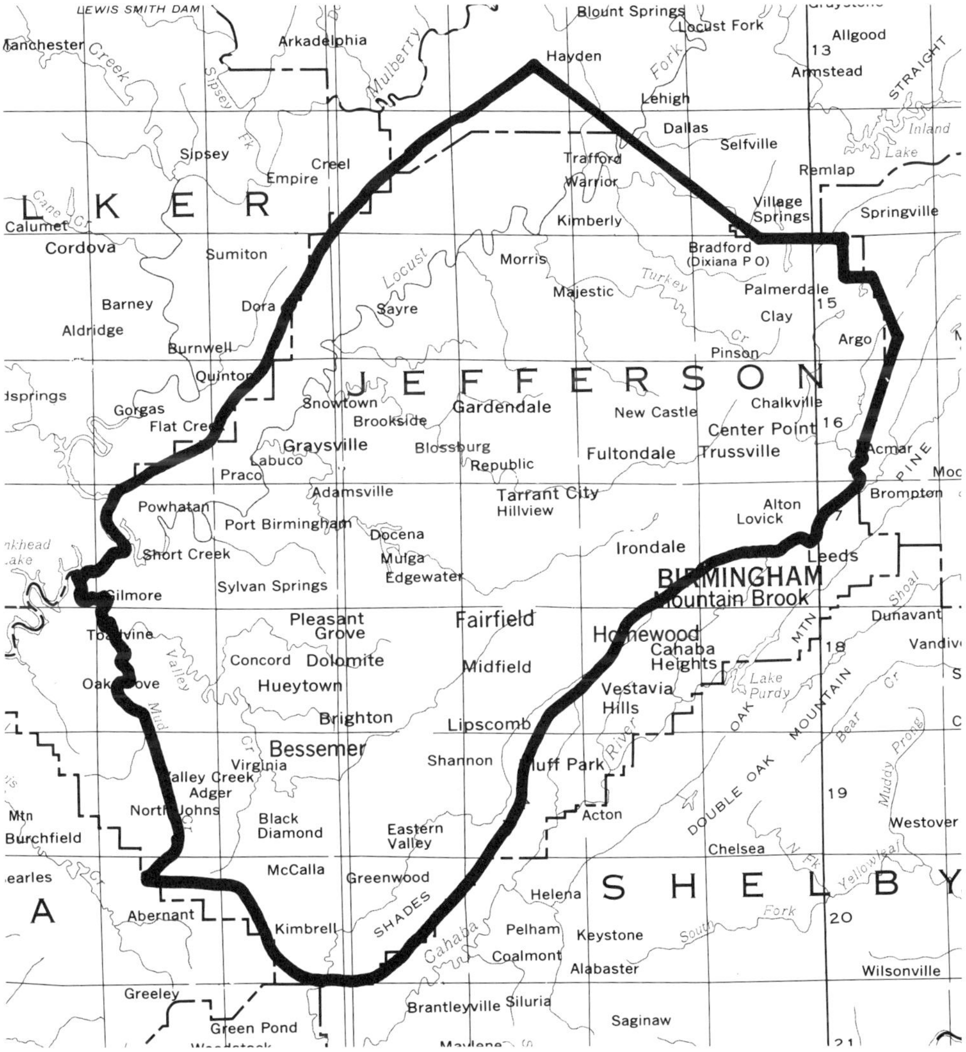

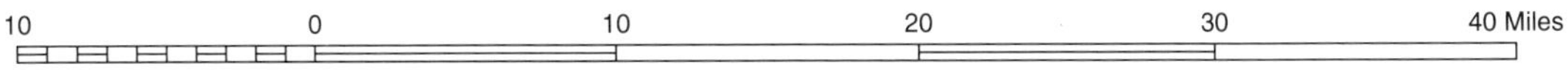

208 ALABAMA

Chronology of JEFFERSON

Map	Date	Event	Resulting Area
❻	after 1 Apr 1833	Gained from SHELBY	1,010 sq mi

(Heavy line depicts historical boundary. Base map shows present-day information.)

❻ c. Apr 1833–2 Feb 1840

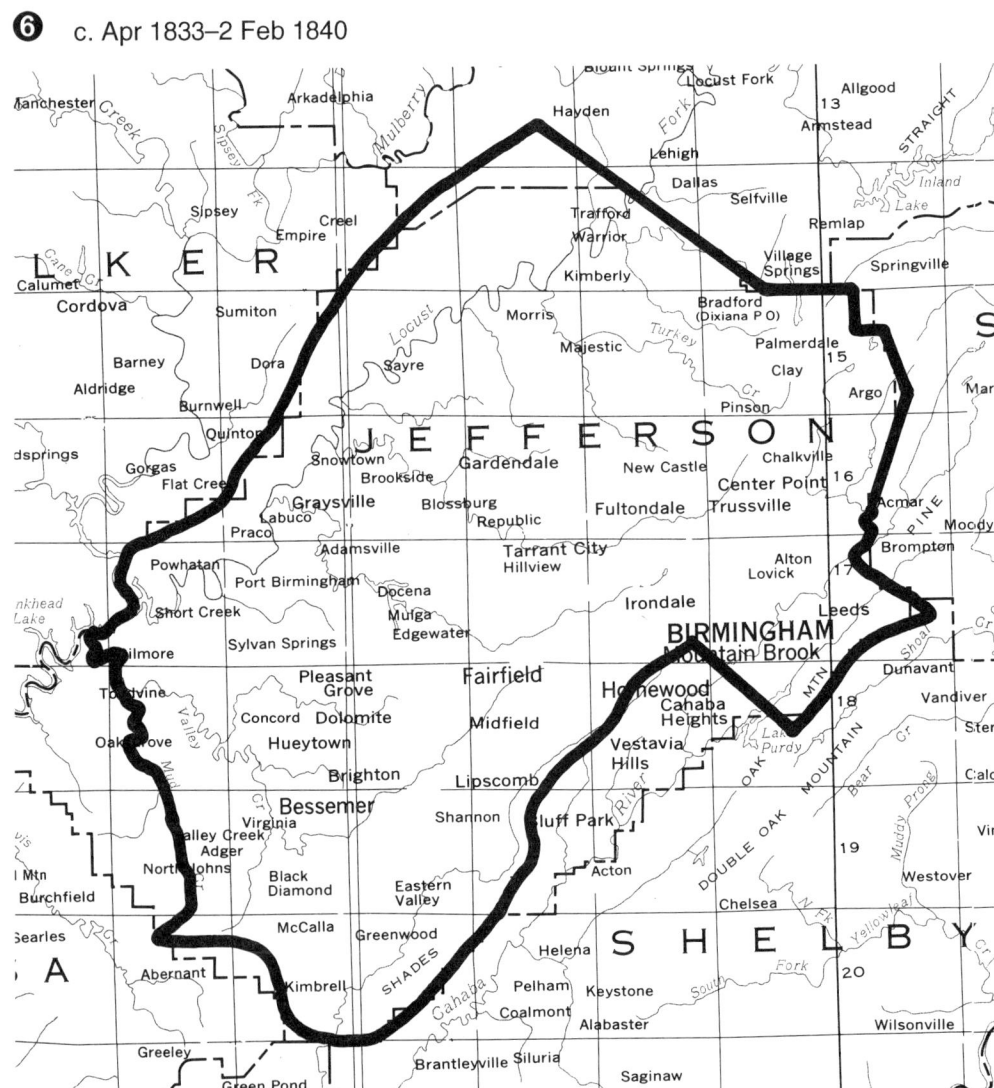

Chronology of JEFFERSON

Map	Date	Event	Resulting Area
❼	3 Feb 1840	Exchanged with TUSCALOOSA	1,070 sq mi
	2 Dec 1841	Gained small area from SHELBY to accommodate local property owner [location unknown, not mapped]	
❼	9 Feb 1852	Gained small area from TUSCALOOSA	1,070 sq mi
❼	8 Feb 1861	Gained from SHELBY	1,080 sq mi
❼	11 Nov 1861	Lost to SHELBY	1,070 sq mi
❼	4 Dec 1862	Gained small area from SHELBY to accommodate local property owner	1,070 sq mi

(Heavy line depicts historical boundary. Base map shows present-day information.)

❼ 3 Feb 1840–5 Mar 1871

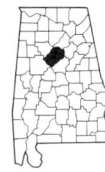

Chronology of JEFFERSON

Map	Date	Event	Resulting Area
❽	6 Mar 1871	Gained from SHELBY	1,080 sq mi

(Heavy line depicts historical boundary. Base map shows present-day information.)

❽ 6 Mar 1871–7 Feb 1877

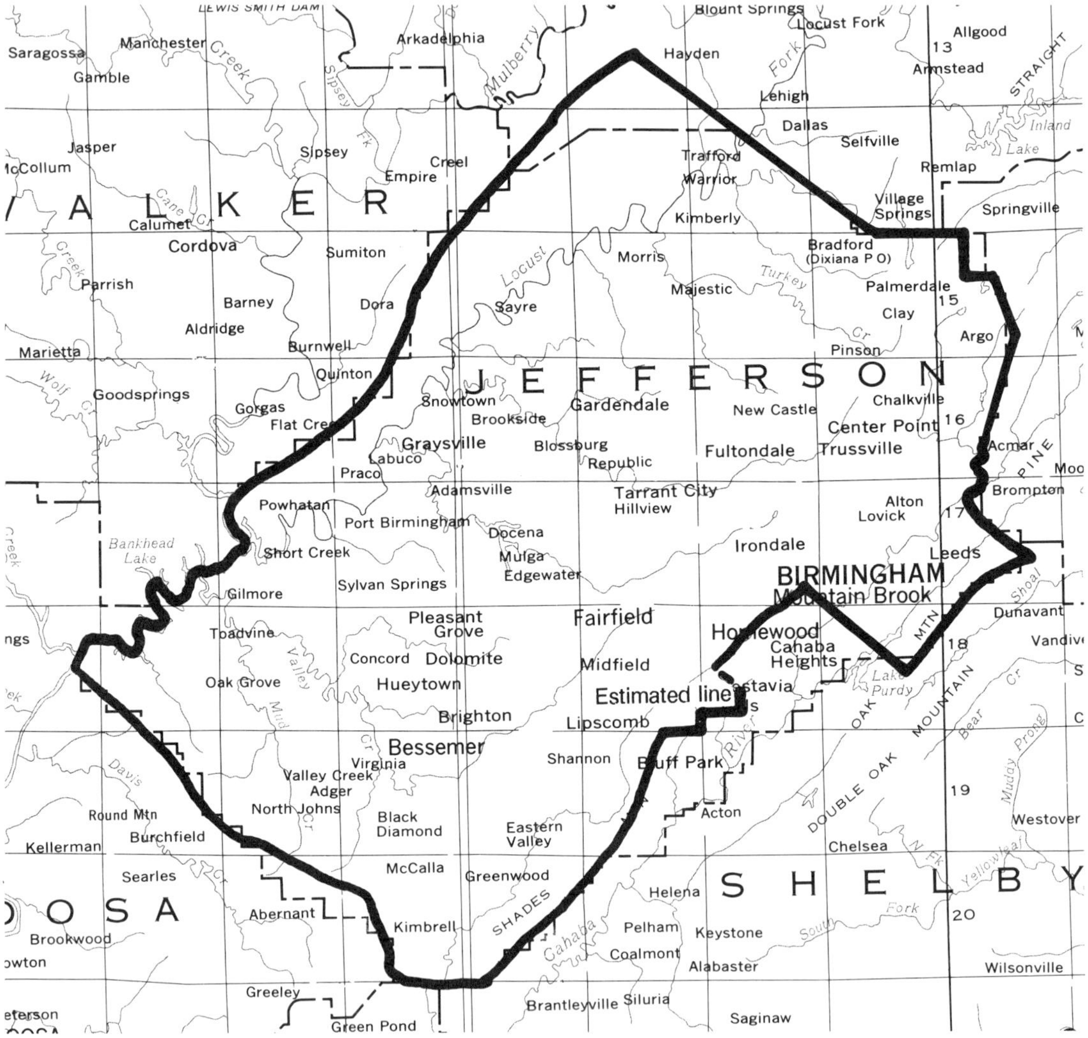

10 0 10 20 30 40 Miles

Individual County Chronologies 211

Chronology of JEFFERSON

Map	Date	Event	Resulting Area
⑨	8 Feb 1877	Lost to BLOUNT	1,060 sq mi
⑨	7 Dec 1878	Gained small area from SHELBY	1,060 sq mi

(Heavy line depicts historical boundary. Base map shows present-day information.)

⑨ 8 Feb 1877–11 Dec 1884

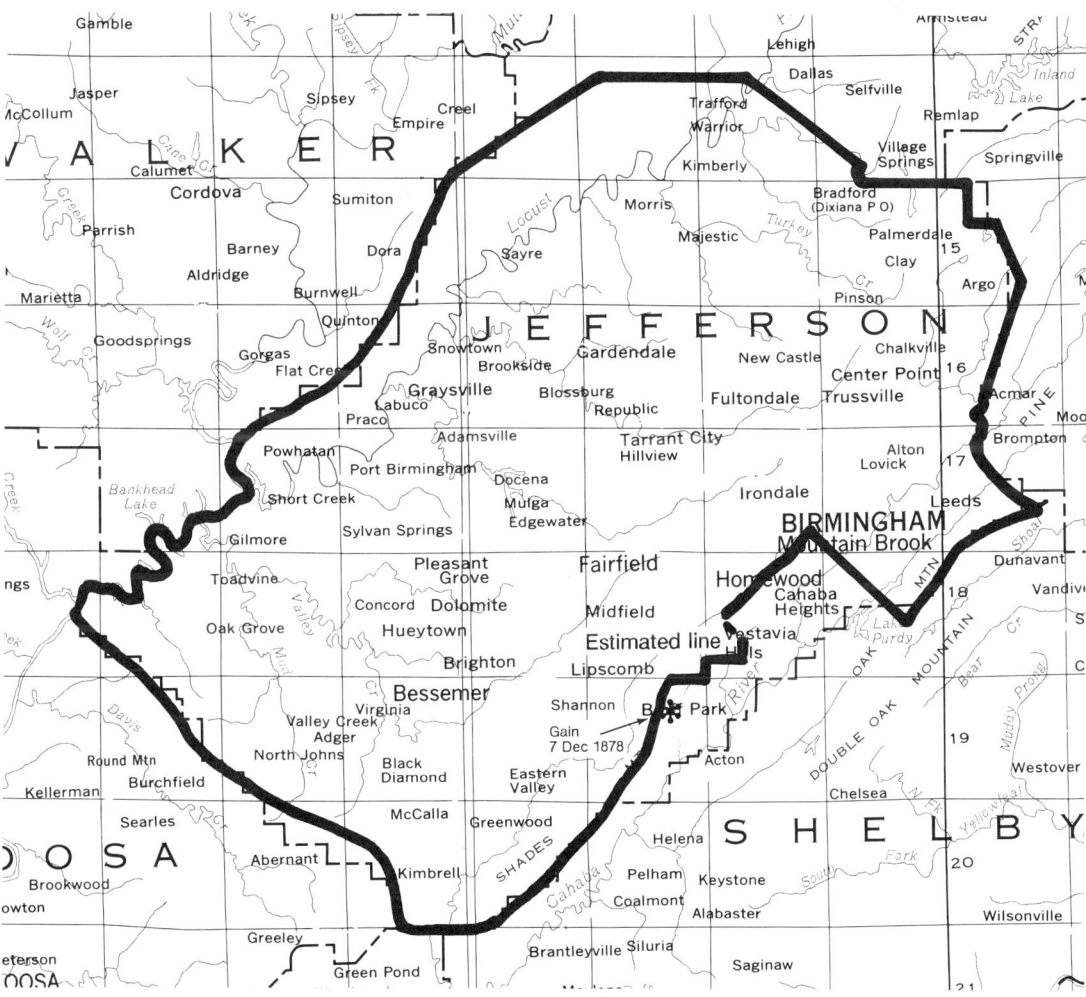

ALABAMA

Chronology of JEFFERSON

Map	Date	Event	Resulting Area
⑩	12 Dec 1884	Gained from SHELBY	1,120 sq mi

(Heavy line depicts historical boundary. Base map shows present-day information.)

⑩ 12 Dec 1884–15 Dec 1898

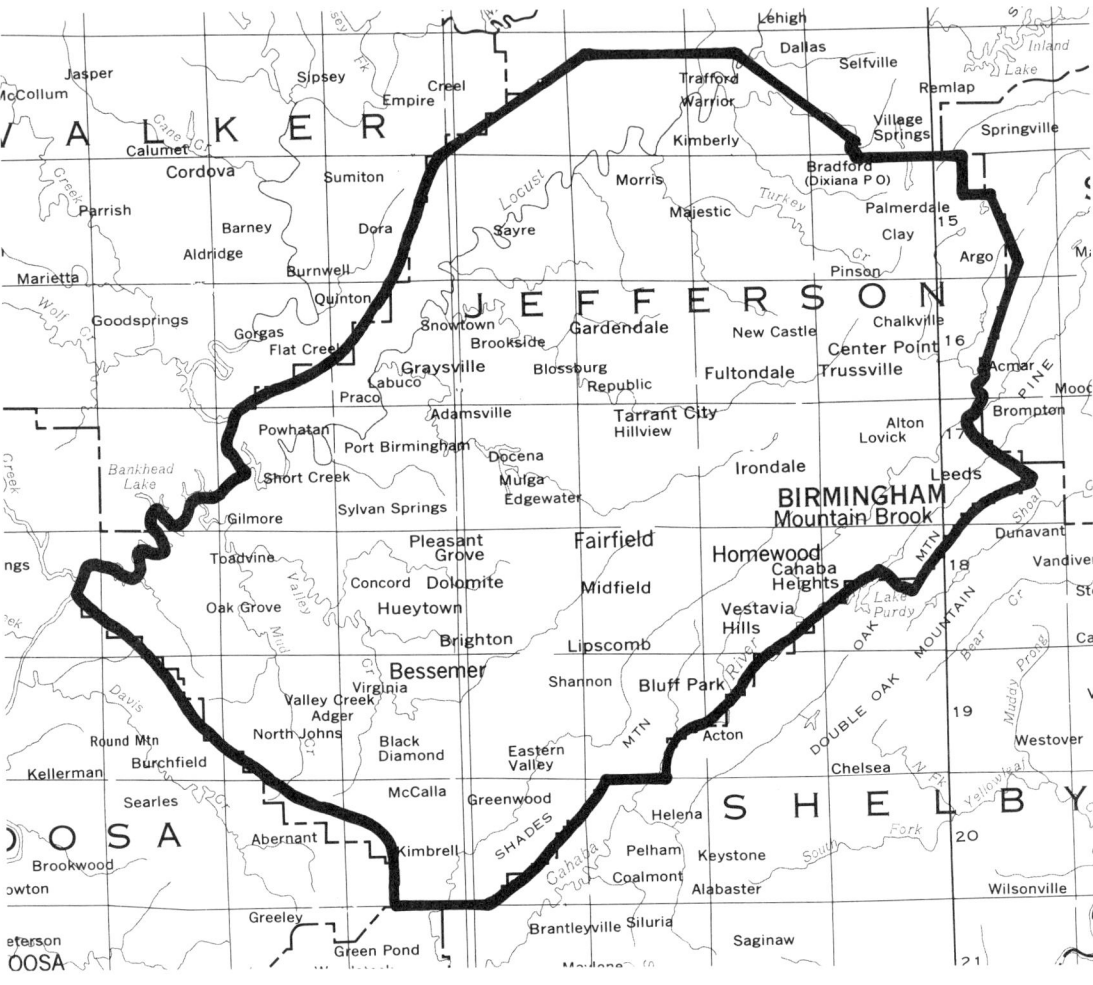

Individual County Chronologies 213

Chronology of JEFFERSON

Map	Date	Event	Resulting Area
⑪	16 Dec 1898	Gained small area from BLOUNT, exchanged with WALKER	1,120 sq mi

(Heavy line depicts historical boundary. Base map shows present-day information.)

⑪ 16 Dec 1898–9 Sep 1915

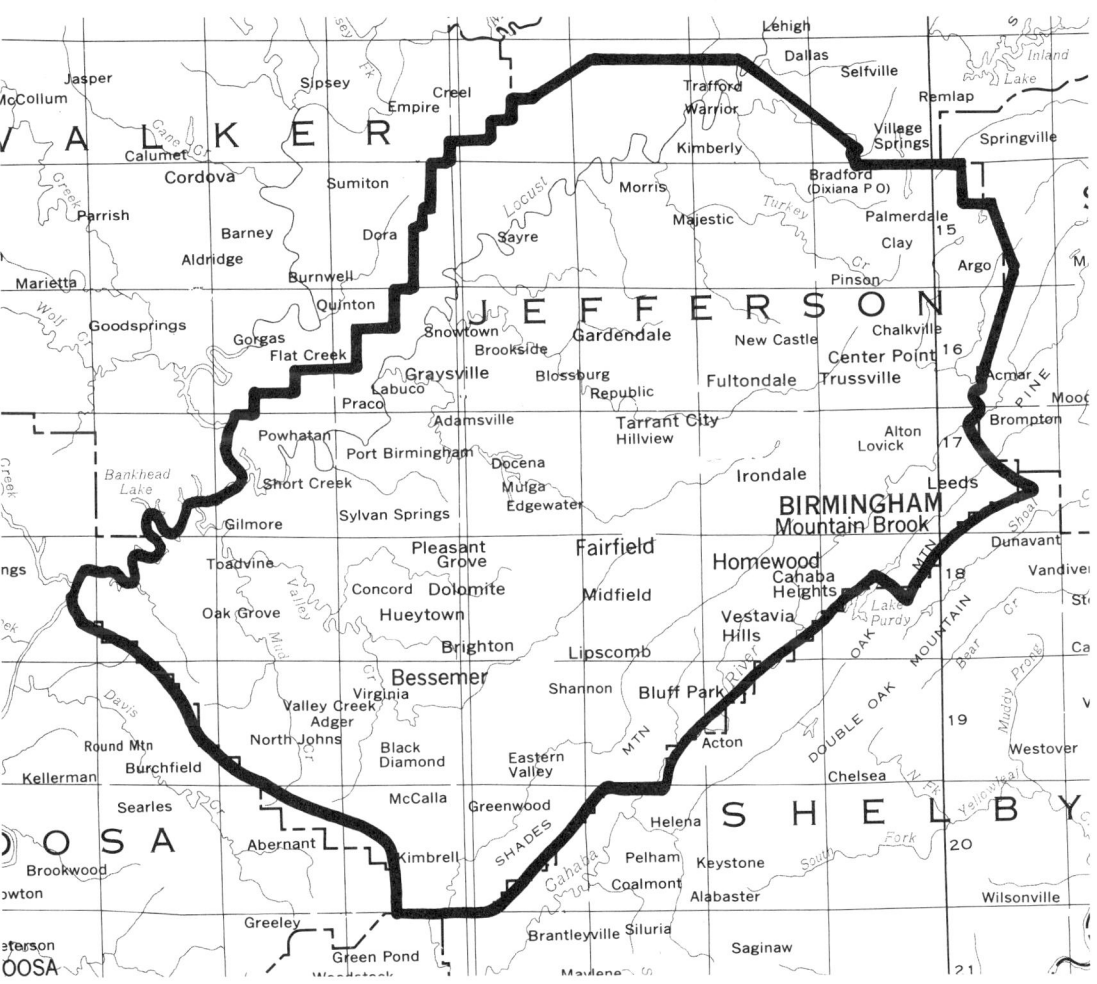

214 ALABAMA

Chronology of JEFFERSON

Map	Date	Event	Resulting Area
⑫	10 Sep 1915	Exchanged with ST. CLAIR	1,120 sq mi

(Heavy line depicts historical boundary. Base map shows present-day information.)

⑫ 10 Sep 1915–27 Sep 1915

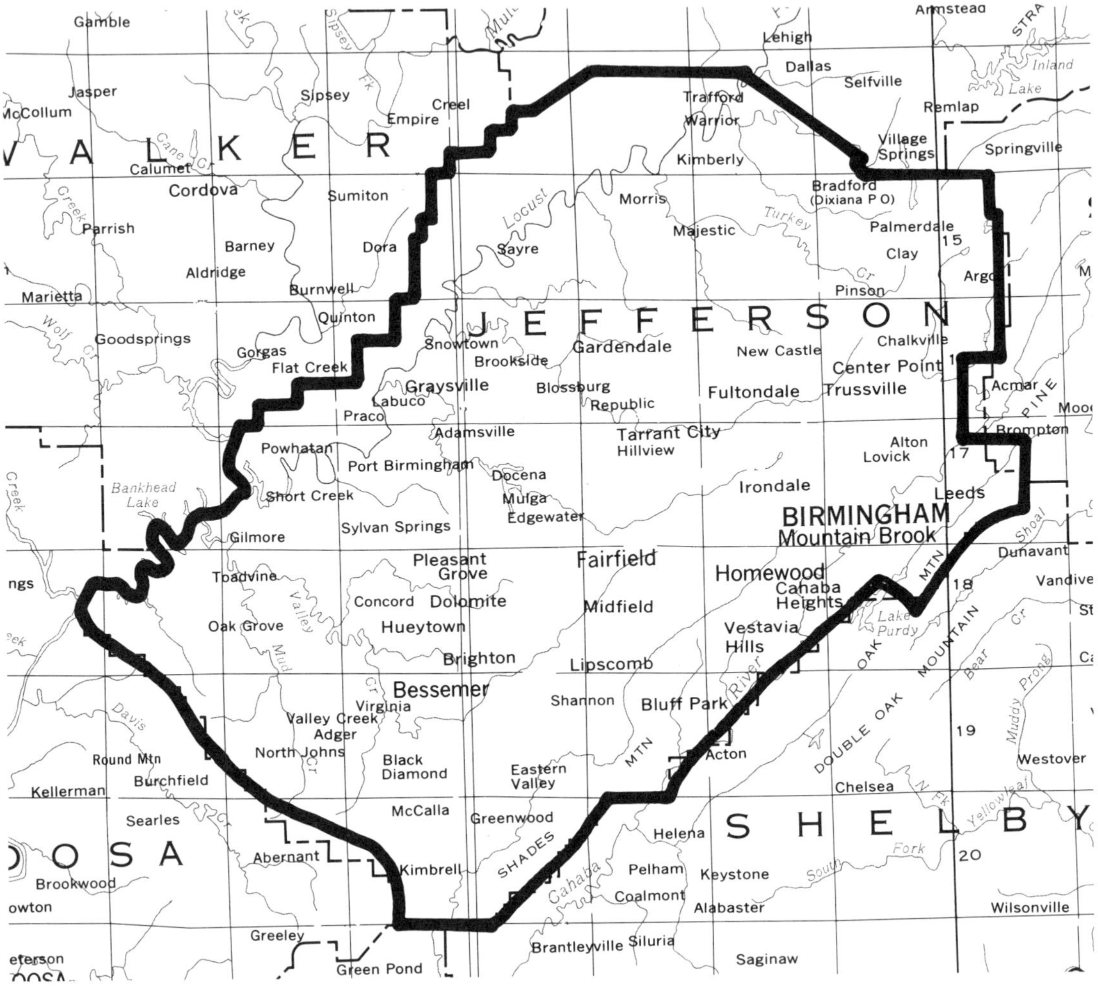

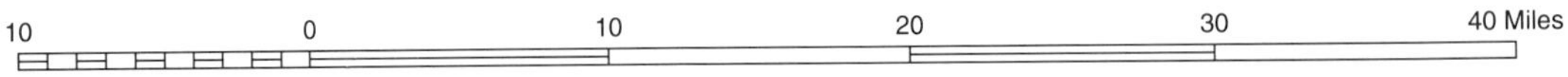

Chronology of JEFFERSON

Map	Date	Event	Resulting Area
⑬	28 Sep 1915	Exchanged with ST. CLAIR and TUSCALOOSA	1,130 sq mi

(Heavy line depicts historical boundary. Base map shows present-day information.)

⑬ 28 Sep 1915–30 Sep 1943

ALABAMA

Chronology of JEFFERSON

Map	Date	Event	Resulting Area
14	1 Oct 1943	Exchanged with SHELBY	1,120 sq mi
14	9 Aug 1979	Gained small area from SHELBY	1,120 sq mi

(Heavy line depicts historical boundary. Base map shows present-day information.)

14 1 Oct 1943–1990

Chronology of JONES (extinct)

Map	Date	Event	Resulting Area
❶	4 Feb 1867	Created from FAYETTE and MARION	590 sq mi
	13 Nov 1867	Lost all territory to FAYETTE and MARION; JONES eliminated [on 8 Oct 1868 SANFORD (now LAMAR) was created with boundaries identical to those of JONES]	

(Heavy line depicts historical boundary. Base map shows present-day information.)

❶ 4 Feb 1867–12 Nov 1867

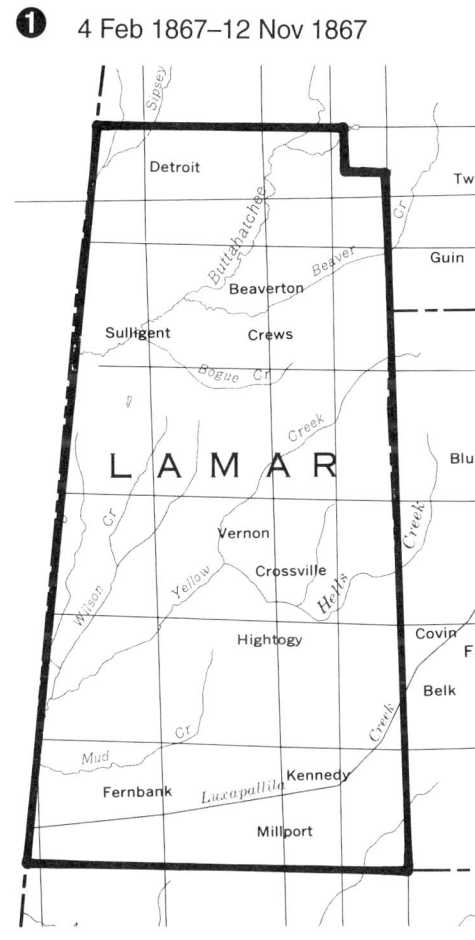

ALABAMA

Chronology of LAMAR (created as SANFORD)

Map	Date	Event	Resulting Area
❶	8 Oct 1868	Created as SANFORD from FAYETTE and MARION; boundaries were identical to those of JONES	590 sq mi
	8 Feb 1877	Renamed LAMAR	

(Heavy line depicts historical boundary. Base map shows present-day information.)

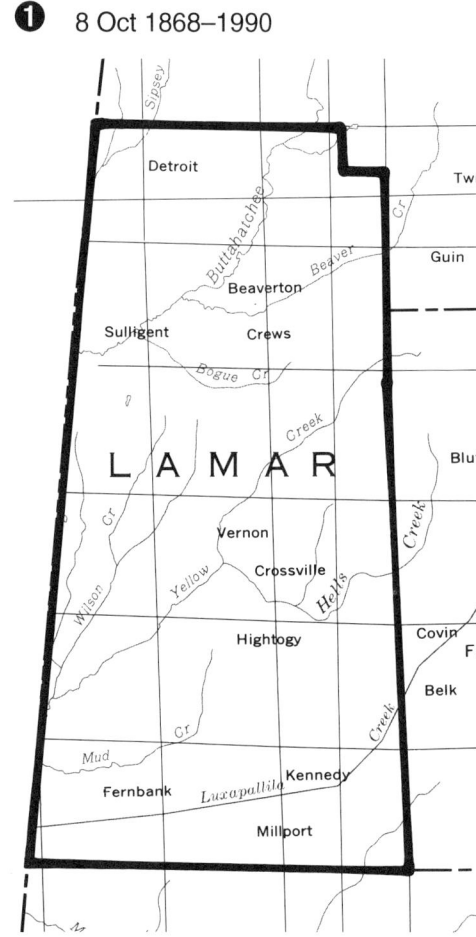

❶ 8 Oct 1868–1990

Individual County Chronologies 219

Chronology of LAUDERDALE

Map	Date	Event	Resulting Area
❶	6 Feb 1818	Created from non-county area	730 sq mi
	9 Feb 1818	County boundary line in Tennessee R. adjusted to run in middle of stream [not mapped]	
❷	27 Nov 1821	Lost to LIMESTONE	720 sq mi

(Heavy line depicts historical boundary. Base map shows present-day information.)

❶ 6 Feb 1818–26 Nov 1821

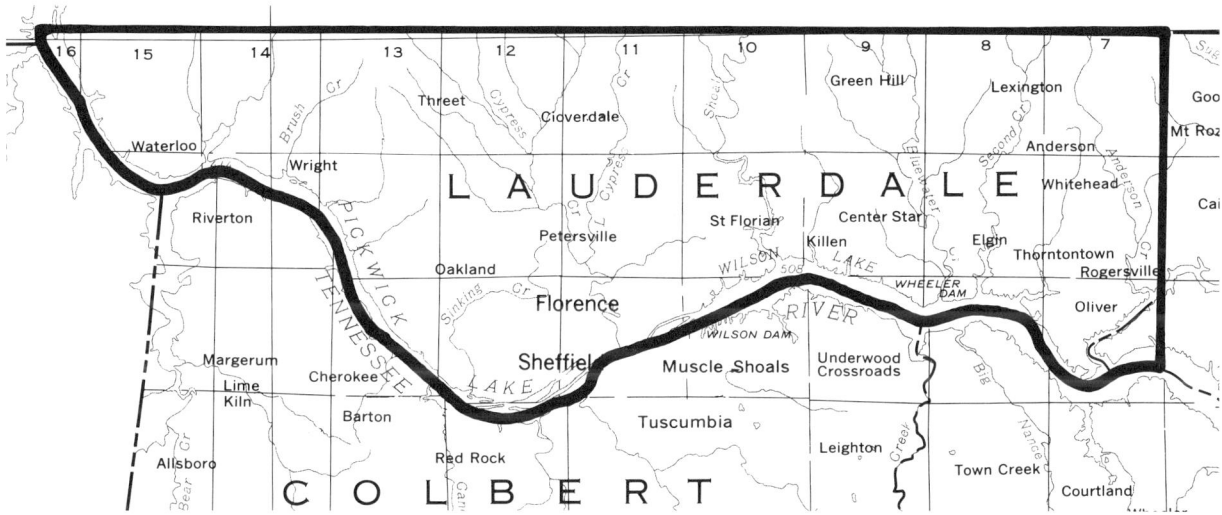

❷ 27 Nov 1821–1990

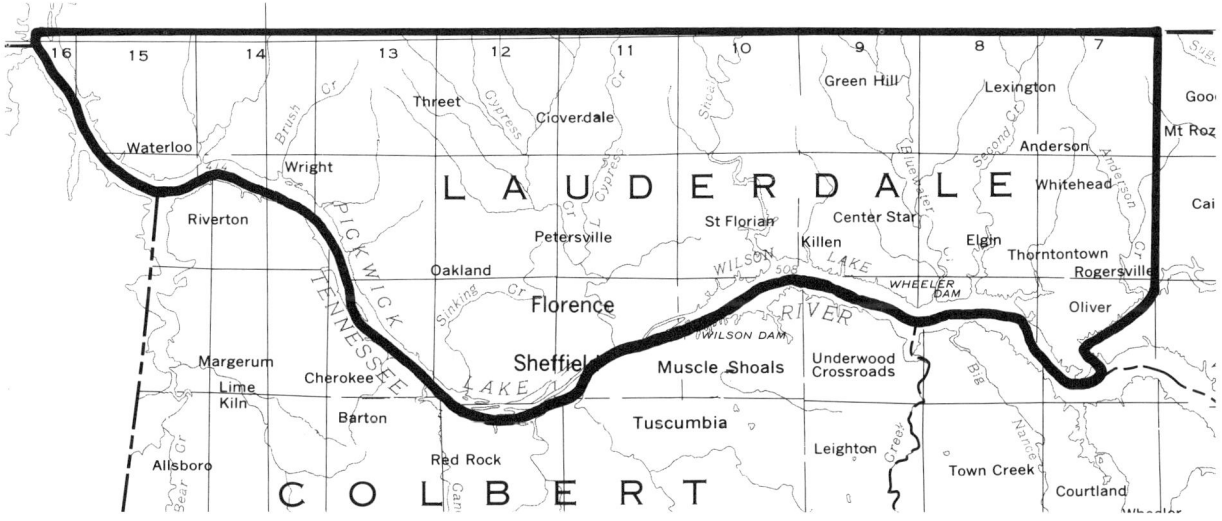

ALABAMA

Chronology of LAWRENCE

Map	Date	Event	Resulting Area
❶	6 Feb 1818	Created from MONTGOMERY and non-county area	780 sq mi
	9 Feb 1818	County boundary line in Tennessee R. adjusted to run in middle of stream [not mapped]	
	21 Nov 1818	Southern boundary clarified [no change]	
❷	6 Feb 1895	Lost to COLBERT	710 sq mi

(Heavy line depicts historical boundary. Base map shows present-day information.)

❶ 6 Feb 1818–5 Feb 1895

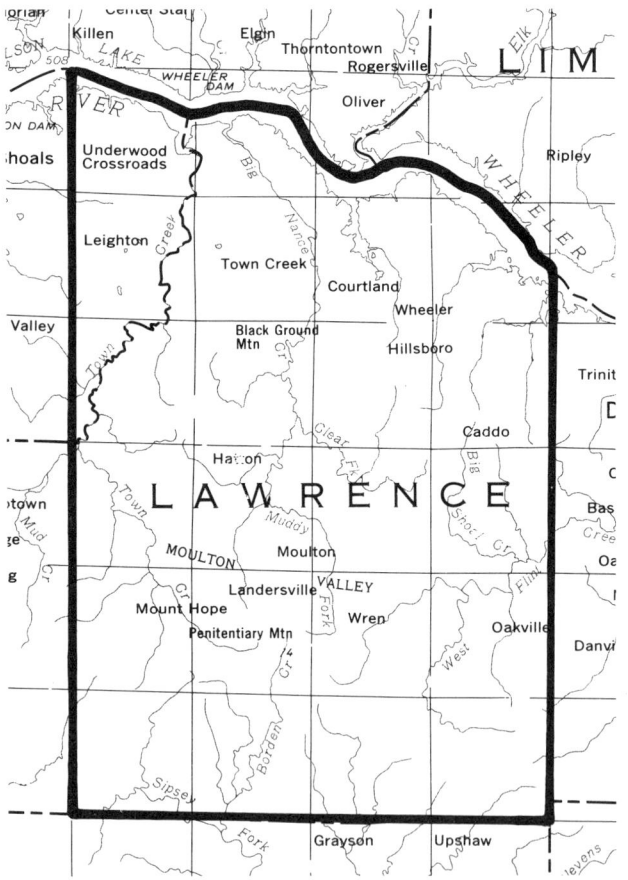

❷ 6 Feb 1895–1990

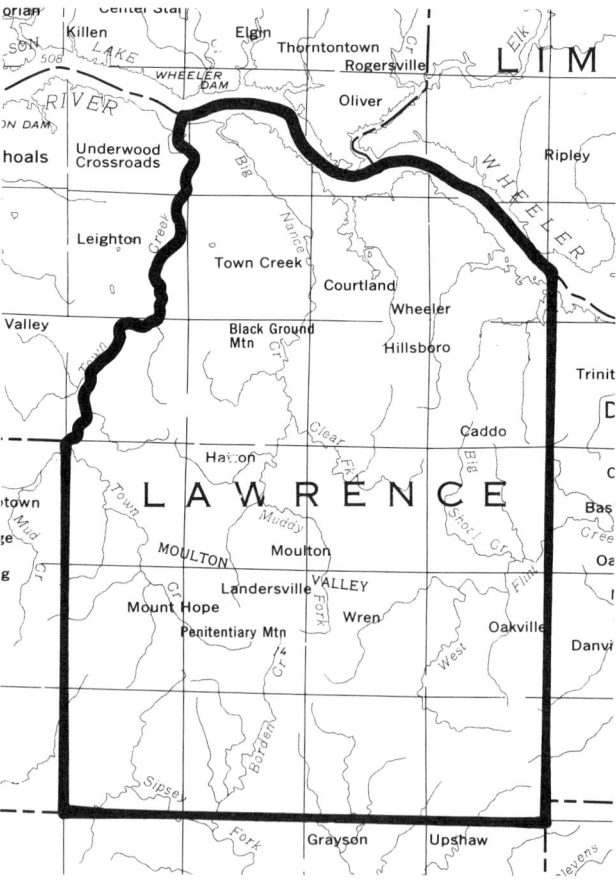

Individual County Chronologies 221

Chronology of LEE

Map	Date	Event	Resulting Area
❶	5 Dec 1866	Created from CHAMBERS, MACON, RUSSELL, and TALLAPOOSA	610 sq mi
❶	17 Jan 1867	Gained small area from CHAMBERS to accommodate local property owner	610 sq mi
❶	4 Feb 1867	Gained small area from CHAMBERS to accommodate local property owner	610 sq mi
❶	16 Feb 1867	Lost small area to TALLAPOOSA	610 sq mi
❶	19 Feb 1867	Gained small area from CHAMBERS to accommodate local property owner	610 sq mi
❶	24 Feb 1872	Gained small area from CHAMBERS to accommodate local property owner	610 sq mi

(Heavy line depicts historical boundary. Base map shows present-day information.)

❶ 5 Dec 1866–12 Feb 1879

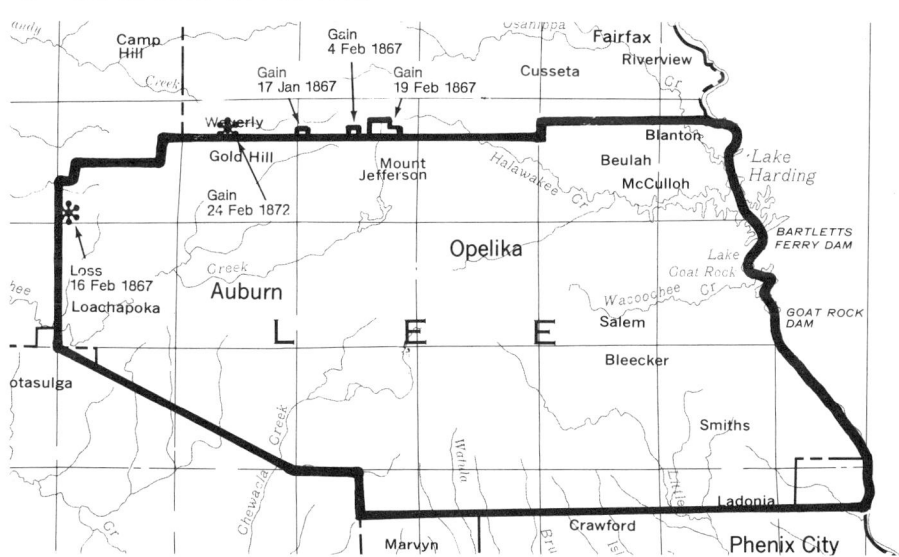

Chronology of LEE

Map	Date	Event	Resulting Area
❷	13 Feb 1879	Lost small area to MACON	610 sq mi
❷	1 Mar 1881	Lost small area to CHAMBERS to accommodate local property owner	610 sq mi
	12 Dec 1888	Boundary with RUSSELL adjusted [location unknown, not mapped]	
❷	6 Aug 1915	Gained small area from TALLAPOOSA	610 sq mi
❸	30 Sep 1932	Exchanged with RUSSELL	620 sq mi

(Heavy line depicts historical boundary. Base map shows present-day information.)

❷ 13 Feb 1879–29 Sep 1932

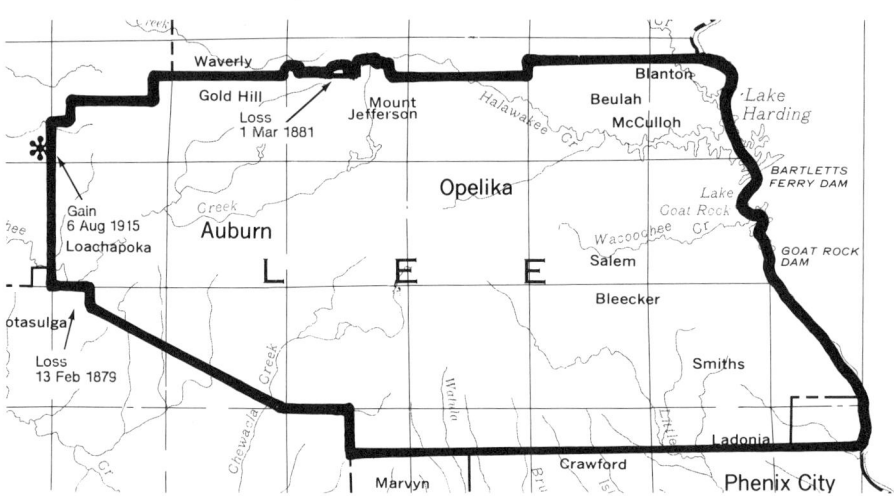

❸ 30 Sep 1932–1990

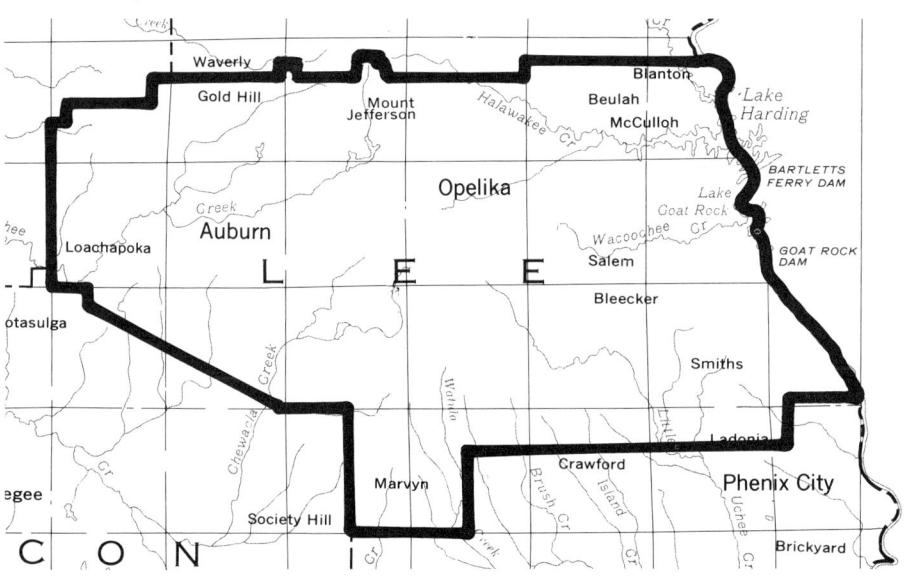

Individual County Chronologies 223

Chronology of LIMESTONE

Map	Date	Event	Resulting Area
❶	6 Feb 1818	Created from MADISON and non-county area	610 sq mi
	9 Feb 1818	County boundary line in Tennessee R. adjusted to run in middle of stream [not mapped]	
❷	27 Nov 1821	Gained from LAUDERDALE	620 sq mi

(Heavy line depicts historical boundary. Base map shows present-day information.)

❶ 6 Feb 1818–26 Nov 1821

❷ 27 Nov 1821–1990

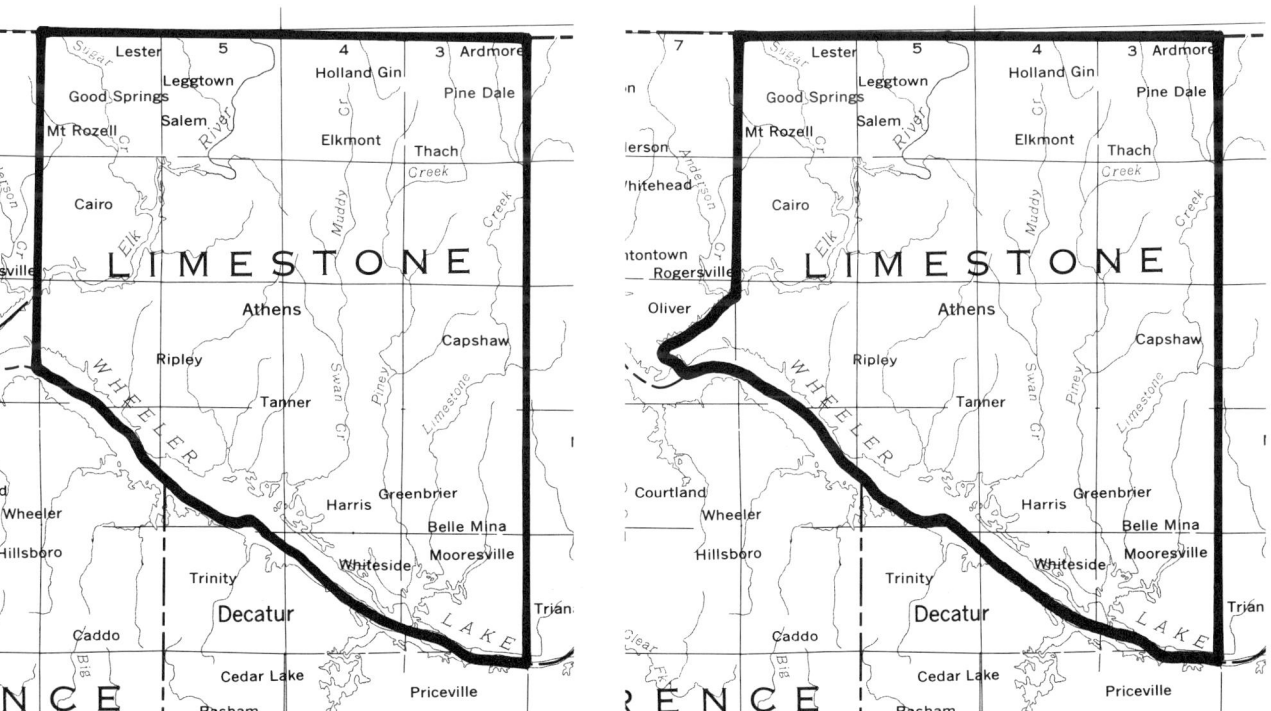

ALABAMA

Chronology of LOWNDES

Map	Date	Event	Resulting Area
❶	20 Jan 1830	Created from BUTLER, DALLAS, MONTGOMERY, PIKE, and WILCOX	860 sq mi
❶	29 Dec 1841	Gained small area from MONTGOMERY	860 sq mi

(Heavy line depicts historical boundary. Base map shows present-day information.)

❶ 20 Jan 1830–23 Nov 1866

Chronology of LOWNDES

Map	Date	Event	Resulting Area
❷	24 Nov 1866	Lost to BUTLER and to creation of CRENSHAW	730 sq mi
❷	19 Feb 1867	Gained small area from CRENSHAW	730 sq mi

(Heavy line depicts historical boundary. Base map shows present-day information.)

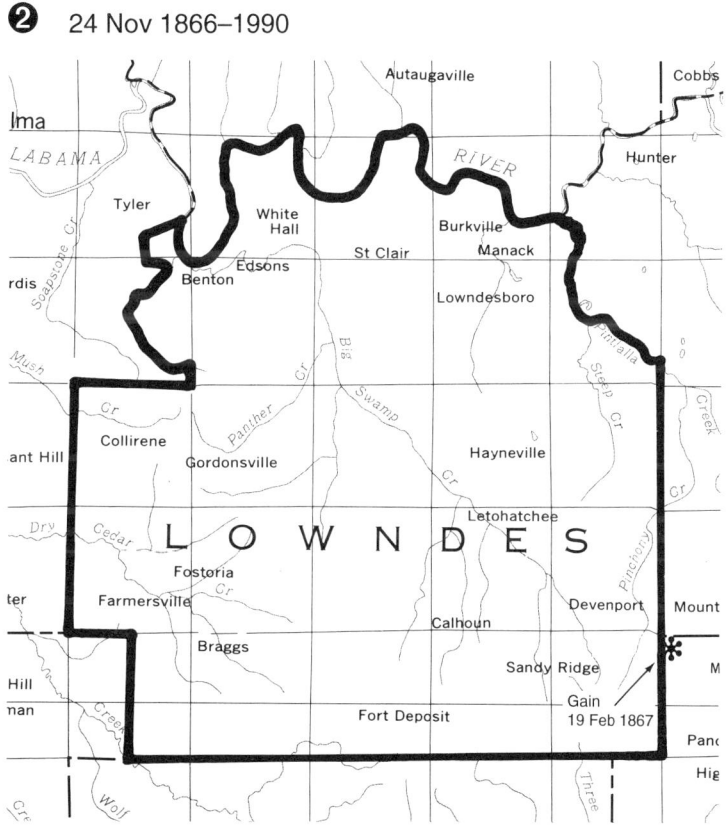

❷ 24 Nov 1866–1990

226 ALABAMA

Chronology of MACON

Map	Date	Event	Resulting Area
❶	18 Dec 1832	Created from MONTGOMERY and PIKE	930 sq mi

(Heavy line depicts historical boundary. Base map shows present-day information.)

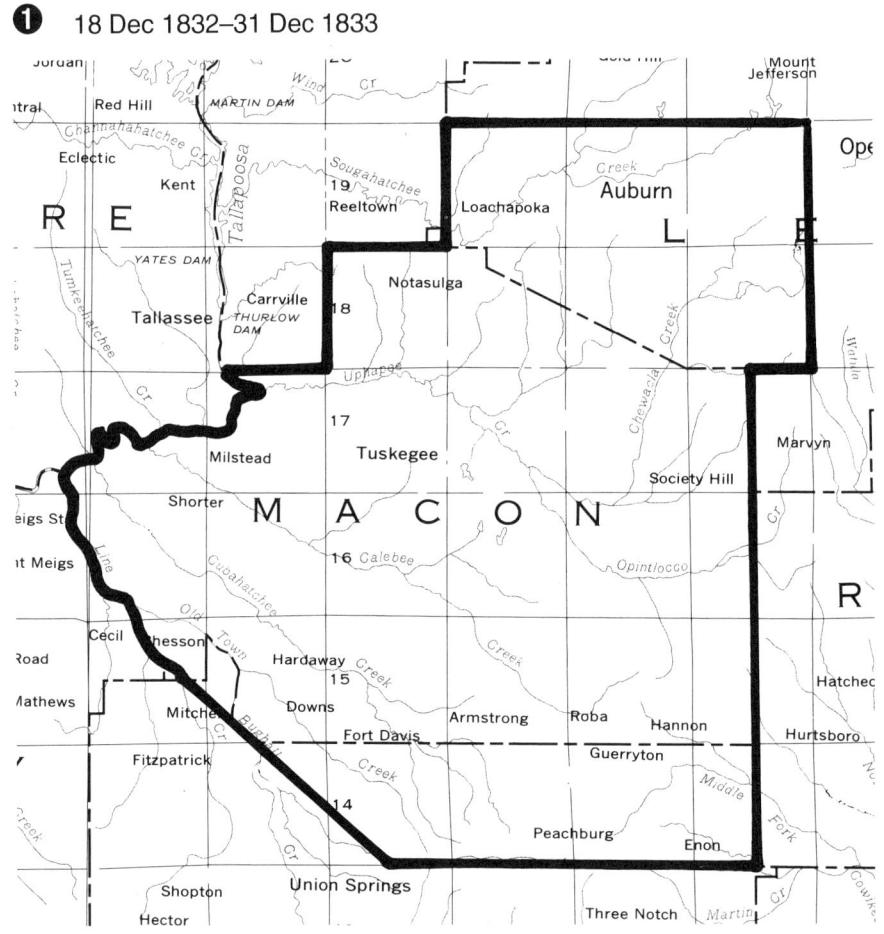

❶ 18 Dec 1832–31 Dec 1833

Chronology of MACON

Map	Date	Event	Resulting Area
❷	1 Jan 1834	Gained from MONTGOMERY	970 sq mi

(Heavy line depicts historical boundary. Base map shows present-day information.)

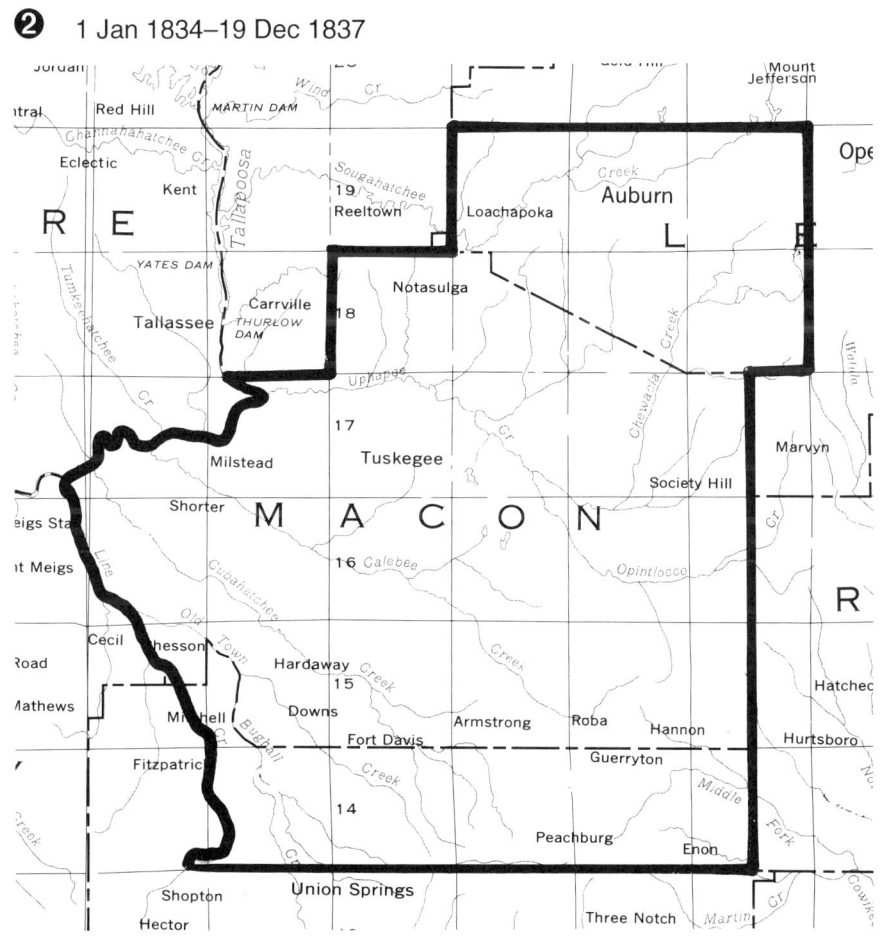

❷ 1 Jan 1834–19 Dec 1837

ALABAMA

Chronology of MACON

Map	Date	Event	Resulting Area
❸	20 Dec 1837	Gained from PIKE	1,040 sq mi
❸	25 Dec 1837	Lost small area to RUSSELL	1,040 sq mi
❸	11 Feb 1843	Gained small area from RUSSELL to accommodate local property owner	1,040 sq mi
❸	27 Jan 1845	Lost to TALLAPOOSA	1,040 sq mi
❸	2 Feb 1846	Gained from TALLAPOOSA	1,040 sq mi

(Heavy line depicts historical boundary. Base map shows present-day information.)

❸ 20 Dec 1837–4 Dec 1866

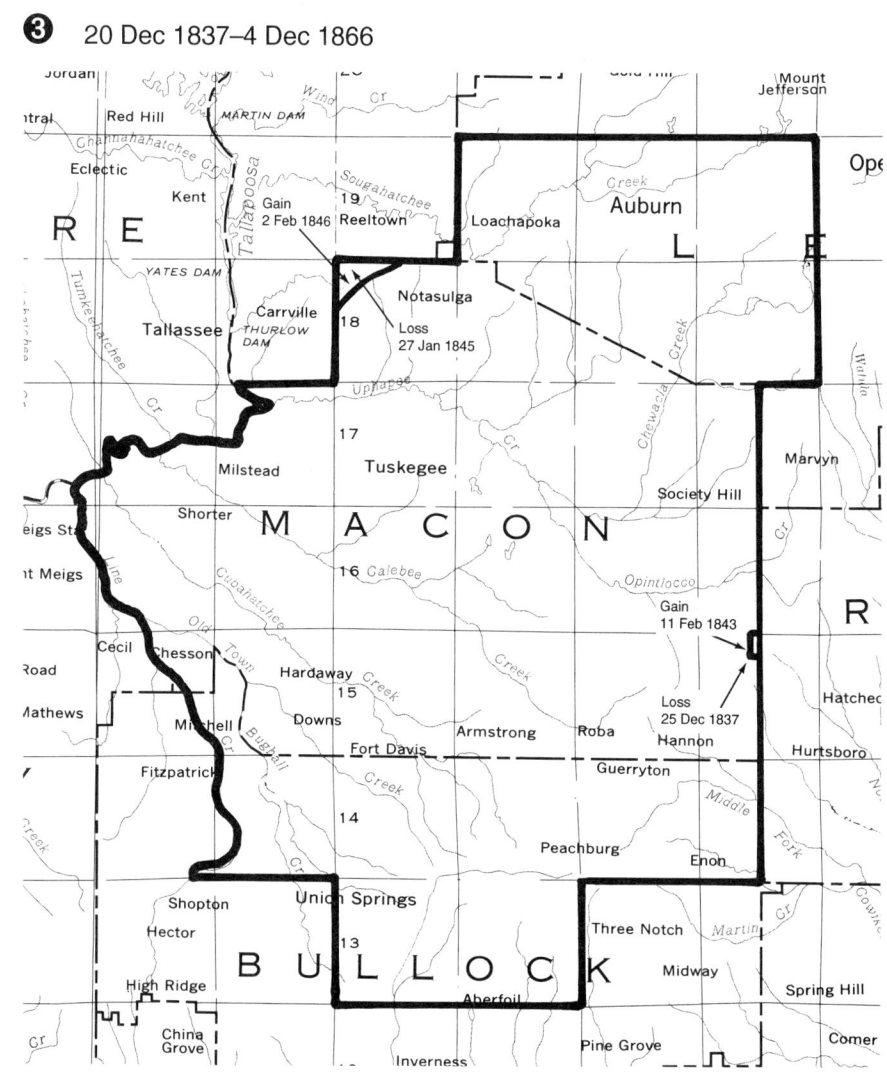

Individual County Chronologies 229

Chronology of MACON

Map	Date	Event	Resulting Area
❹	5 Dec 1866	Lost to creation of both BULLOCK and LEE	610 sq mi
❹	13 Feb 1879	Gained small area from LEE	610 sq mi
❺	17 Feb 1885	Gained small area from TALLAPOOSA	610 sq mi

(Heavy line depicts historical boundary. Base map shows present-day information.)

❹ 5 Dec 1866–16 Feb 1885

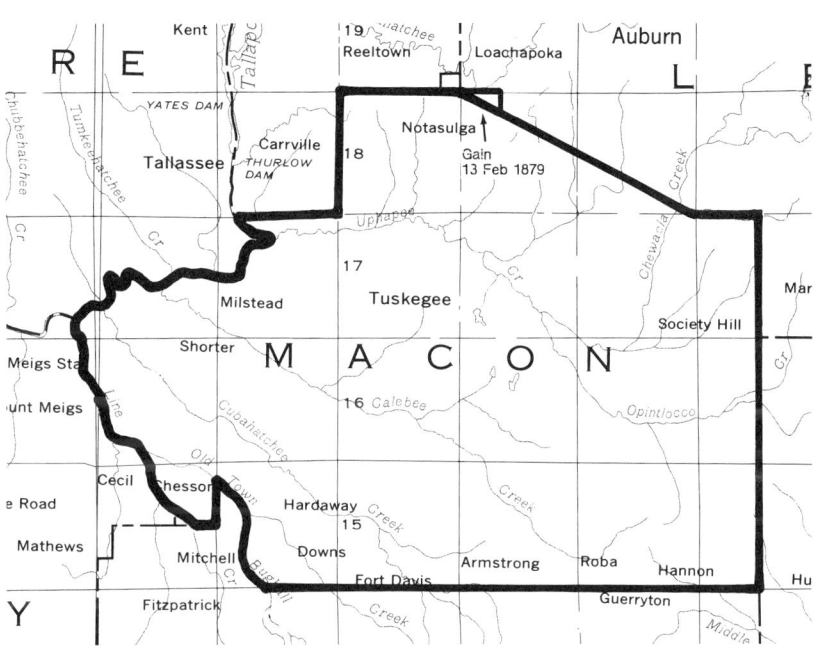

❺ 17 Feb 1885–1990

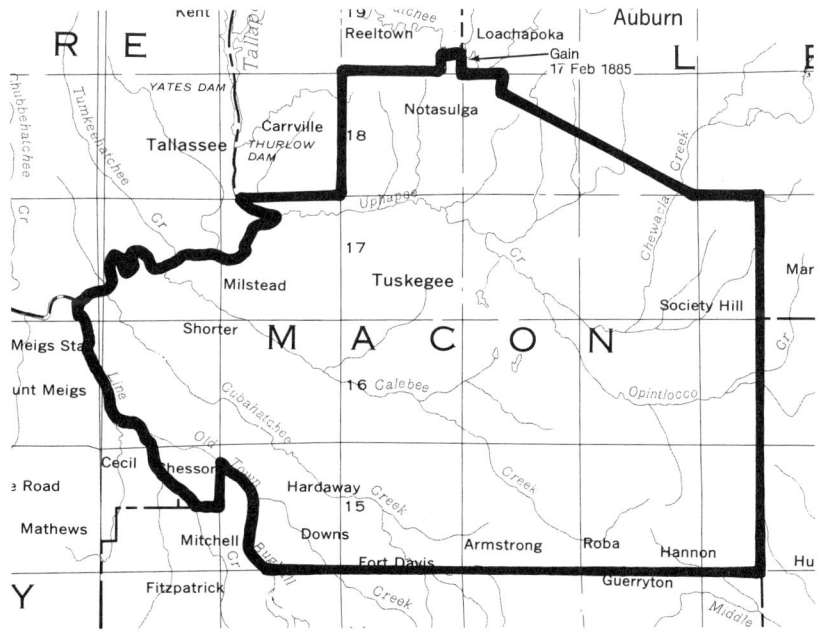

230 ALABAMA

Chronology of MADISON

Map	Date	Event	Resulting Area
❶	13 Dec 1808	Created by Mississippi Territory from non-county area	540 sq mi
	3 Mar 1817	Became part of Alabama Territory	

(Heavy line depicts historical boundary. Base map shows present-day information.)

❶ 13 Dec 1808–5 Feb 1818

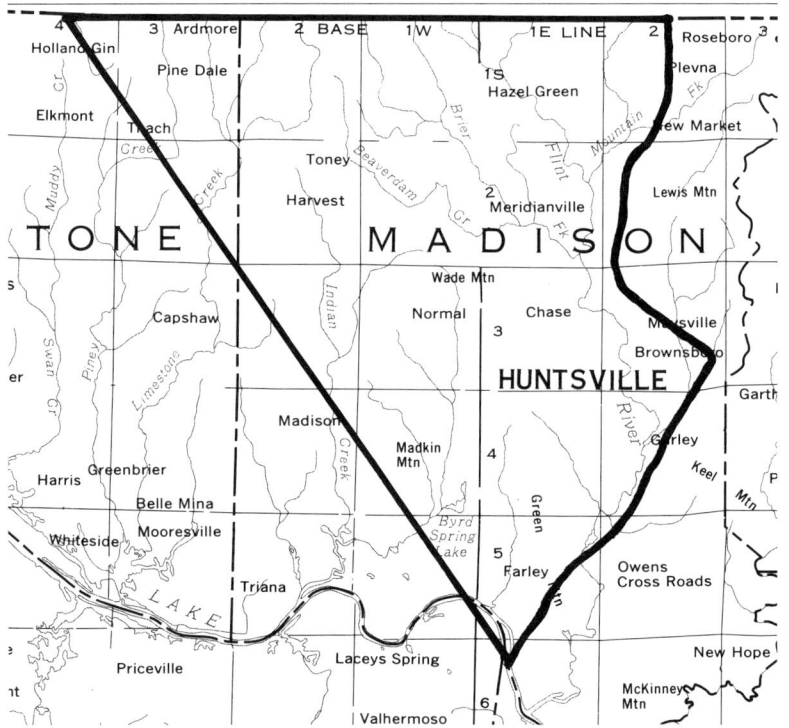

Individual County Chronologies **231**

Chronology of MADISON

Map	Date	Event	Resulting Area
❷	6 Feb 1818	Gained from non-county area, lost to creation of LIMESTONE	600 sq mi
	9 Feb 1818	County boundary line in Tennessee R. adjusted to run in middle of stream [not mapped]	
❸	13 Dec 1819	Gained from non-county area	620 sq mi

(Heavy line depicts historical boundary. Base map shows present-day information.)

❷ 6 Feb 1818–12 Dec 1819

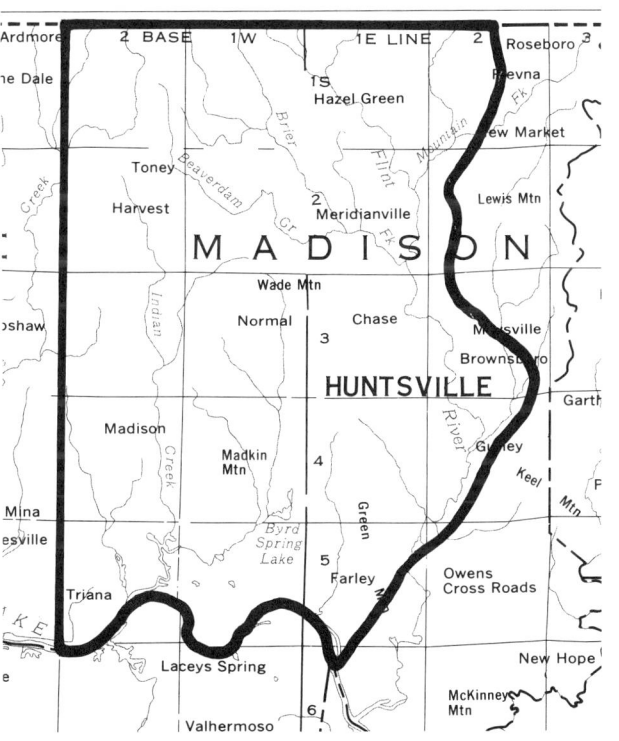

❸ 13 Dec 1819–5 Jan 1826

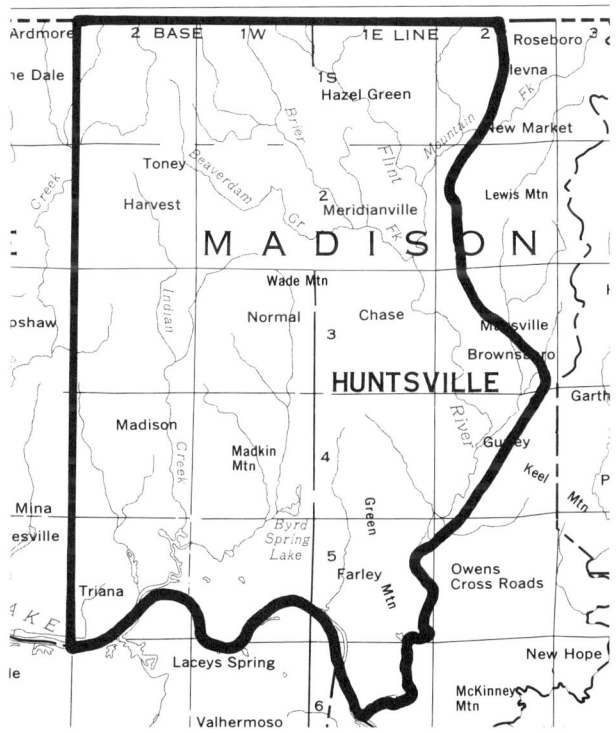

Chronology of MADISON

Map	Date	Event	Resulting Area
❹	6 Jan 1826	Gained from JACKSON	830 sq mi
❺	9 Jan 1836	Gained from JACKSON	840 sq mi

(Heavy line depicts historical boundary. Base map shows present-day information.)

❹ 6 Jan 1826–8 Jan 1836

❺ 9 Jan 1836–22 Dec 1837

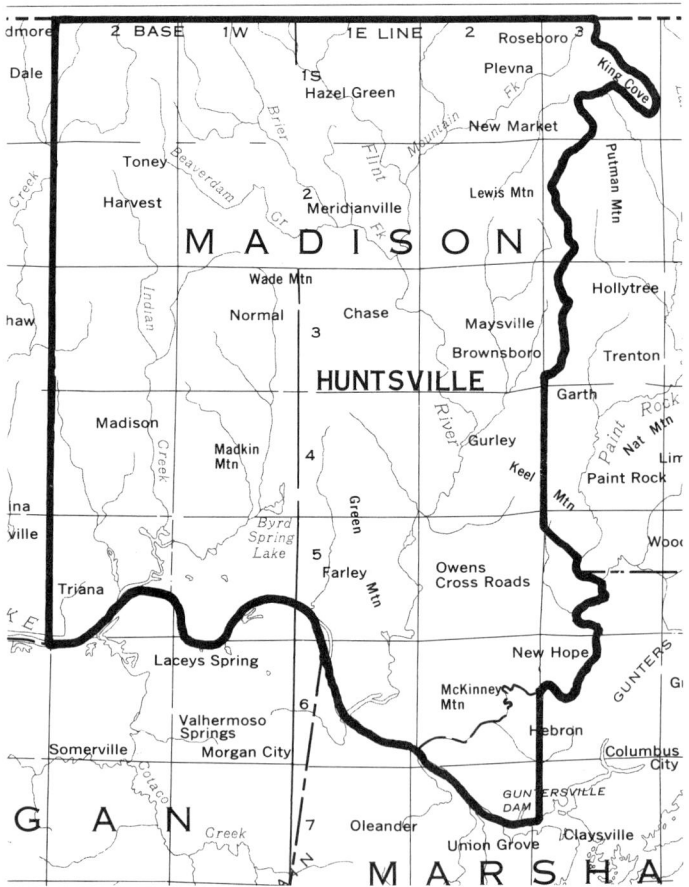

Individual County Chronologies 233

Chronology of MADISON

Map	Date	Event	Resulting Area
❻	23 Dec 1837	Lost to MARSHALL	820 sq mi

(Heavy line depicts historical boundary. Base map shows present-day information.)

❻ 23 Dec 1837–1990

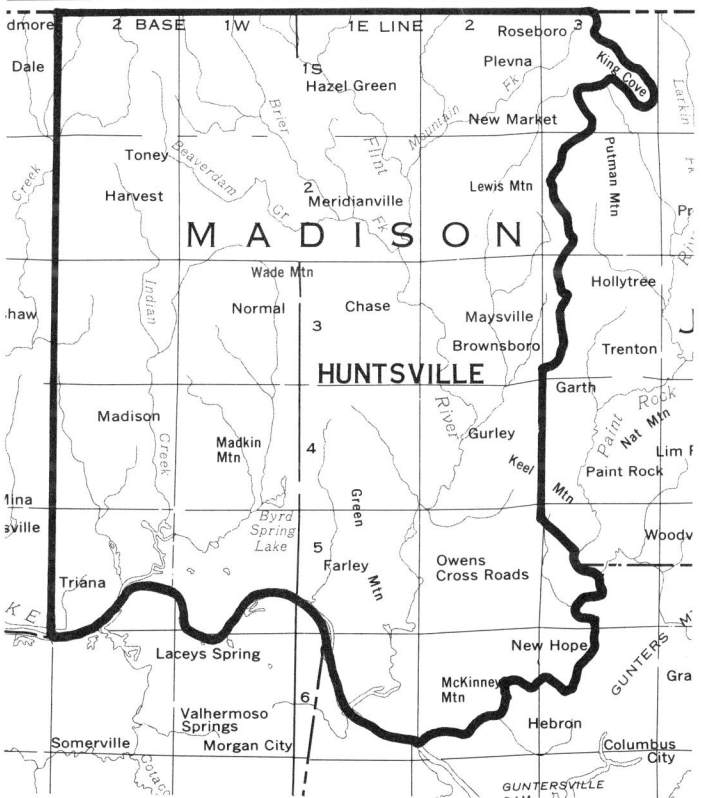

ALABAMA

Chronology of MARENGO

Map	Date	Event	Resulting Area
①	6 Feb 1818	Created from non-county area	1,480 sq mi

(Heavy line depicts historical boundary. Base map shows present-day information.)

① 6 Feb 1818–11 Feb 1818

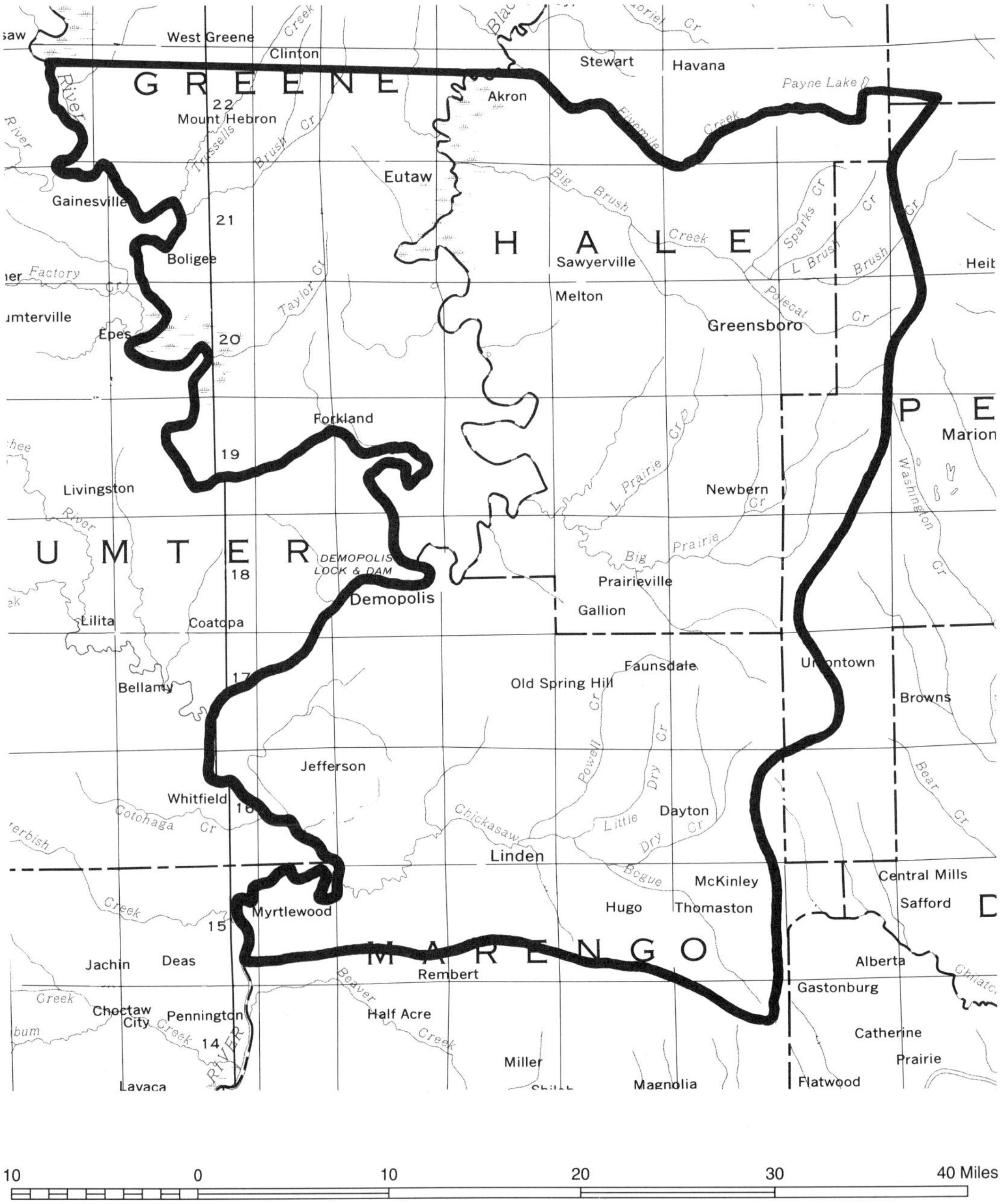

Individual County Chronologies

Chronology of MARENGO

Map	Date	Event	Resulting Area
❷	12 Feb 1818	Gained from non-county area	1,840 sq mi
❸	13 Dec 1819	Gained from DALLAS, lost to creation of GREENE, PERRY, and WILCOX	1,070 sq mi
❹	17 Dec 1819	Non-county area belonging to Choctaw Indians attached to MARENGO	
❸	26 Jan 1829	Gained small area from WILCOX [attachment unchanged; see map 4]	1,070 sq mi
❸	18 Dec 1832	Lost non-county attachment to PICKENS, WASHINGTON, and to creation of SUMTER	

(Heavy line depicts historical boundary. Base map shows present-day information.)

❷ 12 Feb 1818–12 Dec 1819

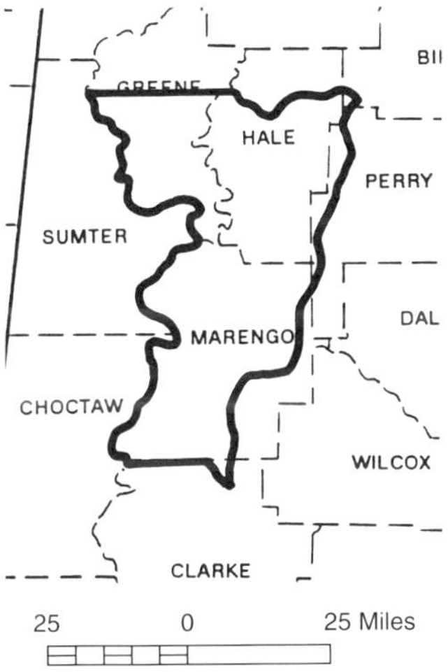

❹ 17 Dec 1819–17 Dec 1832

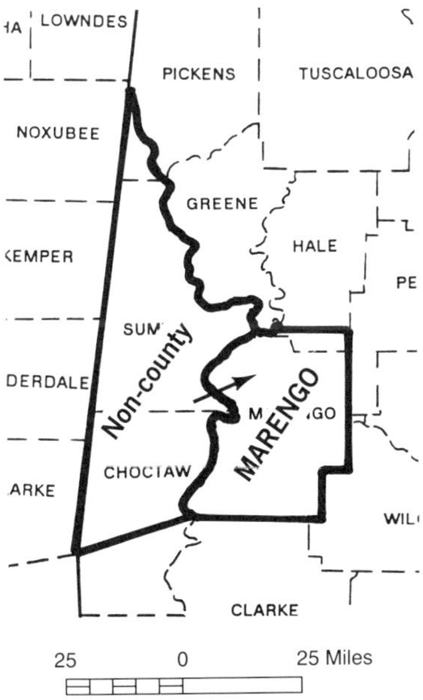

❸ 13 Dec 1819–3 Feb 1840

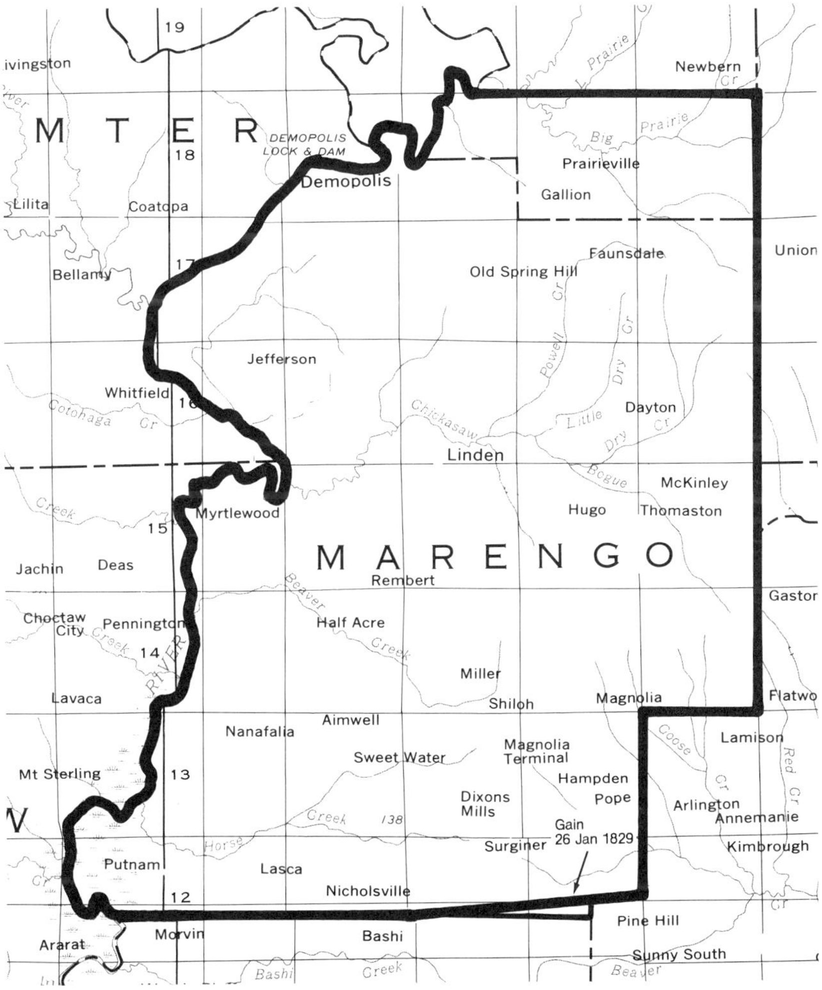

ALABAMA

Chronology of MARENGO

Map	Date	Event	Resulting Area
⑤	4 Feb 1840	Gained from DALLAS	1,080 sq mi
⑤	28 Nov 1863	Gained small area from PERRY to accommodate local property owner	1,080 sq mi
⑤	30 Nov 1863	Lost small area to PERRY to accommodate local property owner	1,080 sq mi
⑤	20 Feb 1866	Gained small area from PERRY to accommodate local property owner	1,080 sq mi

(Heavy line depicts historical boundary. Base map shows present-day information.)

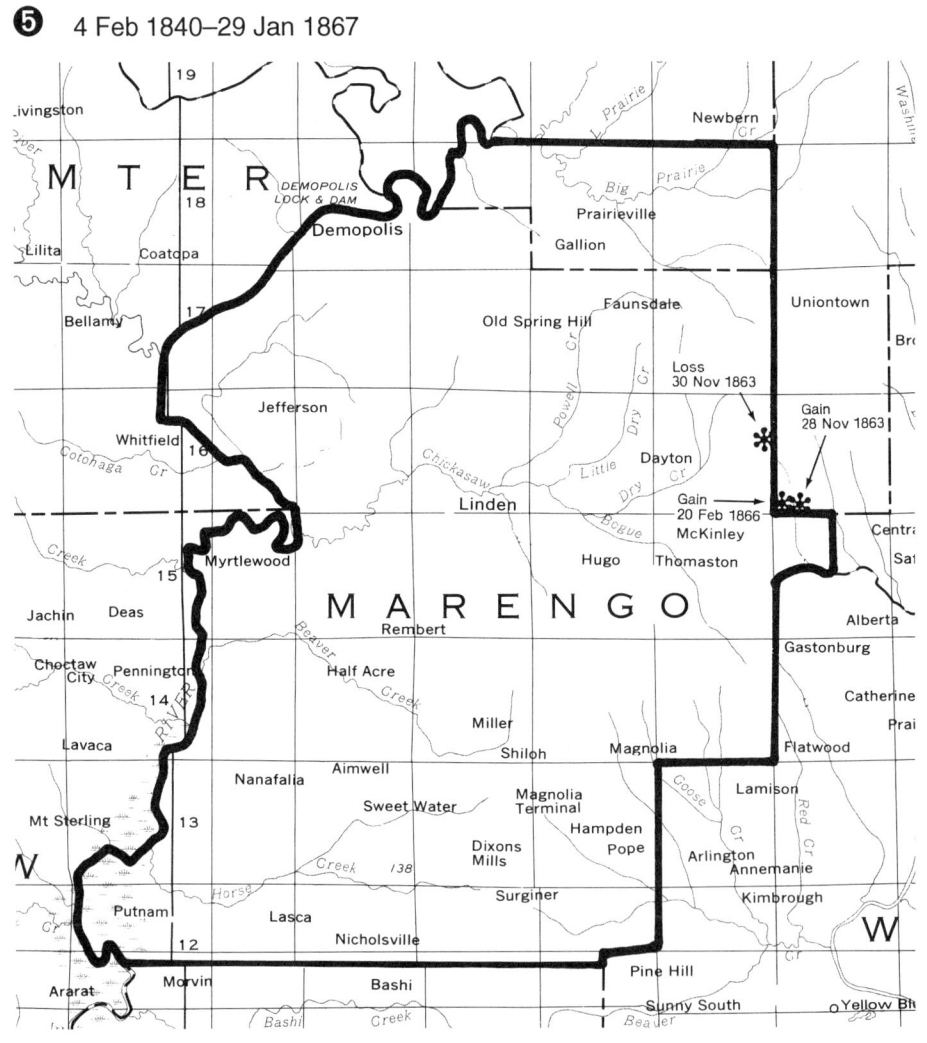

⑤ 4 Feb 1840–29 Jan 1867

Individual County Chronologies 237

Chronology of MARENGO

Map	Date	Event	Resulting Area
❻	30 Jan 1867	Lost to creation of HALE	1,000 sq mi
❻	7 Feb 1870	Gained small area from HALE, and gained small area from PERRY to accommodate local property owner	1,000 sq mi

(Heavy line depicts historical boundary. Base map shows present-day information.)

❻ 30 Jan 1867–1990

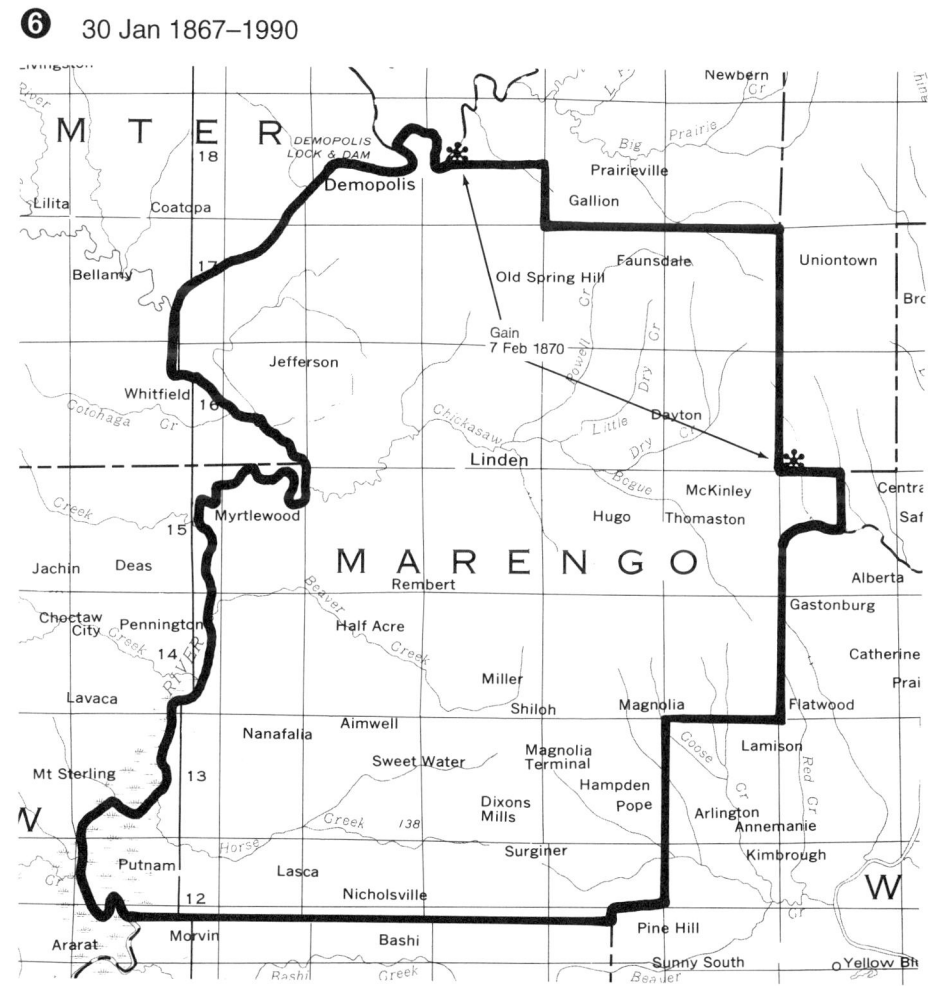

Chronology of MARION

Map	Date	Event	Resulting Area
❶	13 Feb 1818	Created from TUSCALOOSA; included most of TUSCALOOSA's overlap into state of Mississippi	2,640 sq mi
❷	19 Dec 1820	Gained from TUSCALOOSA and from non-county area attached to FRANKLIN, lost overlap of state of Mississippi, lost eastern territory to non-county area, and lost to creation of PICKENS	1,190 sq mi
❸	1 Jan 1823	Gained from non-county area	2,230 sq mi
❷	26 Dec 1823	Lost to creation of WALKER	1,190 sq mi

(Heavy line depicts historical boundary. Base map shows present-day information.)

❶ 13 Feb 1818–18 Dec 1820

❷ 19 Dec 1820–31 Dec 1822
26 Dec 1823–19 Dec 1824

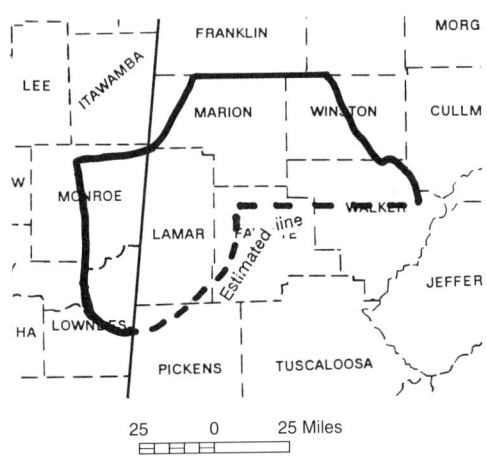

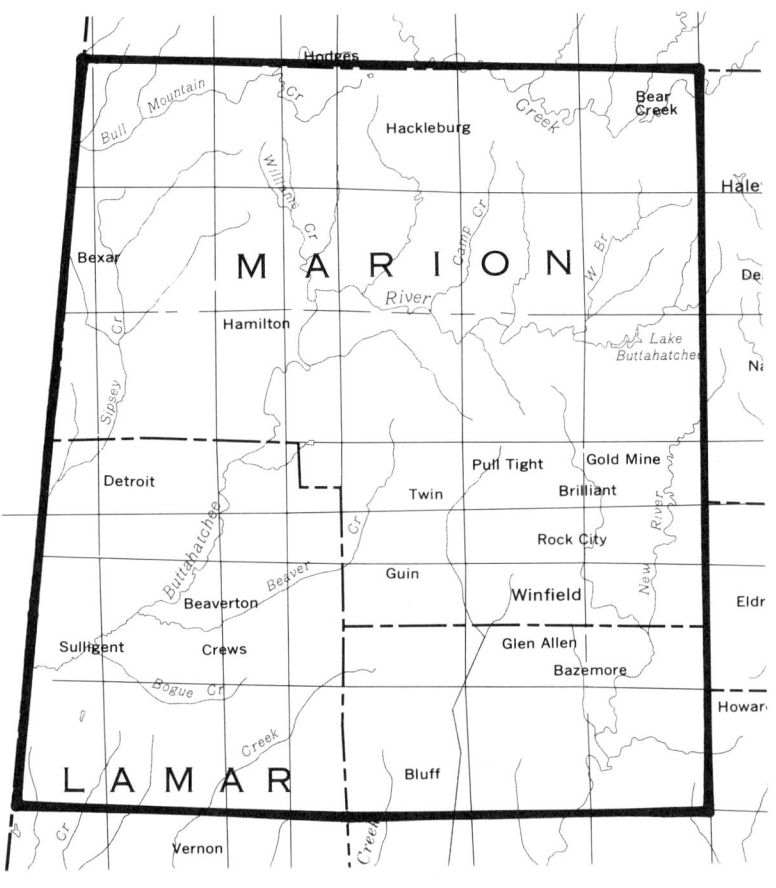

❸ 1 Jan 1823–25 Dec 1823

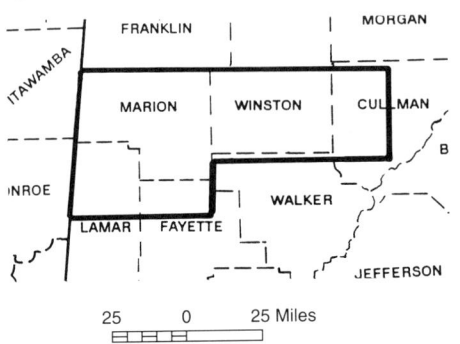

Chronology of MARION

Map	Date	Event	Resulting Area
❹	20 Dec 1824	Lost to creation of FAYETTE	1,100 sq mi

(Heavy line depicts historical boundary. Base map shows present-day information.)

❹ 20 Dec 1824–14 Jan 1831

Chronology of MARION

Map	Date	Event	Resulting Area
❺	15 Jan 1831	Lost to FAYETTE	1,070 sq mi
	18 Dec 1832	Boundaries redefined [no change]	

(Heavy line depicts historical boundary. Base map shows present-day information.)

❺ 15 Jan 1831–22 Dec 1837

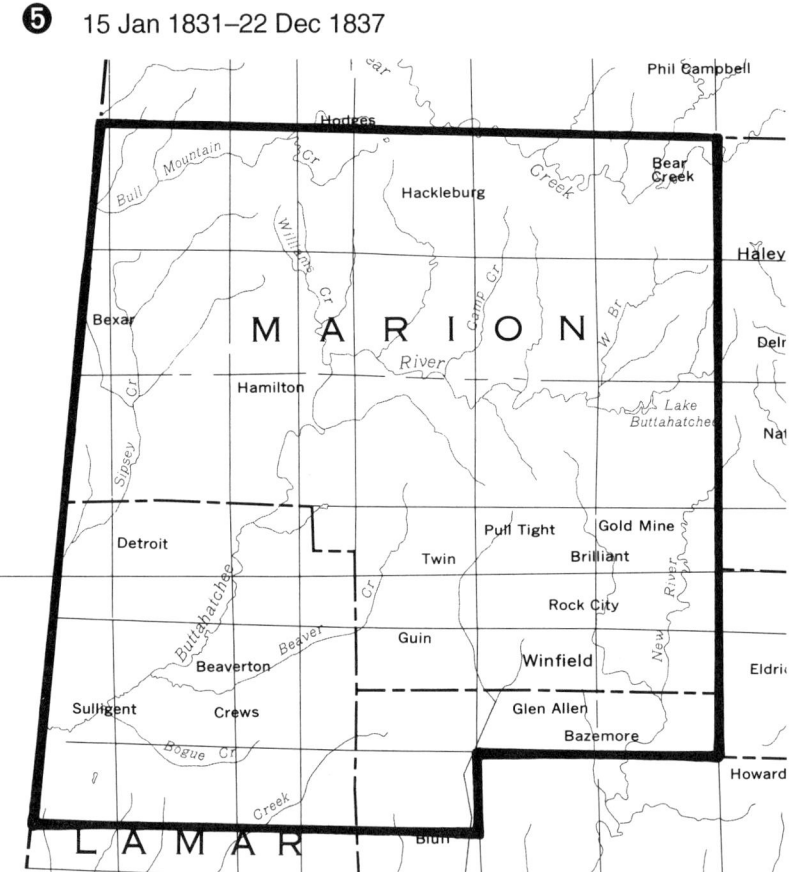

Individual County Chronologies   **241**

Chronology of MARION

Map	Date	Event	Resulting Area
❻	23 Dec 1837	Lost to FAYETTE	1,040 sq mi

(Heavy line depicts historical boundary. Base map shows present-day information.)

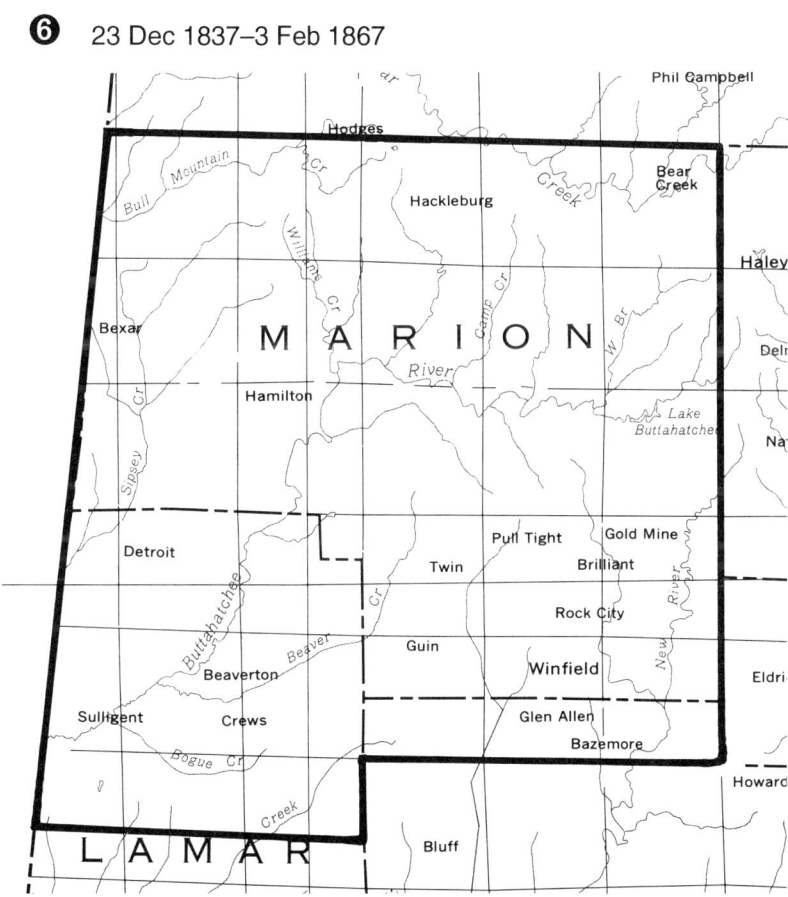

❻   23 Dec 1837–3 Feb 1867

ALABAMA

Chronology of MARION

Map	Date	Event	Resulting Area
❼	4 Feb 1867	Lost to FAYETTE and to creation of JONES	740 sq mi
❽	13 Nov 1867	Gained from JONES; JONES eliminated	990 sq mi
❼	8 Oct 1868	Lost to creation of SANFORD (now LAMAR)	740 sq mi

(Heavy line depicts historical boundary. Base map shows present-day information.)

❼ 4 Feb 1867–12 Nov 1867
8 Oct 1868–1990

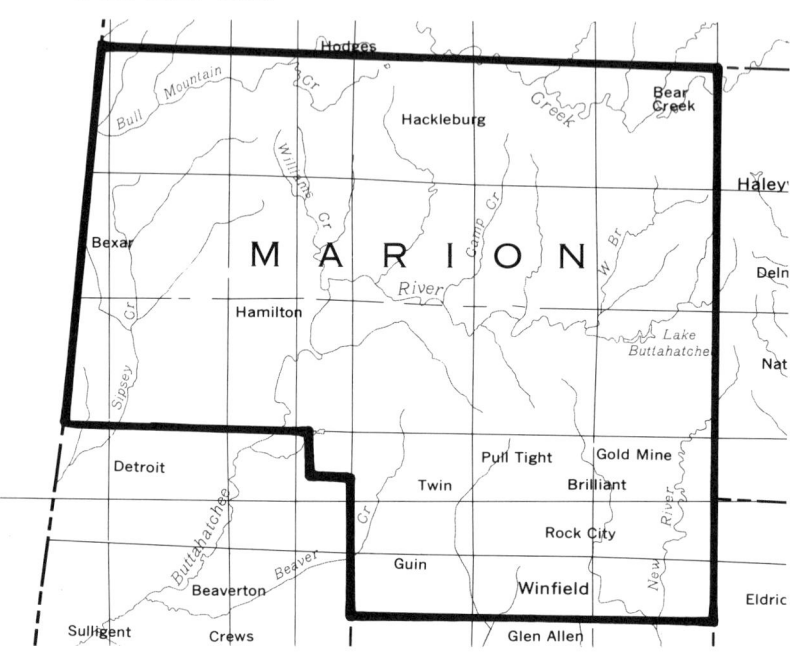

❽ 13 Nov 1867–7 Oct 1868

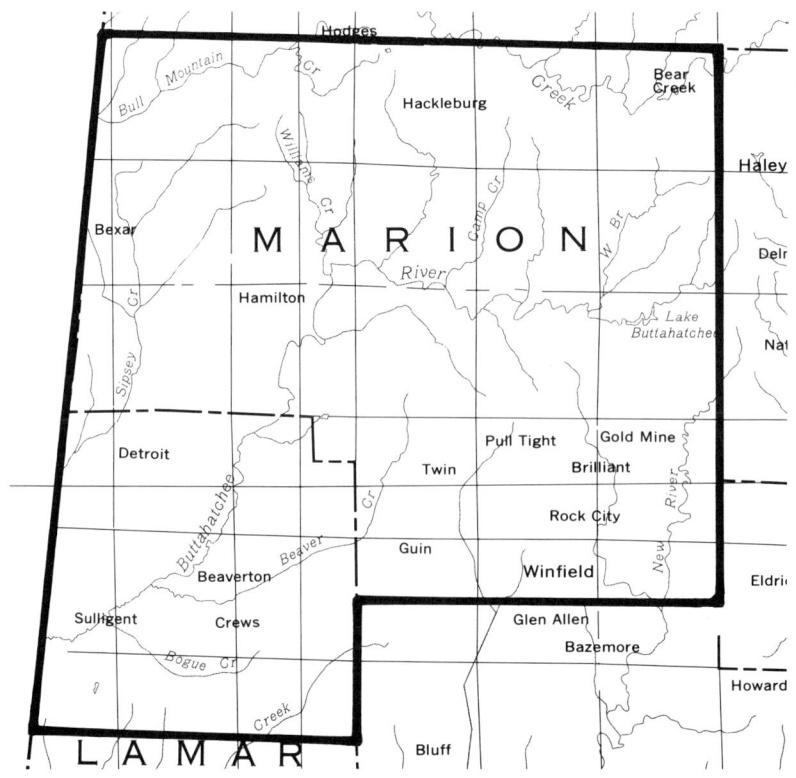

Chronology of MARSHALL

Map	Date	Event	Resulting Area
❶	9 Jan 1836	Created from BLOUNT and JACKSON	630 sq mi

(Heavy line depicts historical boundary. Base map shows present-day information.)

❶ 9 Jan 1836–22 Dec 1837

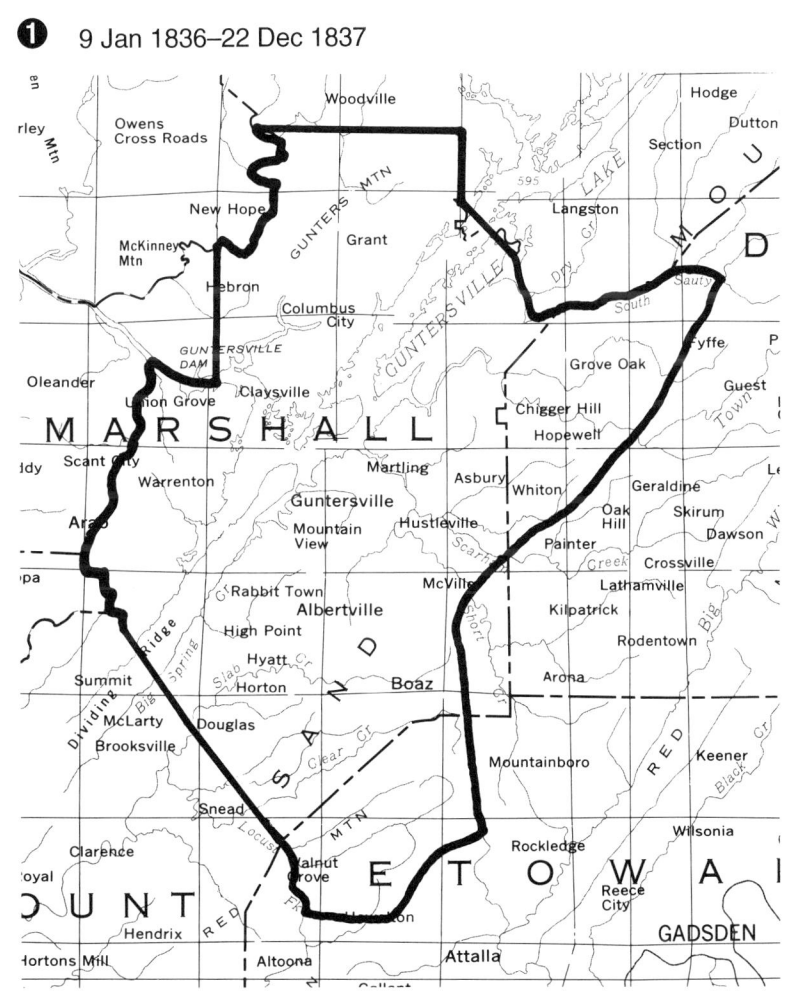

Chronology of MARSHALL

Map	Date	Event	Resulting Area
❷	23 Dec 1837	Gained from MADISON	650 sq mi

(Heavy line depicts historical boundary. Base map shows present-day information.)

❷ 23 Dec 1837–14 Dec 1840

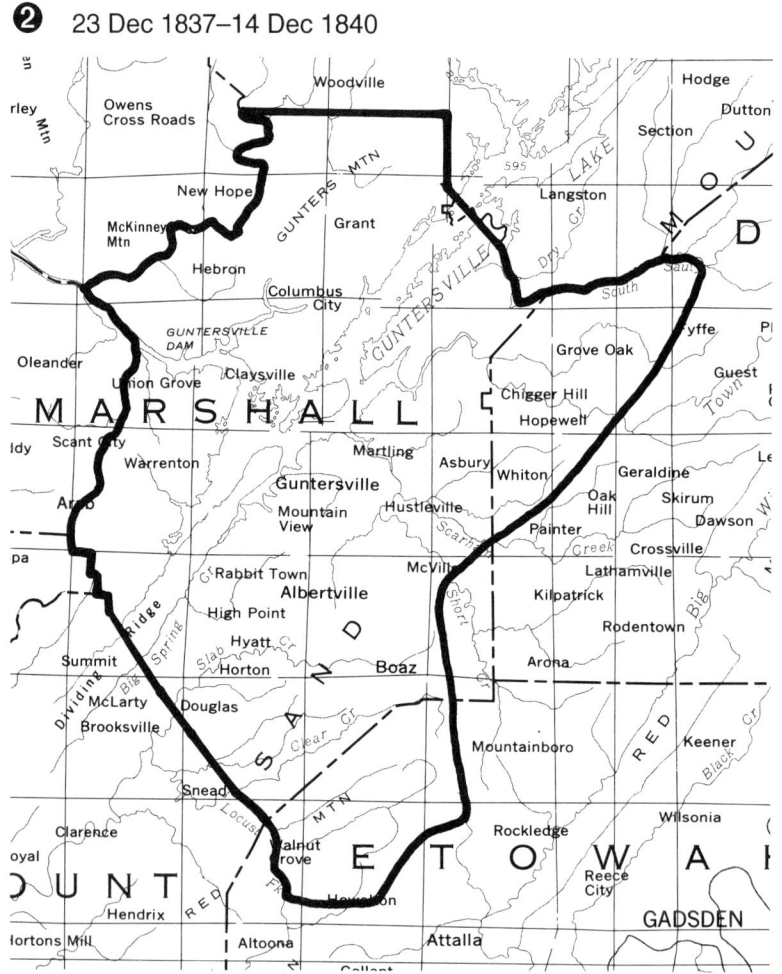

Individual County Chronologies 245

Chronology of MARSHALL

Map	Date	Event	Resulting Area
❸	15 Dec 1840	Gained from MORGAN	750 sq mi

(Heavy line depicts historical boundary. Base map shows present-day information.)

❸ 15 Dec 1840–6 Feb 1843

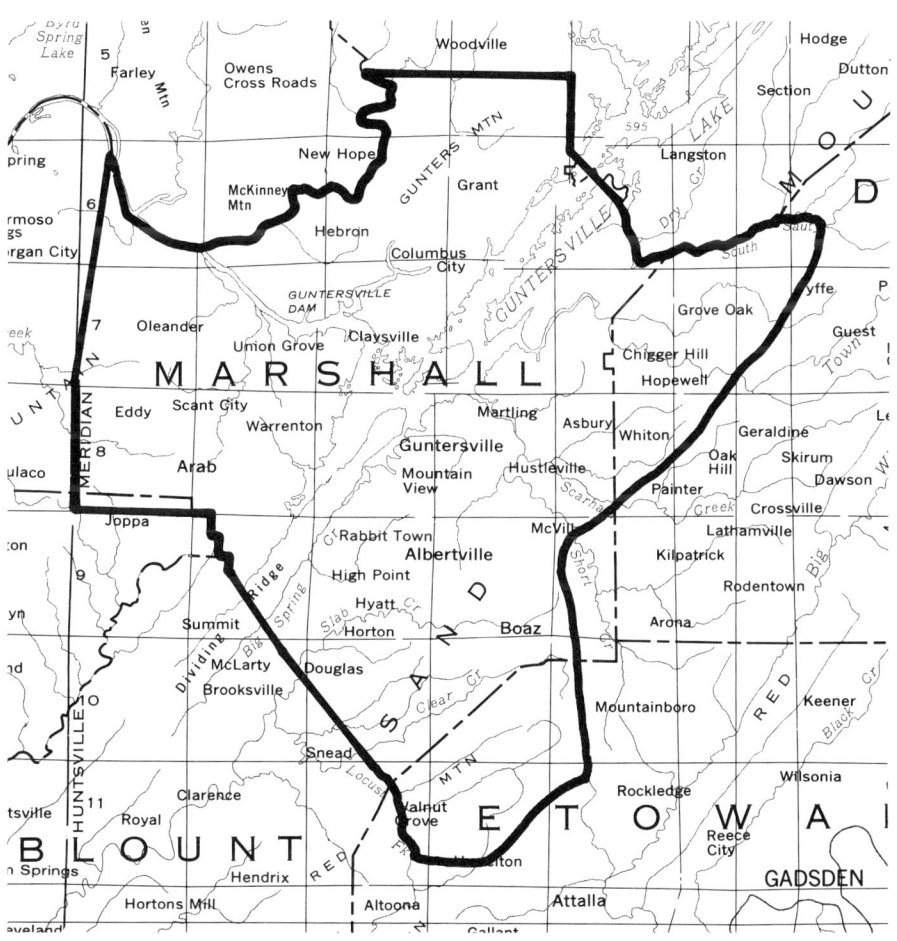

ALABAMA

Chronology of MARSHALL

Map	Date	Event	Resulting Area
4	7 Feb 1843	Exchanged with DE KALB	690 sq mi
4	5 Feb 1852	Lost small area to JACKSON	690 sq mi

(Heavy line depicts historical boundary. Base map shows present-day information.)

4 7 Feb 1843–1 Feb 1858

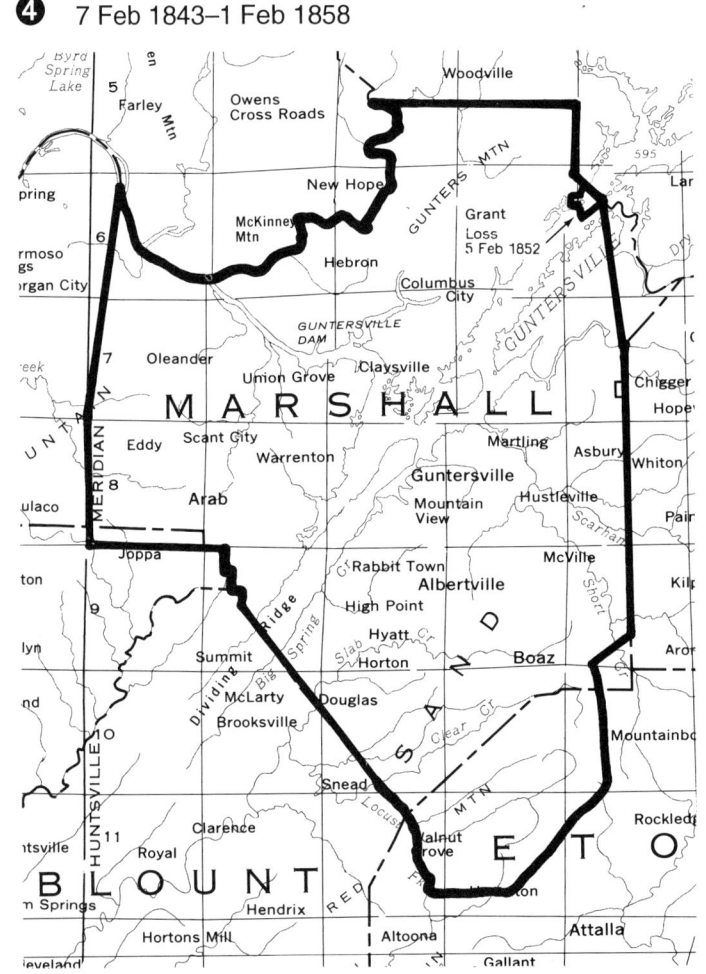

Chronology of MARSHALL

Map	Date	Event	Resulting Area
❺	2 Feb 1858	Gained from DE KALB	700 sq mi

(Heavy line depicts historical boundary. Base map shows present-day information.)

❺ 2 Feb 1858–6 Dec 1866
3 Dec 1867–30 Nov 1868

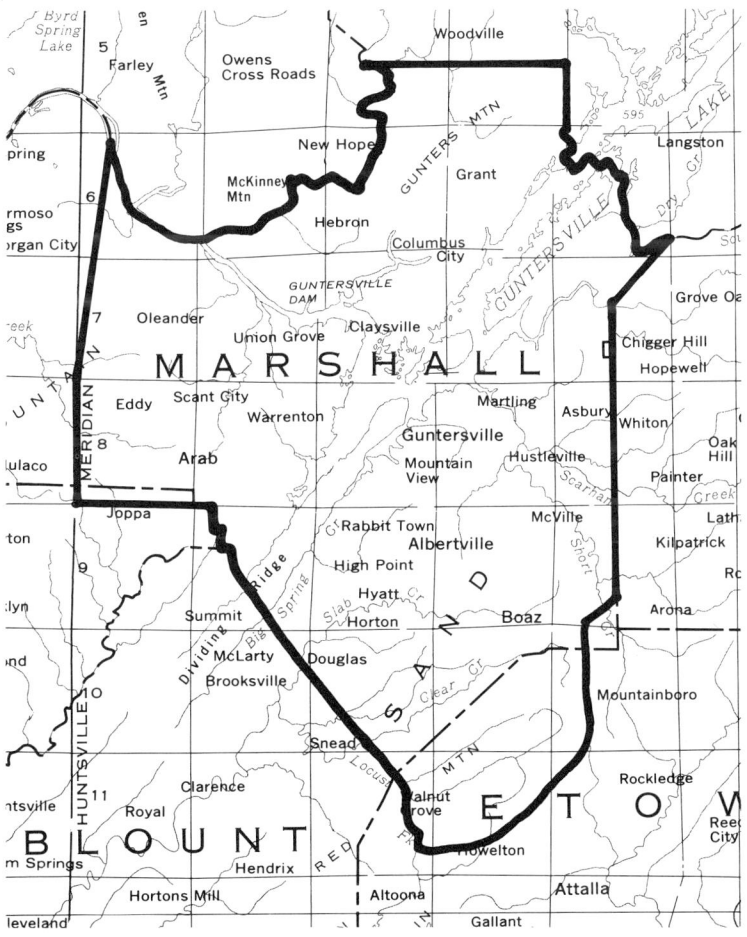

ALABAMA

Chronology of MARSHALL

Map	Date	Event	Resulting Area
❻	7 Dec 1866	Lost to creation of BAINE	600 sq mi

(Heavy line depicts historical boundary. Base map shows present-day information.)

❻ 7 Dec 1866–18 Feb 1867

Chronology of MARSHALL

Map	Date	Event	Resulting Area
❼	19 Feb 1867	Gained from BAINE	610 sq mi
❺	3 Dec 1867	Gained from BAINE; BAINE eliminated	700 sq mi

(Heavy line depicts historical boundary. Base map shows present-day information.)

❼ 19 Feb 1867–2 Dec 1867

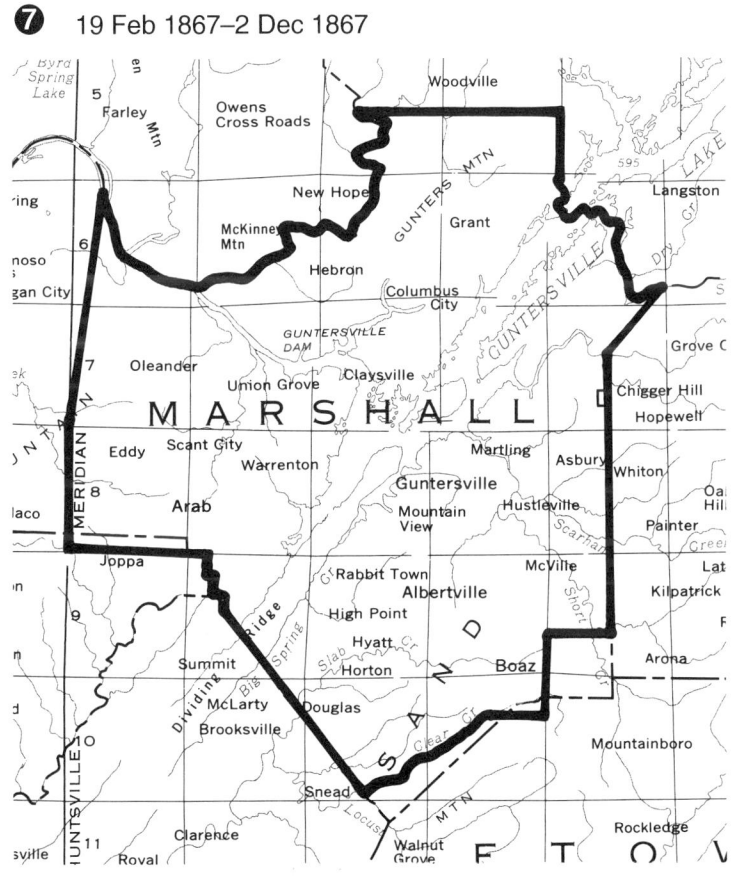

ALABAMA

Chronology of MARSHALL

Map	Date	Event	Resulting Area
8	1 Dec 1868	Apparently gained from DE KALB, lost to creation of ETOWAH	640 sq mi
8	25 Feb 1870	Lost small area to BLOUNT	640 sq mi

(Heavy line depicts historical boundary. Base map shows present-day information.)

8   1 Dec 1868–23 Jan 1877

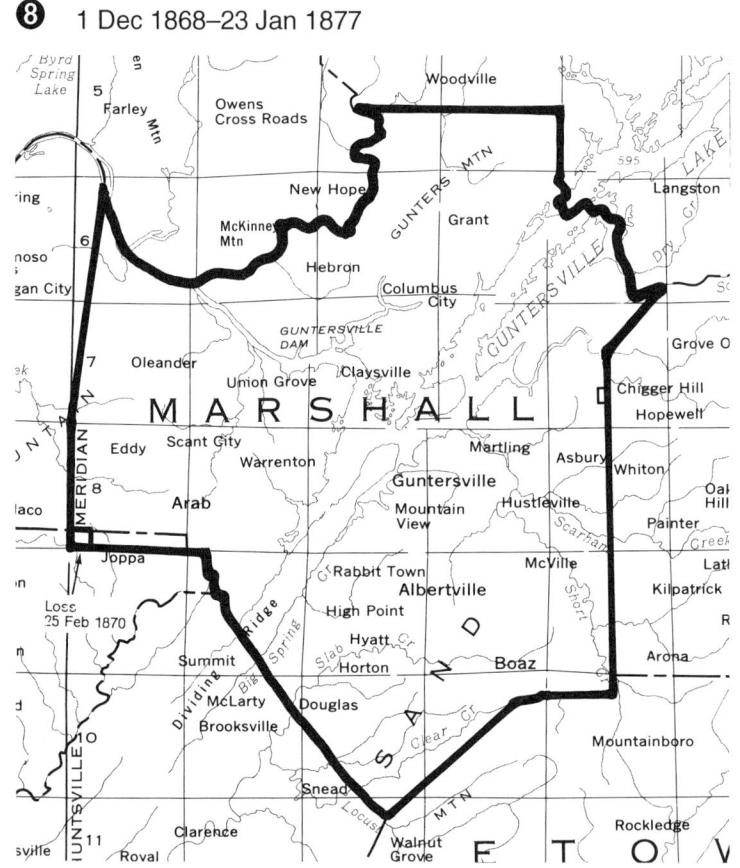

Chronology of MARSHALL

Map	Date	Event	Resulting Area
⑨	24 Jan 1877	Lost to creation of CULLMAN	630 sq mi
⑨	30 Jan 1877	Lost to DE KALB	620 sq mi

(Heavy line depicts historical boundary. Base map shows present-day information.)

⑨ 24 Jan 1877–3 Feb 1879

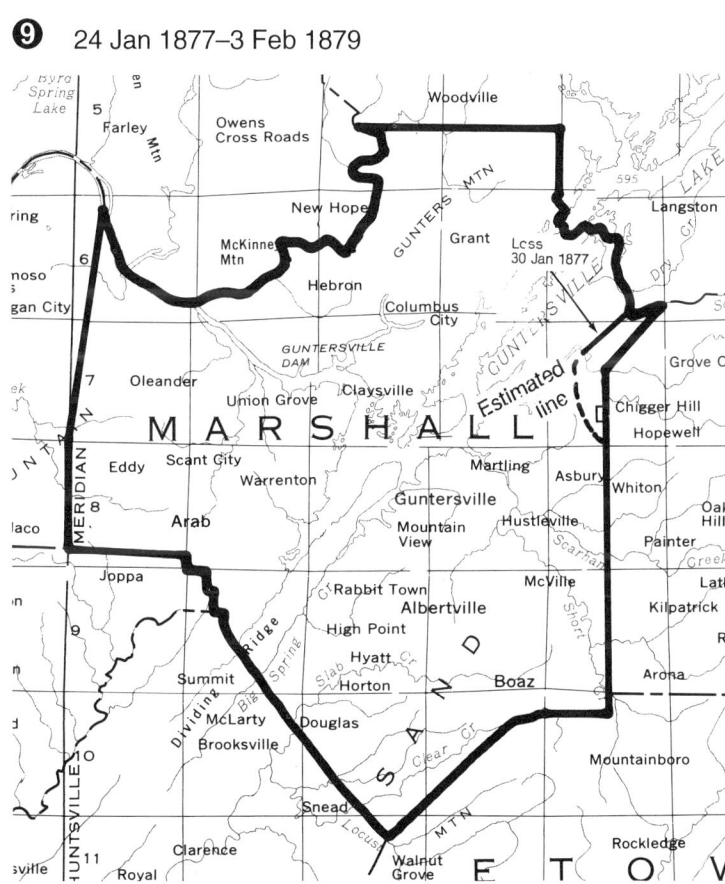

Chronology of MARSHALL

Map	Date	Event	Resulting Area
⑩	4 Feb 1879	Gained from DE KALB	630 sq mi

(Heavy line depicts historical boundary. Base map shows present-day information.)

⑩ 4 Feb 1879–1990

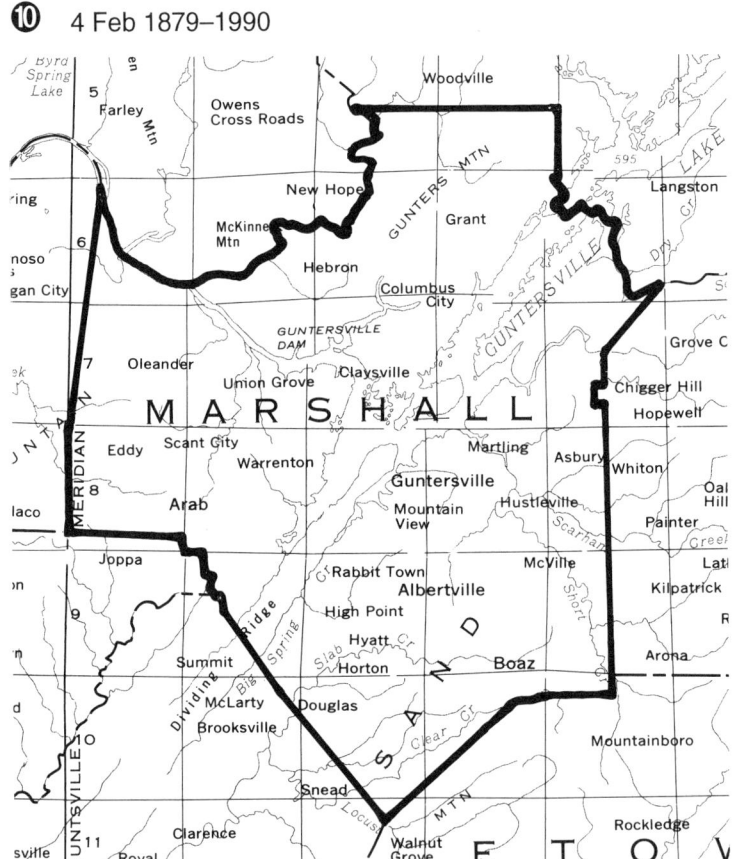

Chronology of MOBILE

Map	Date	Event	Resulting Area
❶	1 Aug 1812	Created by Mississippi Territory from non-county area in present Alabama and Mississippi that was claimed, but not fully controlled, by the United States	6,050 sq mi

(Heavy line depicts historical boundary. Base map shows present-day information.)

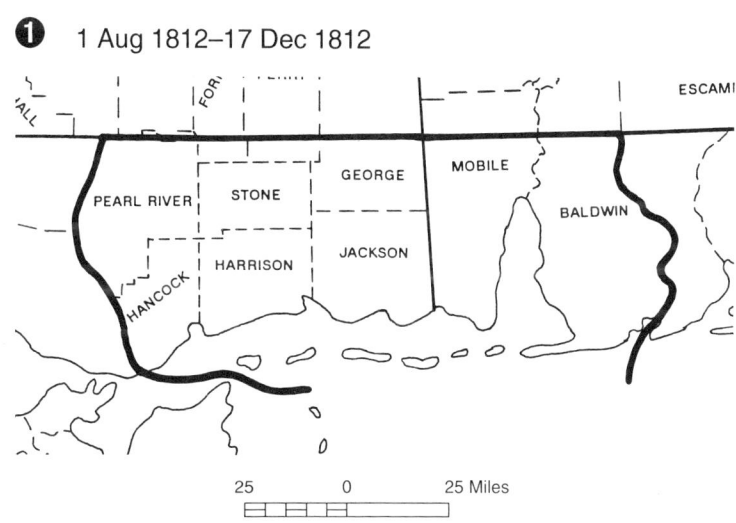

❶ 1 Aug 1812–17 Dec 1812

Chronology of MOBILE

Map	Date	Event	Resulting Area
❷	18 Dec 1812	Lost to creation of HANCOCK (Miss.) and JACKSON (Miss.)	2,000 sq mi
	15 Apr 1813	American forces captured city of Mobile from Spain, effectively adding to the United States the territory between the Pearl and Perdido rivers previously claimed by the United States as part of Louisiana and where MOBILE had been created	
	3 Mar 1817	Became part of Alabama Territory	

(Heavy line depicts historical boundary. Base map shows present-day information.)

❷ 18 Dec 1812–6 Feb 1818

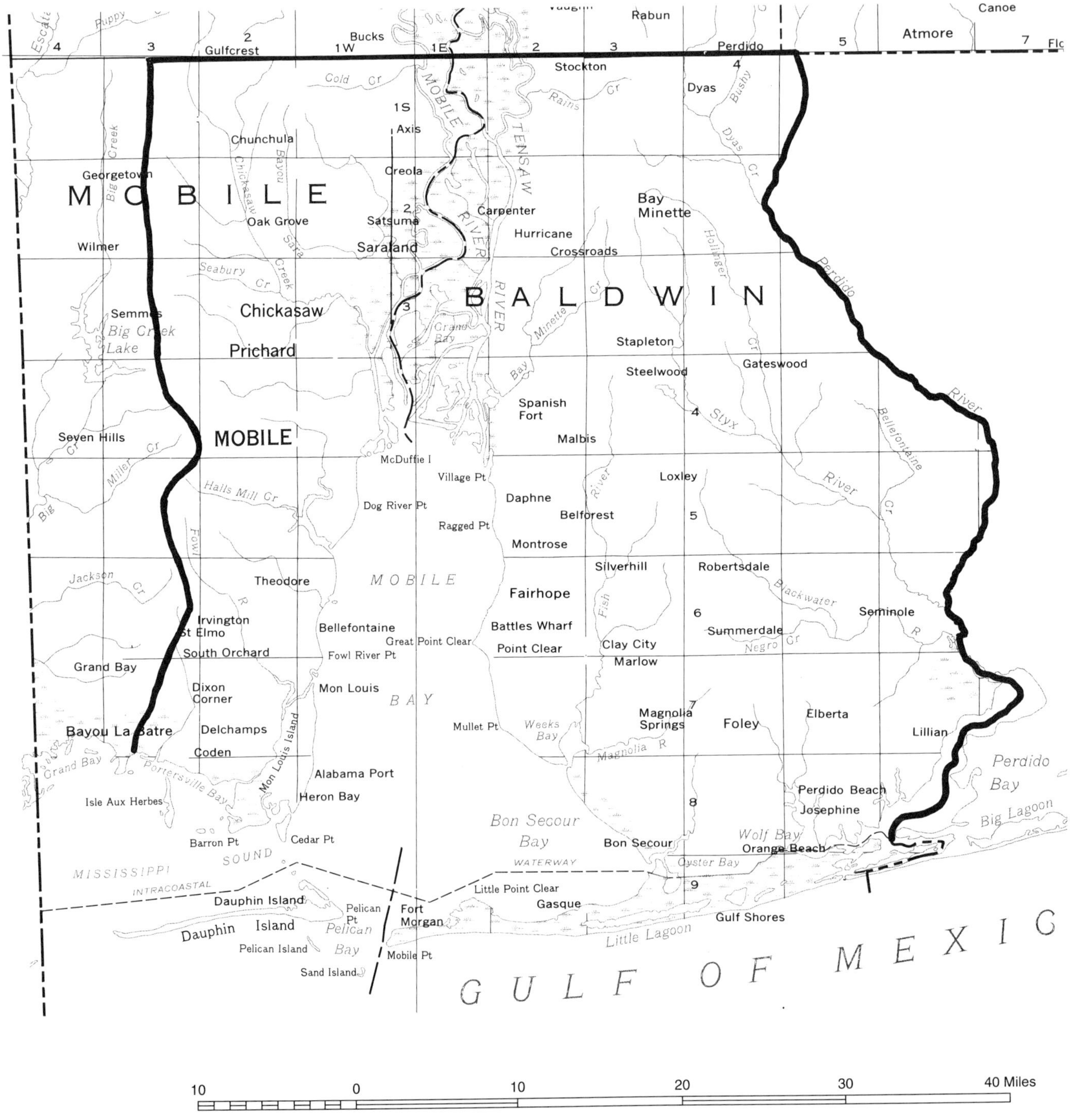

Individual County Chronologies 255

Chronology of MOBILE

Map	Date	Event	Resulting Area
❸	7 Feb 1818	Gained from JACKSON (Miss.)	2,500 sq mi

(Heavy line depicts historical boundary. Base map shows present-day information.)

❸ 7 Feb 1818–before 29 May 1820

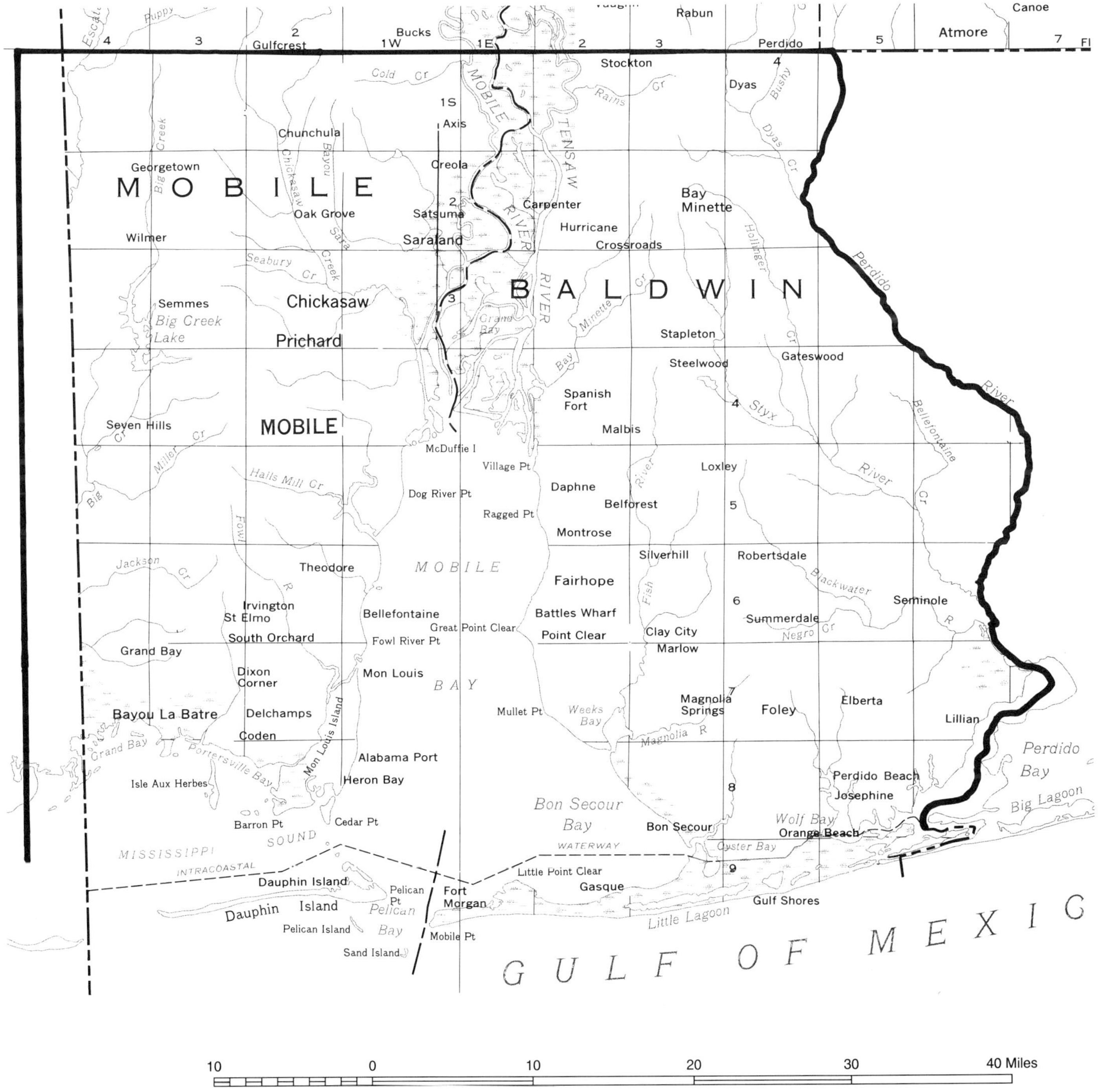

ALABAMA

Chronology of MOBILE

Map	Date	Event	Resulting Area
❹	by 29 May 1820	Lost to Mississippi when surveyors implemented the authorized adjustment of the Mississippi-Alabama line	2,360 sq mi

(Heavy line depicts historical boundary. Base map shows present-day information.)

❹ by 29 May 1820–15 Dec 1820

Individual County Chronologies 257

Chronology of MOBILE

Map	Date	Event	Resulting Area
❺	16 Dec 1820	Exchanged with BALDWIN	1,950 sq mi
❻	27 Jan 1829	Lost to WASHINGTON	1,320 sq mi

(Heavy line depicts historical boundary. Base map shows present-day information.)

❻ 27 Jan 1829–20 Dec 1832

❺ 16 Dec 1820–26 Jan 1829

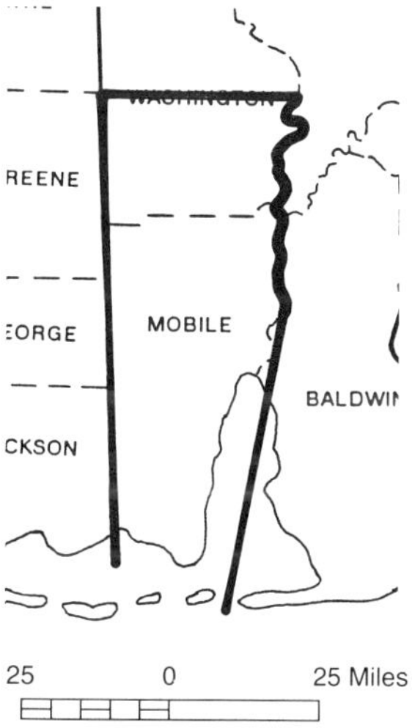

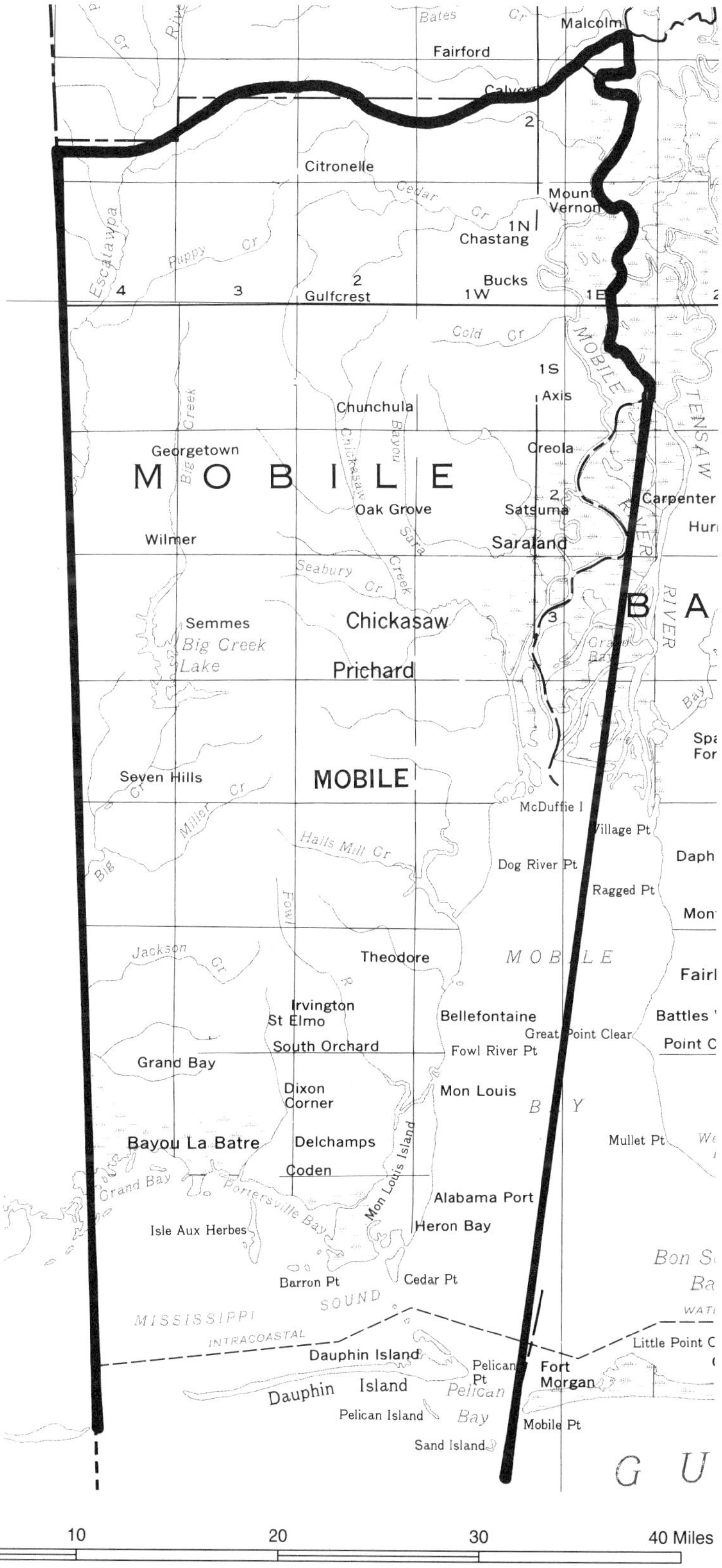

258   ALABAMA

Chronology of MOBILE

Map	Date	Event	Resulting Area
❼	21 Dec 1832	Lost to BALDWIN	1,280 sq mi
❼	21 Feb 1860	Lost small area to WASHINGTON	1,280 sq mi
❼	27 Aug 1863	Gained small area from WASHINGTON to accommodate local property owners	1,280 sq mi

(Heavy line depicts historical boundary. Base map shows present-day information.)

❼ 21 Dec 1832–20 Feb 1893

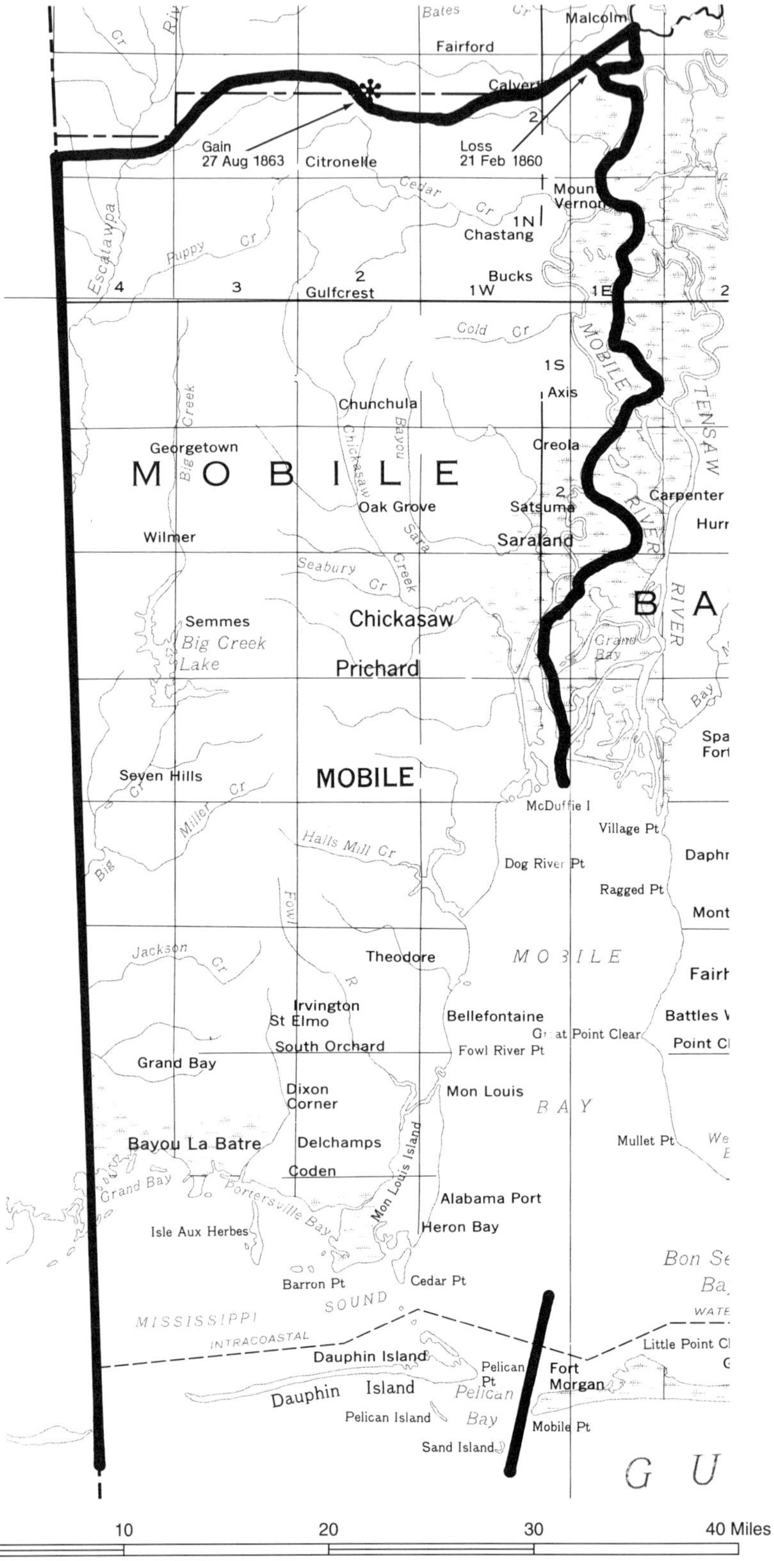

Individual County Chronologies   259

Chronology of MOBILE

Map	Date	Event	Resulting Area
⑧	21 Feb 1893	Exchanged with WASHINGTON	1,280 sq mi
⑧	18 Feb 1895	Lost small area to WASHINGTON	1,280 sq mi
⑧	28 Feb 1901	Gained small area from WASHINGTON	1,280 sq mi
	18 Jul 1983	Boundaries redefined [no change]	

(Heavy line depicts historical boundary. Base map shows present-day information.)

⑧   21 Feb 1893–1990

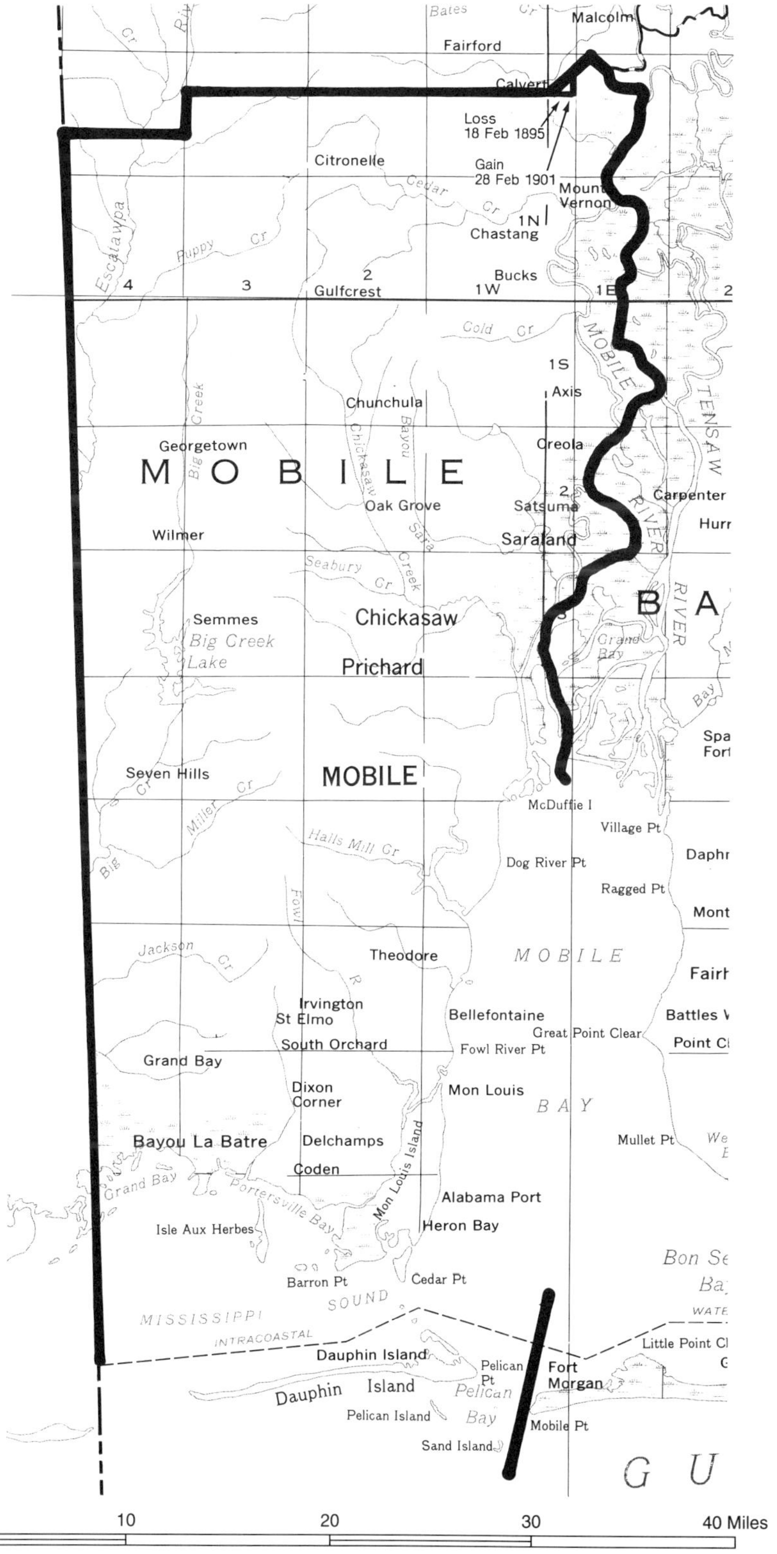

260 ALABAMA

Chronology of MONROE

Map	Date	Event	Resulting Area
❶	29 Jun 1815	Created by Mississippi Territory from non-county area	21,500 sq mi

(Heavy line depicts historical boundary. Base map shows present-day information.)

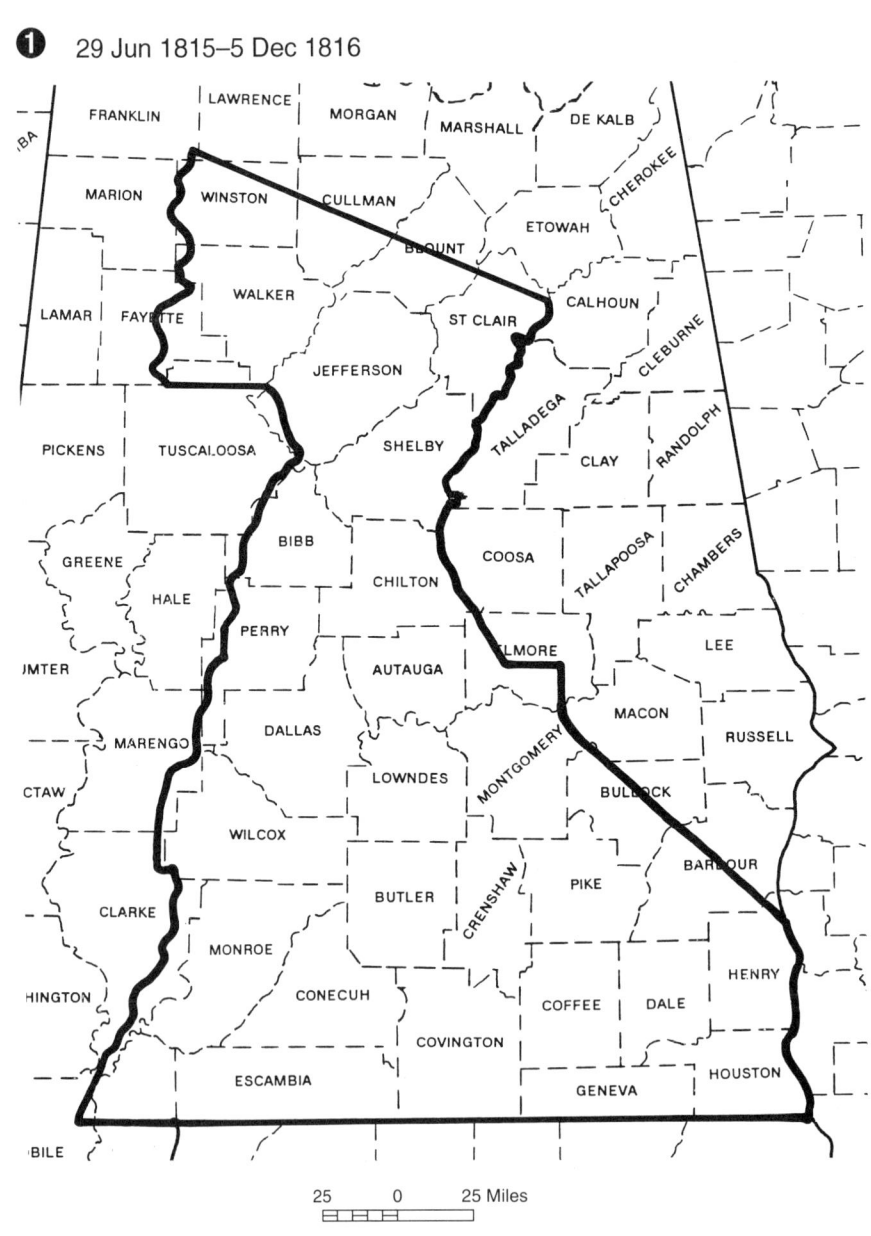

❶ 29 Jun 1815–5 Dec 1816

Individual County Chronologies 261

Chronology of MONROE

Map	Date	Event	Resulting Area
❷	6 Dec 1816	Lost to creation of MONTGOMERY	10,600 sq mi
	3 Mar 1817	Became part of Alabama Territory	
❸	9 Feb 1818	Lost to creation of DALLAS	10,200 sq mi
❹	13 Feb 1818	Lost to creation of CONECUH	2,100 sq mi

(Heavy line depicts historical boundary. Base map shows present-day information.)

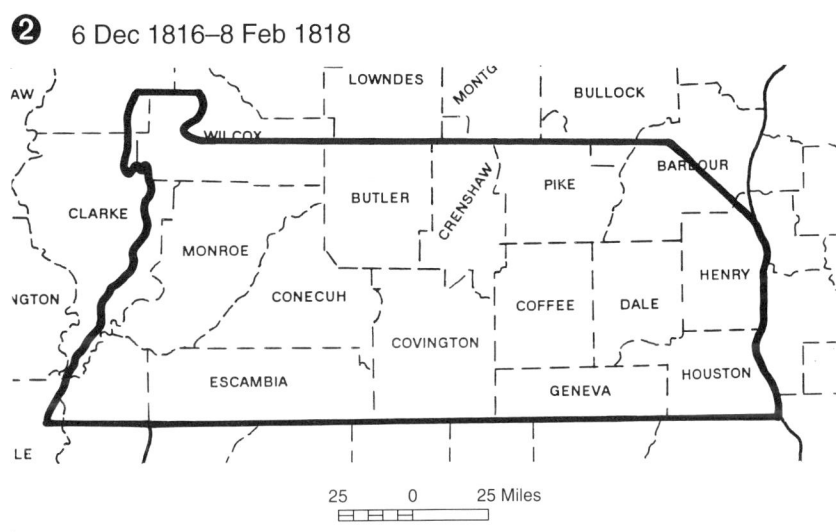

❷ 6 Dec 1816–8 Feb 1818

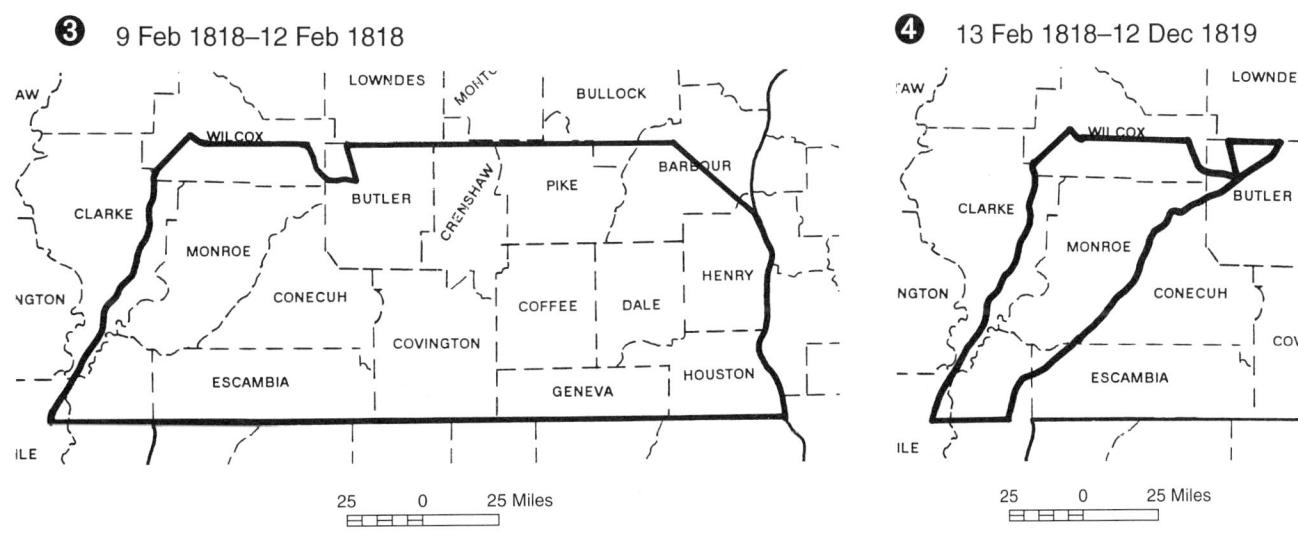

❸ 9 Feb 1818–12 Feb 1818

❹ 13 Feb 1818–12 Dec 1819

262 ALABAMA

Chronology of MONROE

Map	Date	Event	Resulting Area
⑤	13 Dec 1819	Lost to BALDWIN and lost to creation of both BUTLER and WILCOX	1,310 sq mi
⑥	16 Dec 1820	Gained from BALDWIN	1,410 sq mi
⑥	28 Nov 1821	Lost small area to CLARKE	1,410 sq mi

(Heavy line depicts historical boundary. Base map shows present-day information.)

⑤ 13 Dec 1819–15 Dec 1820

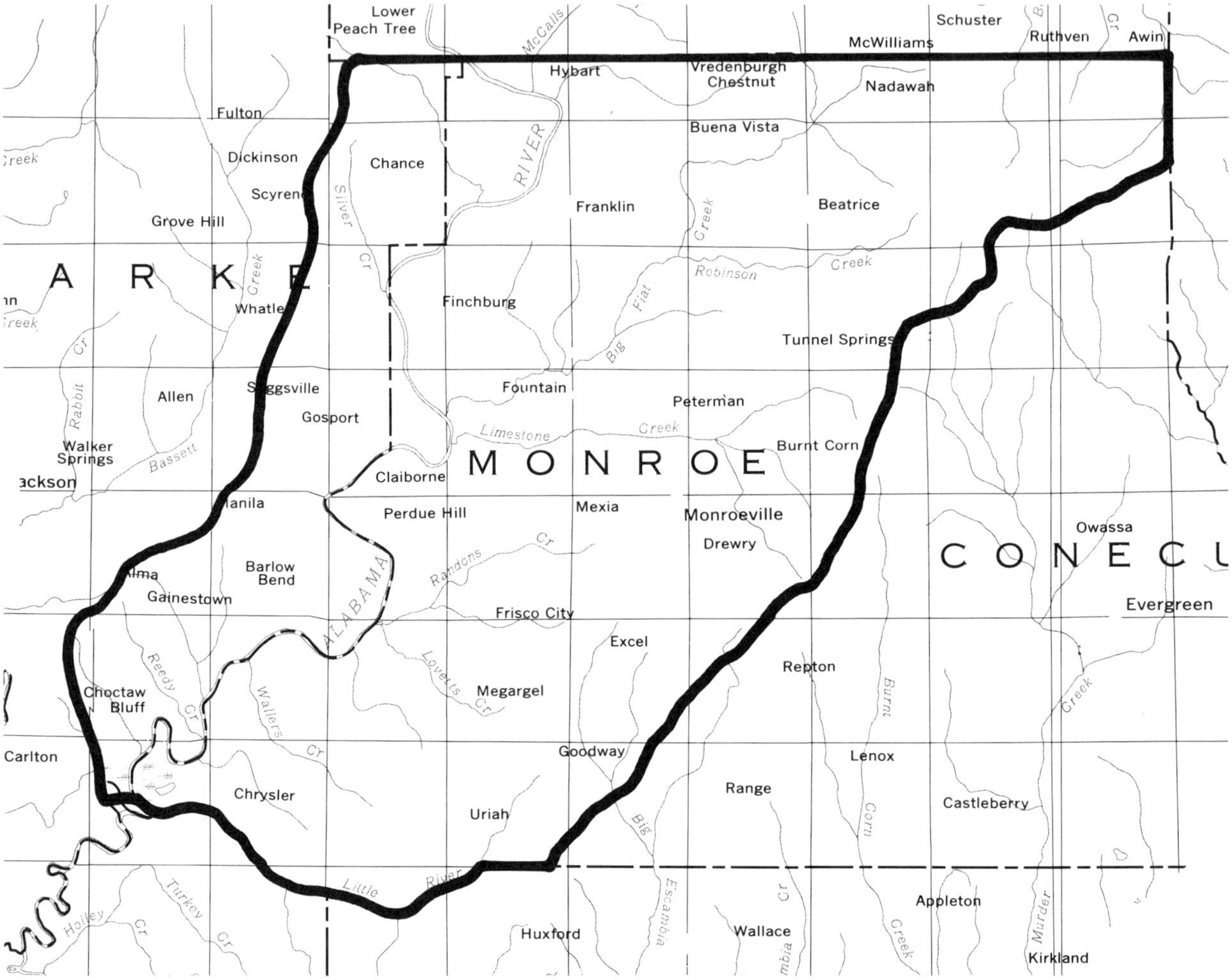

⑥ 16 Dec 1820–25 Jan 1829

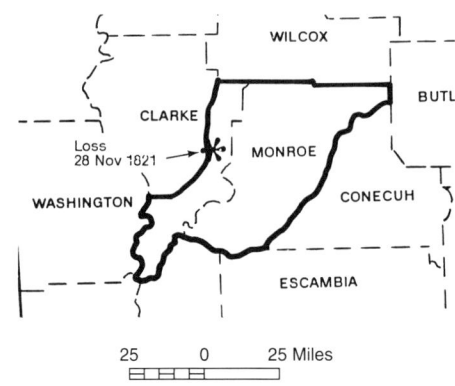

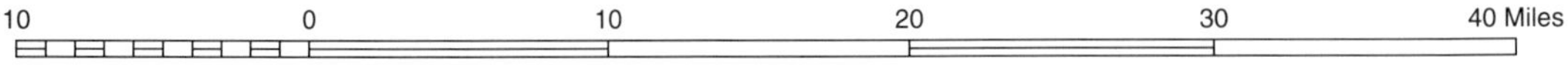

Chronology of MONROE

Map	Date	Event	Resulting Area
❼	26 Jan 1829	Lost to CLARKE	1,080 sq mi
❼	5 Jan 1833	Lost small area to BUTLER	1,080 sq mi
❼	by 1839	Gained small area from BUTLER	1,080 sq mi

(Heavy line depicts historical boundary. Base map shows present-day information.)

❼ 26 Jan 1829–12 Feb 1843

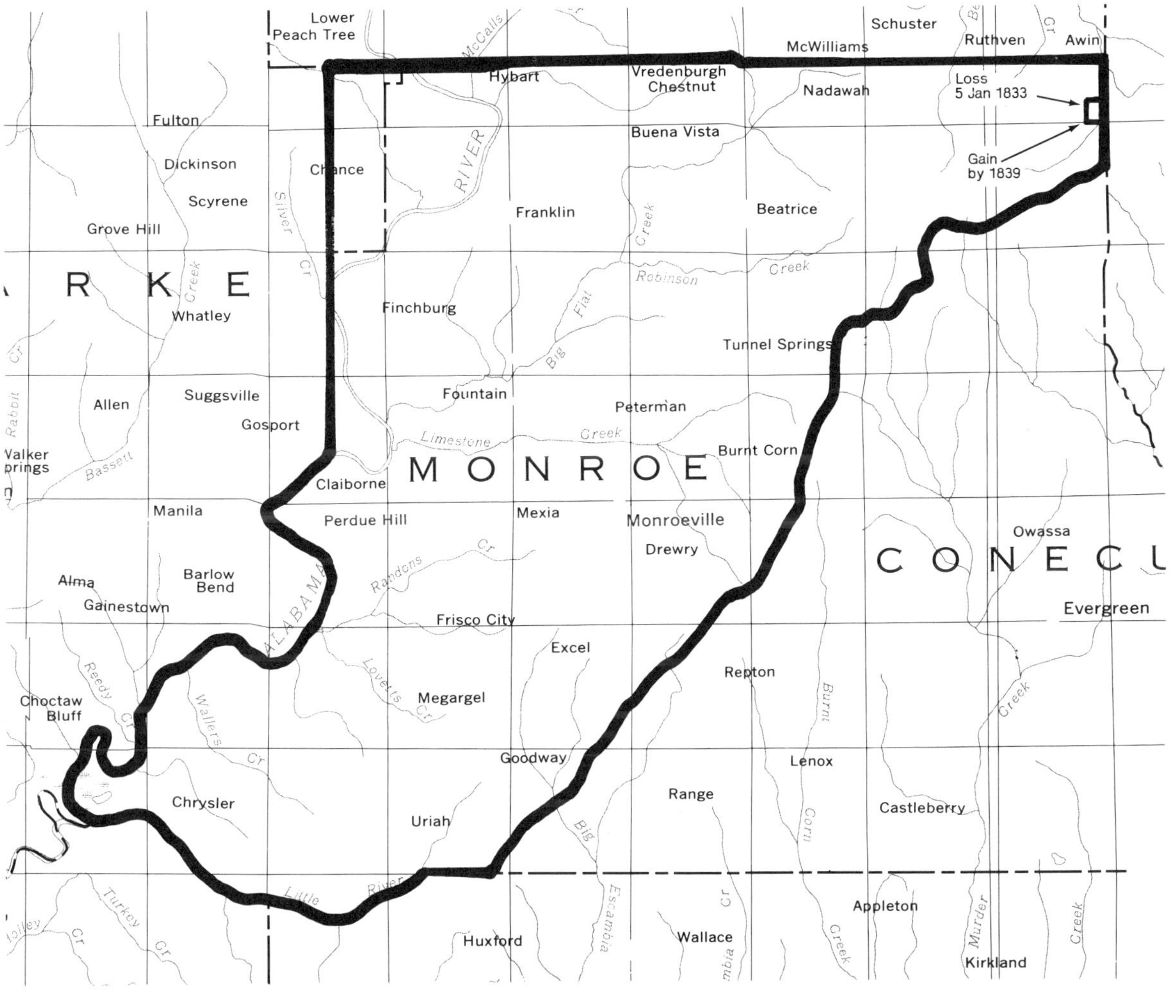

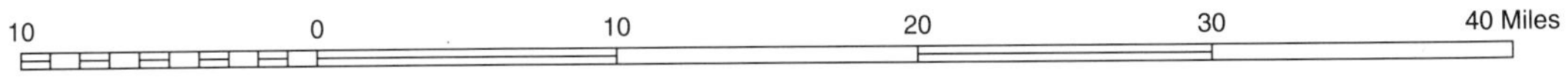

264 ALABAMA

Chronology of MONROE

Map	Date	Event	Resulting Area
⑧	13 Feb 1843	Lost to CLARKE	1,050 sq mi
	10 Feb 1852	Boundary with CONECUH clarified [no change]	
⑧	6 Dec 1861	Lost small area to CLARKE to accommodate local property owner	1,050 sq mi
⑧	11 Dec 1865	Gained small area from CONECUH to accommodate local property owner	1,050 sq mi
⑧	10 Dec 1868	Apparently gained from BALDWIN	1,050 sq mi

(Heavy line depicts historical boundary. Base map shows present-day information.)

⑧ 13 Feb 1843–1990

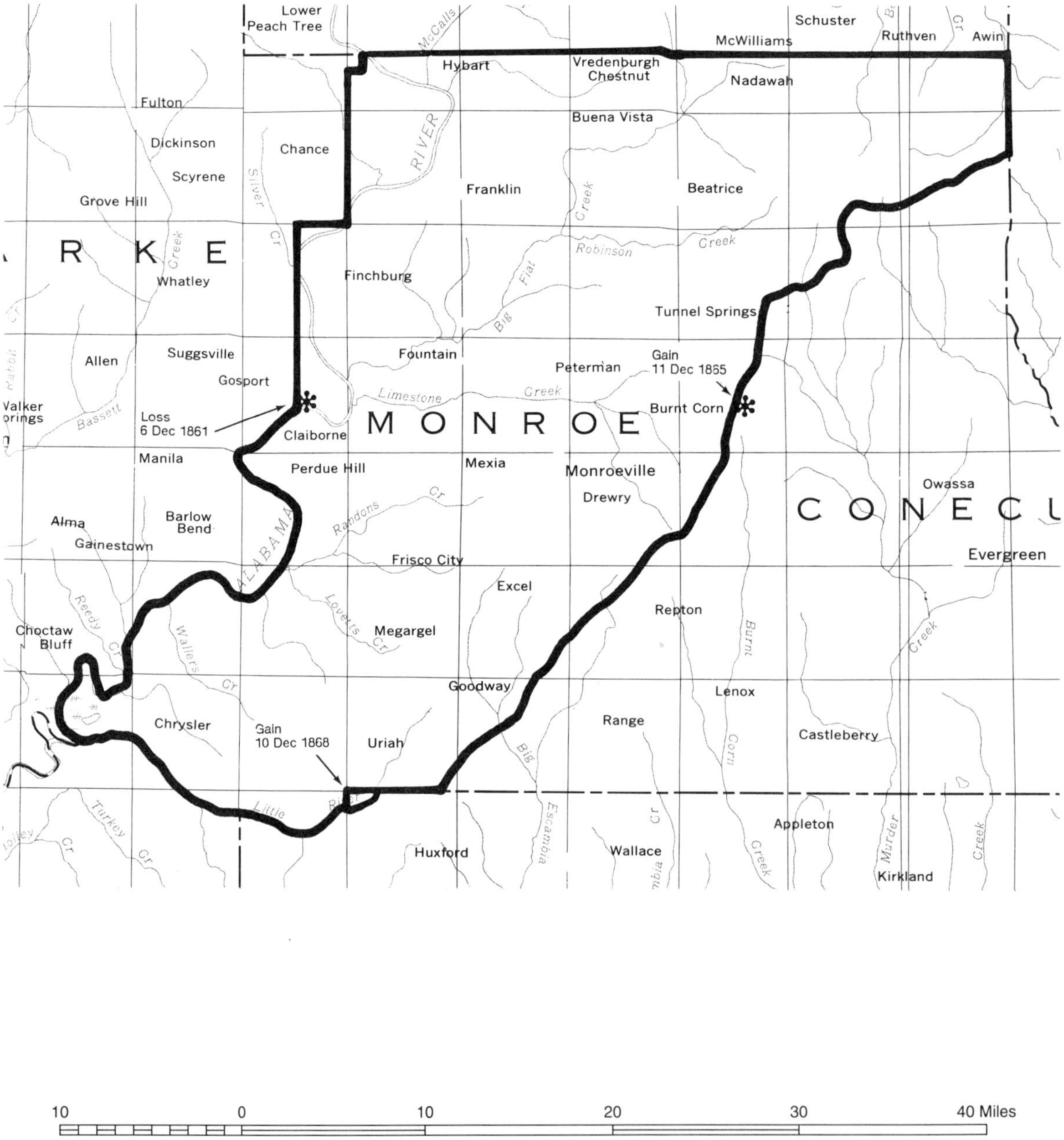

Chronology of MONTGOMERY

Map	Date	Event	Resulting Area
❶	6 Dec 1816	Created by Mississippi Territory from MONROE	10,900 sq mi
	3 Mar 1817	Became part of Alabama Territory	
❷	6 Feb 1818	Lost to creation of BLOUNT, FRANKLIN, LAWRENCE, and TUSCALOOSA	8,030 sq mi
❸	7 Feb 1818	Lost to creation of both CAHAWBA (now BIBB) and SHELBY	5,330 sq mi
❹	9 Feb 1818	Lost to creation of DALLAS	3,470 sq mi

(Heavy line depicts historical boundary. Base map shows present-day information.)

❶ 6 Dec 1816–5 Feb 1818

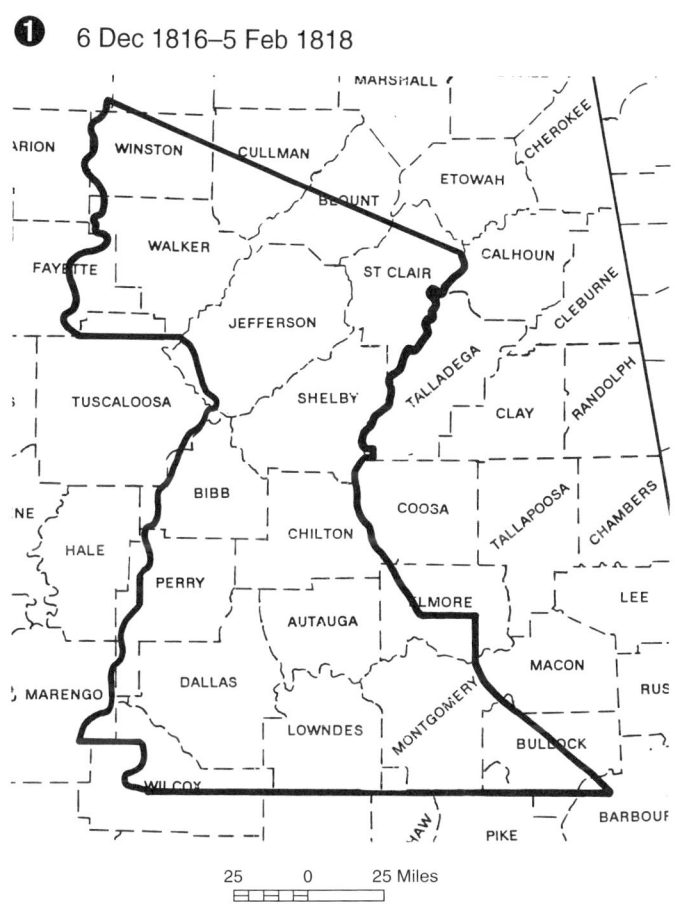

❷ 6 Feb 1818

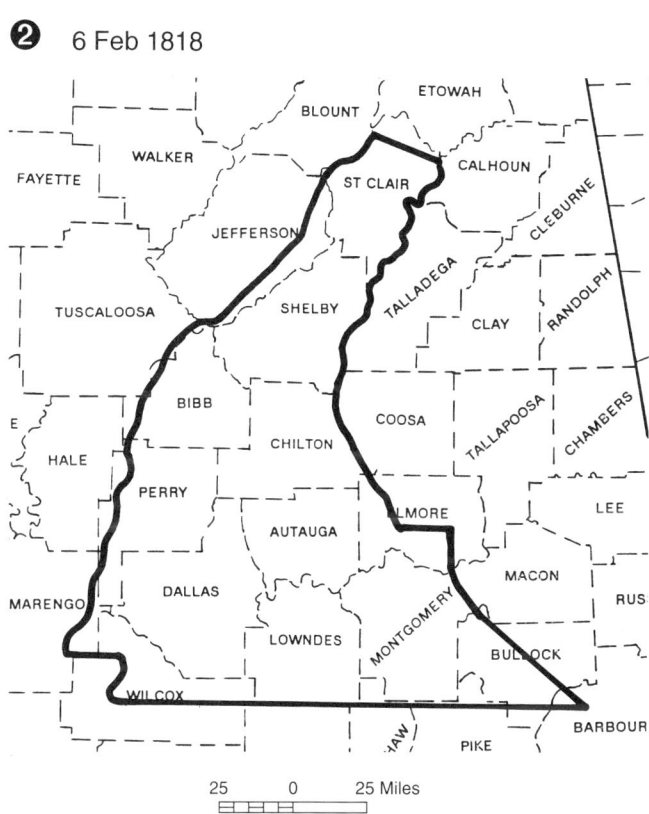

❸ 7 Feb 1818–8 Feb 1818

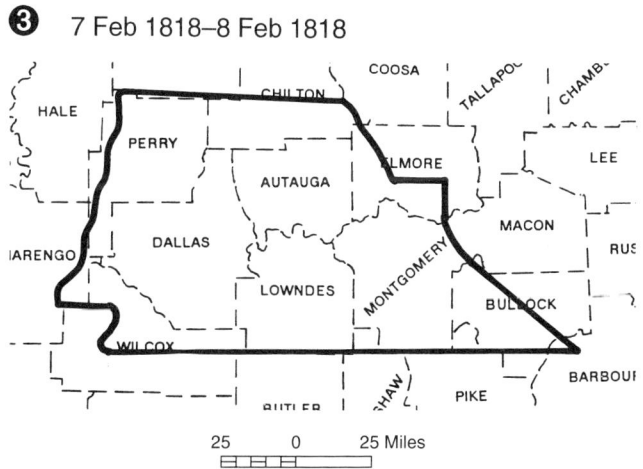

❹ 9 Feb 1818–19 Nov 1818

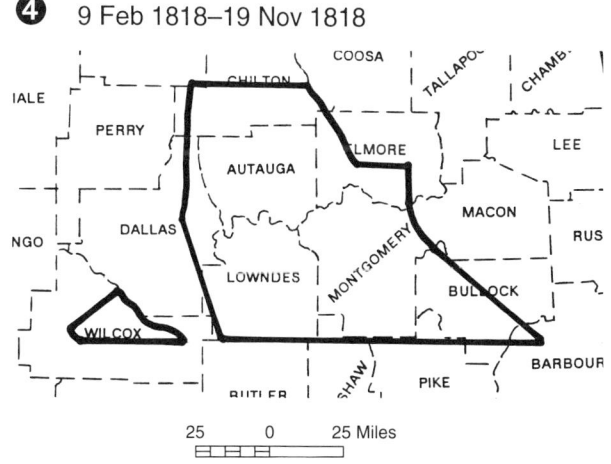

266 ALABAMA

Chronology of MONTGOMERY

Map	Date	Event	Resulting Area
⑤	20 Nov 1818	Lost to CAHAWBA (now BIBB)	3,410 sq mi
⑥	21 Nov 1818	Lost to DALLAS and to creation of AUTAUGA	2,200 sq mi
⑦	13 Dec 1819	Lost to DALLAS and to creation of WILCOX	1,910 sq mi
⑧	17 Dec 1819	Non-county area belonging to Creek Indians attached to MONTGOMERY	

(Heavy line depicts historical boundary. Base map shows present-day information.)

⑤ 20 Nov 1818

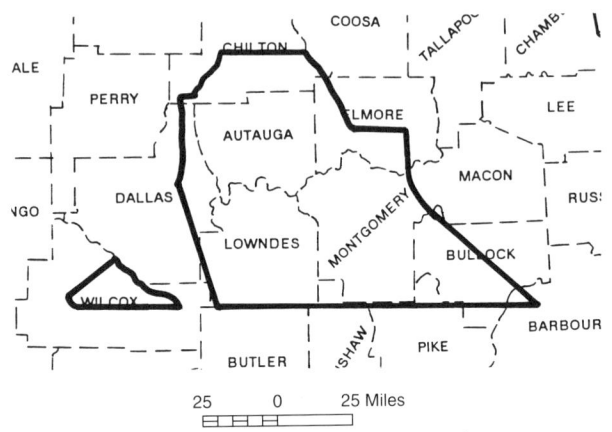

⑥ 21 Nov 1818–12 Dec 1819

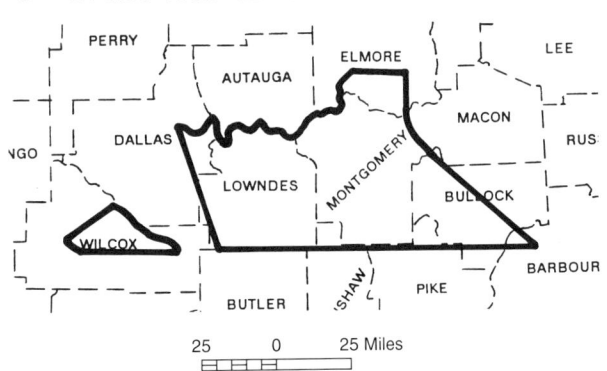

⑦ 13 Dec 1819–6 Dec 1821

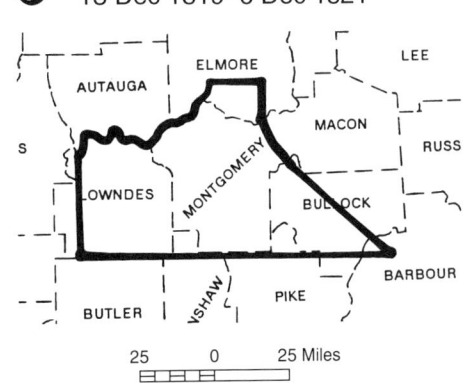

⑧ 17 Dec 1819–28 Feb 1827

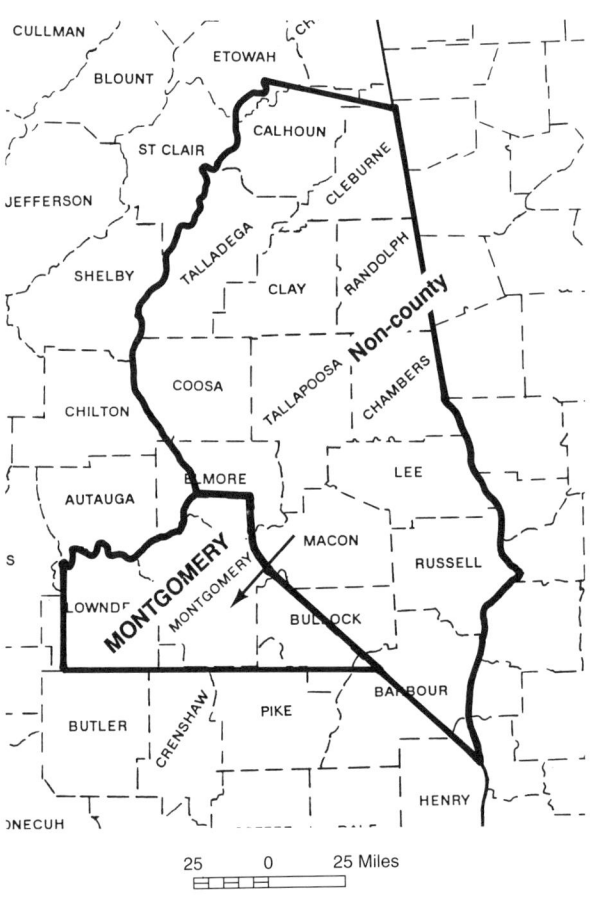

Individual County Chronologies 267

Chronology of MONTGOMERY

Map	Date	Event	Resulting Area
⑨	7 Dec 1821	Lost to creation of PIKE [attachment unchanged; see map 8]	1,550 sq mi
⑩	22 Dec 1824	Gained from PIKE [attachment unchanged; see map 8]	1,660 sq mi

(Heavy line depicts historical boundary. Base map shows present-day information.)

⑨ 7 Dec 1821–21 Dec 1824

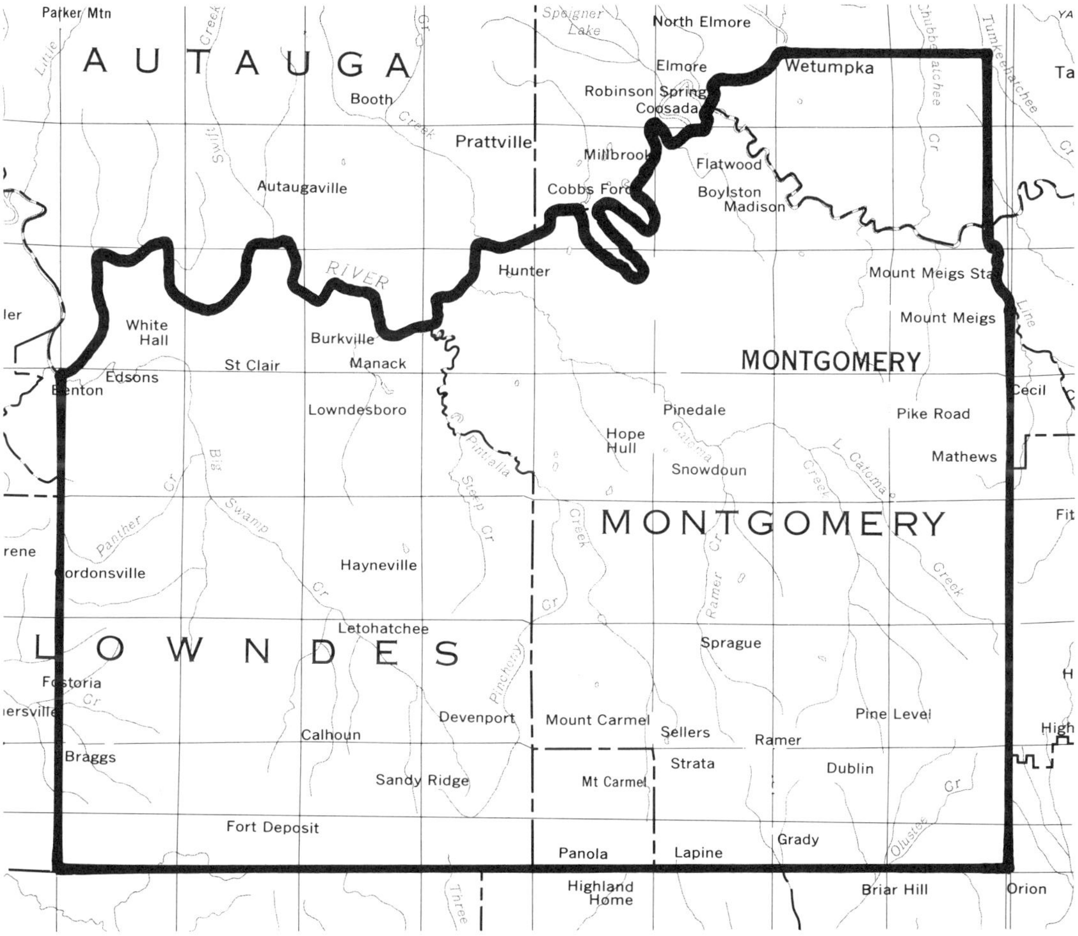

⑩ 22 Dec 1824–28 Jan 1829

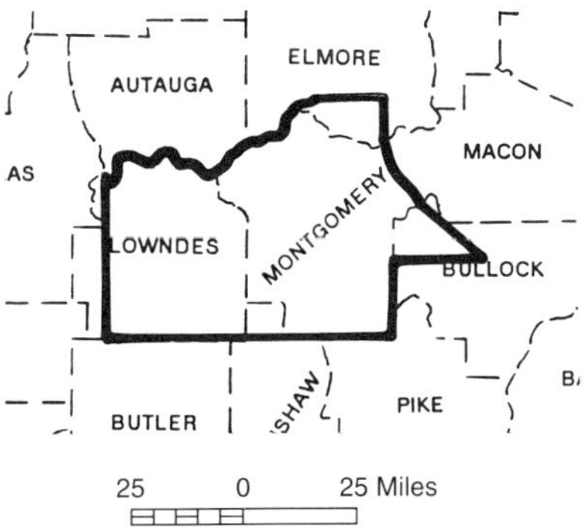

Chronology of MONTGOMERY

Map	Date	Event	Resulting Area
⑪	1 Mar 1827	Part of non-county area detached, attached to AUTAUGA	
⑫	29 Jan 1829	Gained from non-county area that was concurrently attached to AUTAUGA, ST. CLAIR, and SHELBY; gained part of non-county attachment, and lost remaining non-county attachment to PIKE	5,220 sq mi
⑬	20 Jan 1830	Lost to creation of LOWNDES	4,560 sq mi
⑭	15 Jan 1831	Lost to SHELBY	4,090 sq mi

(Heavy line depicts historical boundary. Base map shows present-day information.)

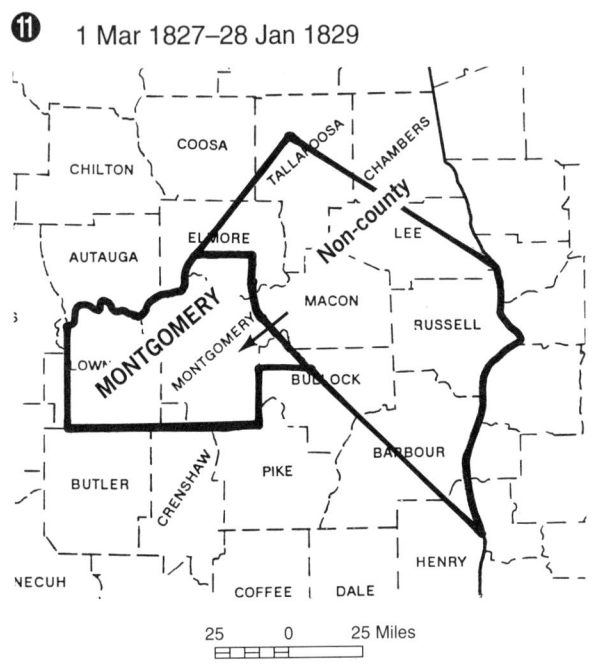

⑪ 1 Mar 1827–28 Jan 1829

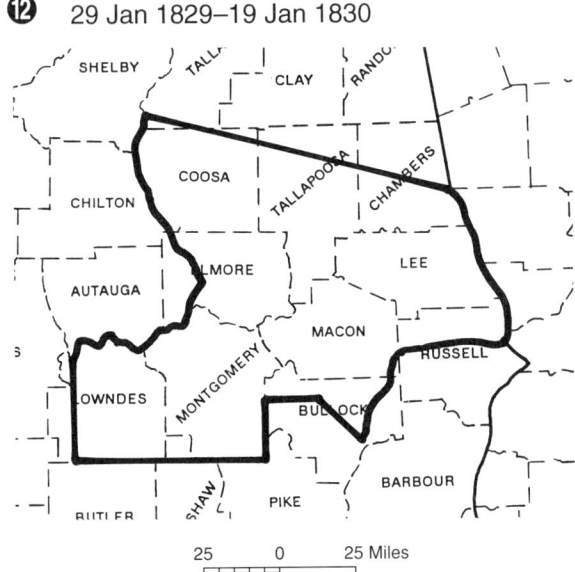

⑫ 29 Jan 1829–19 Jan 1830

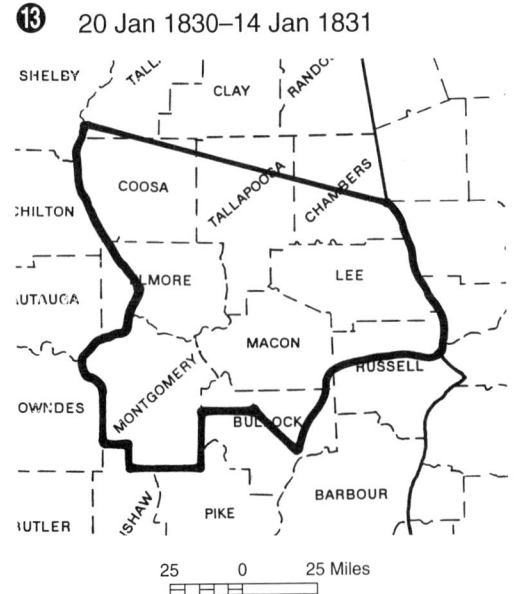

⑬ 20 Jan 1830–14 Jan 1831

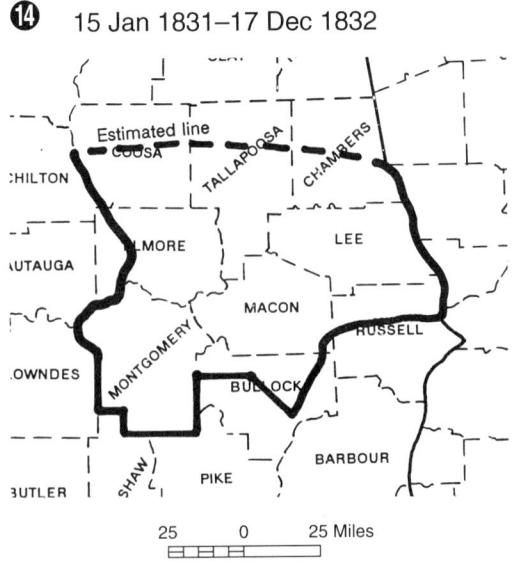

⑭ 15 Jan 1831–17 Dec 1832

Chronology of MONTGOMERY

Map	Date	Event	Resulting Area
⑮	18 Dec 1832	Lost to PIKE and lost to creation of CHAMBERS, COOSA, MACON, RUSSELL, and TALLAPOOSA	990 sq mi

(Heavy line depicts historical boundary. Base map shows present-day information.)

⑮ 18 Dec 1832–31 Dec 1833

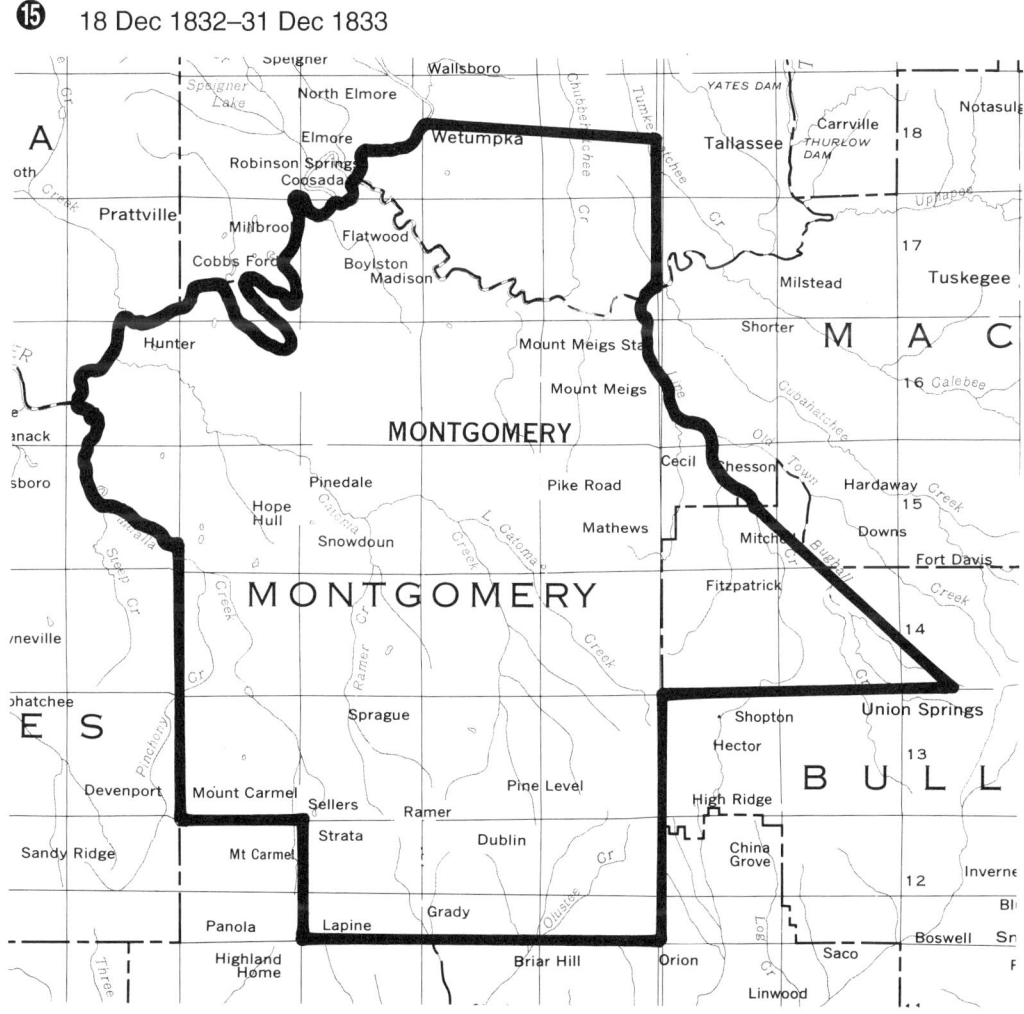

ALABAMA

Chronology of MONTGOMERY

Map	Date	Event	Resulting Area
⑯	1 Jan 1834	Lost to MACON	960 sq mi

(Heavy line depicts historical boundary. Base map shows present-day information.)

⑯ 1 Jan 1834–23 Jun 1837

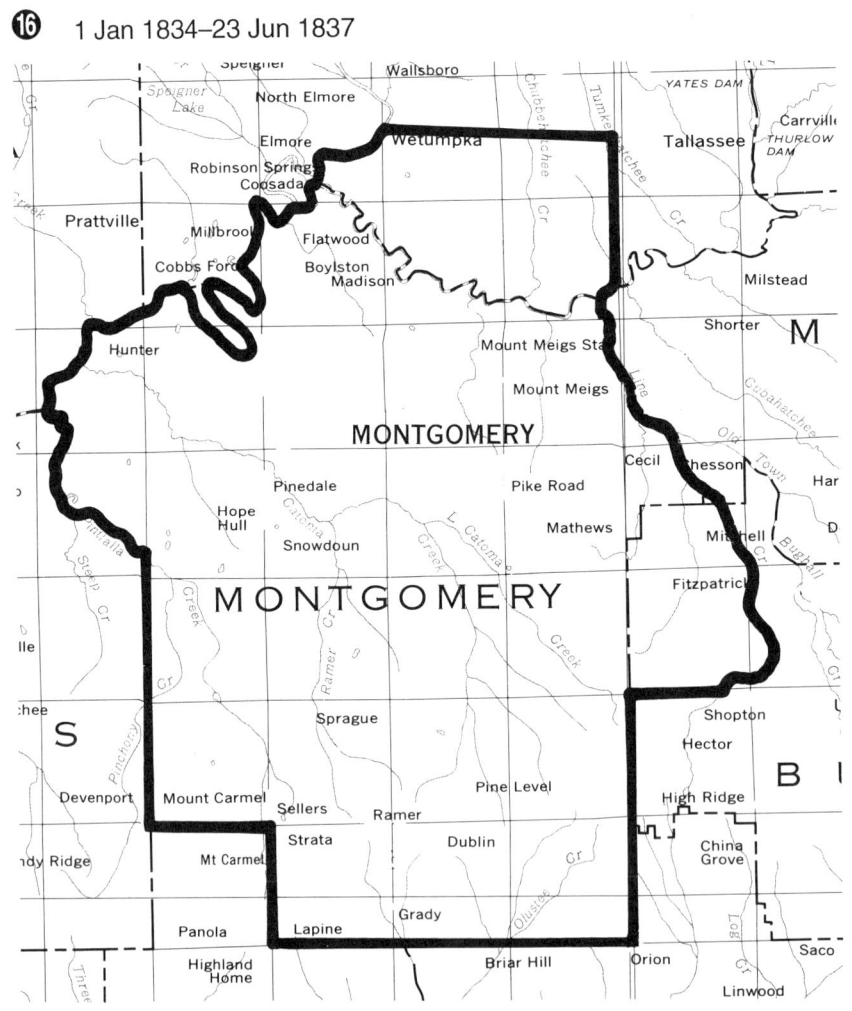

Individual County Chronologies 271

Chronology of MONTGOMERY

Map	Date	Event	Resulting Area
⑰	24 Jun 1837	Exchanged with COOSA	960 sq mi
⑰	21 Dec 1837	Lost to COOSA; remaining boundary with COOSA clarified [no change]	960 sq mi

(Heavy line depicts historical boundary. Base map shows present-day information.)

⑰ 24 Jun 1837–1 Feb 1839

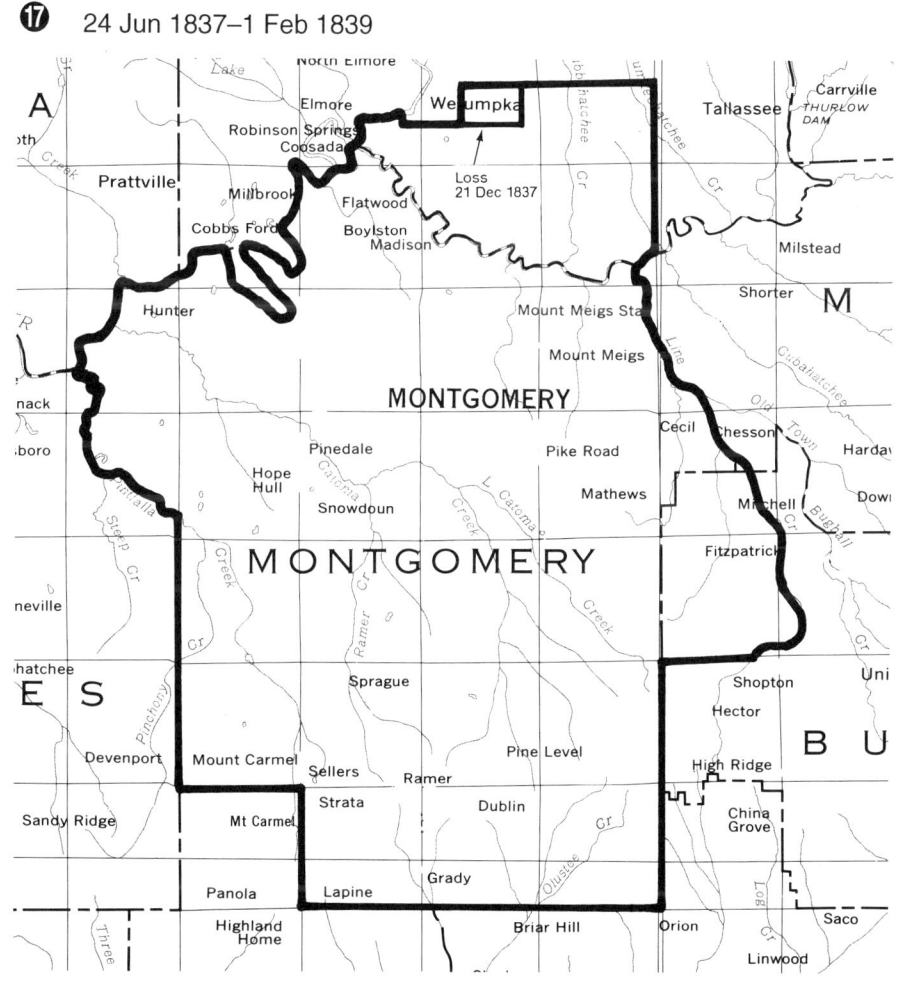

272 ALABAMA

Chronology of MONTGOMERY

Map	Date	Event	Resulting Area
⑱	2 Feb 1839	Gained from TALLAPOOSA	980 sq mi
⑱	29 Dec 1841	Lost small area to LOWNDES	980 sq mi
⑱	28 Nov 1862	Gained small area from PIKE to accommodate local property owner	980 sq mi
	24 Nov 1866	A provision of law creating CRENSHAW would have included part of MONTGOMERY in CRENSHAW but was never implemented [no change]	

(Heavy line depicts historical boundary. Base map shows present-day information.)

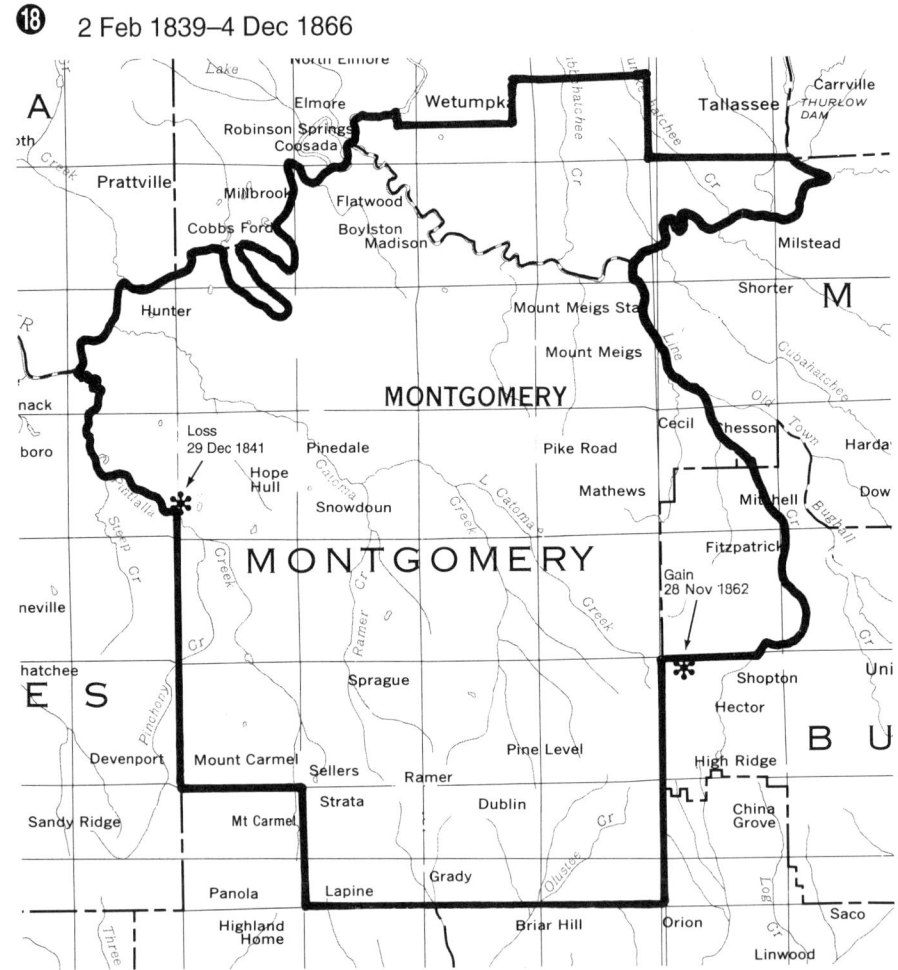

⑱ 2 Feb 1839–4 Dec 1866

Individual County Chronologies 273

Chronology of MONTGOMERY

Map	Date	Event	Resulting Area
⑲	5 Dec 1866	Lost to creation of BULLOCK	920 sq mi

(Heavy line depicts historical boundary. Base map shows present-day information.)

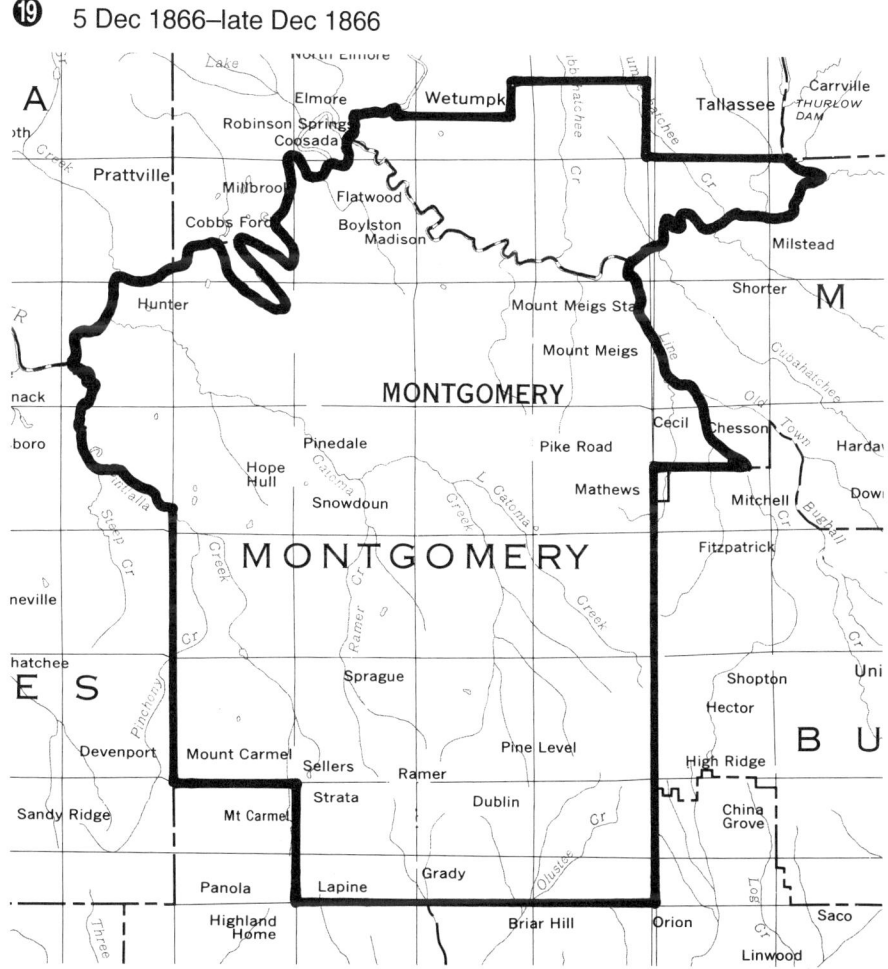

⑲ 5 Dec 1866–late Dec 1866

274 ALABAMA

Chronology of MONTGOMERY

Map	Date	Event	Resulting Area
20	late Dec 1866	Lost to creation of ELMORE	800 sq mi
20	5 Feb 1877	Gained small area from BULLOCK to accommodate local property owner	800 sq mi

(Heavy line depicts historical boundary. Base map shows present-day information.)

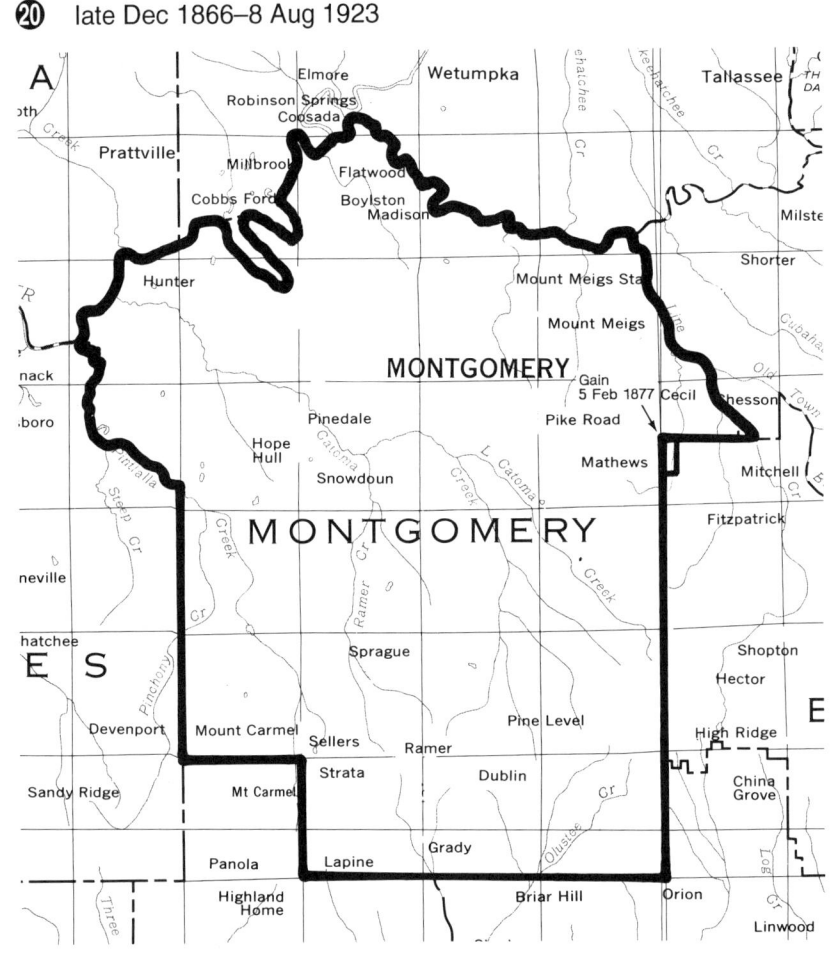

20 late Dec 1866–8 Aug 1923

Chronology of MONTGOMERY

Map	Date	Event	Resulting Area
㉑	9 Aug 1923	Gained from ELMORE	810 sq mi

(Heavy line depicts historical boundary. Base map shows present-day information.)

㉑ 9 Aug 1923–1990

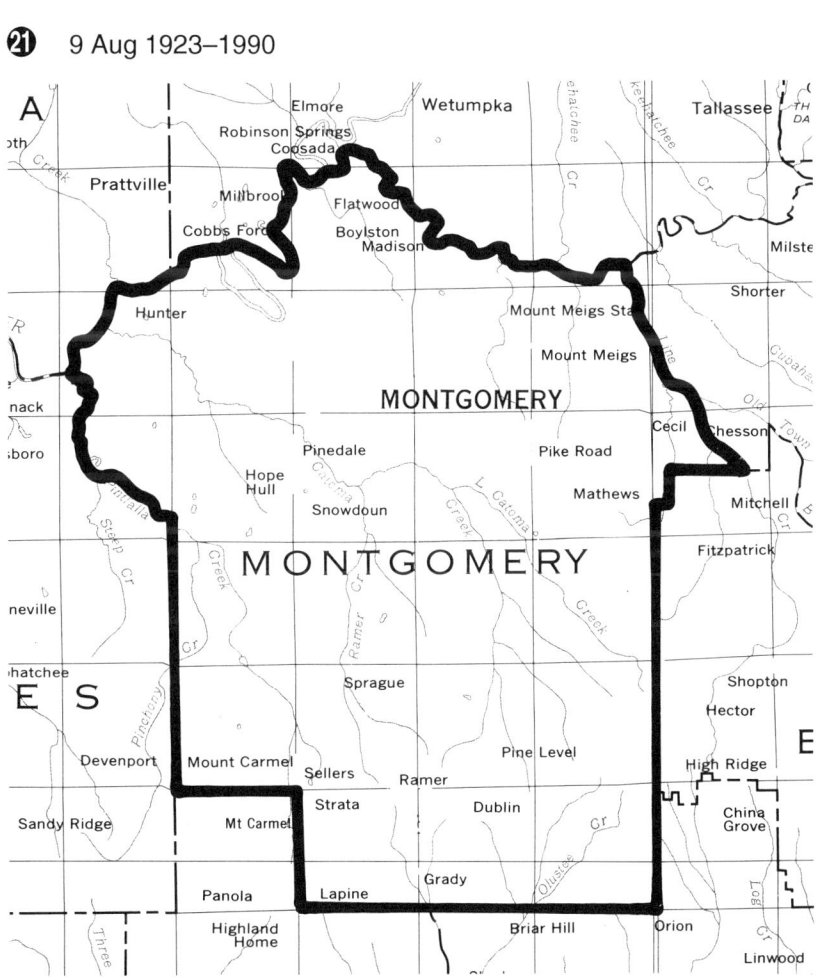

276 ALABAMA

Chronology of MORGAN (created as COTACO)

Map	Date	Event	Resulting Area
❶	6 Feb 1818	Created as COTACO from non-county area	620 sq mi
	9 Feb 1818	County boundary line in Tennessee R. adjusted to run in middle of stream [not mapped]	
	21 Nov 1818	Southern boundary clarified [no change]	
❷	20 Dec 1820	Part of non-county area detached from ST. CLAIR, attached to COTACO (now MORGAN)	
	14 Jun 1821	Renamed MORGAN	
❸	27 Nov 1821	Most of non-county area detached, attached to JACKSON	

(Heavy line depicts historical boundary. Base map shows present-day information.)

❶ 6 Feb 1818–20 Jan 1832

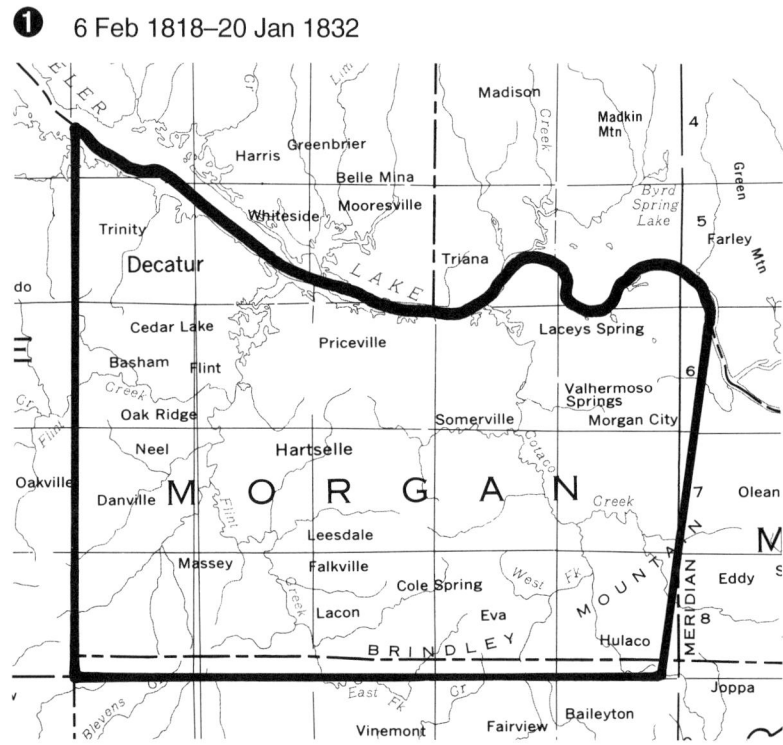

❷ 20 Dec 1820–26 Nov 1821

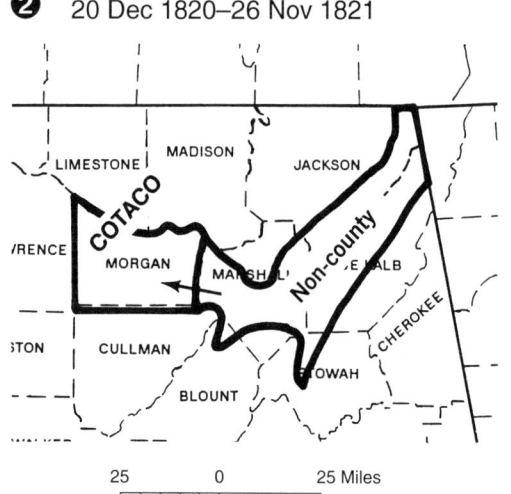

❸ 27 Nov 1821–20 Jan 1832

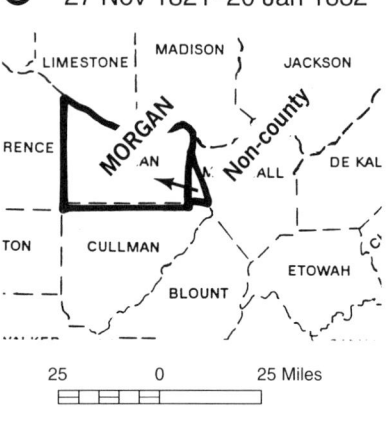

Individual County Chronologies 277

Chronology of MORGAN (created as COTACO)

Map	Date	Event	Resulting Area
❹	21 Jan 1832	Gained from BLOUNT and from non-county areas attached to JACKSON and MORGAN, lost remaining non-county attachment to BLOUNT	740 sq mi

(Heavy line depicts historical boundary. Base map shows present-day information.)

❹ 21 Jan 1832–14 Dec 1840

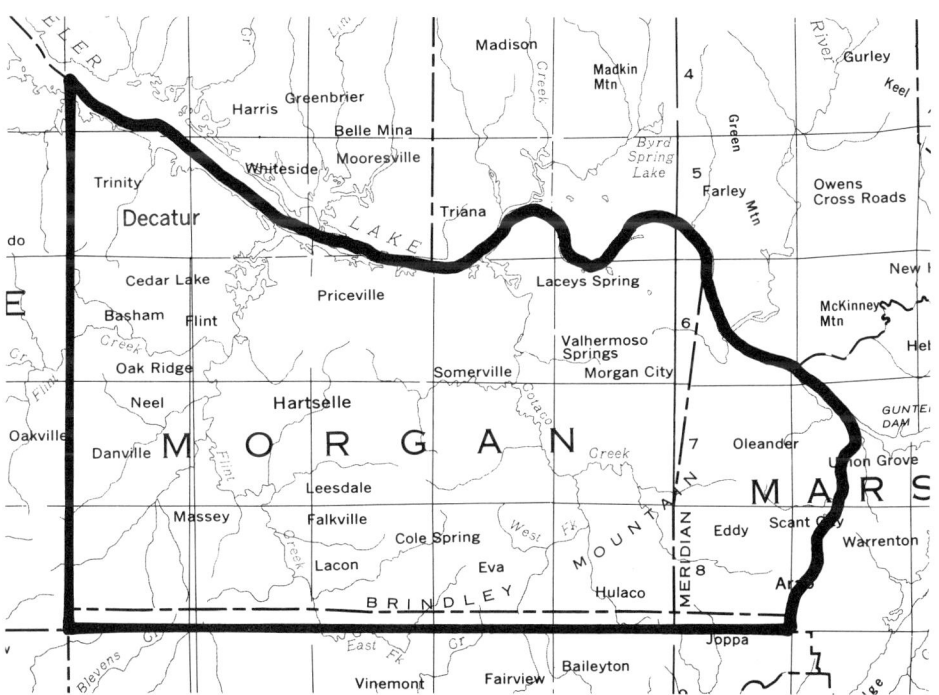

278 ALABAMA

Chronology of MORGAN (created as COTACO)

Map	Date	Event	Resulting Area
❺	15 Dec 1840	Lost to MARSHALL	620 sq mi
❻	24 Jan 1877	Lost to creation of CULLMAN	590 sq mi

(Heavy line depicts historical boundary. Base map shows present-day information.)

❺ 15 Dec 1840–23 Jan 1877

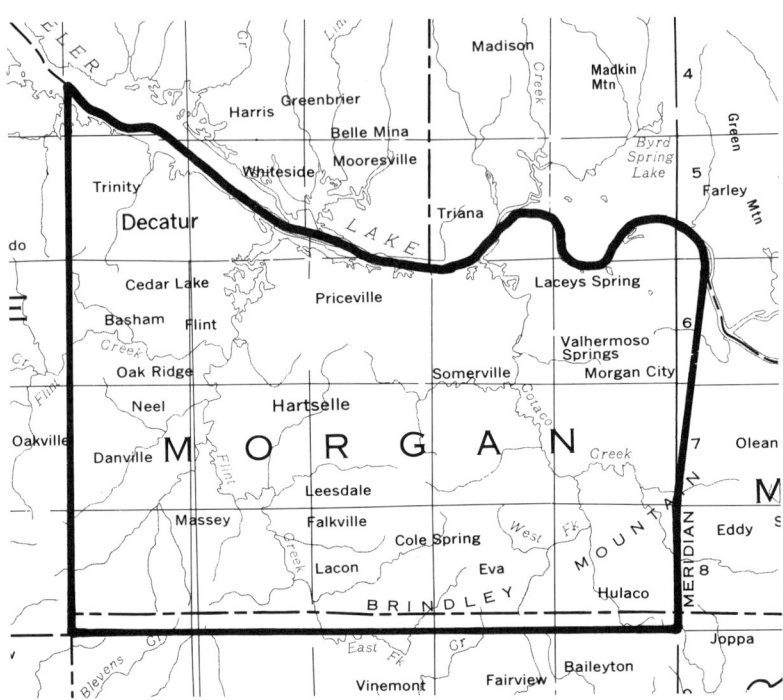

❻ 24 Jan 1877–1990

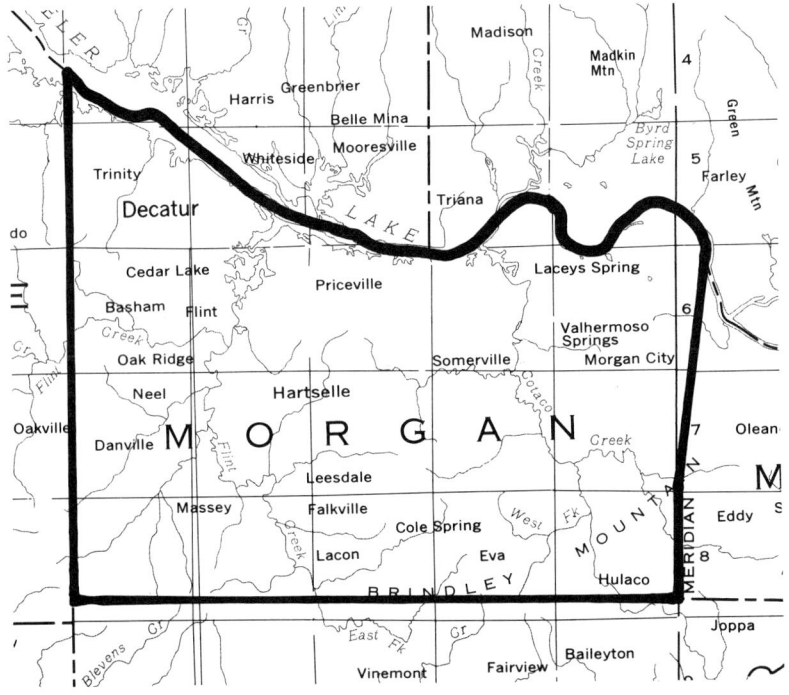

Chronology of PASCAGOULA (Orleans Terr., extinct)

Map	Date	Event	Resulting Area
❶	4 Jan 1811	Created by Orleans Territory as a parish within FELICIANA County (La.); included parts of present Mississippi and Alabama. Spain controlled part of the area until 1813	Indefinite
❷	26 Jan 1811	Gained area within FELICIANA (La.) in present Alabama	Indefinite
❸	24 Apr 1811	Gained area within FELICIANA (La.) in present Alabama	4,450 sq mi
	30 Apr 1812	Eliminated when Louisiana was admitted to the Union	

(Heavy line depicts historical boundary. Base map shows present-day information.)

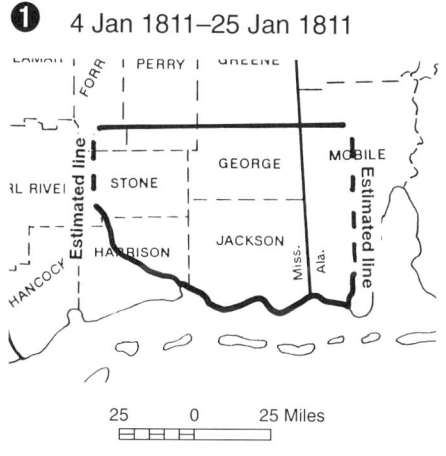

❶ 4 Jan 1811–25 Jan 1811

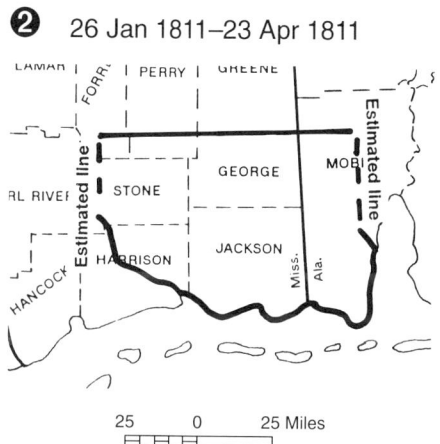

❷ 26 Jan 1811–23 Apr 1811

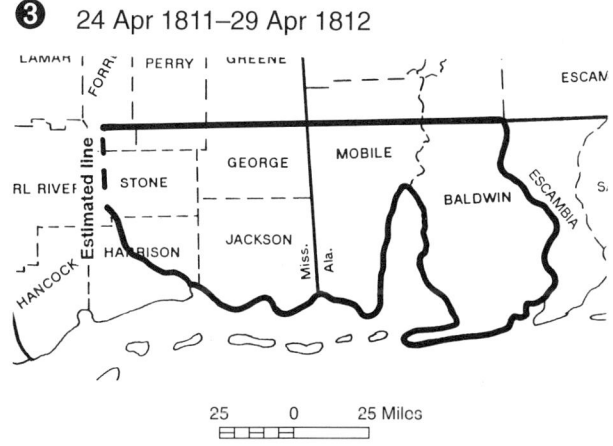

❸ 24 Apr 1811–29 Apr 1812

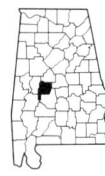

Chronology of PERRY

Map	Date	Event	Resulting Area
❶	13 Dec 1819	Created from CAHAWBA (now BIBB), DALLAS, MARENGO, and TUSCALOOSA	910 sq mi

(Heavy line depicts historical boundary. Base map shows present-day information.)

❶ 13 Dec 1819–19 Dec 1820

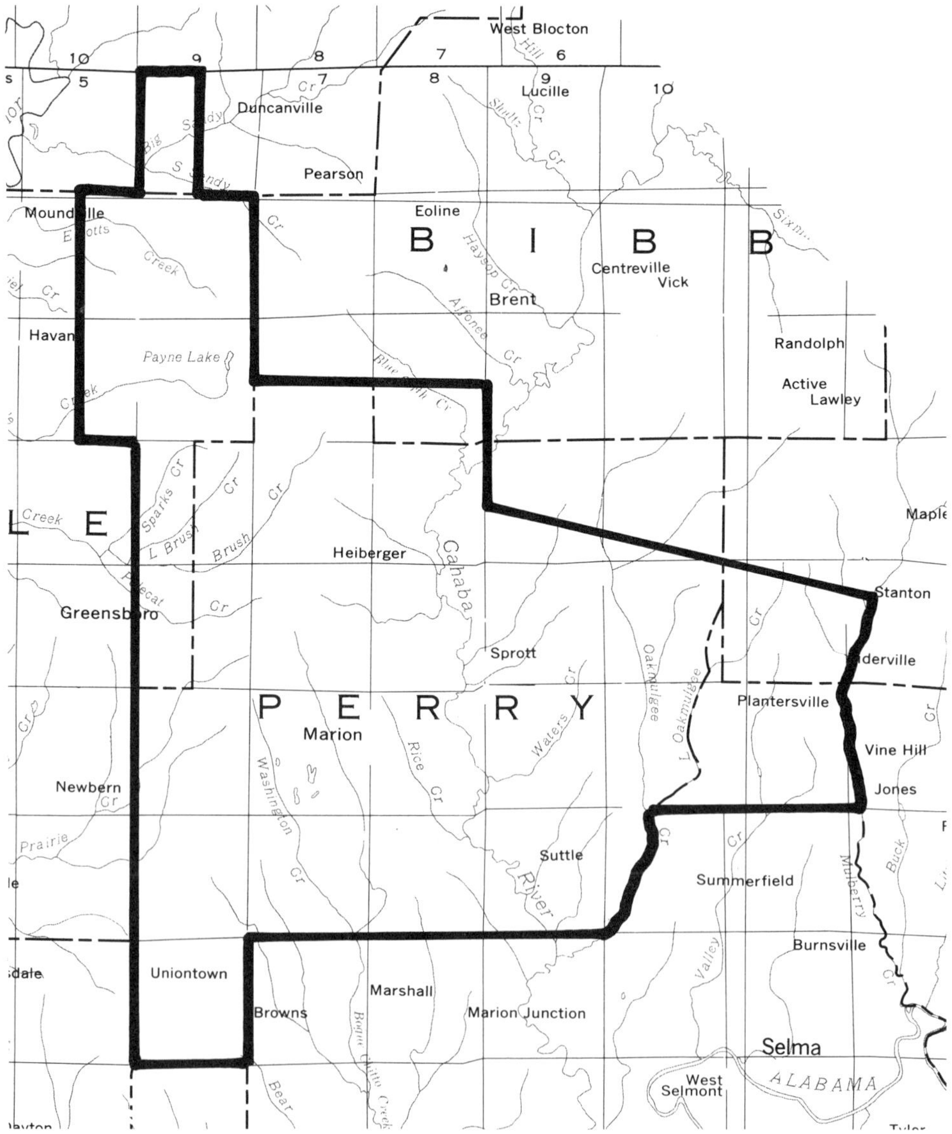

10 0 10 20 30 40 Miles

Individual County Chronologies 281

Chronology of PERRY

Map	Date	Event	Resulting Area
❷	20 Dec 1820	Exchanged with BIBB, lost to GREENE and TUSCALOOSA	910 sq mi

(Heavy line depicts historical boundary. Base map shows present-day information.)

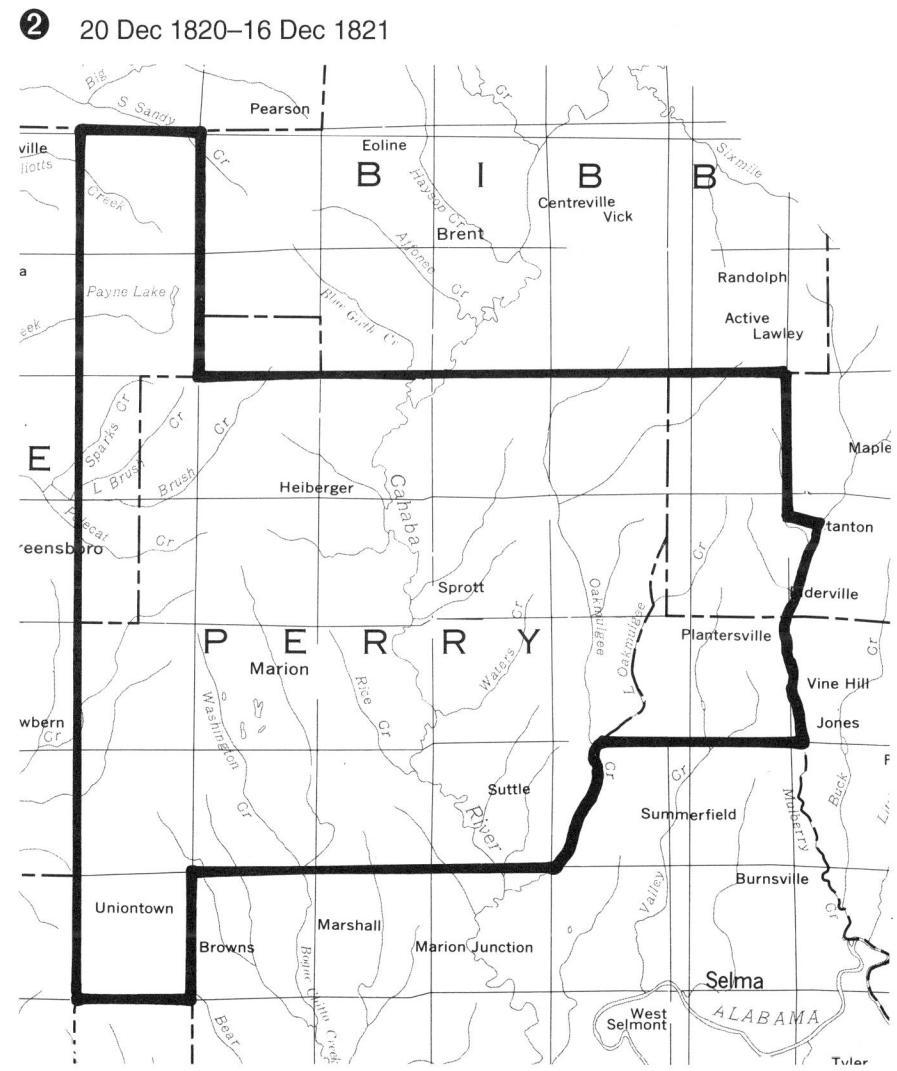

❷ 20 Dec 1820–16 Dec 1821

282 ALABAMA

Chronology of PERRY

Map	Date	Event	Resulting Area
❸	17 Dec 1821	Exchanged with BIBB	910 sq mi

(Heavy line depicts historical boundary. Base map shows present-day information.)

❸ 17 Dec 1821–29 Dec 1822

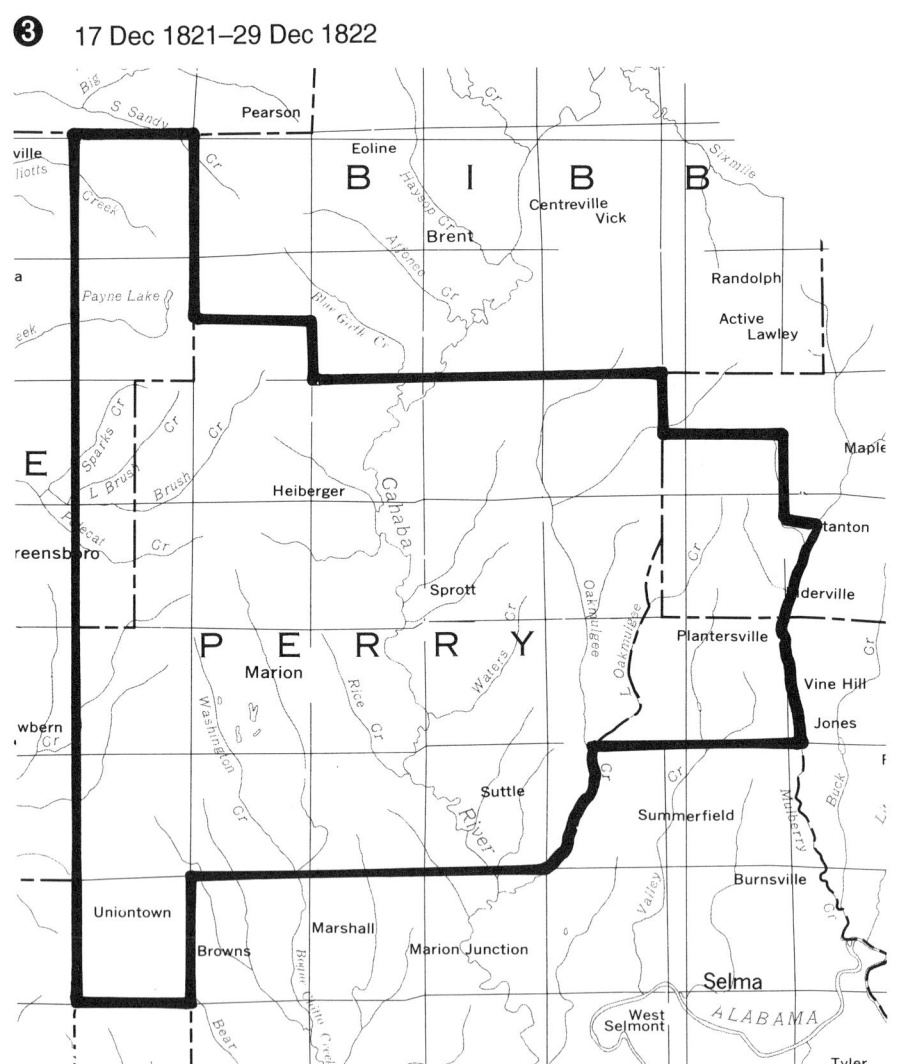

Chronology of PERRY

Map	Date	Event	Resulting Area
❹	30 Dec 1822	Gained from DALLAS	950 sq mi
❹	3 Jan 1828	Lost small area to BIBB	950 sq mi
❹	28 Nov 1863	Lost small area to MARENGO to accommodate local property owner	950 sq mi
❹	30 Nov 1863	Gained small area from MARENGO to accommodate local property owner	950 sq mi
❹	20 Feb 1866	Lost small area to MARENGO to accommodate local property owner	950 sq mi

(Heavy line depicts historical boundary. Base map shows present-day information.)

❹ 30 Dec 1822–29 Jan 1867

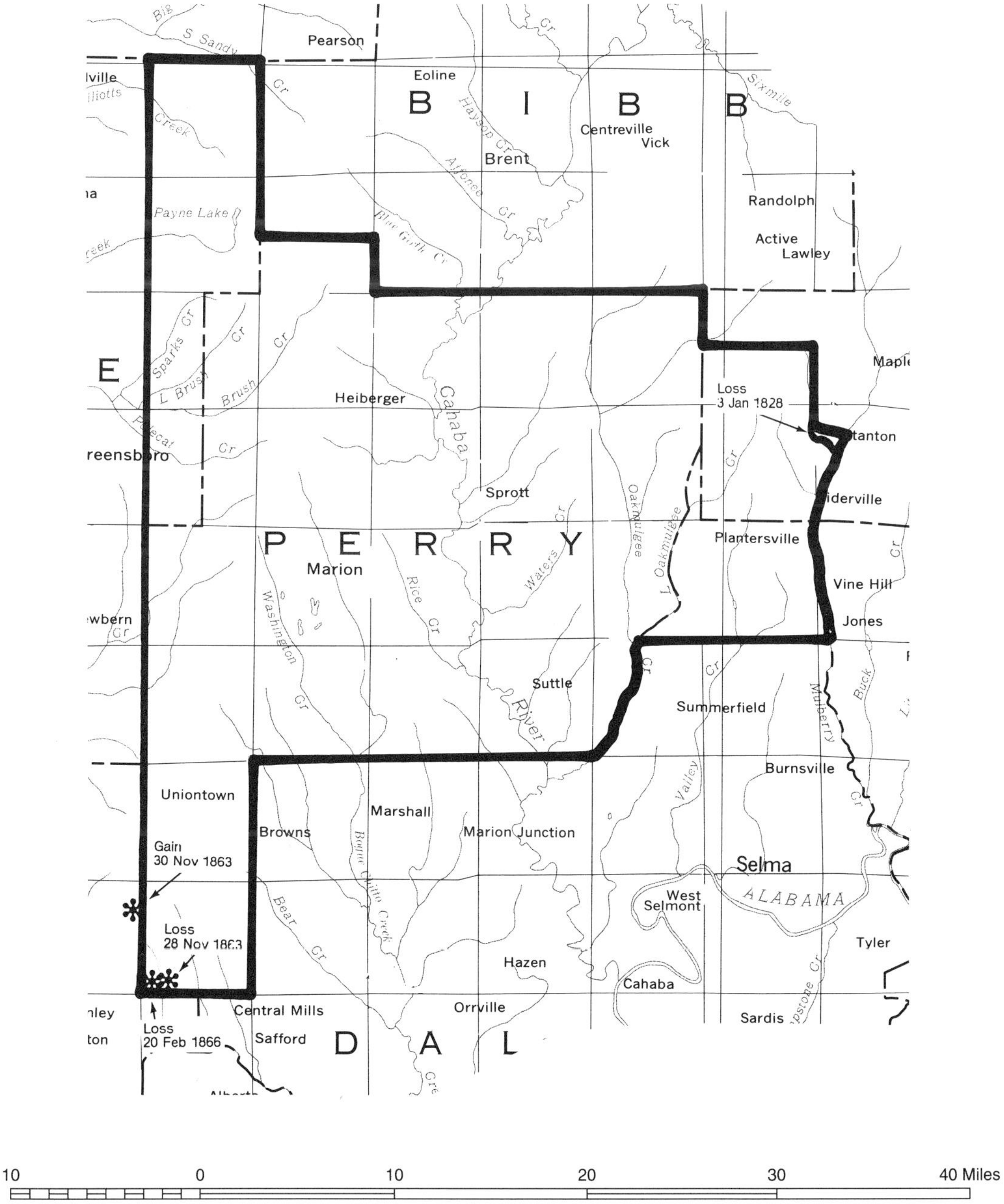

284 ALABAMA

Chronology of PERRY

Map	Date	Event	Resulting Area
⑤	30 Jan 1867	Lost to creation of HALE	850 sq mi

(Heavy line depicts historical boundary. Base map shows present-day information.)

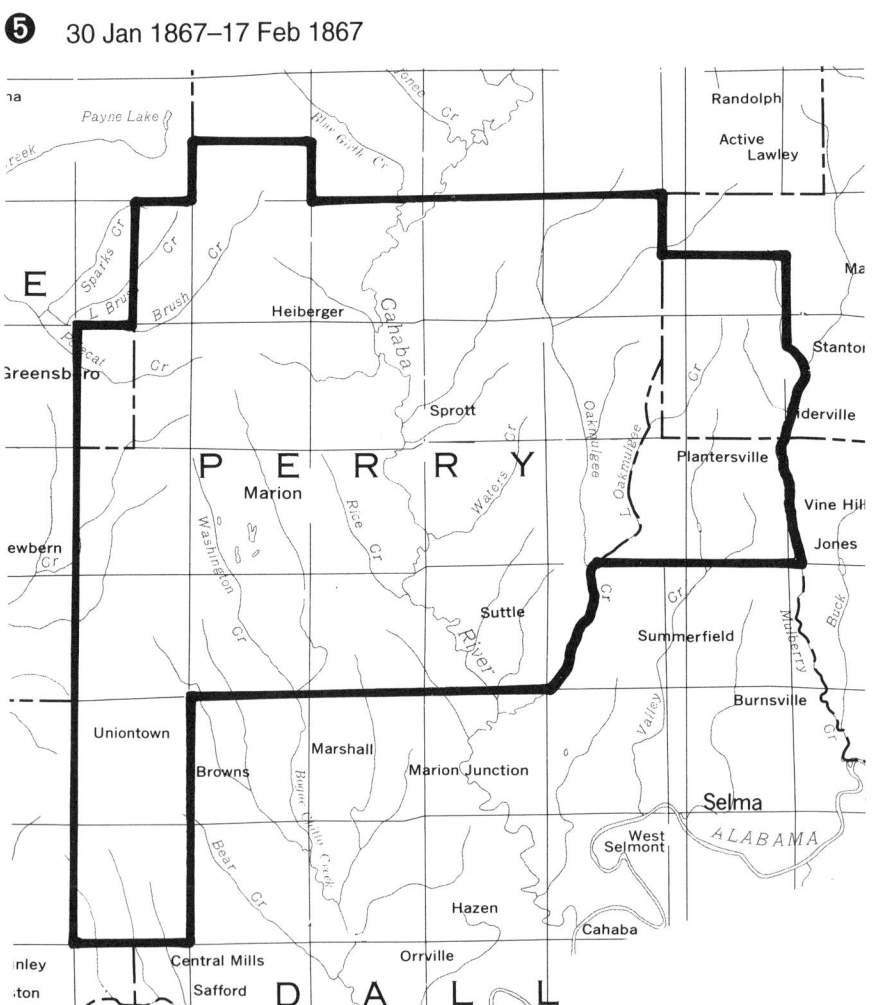

⑤ 30 Jan 1867–17 Feb 1867

Individual County Chronologies 285

Chronology of PERRY

Map	Date	Event	Resulting Area
❻	18 Feb 1867	Lost to DALLAS	740 sq mi
❻	28 Dec 1868	Lost small area to DALLAS [became a DALLAS exclave on 30 Dec 1868 and returned to PERRY 28 Feb 1889]	740 sq mi
	30 Dec 1868	Small area gained by DALLAS from PERRY 2 days earlier became a DALLAS exclave when BAKER (now CHILTON) was created [corrected 28 Feb 1889]	
❻	7 Feb 1870	Lost small area to MARENGO to accommodate local property owner	740 sq mi
❻	7 Dec 1871	Lost small area to BIBB to accommodate local property owners	740 sq mi
❼	13 Jan 1877	Lost to HALE	720 sq mi
❼	28 Feb 1889	Gained the DALLAS exclave of 1868	720 sq mi

(Heavy line depicts historical boundary. Base map shows present-day information.)

❻ 18 Feb 1867–12 Jan 1877

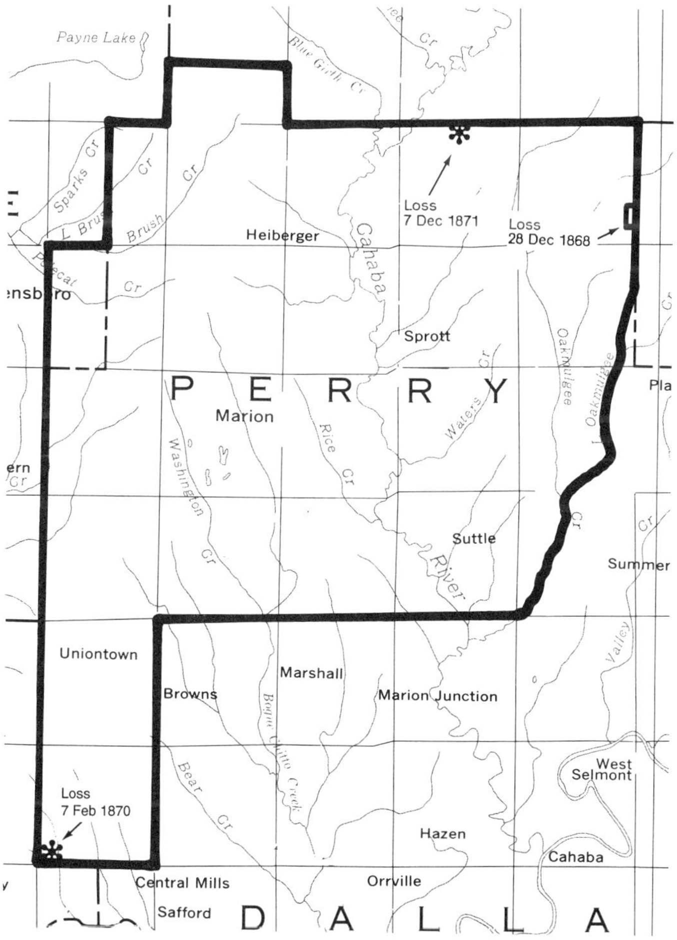

❼ 13 Jan 1877–1990

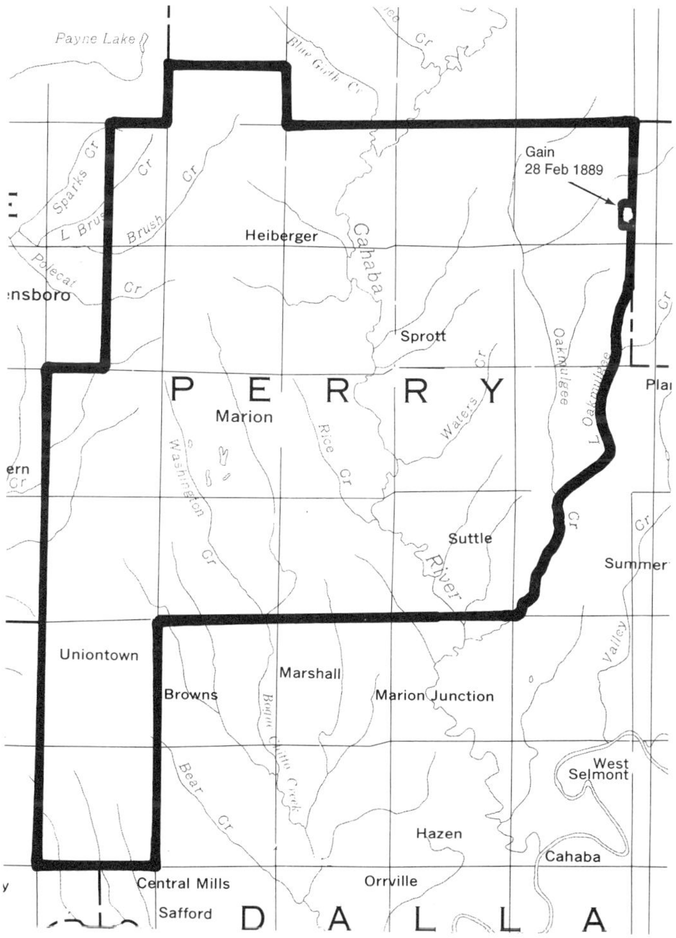

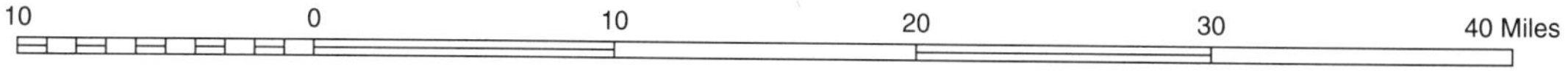

ALABAMA

Chronology of PICKENS

Map	Date	Event	Resulting Area
❶	19 Dec 1820	Created from MARION and TUSCALOOSA	1,290 sq mi
❷	20 Dec 1824	Gained from TUSCALOOSA, lost to creation of FAYETTE	910 sq mi
❷	21 Jan 1832	Gained small area from GREENE; lost narrow strip all along GREENE boundary [not mapped]	910 sq mi

(Heavy line depicts historical boundary. Base map shows present-day information.)

❶ 19 Dec 1820–19 Dec 1824

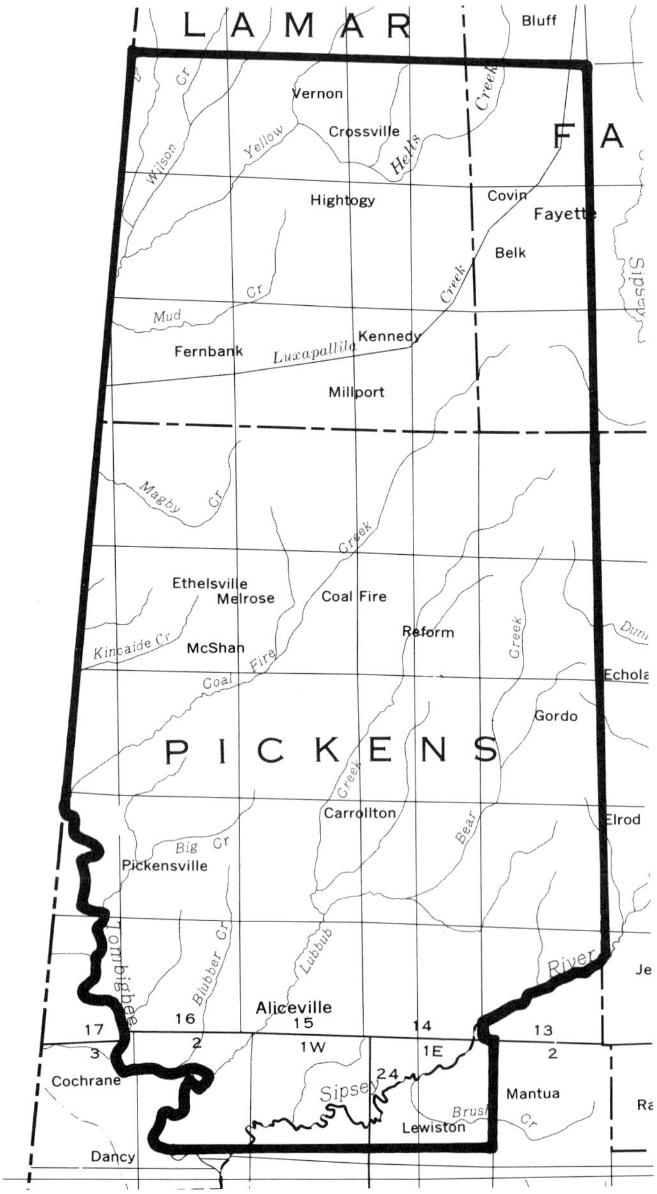

❷ 20 Dec 1824–17 Dec 1832

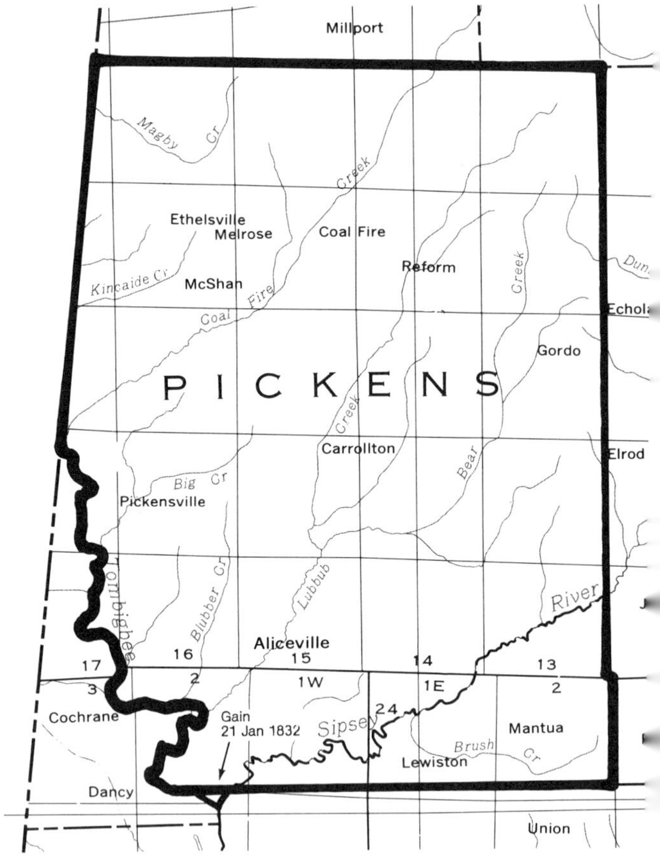

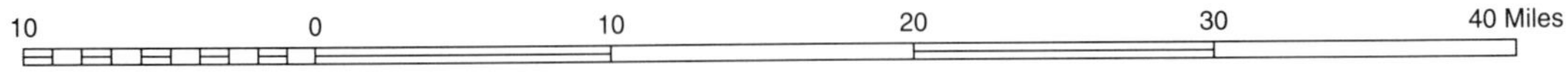

Individual County Chronologies **287**

Chronology of PICKENS

Map	Date	Event	Resulting Area
❸	18 Dec 1832	Gained from non-county area attached to MARENGO	990 sq mi
❸	14 Feb 1843	Lost to GREENE	980 sq mi
❹	30 Jan 1867	Lost to GREENE	890 sq mi

(Heavy line depicts historical boundary. Base map shows present-day information.)

❸ 18 Dec 1832–29 Jan 1867

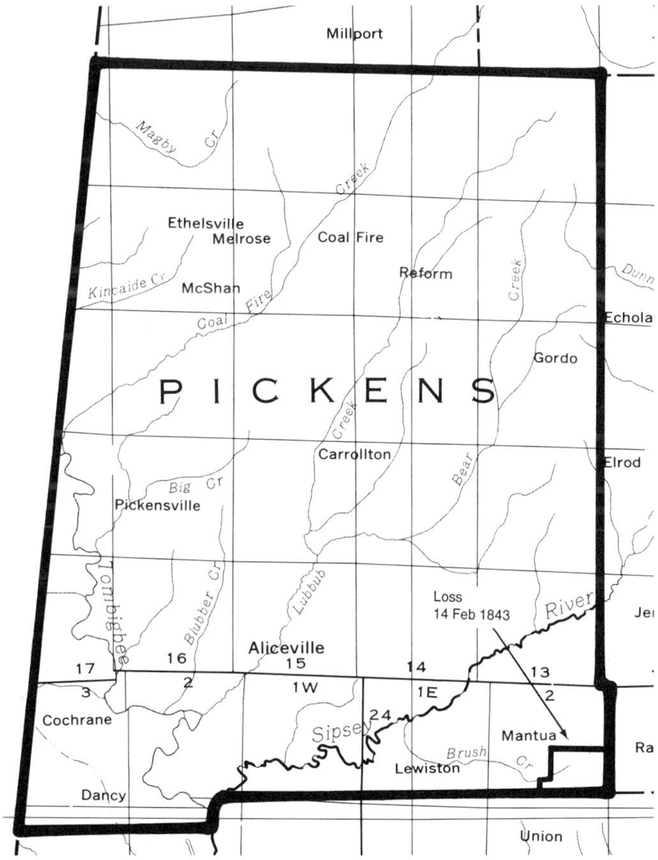

❹ 30 Jan 1867–1990

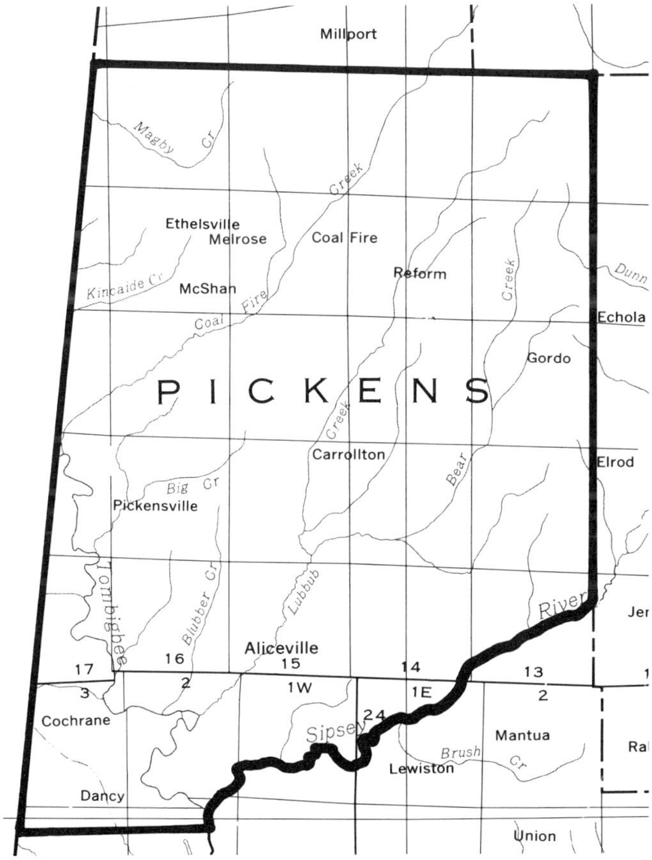

ALABAMA

Chronology of PIKE

Map	Date	Event	Resulting Area
❶	7 Dec 1821	Created from HENRY and MONTGOMERY	1,420 sq mi
❷	22 Dec 1824	Lost to MONTGOMERY	1,280 sq mi
❸	4 Jan 1826	Gained from DALE	1,500 sq mi
❹	3 Jan 1828	Lost to BUTLER	1,440 sq mi
❺	20 Dec 1828	Gained from DALE	1,500 sq mi
❻	27 Jan 1829	Gained from BUTLER and COVINGTON	1,550 sq mi
❼	29 Jan 1829	Gained from non-county area attached to MONTGOMERY	2,560 sq mi
❽	20 Jan 1830	Lost to creation of LOWNDES	2,530 sq mi

(Heavy line depicts historical boundary. Base map shows present-day information.)

❶ 7 Dec 1821–21 Dec 1824

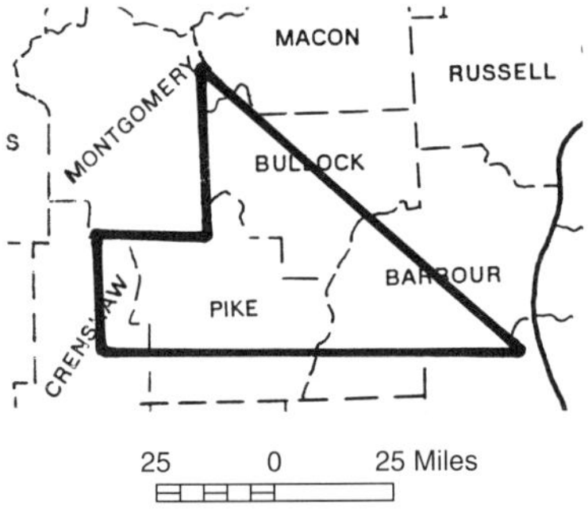

❷ 22 Dec 1824–3 Jan 1826

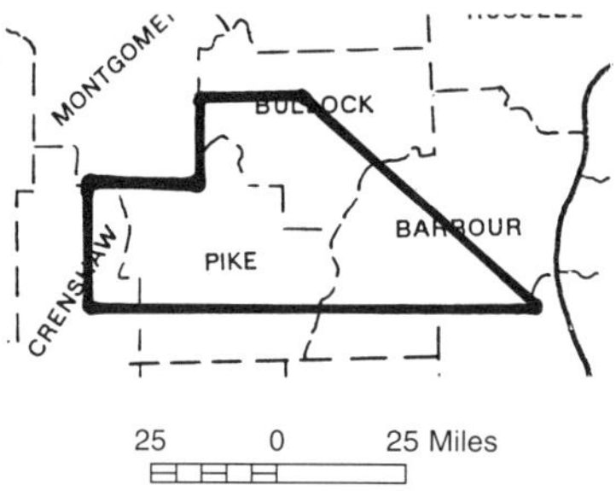

❸ 4 Jan 1826–2 Jan 1828

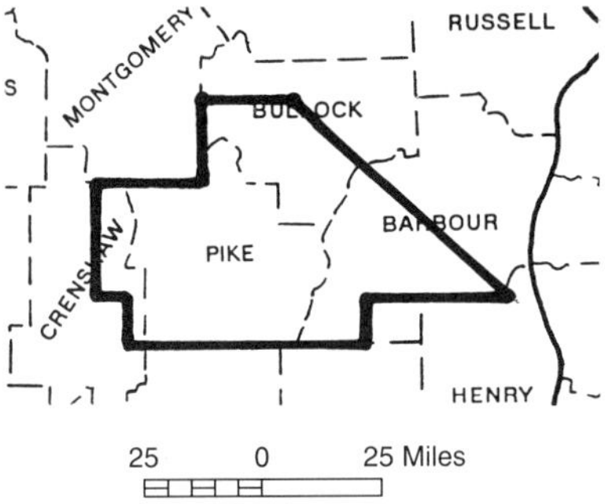

❹ 3 Jan 1828–19 Dec 1828

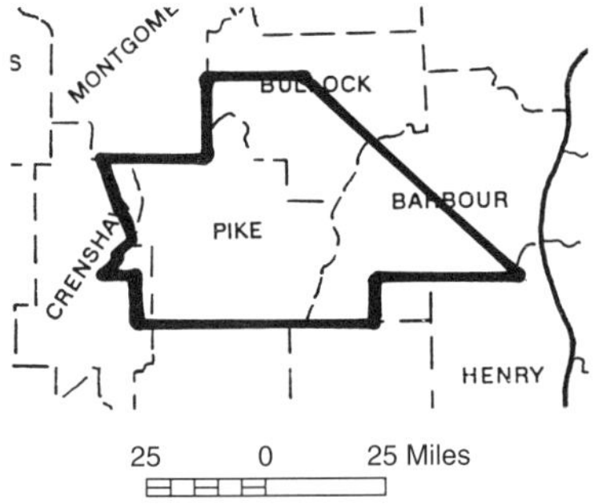

❺ 20 Dec 1828–26 Jan 1829

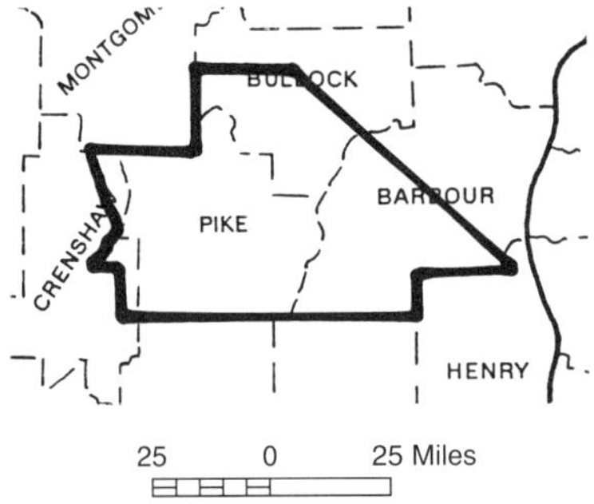

❻ 27 Jan 1829–28 Jan 1829

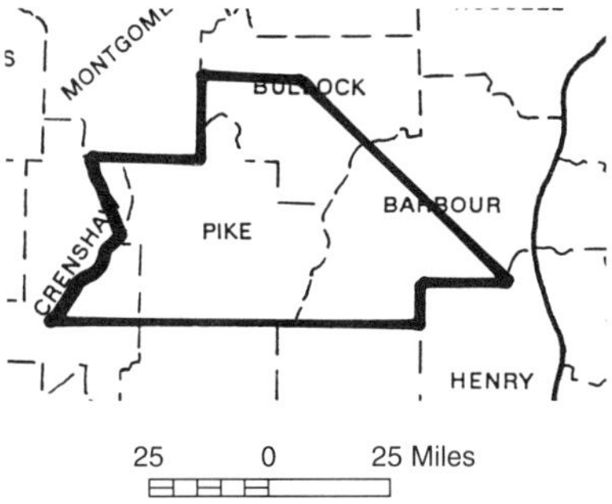

❼ 29 Jan 1829–19 Jan 1830

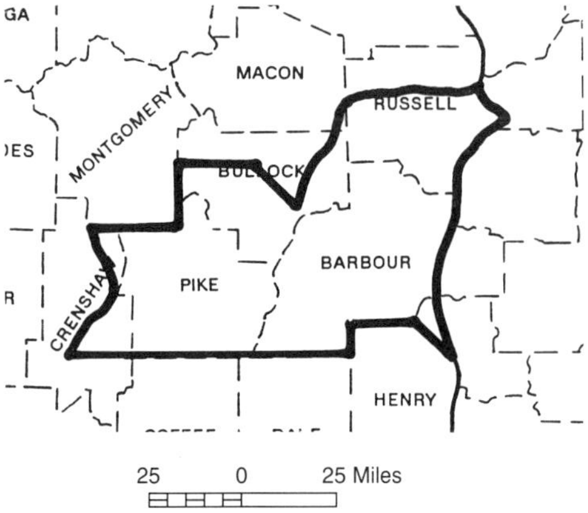

❽ 20 Jan 1830–27 Dec 1831

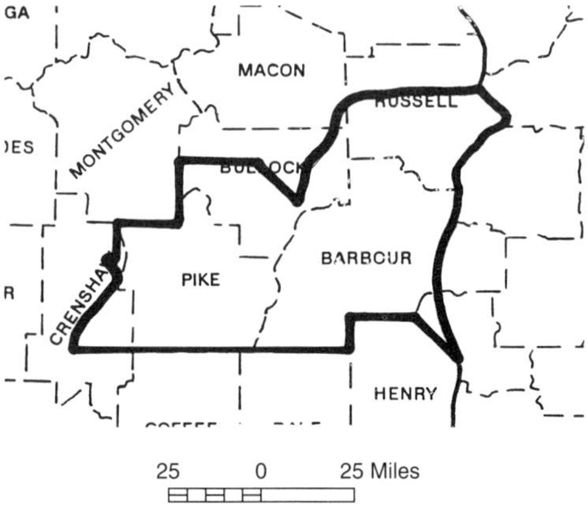

Individual County Chronologies 289

Chronology of PIKE

Map	Date	Event	Resulting Area
⑨	28 Dec 1831	Lost to HENRY	2,500 sq mi
	15 Dec 1832	Boundary with HENRY clarified [no change]	
⑩	18 Dec 1832	Gained from MONTGOMERY, lost to creation of BARBOUR, MACON, and RUSSELL	1,140 sq mi

(Heavy line depicts historical boundary. Base map shows present-day information.)

⑨ 28 Dec 1831–17 Dec 1832

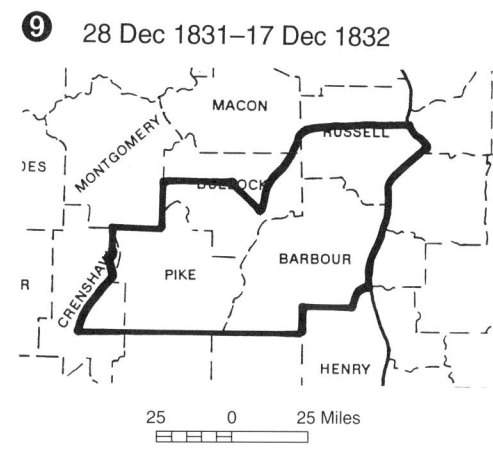

⑩ 18 Dec 1832–19 Dec 1837

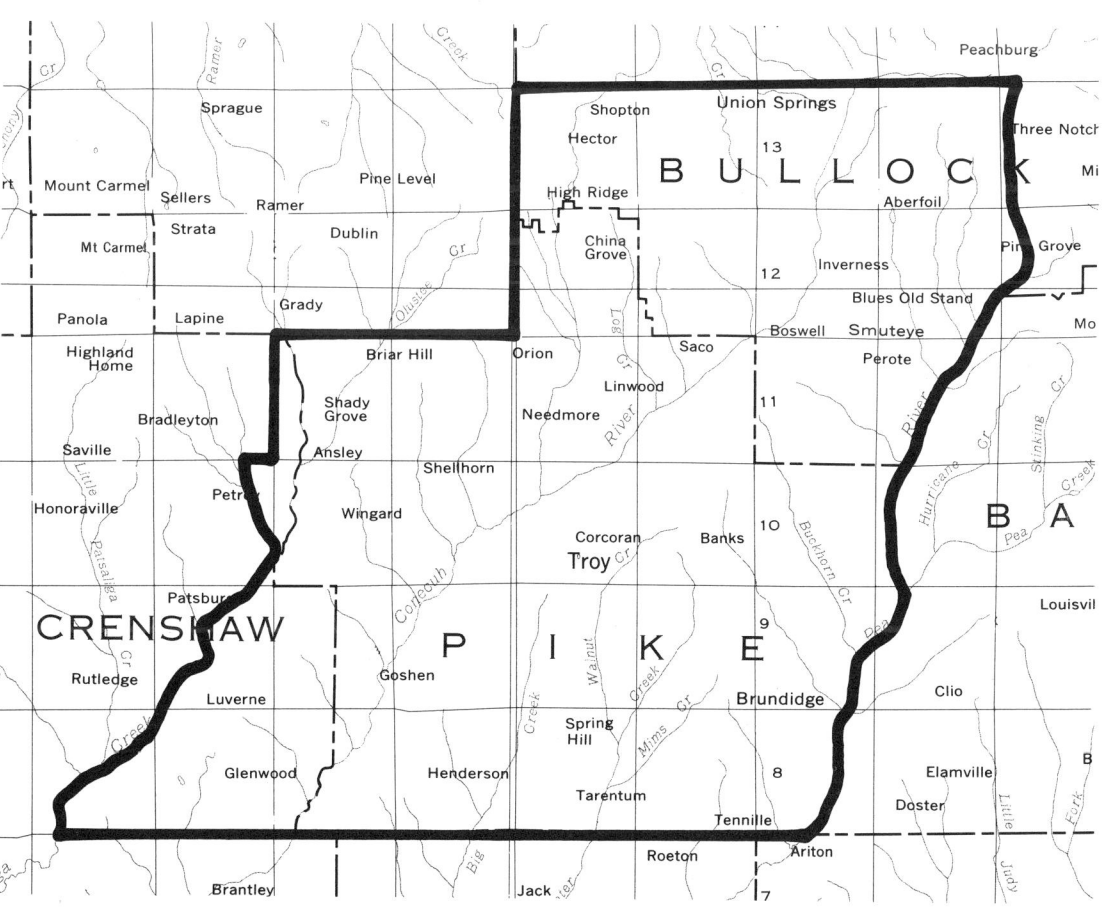

ALABAMA

Chronology of PIKE

Map	Date	Event	Resulting Area
⑪	20 Dec 1837	Lost to MACON	1,070 sq mi
⑪	29 Jan 1840	Gained small area from DALE	1,070 sq mi
⑪	28 Nov 1862	Lost small area to MONTGOMERY to accommodate local property owner	1,070 sq mi

(Heavy line depicts historical boundary. Base map shows present-day information.)

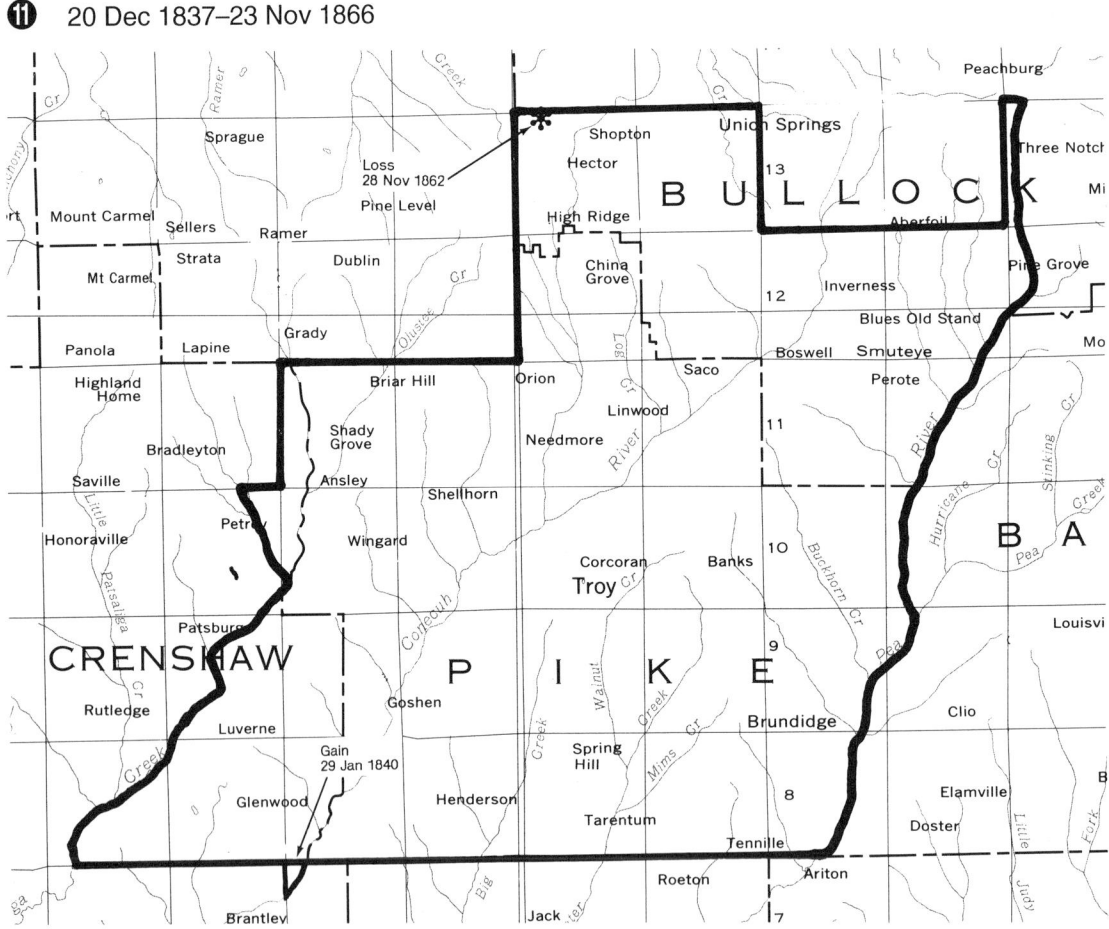

⑪ 20 Dec 1837–23 Nov 1866

Individual County Chronologies **291**

Chronology of PIKE

Map	Date	Event	Resulting Area
⑫	24 Nov 1866	Lost to creation of CRENSHAW	950 sq mi

(Heavy line depicts historical boundary. Base map shows present-day information.)

⑫ 24 Nov 1866–4 Dec 1866

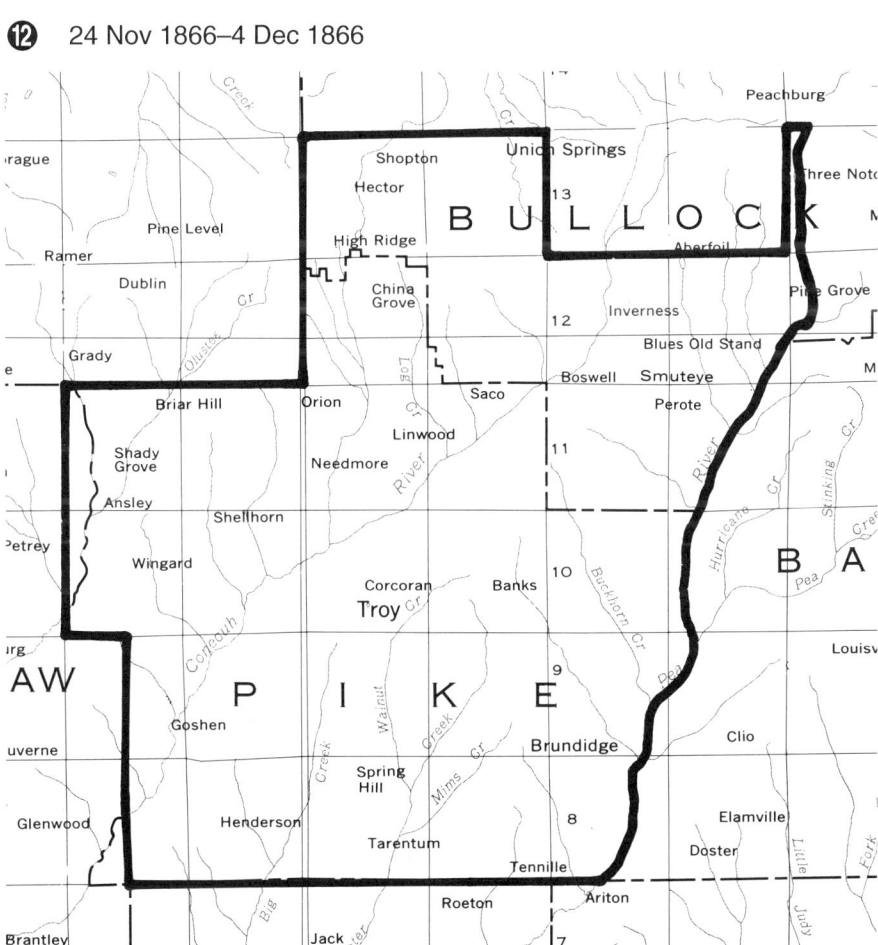

Chronology of PIKE

Map	Date	Event	Resulting Area
⑬	5 Dec 1866	Lost to creation of BULLOCK	690 sq mi
⑬	4 Feb 1867	Gained small area from BULLOCK to accommodate local property owner	690 sq mi

(Heavy line depicts historical boundary. Base map shows present-day information.)

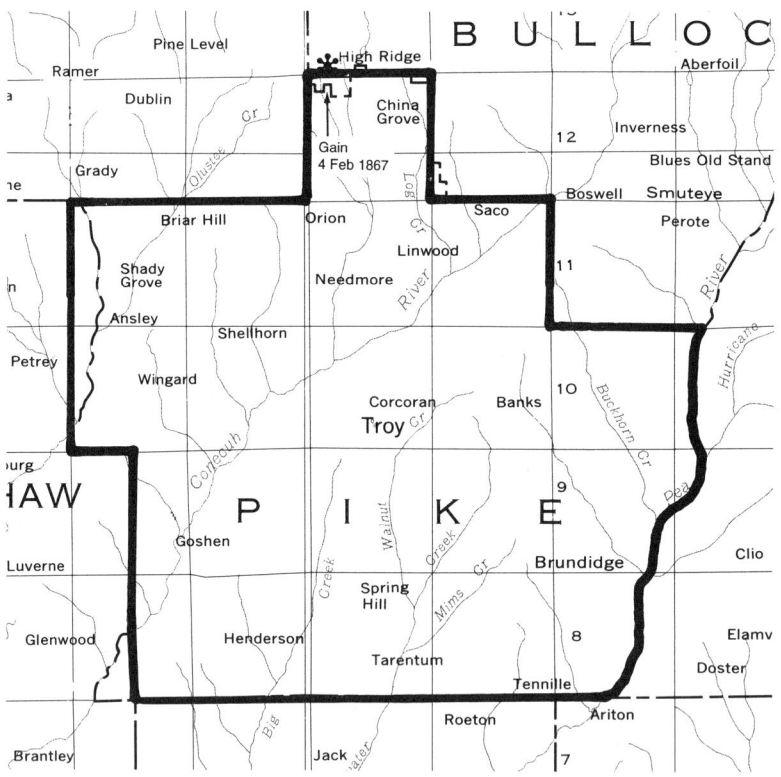

⑬ 5 Dec 1866–18 Feb 1867

Individual County Chronologies **293**

Chronology of PIKE

Map	Date	Event	Resulting Area
⑭	19 Feb 1867	Gained from CRENSHAW	690 sq mi
⑭	11 Dec 1871	Gained small area from BULLOCK to accommodate local property owner	690 sq mi
⑭	14 Dec 1874	Gained small area from BULLOCK	690 sq mi

(Heavy line depicts historical boundary. Base map shows present-day information.)

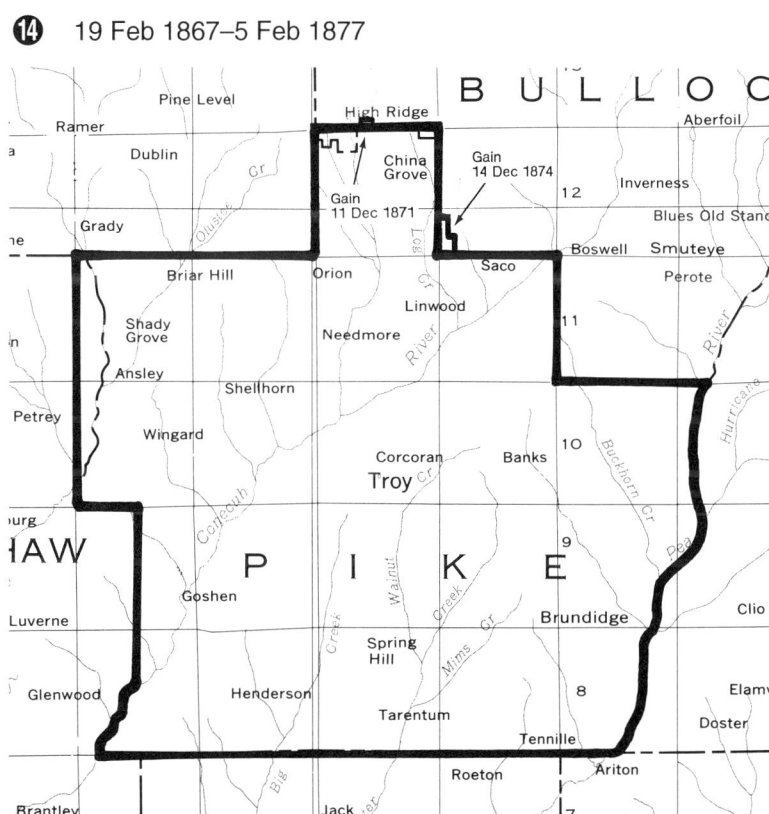

⑭ 19 Feb 1867–5 Feb 1877

ALABAMA

Chronology of PIKE

Map	Date	Event	Resulting Area
15	6 Feb 1877	Lost to CRENSHAW	680 sq mi
15	22 Feb 1887	Lost small area to BULLOCK to accommodate local property owners	680 sq mi
15	7 Feb 1889	Lost small area to BULLOCK to accommodate local property owners	680 sq mi

(Heavy line depicts historical boundary. Base map shows present-day information.)

15 6 Feb 1877–12 Feb 1897

Individual County Chronologies **295**

Chronology of PIKE

Map	Date	Event	Resulting Area
⑯	13 Feb 1897	Lost small area to BULLOCK	680 sq mi

(Heavy line depicts historical boundary. Base map shows present-day information.)

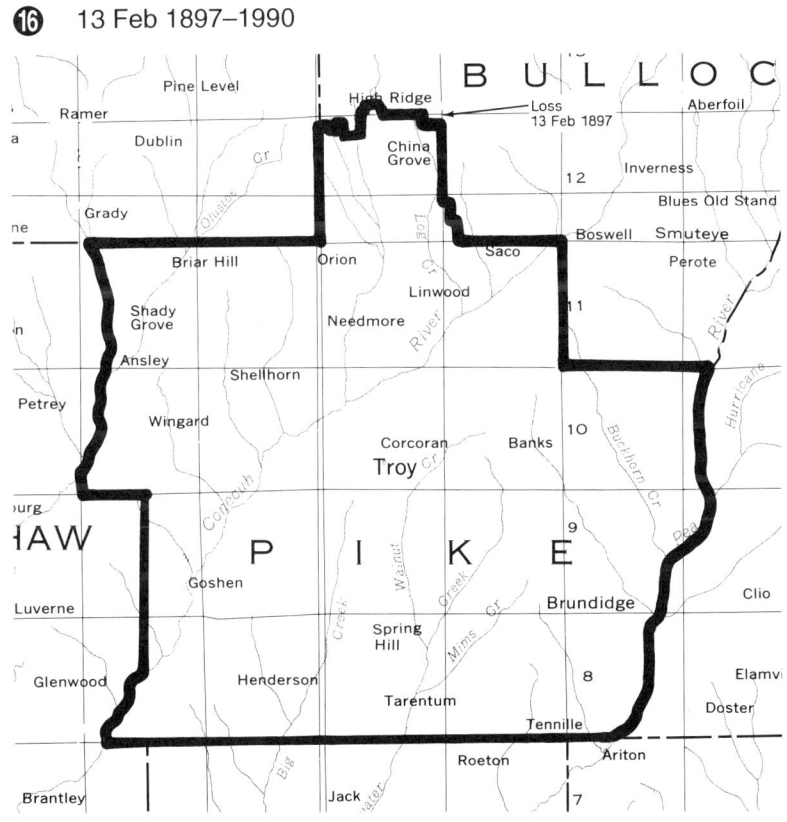

⑯ 13 Feb 1897–1990

ALABAMA

Chronology of RANDOLPH

Map	Date	Event	Resulting Area
❶	18 Dec 1832	Created from ST. CLAIR and SHELBY	910 sq mi
❷	6 Dec 1866	Lost to creation of CLEBURNE	750 sq mi

(Heavy line depicts historical boundary. Base map shows present-day information.)

❶ 18 Dec 1832–5 Dec 1866

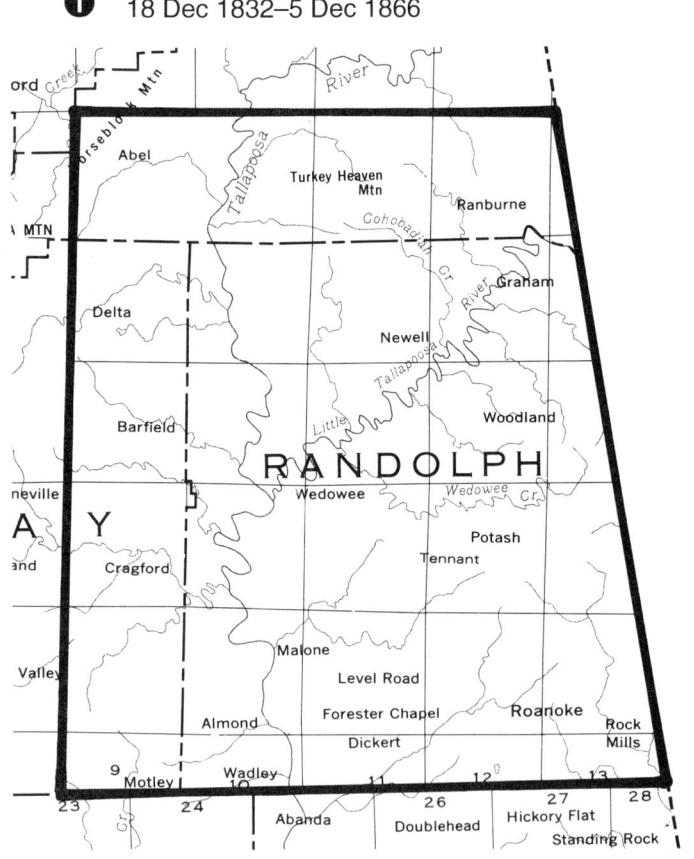

❷ 6 Dec 1866

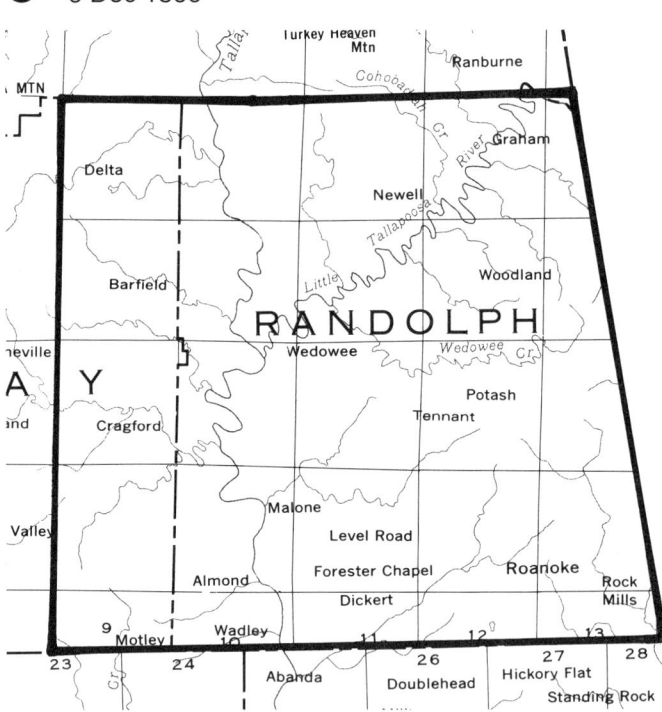

Individual County Chronologies **297**

Chronology of RANDOLPH

Map	Date	Event	Resulting Area
❸	7 Dec 1866	Lost to creation of CLAY	580 sq mi
	16 Dec 1871	CLAY authorized to gain from RANDOLPH [cannot be demarcated as described, no change]	
❸	17 Mar 1873	Lost small area to CLAY	580 sq mi
❹	29 Jul 1907	Exchanged small areas with CLEBURNE	580 sq mi

(Heavy line depicts historical boundary. Base map shows present-day information.)

❸ 7 Dec 1866–28 Jul 1907

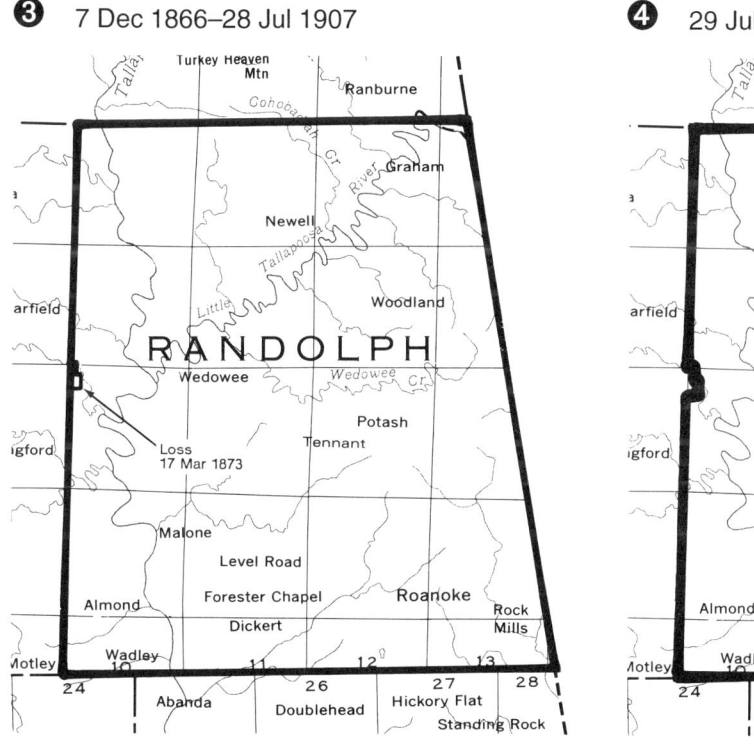

❹ 29 Jul 1907–1990

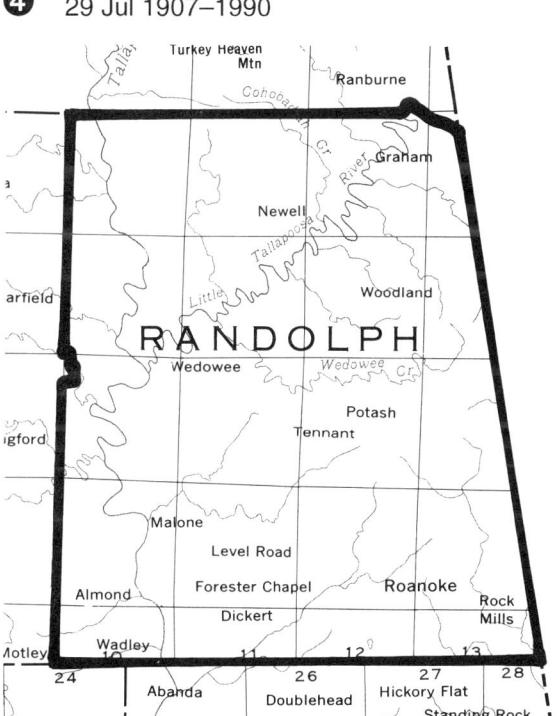

298　ALABAMA

Chronology of RUSSELL

Map	Date	Event	Resulting Area
❶	18 Dec 1832	Created from MONTGOMERY and PIKE	890 sq mi
❶	25 Dec 1837	Gained small area from MACON	890 sq mi
❶	11 Feb 1843	Lost small area to MACON to accommodate local property owner	890 sq mi
❷	5 Dec 1866	Lost to creation of LEE	600 sq mi

(Heavy line depicts historical boundary. Base map shows present-day information.)

❶ 18 Dec 1832–4 Dec 1866

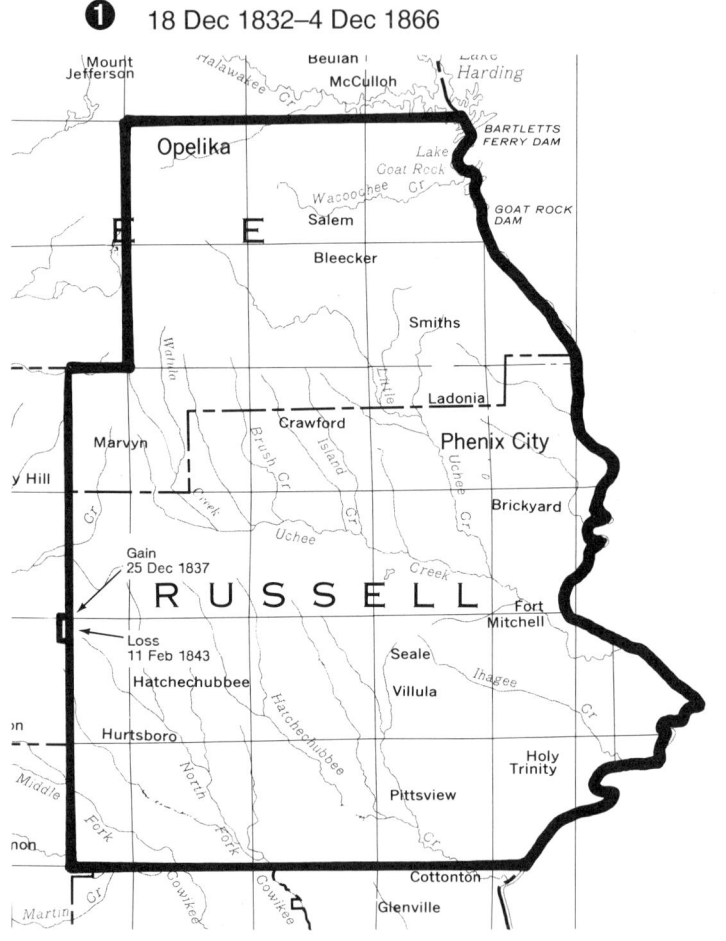

❷ 5 Dec 1866–30 Dec 1868

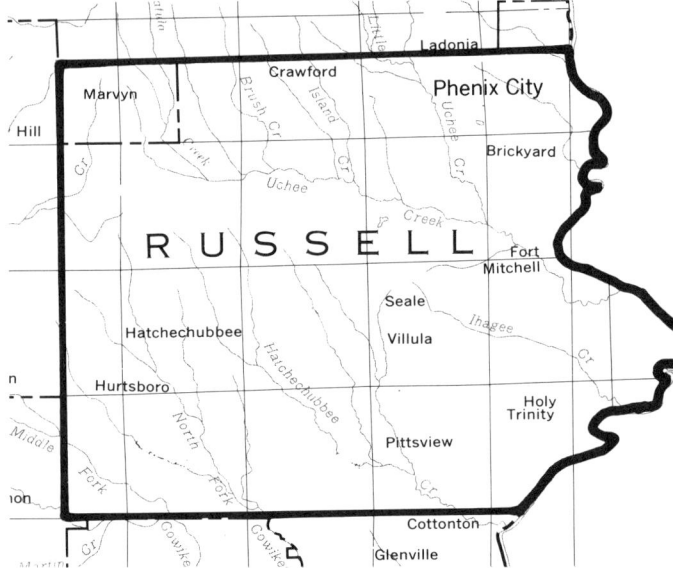

Individual County Chronologies

Chronology of RUSSELL

Map	Date	Event	Resulting Area
❸	31 Dec 1868	Gained from BARBOUR	650 sq mi
❸	15 Mar 1873	Lost small area to BARBOUR to accommodate local property owner	650 sq mi
❸	10 Feb 1875	Gained small area from BARBOUR to accommodate local property owner	650 sq mi
	12 Dec 1888	Boundary with LEE adjusted [location unknown, not mapped]	
❹	30 Sep 1932	Exchanged with LEE	640 sq mi

(Heavy line depicts historical boundary. Base map shows present-day information.)

❸ 31 Dec 1868–29 Sep 1932

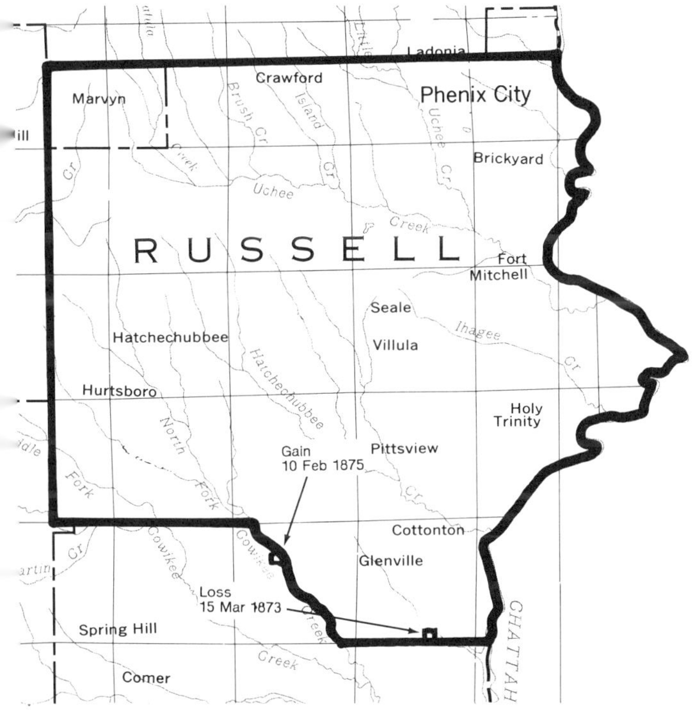

❹ 30 Sep 1932–1990

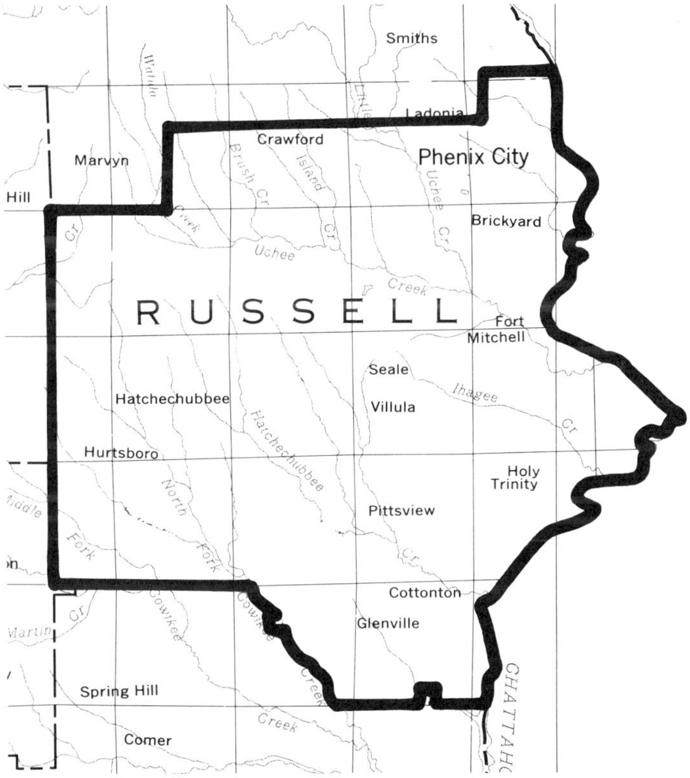

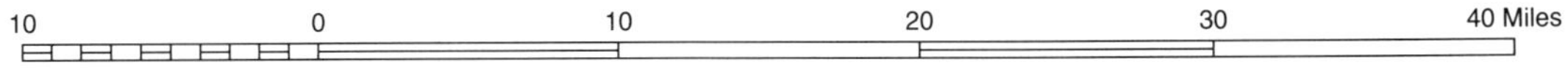

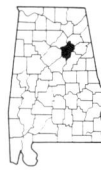

Chronology of ST. CLAIR

Map	Date	Event	Resulting Area
❶	20 Nov 1818	Created from SHELBY	890 sq mi

(Heavy line depicts historical boundary. Base map shows present-day information.)

❶ 20 Nov 1818–12 Dec 1819

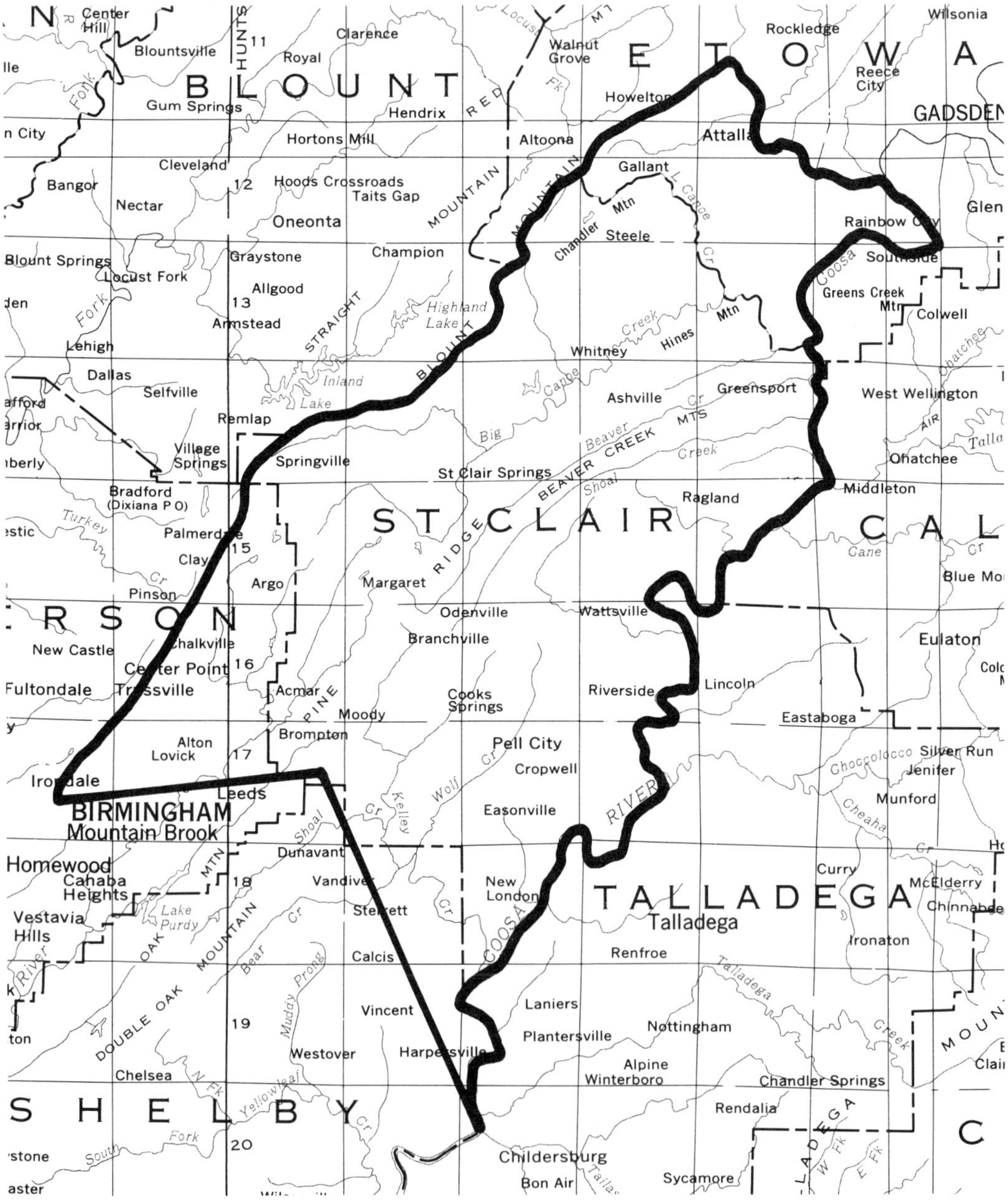

10 0 10 20 30 40 Miles

Individual County Chronologies 301

Chronology of ST. CLAIR

Map	Date	Event	Resulting Area
❷	13 Dec 1819	Lost to creation of JEFFERSON	840 sq mi

(Heavy line depicts historical boundary. Base map shows present-day information.)

❷ 13 Dec 1819–31 Mar 1821

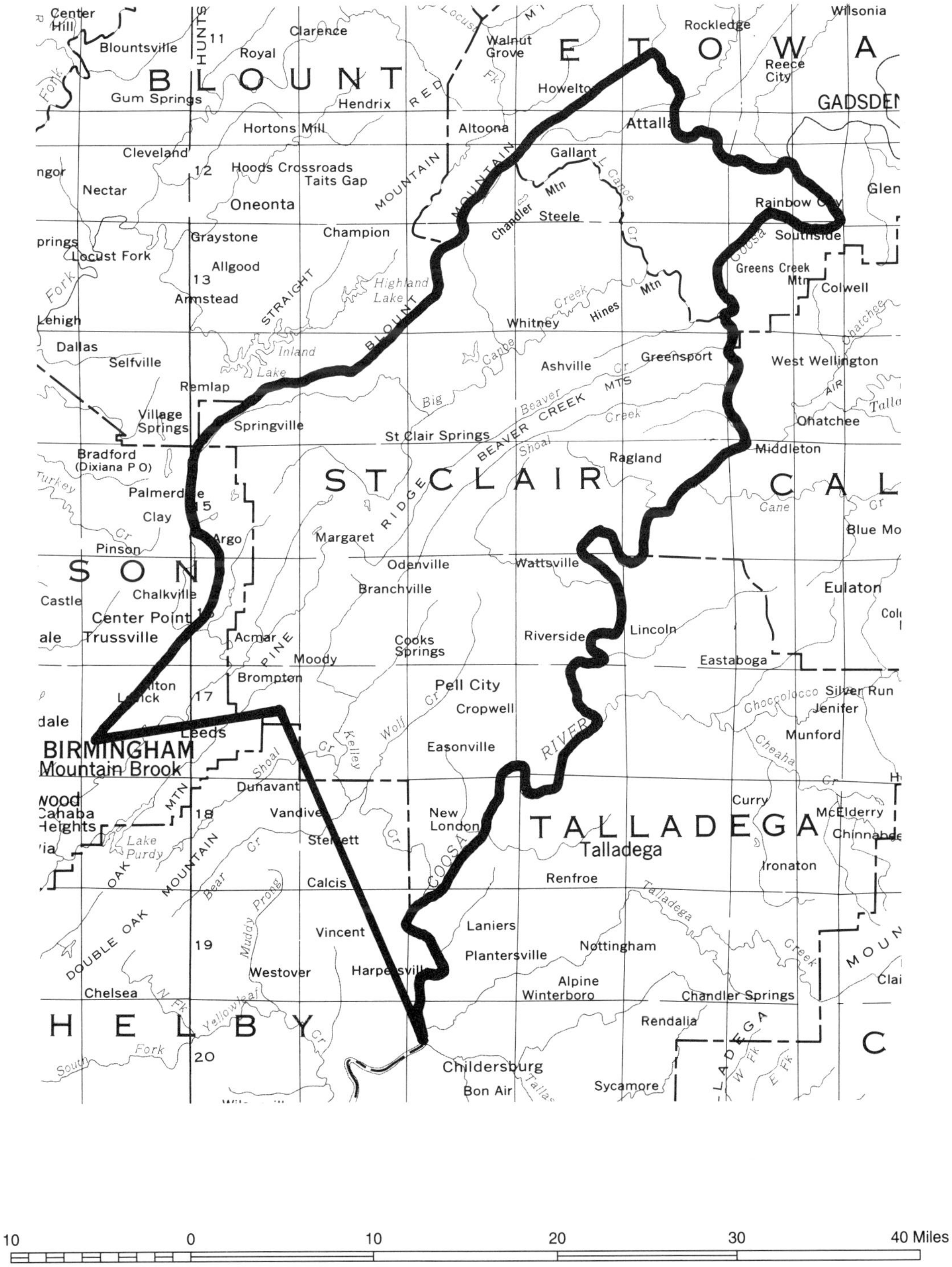

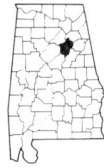

Chronology of ST. CLAIR

Map	Date	Event	Resulting Area
❸	17 Dec 1819	Non-county area belonging to Cherokee Indians attached to ST. CLAIR	
❹	20 Dec 1820	Part of non-county area detached, attached to COTACO (now MORGAN)	
❺	1 Apr 1821	Exchanged with JEFFERSON [attachment unchanged; see map 4]	810 sq mi

(Heavy line depicts historical boundary. Base map shows present-day information.)

❸ 17 Dec 1819–19 Dec 1820

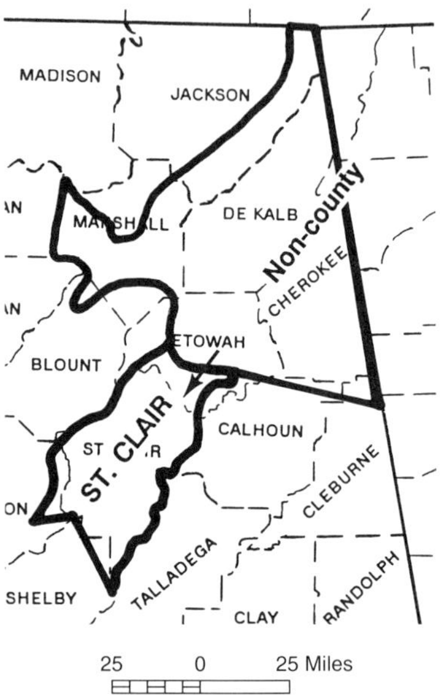

❹ 20 Dec 1820–20 Jan 1832

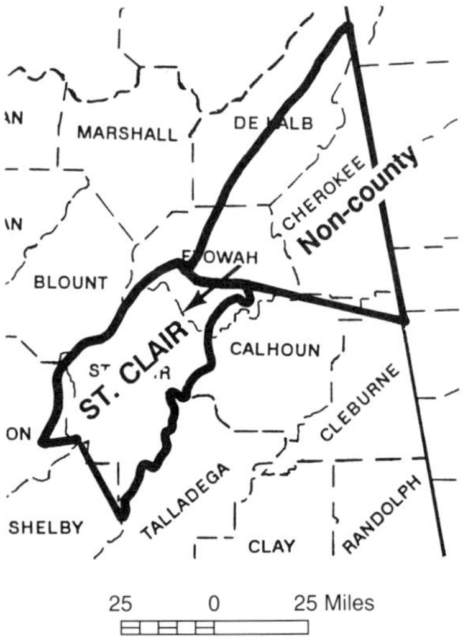

❺ 1 Apr 1821–18 Dec 1823

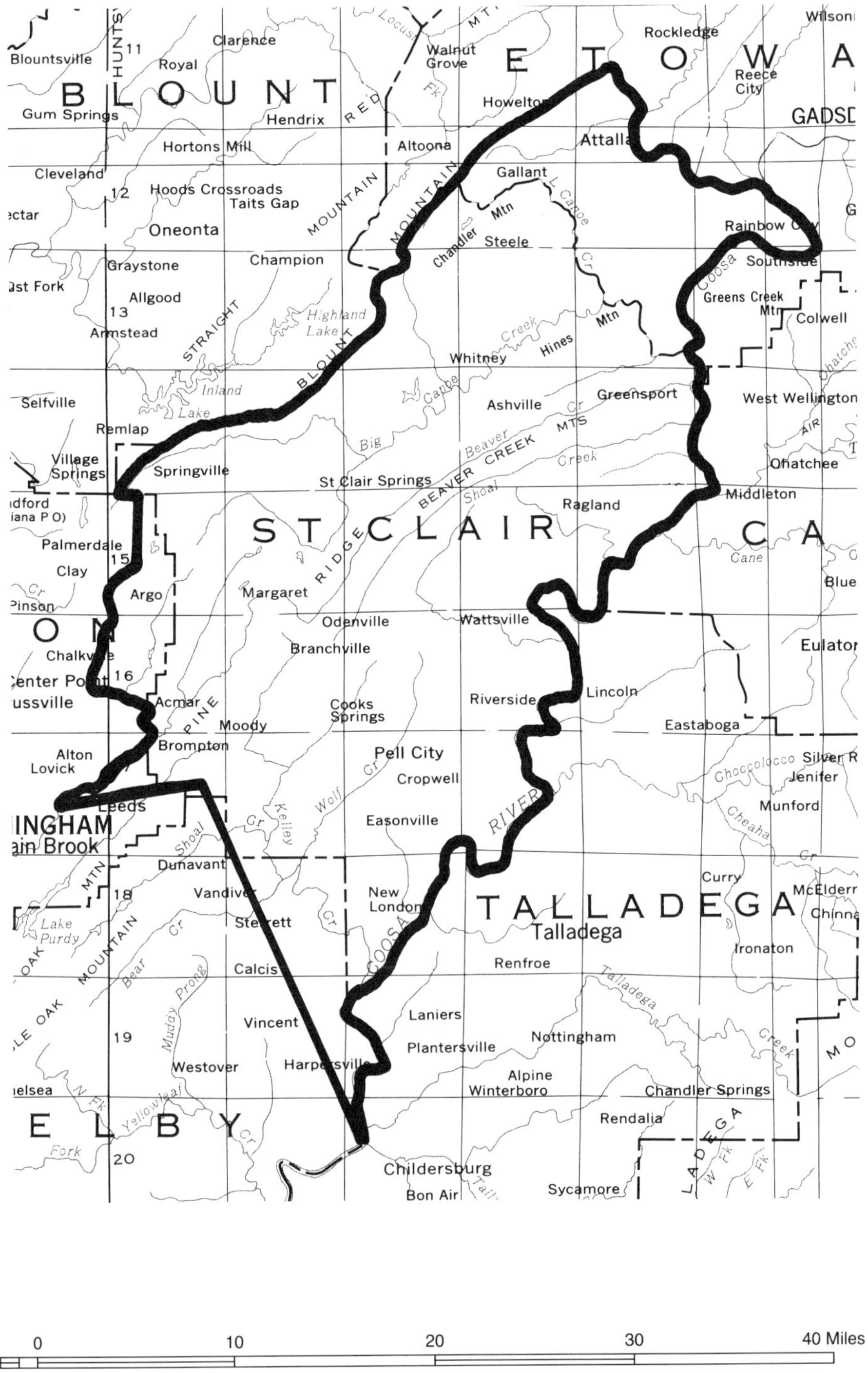

Chronology of ST. CLAIR

Map	Date	Event	Resulting Area
❻	19 Dec 1823	Lost to JEFFERSON [attachment unchanged; see map 4]	790 sq mi

(Heavy line depicts historical boundary. Base map shows present-day information.)

❻ 19 Dec 1823–28 Jan 1829

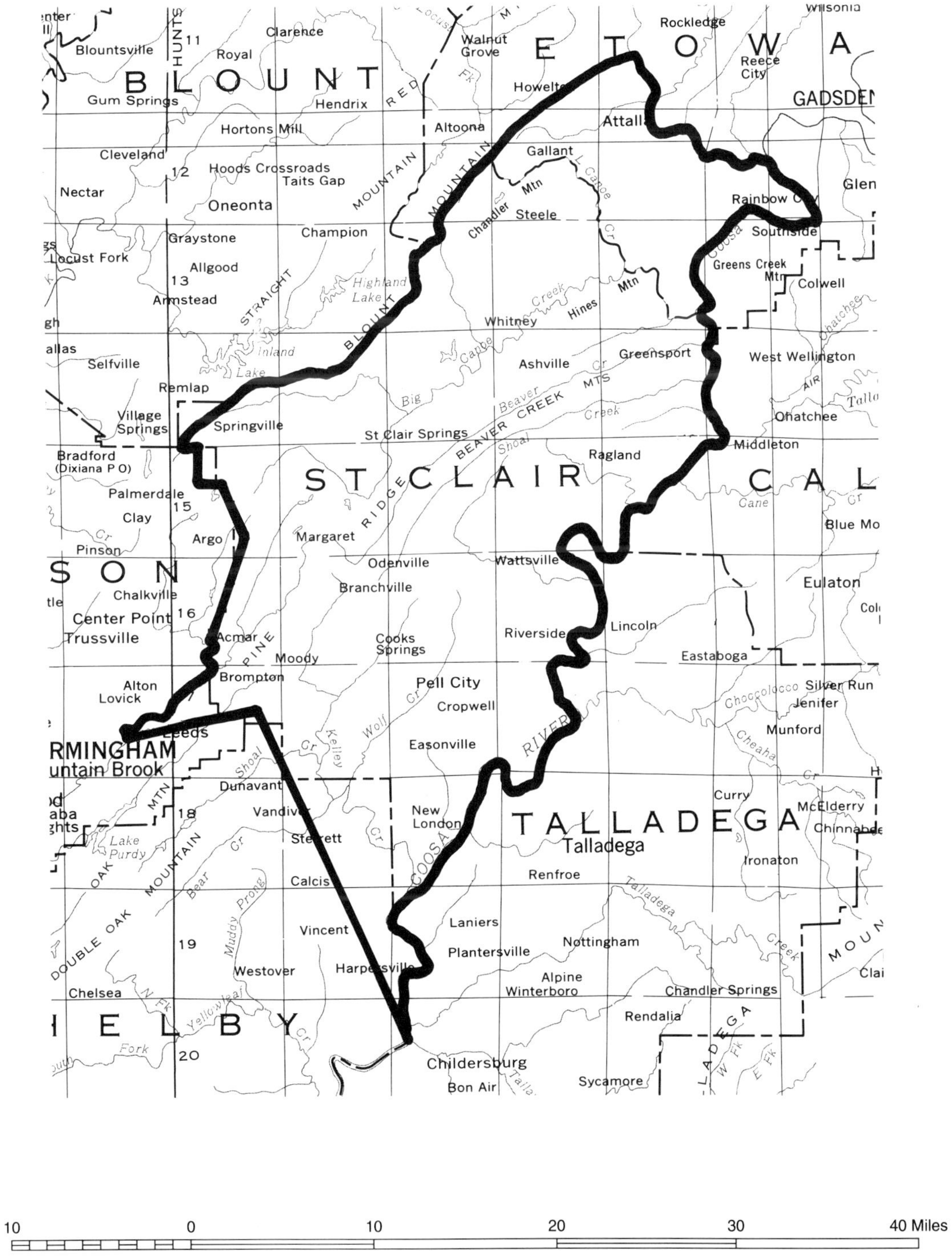

Chronology of ST. CLAIR

Map	Date	Event	Resulting Area
❼	9 Jan 1828	Given concurrent jurisdiction with AUTAUGA and SHELBY over non-county area attached to AUTAUGA on 1 Mar 1827	
❽	29 Jan 1829	Gained from non-county area that was concurrently attached to AUTAUGA, ST. CLAIR, and SHELBY [original attachment remained unchanged; see map 4]	2,750 sq mi
❾	15 Jan 1831	Exchanged with SHELBY [attachment unchanged; see map 4]	2,710 sq mi

(Heavy line depicts historical boundary. Base map shows present-day information.)

❼ 9 Jan 1828–28 Jan 1829

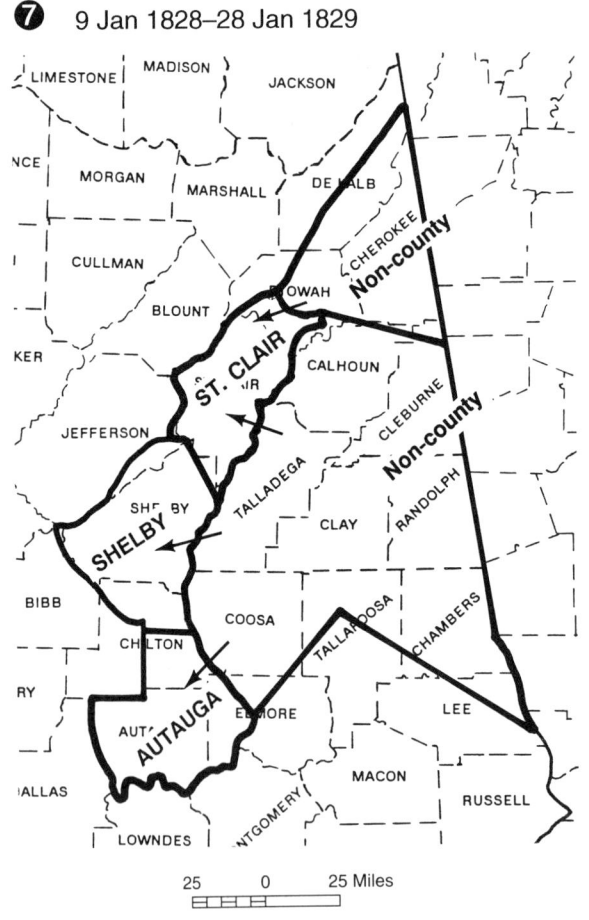

❽ 29 Jan 1829–14 Jan 1831

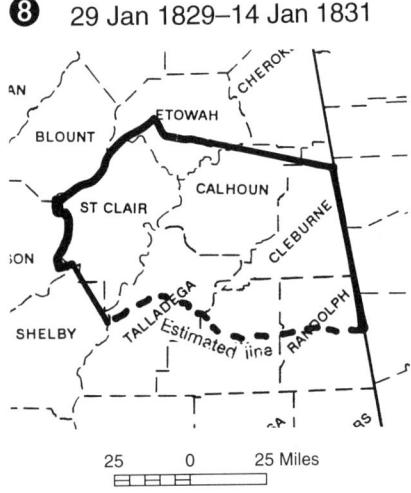

❾ 15 Jan 1831–20 Jan 1832

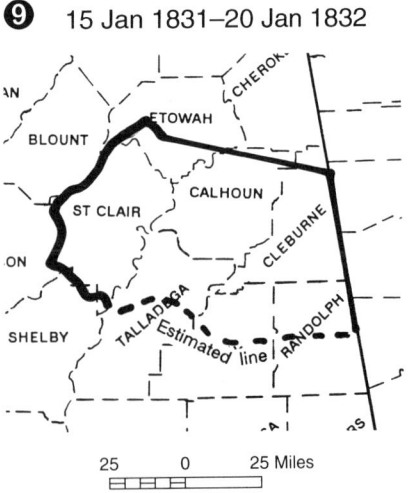

Chronology of ST. CLAIR

Map	Date	Event	Resulting Area
⑩	21 Jan 1832	Gained non-county attachment and gained from non-county area attached to JACKSON	4,380 sq mi
⑪	18 Dec 1832	Lost to creation of BENTON (now CALHOUN), RANDOLPH, and TALLADEGA	2,310 sq mi
⑫	14 Jan 1834	Lost to JACKSON	1,560 sq mi
⑬	30 Dec 1834	Part of ST. CLAIR attached to BENTON (now CALHOUN)	

(Heavy line depicts historical boundary. Base map shows present-day information.)

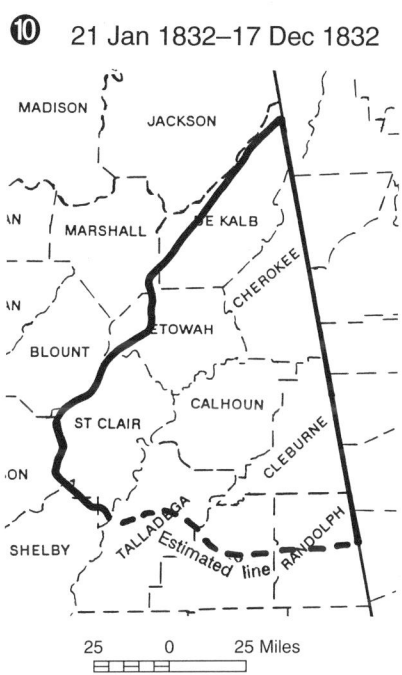

⑩ 21 Jan 1832–17 Dec 1832

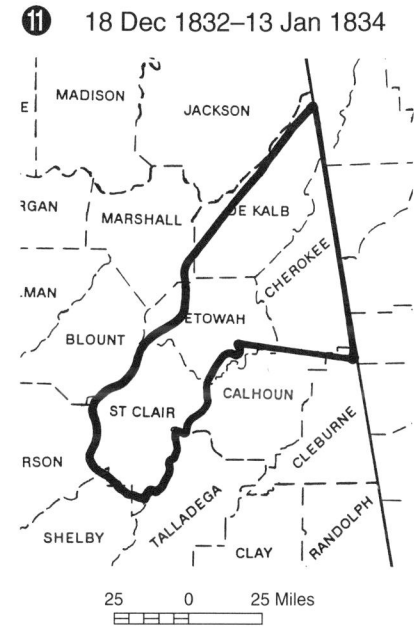

⑪ 18 Dec 1832–13 Jan 1834

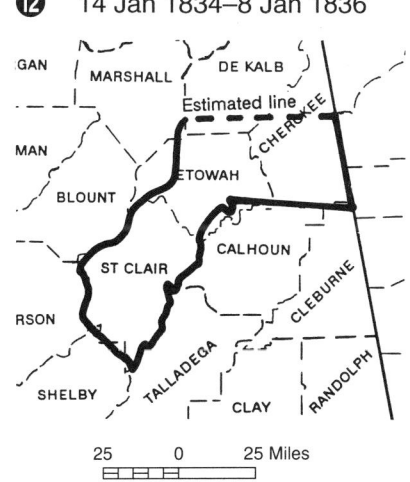

⑫ 14 Jan 1834–8 Jan 1836

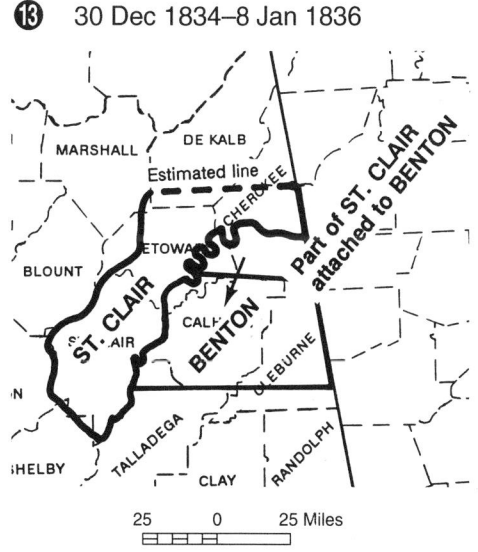

⑬ 30 Dec 1834–8 Jan 1836

Chronology of ST. CLAIR

Map	Date	Event	Resulting Area
⑭	9 Jan 1836	Lost to creation of DE KALB; lost to creation of CHEROKEE, including the part that was attached to BENTON (now CALHOUN)	760 sq mi

(Heavy line depicts historical boundary. Base map shows present-day information.)

⑭ 9 Jan 1836–6 Dec 1866
3 Dec 1867–30 Nov 1868

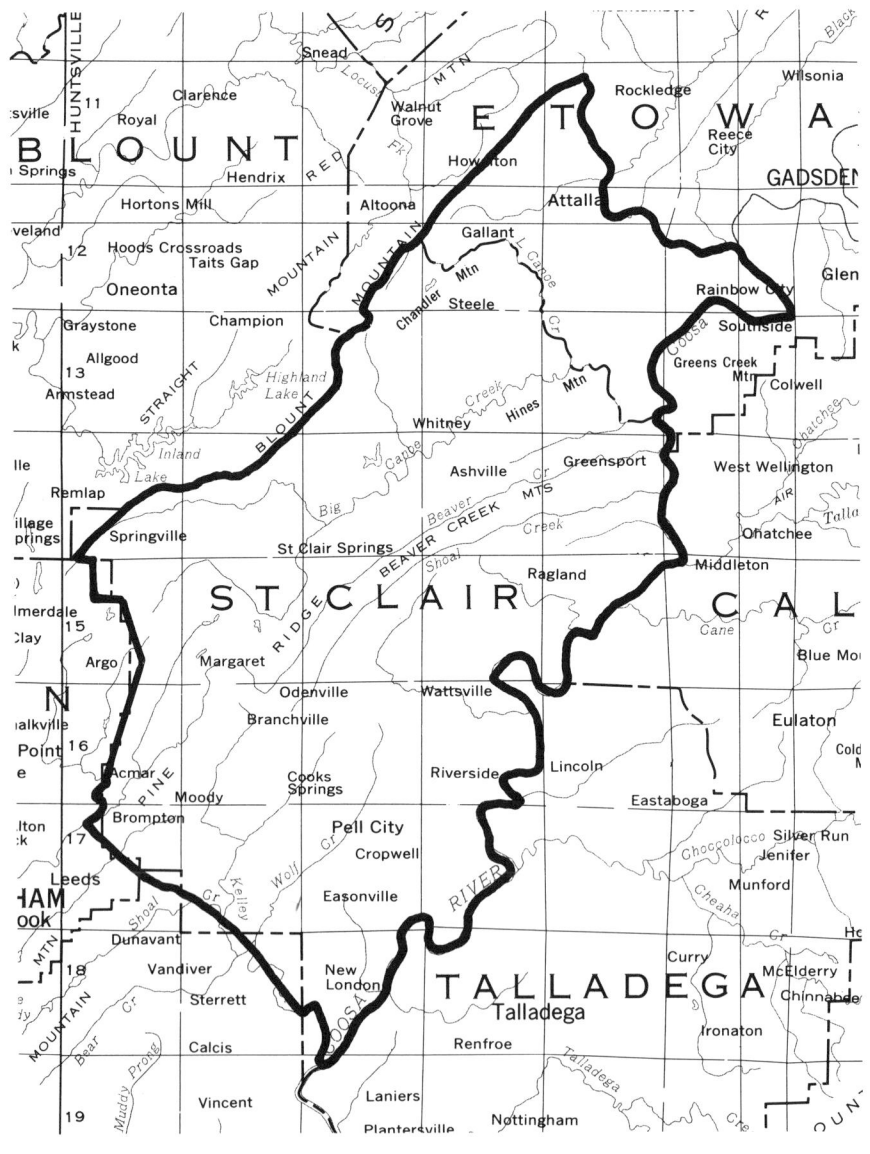

Chronology of ST. CLAIR

Map	Date	Event	Resulting Area
⑮	7 Dec 1866	Lost to creation of BAINE	640 sq mi
	19 Feb 1867	Change in boundary with BAINE and BLOUNT authorized [cannot be demarcated as described, no change]	
⑭	3 Dec 1867	Gained from BAINE; BAINE eliminated	760 sq mi
⑮	1 Dec 1868	Lost to creation of ETOWAH	640 sq mi
	17 Dec 1868	Gained small area from ETOWAH to accommodate local property owner [location unknown, not mapped]	

(Heavy line depicts historical boundary. Base map shows present-day information.)

⑮ 7 Dec 1866–2 Dec 1867
1 Dec 1868–6 Feb 1870

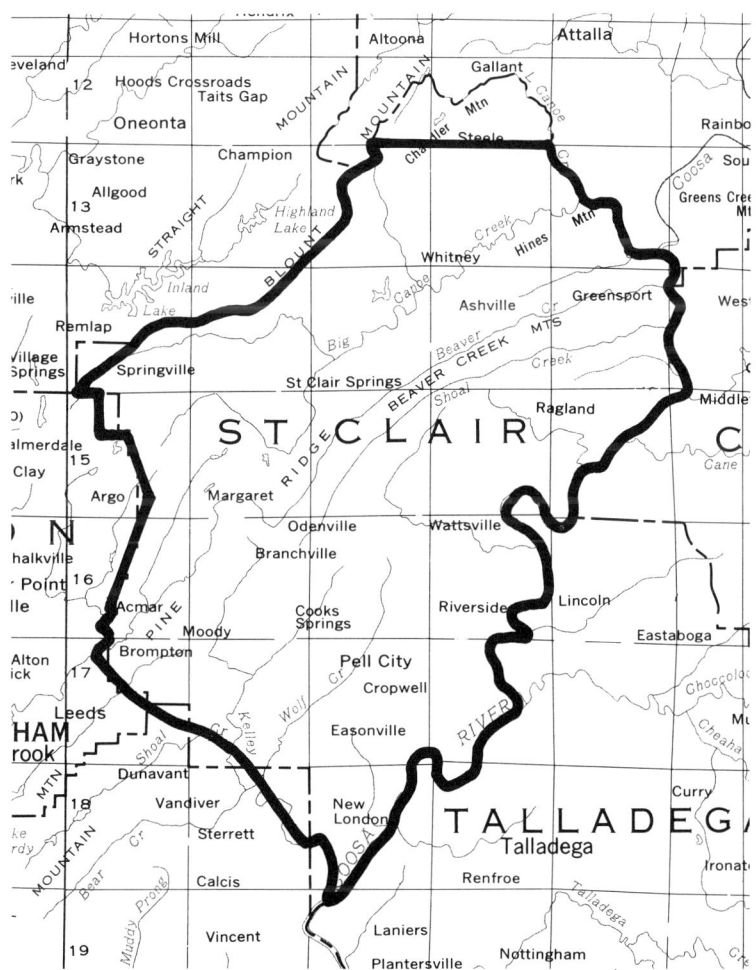

ALABAMA

Chronology of ST. CLAIR

Map	Date	Event	Resulting Area
⓰	7 Feb 1870	Gained from ETOWAH	660 sq mi
⓰	11 Feb 1887	Gained from BLOUNT	660 sq mi

(Heavy line depicts historical boundary. Base map shows present-day information.)

⓰ 7 Feb 1870–6 Feb 1899

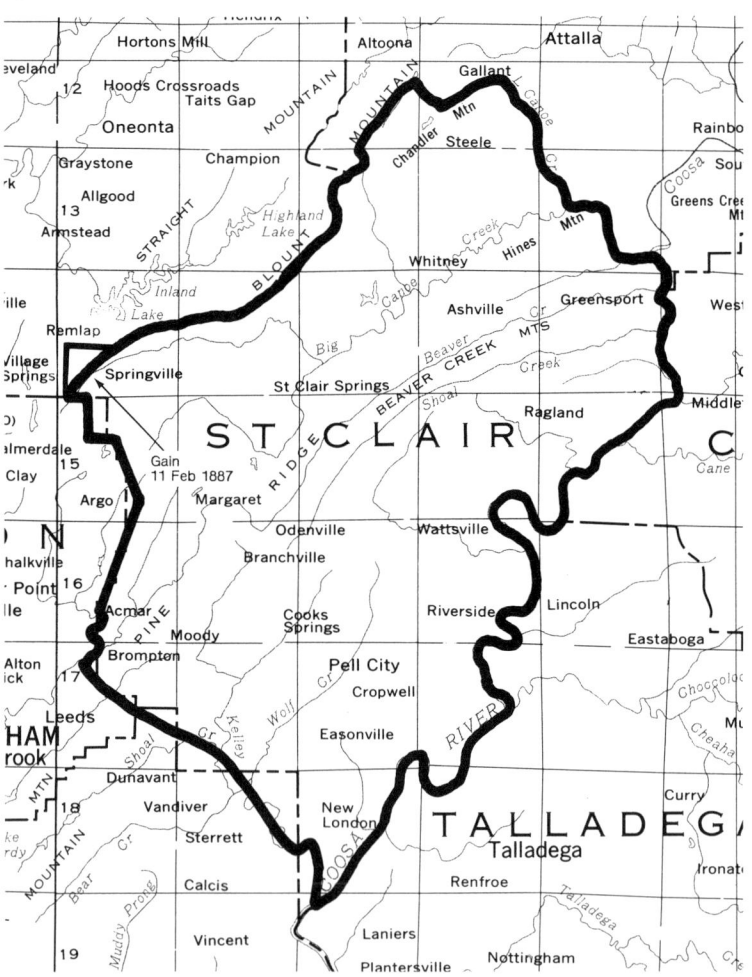

Chronology of ST. CLAIR

Map	Date	Event	Resulting Area
⑰	7 Feb 1899	Exchanged with SHELBY	650 sq mi

(Heavy line depicts historical boundary. Base map shows present-day information.)

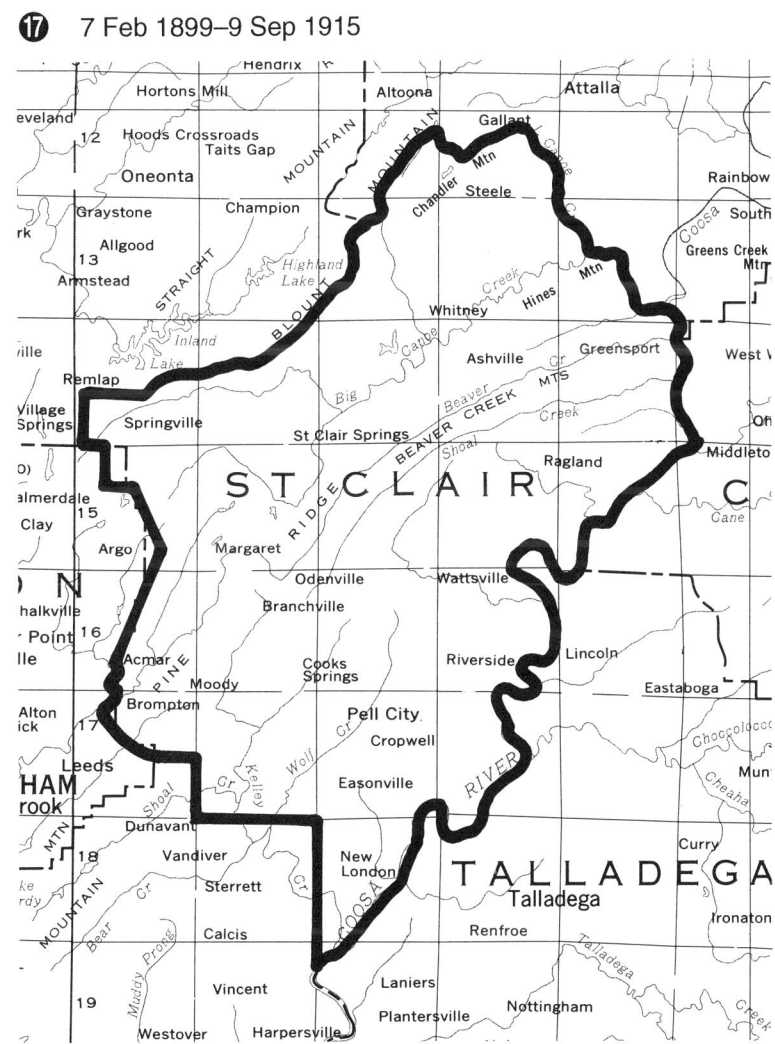

⑰ 7 Feb 1899–9 Sep 1915

Chronology of ST. CLAIR

Map	Date	Event	Resulting Area
⑱	10 Sep 1915	Exchanged with JEFFERSON	630 sq mi

(Heavy line depicts historical boundary. Base map shows present-day information.)

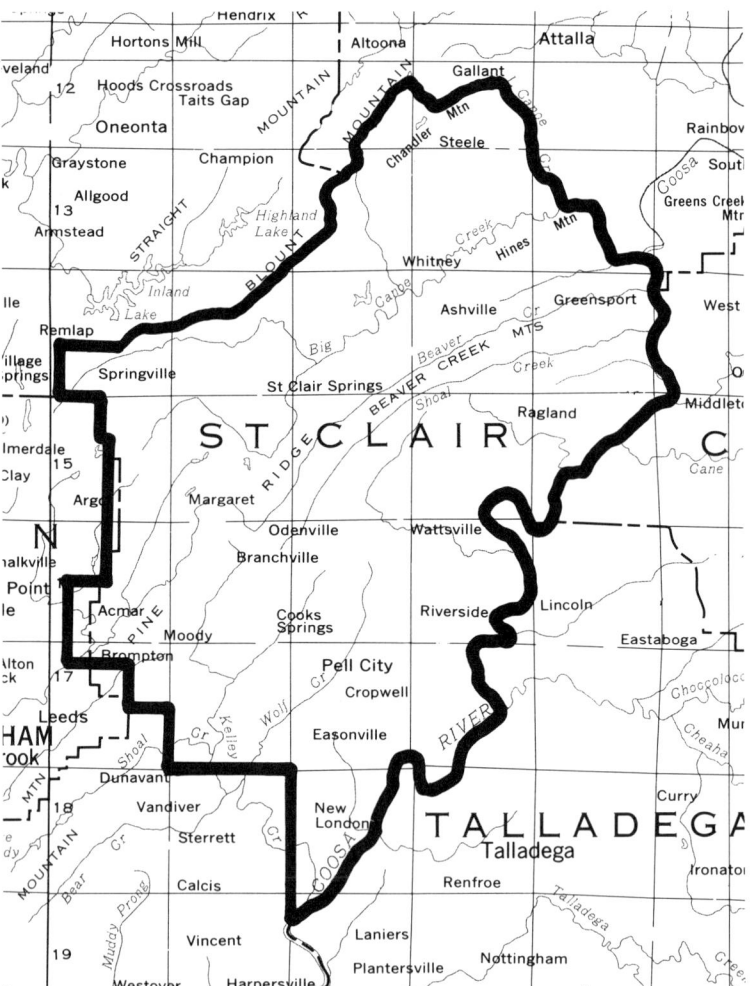

⑱ 10 Sep 1915–27 Sep 1915

Chronology of ST. CLAIR

Map	Date	Event	Resulting Area
⑲	28 Sep 1915	Exchanged with JEFFERSON	640 sq mi

(Heavy line depicts historical boundary. Base map shows present-day information.)

⑲ 28 Sep 1915–1990

Chronology of SHELBY

Map	Date	Event	Resulting Area
❶	7 Feb 1818	Created from MONTGOMERY and non-county area	1,370 sq mi
❷	20 Nov 1818	Gained from CAHAWBA (now BIBB) and from non-county area, lost to creation of ST. CLAIR	1,130 sq mi

(Heavy line depicts historical boundary. Base map shows present-day information.)

❶ 7 Feb 1818–19 Nov 1818

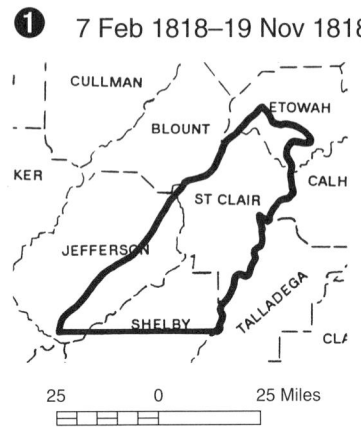

❷ 20 Nov 1818–12 Dec 1819

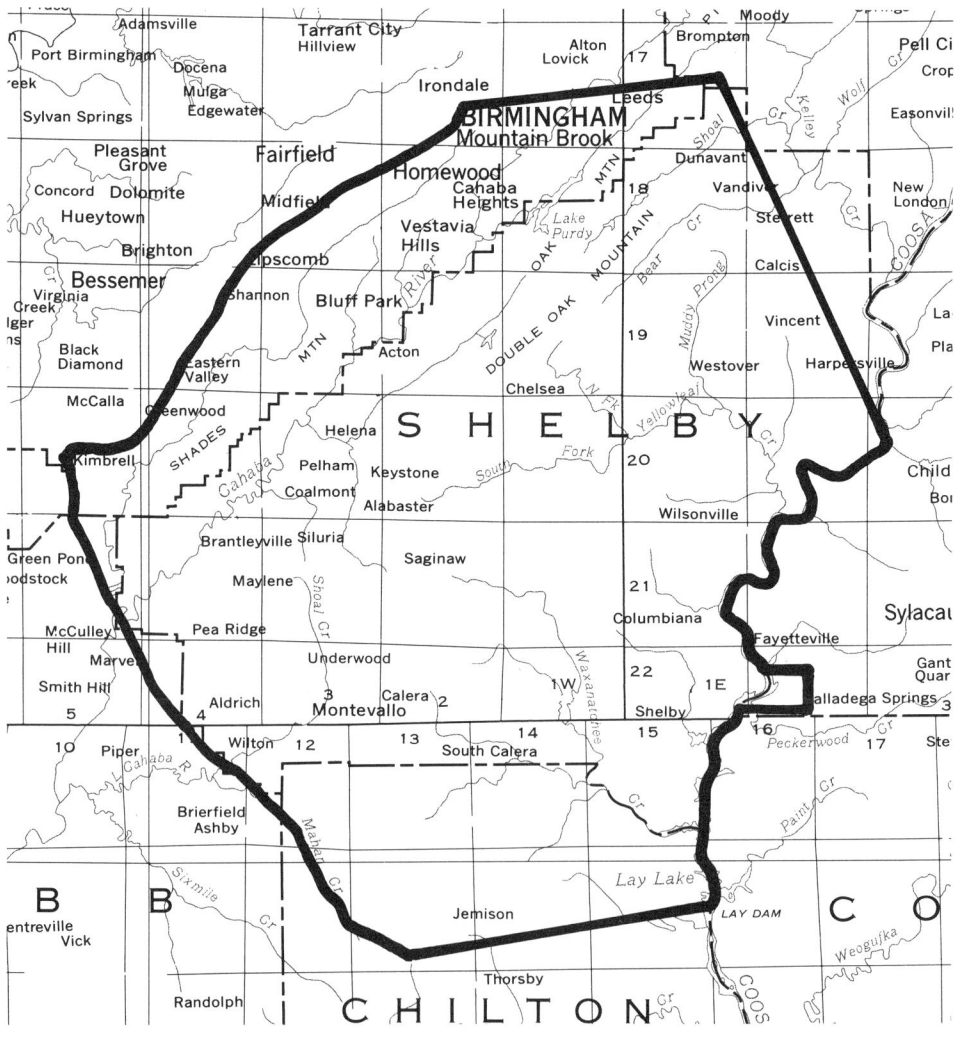

Individual County Chronologies 313

Chronology of SHELBY

Map	Date	Event	Resulting Area
❸	13 Dec 1819	Lost to creation of JEFFERSON	1,030 sq mi

(Heavy line depicts historical boundary. Base map shows present-day information.)

❸ 13 Dec 1819–11 Jan 1827

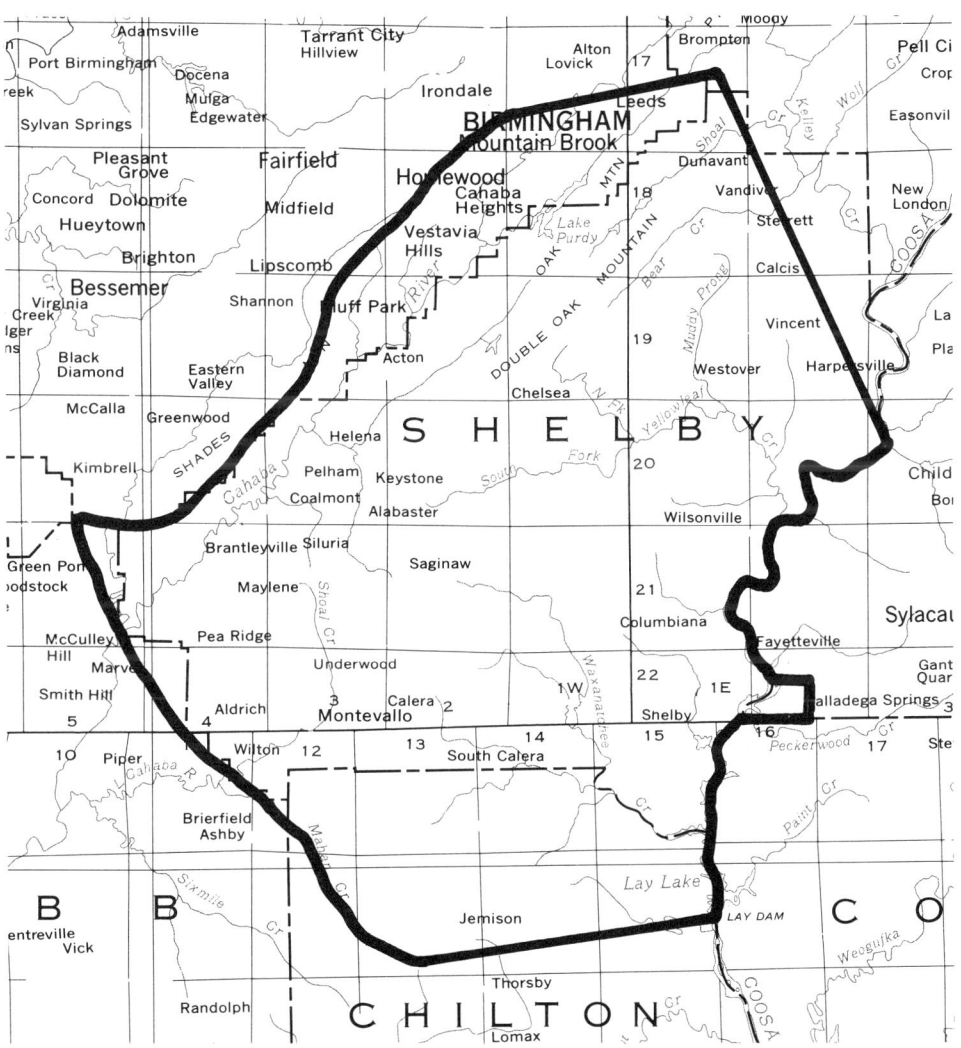

314   ALABAMA

Chronology of SHELBY

Map	Date	Event	Resulting Area
❹	12 Jan 1827	Gained from AUTAUGA	1,070 sq mi

(Heavy line depicts historical boundary. Base map shows present-day information.)

❹ 12 Jan 1827–27 Dec 1827

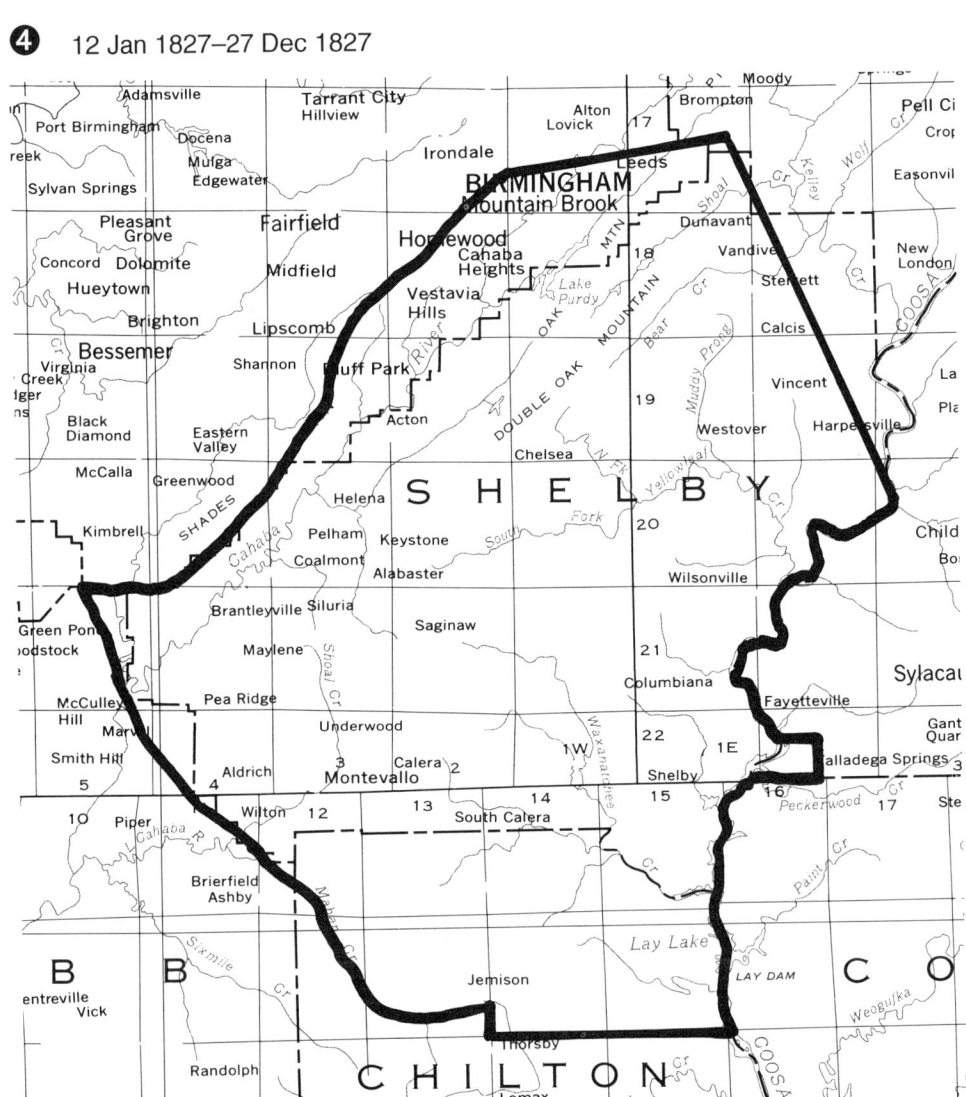

Individual County Chronologies 315

Chronology of SHELBY

Map	Date	Event	Resulting Area
❺	28 Dec 1827	Gained from AUTAUGA	1,080 sq mi

(Heavy line depicts historical boundary. Base map shows present-day information.)

❺ 28 Dec 1827–28 Jan 1829

Chronology of SHELBY

Map	Date	Event	Resulting Area
❻	9 Jan 1828	Given concurrent jurisdiction with AUTAUGA and ST. CLAIR over non-county area attached to AUTAUGA on 1 Mar 1827	
❼	29 Jan 1829	Gained from non-county area that was concurrently attached to AUTAUGA, ST. CLAIR, and SHELBY	2,660 sq mi
❽	15 Jan 1831	Gained from MONTGOMERY, exchanged with ST. CLAIR	3,170 sq mi
❽	18 Jan 1832	Lost to BIBB [see also BIBB, map 8]	3,160 sq mi

(Heavy line depicts historical boundary. Base map shows present-day information.)

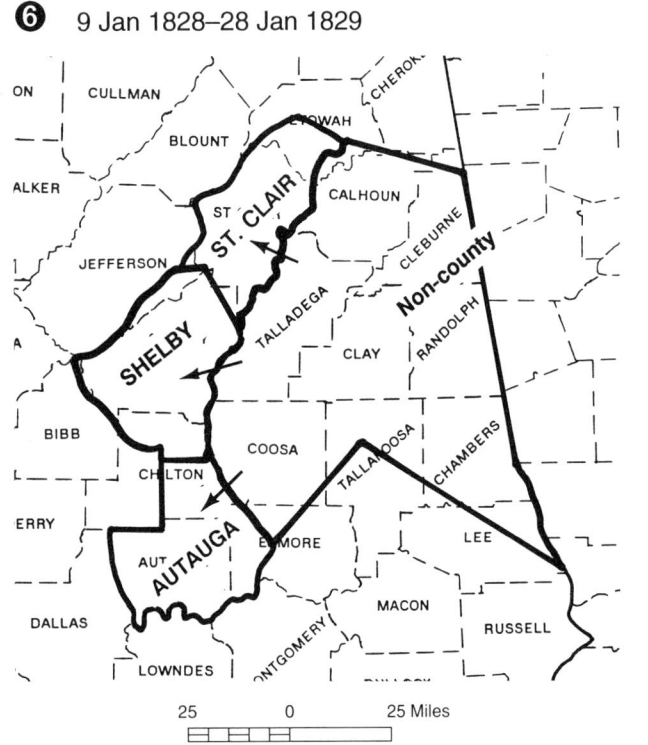

❻ 9 Jan 1828–28 Jan 1829

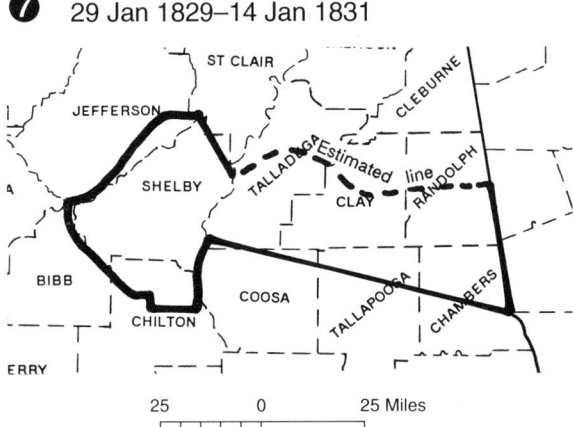

❼ 29 Jan 1829–14 Jan 1831

❽ 15 Jan 1831–17 Dec 1832

Individual County Chronologies 317

Chronology of SHELBY

Map	Date	Event	Resulting Area
9	18 Dec 1832	Lost to creation of CHAMBERS, COOSA, RANDOLPH, TALLADEGA, and TALLAPOOSA	1,130 sq mi

(Heavy line depicts historical boundary. Base map shows present-day information.)

9   18 Dec 1832–c. Apr 1833

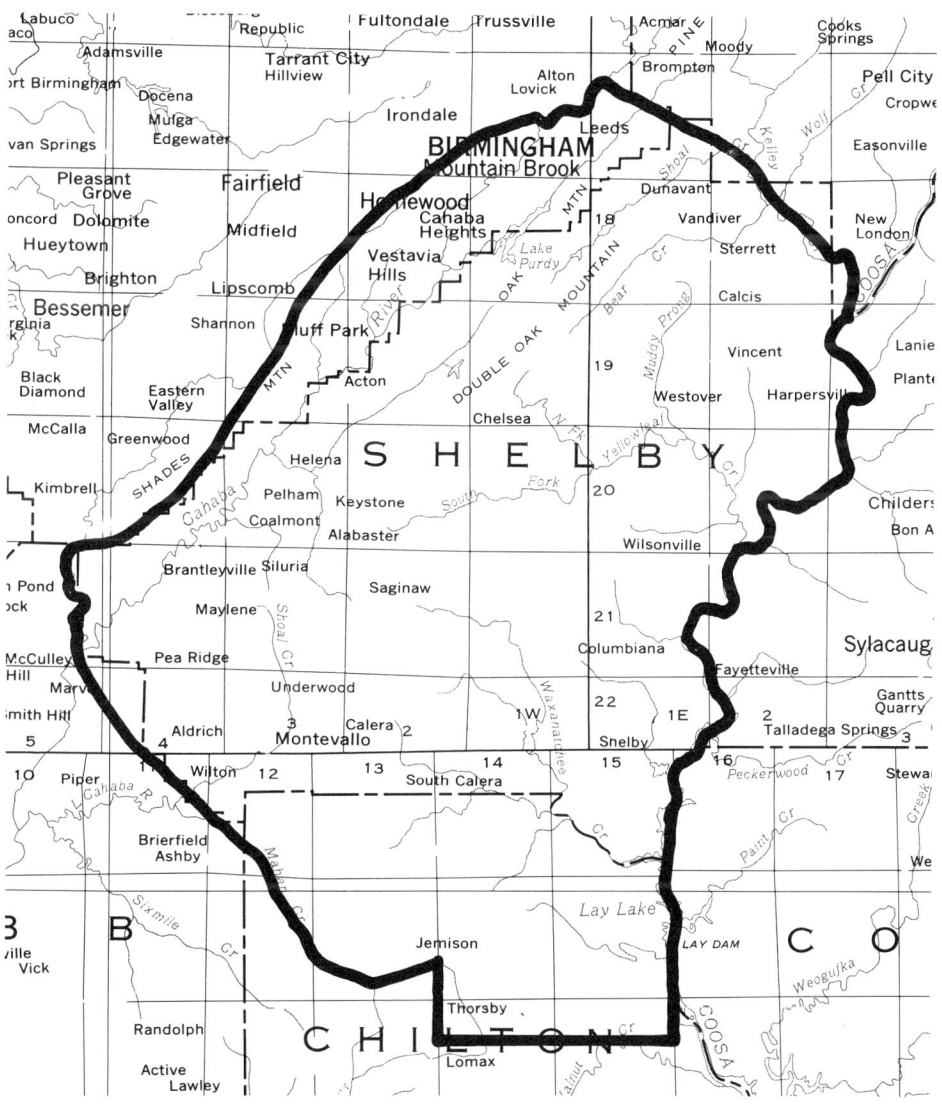

318 ALABAMA

Chronology of SHELBY

Map	Date	Event	Resulting Area
⑩	after 1 Apr 1833	Lost to JEFFERSON	1,090 sq mi
	2 Dec 1841	Lost small area to JEFFERSON to accommodate local property owner [location unknown, not mapped]	
⑩	8 Feb 1861	Lost to JEFFERSON	1,090 sq mi
⑩	11 Nov 1861	Gained from JEFFERSON	1,090 sq mi
⑩	4 Dec 1862	Lost small area to JEFFERSON to accommodate local property owner	1,090 sq mi

(Heavy line depicts historical boundary. Base map shows present-day information.)

⑩ c. Apr 1833–29 Dec 1868

Individual County Chronologies 319

Chronology of SHELBY

Map	Date	Event	Resulting Area
⑪	30 Dec 1868	Lost to creation of BAKER (now CHILTON)	870 sq mi
⑪	6 Mar 1871	Lost to JEFFERSON	870 sq mi

(Heavy line depicts historical boundary. Base map shows present-day information.)

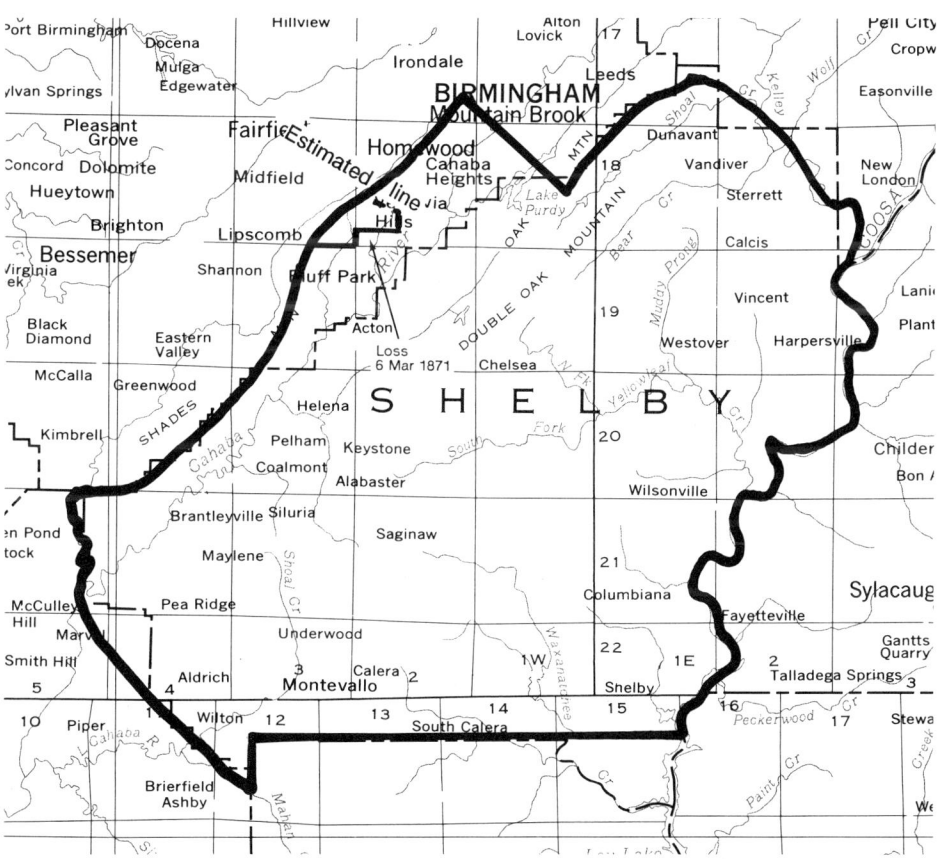

⑪   30 Dec 1868–22 Apr 1873

320 ALABAMA

Chronology of SHELBY

Map	Date	Event	Resulting Area
⑫	23 Apr 1873	Gained from BAKER (now CHILTON)	880 sq mi
⑫	7 Dec 1878	Lost small area to JEFFERSON	880 sq mi

(Heavy line depicts historical boundary. Base map shows present-day information.)

⑫ 23 Apr 1873–11 Dec 1884

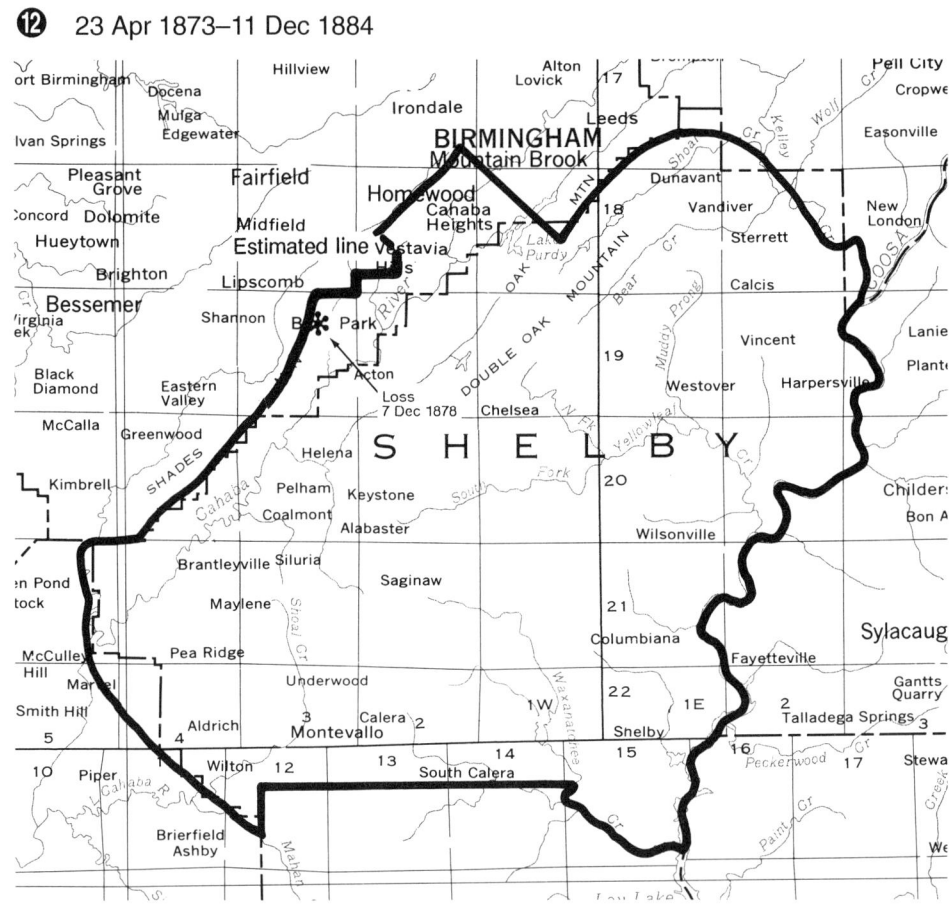

Individual County Chronologies 321

Chronology of SHELBY

Map	Date	Event	Resulting Area
⑬	12 Dec 1884	Lost to JEFFERSON	840 sq mi

(Heavy line depicts historical boundary. Base map shows present-day information.)

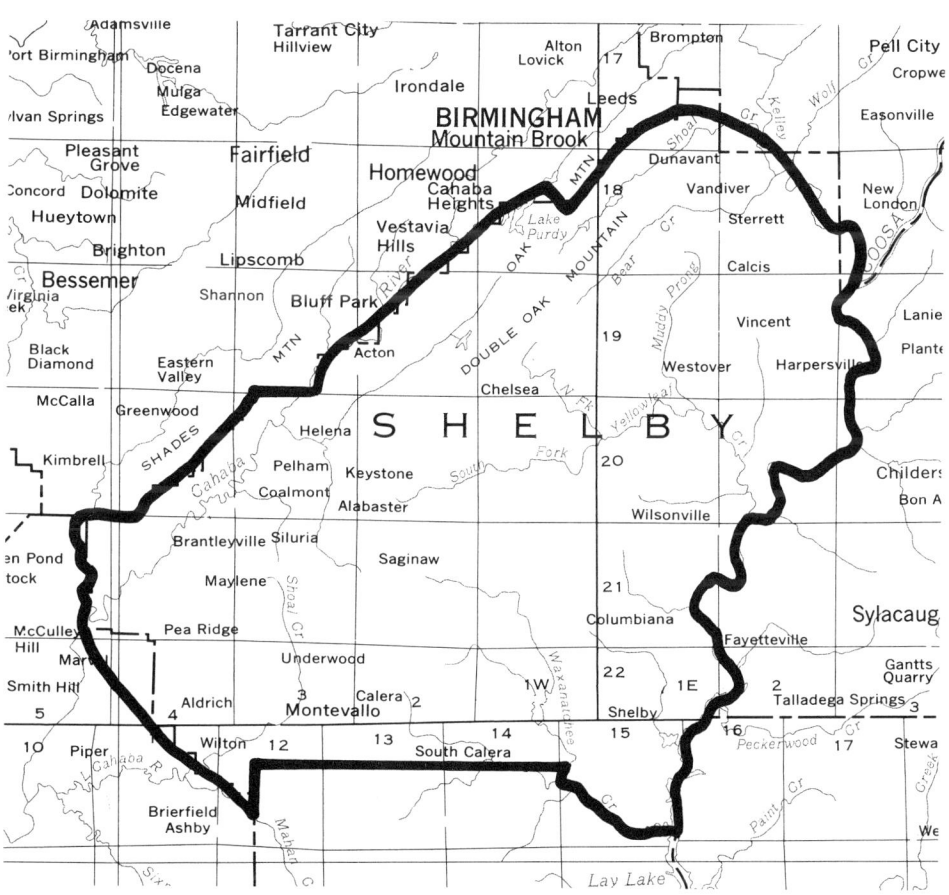

⑬ 12 Dec 1884–6 Feb 1899

322　ALABAMA

Chronology of SHELBY

Map	Date	Event	Resulting Area
⑭	7 Feb 1899	Exchanged with ST. CLAIR	840 sq mi

(Heavy line depicts historical boundary. Base map shows present-day information.)

⑭ 7 Feb 1899–30 Sep 1899

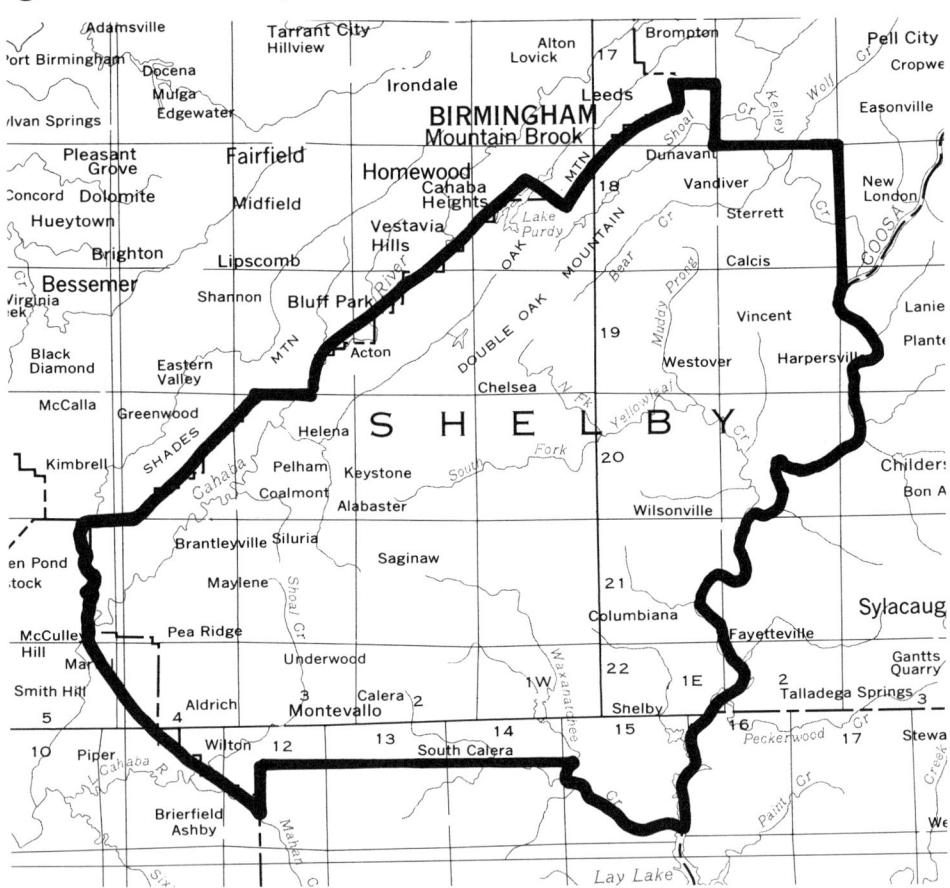

Chronology of SHELBY

Map	Date	Event	Resulting Area
⑮	1 Oct 1899	Exchanged with BIBB	820 sq mi

(Heavy line depicts historical boundary. Base map shows present-day information.)

⑮ 1 Oct 1899–1 Mar 1907

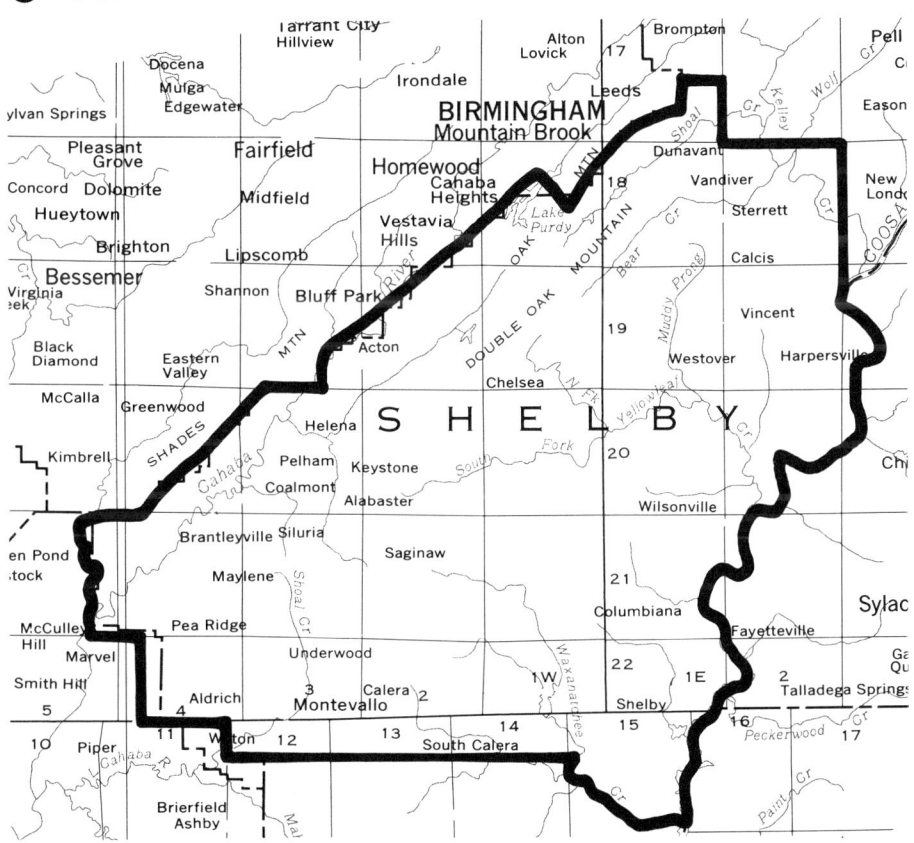

ALABAMA

Chronology of SHELBY

Map	Date	Event	Resulting Area
⓰	2 Mar 1907	Exchanged with BIBB	820 sq mi

(Heavy line depicts historical boundary. Base map shows present-day information.)

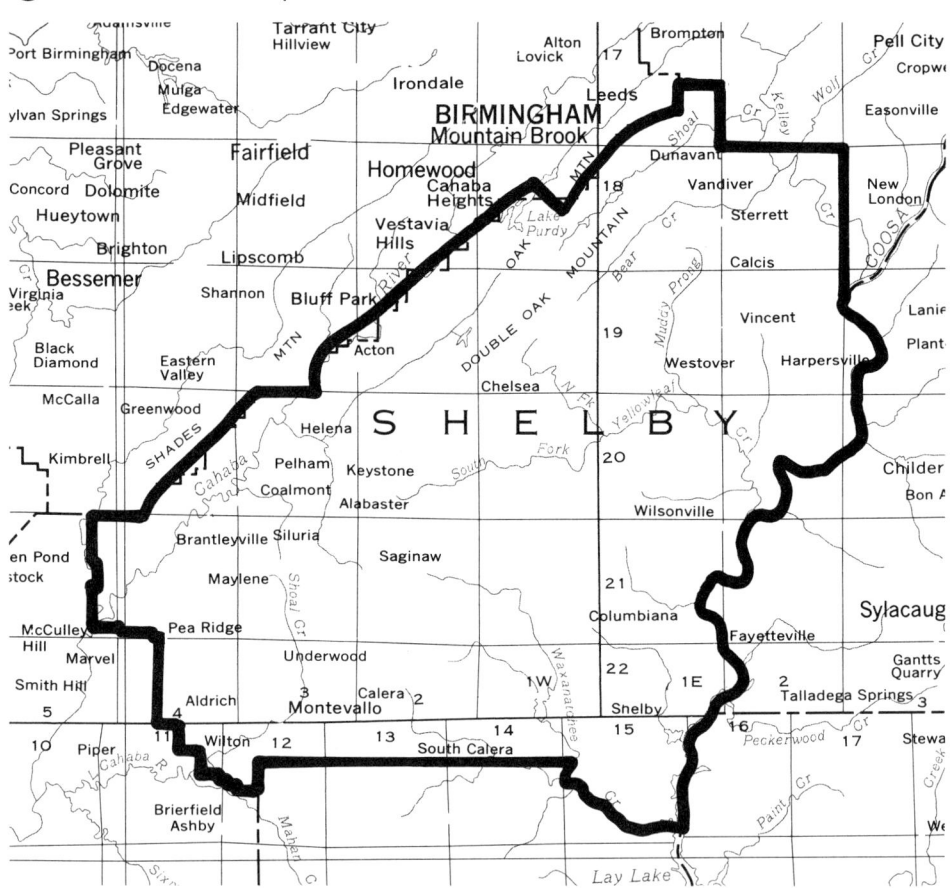

⓰ 2 Mar 1907–30 Sep 1943

Individual County Chronologies   325

Chronology of SHELBY

Map	Date	Event	Resulting Area
⑰	1 Oct 1943	Exchanged with JEFFERSON	810 sq mi
⑰	9 Aug 1979	Lost small area to JEFFERSON	810 sq mi

(Heavy line depicts historical boundary. Base map shows present-day information.)

⑰ 1 Oct 1943–1990

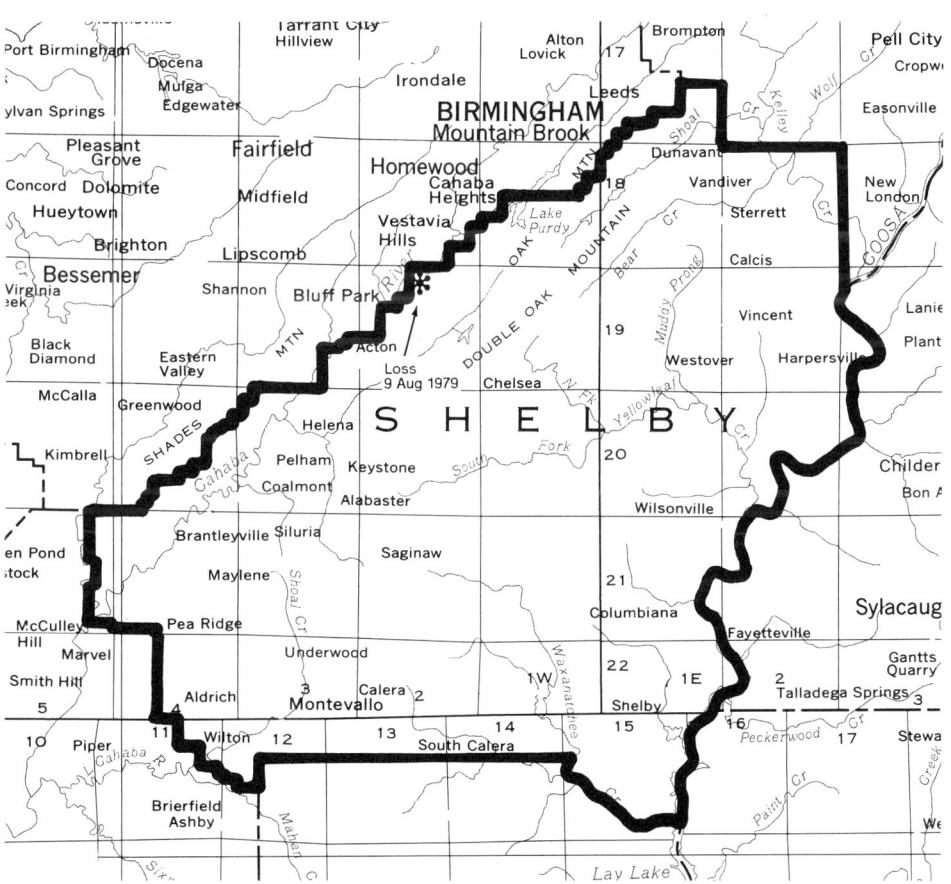

ALABAMA

Chronology of SUMTER

Map	Date	Event	Resulting Area
❶	18 Dec 1832	Created from non-county area attached to MARENGO	1,240 sq mi

(Heavy line depicts historical boundary. Base map shows present-day information.)

❶ 18 Dec 1832–28 Dec 1847

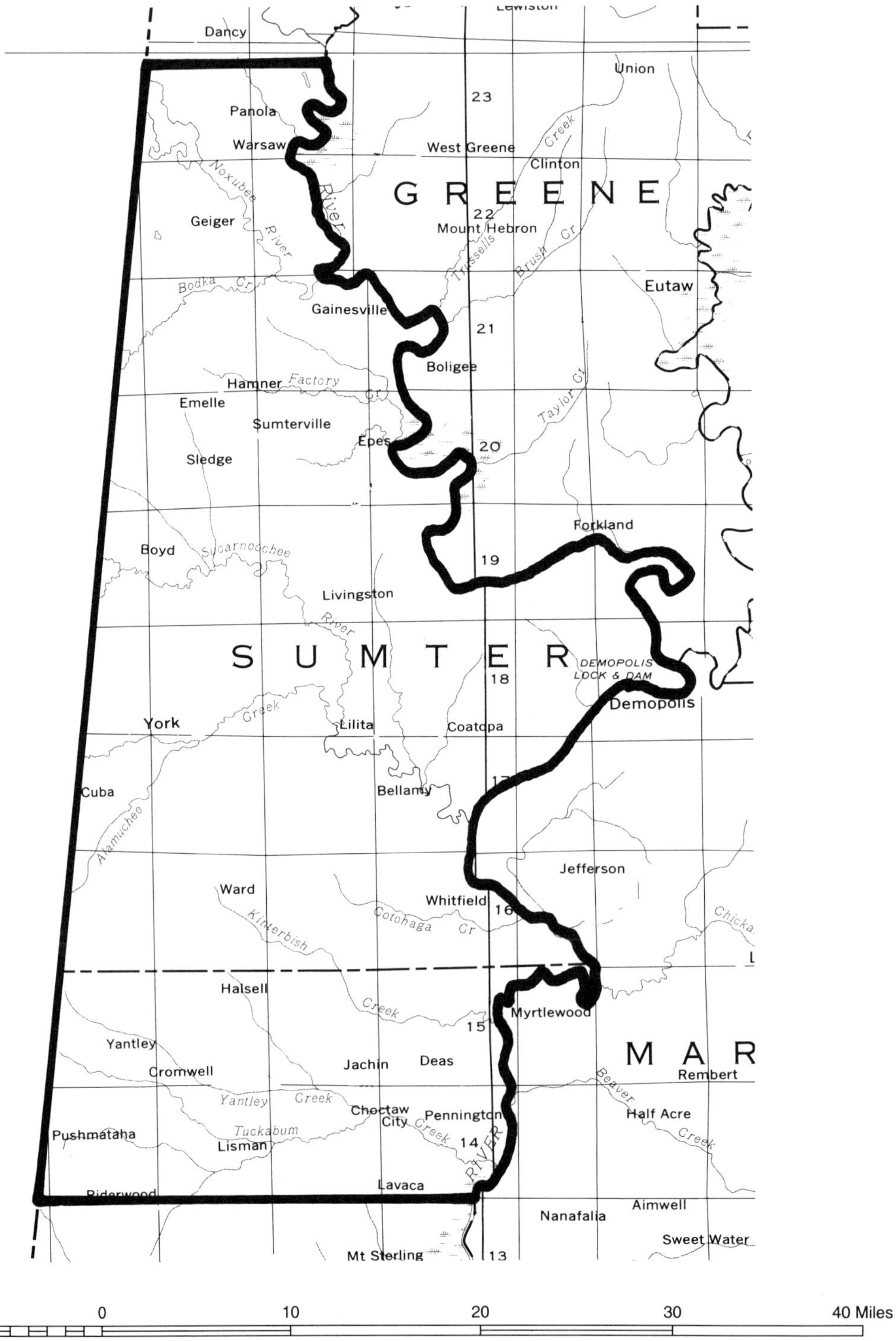

Chronology of SUMTER

Map	Date	Event	Resulting Area
❷	29 Dec 1847	Lost to creation of CHOCTAW	920 sq mi
	1 Mar 1870	CHOCTAW authorized to gain from SUMTER, dependent on local referendum [local action unknown, no change]	

(Heavy line depicts historical boundary. Base map shows present-day information.)

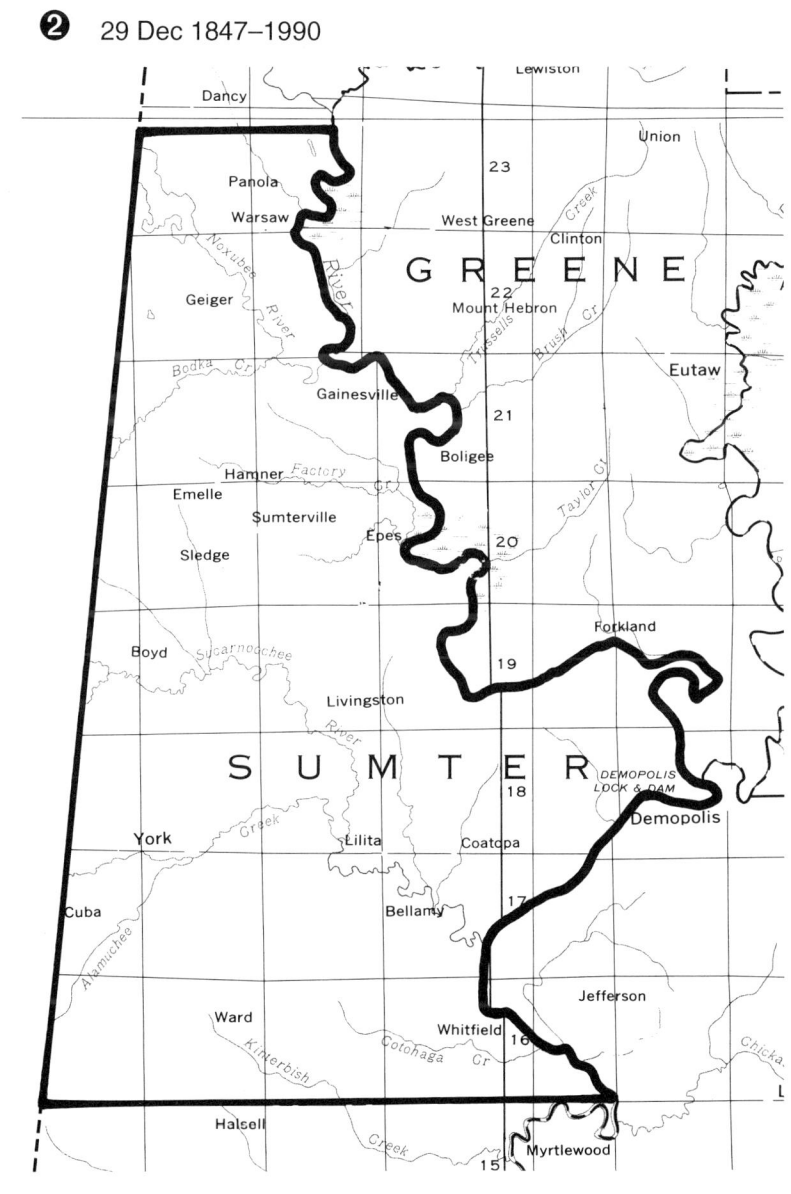

❷ 29 Dec 1847–1990

ALABAMA

Chronology of TALLADEGA

Map	Date	Event	Resulting Area
❶	18 Dec 1832	Created from ST. CLAIR and SHELBY	1,200 sq mi

(Heavy line depicts historical boundary. Base map shows present-day information.)

❶ 18 Dec 1832–22 Dec 1836

Individual County Chronologies **329**

Chronology of TALLADEGA

Map	Date	Event	Resulting Area
❷	23 Dec 1836	Gained from BENTON (now CALHOUN)	1,250 sq mi
❷	27 Jan 1845	Gained small area from BENTON (now CALHOUN)	1,250 sq mi
❷	5 Feb 1850	Gained small area from BENTON (now CALHOUN)	1,250 sq mi

(Heavy line depicts historical boundary. Base map shows present-day information.)

❷ 23 Dec 1836–5 Dec 1866

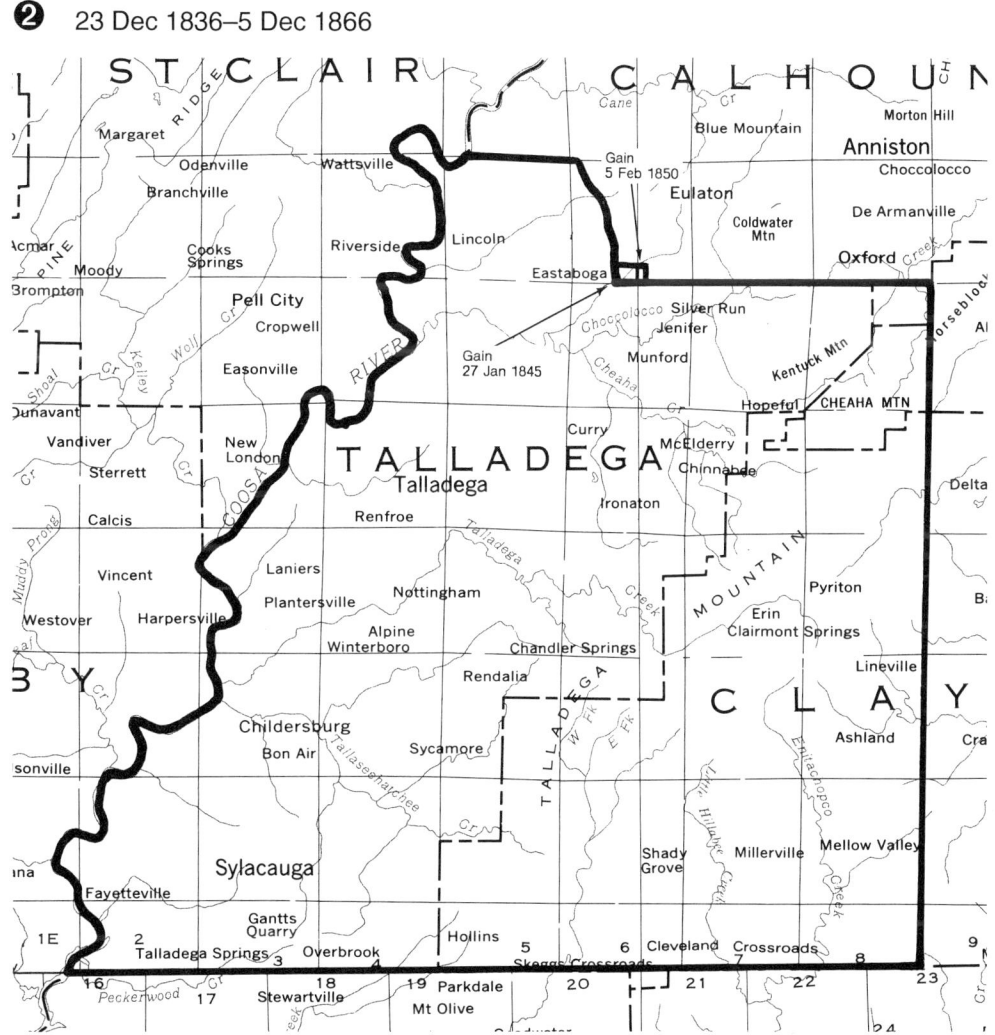

ALABAMA

Chronology of TALLADEGA

Map	Date	Event	Resulting Area
❸	6 Dec 1866	Lost to creation of CLEBURNE	1,220 sq mi

(Heavy line depicts historical boundary. Base map shows present-day information.)

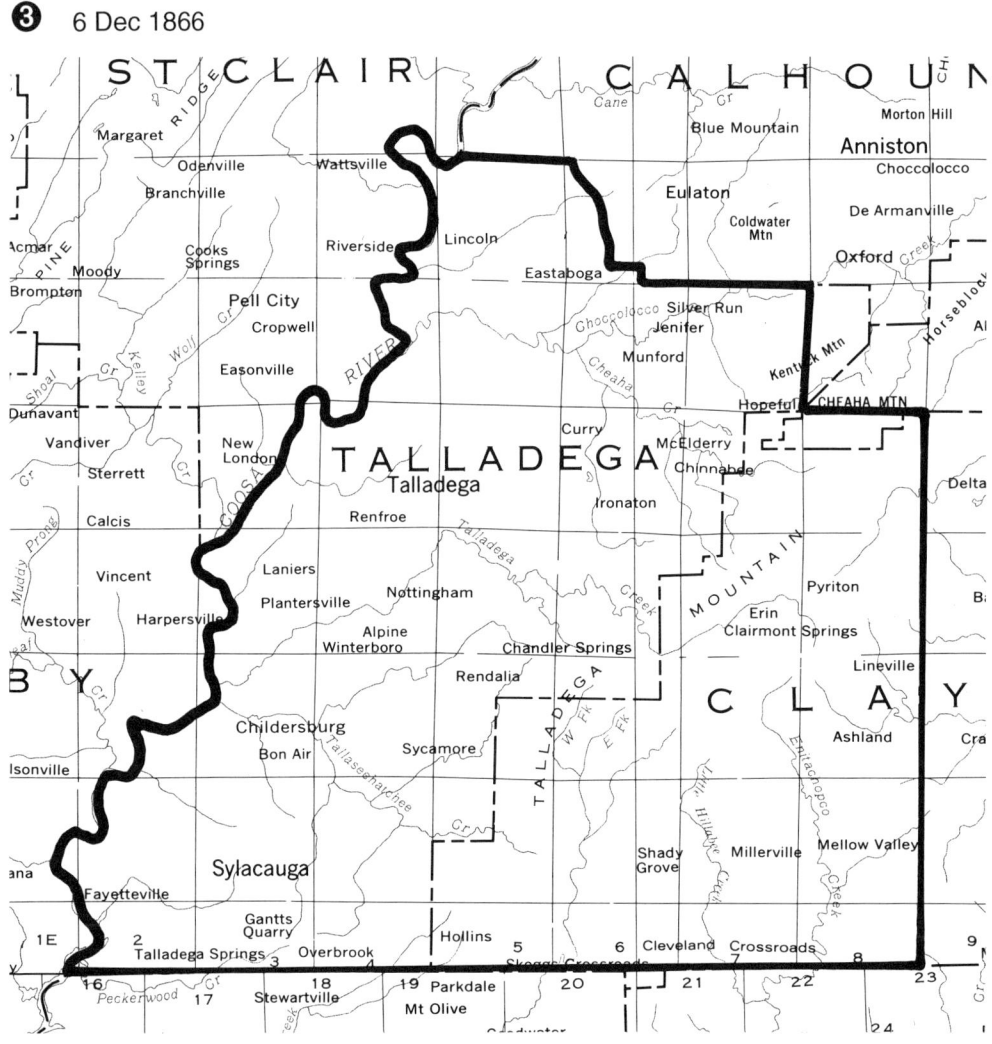

❸ 6 Dec 1866

Individual County Chronologies 331

Chronology of TALLADEGA

Map	Date	Event	Resulting Area
❹	7 Dec 1866	Lost to creation of CLAY	760 sq mi

(Heavy line depicts historical boundary. Base map shows present-day information.)

❹ 7 Dec 1866–13 Feb 1867

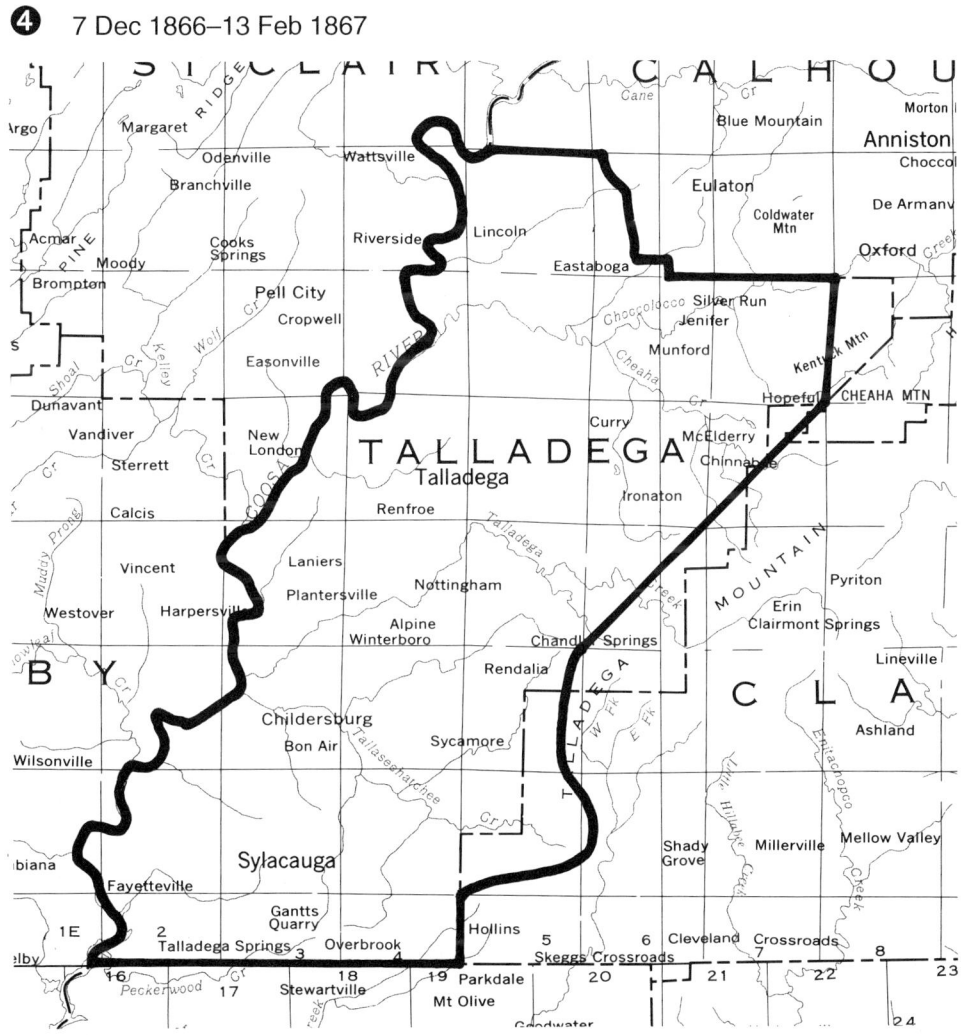

ALABAMA

Chronology of TALLADEGA

Map	Date	Event	Resulting Area
❺	14 Feb 1867	Gained from CLEBURNE	770 sq mi
❺	15 Feb 1867	Gained from CLAY, lost to CLEBURNE	770 sq mi

(Heavy line depicts historical boundary. Base map shows present-day information.)

❺ 14 Feb 1867–15 Feb 1867

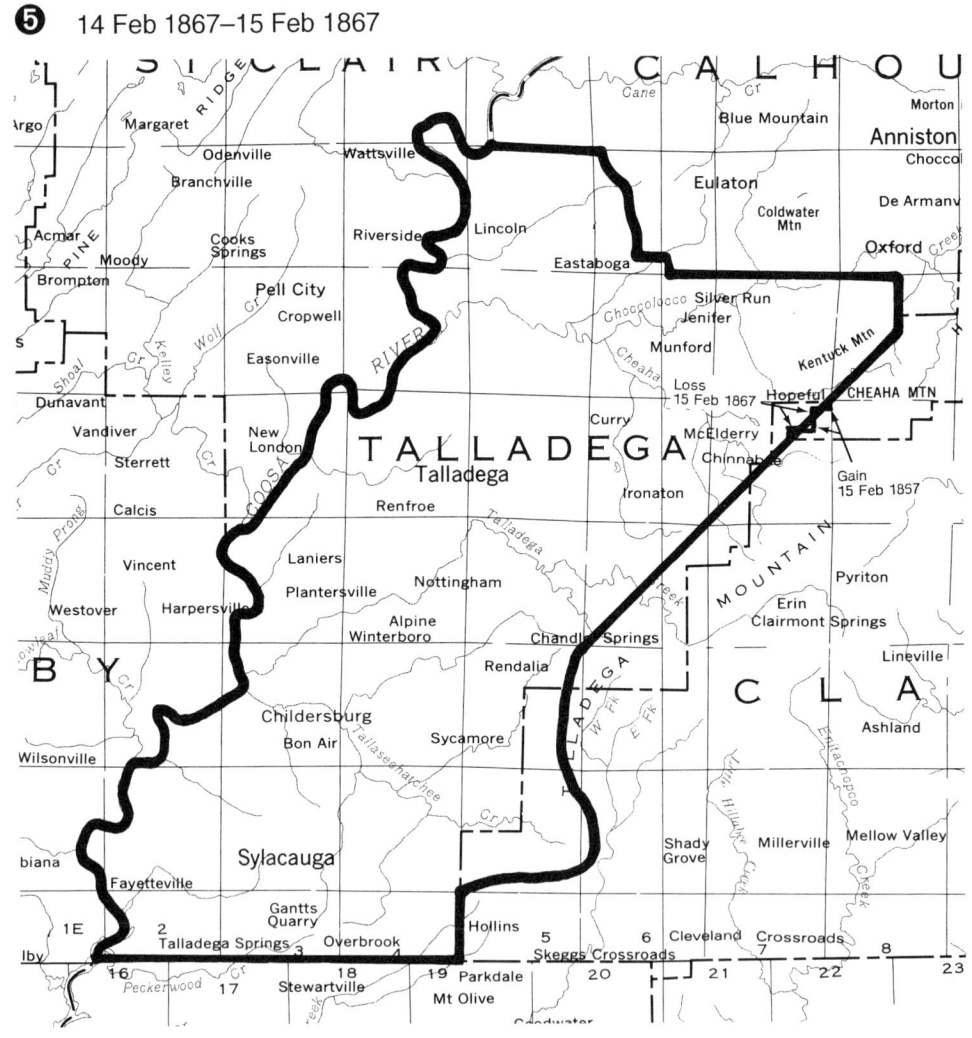

Chronology of TALLADEGA

Map	Date	Event	Resulting Area
❻	16 Feb 1867	Gained from CLAY	790 sq mi

(Heavy line depicts historical boundary. Base map shows present-day information.)

❻ 16 Feb 1867–9 Jan 1877
9 Feb 1893–11 Dec 1894

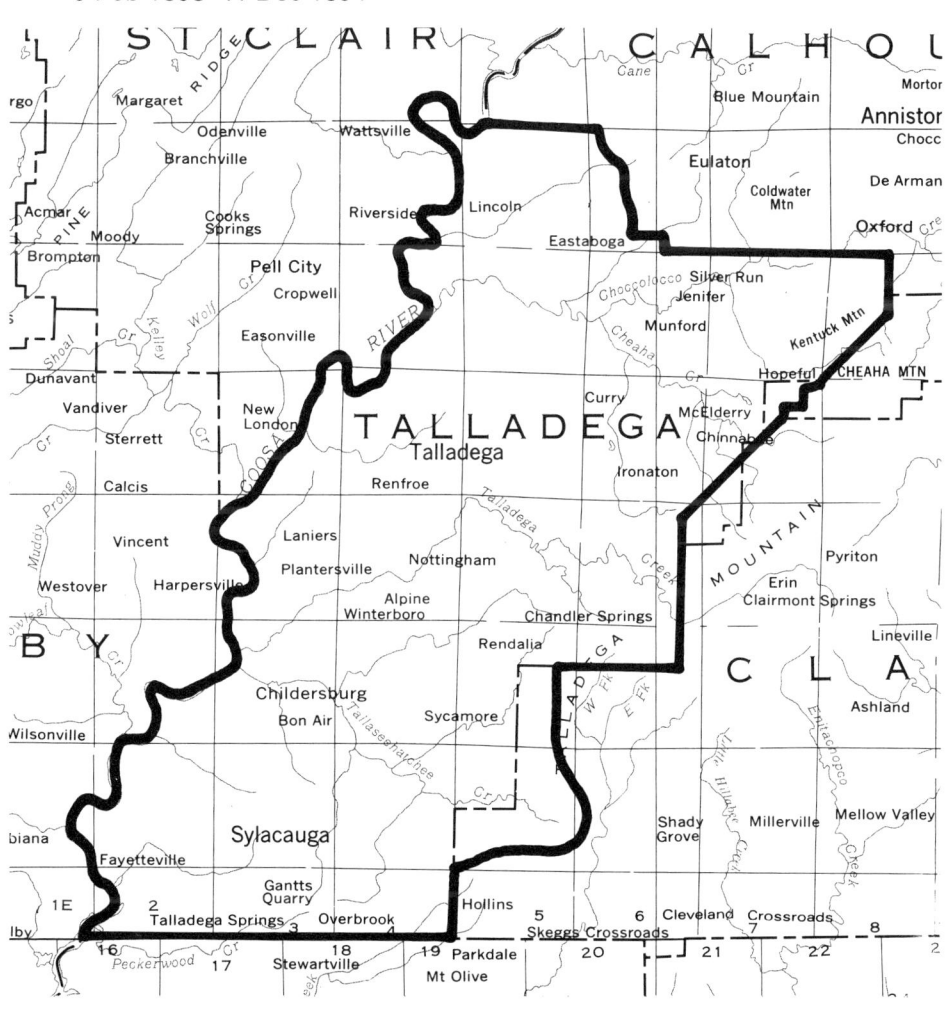

Chronology of TALLADEGA

Map	Date	Event	Resulting Area
❼	10 Jan 1877	Gained from CLAY	840 sq mi
❻	9 Feb 1893	Lost to CLAY	790 sq mi

(Heavy line depicts historical boundary. Base map shows present-day information.)

❼ 10 Jan 1877–8 Feb 1893

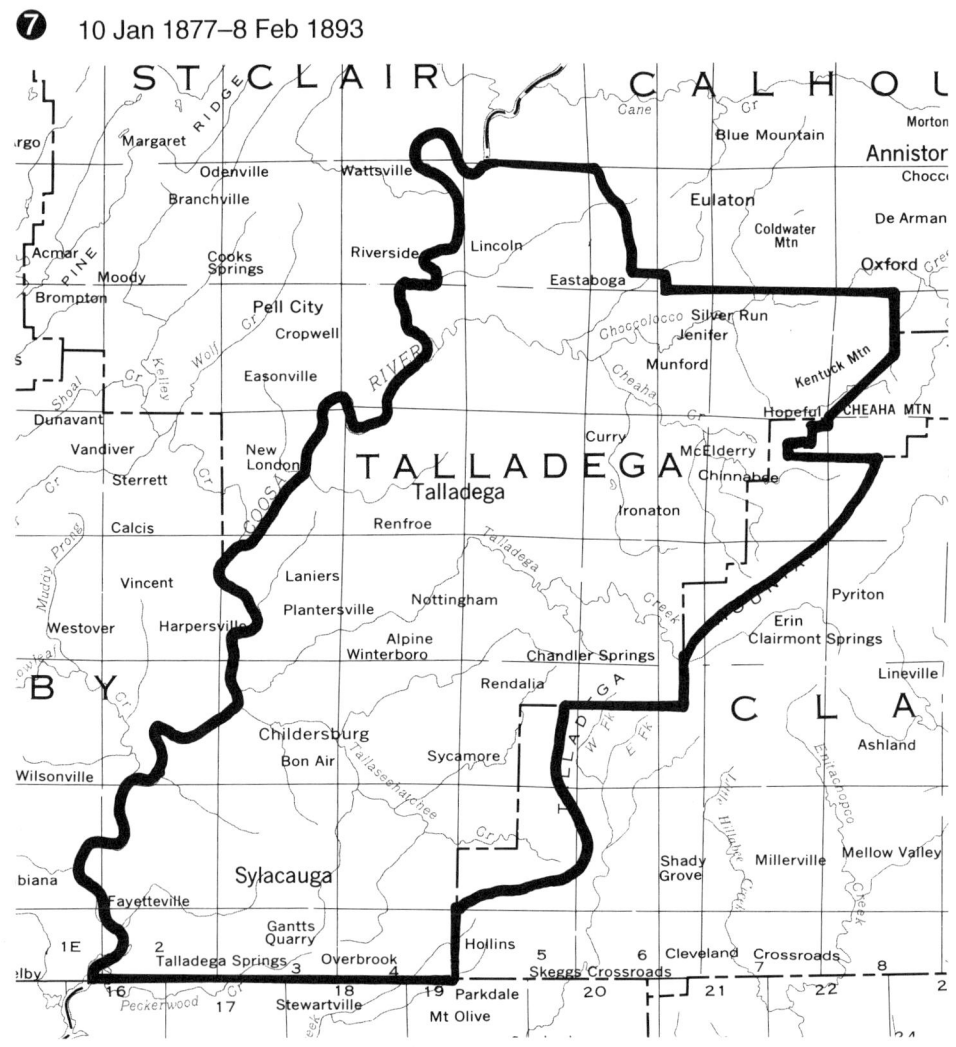

Chronology of TALLADEGA

Map	Date	Event	Resulting Area
❽	12 Dec 1894	Exchanged with CLAY	750 sq mi

(Heavy line depicts historical boundary. Base map shows present-day information.)

❽ 12 Dec 1894–1990

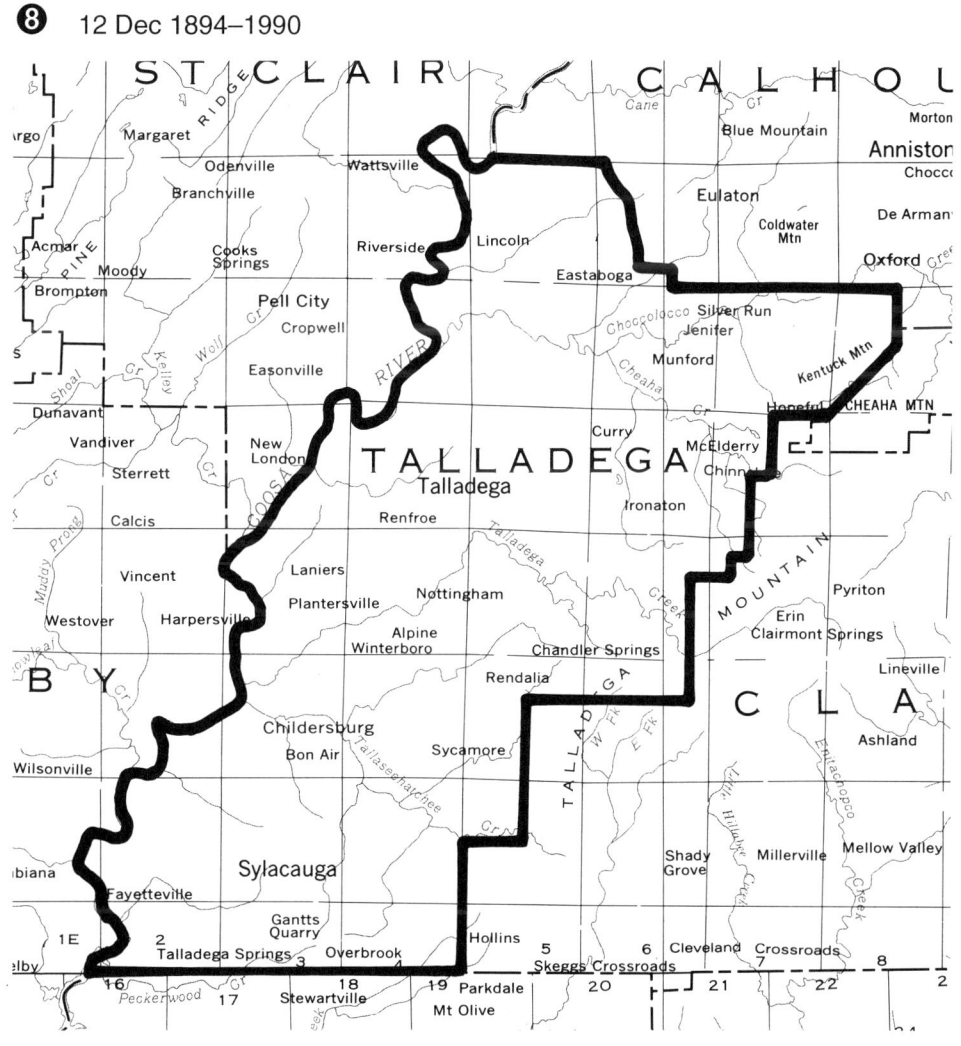

Chronology of TALLAPOOSA

Map	Date	Event	Resulting Area
❶	18 Dec 1832	Created from MONTGOMERY and SHELBY	930 sq mi
❷	2 Feb 1839	Lost to MONTGOMERY	910 sq mi
❷	27 Jan 1845	Gained from MACON	910 sq mi
❷	2 Feb 1846	Lost to MACON	910 sq mi
❷	10 Feb 1866	Lost small area to CHAMBERS to accommodate local property owner	910 sq mi

(Heavy line depicts historical boundary. Base map shows present-day information.)

❶ 18 Dec 1832–1 Feb 1839

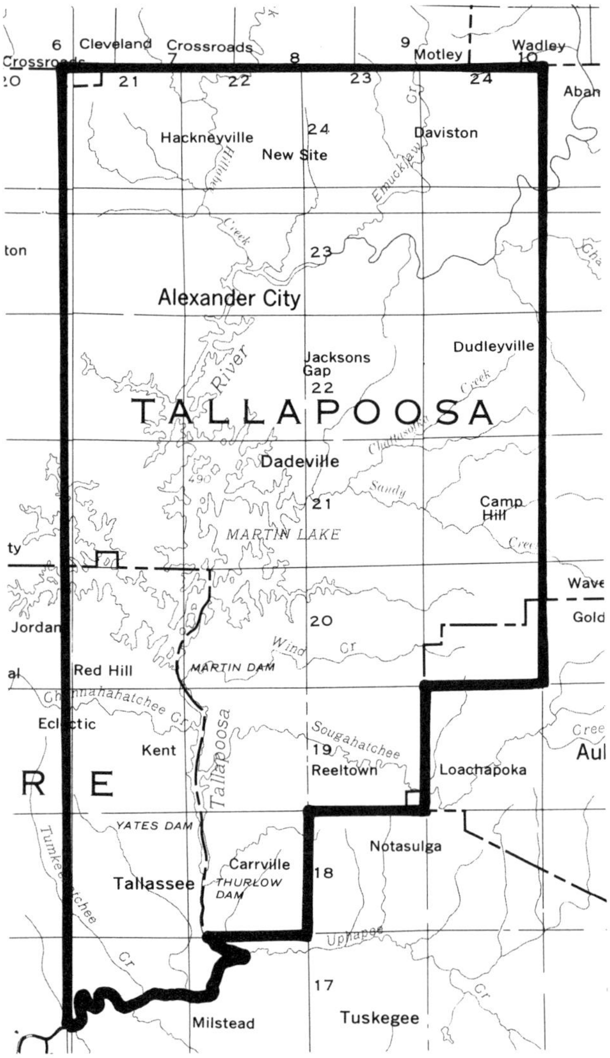

❷ 2 Feb 1839–4 Dec 1866

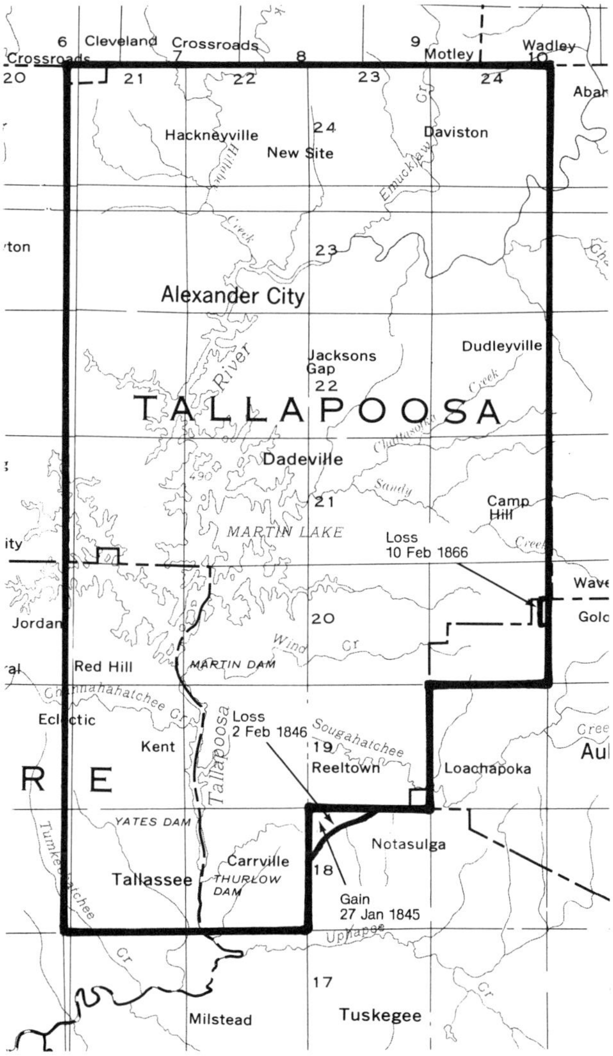

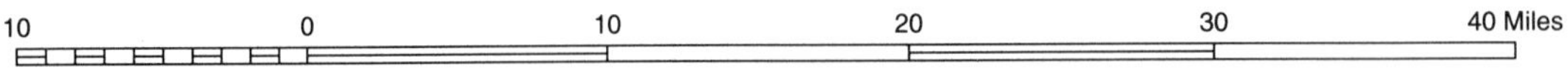

Chronology of TALLAPOOSA

Map	Date	Event	Resulting Area
❸	5 Dec 1866	Lost to creation of LEE	890 sq mi
❹	late Dec 1866	Lost to creation of ELMORE	780 sq mi
❹	16 Feb 1867	Gained small area from LEE	780 sq mi
❹	14 Feb 1870	Lost small area to ELMORE to accommodate local property owners	780 sq mi
❹	9 Feb 1877	Lost small area to CLAY	780 sq mi

(Heavy line depicts historical boundary. Base map shows present-day information.)

❸ 5 Dec 1866–late Dec 1866

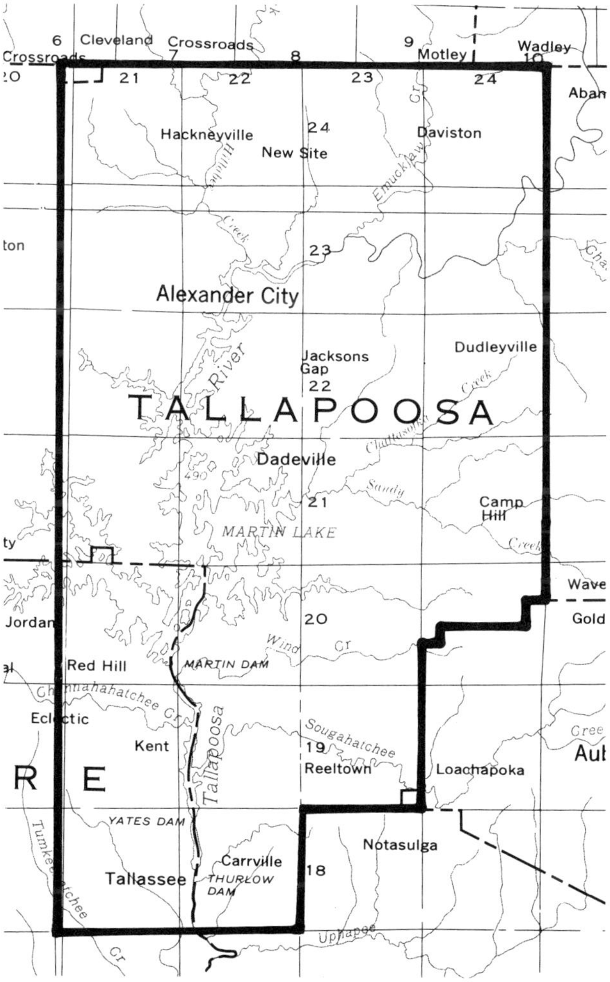

❹ late Dec 1866–16 Feb 1885

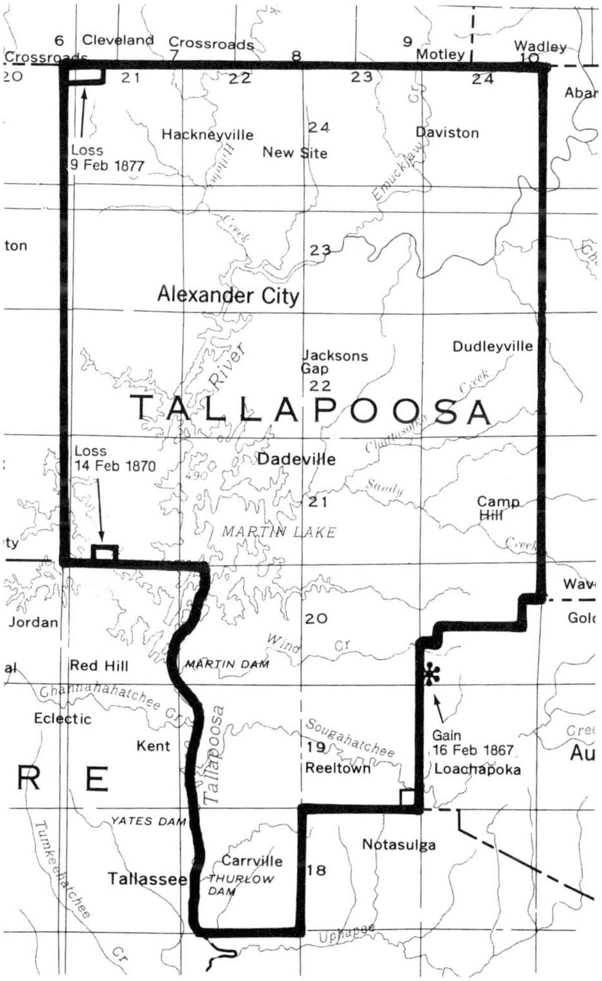

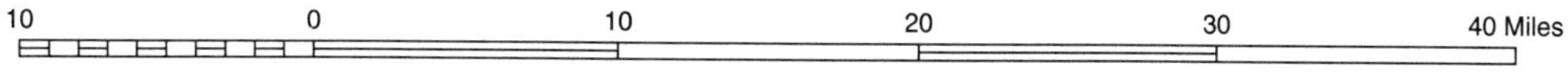

ALABAMA

Chronology of TALLAPOOSA

Map	Date	Event	Resulting Area
❺	17 Feb 1885	Lost small area to MACON	770 sq mi
❺	6 Aug 1915	Lost small area to LEE	770 sq mi
❺	14 Sep 1963	Exchanged small areas with COOSA [mistake in description corrected 20 Apr 1965]	770 sq mi
	20 Apr 1965	Boundary with COOSA redefined, correcting mistake of 14 Sep 1963 [no change]	

(Heavy line depicts historical boundary. Base map shows present-day information.)

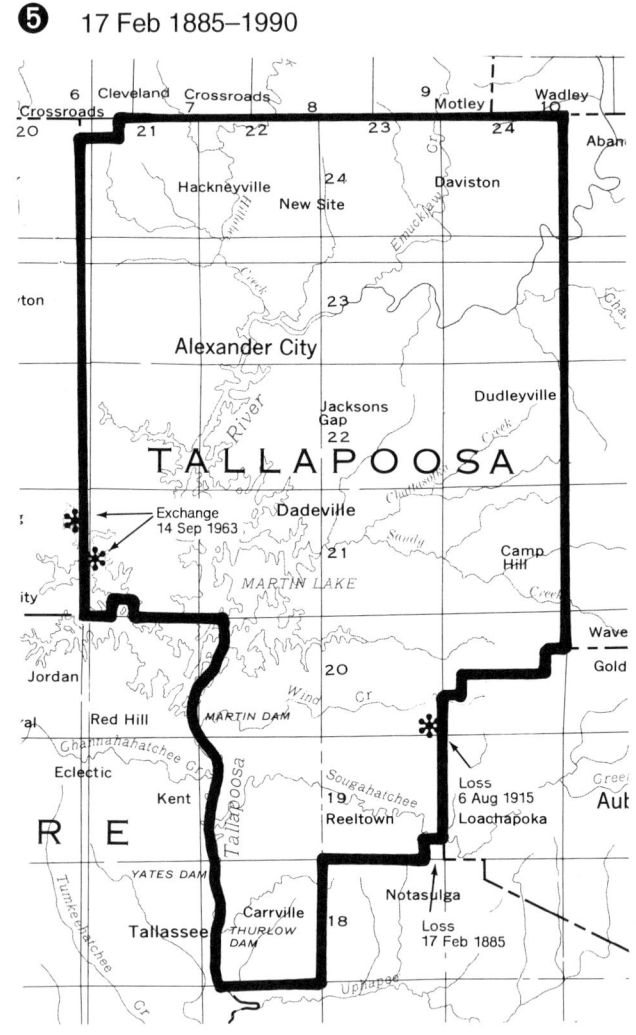

❺ 17 Feb 1885–1990

Chronology of TUSCALOOSA

Map	Date	Event	Resulting Area
❶	6 Feb 1818	Created from MONTGOMERY and non-county area; overlapped state of Mississippi	6,120 sq mi
❷	13 Feb 1818	Lost to creation of MARION; loss included most of overlap of Mississippi	3,480 sq mi
❷	20 Nov 1818	Gained from CAHAWBA (now BIBB) [see also BIBB, map 2]	3,480 sq mi
❸	13 Dec 1819	Lost to creation of both GREENE and PERRY	3,160 sq mi

(Heavy line depicts historical boundary. Base map shows present-day information.)

❶ 6 Feb 1818–12 Feb 1818

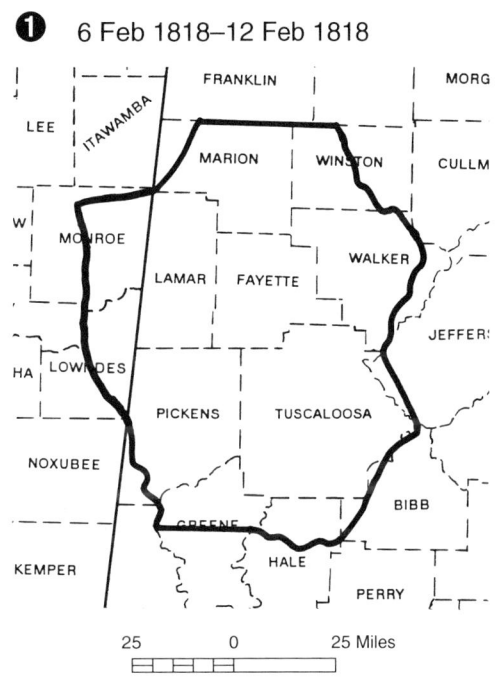

❷ 13 Feb 1818–12 Dec 1819

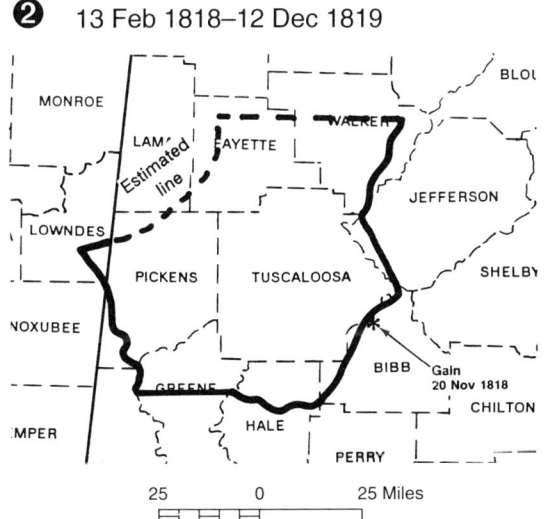

❸ 13 Dec 1819–18 Dec 1820

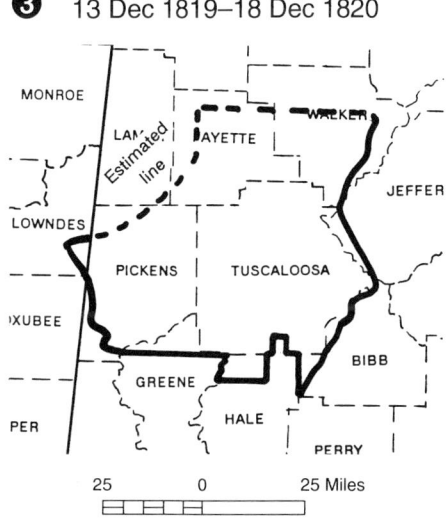

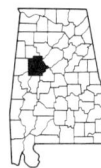

Chronology of TUSCALOOSA

Map	Date	Event	Resulting Area
❹	19 Dec 1820	Lost to MARION and to creation of PICKENS; overlap of state of Mississippi ended	2,240 sq mi

(Heavy line depicts historical boundary. Base map shows present-day information.)

❹ 19 Dec 1820

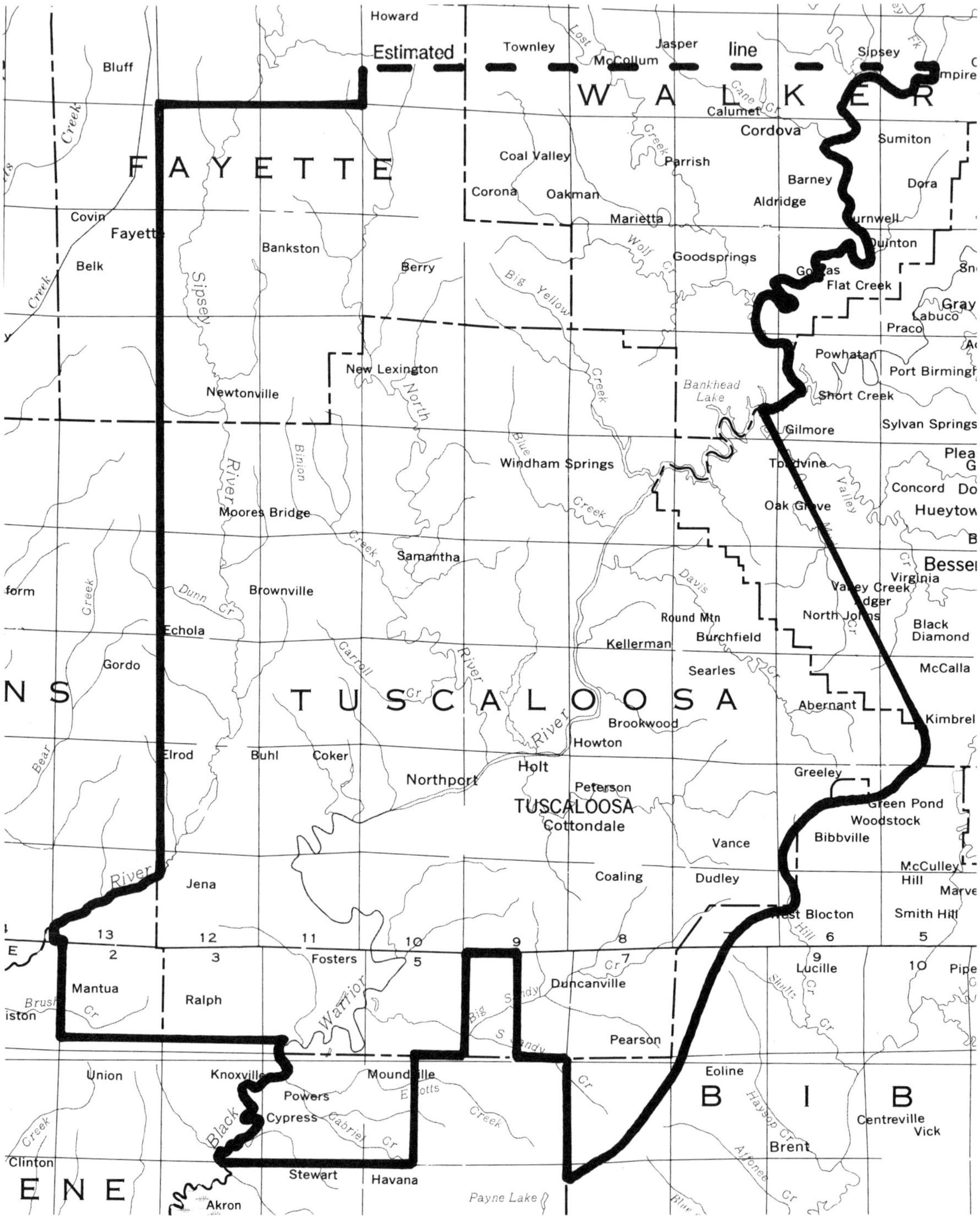

10	0	10	20	30	40 Miles

Individual County Chronologies 341

Chronology of TUSCALOOSA

Map	Date	Event	Resulting Area
❺	20 Dec 1820	Gained from PERRY, lost to BIBB	2,210 sq mi

(Heavy line depicts historical boundary. Base map shows present-day information.)

❺ 20 Dec 1820–31 Dec 1822

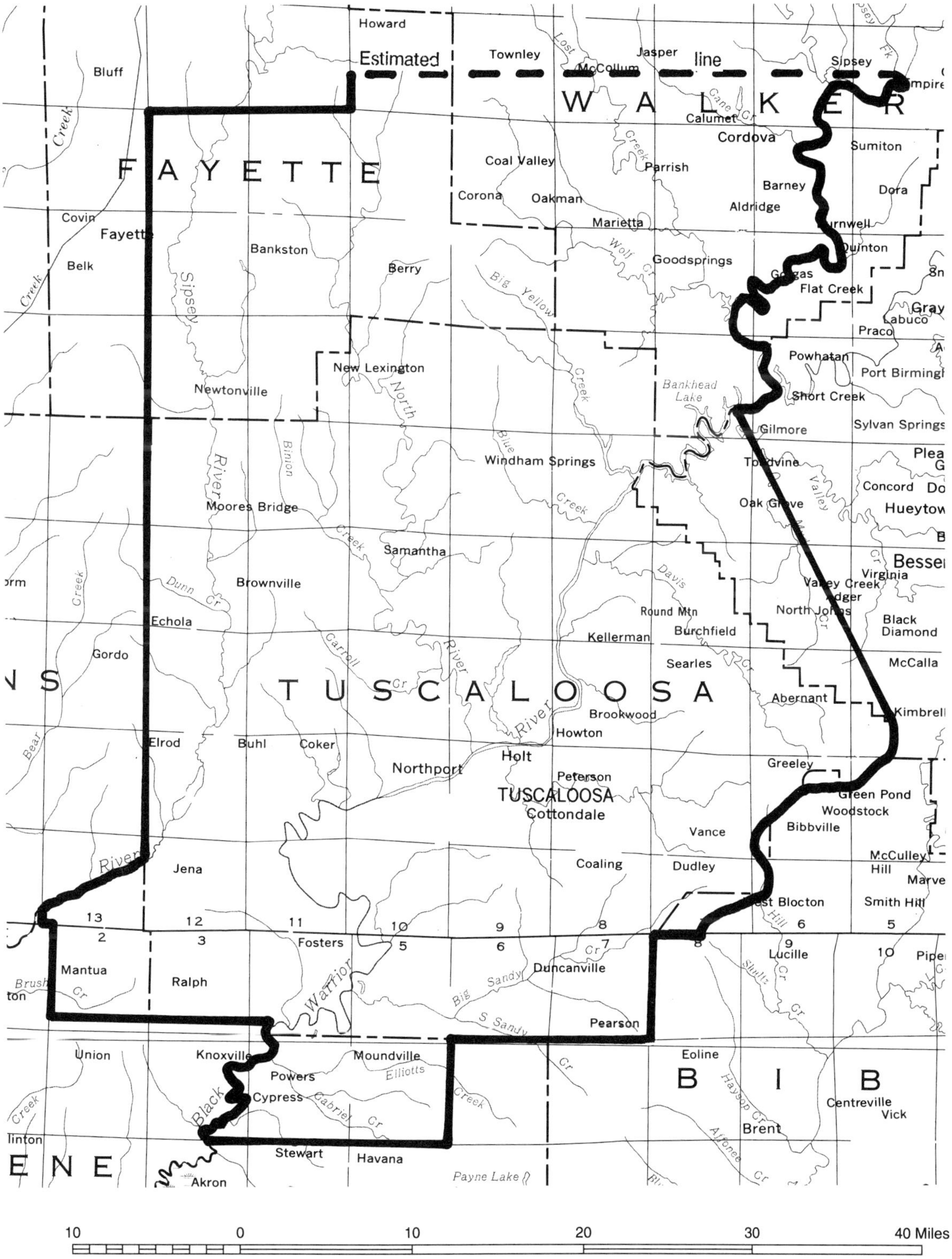

Chronology of TUSCALOOSA

Map	Date	Event	Resulting Area
❻	1 Jan 1823	Gained from non-county area	2,540 sq mi

(Heavy line depicts historical boundary. Base map shows present-day information.)

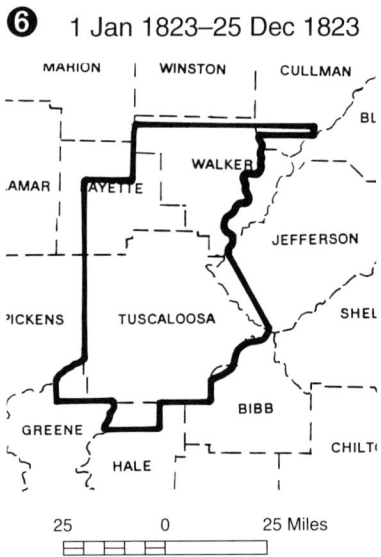

❻ 1 Jan 1823–25 Dec 1823

Chronology of TUSCALOOSA

Map	Date	Event	Resulting Area
❼	26 Dec 1823	Lost to creation of WALKER	1,900 sq mi

(Heavy line depicts historical boundary. Base map shows present-day information.)

❼ 26 Dec 1823–19 Dec 1824

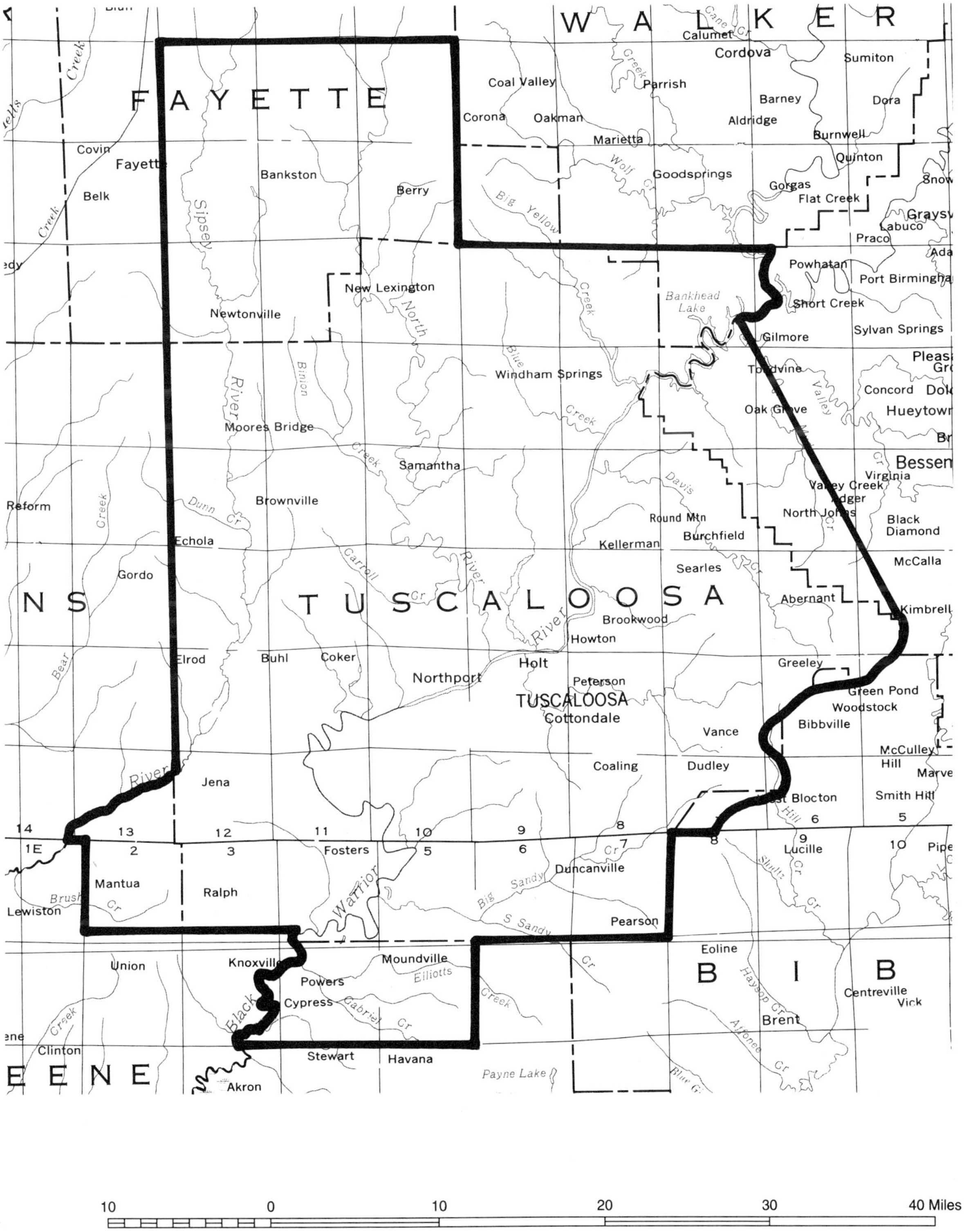

ALABAMA

Chronology of TUSCALOOSA

Map	Date	Event	Resulting Area
8	20 Dec 1824	Lost to PICKENS and to creation of FAYETTE	1,600 sq mi

(Heavy line depicts historical boundary. Base map shows present-day information.)

8 20 Dec 1824–21 Dec 1824

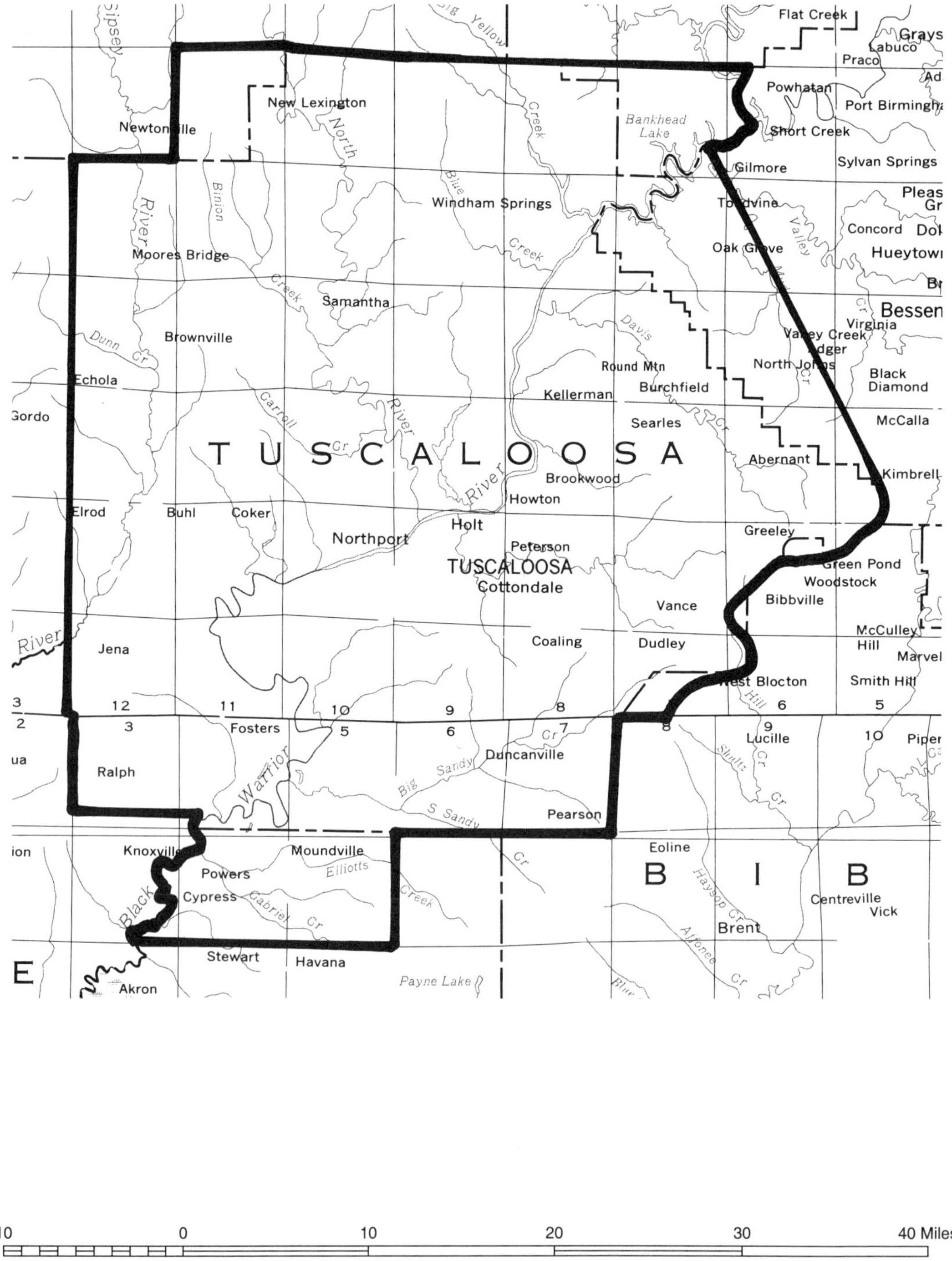

Individual County Chronologies 345

Chronology of TUSCALOOSA

Map	Date	Event	Resulting Area
⑨	22 Dec 1824	Lost to WALKER	1,560 sq mi

(Heavy line depicts historical boundary. Base map shows present-day information.)

⑨ 22 Dec 1824–30 Dec 1827

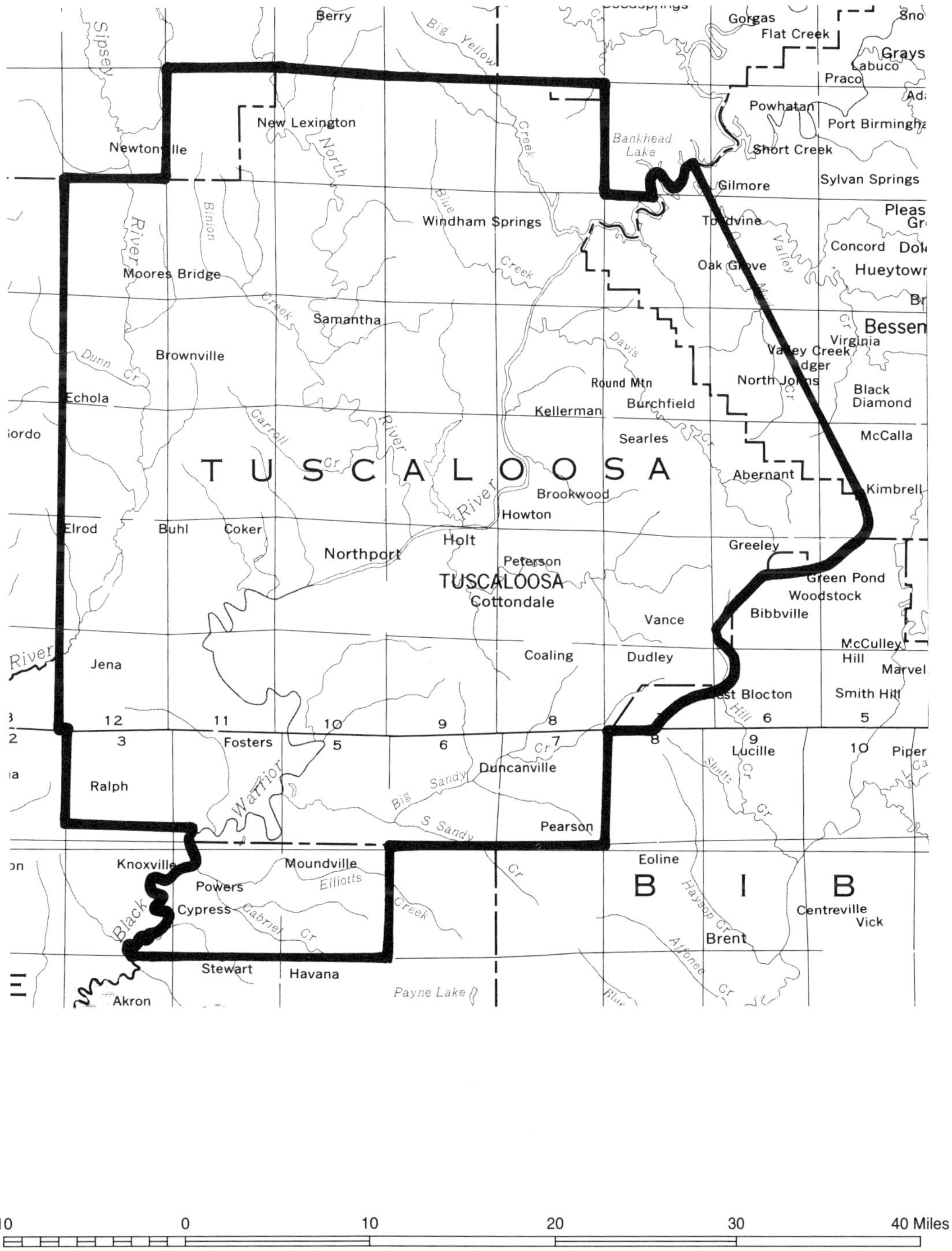

346 ALABAMA

Chronology of TUSCALOOSA

Map	Date	Event	Resulting Area
⑩	31 Dec 1827	Exchanged with JEFFERSON	1,550 sq mi
	15 Jan 1828	Boundary with BIBB clarified [no change]	

(Heavy line depicts historical boundary. Base map shows present-day information.)

⑩ 31 Dec 1827–14 Jan 1831

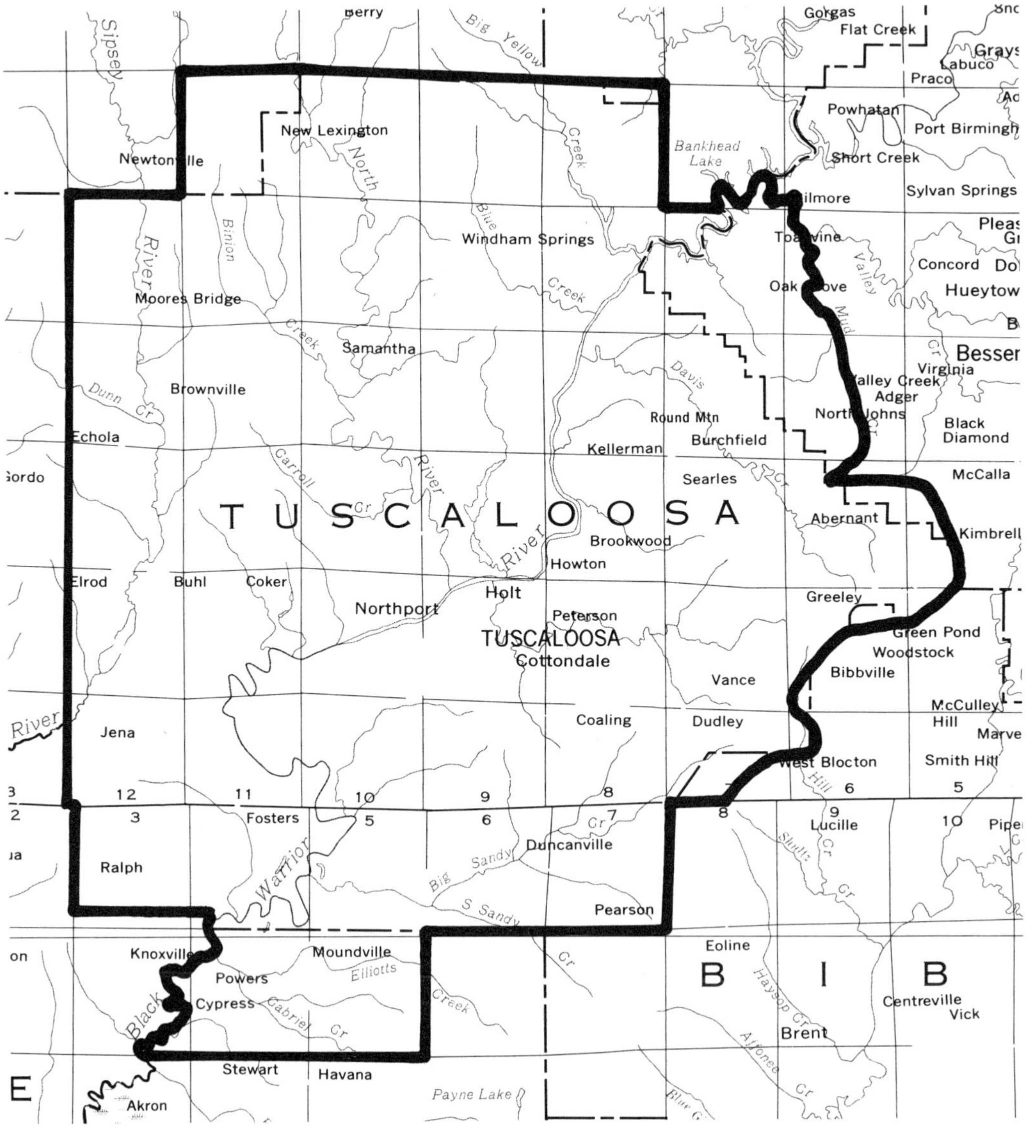

Individual County Chronologies **347**

Chronology of TUSCALOOSA

Map	Date	Event	Resulting Area
⑪	15 Jan 1831	Exchanged with BIBB	1,550 sq mi

(Heavy line depicts historical boundary. Base map shows present-day information.)

⑪ 15 Jan 1831–19 Jan 1832

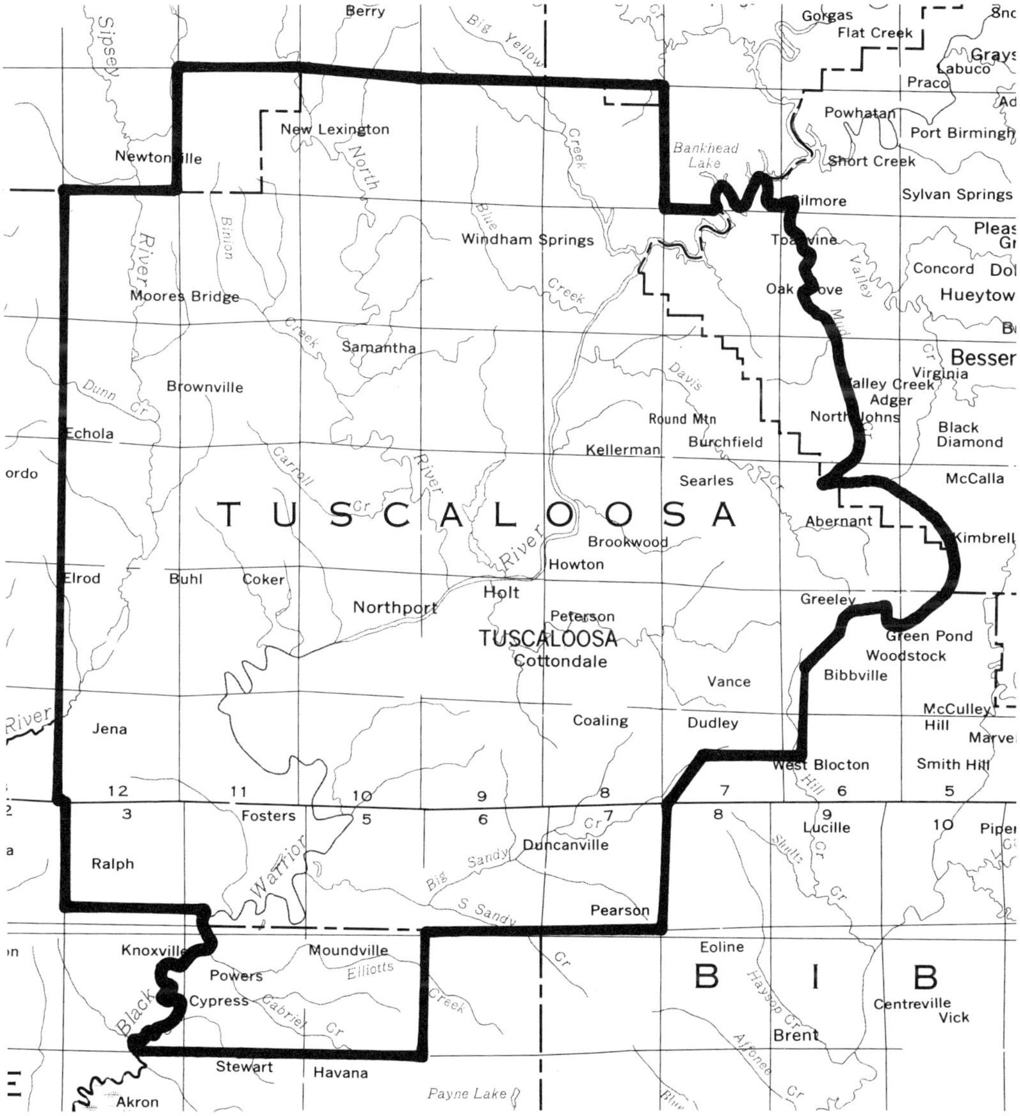

ALABAMA

Chronology of TUSCALOOSA

Map	Date	Event	Resulting Area
⑫	20 Jan 1832	Lost to FAYETTE	1,520 sq mi
⑫	21 Jan 1832	Gained small area from GREENE	1,520 sq mi

(Heavy line depicts historical boundary. Base map shows present-day information.)

⑫ 20 Jan 1832–2 Feb 1840

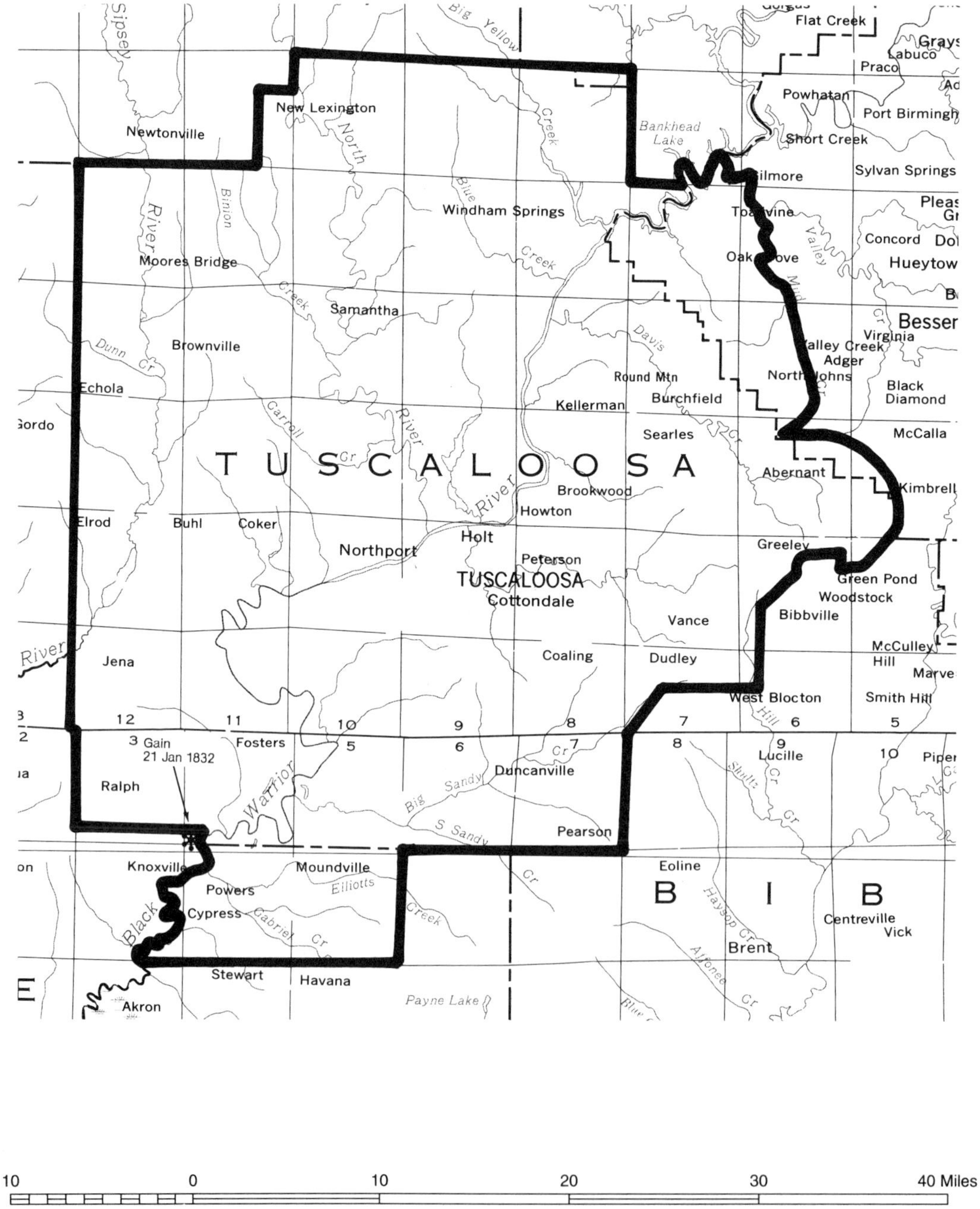

Chronology of TUSCALOOSA

Map	Date	Event	Resulting Area
⑬	3 Feb 1840	Exchanged with JEFFERSON	1,440 sq mi
	12 Feb 1850	WALKER authorized to gain from TUSCALOOSA, but apparently faulty description was never implemented [no change]	
⑬	9 Feb 1852	Lost small area to JEFFERSON	1,440 sq mi
	3 Oct 1864	Lost small area to GREENE to accommodate local property owner [location unknown, not mapped]	

(Heavy line depicts historical boundary. Base map shows present-day information.)

⑬ 3 Feb 1840–29 Jan 1867

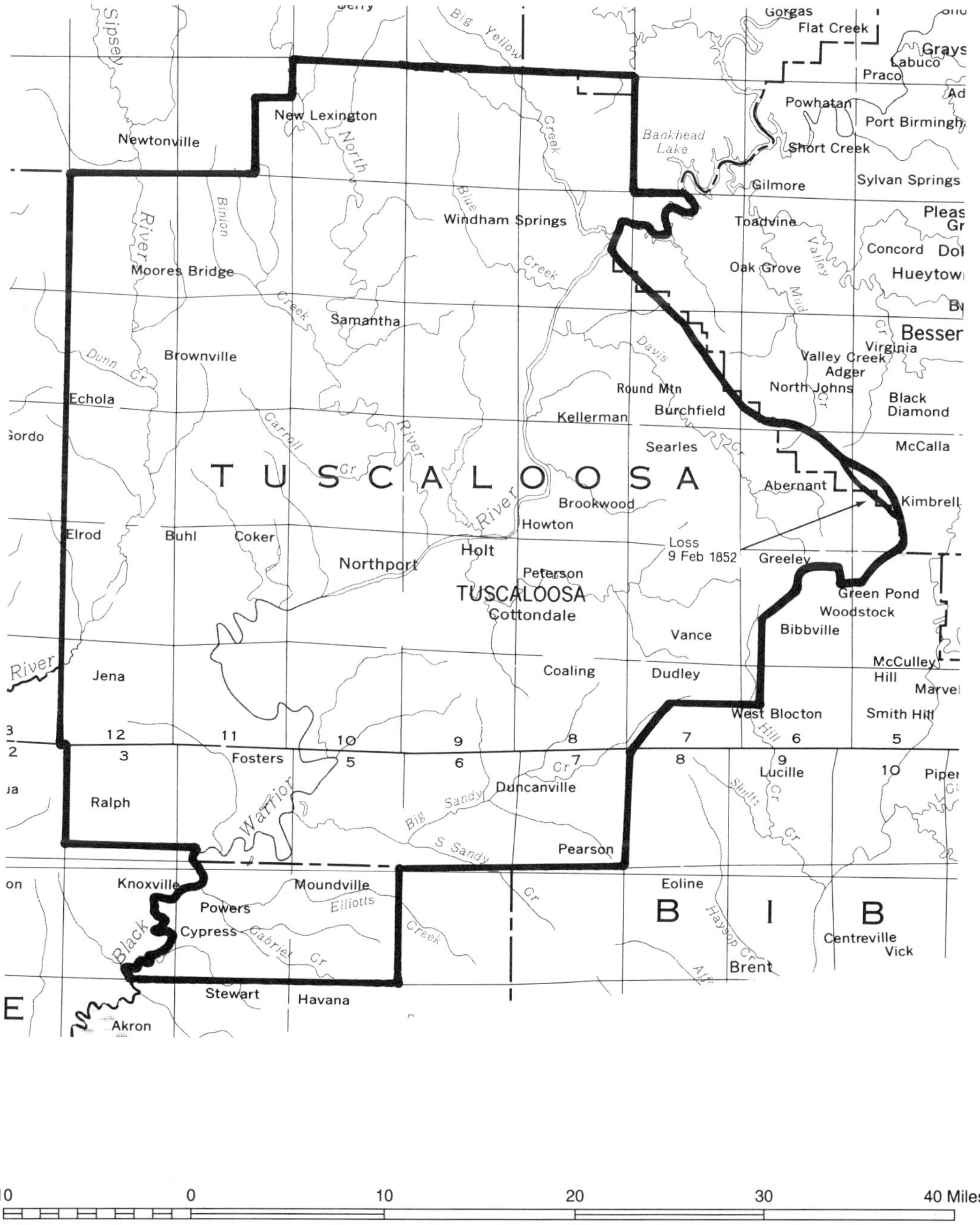

ALABAMA

Chronology of TUSCALOOSA

Map	Date	Event	Resulting Area
⑭	30 Jan 1867	Lost to creation of HALE	1,370 sq mi

(Heavy line depicts historical boundary. Base map shows present-day information.)

⑭ 30 Jan 1867–27 Sep 1915

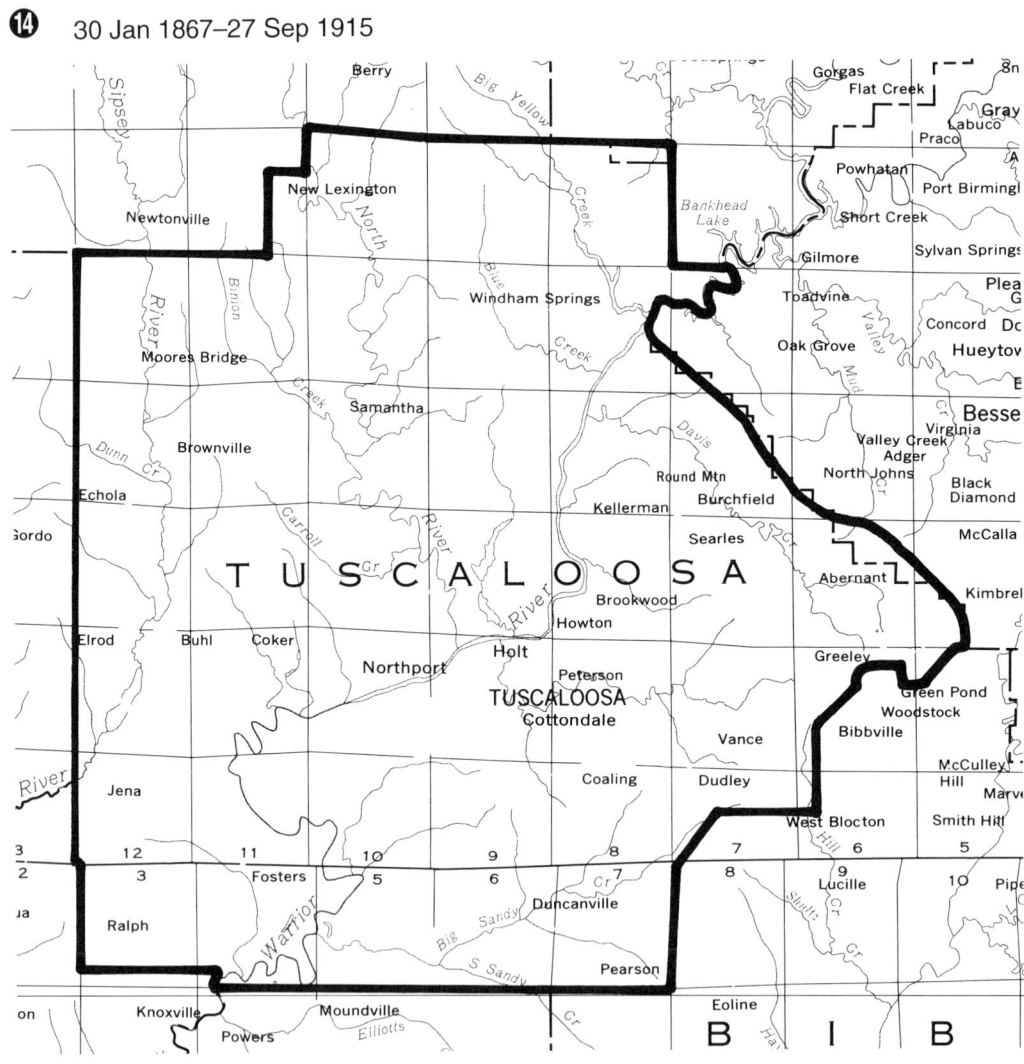

Individual County Chronologies 351

Chronology of TUSCALOOSA

Map	Date	Event	Resulting Area
⑮	28 Sep 1915	Exchanged with JEFFERSON	1,360 sq mi

(Heavy line depicts historical boundary. Base map shows present-day information.)

⑮ 28 Sep 1915–c. 1927

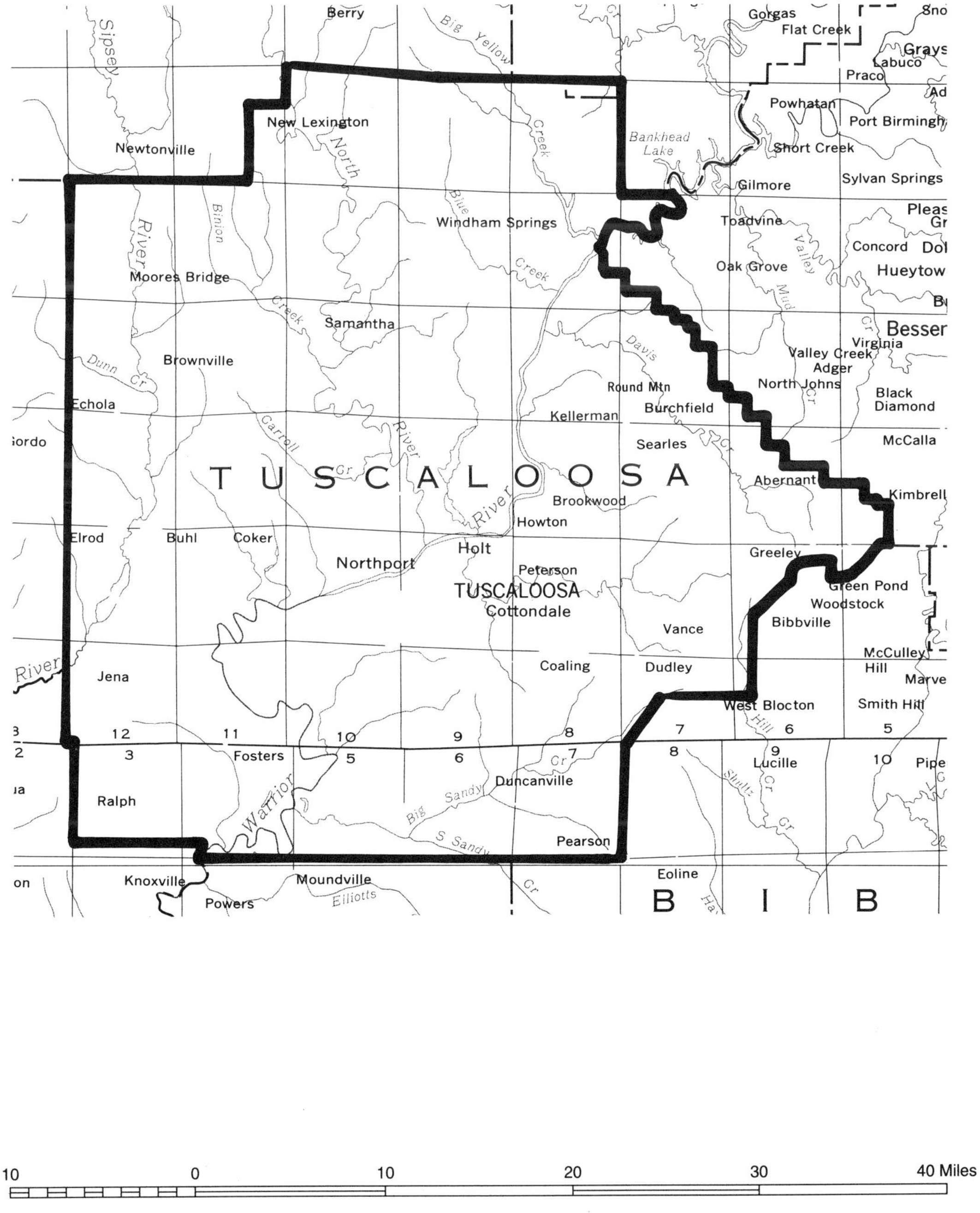

Chronology of TUSCALOOSA

Map	Date	Event	Resulting Area
⑯	c. 1927	Lost small area to WALKER, ending boundary dispute dating from nineteenth century	1,360 sq mi
⑯	28 May 1980	Exchanged small areas with BIBB [area gained from BIBB is too small to map at our scale]	1,350 sq mi

(Heavy line depicts historical boundary. Base map shows present-day information.)

⑯ c. 1927–1990

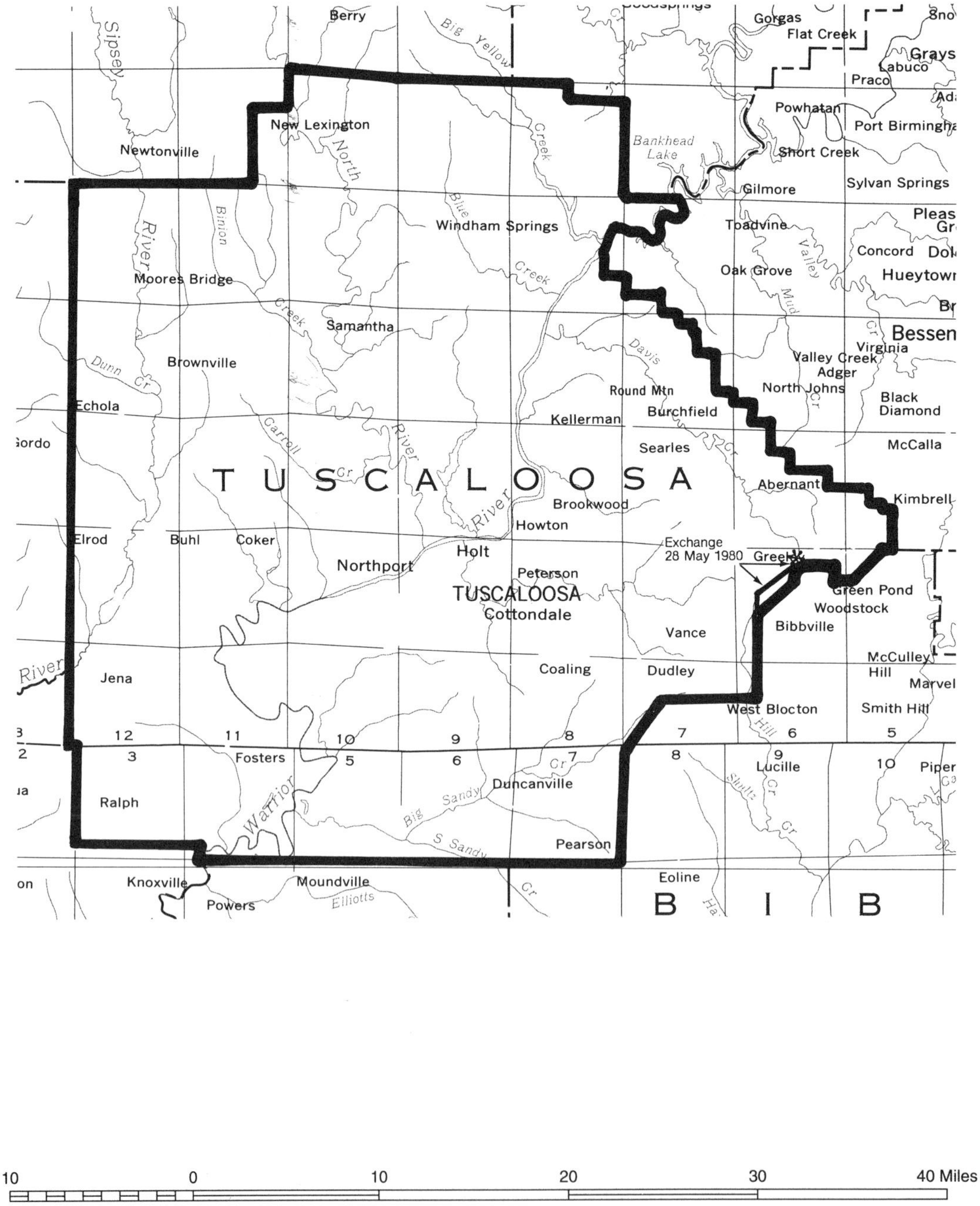

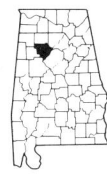

Chronology of WALKER

Map	Date	Event	Resulting Area
❶	26 Dec 1823	Created from JEFFERSON, MARION, and TUSCALOOSA	1,870 sq mi

(Heavy line depicts historical boundary. Base map shows present-day information.)

❶ 26 Dec 1823–19 Dec 1824

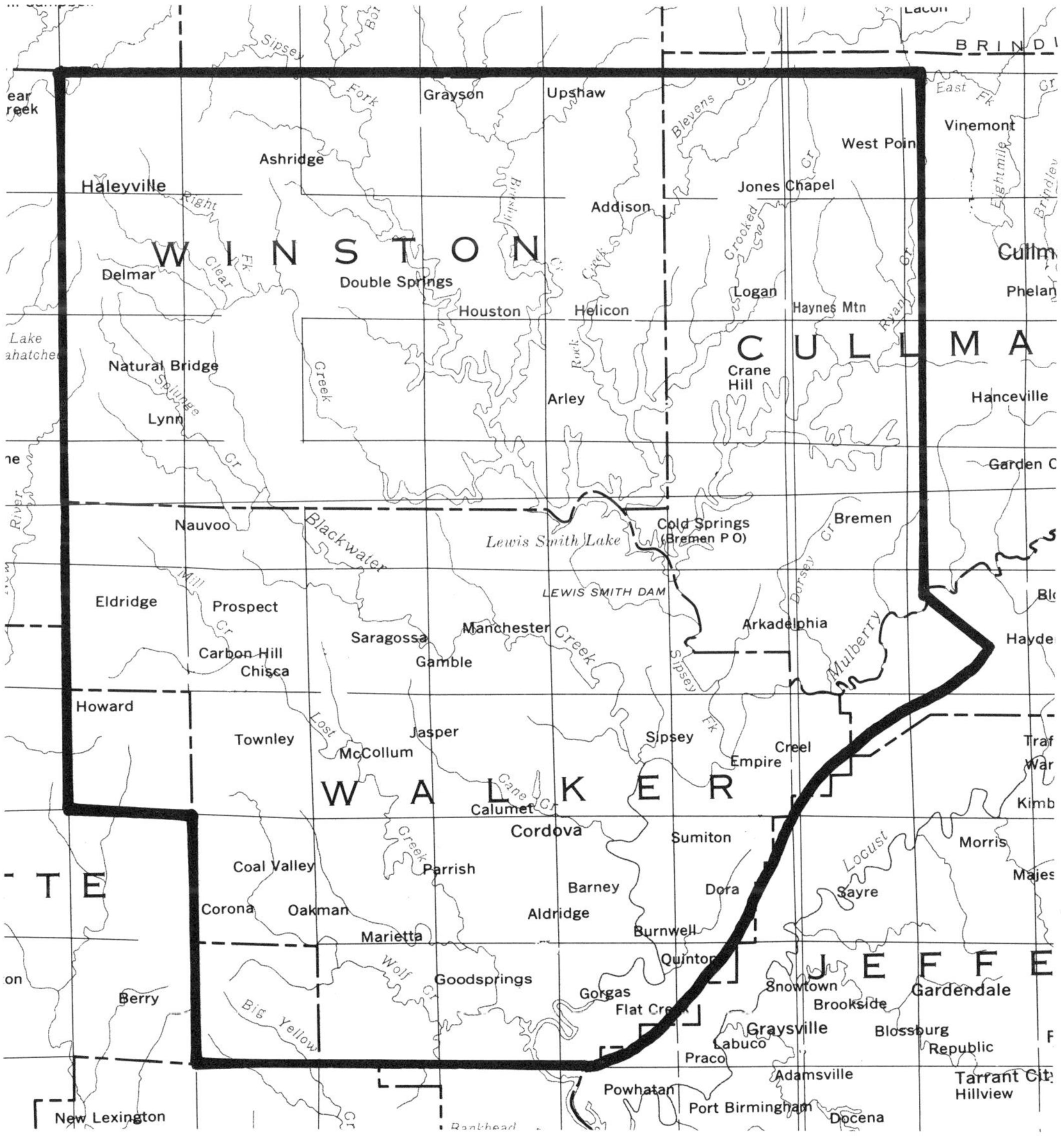

10 0 10 20 30 40 Miles

ALABAMA

Chronology of WALKER

Map	Date	Event	Resulting Area
❷	20 Dec 1824	Lost to creation of FAYETTE	1,720 sq mi

(Heavy line depicts historical boundary. Base map shows present-day information.)

❷ 20 Dec 1824–21 Dec 1824

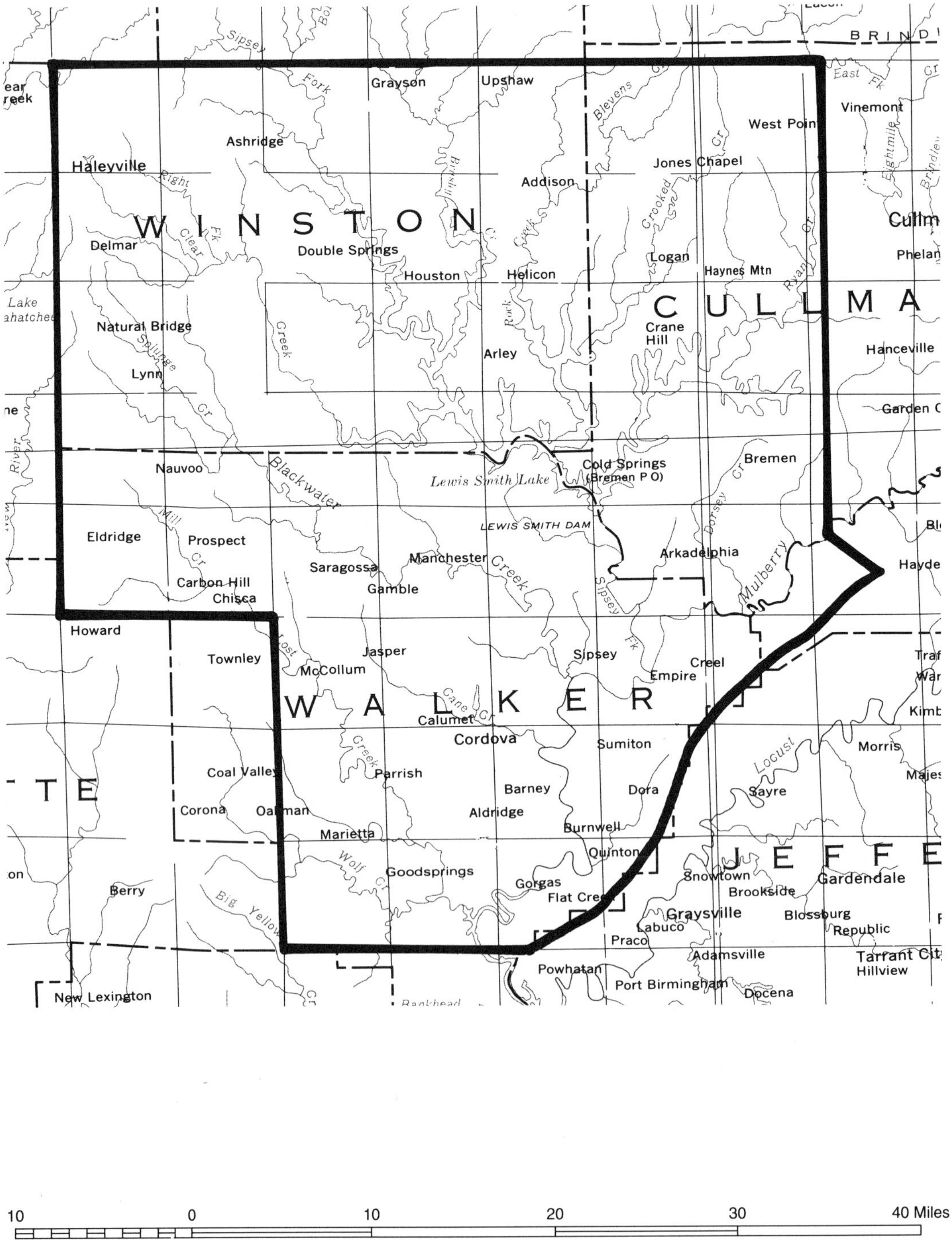

Individual County Chronologies 355

Chronology of WALKER

Map	Date	Event	Resulting Area
❸	22 Dec 1824	Gained from TUSCALOOSA	1,750 sq mi

(Heavy line depicts historical boundary. Base map shows present-day information.)

❸ 22 Dec 1824–8 Jan 1843

Chronology of WALKER

Map	Date	Event	Resulting Area
❹	9 Jan 1843	Gained from FAYETTE	1,830 sq mi

(Heavy line depicts historical boundary. Base map shows present-day information.)

❹ 9 Jan 1843–11 Feb 1850

Chronology of WALKER

Map	Date	Event	Resulting Area
❺	12 Feb 1850	Lost to creation of HANCOCK (now WINSTON) Gain from TUSCALOOSA authorized, but apparently faulty description was never implemented [no change]	920 sq mi

(Heavy line depicts historical boundary. Base map shows present-day information.)

❺ 12 Feb 1850–7 Feb 1877

ALABAMA

Chronology of WALKER

Map	Date	Event	Resulting Area
❻	8 Feb 1877	Lost to BLOUNT	830 sq mi

(Heavy line depicts historical boundary. Base map shows present-day information.)

❻ 8 Feb 1877–28 Jan 1879

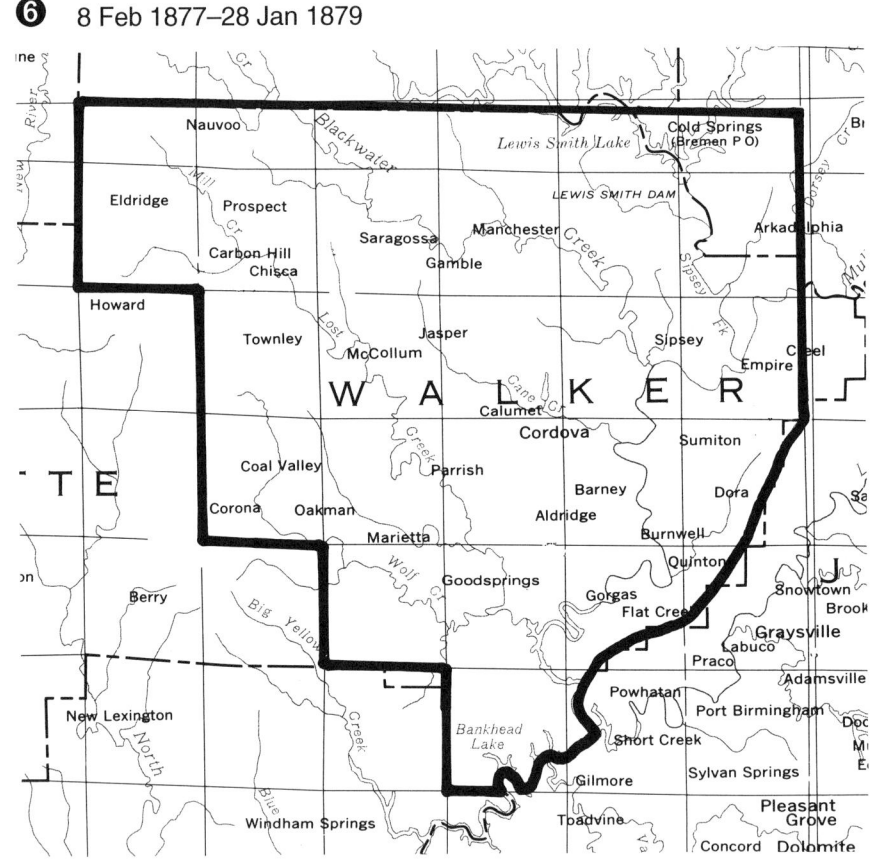

Individual County Chronologies 359

Chronology of WALKER

Map	Date	Event	Resulting Area
❼	29 Jan 1879	Exchanged with BLOUNT	800 sq mi
❼	18 Feb 1895	Lost small area to BLOUNT	800 sq mi

(Heavy line depicts historical boundary. Base map shows present-day information.)

❼ 29 Jan 1879–15 Dec 1898

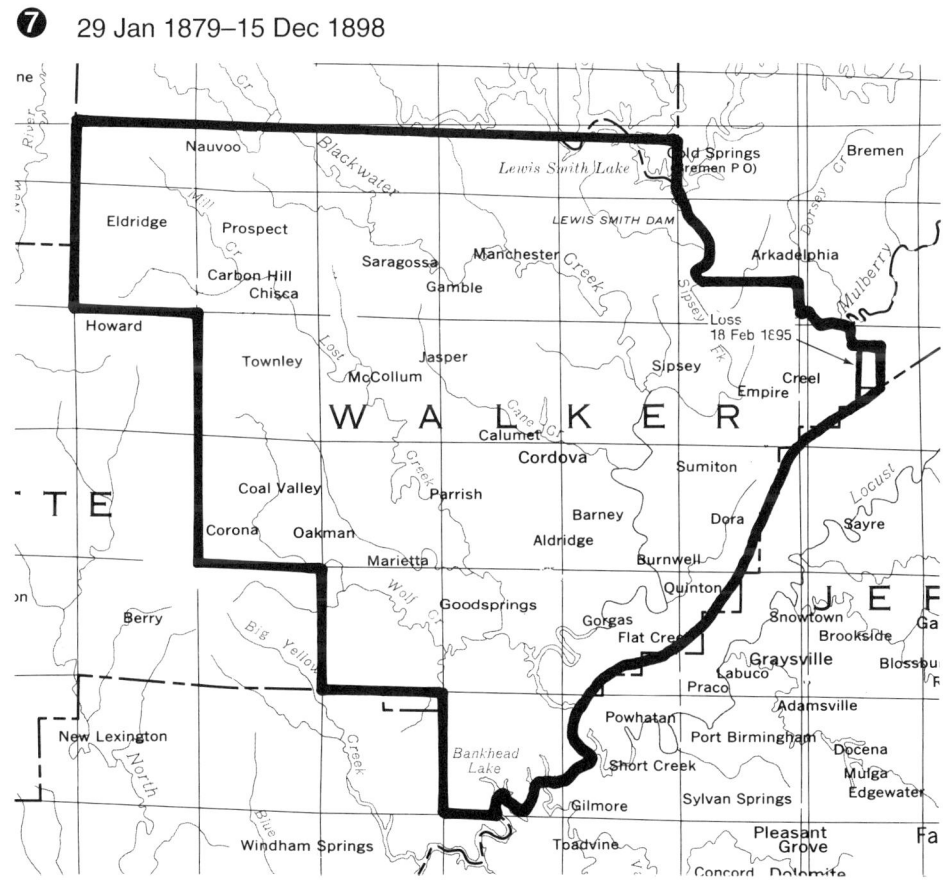

360 ALABAMA

Chronology of WALKER

Map	Date	Event	Resulting Area
❽	16 Dec 1898	Exchanged with JEFFERSON	800 sq mi

(Heavy line depicts historical boundary. Base map shows present-day information.)

❽ 16 Dec 1898–4 Mar 1901

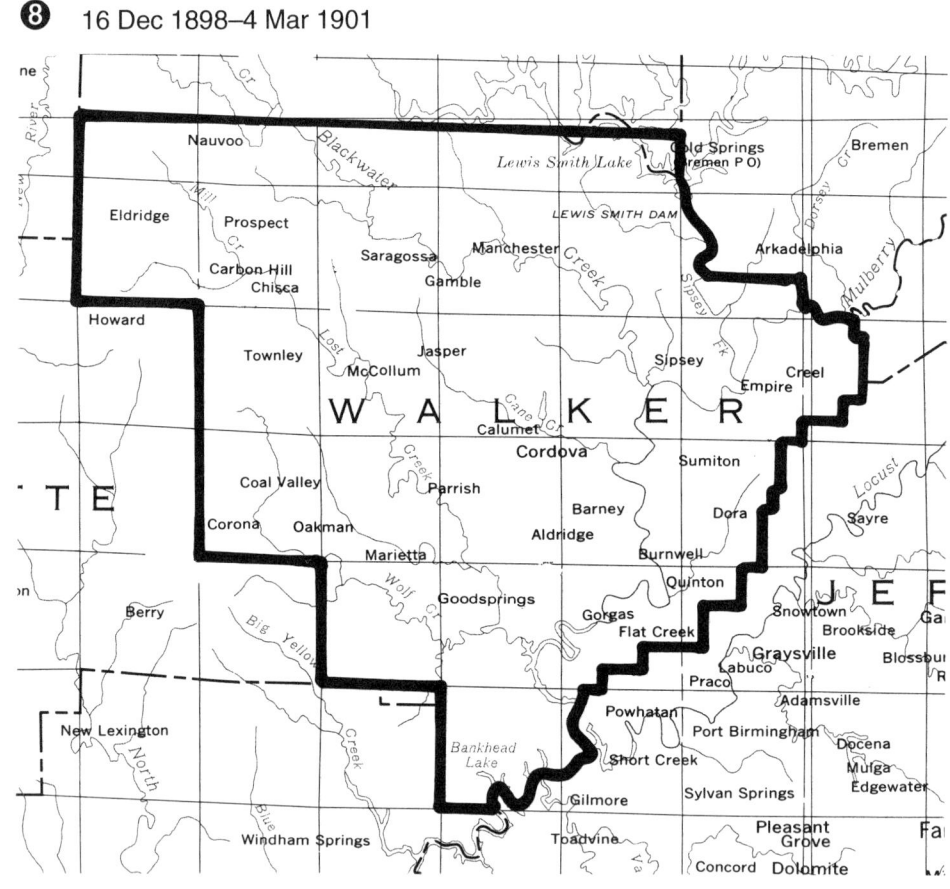

Individual County Chronologies 361

Chronology of WALKER

Map	Date	Event	Resulting Area
⑨	5 Mar 1901	Exchanged with WINSTON	800 sq mi
⑨	c. 1927	Gained small area from TUSCALOOSA, ending boundary dispute dating from nineteenth century	800 sq mi

(Heavy line depicts historical boundary. Base map shows present-day information.)

⑨ 5 Mar 1901–14 Sep 1953

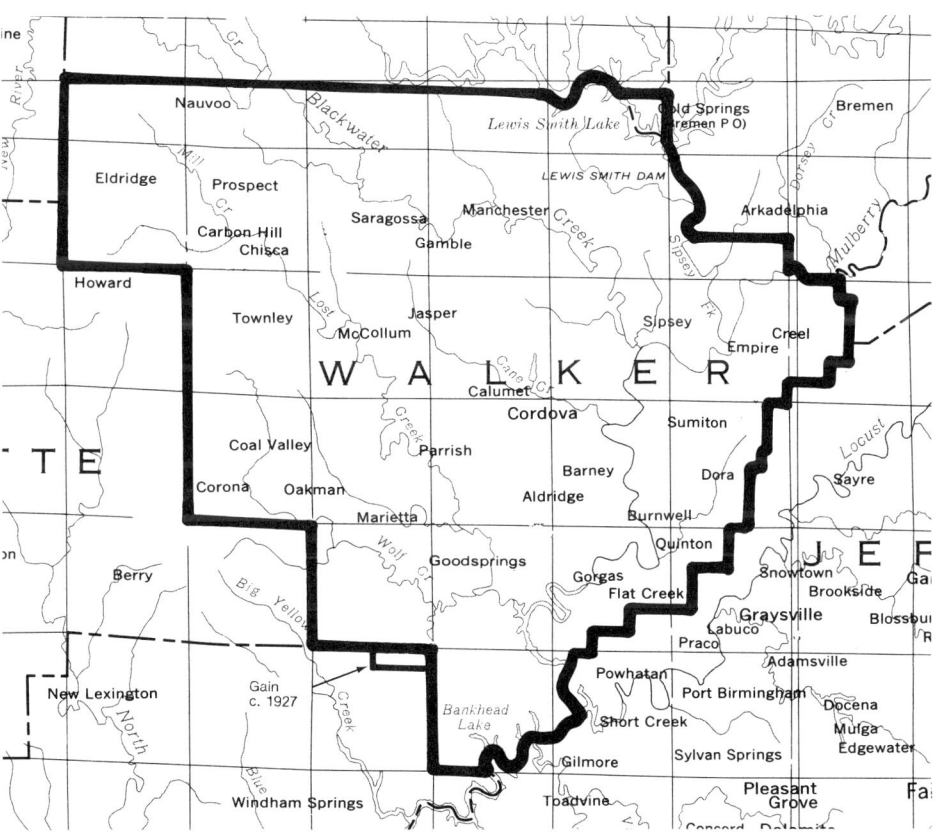

Chronology of WALKER

Map	Date	Event	Resulting Area
⑩	15 Sep 1953	Lost to CULLMAN	800 sq mi

(Heavy line depicts historical boundary. Base map shows present-day information.)

⑩ 15 Sep 1953–1990

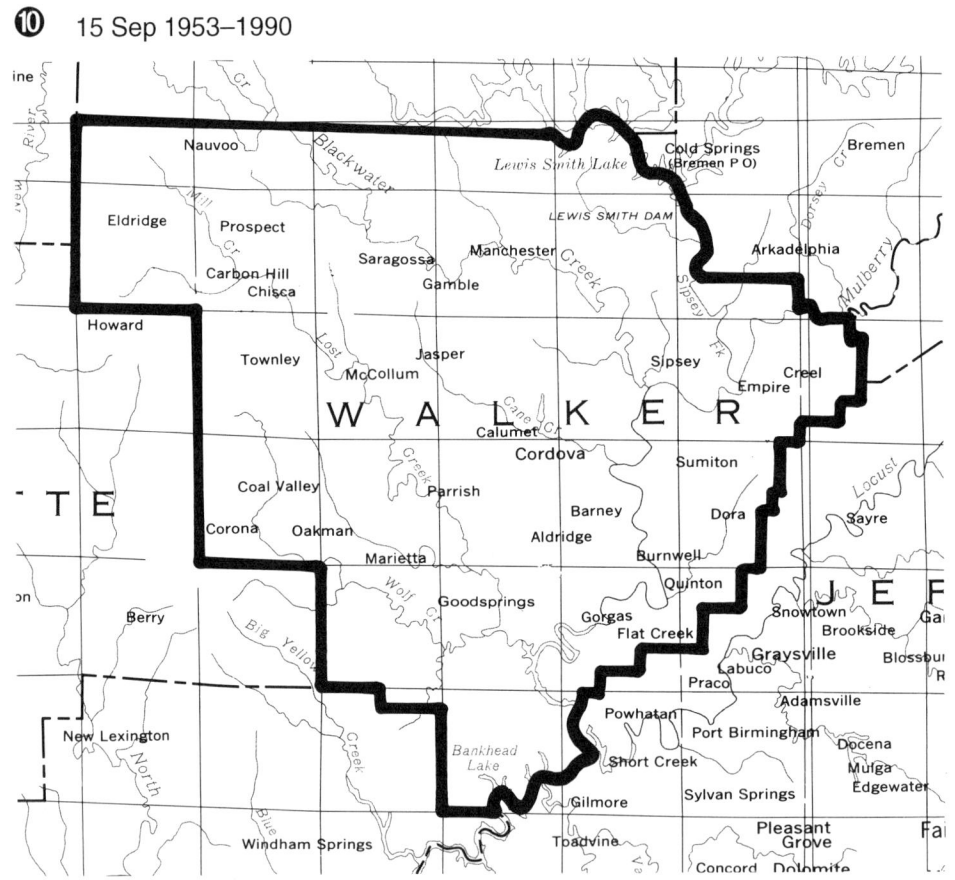

Chronology of WASHINGTON

Map	Date	Event	Resulting Area
❶	4 Jun 1800	Created by Mississippi Territory from ADAMS (Miss.) and PICKERING (now JEFFERSON, Miss.); included part of present Mississippi	27,500 sq mi
	27 Jan 1802	Overlapped by CLAIBORNE (Miss.) [not mapped; see CLAIBORNE (Miss.), map 1]	
❶	30 Jan 1802	Overlap by CLAIBORNE (Miss.) ended	27,500 sq mi
	12 Mar 1803	Again overlapped by CLAIBORNE (Miss.), apparently by mistake [not mapped]	
❶	7 Feb 1807	Boundary with CLAIBORNE (Miss.) clarified, eliminating overlap of 1803	27,500 sq mi

(Heavy line depicts historical boundary. Base map shows present-day information.)

❶ 4 Jun 1800–20 Dec 1809

Chronology of WASHINGTON

Map	Date	Event	Resulting Area
❷	21 Dec 1809	Lost to non-county area and lost to creation of both BALDWIN and WAYNE (Miss.)	1,640 sq mi

(Heavy line depicts historical boundary. Base map shows present-day information.)

❷ 21 Dec 1809–9 Dec 1812

Chronology of WASHINGTON

Map	Date	Event	Resulting Area
❸	10 Dec 1812	Lost to creation of CLARKE	770 sq mi
	3 Mar 1817	Became part of Alabama Territory	

(Heavy line depicts historical boundary. Base map shows present-day information.)

❸ 10 Dec 1812–6 Feb 1818

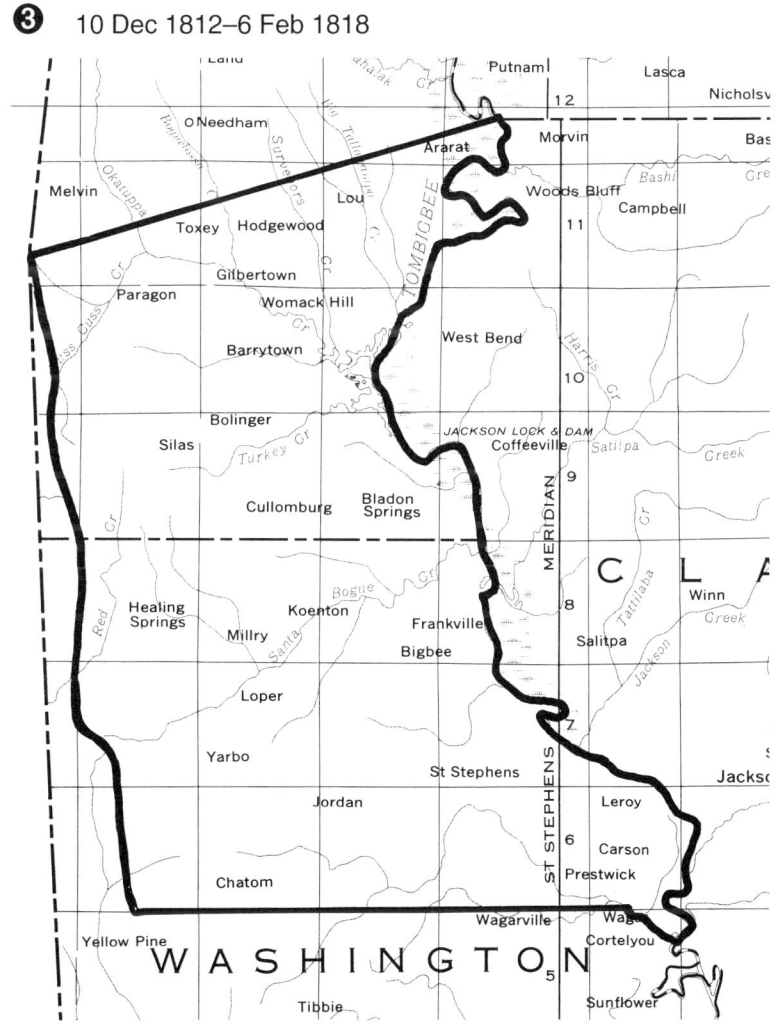

366   ALABAMA

Chronology of WASHINGTON

Map	Date	Event	Resulting Area
❹	7 Feb 1818	Gained from WAYNE (Miss.)	840 sq mi

(Heavy line depicts historical boundary. Base map shows present-day information.)

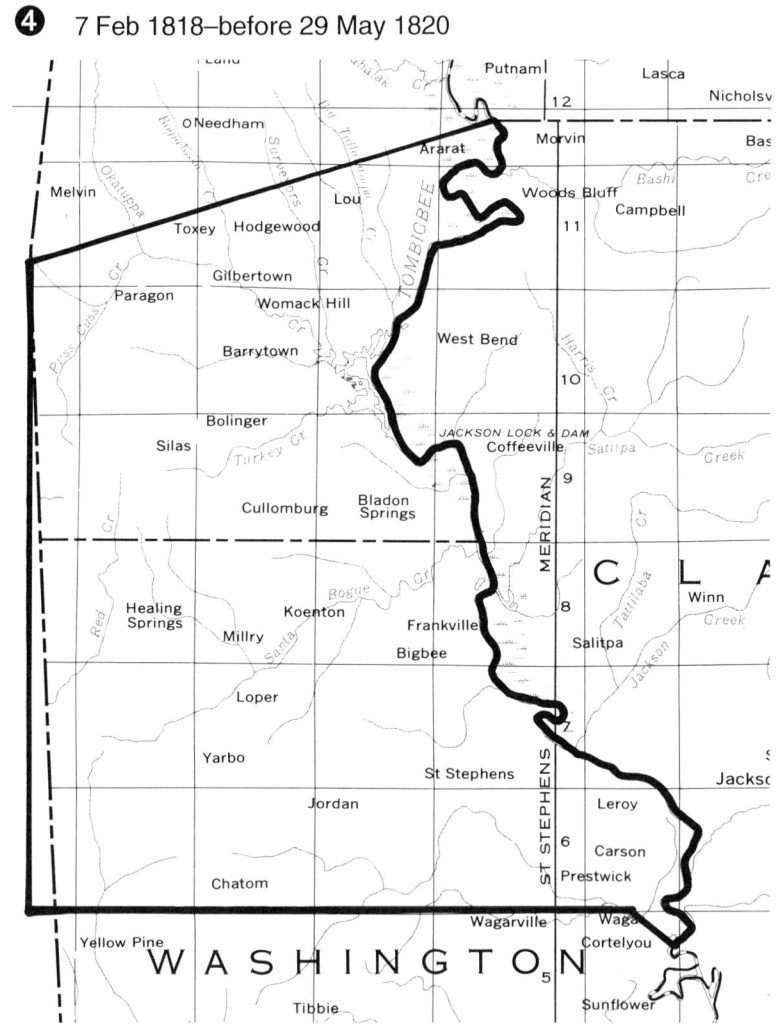

❹ 7 Feb 1818–before 29 May 1820

Individual County Chronologies   367

Chronology of WASHINGTON

Map	Date	Event	Resulting Area
❺	by 29 May 1820	Lost to Mississippi when surveyors implemented the authorized adjustment of the Mississippi-Alabama line	820 sq mi

(Heavy line depicts historical boundary. Base map shows present-day information.)

❺   by 29 May 1820–26 Jan 1829

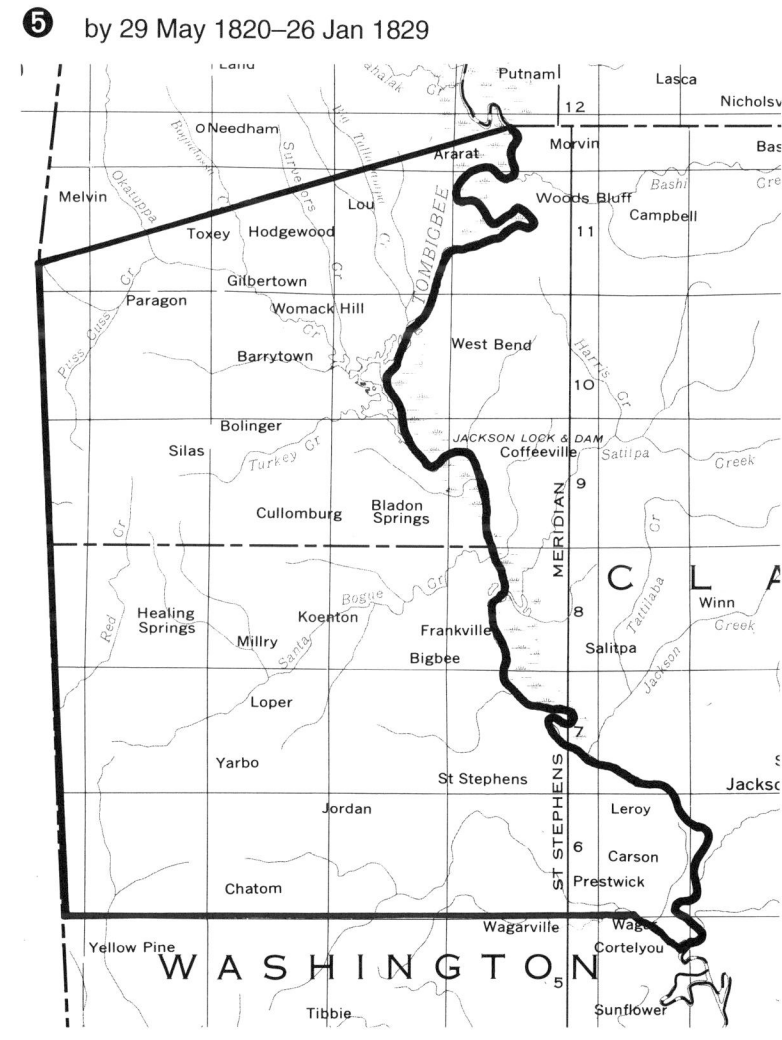

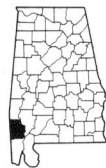

Chronology of WASHINGTON

Map	Date	Event	Resulting Area
❻	27 Jan 1829	Gained from MOBILE	1,440 sq mi
❼	18 Dec 1832	Gained from non-county area attached to MARENGO	1,740 sq mi

(Heavy line depicts historical boundary. Base map shows present-day information.)

❻ 27 Jan 1829–17 Dec 1832

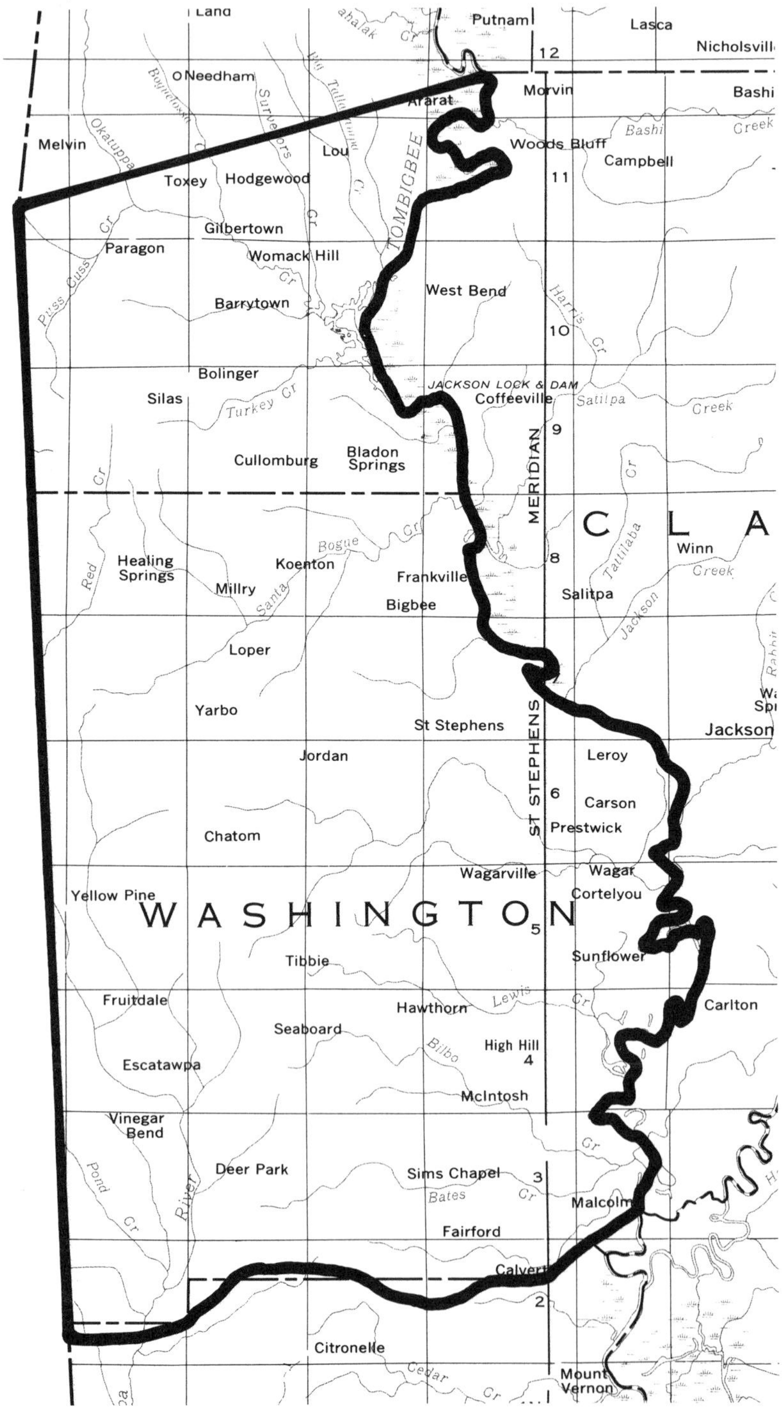

10 0 10 20 30 40 Miles

❼ 18 Dec 1832–28 Dec 1847

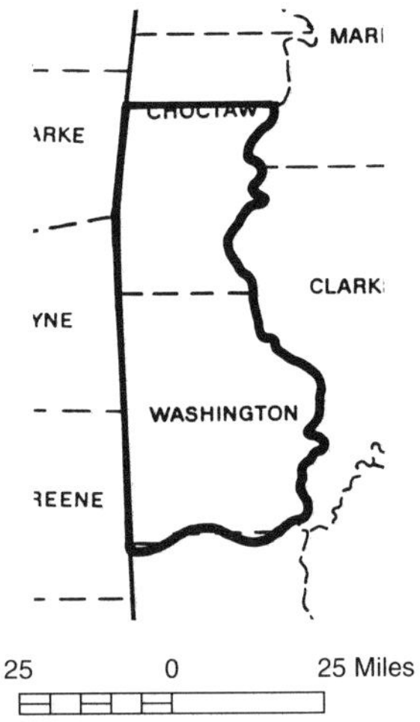

Chronology of WASHINGTON

Map	Date	Event	Resulting Area
8	29 Dec 1847	Lost to creation of CHOCTAW	1,090 sq mi
8	21 Feb 1860	Gained small area from MOBILE	1,090 sq mi
8	27 Aug 1863	Lost small area to MOBILE to accommodate local property owners	1,090 sq mi
	1 Mar 1870	Gain from CHOCTAW authorized, dependent on local referendum [local action unknown, no change]	

(Heavy line depicts historical boundary. Base map shows present-day information.)

8   29 Dec 1847–20 Feb 1893

Chronology of WASHINGTON

Map	Date	Event	Resulting Area
⑨	21 Feb 1893	Exchanged with MOBILE	1,090 sq mi
⑨	18 Feb 1895	Gained small area from MOBILE	1,090 sq mi
⑨	28 Feb 1901	Lost small area to MOBILE	1,090 sq mi

(Heavy line depicts historical boundary. Base map shows present-day information.)

⑨ 21 Feb 1893–1990

Individual County Chronologies 371

Chronology of WAYNE (Miss.)

Map	Date	Event	Resulting Area
❶	21 Dec 1809	Created by Mississippi Territory from WASHINGTON; included part of present Alabama	5,230 sq mi
❷	9 Dec 1811	Lost to creation of both GREENE (Miss.) and MARION (Miss.)	1,460 sq mi
	3 Mar 1817	Eliminated from present Alabama when Alabama Territory was created; eastern end fell within Alabama Territory and became non-county area	
	7 Feb 1818	Remnant in Alabama Territory added to WASHINGTON	

(Heavy line depicts historical boundary. Base map shows present-day information.)

❶ 21 Dec 1809–8 Dec 1811

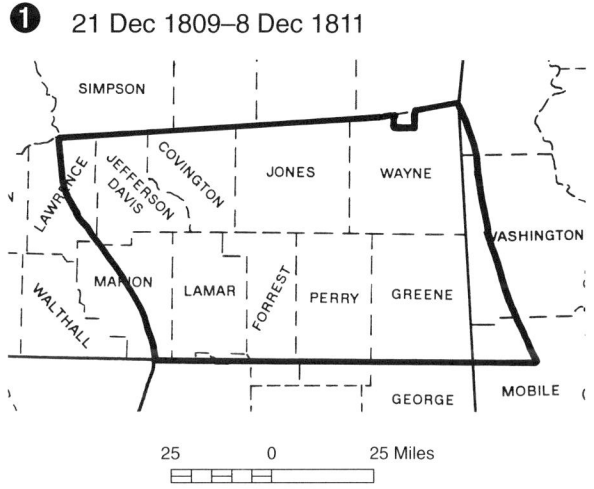

❷ 9 Dec 1811–2 Mar 1817

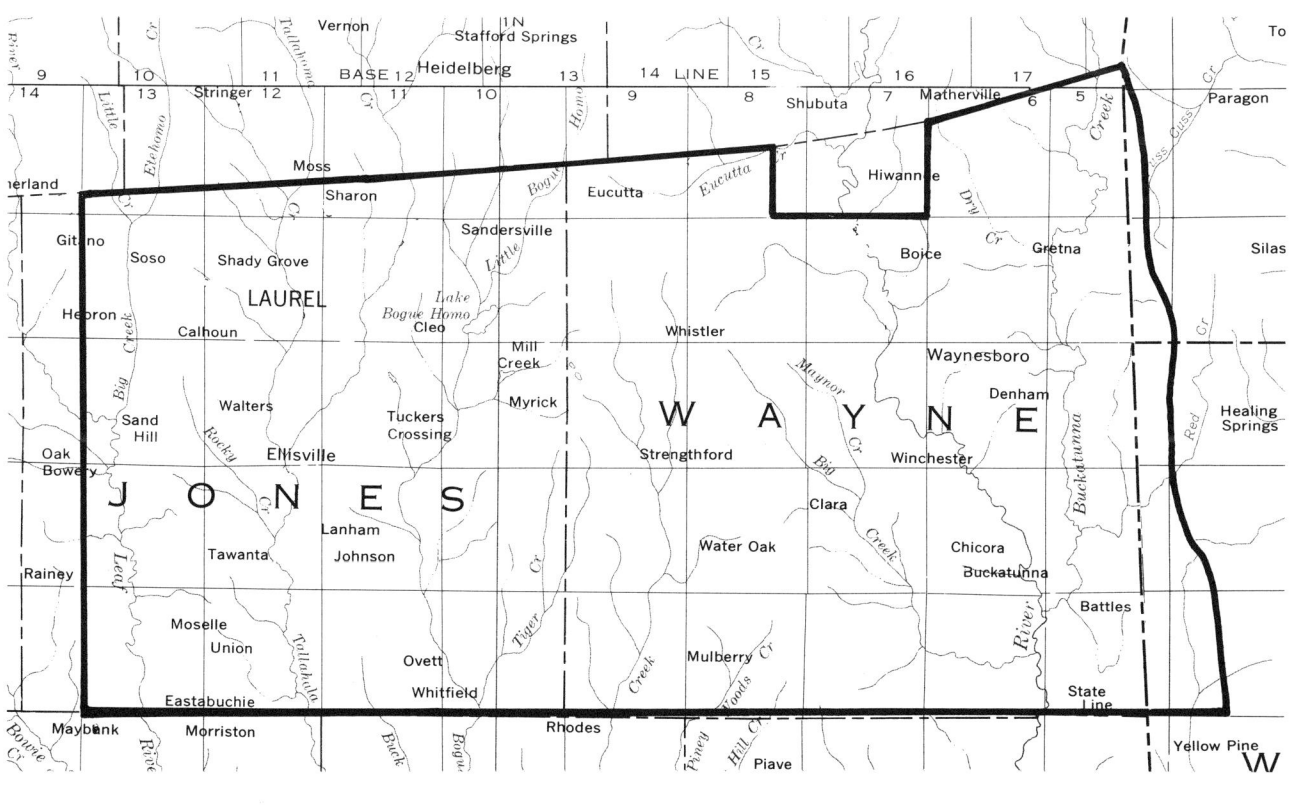

372 ALABAMA

Chronology of WILCOX

Map	Date	Event	Resulting Area
❶	13 Dec 1819	Created from DALLAS, MARENGO, MONROE, and MONTGOMERY	960 sq mi

(Heavy line depicts historical boundary. Base map shows present-day information.)

❶ 13 Dec 1819–26 Dec 1822

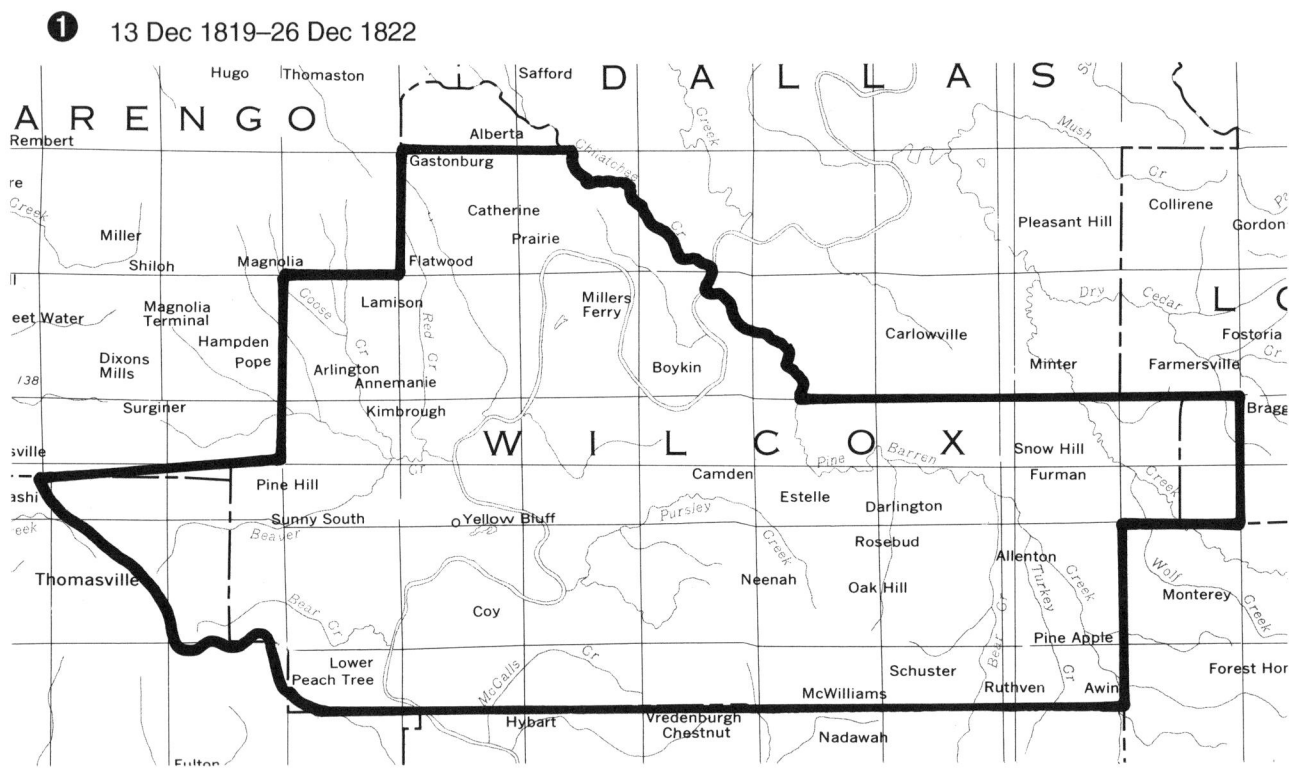

Individual County Chronologies 373

Chronology of WILCOX

Map	Date	Event	Resulting Area
❷	27 Dec 1822	Gained from DALLAS	980 sq mi

(Heavy line depicts historical boundary. Base map shows present-day information.)

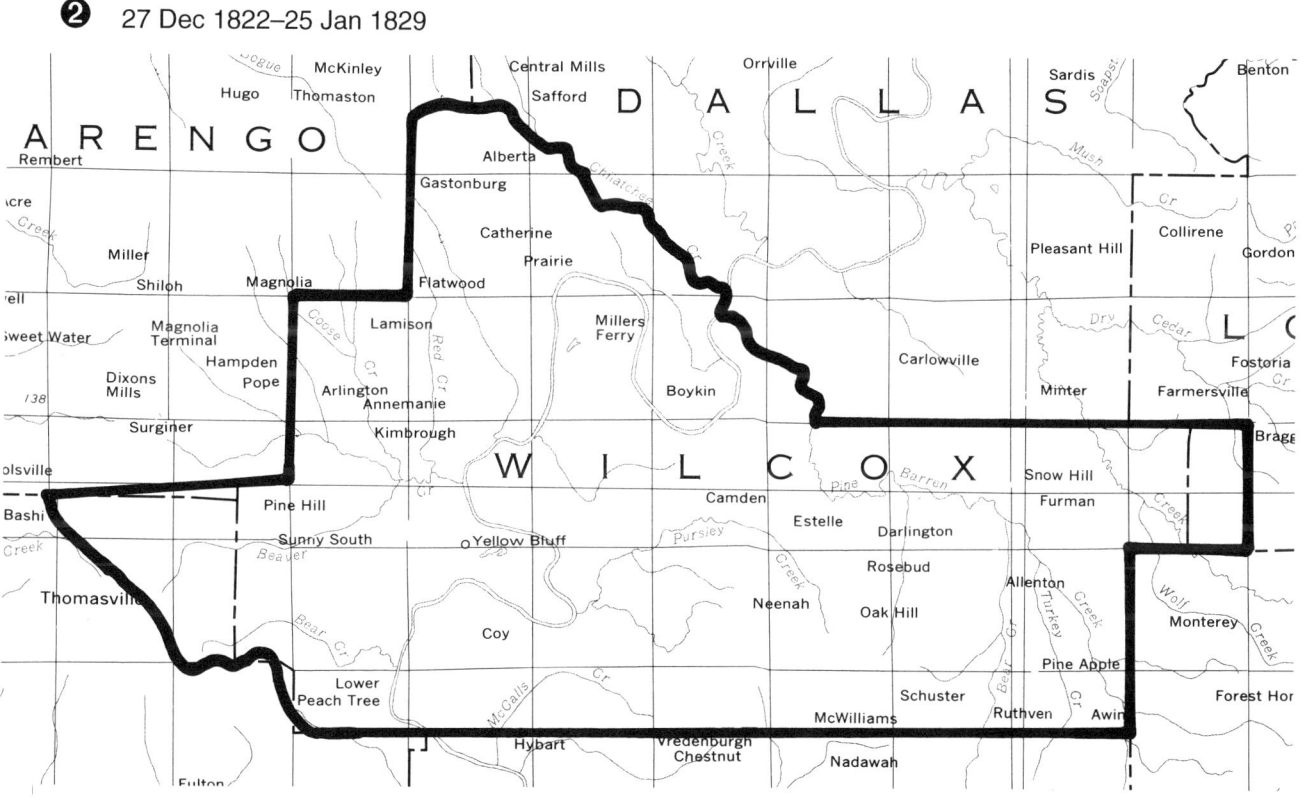

❷ 27 Dec 1822–25 Jan 1829

ALABAMA

Chronology of WILCOX

Map	Date	Event	Resulting Area
❸	26 Jan 1829	Lost to CLARKE and MARENGO	930 sq mi

(Heavy line depicts historical boundary. Base map shows present-day information.)

❸ 26 Jan 1829–19 Jan 1830

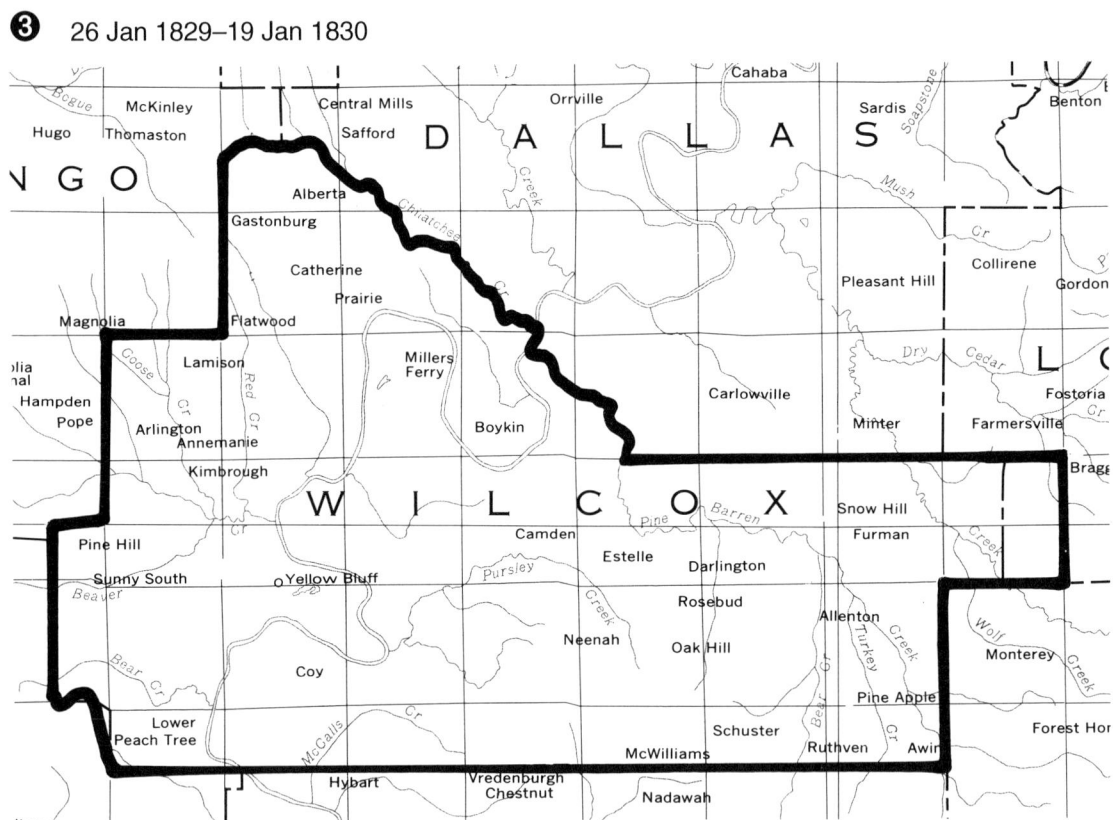

Individual County Chronologies 375

Chronology of WILCOX

Map	Date	Event	Resulting Area
❹	20 Jan 1830	Gained from CLARKE, lost to creation of LOWNDES	960 sq mi

(Heavy line depicts historical boundary. Base map shows present-day information.)

❹ 20 Jan 1830–14 Jan 1831

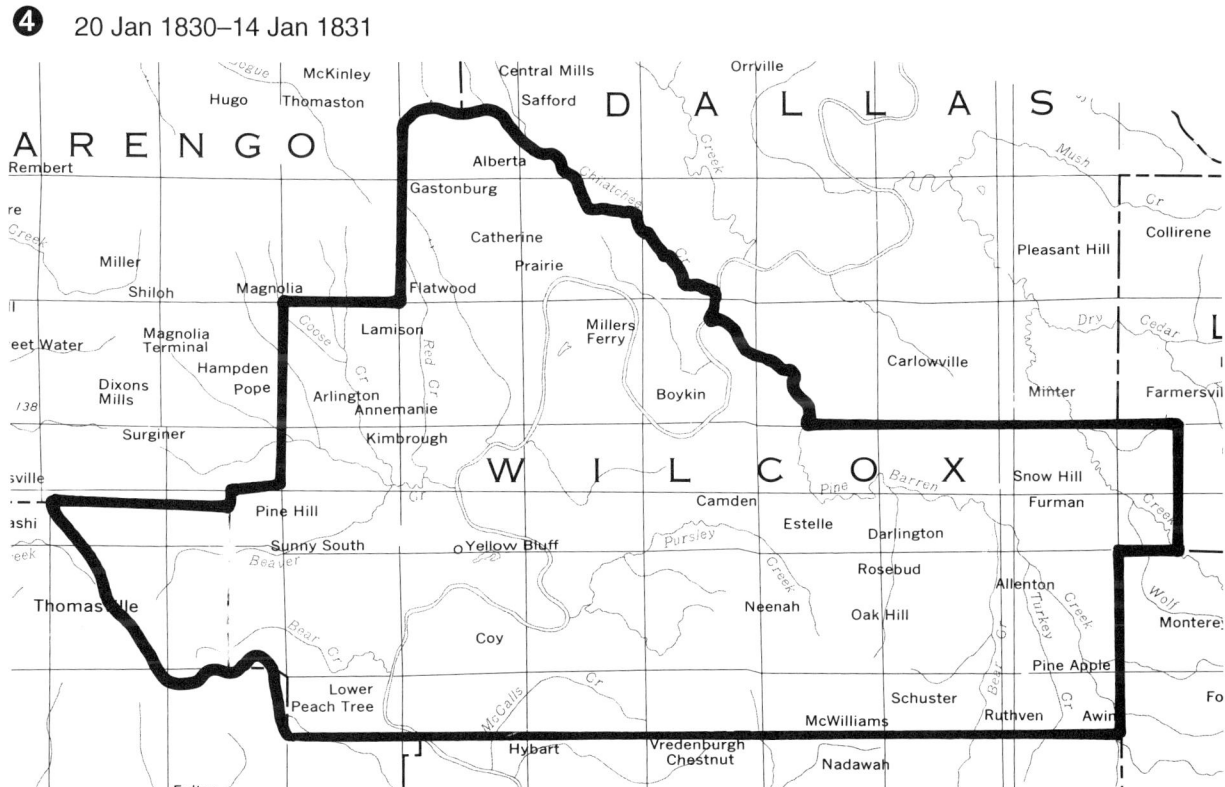

Chronology of WILCOX

Map	Date	Event	Resulting Area
⑤	15 Jan 1831	Lost to CLARKE	910 sq mi
⑤	18 Dec 1840	Lost small area to BUTLER	910 sq mi
⑤	1901	Exchanged small areas with CLARKE	910 sq mi

(Heavy line depicts historical boundary. Base map shows present-day information.)

⑤ 15 Jan 1831–1990

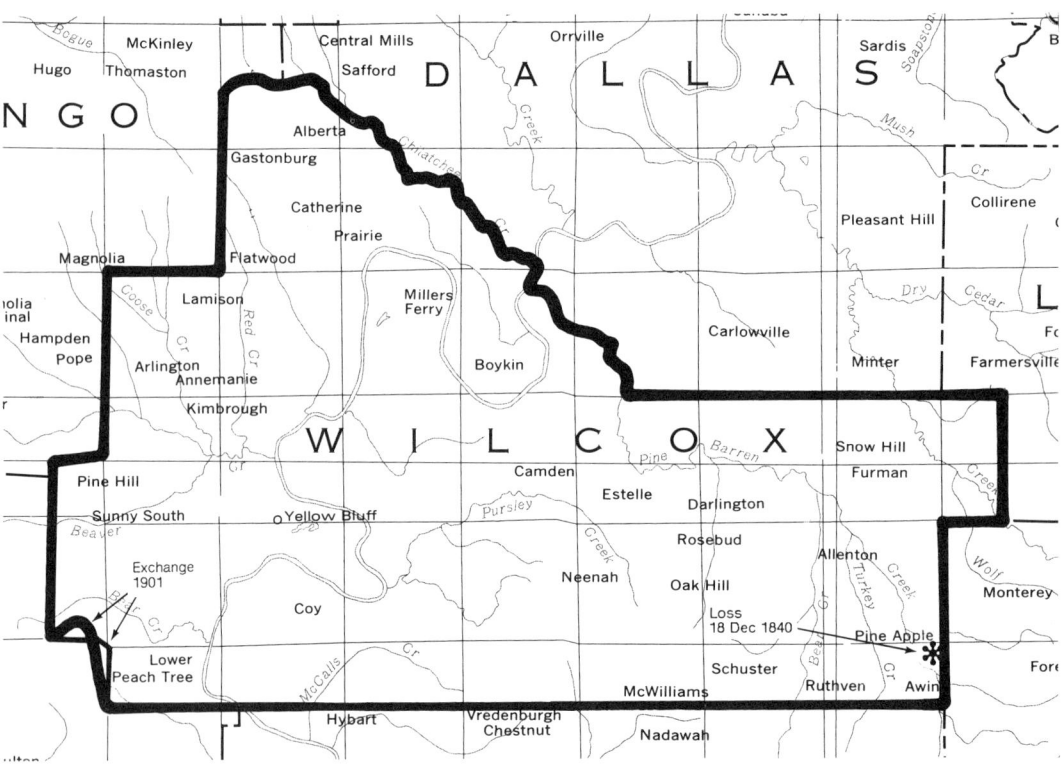

Individual County Chronologies   377

Chronology of WINSTON (created as HANCOCK)

Map	Date	Event	Resulting Area
❶	12 Feb 1850	Created as HANCOCK from WALKER	900 sq mi
	22 Jan 1858	Renamed WINSTON	
❷	24 Jan 1877	Lost to creation of CULLMAN	630 sq mi
❸	5 Mar 1901	Exchanged with WALKER	630 sq mi

(Heavy line depicts historical boundary. Base map shows present-day information.)

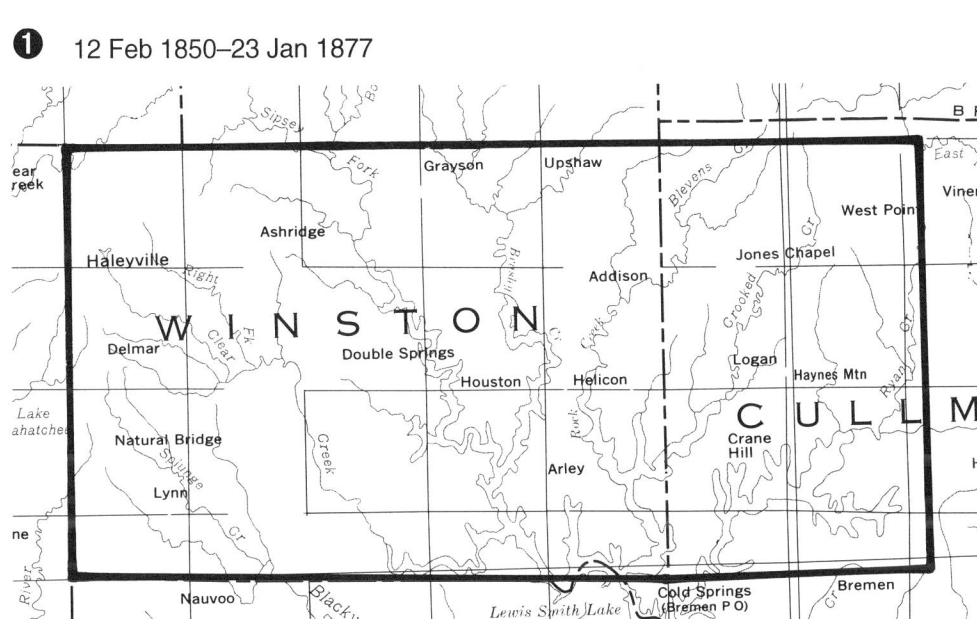

❶ 12 Feb 1850–23 Jan 1877

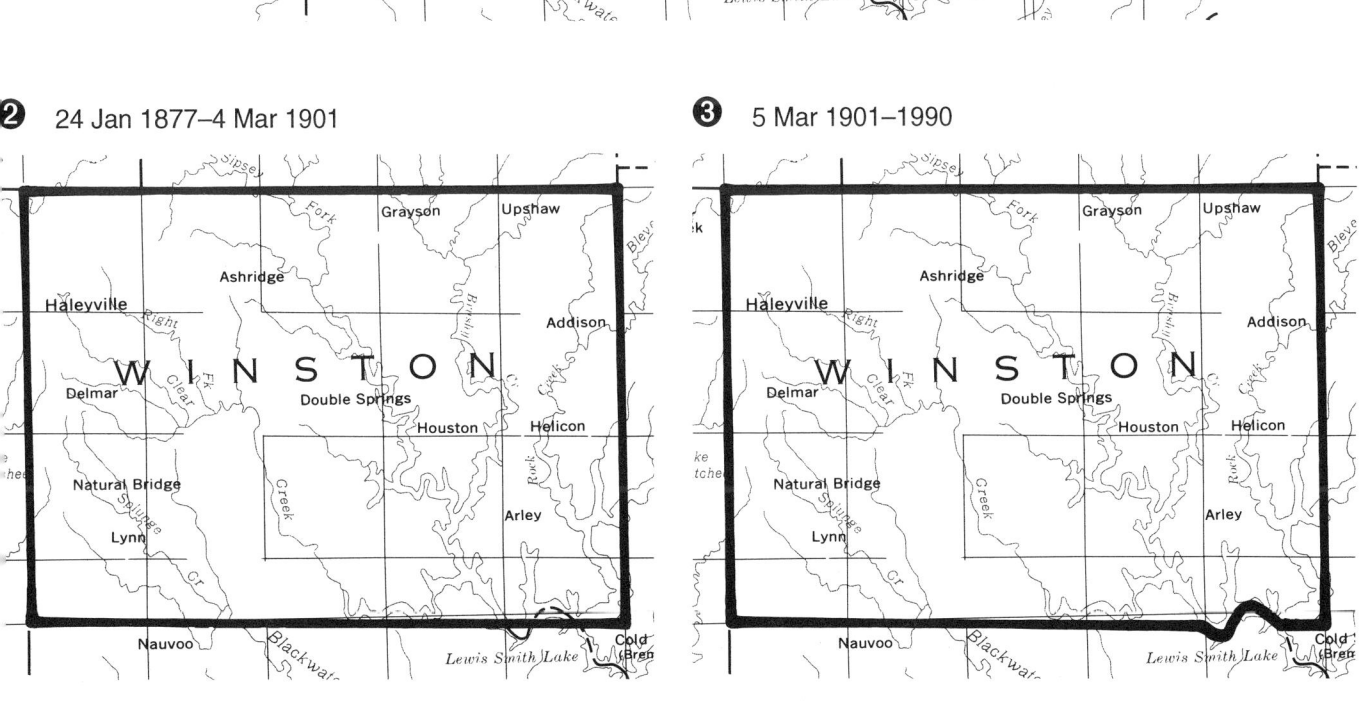

❷ 24 Jan 1877–4 Mar 1901

❸ 5 Mar 1901–1990

Territorial, State, and Federal Censuses in Alabama

Date	Census
4 Aug 1800	Federal census [not mapped]. Statistics for WASHINGTON included with Mississippi Territory; no names.
after 1 Mar 1808	Territorial census [not mapped]. No statistics; names for WASHINGTON (*Ala. Geneal. Reg.* 9 [Sep 1967]: 124–126).
6 Aug 1810	Federal census. Statistics for BALDWIN, MADISON, and WASHINGTON included with Mississippi Territory; names for BALDWIN and WASHINGTON (*Ala. Geneal. Reg.* 9 [Jun and Sep 1967]: 63–66, 126–135).
1816	Territorial census. Statistics (*Terr. Papers U.S.*, 6:719–720, 730); names for BALDWIN, CLARKE, and MONROE (*Ala. Geneal. Reg.* 9 [Jun and Dec 1967]: 67–69, 186–196 and *Ala. Geneal. Reg.* 10 [Jun-Sep 1968]: 51–52, 123–134).
after Feb 1818	Territorial census. Statistics for all counties except LAWRENCE and MARION (*Terr. Papers U.S.*, 18:462); no names.
7 Aug 1820	Federal census. Statistics; names for 8 of 25 counties (*Ala. Hist. Quart.* 6 [Fall 1944]).
1820	State census. No statistics; names for LAWRENCE at Ala. Dept. of Arch. and Hist.
by 6 Aug 1821	State census [not mapped]. No extant statistics or names.
1824	State census [not mapped]. No extant statistics or names.
1827	State census [not mapped]. No extant statistics or names.
1 Jun 1830	Federal census. Statistics and names.
1 Apr 1833	State census [not mapped]. Fragmentary records at Ala. Dept. of Arch. and Hist.
1 Apr 1838	State census. Statistics (Dubester, 1); no names.
1 Jun 1840	Federal census. Statistics and names.
1 Apr 1844	State census. Statistics for all counties except BALDWIN and SUMTER (Dubester, 1); no names.
1 Apr 1850	State census. No extant statistics or names.
1 Jun 1850	Federal census. Statistics and names.
1 Apr 1855	State census [not mapped]. No statistics; names for 12 of 52 counties (Jackson, *Alabama 1855 Census Index*).
1 Jun 1860	Federal census. Statistics and names.
1 Apr 1866	State census. No statistics; names for 44 of 52 counties at Ala. Dept. of Arch. and Hist.
1 Jun 1870	Federal census. Statistics and names.
1875	State census [not mapped]. Authorization rescinded (Dubester, 2).
1 Jun 1880	Federal census. Statistics and names.
2 Jun 1890	Federal census. Statistics; some names from PERRY only.

1 Jun 1900	Federal census. Statistics and names.
1907	Census of Confederate Veterans. No statistics; names for most counties at Ala. Dept. of Arch. and Hist.
15 Apr 1910	Federal census. Statistics and names.
1 Jan 1920	Federal census. Statistics and names.
1 Apr 1930	Federal census. Statistics; names not available until 2002.
1 Apr 1940	Federal census. Statistics; names not available until 2012.
1 Apr 1950	Federal census. Statistics; names not available until 2022.
1 Apr 1960	Federal census. Statistics; names not available until 2032.
1 Apr 1970	Federal census. Statistics; names not available until 2042.
1 Apr 1980	Federal census. Statistics; names not available until 2052.
1 Apr 1990	Federal census. Statistics; names not available until 2062.

Sources

Alabama Genealogical Register 9 (1967): 63–69, 124–135, 186–196; 10 (1968): 51–52, 123–124. Cited as *Ala. Geneal. Reg.*

Alabama Historical Quarterly 6 (Fall 1944). Cited as *Ala. Hist. Quart.*

Dubester, Henry J. *State Censuses: An Annotated Bibliography of Censuses of Population Taken after the Year 1790 by States and Territories of the United States.* 1948. Reprint. New York: Burt Franklin, 1969.

Jackson, Ronald Vern, comp. *Alabama 1855 Census Index.* Bountiful, Utah: Accelerated Indexing Systems, 1981.

Lainhart, Ann S. *State Census Records.* [Baltimore]: Genealogical Publishing Co., 1992.

Territorial Papers of the United States. Vols. 1–26 edited by Clarence E. Carter; vols. 27–28 edited by John P. Bloom. Washington, D.C.: Government Printing Office, 1934–1975. Cited as *Terr. Papers U.S.*

Census Outline Maps for Alabama

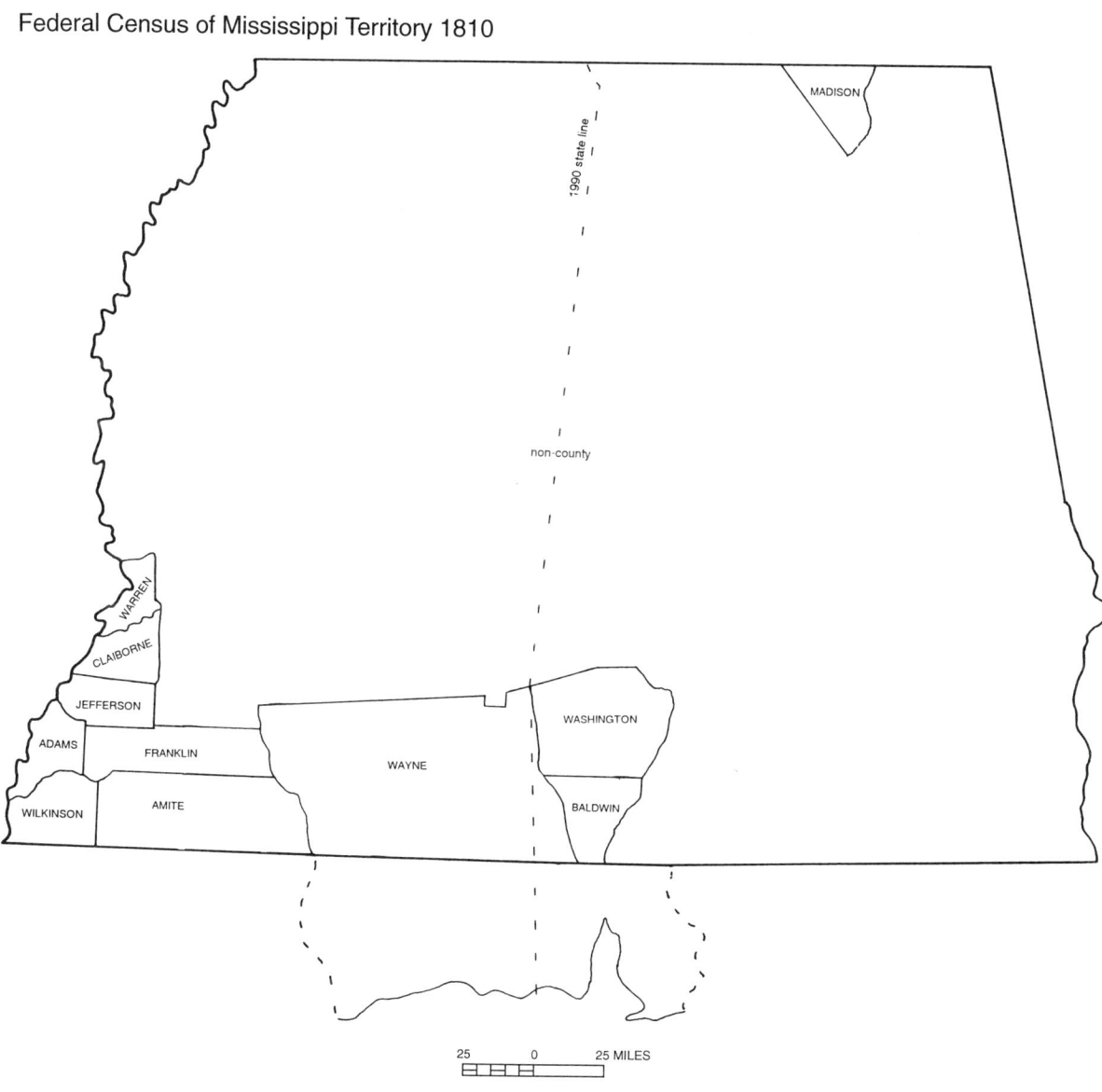

Federal Census of Mississippi Territory 1810

ALABAMA

Mississippi Territorial Census 1816

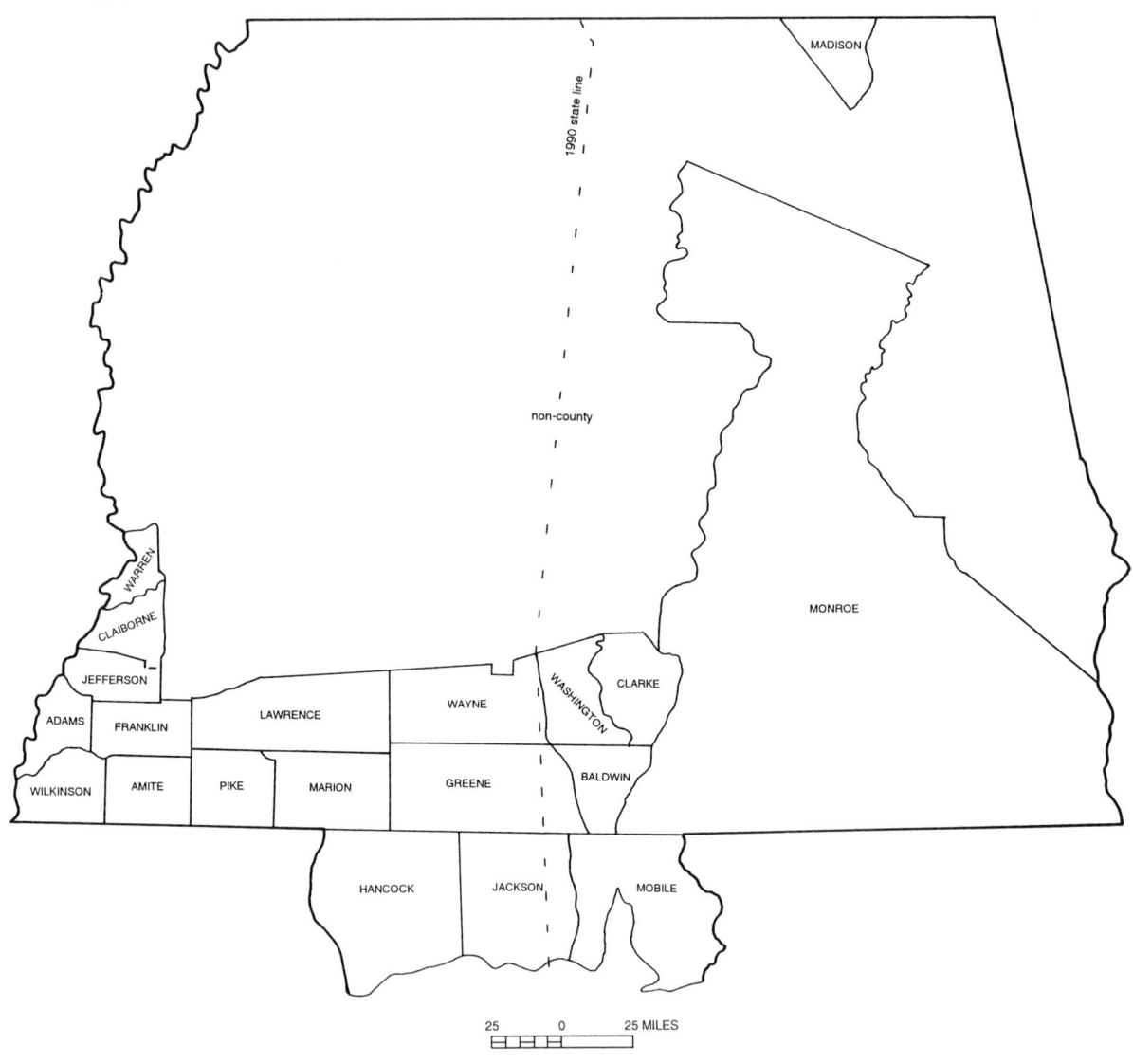

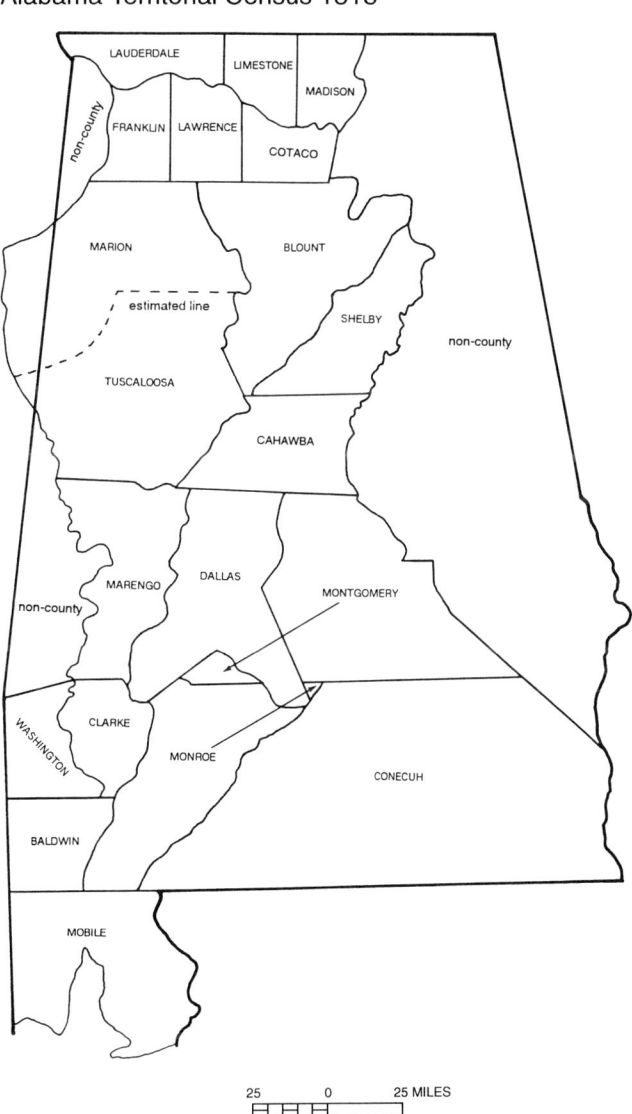

Federal and State Censuses 1820

Federal Census 1830

State Census 1838

Federal Census 1840

State Census 1844

Federal and State Censuses 1850

Census Outline Maps 391

Federal Census 1870

ALABAMA

Federal Census 1880

Federal Census 1890

ALABAMA

Federal Censuses 1900–1920
Census of Confederate Veterans 1907

Federal Census 1930

ALABAMA

Federal Censuses 1940–1990

Bibliography

Abrams, Ulysses Huey. *History of Early Bibb County, Alabama, 1820–1870.* Edited by Mattie Sandford Johnson. N.p.: [Mattie Sandford Johnson], 1981.

Alabama. *Acts of Alabama.* Tuscaloosa et al., 1819–. Cited as Ala. Acts.

Alabama Genealogical Register 9 (1967): 63–69, 124–135, 186–196; 10 (1968): 51–52, 123–124. Contains transcripts of territorial censuses. Cited as *Ala. Geneal. Reg.*

Alabama Historical Quarterly 6 (Fall 1944): 333–515. Reprint. Tuscaloosa, Ala.: Willo Publishing Co., 1960. Entire issue devoted to 1820 and 1830 Alabama censuses. Cited as *Ala. Hist. Quart.*

Alabama Supreme Court. *Alabama Reports.* 295 vols. 1841–1977. Reports of cases heard before the Supreme Court of Alabama. Cited as *Ala. Rpts.*

Alabama Territory. *Acts of Alabama Territory.* 1st and 2d sessions, Jan. and Nov. 1818. St. Stephens, Ala., 1818. Cited as Ala. Terr. Acts.

Anthony, J. D. "Reminiscences of Cherokee County, 1835–1875." In *Early History of Northeast Alabama, and Incidentally of Northwest Georgia*, edited by W. Stanley Hoole and Addie S. Hoole. University, Ala.: Confederate Publishing Co., 1979.

Ball, T. H. *Glance into the Great South-East, or, Clarke County, Alabama, and Its Surroundings, from 1540 to 1877.* Grove Hill, Ala., 1882.

Barefield, Marilyn Davis, comp. *Old Huntsville Land Office Records and Military Warrants, 1810–1854.* Easley, S.C.: Southern Historical Press, 1985.

Barefield, Marilyn Davis, comp. *Old Mardisville, Lebanon and Centre Land Office Records and Military Warrants, 1834–1860.* Greenville, S.C.: Southern Historical Press, 1990.

Barefield, Marilyn Davis, comp. *Old Tuskaloosa Land Office Records and Military Warrants, 1821–1855.* Easley, S.C.: Southern Historical Press, 1984.

Barefield, Marilyn Davis. *Researching in Alabama: A Genealogical Guide.* Edited by Yvonne Shelton Crumpler. Easley, S.C.: Southern Historical Press, 1987.

Bennett, James R. *Old Tannehill: A History of the Pioneer Ironworks in Roupes Valley (1829–1865).* [Birmingham]: Jefferson County Historical Commission, 1986.

Birmingham Public Library. *List of Nineteenth Century Maps of the State of Alabama.* Birmingham, 1973.

Brannon, Peter A. "Tennessee State Line: An Historical Interpretation." *Alabama Historical Quarterly* 18 (1956): 412–420.

Brannon, Peter A. "Western Boundary Line of Alabama, A Comment." *Alabama Historical Quarterly* 20 (1958): 571–580.

Brown, Virginia Pounds, and Jane Porter Nabers. "Origin of Certain Place Names in Jefferson County, Alabama." *Alabama Review* 5 (1952): 177–202.

Bryant, Pat, comp. *Georgia Counties: Their Changing Boundaries.* 2d ed. Revised by Ingrid Shields. Atlanta: State Printing Office, 1983.

Calhoun, Robert Dabney. "Origin and Early Development of County-Parish Government in Louisiana (1805–1845)." *Louisiana Historical Quarterly* 18 (1935): 56–160.

Candler, Allen D., comp. *Revolutionary Records of the State of Georgia.* Vol. 3, pt. 2, *Journal of the House of Assembly from August 17, 1781, to February 26, 1784.* Atlanta: Franklin-Turner Co., 1908.

Cappon, Lester J., Barbara Bartz Petchenik, and John Hamilton Long, eds. *Atlas of Early American History: The Revolutionary Era, 1760–1790.* Princeton, N.J.: Princeton University Press, 1976. Section on boundaries is thoroughly documented.

Coleman, Kenneth. *American Revolution in Georgia, 1763–1789.* Athens, Ga.: University of Georgia Press, 1958.

Cotterill, R. S. "National Land System in the South: 1803–1812." *Mississippi Valley Historical Review* 16 (1929–1930): 495–506.

Cox, Isaac Joslin. *West Florida Controversy, 1798–1813: A Study in American Diplomacy.* Baltimore: Johns Hopkins Press, 1918.

Crow, Mattie Lou Teague. *History of St. Clair County [Alabama].* Huntsville, Ala.: Strode Publishers, 1973.

Davis, George B., et al. *Atlas to Accompany the Official Records of the Union and Confederate Armies.* 1891–1895. Reprinted as *Official Military Atlas of the Civil War.* New York: Fairfax Press, 1983. Coverage limited to areas of military activity during the Civil War, but affords accurate detail of landmarks and other geographic features before and after the war.

Doster, James F. "Land Titles and Public Land Sales in Early Alabama." *Alabama Review* 16 (1963): 108–124.

Du Bose, John Witherspoon. *Jefferson County and Birmingham, Alabama, Historical and Biographical.* 1887. Reprint. [Easley, S.C.: Southern Historical Press], n.d.

Dubester, Henry J. *State Censuses: An Annotated Bibliography of Censuses of Population Taken after the Year 1790 by States and Territories of the United States.* 1948. Reprint. New York: Burt Franklin, 1969. The standard guide for its subject.

Duffee, Mary Gordon. *Sketches of Alabama: Being an Account of the Journey from Tuscaloosa to Blount Springs through Jefferson County on the Old Stage Roads.* Edited by Virginia Pounds Brown and Jane Porter Nabers. University, Ala.: University of Alabama Press, 1970.

Duncan, Katherine McKinstry, and Larry Joe Smith. *History of Marshall County, Alabama.* Vol. 1. Albertville, Ala.: Thompson Printing, 1969.

Elliott, Carl, comp. *Annals of Northwest Alabama.* 4 vols. Tuscaloosa, Ala.: Carl Elliott, 1958–1972.

Ellison, Rhoda Coleman. *Bibb County, Alabama: The First Hundred Years, 1818–1918.* University, Ala.: University of Alabama Press, 1984.

"Establishment of the Alabama Territory." *Alabama Historical Quarterly* 24 (1962): 97–128.

Filby, P. William, comp. *American and British Genealogy and Heraldry: A Selected List of Books.* 3d ed. Boston: New England Historic Genealogical Society, 1983.

Filby, P. William, comp. *American and British Genealogy and Heraldry: 1982–1985 Supplement.* Boston: New England Historic Genealogical Society, 1987.

Filby, P. William, comp. *Bibliography of American County Histories.* Baltimore: Genealogical Publishing Co., 1985.

Fleming, Walter L. *Civil War and Reconstruction in Alabama.* 1905. Reprint. Cleveland: Arthur H. Clark Co., 1911.

Fonde, Henry. *Township and Sectional Map of Mobile County, State of Alabama.* St. Louis, 1895.

Foscue, Virginia O. *Place Names in Alabama.* Tuscaloosa: University of Alabama Press, 1989.

Foscue, Virginia O. "Sumter County Place-Names: A Selection." *Alabama Review* 13 (1960): 52–67.

Fuller, Hubert Bruce. *Purchase of Florida: Its History and Diplomacy.* Cleveland: Burrows Brothers Co., 1906.

Graham, John Simpson. *History of Clarke County [Alabama].* Birmingham: Birmingham Printing Co., 1923.

Griffith, Lucille. *Alabama: A Documentary History to 1900.* Rev. ed. University, Ala.: University of Alabama Press, 1972.

Hahn, Marilyn Davis, comp. *Old Cahaba Land Office Records and Military Warrants, 1817–1853.* Rev. ed. Birmingham: Southern University Press, 1986.

Hahn, Marilyn Davis, comp. *Old St. Stephen's Land Office Records and American State Papers, Public Lands.* Vol. 1, *1768–1888.* Easley, S.C.: Southern Historical Press, 1983.

Hahn, Marilyn Davis, comp. *Old Sparta and Elba Land Office Records and Military Warrants, 1822–1860.* Easley, S.C.: Southern Historical Press, 1983.

Halbert, Henry Sale. "Choctaw Indian Names in Alabama and Mississippi." *Transactions of the Alabama Historical Society* 3 (1898–1899): 64–77.

Hamilton, Peter J. *Colonial Mobile.* Rev. ed. 1910. Reprint. Edited by Charles G. Summersell. Southern Historical Publications, no. 20. University, Ala.: University of Alabama Press, 1976.

Hamilton, Peter J. "Early Roads of Alabama." *Transactions of the Alabama Historical Society* 2 (1897–1898): 39–56.

Harris, W. Stuart. *Dead Towns of Alabama.* University, Ala.: University of Alabama Press, 1977.

Haynes, Robert V. "Disposal of Lands in the Mississippi Territory." *Journal of Mississippi History* 24 (1962): 226–252.

Higginbotham, Jay. *Old Mobile: Fort Louis de la Louisiane, 1702–1711.* Museum of the City of Mobile, Museum Publication no. 4. [Mobile], 1977.

Historical Records Survey, Alabama. *Colbert County (Tuscumbia).* Inventory of the County Archives of Alabama, no. 17. Birmingham: Alabama Historical Records Survey, 1939. Cited as HRS Ala., *Colbert.*

Historical Records Survey, Alabama. *Lowndes County (Hayneville).* Inventory of the County Archives of Alabama, no. 43. Birmingham: Alabama Historical Records Survey, 1939.

Historical Records Survey, Mississippi. *Sargent's Code: A Collection of the Original Laws of the Mississippi Territory Enacted 1799–1800 by Governor Winthrop Sargent and the Territorial Judges.* Jackson: Mississippi Historical Records Survey, 1939.

Historical Records Survey, Mississippi. *State and County Boundaries of Mississippi.* Preliminary ed. Jackson: Mississippi Historical Records Survey, 1942. A convenient and reliable collection of boundary descriptions excerpted from the laws.

Jackson, Ronald Vern, comp. *Alabama 1855 Census Index.* Bountiful, Utah: Accelerated Indexing Systems, 1981.

Jacoway, W. V. "History of DeKalb County, 1836–1925." In *Early History of Northeast Alabama, and Incidentally of Northwest Georgia*, edited by W. Stanley Hoole and Addie S. Hoole. University, Ala.: Confederate Publishing Co., 1979.

Kane, Joseph Nathan. *American Counties: Origins of Names, Dates of Creation and Organization, Area, Population, Historical Data, and Published Sources.* 3d ed. Metuchen, N.J.: Scarecrow Press, 1972.

Kennamer, John Robert. *History of Jackson County [Alabama].* Winchester, Tenn.: Southern Printing and Publishing Co., 1935.

Lainhart, Ann S. *State Census Records.* [Baltimore]: Genealogical Publishing Co., 1992.

Lambert, Alton. *History of Tuscaloosa County, Alabama.* 3 vols. Centre, Ala.: Stewart University Press, 1977–1979.

Little, John Buckner. *History of Butler County, Alabama, from 1815 to 1885.* Cincinnati, 1885.

Long, John H. "A Case Study in Utilizing Computer Technology: The Atlas of Historical County Boundaries." *Perspectives: American Historical Association Newsletter* 30, no. 3 (March 1992): 16–17. Describes how computers have been employed in the making of this atlas.

McCalley, Henry. *Report on the Valley Regions of Alabama (Paleozoic Strata).* 2 vols. Geological Survey of Alabama, Alabama State Geologist, Special Report, nos. 8–9. Montgomery, 1896–1897.

MacDonald, Grace E., comp. *Check-List of Session Laws.* New York: H.W. Wilson Co., 1936. Complemented by Pollack (below), this guide lists all state session laws through 1935.

MacDonald, Grace E., comp. *Check-List of Statutes of States of the United States of America, Including Revisions, Compilations, Digests, Codes and Indexes.* Providence: Oxford Press, 1937. The most complete guide to state codes through 1937.

McLemore, Richard A. "Division of Mississippi Territory." *Journal of Mississippi History* 5 (1943): 79–82.

McMillan, Malcolm Cook. *Constitutional Development in Alabama, 1798–1901: A Study in Politics, the Negro, and Sectionalism.* University of North Carolina Departments of History and Political Sciences, James Sprunt Studies in History and Political Science, vol. 37. Chapel Hill, 1955.

["Map of the State of Louisiana, and Adjacent Countries."] Frontispiece to *Geographical Description of the State of Louisiana, the Southern Part of the State of Mississippi, and Territory of Alabama,* 2d ed., by William Darby. New York, 1817.

Mayhew, James H. *Map of Madison County, Alabama.* Cincinnati, 1875.

Melish, John. *Map of Alabama.* Philadelphia, 1819. Very accurate for its time.

Mississippi Territory [map]. [c. 1816]. Reprinted as "Mississippi Territory, ca. 1816" in *Mississippi Maps, 1816–1873.* Jackson: Mississippi Historical Society, 1969. Part of a portfolio of map reproductions; no supporting text or documentation.

Mississippi Territory. *Statutes of the Mississippi Territory.* Natchez, 1816. Compilation of this digest often attributed to Edward Turner; cited as Miss. Terr. Stat.

Moore, Albert Burton. *History of Alabama and Her People.* 3 vols. Chicago and New York: American Historical Society, 1927.

Morse, Sidney Edward. "Alabama" [map]. In *North American Atlas,* compiled by Sidney Edward Morse, [pl. 33]. New York, 1842.

New Map of Alabama with its Roads and Distances, From Place to Place, Along the Stage and Steam Boat Routes. Philadelphia: Thomas, Cowperthwait and Co., 1854.

1989–90 County and State Officials Directory [Alabama]. Birmingham: Roberts and Son, [1989?].

Northern Alabama, Historical and Biographical. Birmingham: Smith and De Land, 1888.

Orleans Territory. *Acts of the Territory of Orleans.* Legislative Council and 1st–3d legislatures, December 1804–January 1811. New Orleans, 1805–1811. The session laws of Orleans Territory.

Owen, Thomas McAdory. *History of Alabama and Dictionary of Alabama Biography.* 4 vols. Chicago: S.J. Clarke Publishing Co., 1921.

Parry, Clive, ed. *Consolidated Treaty Series.* 231 vols. Dobbs Ferry, N.Y.: Oceana Publications, 1969–1981.

Paullin, Charles O. *Atlas of the Historical Geography of the United States.* Edited by John K. Wright. Washington, D.C., and New York: Carnegie Institution of Washington and American Geographical Society of New York, 1932. Excellent section on international and interstate boundary disputes.

"Pike County Alabama Tomb Records." *Alabama Historical Quarterly* 35 (1973): 1–416. Good county map at back of volume.

Pollack, Ervin H., comp. *Supplement with Bibliographical Notes, Emendations, and Additions to the Check List of Session Laws, Compiled by Grace E. MacDonald.* Preliminary ed. Boston: National Association of State Libraries, 1941. Fills gaps in MacDonald's 1935 compilation (above) to produce the most complete list of state session laws through 1935.

Powell, George. "Description and History of Blount County." *Alabama Historical Quarterly* 27 (1965): 95–132.

Rand, McNally, and Company. "Alabama" [map]. In *Rand, McNally and Co.'s Enlarged Business Atlas and Shippers' Guide,* 154–155. Chicago, 1902.

Read, William A. *Indian Place Names in Alabama.* Louisiana State University Studies, no. 29. 1937. Rev. ed. Edited by James B. McMillan. University, Ala.: University of Alabama Press, 1984.

Riley, Benjamin Franklin. *History of Conecuh County, Alabama: Embracing a Detailed Record of Events from the Earliest Period to the Present; Biographical Sketches of Those Who Have Been Most Conspicuous in the Annals of the County; A Complete List of the Officials of Conecuh, Besides Much Valuable Information Relative to the Internal Resources of the County.* 1881. Reprint. Edited by J. Vernon Brantley. [Washington, D.C.: J. Vernon Brantley], 1964.

Rowland, Dunbar, ed. *Mississippi Provincial Archives, 1763–1766: English Dominion.* Nashville: Brandon Printing Co., 1911. Only volume published in a projected multi-volume series.

Rowland, Dunbar, ed. *Mississippi Territorial Archives, 1798–1803.* Nashville: Brandon Printing Co., 1905. Cited as Rowland, *Miss. Terr. Arch.*

Royce, Charles C., comp. "Indian Land Cessions in the United States." Part 2 of *Eighteenth Annual Report of the Bureau of American Ethnology, 1896–1897.* Washington, D.C., 1899. The standard authority in its field; state maps detail all Indian land-cession treaties with the federal government.

Sealock, Richard B., Margaret M. Sealock, and Margaret S. Powell. *Bibliography of Place-Name Literature: United States and Canada.* 3d ed. Chicago: American Library Association, 1982.

Shortt, Adam, and Arthur G. Doughty, eds. *Documents Relating to the Constitutional History of Canada.* Vol. 1, *1759–1791.* Canadian Archives, Sessional Paper no. 18. Ottawa, 1907. Contains full text of King George III's Proclamation of 1763, including boundary descriptions.

Sinko, Peggy Tuck. *Guide to Local and Family History at the Newberry Library.* Salt Lake City: Ancestry Publishing, 1987.

Smith, Charles P. "History of Gadsden, 1836–1900." In *Early History of Northeast Alabama, and Incidentally of Northwest Georgia,* edited by W. Stanley Hoole and Addie S. Hoole. University, Ala.: Confederate Publishing Co., 1979.

Snedecor, V. Gayle. *Directory of Greene County [Alabama] for 1855–6.* 1856. Reprint. Edited by Franklin Schackelford Moseley. Eutaw, Ala.: Franklin Schackelford Moseley, 1963.

Snedecor, V. Gayle. *Snedecor's Map of Greene County, Alabama.* N.p., 1856.

Snedecor, V. Gayle. *Snedecor's Map of Hale County, Alabama.* Boston, 1870.

Southerland, Henry DeLeon, Jr. "Federal Road, Gateway to Alabama, 1806–1836." *Alabama Review* 39 (1986): 96–109.

Stephenson, Richard W., comp. *Land Ownership Maps: A Checklist of Nineteenth Century United States County Maps in the Library of Congress.* Washington, D.C.: Library of Congress, 1967. Most of the maps listed here have been reproduced on microfiche by the Library of Congress.

Stewart, Mrs. Frank Ross. *Alabama's Pike County.* 2 vols. Centre, Ala.: Stewart University Press, 1976–1978.

Stewart, Mrs. Frank Ross. *Cherokee County [Alabama] History, 1836–1956.* 2 vols. Centre, Ala., 1958–1959.

Swindler, William F., ed. *Sources and Documents of United States Constitutions.* 10 vols. Dobbs Ferry, N.Y.: Oceana Publications, 1973–1979. The most complete and up-to-date compilation for the states.

Tanner, Henry S. *New American Atlas Containing Maps of the Several States of the North American Union, Projected and Drawn on a Uniform Scale from Documents Found in the Public Offices of the United States and State Governments, and Other Original and Authentic Information.* Philadelphia, [c. 1823]. Map of Georgia and Alabama was especially helpful.

Tanner, Henry S. *United States of America* [map]. Philadelphia, 1829. A useful map, despite its relative lack of detail.

Taylor, Thomas Jones. *History of Madison County, and Incidentally of North Alabama, 1732–1840.* Edited by W. Stanley Hoole and Addie S. Hoole. University, Ala.: Confederate Publishing Co., 1976.

Territorial Papers of the United States. Vols. 1–26 edited by Clarence E. Carter; vols. 27–28 edited by John P. Bloom. Washington, D.C.: Government Printing Office, 1934–1975. Cited as *Terr. Papers U.S.*

Tharin, W. C. *Directory of Marengo County [Alabama] for 1860–61.* Mobile, 1861.

Thorndale, William, and William Dollarhide. *Map Guide to the U.S. Federal Censuses, 1790–1920.* Baltimore: Genealogical Publishing Co., 1987. An atlas of well-designed county outline maps for each state, accompanied by a bibliography and an explanation of methodology.

Toulmin, Harry, comp. *Digest of the Laws of the State of Alabama: Containing the Statutes and Resolutions in Force at the End of the General Assembly in January 1823.* Cahawba, Ala., 1823.

Toulmin, Harry, ed. *Statutes of the Mississippi Territory, Revised and Digested by the Authority of the General Assembly.* Natchez, 1807.

Tuscaloosa Genealogical Society. *Pioneers of Tuscaloosa County, Alabama, Prior to 1830.* Montgomery: Herff Jones Division, 1981.

United States. *Statutes at Large of the United States of America, 1789–1873.* 17 vols. Boston: Little, Brown, 1845–1874. Cited as U.S. Stat.

U.S. General Land Office. "Diagram of the State of Alabama." In *Annual Report of the Commissioner of the General Land Office.* 29th Congress, 1st sess., 1845–1846. Senate Document 16. Serial 472.

U.S. National Park Service. *Natchez Trace Parkway Survey.* Washington, D.C.: Government Printing Office, 1941. Also published in 76th Congress, 3d sess., 1940–1941. Senate Document 148. Serial 10450. Very useful modern survey of old roads and landmarks, many of which no longer exist.

Van Zandt, Franklin K. *Boundaries of the United States and the Several States.* Geological Survey Professional Paper 909. Washington, D.C.: Government Printing Office, 1976. The standard compilation for its subject.

Whitaker, A[rthur] P[reston]. "Muscle Shoals Speculation, 1783–1789." *Mississippi Valley Historical Review* 13 (1926–1927): 365–386.

Whitaker, Arthur Preston. *Spanish-American Frontier: 1783–1795.* Boston and New York: Houghton Mifflin Co., 1927.

Wiggins, Sarah Woolfolk. *Scalawag in Alabama Politics, 1865–1881.* University, Ala.: University of Alabama Press, 1977.